S

Protestant Theological Education in America: A Bibliography

by
HEATHER F. DAY

ATLA Bibliography Series, No. 15

The American Theological
Library Association
and
The Scarecrow Press, Inc.
Metuchen, N.J., & London
1985

Library of Congress Cataloging-in-Publication Data

Day, Heather F.
    Protestant theological education in America.

    (ATLA bibliography series ; no. 15)
    Includes index.
    1. Theology--Study and teaching--United States--Bibli-
ography. 2. Theological seminaries, Protestant--Bibliog-
raphy. 3. Theological seminaries--United States--Bibliog-
raphy. I. Title. II. Series.
    Z7848.D39 1985   [BV4030]   016.207'73   85-18300
    ISBN 0-8108-1842-6

CONTENTS

iii

EDITOR'S NOTE

The American Theological Library Association Bibliography series is designed to stimulate and encourage the preparation of reliable bibliographies and guides to the literature of religious studies in all of its scope and variety. Compilers are free to define their field, make their own selections, and work out internal organization as the unique demands of the subject require. We are pleased to publish Heather F. Day's Protestant Theological Education in America as number fifteen in our series.

Heather F. Day received a B.A. in French from Taylor University in 1971, an M.A. in Library Science from Indiana University in 1974, and an M.A. in Church History from Butler University (in conjunction with Christian Theological Seminary) in 1982. She served as librarian at Lilly Endowment from 1974 to 1980 and is currently engaged in homemaking, free-lance writing and bibliographic projects, and volunteer work with internationals. She is also an active member of the Reformed Presbyterian Church of West Lafayette, Indiana.

Kenneth E. Rowe
Series Editor

Drew University Library
Madison, NJ   07940

INTRODUCTION

I. How the Bibliography Began

This book owes its origins to an earlier project carried out at Auburn Theological Seminary in New York City. In 1974, Lilly Endowment, Inc. made a grant to Auburn for a study of reform in Protestant seminaries from 1890 to 1970. In due course, this project fed into a larger study of the history of Protestant theological education in America over a 200-year time span.

In preparation for this work, Glenn Miller spent 2 1/2 months combing through the card catalogue and various indexes at the Library of Congress, Union Theological Seminary in New York City, the University of Chicago and Duke University. He amassed several hundred cards referring to works dealing with theological education. Christa Klein, who was writing the section on Lutheran education, obtained more citations from the Lutheran Theological Seminary at Gettysburg. Virginia Brereton, James Fraser and Robert Lynn all together added a few hundred more cards to the bibliography from their researches. Barbara Wheeler was, at the time, involved in organizing and distributing the cards among the writers.

In 1978, I first became involved in the "history project" while working as librarian at Lilly Endowment. I inherited the 2500 or so cards which had already been gathered together, and I spent considerable time checking each one of the entries for accuracy and completeness of bibliographic information. If the entry could not be found in an index, then an attempt was made to look at the original source. If the original source was not available locally, the libraries which owned the sources were contacted to obtain their help in verification. Hence entries were not put into the final bibliography until they had been checked for accuracy and found to be accessible to anyone researching the subject.

The bibliography lay dormant for two years until I began working on it again in 1982, and the decision was made to make the bibliography as comprehensive as possible in the field of Protestant theological education in America, and to bring it up to date. It became obvious then that the bibliography was becoming too extensive to attach to a larger work, so it would have to be published separately.

II. Scope

Since much of the bibliography was first gathered to support the writing of a history of Protestant theological education in America, many of the materials were gathered to contribute to a general understanding of the subject. Therefore, a number of items appear under general headings such as "United States - Religious History - 19th Century" in the index. These background materials appear in Section I of the index. Also, the writers felt that it was necessary to an understanding of American thelogical education to familiarize themselves with theological education in Germany and Great Britain in particular, so headings appear under the names of these countries. The writers also looked at works concerning Roman Catholic theological education, either to determine the influence of Catholic upon Protestant education or to gain a better understanding of Protestant education by way of comparison. So some items on Roman Catholic theological education have been included in the bibliography.

Several works have been listed under the heading "Private Theological Instruction." This heading covers the entries which deal with the early years of theological education when it was conducted privately under individual ministers before theological schools were conceived.

Some church groups, notably the Baptists, Methodists and Christian Churches, continued to educate their ministers in church colleges when other denominations were establishing seminaries. Thus, quite a number of works on church colleges have been included in the bibliography, especially colleges operated by the churches mentioned above. Other denominations educated their ministers primarily in Bible colleges. Attempts were made to cover all Protestant denominations, no matter how small, though these efforts were constrained somewhat due to the limited scope of some indexing and abstracting services.

The kinds of terms used in the search were: Theological Seminaries, Theological Education, Theology - Study and Teaching, Seminarians, Ministers - Training, Clergy - Training, Church and Colleges, Bible Colleges, Missionary Education, Pastors - Training, etc. Where individual seminaries were indexed separately, these entries were searched individually. In the case of Writings on American History, the indexing was sketchy enough that I had to look under names of individual seminaries and denominations to find works on theological education.

The Archivist-Historian of the Episcopal Church Historical Society kindly sent entries from the Historical Magazine of the Protestant Episcopal Church prior to 1973, when indexing on this periodical began in Religion Index.

III. Indexes, Abstracts and Libraries Searched

1. America: History and Life (1963-1982, Issue 19A3. Conducted by computer.)

2. Christian Periodical Index (1956 - September 1982).

3. Combined Retrospective Index to Journals in History (1838-1974).

4. Comprehensive Dissertation Index (1861-1972).

5. Cumulative Book Index (1928-1952).

6. Dissertation Abstracts Online (1861 - February 1984. Conducted by computer.)

7. Education Index (1929 - September 1982).

8. Education Literature (1907-1932).

9. ERIC (Educational Resources Information Center) (1966 - January 1983. Conducted by computer.)

10. Essay and General Literature Index (1900-1982).

11. Historical Abstracts (not indexing U.S. after 1963) (1955-1963).

12. Humanities Index (1974 - September 1982).

13. International Index to Periodicals (later Social Sciences and Humanities Index - 1907-1974).

14. Library of Congress Catalog, Books: Subjects (1950-1982).

15. Magazine Index (1977 - July 1982).

16. National Newspaper Index (includes Christian Science Monitor, New York Times, Wall Street Journal since 1983, Los Angeles Times and Washington Post. 1979 - January 1983. Conducted by computer.)

17. Peabody Institute, Baltimore. Catalogue of the Library (1883-1905).

18. Philosopher's Index (1940 - February 1983. Conducted by computer.)

19. Poole's Index to Periodical Literature (1802-1906).

20. Public Affairs Information Service (1976 - July 1983. Conducted by computer.)

21. Readers' Guide to Periodical Literature (1890 - September 16, 1983).

22. Religion and Society in North America: An Annotated Bibliography, edited by Robert deV. Brunkow. 1983.

23. Religious and Theological Abstracts (1958 - Fall 1983).

24. Religion Index One: Periodicals (formerly Index to Religious Periodical Literature 1949-1969) (1970 - January 1983. Conducted by computer.)

25. Religion Index Two: Multi-Author Works (1960-1980. Conducted by computer.)

26. Social Sciences Citation Index (1977-1982).

27. Social Sciences Index (1974 - September 1982).

28. Sociological Abstracts (1963-1983. Conducted by computer.)

29. Subject Guide to Books in Print (1981-1984).

30. United States Catalog (1898-1927).

31. Writings on American History (1902-1973).

As indicated in the list of services, computer searches were run whenever possible.

Searches were made of state historical journals, even though some of these are indexed in the historical indexing services. Letters were written to several church historical societies to see if they had

citations dealing with theological education in their
denominations which might not have been listed in the
general sources. Responses were gratefully received
from the following denominations: American Lutheran,
Congregational Christian, Disciples of Christ,
Episcopalian, Evangelical and Reformed, Reformed
Presbyterian, Southern Baptist, Unitarian/Universalist
and United Methodist.

IV. Services Not Searched

It lay beyond the scope of this bibliography to
go to denominational indexes, such as the United
Methodist Periodical Index and the Southern Baptist
Periodical Index. Since the major periodicals from
these denominations are indexed in Religion Index One,
articles of greatest significance from these denominations should be found in the bibliography. However,
researchers who are interested in articles on a
particular denomination that appear in smaller
denominational publications should look at the
appropriate denominational index.

Other services or indexes which were not
searched, but may prove helpful, are Pastoral Care and
Counseling Abstracts, Psychological Abstracts,
Shelflist of the Widener Library of Harvard
University, catalog of the New York Public Library
Research Libraries, and computerized subject coverage

of the libraries participating in the Research
Libraries Network. <u>American Imprints</u> (1820-1831),
<u>American Bibliography</u> (1801-1819), and <u>Evans American
Bibliography</u> (1639-1800) have little or no subject
index, so were not searched. It remains for a
bibliographer to make these works more accessible to
the user.

V. <u>Format</u>

Turabian format has been followed in general.
However, there are a few variations. All works by
individual authors are listed in alphabetical order by
title (whether or not he or she has written it with
other authors). Where an author's full name did not
appear in the index from which it was taken, the name
has been left as it was found. If, however, it
appears obvious that "Marty, M.", for instance, is the
same author as "Marty, Martin," the works are
alphabetized together. Titles appearing in <u>Poole's
Index</u> are often not exact titles, so these have been
placed in parentheses.

VI. <u>Acknowledgments</u>

The librarians at Christian Theological Seminary,
the Indiana State Library, Indiana University/Purdue
University at Indianapolis, and Purdue University were
most helpful as the project progressed. Les
Galbraith, librarian at Christian Theological Seminary

and Director of the project for the last two years, enabled the project to go more smoothly and to reach completion.

Virginia Brereton, James Fraser, Christa Klein and Barbara Wheeler, all original members of the "Auburn History Project," contributed many citations to the initial bibliography, and Christa Klein remained involved with the bibliography project beyond the initial period.

Bibliographies compiled by Norman Kansfield, Kenneth Rowe and Gerald Winkleman yielded valuable additions to the bibliography. Norman Kansfield consulted with us on the project and Kenneth Rowe first encouraged me to submit the bibliography to the American Theological Library Association as part of the ATLA Bibliography Series, which he edits.

Theresa Caruso was the most able typist on the word processor, handling the careful details of this kind of typing with great ease and cheerfulness. Her husband, Philip, assisted in the technical side of computerizing the data.

This bibliography would not have been possible without the initial foundation work of Glenn Miller of Southeastern Baptist Theological Seminary. He assisted me throughout the work of checking, expanding and indexing the bibliography.

Robert Lynn, Senior Vice President of Lilly Endowment, first conceived of the entire project. His vision of the possibilities for theological education in America is being carried out in many ways through projects supported by Lilly Endowment. Dr. Lynn's certainty that this bibliographic project might contribute to further research and understanding of theological education has been a great encouragement to me personally.

Last of all, my husband, Harlan Day, has taken a great interest in the bibliography, to the extent of trying to understand the most mundane aspects of the work as I have felt the need to discuss it. Our sons, Stephen, Peter and Timothy have never understood the importance of all the cards they saw or why these cards had to stay in a certain order. All were born while the bibliography was in progress. Were it not for these three, the bibliography would have been finished sooner. Yet it had to take a secondary place to the more important task of raising them. Maybe one day they will use it in their own study of theological education in America!

May the glory for this work go to God Himself, for Whose glory all of the institutions listed in it were founded.

1. Aaron, Daniel. Men of Good Hope: A Story of American Progressives. New York: Oxford University Press, 1951.

2. Abbott, E. H. "Should Ministers Be Educated?" Outlook 141 (December 23, 1925):625-6; "Discussion." Outlook 142 (February 10-17, 1926):205-7, 244-6.

3. Abbott, L. "Autobiographical." Outlook 87 (November 2, 1907):469-72.

4. Abbott, Lyman. The Christian Ministry. Boston and New York: Houghton, Mifflin Co., 1905.

5. Abbott, Lyman. Reminiscences. Boston and New York: Houghton, Mifflin Co., 1915.

6. Abel, Paul Frederick. "An Historical Study of the Origin and Development of Asbury Theological Seminary." M.A. thesis, Columbia University, 1951.

7. Aberly, John. "New Tasks of the Seminary at the Beginning of the New Century." Lutheran Quarterly 56 (October 1926):441-51.

8. Aberly, John. "Theological Education and the World Mission of the Church." Lutheran Church Quarterly 3 (January 1930):15-28.

9. "Academic Freedom and Tenure: Concordia Seminary (Missouri) American Association of University Professors. Committee on Academic Freedom and Tenure." AAUP Bulletin 61 (April 1975):49-59.

10. "Academy of Parish Clergy Founded." Christian Century 86 (May 21, 1969):704.

11. Accrediting Association of Bible Colleges. Official Listing of Member Schools and Officers of the Executive Committee. Providence, 1959?

12. "Accrediting Bible Colleges." School and Society 89 (May 6, 1961):219.

13. "Across Borderlines [Cooperative Program in Graduate Courses of Theology]." Christian Century 83 (April 27, 1966):562.

1

14. "Act for Establishing a Theological Seminary."
Panoplist 1 (January 1806):357-61.

15. "Action of the General Conferences of 1866 and
1870 on Ministerial Education." Christian
Advocate (Nashville) 32 (New Series)
(March 9, 1872):10.

16. Adamo, S. J. "Philadelphia Story: Expulsion
of Five Seminarians from St. Charles
Seminary, Overbrook, Pa." America 115
(December 3, 1966):756-8.

17. Adams, Arthur. "The Founding of Trinity
College [Washington College, 1823-1845]."
Historical Magazine of the Protestant
Episcopal Church 14 (March 1945):53-65.

18. Adams, Arthur Merrihew. "Theological Field
Education." Princeton Seminary Bulletin 58
(October 1964):5-19.

19. Adams, H. B. "Doctoral Studies for Pastors:
In-Service Doctoral Program." Christian
Century 82 (April 28, 1965):560+.

20. Adams, H. B. "Major Issues in the Lilly Study
[Pre-Seminary Education]." Journal of
Bible and Religion 34 (April 1966).

21. Adams, H. B. "Patterns of Continuing
Education: S. T. D. Education at San
Francisco." Theological Education 1
(Summer 1965):223-5.

22. Adams, H. B. "(Seminary Libraries and
University Extension)." Johns Hopkins
University Studies in Historical and
Political Science 5 (1887):no. 11.

23. Adams, Henry Babcock. "Advanced Pastoral
Studies: A New Need." Encounter 26
(Summer 1965):340-8.

24. Adams, Henry Babcock. Christian Mission: Its
Nature and Implications. New York:
National Council of Churches, 1966.

25. Adams, Henry Babcok. "Consultation: An
Alternative to Supervision." Journal of
Pastoral Care 25, no. 3 (1971):157-64.

2

26. Adams, Henry Babcock. "Continuous Education
    for Ministers." 1966. (ERIC Document)

27. Adams, Henry Babcock. "The Emergence of
    Continuing Education." 1966. (ERIC Doc-
    ument)

28. Adams, Henry Babcock. An Incentive Fund for
    the Continuing Education of Ministers. New
    York: National Council of Churches, 1966.

29. Adams, Henry Babcock. The Needs of
    Professionals in Continuing Education for
    Ministers. New York: National Council of
    Churches, 1966.

30. Adams, Henry Babcock. "Performance Evaluation
    in Ministry." Theological Education 7
    (Winter 1971):102-8.

31. Adams, Henry B., ed. "Proceedings of the
    Adult Learning Seminar, Syracuse Uni-
    versity, N.Y., June 12-16, 1967." (ERIC
    Document)

32. Adams, Herbert B. Seminary Notes on Recent
    Historical Literature. Johns Hopkins
    University Studies in the Social Sciences.
    8th series 1890, nos. 11-12. New York:
    Johnson Reprint Corp., 1973.

33. Adams, J. E. "Seed of Schism: A Seminary in
    Exile." Christian Century 91 (March 6,
    1974):252-4; "Discussion." 91 (March
    27):350; (May 8):518.

34. Adams, James Edward. Need of Specific and
    Thorough Training of Theological Students
    Concerning the Church's Missionary Work.
    N.p., 1895.

35. Adams, J. L. "Study of Christian Social
    Ethics at the Divinity School." Harvard
    Divinity Bulletin 26 (April 1962):11-21.

36. Adams, James Luther. "Uses of Diversity [in a
    Divinity School]." Harvard Divinity Bul-
    letin 23 (1957-58):47-64.

37. Adams, John Quincy. A History of Auburn
    Theological Seminary, 1818-1918. Auburn,
    N.Y.: Auburn Seminary Press, 1918.

3

38. Adams, L. C. "Clinical Pastoral Education as a Clinical Trainee." Duke Divinity School Review 33 (Autumn 1968):178-81.

39. Adams, R. S. "Why Summer Schools for Rural Pastors?" Missionary Review of the World 52 (June 1929):464-5.

40. Adams, Robert L. "Conflict over Charges of Heresy in American Protestant Seminaries." Social Compass 17, no. 2 (1970):243-62.

41. Adams, Robert Lynn. "The Process of Ideological Change in American Protestant Seminaries." Ph.D. dissertation, Vanderbilt University, 1969.

42. Adams, William. A Discourse on the Life and Services of Professor Moses Stuart. New York: J. F. Trow, Printer, 1852.

43. Adams, William. Theological Seminaries: A Discourse Delivered in the Madison Square Presbyterian Church. New York: Trow & Smith, 1870.

44. Addison, James Thayer. "A New Departure in Theological Education." Harvard Alumni Bulletin 32 (November 21, 1929):246-50.

45. Adger, John Bailey. My Life and Times, 1810-1899. Richmond, Va.: Presbyterian Committee of Publication, 1899.

46. Adler, B. "Who Goes into Religious Life?" Cosmopolitan 145 (December 1958):42-53.

47. Adolphus, Otto. Compendium Theologicum: Or, Manual for Student. Cambridge [Eng.]: Printed by Hall & Son, 1852.

48. "Advantages of Private Instruction." Bibliotheca Sacra 38 (1881):707-22.

49. "Advice to a Theological Student." New Englander 5 (1847):505-13.

50. "Advice to College Students Intending to Enter the Ministry." Biblical World 29 (May 1907):323-6.

51. Aeschbacher, Joseph Edmond. Sandhill Preacher. Versailles, Mo., 1971.

52. African Methodist Episcopal Church. Survey of the Colleges and Schools of the Colored Methodist Episcopal Church. Compiled by J. A. Bray. N.p.:J. W. Perry, n.d.

53. After Fifty Years: A Record of God's Working through the Christian and Missionary Alliance. Harrisburg, Pa.: Christian Publications, 1939.

54. After Seventy-Five Years 1860-1935 [Augustana College and Theological Seminary]. Rock Island, Ill.: Augustana Book Concern, 1935.

55. Agrimson, J. E. "Value of Clinical Pastoral Education for the Parish Ministry." Lutheran Quarterly 19 (May 1967):133-41.

56. Ahlstrom, Sydney Eckman. "Facing the New World: Augustana and the American Challenge." In Centennial Essays: Augustana Lutheran Church 1860-1960, pp. 1-27. By Augustana Evangelical Lutheran Church. Centennial Publication Committee. Rock Island, Ill.: Augustana Press, 1960.

57. Ahlstrom, Sydney E. "National Trauma and Changing Religious Values." Daedalus 107 (Winter 1978):13-29.

58. "Ailing Seminaries: Unfit to be Tied? United Presbyterian Schools." Christianity Today 15 (March 12, 1971):39-40.

59. Aitken, P. W. "Clinical Pastoral Education." Duke Divinity School Review 32 (Winter 1967):14-19.

60. Aitken, P. W. "Clinical Pastoral Education as a Clinical Training Supervisor." Duke Divinity School Review 33 (Autumn 1968):174-8.

61. Alban Institute, Washington, D.C. Planned Continuing Education: A Study of Needs Assessment Processes. Collegeville, Pa.: Society for the Advancement of Continuing Education for Ministry, 1978.

62. Albee, Lowell C. "Can These Bones Live: Place of Rare Books in a Denominational Theological Seminary (Collections of the

Jesuit-Krauss-McCormick Library; Plates)."
In Essays on Theological Librarianship, to
C. H. Schmitt. Edited by P. De Klerk.
1980.

63. Albert, L. E. "(Education for Ministry.)"
Evangelical Review 9 (1858):412+.

64. Albrecht, Esther Andreen. "Gustav [Albert]
Andreen [1864-1940] and the Growth of
Augustana College and Theological Seminary
[founded in 1860]." M.A. thesis,
University of Illinois, 1950.

65. Albright, Raymond Wolf. "A Not Impossible
Theological Education." Christian Century
58 (September 3, 1941):1074-6.

66. Albus, Harry J. "Christian Education Today."
Christian Life 10 (September 1948):26.

67. Alcorn, Wallace. "The Biblical Concept of
Discipleship as Education for Ministry."
Ph.D. dissertation, New York University,
1974.

68. Aldrich, W. M. "Basic Concepts of Bible
College Education." Bibliotheca Sacra 119
(July 1962):244-50.

69. Alexander, Archibald. Biographical Sketches
of the Founder and Principal Alumni of the
Log College. Together with an Account of
the Revivals of Religion under Their
Ministry. Philadelphia: Presbyterian
Board of Publication, 1851.

70. Alexander, Archibald. "The Education of
Presbyterian Theological Students. A
Letter of Dr. Archibald Alexander, with a
Historical Note by Edward B. Hodge, D.D."
Journal of the Presbyterian Historical
Society 2 (1903-1904):287-91.

71. Alexander, J. B. "Religion in the Program of
the Church-Related Colleges: For the Pre-
Theological Student." Christian Education
29 (December 1946):406-10.

72. Alexander, J. W. "Education for the Ministry." Princeton Review 15 (October
1843):587-604.

6

73. Alexander, James E. "New Formula for Theological Education." Religion in Life 35 (Winter, 1965-6):30-44.

74. Alexander, James Waddell. The Life of Archibald Alexander, D.D., First Professor in the Theological Seminary at Princeton, New Jersey. New York: Charles Scribner's Sons, 1854.

75. Aliotta, Antonio. "Science and Religion in the Nineteenth Century." In Science, Religion and Reality. Edited by Joseph Needham. New York: Macmillan & Co., 1925.

76. Allbeck, Willard Dow. A Century of Lutherans in Ohio. Yellow Springs, Ohio: Antioch Press, 1966.

77. Allbeck, Willard Dow. Theology at Wittenberg, 1845-1945. Springfield, Ohio: Wittenberg Press, 1946.

78. Allen, Alexander Viets Griswold. Life and Letters of Phillips Brooks. New York: E. P. Dutton & Co., 1901.

79. Allen, Diarca Howe. The Life and Services of Rev. Lyman Beecher, D.D. as President and Professor of Theology in Lane Seminary: A Commemorative Discourse. Cincinnati: Johnson, Stephens & Co., Printers, 1863.

80. Allen, Elliott B. "Roman Catholic Seminary: Changing Perspectives in Theological Education." Canadian Journal of Theology 14 (July 1968):159-68.

81. Allen, Henry F., Berry, George P., Nemiah, John C. and Tullis, James L. "Discussion of the Paper." Theological Education 5 (Spring 1969):215-21.

82. Allen, James E. and Cole, Lynda P. "Clergy Skills in Family-Planning Education and Counseling." Journal of Religion and Health 14 (July 1975):198-205.

83. Allen, James E. and Cole, Lynda P. "Differences in Predominant Family Planning Attitudes and Experiences of Seminary Students: A Ten-Year Assessment." Review of Religious Research 17 (Fall 1975):68-73.

7

84. Allen, James Elmore. "Family Planning
    Attitudes of Methodist Seminary Husbands
    and Wives." Ph.D. dissertation, Boston
    University Graduate School, 1964.

85. Allen, James E. "Family Planning Attitudes of
    Seminary Students." Review of Religious
    Research 9 (Fall 1967):52-5.

86. Allen, Joseph L. "The Policy Process at
    Perkins in the Quillian Years." Perkins
    School of Theology: Journal 34 (Spring
    1981):15-24.

87. Allen, T. Scott, and Hartsig, Jo C.
    "Seminarians Protest 'Corpus Christi' Sub."
    Witness 64 (December 1981):8-9.

88. Allen, Yorke. A Seminary Survey: A Listing
    and Review of the Activities of the
    Theological Schools and Major Seminaries
    Located in Africa, Asia and Latin
    America.... New York: Harper & Row, 1960.

89. Alley, Reuben E. "The Relation of Social
    Science to Ministerial Training." Ph.D.
    dissertation, Southern Baptist Theological
    Seminary, 1928.

90. Alley, Reuben E. "Southern Baptist Seminaries
    and Academic Freedom." Review and
    Expositor 61 (Winter 1964):555-67.

91. Allison, Charles Elmer. A Historical Sketch
    of Hamilton College, Clinton, New York.
    Yonkers, N.Y., 1889.

92. Allmendinger, David. Paupers and Scholars:
    The Transformation of Student Life in
    Nineteenth-Century New England. New York:
    St. Martin's Press, 1975.

93. Allmendinger, David F., Jr. "Strangeness of
    the American Education Society: Indigent
    Students and the New Charity, 1815-1840
    [bibliog.]." History of Education
    Quarterly 11 (Spring 1971):3-22.

94. Alsdurf, P. "Fuller's Problems are
    Psychological but Real: Reaccreditation."
    Christianity Today 23 (July 20, 1979):34+.

8

95. Altholz, Josef Lewis. The Churches in the
    Nineteenth Century. Indianapolis: Bobbs-
    Merrill Co., 1967.

96. American Academy of Political and Social
    Science, Philadelphia. Religion in
    American Society. Philadelphia: American
    Academy of Political and Social Science,
    1960.

97. American Association of Theological Schools.
    Horizons of Theological Education: Essays
    in Honor of Charles L. Taylor. Edited by
    John B. Coburn, Walter D. Wagoner and Jesse
    H. Ziegler. Dayton, Ohio, 1966.

98. American Association of Theological Schools.
    Library Check List, Consisting of Selected
    Basic Reference Books, Periodicals and
    Check Sheets for Self-Study and Evaluation
    of Seminary Libraries. Louisville? Ky.,
    1954.

99. American Association of Theological Schools.
    Theological Education in the 1970's: A
    Report of the Resources Planning
    Commission. Dayton, Ohio: American
    Association of Theological Schools in the
    U.S. and Canada, 1969.

100. American Association of Theological Schools.
    Resources Planning Commission. "Resources
    Planning in Theological Education." Theo-
    logical Education 4 (Summer 1968):751-833.

101. American Association of Theological Schools.
    Task Force of Spiritual Development.
    Voyage, Vision, Venture. Dayton, Ohio:
    American Association of Theological
    Schools, 1972.

102. "The American Association of Theological
    Schools." Christian Education 32 (1949):
    44-7.

103. American Baptist Convention. "Theological
    Education in the American Baptist
    Convention." Report by the Committee of
    Seventeen. (Mimeographed)

104. American Baptist Convention. Board of
    Education. Theological Education in the
    Northern Baptist Convention: A Survey.

Prepared by Hugh Hartshorne and Milton C.
Froyd for the Commission on a Survey of
Theological Education of the Board of
Education of the Northern Baptist
Convention, 1944-45. Philadelphia: Judson
Press, 1954.

105. American Education Society. Constitution &
Address of the American Society for
Educating Pious Youth. Boston, 1816.

106. American Historical Association. Committee on
Graduate Education. The Education of
Historians in the United States. New York:
McGraw-Hill Book Co., 1962.

107. American Lutheran Church. Division of
Theological Education. Our Theological
Seminaries in the 1970's. Minneapolis:
American Lutheran Church, 1970?

108. "The American Psychological Association Has
Granted a Five-Year Renewal of
Accreditation to Fuller Seminary's School
of Psychology." Christianity Today 24
(August 8, 1980):50.

109. American Theological Library Association.
Second Annual Conference, June 14-15, 1948.
Bonebrake Theological Seminary, Dayton,
Ohio. Summary of Proceedings. American
Theological Library Association, 1948.

110. American Theological Library Association.
"Summary of Proceedings: Twenty-Ninth
Annual Conference, Gordon-Conwell Theo-
logical Seminary, South Hamilton, Mass.,
June 16-20, 1975." ATLA Proceedings 29
(1975):1-204.

111. American Unitarian Association. Commission of
Appraisal. Unitarians Face a New Age, pp.
99-110. Boston: American Unitarian
Association, 1936.

112. Ames, Charles Gordon. Charles Gordon Ames: A
Spiritual Autobiography. Boston and New
York: Houghton, Mifflin Co., 1913.

113. Ames, David A. "Science and Religion: Toward
Understanding and Collaboration in the
University Setting." Anglican Theological
Review 63 (October 1981):465-71.

114. Ames, Edward Scribner. *Beyond Theology: The Autobiography of Edward Scribner Ames.* Edited by Van Meter Ames. Chicago: University of Chicago Press, 1959.

115. Amicus. "On the Importance of Placing Biblical Literature and Antiquities on an Equality, at Least, with the Heathen Classics." *Quarterly Review of the Methodist Episcopal Church, South* 1 (July 1847):475-7.

116. Anders, Sarah F. "Woman's Role in the Southern Baptist Convention and Its Churches as Compared with Selected Other Denominations." *Review and Expositor* 72 (Winter 1975):31-9.

117. Andersen, Francis I. "The Seminaries' Responsibility in Overseas Theological Training." *Theological Education* 5 (Summer 1969):380-90.

118. Anderson, Abraham. *An Address Delivered to the Students of the Associate Theological Seminary... Together with a Catalogue of the Officers, Alumni, and Students of the Institution, Canonsburg, Pa.* Washington, Pa.: Printed at the Commonwealth Office, 1852.

119. Anderson, Bernhard W. and Imler, William A. "Drew's 'C.T.E.' Project." *Christian Century* 79 (April 25, 1962):518-20.

120. Anderson, Bernhard Word. "A Look at Theological Education Today." *Drew Gateway* 31 (Winter 1961):88-97.

121. Anderson, Charles A., ed. "San Francisco Journal of George Burrowes, 1858-1875. With a Biographical Sketch by Clifford M. Drury." *Journal of the Presbyterian Historical Society* 33, no. 2 (1955):93-120; no. 3 (1955):157-80; no. 4 (1955):257-78.

122. Anderson, Charles S. "Looking to the Future in Theological Education." In *Striving for Ministry: Centennial Essays Interpreting the Heritage of Luther Theological Seminary,* pp. 186-200. Edited by Warren A. Quanbeck, Eugene L. Fevold, and Gerhard E. Frost. Minneapolis: Augsburg Pub. House, 1977.

11

123. Anderson, F. I. "Seminaries' Responsibility in Overseas Theological Training." Theological Education 5 (Summer 1969):380-90.

124. Anderson, H. George. "Challenge and Change within German Protestant Theological Education during the Nineteenth Century." Church History 39 (March 1970):36-48.

125. Anderson, Harry H., ed. "Remembrances of Nashotah Days: Two Letters of Gustaf Unonius." Swedish Pioneer Historical Quarterly 27, no. 2 (1976):111-15.

126. Anderson, Herbert. "Learning and Teaching about Death and Dying." Princeton Theological Seminary, 1972. (ERIC Document)

127. Anderson, Herbert. "What Do Seminaries Expect of Clinical Pastoral Education?" Journal of Pastoral Care 34 (March 1980):54-61.

128. Anderson, Hugh. "Some Impressions of Theological Education in America Today." Expository Times 70 (September 1959):356-60.

129. Anderson, James Maitland. Handbook to the City and University of St. Andrews. St. Andrews [Scot]: W. C. Henderson & Sons, University Press, 1911.

130. Anderson, Robert Charles. "Denominationalism, Higher Education and Interrelationships: A Study of a Theologically Conservative Protestant Denomination and Its Three Institutions of Higher Education." Ph.D. dissertation, University of Iowa, 1972.

131. Anderson, S. T. "(Education for Christian Ministry.)" Cumberland Presbyterian Quarterly Review 2 (1881):129+.

132. Anderson, Terence R. "The Seminary as Part of a University Community." Theological Education 2 (Autumn 1965):34-41.

133. "Andover and the Dead Hand." Christian Century 43 (June 3, 1926):703-4.

134. "Andover at Cambridge." Outlook 88 (March 28, 1908):675-6.

135. "Andover Question Settled." Independent 65
     (December 31, 1908):1631.

136. Andover Theological Seminary. The Andover
     Case: With an Introductory Historical
     Statement. Boston: Stanley & Usher, 1887.

137. Andover Theological Seminary. The Constitution
     and Associate Statutes of the Theological
     Seminary in Andover. Andover: Printed by
     Flagg & Gould, 1817.

138. Andover Theological Seminary. The Constitution
     and Associate Statutes of the Theological
     Seminary in Andover: With a Sketch of Its
     Rise and Progress. Boston, Mass.: Farr &
     Mallory & Co., 1808.

139. Andover Theological Seminary. General
     Catalogue (1808-1908). Boston: T. Tod,
     Printer, 1909.

140. Andover Theological Seminary. A Memorial of
     the Semi-Centennial Celebration of the
     Founding of the Theological Seminary at
     Andover. Andover: Warren F. Draper, 1859.

141. Andover Theological Seminary. An Outline of
     the Course of Study in the Department of
     Christian Theology. Andover: Printed by
     Flagg & Gould, 1822.

142. "Andover Theological Seminary and Harvard
     University." School and Society 22
     (September 26, 1925):394-5.

143. Andrews, E. Benjamin. "How Can Economic
     Studies Help the Ministry?" Homiletic
     Review 22 (November 1981):408-12.

144. Andrews, Kenneth R. "The Progress of
     Professional Education for Business."
     Theological Education 5 (Spring 1969):144-
     66.

145. "Angels in Outer Space." America 107 (May 26,
     1962):288-9.

146. "Answering the Call after Thirty." Time 85
     (April 30, 1965):88.

147. Appel, Theodore. The Beginnings of the
     Theological Seminary of the Reformed Church

in the United States, from 1817 to 1832.
Philadelphia: Reformed Church Publication
Board, 1866.

148. Appel, Theodore. "A Chapter on the Beginnings
of the Theological Seminary of the Reformed
Church." Reformed Quarterly Review 33
(1886):388-414.

149. Apple, T. G. "(Internal History of German
Reformed Church.)" Mercersburg Review 23
(1876):59+.

150. Appleby, R. Scott. "The Divinity School Deans
1892-1960." Criterion 19 (Autumn 1980):17-
22.

151. Arden, Gothard Everett. Augustana Heritage:
A History of the Augustana Lutheran Church.
Rock Island, Ill.: Augustana Press, 1963.

152. Arden, Gothard Everett. The School of the
Prophets: The Background and History of
Augustana Theological Seminary, 1860-1960.
Rock Island, Ill.: Augustana Theological
Seminary, 1960.

153. "Are the Results Accomplished by Our
Theological Seminaries Satisfactory?" Old
Testament Student 5 (January 1886):235.

154. Armentrout, Donald S. "The Beginnings of
Theological Education at the University of
the South: The Role of John Austin
Merrick." Historical Magazine of the
Protestant Episcopal Church 51 (Summer
1982):253-67.

155. Armstrong, Marjorie Moore. "Turns Down Bible
Courses: Missouri Attorney General Rules
State College Chair Unconstitutional."
Christian Century 67 (September 20,
1950):1118.

156. Armstrong, O. K. and Armstrong, Marjorie M.
The Indomitable Baptists: A Narrative of
Their Role in Shaping American History.
Garden City, N.Y.: Doubleday & Co., 1967.

157. Arnett, Benjamin William, comp. The Wilberforce Alumnal: A Comprehensive Review of
the Origin, Development and Present Status
of Wilberforce University. Xenia, Ohio:

14

Printed at the Gazette Office, 1885.

158. Arnold, Charles Harvey. God before You and behind You: The Hyde Park Union Church Through a Century, 1874-1974. Chicago: Hyde Park Union Church, 1974.

159. Arnold, Charles Harvey. "A Religion that Walks the Earth: Edward Scribner Ames and the Chicago School of Theology." Encounter 30 (Fall 1969):314-39.

160. Arnold, Glenn Freeman. "A Comparative Study of the Present Doctrinal Positions and Christian Conduct Codes of Selected Alumni of Moody Bible Institute: 1945-1971." Ph.D. dissertation, New York University, 1977.

161. Arnold, Harvey. "A Religion that Walks the Earth [University of Chicago Divinity School and Edward Scribner Ames]." Encounter 30, no. 4 (1969):314-39.

162. Arnold, T. "'Harriet' Beecher Lectures." Christian Century 97 (July 2-9, 1980):702-4.

163. Arnold, William Van. "Husband-Wife Interaction of Selected Theological Students." Th.D. dissertation, Southern Baptist Theological Seminary, 1970.

164. Asbury, Beverly A. "A Critical Look at Seminary Curriculum by a U.S. Pastor." Theological Education 2:(Spring 1966):173-6.

165. Ash, J. L., Jr. "American Religion and the Academy in the Early Twentieth Century: The Chicago Years of William Warren Sweet." Church History 50 (December 1981):450-64.

166. Ashbrook, J. A. "Limitation of the Older Medical Model in Training Pastoral Counselors." Journal of Pastoral Care 22 (December 1968):232-4.

167. Ashbrook, James B. and Harvey, Louis C. "Black Pastors and White Professors: Report on Collaboration and Challenge." Religion in Life 49 (Spring 1980):35-48.

168. Ashbrook, James B. "Clinical Training: For What Kind of Ministry?" Journal of Pastoral Care 16 (Autumn 1962):139-48.

169. Ashbrook, J. B. and Powell, R. K. "Comparison of Graduating and Non-Graduating Theological Students on the Minnesota Multiphasic Personality Inventory [bibliog.]." Journal of Counseling Psychology 14 (March 1967): 171-4.

170. Ashbrook, James B. "Two Kinds of Learning in Theological Education." Theological Education 2 (Spring 1966):197-202.

171. Ashby, Homer U., Jr., et al. "CPE and Academic Credit: Three Criteria of Eligibility." Journal of Pastoral Care 35 (June 1981):99-105.

172. Ashley, Benedict M. "The Discipline of Theology: Seminary and University." In Does the Church Know How To Teach. Edited by K. Cully. New York: Macmillan, 1970.

173. Ashlock, Marvin. "The Problem of Coordination of Baptist College and Seminary Curricula." Ph.D. dissertation, Southern Baptist Theological Seminary, 1949.

174. Ashworth, Robert Archibald. "The Fundamentalist Movement among the Baptists." Journal of Religion 4 (November 1924):611-31.

175. "Aspects of Management and Governance [American Association of Seminary Staff Officers]." Theological Education 7 (Autumn 1970):7-56.

176. Asquith, Glenn H., Jr. "Anton T. Boisen and the Study of 'Living Human Documents.'" Journal of Presbyterian History 60, no. 3 (1982):244-65.

177. "Assessing the Current Crop of Seminarians: American Association of Theological Schools Report Findings." Christian Century 91 (February 6, 1974):116.

178. Associate Reformed Church in North America. The History, Catalogue, and Arrangements of the Theological Seminary of the Associate

Reformed Synod of New York, at Newburgh:
To Which is Added the Address of the Rev.
J. McCarrell, D.D. at the Opening of the
Session, 1839-1840. Newburgh: J.D.
Spalding, 1840.

179. Association for Clinical Pastoral Education.
Directory of Accredited Clinical Pastoral
Education Centers and Member Seminaries.
New York, 1975.

180. Athearn, Walter Scott. An Adventure in
Religious Education: The Story of a Decade
of Experimentation and Professional
Training of Christian Workers. New York
and London: Century Co., 1930.

181. Atkinson, Henry A. The Church and the
People's Play. Boston: Pilgrim Press,
1915.

182. Atwood, A. "Theological Seminaries."
Christian Advocate and Journal (New York)
29 (February 23, 1854):1.

183. Auburn Affirmation. An Affirmation Designed
to Safeguard the Unity and Liberty of the
Presbyterian Church in the U.S.A. Auburn,
N.Y.: Jacobs Press, 1924.

184. Auburn Theological Seminary, Auburn, N.Y.
"Addresses at the Inauguration of the Rev.
Timothy G. Darling, D.D., as Professor of
Sacred Rhetoric and Pastoral Theology,
Auburn Theological Seminary, Auburn, N.Y.,
September 5, 1888. Auburn: Knapp, Peck &
Thomson, 1889.

185. Auburn Theological Seminary, Auburn, N.Y.
Appeal in Behalf of the Auburn Theological
Seminary. Auburn, Recorder Office, n.d.

186. Auburn Theological Seminary, Auburn, N.Y.
Exercises Connected with the Inauguration
of Rev. Ransom B. Welch, D.D., LL.D., as
Professor of Christian Theology, in Auburn
Theological Seminary, Auburn, New York,
Wednesday, October 3, 1877. Auburn, N.Y.:
Benton & Reynolds, 1878.

187. Auburn Theological Seminary, Auburn, N.Y. For
Truth and Freedom. Auburn, N.Y.: Auburn
Theological Seminary, 1929.

188. Auburn Theological Seminary, Auburn, N.Y. The Inauguration of George Black Stewart as President of the Theological Seminary of Auburn in the State of New York, and as Professor of Practical Theology. Auburn: For the Seminary, 1899.

189. Auburn Theological Seminary, Auburn, N.Y. Inauguration of Henry M. Booth, D.D., as President and Professor of Practical Theology. Auburn Theological Seminary, 1893.

190. Augustana College and Theological Seminary, Rock Island, Ill. Denkmann Memorial Library. The Augustana College Library: A Description of the Building, Its Collection and Services. Rock Island, 1950.

191. Augustana Evangelical Lutheran Church. After Seventy-Five Years, 1860-1935: A Jubilee Publication, Seventy-Fifth Anniversary of the Augustana Synod and Augustana College and Theological Seminary. Rock Island, Ill.: Augustana Book Concern, 1935.

192. Augustana Evangelical Lutheran Church. The Story of Augustana College and Theological Seminary, After Seventy-five Years, 1860-1935. Rock Island, Ill.: Augustana Book Concern, 1935.

193. Ault, J. M. "Address of Response: On the Occasion of His Installation as Dean of the Theological School of Drew University." Drew Gateway 39 (Autumn 1968):12-15.

194. Ault, James M. "Community within Diversity in a Large School." Theological Education 2 (Autumn 1965):16-22.

195. Ault, James M. "Education for Change [Union, N.Y.]" Union Seminary Quarterly Review 20 (January 1965):165-75.

196. Austin, Charles. "Poll Finds Conservatism by Seminary Teachers." New York Times 131 (June 11, 1982):15 (national ed.), D20 (late city ed.)

197. Austin, Charles. "Seminary Professors and Politics." Worldview 25 (August 1982):13-14.

198. Axel, Larry E. "The 'Chicago School' of
     Theology and Henry Nelson Wieman."
     Encounter 40, no. 4 (1979):341-58.

199. Babb, Wylie Sherrill. "Legal Bases,
     Regulations, and Procedures for the
     Chartering and Approval of Private,
     Nonprofit Degree-Granting Colleges,
     Universities and Seminaries in
     Pennsylvania." Ph.D. dissertation,
     University of Pittsburgh, 1979.

200. Bachmann, E. Theodore. "Curricular Offerings
     on the History of Lutheranism." Concordia
     Historical Institute Quarterly 37, no. 4
     (1966):197-203.

201. Bachmann, E. Theodore. "Curricular Offerings
     on the History of Lutheranism." Lutheran
     Historical Conference 1 (1966):145-57.

202. Bachmann, E. Theodore. "The Future of
     Seminaries in the Light of Continuing
     Education: The LCA Experience." Lutheran
     Quarterly 18 (November 1966):337-50.

203. Bachmann, E. Theodore. "Samuel Simon
     Schmucker (1799-1873): Lutheran Educator."
     In Sons of the Prophets: Leaders in
     Protestantism from Princeton Seminary, pp.
     39-68. Edited by Hugh Thomson Kerr.
     Princeton: Princeton University Press,
     1963.

204. Bacon, Benjamin W. "Is Theology Scientific?"
     New Englander 46 (January 1887):57-66.

205. Bacon, Benjamin W. The Teaching Ministry for
     Tomorrow. New Haven: Yale University
     Press, 1923.

206. Bacon, Benjamin Wisner. Theodore Thornton
     Munger, New England Minister. New Haven:
     Yale University Press, 1913.

207. Bacon, E. M. "On Andover Hill." In his
     Literary Pilgrimages in New England, pp. 7-
     10. Silver, 1902.

208. Bacon, Ernest Wallace. Spurgeon: Heir of the
     Puritans. London: Allen & Unwin, 1967.

209. Bacon, Leonard. *A Commemorative Discourse, on the Completion of Fifty Years from the Founding of the Theological Seminary at Andover.* Andover: Printed by W. F. Draper, 1858.

210. Bacon, Leonard Woolsey. *Young People's Societies.* New York: Lentilhon & Co., 1900.

211. Bacon, Theodore Davenport. *Leonard Bacon: A Statesman in the Church.* New Haven: Yale University Press, 1931.

212. Baer, Paul. "Potential Stress and Individual Adaptation: A Study of a Seminary." Ph.D. dissertation, University of Chicago, 1954.

213. Bagger, Henry H. "The Problem of Our Theological Seminaries." *Lutheran Church Quarterly* 1 (July 1928):336-45.

214. Bagnell, K. "Comfortable Pulpits, Uncomfortable Pews: Rise in Enrollment." *Macleans* (October 9, 1978):54-5.

215. Bailey, Donald Randall. "Factors Affecting Racial Attitudes and Overt Behavior of Seminary-Trained Methodist Ministers: A Panel Study." Ph.D. dissertation, Emory University, 1972.

216. Bailey, Kenneth K. "Southern White Protestantism at the Turn of the Century." *American Historical Review* 68, no. 3 (1963):618-35.

217. Bailey, M. "What If It All Had To Be Done Again! [Hartford Seminary Foundation]" *Hartford Quarterly* 3 (Autumn 1962):15-22.

218. Baillie, John. "Some Reflections on the Changing Theological Scene." *Union Seminary Quarterly Review* 12 (January 1957):3-9.

219. Baillie, John. "The Theological Course as a Preparation for the Missionary." *International Review of Missions* 28 (October 1939):535-48.

220. Bain, Read. "Educational Plans and Efforts by Methodists in Oregon to 1860." *Oregon*

Historical Society. Quarterly 21 (June 1920):63-94.

221. Bainton, Roland H. "Yale and German Theology in the Middle of the Nineteenth Century." Zeitschrift für Kirchengeschichte 66 (1954):294-302.

222. Bainton, Roland Herbert. Yale and the Ministry: A History of Education for the Christian Ministry at Yale from the Founding in 1701. New York: Harper, 1957.

223. Baird, Joseph Arthur. "Lilly Endowment Study of Pre-Seminary Education." Journal of Bible and Religion 29 (January 1961):16-19.

224. Baird, J. A. "Maturity in Theological Education and the College Teaching of Religion." Journal of Bible and Religion 34 (April 1966).

225. Baird, J. Arthur. "Pre-Theological Training: An Empirical Study." Journal of Bible and Religion 27 (1959):303-10.

226. Baird, Robert. Religion in the United States of America, or an Account of the Origin, Progress, Relations to the State, and Present Condition of the Evangelical Churches in the United States. Glasgow & Edinburgh: Blackie & Son, 1844.

227. Baird, Samuel John. A History of the Early Policy of the Presbyterian Church in the Training of Her Ministry: And of the First Years of the Board of Education. Philadelphia, 1865.

228. Baker, John W. "Government Aid - Hidden Curse." Theological Education 16 (Spring 1980):445-7.

229. Baker, O. H. "Scholarly Pastor." Criterion 2 (Spring 1963):14+.

230. Baker, Oren Huling. "Protestant Theological Education." Higher Education 9 (May 15, 1953):207+.

231. Baker, Robert Andrew. "First Year on the Hill." Southwestern Journal of Theology 8 (October 1965):89-101.

21

232. Baker, Robert A. "Retirement of President Robert E. Naylor." *Southwestern Journal of Theology* 20 (Spring 1978):7-14.

233. Baker, Robert A. "William W. Barnes and Southwestern Baptist Theological Seminary." *Southwestern Journal of Theology* 18 (Fall 1975):72-81.

234. Baketel, Olivers S. "The First Educational Institutions of the Methodist Episcopal Church." *Methodist Review* 97 (May 1915): 404-8.

235. Baldinger, Albert Henry. *May We Introduce Pittsburgh-Xenia Theological Seminary.* Board of Christian Education of the United Presbyterian Church, 1954.

236. Baldwin, George W. et al. "Theological Field Education for Ministry." *Theological Education* 11 (Summer 1975):265-328.

237. Balleine, George Reginald. *A History of the Evangelical Party in the Church of England.* London, New York: Longmans, 1933.

238. Balmer, Randall H. "The Princetonians, Scripture, and Recent Scholarship." *Journal of Presbyterian History* 60 (Fall 1982):267-70.

239. Baltzell, Edward Digby. *The Protestant Establishment: Aristocracy and Caste in America.* New York: Random House, 1964.

240. Bangs, Nathan. "The Importance of Study to a Minister of the Gospel." *Methodist Magazine* 5 (1822):345-7; 377-82; 417-21; 454-7; 6 (1823):30-4; 63-6; 102-6; 141-5; 189-96; 216-20; 264-7; 302-6.

241. Bangs, Nathan. *Letters to Young Ministers of the Gospel, on the Importance and Method of Study.* New York: N. Bangs & J. Emory for the Methodist Episcopal Church, 1826.

242. Bangs, Nathan. *The Present State, Prospects, and Responsibilities of the Methodist Episcopal Church.* New York: Lane & Scott, 1850.

243. Banks, Robert. "Interim Report on the Ad Hoc Committee on Academic Freedom." In Canon Law Society of America: Proceedings of the 32nd Annual Convention, New Orleans, October 1970. By Thomas F. O'Meara, et al. Hartford, Conn.: Canon Law Society of America, 1971.

244. Banner, Lois W. "Religion and Reform in the Early Republic: The Role of Youth." American Quarterly 23 (1971):677-95.

245. Bannister, Henry. "John Dempster, D.D." Methodist Quarterly Review 46 (1864):357-79.

246. "Baptist Split." Time 80 (November 9, 1962):58.

247. Baptist Theological Faculties' Union. Minutes of the Sixth Annual Meeting, March 25, 1909. Chicago, n.d.

248. Baptist Theological Faculties' Union. Minutes of the Seventh Annual Meeting, March 15, 1910. Chicago, n.d.

249. Baptist Theological Faculties' Union. Minutes of a Special Meeting, May 17-19. N.p., n.d.

250. Baptists, Pennsylvania. Philadelphia Association. Minutes of the Philadelphia Baptist Association, from A.D. 1707, to A.D. 1807: Being the First One Hundred Years of Its Existence. Philadelphia: American Baptist Publication Society, 1851.

251. Baptists, Rhode Island. Warren Association. Education Society. Constitution of the Education Society of the Warren Baptist Association: And Circular Letter to the Ministers and Churches on the Importance of Education to Ministers of the Gospel. Boston: Printed by James Loring, 1817.

252. Barbour, D. D. "Has Missionary Training Missed the Mark?" Religious Education 22 (January 1927):23-7.

253. Barclay, Wade Crawford. History of Methodist Missions. 4 vols. New York: Board of Missions and Church Extension of the Methodist Church, 1949- .

254. Barker, Catherine Finney. "The Relationship between Marital Adjustment and Selected Variables for Student Couples at a Theological Seminary and Graduate School." Ph.D. dissertation, Fuller Theological Seminary, School of Psychology, 1981.

255. Barker, E. "Accreditation of Theological Schools [bibliog.]." Peabody Journal of Education 14 (January 1937):169-77.

256. Barker, Earl Pickett. "The Contribution of Methodism to Education in Kentucky." Ph.D. dissertation, George Peabody College for Teachers, 1937.

257. "Barnabas up to Date [Theological Students]." Time 53 (January 3, 1949):48.

258. Barnard, A. N. "What Should Happen to the Ordinand?" Theology 72 (December 1969):551-3.

259. Barnard, John. From Evangelicalism to Progressivism at Oberlin College, 1866-1917. Columbus: Ohio State University Press, 1969.

260. Barnes, C. "Matthew Parker's Pastoral Training and Marlowe's Doctor Faustus." Comparative Drama 15 (Fall 1981):258-67.

261. Barnes, Gilbert Hobbs. The Anti-Slavery Impulse, 1830-1844. New York: D. Appleton-Century Co., 1933.

262. Barnes, William Wright. The Southern Baptist Convention, 1845-1953. Nashville: Broadman Press, 1954.

263. Barnette, Henlee. "Negro Students in Southern Baptist Seminaries [Louisville, Fort Worth, New Orleans, and San Francisco, since 1941]." Review and Expositor 53 (April 1956):207-10.

264. Barr, Browne. "Lineaments of Seminary Renewal." Christian Century 88 (January 27, 1971):97-101.

265. Barr, James. "Position of Hebrew Language in Theological Education?" Princeton Seminary Bulletin 55 (April 1962):16-24.

266. Barrabee, Susan Copenhaver. "Education for Liberation: Women in the Seminary." In Women's Liberation and the Church. Edited by S. Doely. 1970.

267. Barrick, William E. "Field Education in Protestant Theological Seminaries in the United States: An Interpretation of Major Trends, 1920-1970." Ed.D. dissertation, Columbia University. Under the Fac. of U.T.S. in the City of N.Y., 1975.

268. Barrois, Georges A. "Medieval Studies in a Program of Reformed Theology." Princeton Seminary Bulletin 55 (September 1961):17-24.

269. Barrows, M. "Bible in the Theological Curriculum." Journal of Religion 15 (October 1935):379-88.

270. Barrus, Ben M., Baughn, Milton L. and Campbell, Thomas H. A People Called Cumberland Presbyterians. Memphis: Frontier Press, 1972.

271. Barrymore, Henry J. "The Paradoxical Profession." Forum 29 (1900):188-202.

272. Barth, Eugene. "Schuylkill College: The Early Years." Historical Review of Berks County 35, no. 1 (1970):9-11, 24-31.

273. Barth, Karl, et al. "In Honor of Karl Barth." Chicago Theological Seminary Register 52 (April 1962):29.

274. Barth, Karl. Protestant Theology in the Nineteenth Century: Its Background and History. Translated from the German. London: SCM Press, 1972.

275. Bartholomew, Allen R. Our Reformed Church, 1725 - Then and Now - 1925. Philadelphia: Board of Foreign Missions, Reformed Church in the United States, 1926?

276. Bartlett, E. R. "Religious Education in Church Colleges and Theological Schools [bibliog.]." In Orientation in Religious Education, pp. 352-64. Edited by Philip Henry Lotz. New York: Abingdon-Cokesbury Press, 1950.

277. Bartlett, G. E. "Clinical Training in One
      Church." Christian Century 57 (July 24,
      1940):927.

278. Bartlett, Josiah R. Report of Unitarian
      Universalist Ministerial Shifts Study.
      Berkeley: Wright Institute, 1969.

279. Barton, George Aaron. American Schools of
      Oriental Research. N.p., 1923?

280. Barton, J. L. "(Work, Needs and Claims of New
      England Congregational Theological Semi-
      naries.)" Hartford Seminary Record 15
      (1905):24+.

281. Bartow, Charles Louis. "An Evaluation of
      Student Preaching in the Basic Homiletics
      Courses at Princeton Theological Seminary:
      A Farmerian Approach to Homiletical
      Criticism." Ph.D. dissertation, New York
      University, 1971.

282. Battles, F. L. and Bodine, J. J. "Some
      Thoughts on Church History." Hartford
      Quarterly 4 (Spring 1964).

283. [Baugher, Henry Louis] "Theological Education
      in the Lutheran Church in the United
      States." Evangelical Review 1 (July
      1849):19-39.

284. Baughman, Harry Fridley. "That the Man of God
      May be Adequate." Lutheran Quarterly 4
      (May 1952):191-205.

285. Baumgaertner, W. "Communications and Pastoral
      Studies." Momentum 13 (February 1982):18-
      19.

286. Baumgaertner, William L. "States and Accred-
      itation: A Case Study [in Minnesota]."
      Theological Education 14 (Autumn 1977):38-
      42.

287. Baur, John C. "For Christ and His Kingdom,
      1923." Concordia Historical Institute
      Quarterly 50 (Fall 1977):99-105.

288. Baxter, Richard. Gildas Salvianus: The
      Reformed Pastor. 2d ed. London: Epworth
      Press, 1955. (Originally published 1656).

289. Beach, David Nelson. "Primary Qualifications
      for the Ministry." Andover Review 19 (May
      1893):288-309.

290. Beach, Harlan P. "The Preparation of
      Missionaries at Home and on the Mission
      Field." International Review of Missions 2
      (1913):733-50.

291. Beach, Mark. "Professional Versus Profes-
      sorial Control of Higher Education."
      Educational Record 49 (Summer 1968):263-73.

292. Beach, R. F. "Ecumenism and Inter-Library
      Cooperation." Theological Education 1
      (Spring 1965):189-90.

293. Beals, Carleton. The Great Revolt and Its
      Leaders: The History of Popular American
      Uprisings in the 1890's. London, New York:
      Abelard-Schuman, 1968.

294. Beam, Richard Kenneth. "A Comparative Study
      of Three Categories of American Protestant
      Seminaries." Ed.D. dissertation, Univer-
      sity of Kentucky, 1981.

295. Beaman, Robert S. "Alexander Hall at the
      Princeton Theological Seminary." Princeton
      History no. 2 (1977):45-60.

296. Bearden, Donald Roland. "Competencies for a
      Minister of Music in a Southern Baptist
      Church: Implications for Curriculum
      Development." Ph.D. dissertation,
      Louisiana State University and Agricultural
      and Mechanical College, 1980.

297. Beardslee, W. A. "The Background of the Lilly
      Endowment Study of Pre-Seminary Education."
      Journal of Bible and Religion 34 (April
      1966).

298. Beardsley, William A. "Episcopal Academy of
      Connecticut." Historical Magazine of the
      Protestant Episcopal Church 13 (September
      1944):193-215.

299. Beatty, Donald C. "Reflections on the Early
      Beginnings of the Clinical Training
      Movement." Pastoral Psychology 16 (May
      1965):27-30.

300. Beaven, A. W. "Should Theological Seminaries Prepare Their Students to Deal with Parish Family Problems?" Journal of Educational Sociology 8 (April 1935):489-504.

301. Beaven, Albert William. "The Colgate-Rochester Divinity School." Rochester Historical Society Publication 13 (1934): 165-9.

302. Beaver, R. Pierce. "The American Protestant Theological Seminary and Missions: An Historical Survey." Missiology 4 (January 1976):75-87.

303. Becgelhymer, H. "I Look Like I Belong up There: Use of Videotape Recorders for Student Preachers." Christian Century 95 (February 1, 1978):123-6.

304. Beck, Kenneth Nathaniel. "The American Institute of Sacred Literature: A Historical Analysis of an Adult Education Institution." Ph.D. dissertation, University of Chicago, 1968.

305. Becker, Edwin L. "The Contribution of Religious Field Work to the Seminary Student's Self Knowledge." Religious Education 57 (May 1962):203-8.

306. Becker, Edwin Lewis. "Religious Field Work as Experience in the Social Roles of the Minister: A Sociological Study of the Meaning of Religious Field Work in the Divinity School of Yale University." Ph.D. dissertation, Yale University, 1956.

307. Becker, Edwin L. "Theological Education as Education for Church Occupations." Theological Education 7 (Spring 1971):163-70.

308. Becker, Howard S. "The Professional Dance Musician and His Audience." American Journal of Sociology 57 (September 1951): 136-44.

309. Becker, Russell J. "Can Seminaries Train Pastors?" Christian Century 78 (April 26, 1961):513-15.

310. Becker, Russell, J. "In-Parish Pastoral Studies 1960-1966." Theological Education

3 (Spring 1967):403-18.

311. Becker, Russell James. "Place of the Parish in Theological Education." Journal of Pastoral Care 21 (Spring 1967):163-70.

312. Bedell, Gregory Thurston. The Pastor: Pastoral Theology. Philadelphia: J.B. Lippincott & Co., 1880.

313. Beech, L. A. "Supervision in Pastoral Care and Counseling: A Prerequisite for Effective Ministry." Journal of Pastoral Care 24 (December 1970):233-9.

314. Beecher, Henry Ward. "The Study of Human Nature." Popular Science Monthly 1 (July 1872):327-35.

315. Beecher, Lyman. An Address of the Charitable Society for the Education of Indigent Pious Young Men, for the Ministry of the Gospel. Concord: Printed by Hill & Moore, 1820.

316. Beecher, Lyman. Autobiography. 2 vols. Edited by Barbara M. Cross. Cambridge: Belknap Press of Harvard University Press, 1961. (Original edition, Charles Beecher, 1864).

317. Beecher, Lyman. A Plea for the West. Cincinnati: Truman & Smith, 1835.

318. Beecher, Willis Judson. "A Few Thoughts on New Departures in Religious Doctrine." An Address [January 21, 188?] Auburn, N.Y.: Knapp, Peck & Thomson, 1880.

319. Beekmann, Darold, Burtness, James, Fretheim, Terence and Sundberg, W. "Ten Faces of Ministry: A Conversation." Word and World: Theology for Christian Ministry 1 (Fall 1981):382-90.

320. Beeson, T. "Coventry's Pilot Program: Further Training for the Clergy." Christian Century 87 (September 23, 1970): 1113.

321. Behan, Walter Palmer. "The Department of Religious Education in Lay and Missionary Training Schools." Religious Education 10 (October 1915):442-4.

29

322. Behan, Warren Palmer. "An Introductory Survey of the Lay Training School Field." <u>Religious Education</u> 11 (February 1916):47-52.

323. Behney, J. Bruce and Eller, Paul H. <u>The History of the Evangelical United Brethren Church</u>. Edited by Kenneth W. Krueger. Nashville: Abingdon, 1979.

324. Belcher, Joseph. <u>The Clergy of America: Anecdotes Illustrative of the Character of Ministers of Religion in the United States</u>. Philadelphia: J.B. Lippincott & Co., 1849.

325. Belgum, David. "The Office of the Presidency in Denominational Theological Seminaries." <u>Theological Education</u> 6 (Summer 1970):294-302.

326. Bell, M. M. "Speaking for the Class of 1964." <u>Harvard Divinity Bulletin</u> 28 (July 1964): 113-15.

327. Bell, W. Herman. "Early Massachusetts Aid to 'Destitute' Regions of Virginia [Union Theological Seminary in Virginia]." <u>Essex Institute Historical Collections</u> 88 (July 1952):271-5.

328. Bellows, Henry Whitney. <u>An Appeal in Behalf of the Further Endowment of the Divinity School of Harvard University</u>. Cambridge: J. Wilson & Son, 1879.

329. Belsheim, David John. "Continuing Professional Education Centers for Ministry, Law, Education and Health Professions: An Analysis of the Relationship between Organizations and Their Environments." Ph.D. dissertation, University of Illinois at Urbana-Champaign, 1982.

330. Beman, Nathan Sidney Smith. <u>Collegiate and Theological Education at the West: A Discourse Delivered before the Society for the Promotion of Collegiate and Theological Education at the West, at its Annual Meeting at Springfield, Mass., Oct. 28, 1846</u>. New York: Printed by S. W. Benedict, 1847.

331. Bender, R. "Christian Education in Theological Education." Religious Education 62 (January 1967):18-24+.

332. Bender, R. T. "Seminary and Congregation: Communities of Discernment." Mennonite Quarterly Review 39 (July 1965):163-80.

333. Bender, Ross Thomas. The People of God: Report of the Study Project to Develop a Model for Theological Education in the Free Church Tradition. Scottsdale, Pa.: Herald Press, 1971.

334. Bennetch, John Henry. "The Advantage in Knowing the Biblical Languages." Bibliotheca Sacra 100 (January 1943):177-87.

335. Bennett, John Coleman. "Change and Continuity in the Theological Climate at Union Seminary." Union Seminary Quarterly Review 18 (May 1963):357-67.

336. Bennett, John C. "Comments on 'The Office of the Presidency.'" Theological Education 6 (Summer 1970):303-5.

337. Bennett, John C. et al. "Discussion: The Seminary in Ten Years." Union Seminary Quarterly Review 22, no. 4 (1967):329-45.

338. Bennett, John Coleman. "Faculty [of Union] Re-examines Its Work." Union Seminary Quarterly Review 12 (January 1957):25-9.

339. Bennett, John Coleman. "Inaugural Address." Union Seminary Quarterly Review 19 (May 1964):397-408.

340. Bennett, John Coleman. "Priorities in Theological Education." Christianity and Crisis 29 (April 14, 1969):87-90.

341. Bennett, John C. "Theological Education and Social Revolution." Theological Education 3 (Winter 1967):283-90.

342. Bennett, Margaret. The Ministry of the Methodist Episcopal Church: Educational Status and Numerical Strength. Chicago: Methodist Episcopal Church, Commission on Life Service, 192-.

343. Bennett, Rollo James. "History of the Founding of Educational Institutions by the Disciples of Christ in Virginia and West Virginia." University of Pittsburgh Bulletin 29 (January 1933).

344. "Bennett Elected Union President." Christian Century 81 (January 1, 1964):7.

345. Benson, G. A. "Church Needs Christian Lovers, Not Oedipal Boys: Ordination Sermon." Christian Century 88 (January 27, 1971):101-4.

346. Benson, J. Kenneth et al. "Theological Stance and the Positions of Pastors on Public Issues: Social and Organizational Contexts." Paper presented at the 1973 Annual Meeting of the Rural Sociological Society, College Park, Md., August 23-6, 1973. (ERIC Document)

347. Benson, John E. "Bad Time for Giants." Dialog 15 (Winter 1976):8-9.

348. Bentley-Doely, Sarah. "Woman Minister?" Theological Education 8 (Summer 1972):247-51.

349. Benton, Allen R. "Early Educational Conditions [in Indiana] and Founding of a Denominational College [Butler College]." Indiana Magazine of History 4 (March 1908):13-17.

350. Berelson, Bernard. Graduate Education in the United States. New York: McGraw Hill, 1960.

351. Berg, P. L. "Professionalism and Lutheran Seminarians." Lutheran Quarterly 20 (November 1968):406-11.

352. Berg, Philip L. "Self-Identified Fundamentalism among Protestant Seminarians: A Study of Persistence and Change in Value Orientations." Review of Religious Research 12 (Winter 1971):88-94.

353. Bergendoff, Conrad. "An Ancient Culture in a New Land." Swedish Pioneer Historical Quarterly 27, no. 2 (1976):127-34.

354. Bergendoff, Conrad. "Augustana: An Approaching Centennial." American-Scandinavian Review 32 (December 1944):294-303.

355. Bergendoff, Conrad. "The Augustana Four-Year Plan of Theological Education." Christian Education 19 (1935):120-5.

356. Bergendoff, Conrad. The Lutheran Church in America and Theological Education: A Report to the Board of Theological Education. N.p., 1963.

357. Bergendoff, Conrad. "Religious Resources and Obligations of the Church-Related College. Part VI. Theological Education." Christian Education 22 (February 1939):188-90.

358. Bergendoff, C. J. I. "Tenure at Augustana College." Bulletin of the American Association of University Professors 24 (May 1938):449-50.

359. Bergendoff, C. J. I. "Theological Education." Christian Education 22 (February 1939):188-90.

360. Bergendoff, Conrad. "Theology, the Church and the University." Lutheran Quarterly 13 (February 1961):3-18.

361. Berger, Peter L. "Religious Establishment and Theological Education." Theology Today 19 (July 1962):178-91.

362. Berger, Peter Ludwig. "Some Sociological Comments on Theological Education." Perspective 9 (Summer 1968):127-38.

363. Berger, Peter L. "Toward a More Scholarly Ministry." Christian Century 80 (April 24, 1963):524-7.

364. Berger, William Robert. "A Study of Student Values as an Index for Determination of the Feasibility of Adding Liberal Arts Major and Minor Programs to the Bible College Curriculum." Ed.D. dissertation, Oregon State University, 1976.

365. Bergland, James W. "Field Education as Locus for 'Theological Reflection.'" Theological Education 5 (Summer 1969):338-45.

366. Bergland, James Welsey. "The Nature of Theological Inquiry in Henry Nelson Wieman: A Critical Exposition of Wieman's Theological Position with an Exploration of some Implications for Theological Education in America." Th.D. dissertation, Union Theological Seminary in the City of New York, 1972.

367. Bergland, James W. "When Field Education Radicalizes: Reflection on New Pedagogies for the 70's." Theological Education 7 (Summer 1971):245-54.

368. Bergstresser, P. "Education for Ministry." Evangelical Quarterly Review 19 (1868):466-76.

369. Berk, Robert Jay. "The Assessment and Prediction of Certain Personality and Attitude Changes in Pastoral Counseling Trainees." Ph.D. dissertation, New York University, 1972.

370. Berle, A. A. "The Education of a Minister." Bibliotheca Sacra 64 (1907):283-98.

371. Berle, A. A. "Professor Moore on Ministerial Training." Bibliotheca Sacra 65 (July 1908):445-51.

372. Berle, A. A. "The Rout of the Theological Schools." Bibliotheca Sacra 64 (July 1907) 566-87.

373. Bernard, L. L. "Education of the Rural Ministry." School and Society 11 (January 17, 1920):68-73.

374. Bernards, Solomon S. "Theological Education for a Pluralistic Society: What we Teach about Each Other." Encounter 25 (Summer 1964):283-90.

375. Berry, P. "(Education for Ministry for the Times.)" Mercersburg Quarterly Review 7 (1855):614+.

376. Best, G. F. A. "Church Parties and Charities: The Experiences of Three American Visitors to England, 1823-1824 [Origins of General Theological Seminary]." English Historical Review 78, no. 307 (1963):243-62.

34

377. "Better Seminaries but Not in a Day."
     Christian Century 74 (April 24, 1957):507.

378. "Better Training for a Better Clergy?:
     American Association of Theological Schools
     Study." Time 89 (February 3, 1967):50.

379. Beverly, Urias H. "Blacks in Clinical
     Pastoral Education." Journal of Pastoral
     Care 36 (Summer 1982):203-8.

380. "Bible Colleges Search for Identity."
     Christian Life 25 (June 1964):23+.

381. "Bible Schools." In Patterson's American
     Education, pp. 452-3. North Chicago:
     Educational Directories, 1956-57.

382. "Bible Schools." In Patterson's American
     Educational Directory, 1951, p. 457. North
     Chicago: Educational Directories.

383. "Bible Study in Theological Seminaries." Old
     Testament Student 5 (March 1886):289-92.

384. Bibliography of Bible Study for Theological
     Students. Princeton, N.J.: Princeton
     Theological Seminary Library, 1948.

385. Bickersteth, Edward. Christian Student. 2
     vols. 5th ed. London: Seeleys, 1852-1853.

386. Biersdorf, John E. "Patterns: The 1967
     Consultation in Perspective." Theological
     Education 4 (Autumn 1967):566-72.

387. Bigelow, Dana W. "Whitestown Seminary." New
     York State Historical Association. Pro-
     ceedings 14 (1915):207-13.

388. Bikle, P. M. "Educating Men for the
     Ministry." Lutheran Quarterly Review 17
     (January 1887):60-79.

389. Binkley, Luther J. The Mercersburg Theology.
     Lancaster? Pa., 1953.

390. Binkley, Olin T. "The Education of Ministers
     in Contemporary Society." Theological
     Education 3 (Winter 1967):265-9.

391. Binkley, Olin T. "Southern Baptist Semina-
     ries." Christian Century 80 (June 12,

1963):774-5.

392. Binns, Walter Pope. "The Work They Sought To
Do [Southern Baptist Theological Seminary,
1859-1957]." Review and Expositor 54
(April 1957):223-32.

393. Birtch, George M. "Theological Education: A
Canadian Minister's View." Theological
Education 2 (Spring 1966):168-72.

394. The Bishops' Advice on Training for the
Ministry: A Symposium of Opinion.
Philadelphia: Philadelphia Divinity
School, 1932.

395. Bittenger, Emmert F. "Marking One Hundred
Years of Brethren Higher Education."
Brethren Life and Thought 25 (Spring
1980):71-82.

396. Black, H. "Classical Studies as a Preparation
for the Study of Theology, from the Point
of View of the Profession." School Review
16 (October 1908):533-7.

397. Black, Hugh. "The Value of Humanistic,
Particularly Classical, Studies as a
Preparation for the Study of Theology, from
the Point of View of the Profession."
School Review 16 (October 1908):533-7.

398. Black, Robert Eugene. The Story of Johnson
Bible College. Kimberlin Heights, Tenn.:
Tennessee Valley Printing Co., 1951.

399. Blackburn, William M. Church History: The
Exponent of Godly Life and Doctrine: A
Lecture. Chicago: Church, Goodman &
Donnelley, Printers, 1868.

400. Blackman, George L. Faith and Freedom: A
Study of Theological Education and the
Episcopal Theological School. New York:
Seabury Press, 1967.

401. Blackstone, William E. Jesus is Coming. New
York: Fleming H. Revell Co., 1908.

402. Blackwood, James R. "Enter the Seminary
Intern!" Christian Century 62 (July 18,
1945):836-7.

403. Blaikie, William Garden. The Colleges and
Theological Institutions of America.
Edinburgh: Andrew Elliot, 1870.

404. Blaikie, William Garden. For the Work of the
Ministry: A Manual of Homiletical and
Pastoral Theology. London: Strahan & Co.,
1873.

405. Blake, Eugene Carson. "The Ministry and
Church Union." McCormick Quarterly 17
(March 1964):30-4.

406. Blakemore, W. Barnett. "The Nature and
Structure of the Practical Field." Journal
of Religion 29 (October 1949):284-300.

407. Blanchard, Dallas A. "Seminary Effects on
Professional Role Orientations." Review of
Religious Research 22 (June 1981):346-61.

408. Blandy, Gray M. and Brown, Lawrence L. The
Story of the First Twenty-Five Years of the
Episcopal Theological Seminary of the
Southwest. Austin, Tex.: Episcopal
Theological Seminary of the Southwest,
1976.

409. Blanton, Robert J. "The Future of Higher
Education for Negroes." Journal of Negro
Education 9 (April 1940):177-82.

410. Blau, Peter M., Cullen, John B., Margulies,
Rebecca Z., and Silver, Hilary.
"Dissecting Types of Professional Schools."
Sociology of Education 52 (January 1979):7-
19.

411. Bledstein, Burton J. The Culture of Profes-
sionalism: The Middle Class and the
Development of Higher Education in America.
New York: W. W. Norton & Co., 1976.

412. Blizzard, Samuel W. "The Minister's Dilemma."
Christian Century 73 (April 25, 1956):508-
10.

413. Blizzard, Samuel W. "The Roles of the Rural
Parish Minister, the Protestant Seminaries,
and the Sciences of Social Behavior."
Religious Education 50 (November-December
1955):383-92.

414. Blizzard, S. W. "Training of the Parish
     Minister." Union Seminary Quarterly Review
     11 (January 1956):45-50.

415. Bloomquist, Karen L. "Women's Rising Con-
     sciousness: Implications for the Curric-
     ulum." Theological Education 8 (Summer
     1972):233-40.

416. Blount, L. F. and Boyle, J. H. "Theological
     Seminary and the Pastor's Wife." Pastoral
     Psychology 12 (December 1961):40-5+.

417. Board, C. S. "Second Thoughts on the Bible
     College." Eternity (June 1967):20-2+.

418. Board of Higher Education. Higher Education
     for Disciples of Christ. Indianapolis:
     Board of Higher Education, 19?

419. Board of Missionary Preparation (for North
     America). The Report of a Conference on
     the Preparation of Women for Foreign
     Missionary Service Dec. 5-7, 1915. New
     York: Board of Missionary Preparation,
     1915.

420. Boardman, M. T. "Correlation between the
     Church College and the Theological
     Seminary." Christian Education 17
     (December 1933):107-10.

421. Bodine, William B., ed. Statement of Facts
     Bearing upon the Proposed Changes in the
     Constitution of the Theological Seminary of
     the Protestant Episcopal Church in the
     Diocese of Ohio, and of Other facts Bearing
     upon the Welfare of the Institution.
     Prepared by a committee of the Board of
     Trustees. Columbus, Ohio: Nitschke Bros.,
     1890.

422. Bohlmann, Ralph A. "Closing the Academic
     Year." Concordia Journal 7 (September
     1981):186-7.

423. Bohn, Carole R. "Women in Theological
     Education: Realities and Implications."
     Ed.D. dissertation, Boston University
     School of Education, 1981.

424. Boice, James M. "Church and Seminary: A
     Reciprocal Relationship." Christianity

Today 23 (February 2, 1979):14-15.

425. Boisen, Anton Theophilus. "The Challenge to
     Our Seminaries." Journal of Pastoral Care
     5 (Spring 1951):8-12.

426. Boisen, A. T. "Cooperative Inquiry in
     Religion." Journal of Pastoral Care 5, no.
     1 (1951):17-26.

427. Boisen, A. T. "Ideas of Prophetic Mission
     [Theological Students]." Journal of
     Pastoral Care 15 (Spring 1961):1-6.

428. Boisen, A. T. "Period of Beginnings."
     Journal of Pastoral Care 5, no. 1
     (1951):13-16.

429. Boisen, A. T. "Theological Education via the
     Clinic." Religious Education 25 (March
     1930):235-9.

430. Boles, John B. The Great Revival 1787-1805:
     The Origins of the Southern Evangelical
     Mind. Lexington: University Press of
     Kentucky, 1972.

431. Bollinger, Richard A. "Brethren and the
     Church: Second Theological Study Con-
     ference." Christian Century 81 (August 26,
     1964):1062-3.

432. "Bolshevism at Middletown [Berkeley Divinity
     School]." Nation 111 (July 24, 1920):90-1.

433. Bolster, Arthur Stanley. James Freeman
     Clarke: Disciple to Advancing Truth.
     Boston: Beacon Press, 1954.

434. Bonacker, R. D. "Clinical Training for the
     Pastoral Ministry: Purposes and Methods."
     Journal of Pastoral Care 14 (Spring 1960):
     1-12.

435. Bonfils, E. "Practical Professorship in
     Theological Seminaries." Outlook 52
     (December 14, 1895):1022-3.

436. Bonthius, Robert H. and Brown, Jon K. "The
     Metropolis as the Context for Theological
     Education." In Explorations in Ministry.
     Edited by G. Douglass Lewis. New York:
     IDOC North America, 1971.

437. Bonthius, Robert Harold. "Resources Planning in Theological Education: A Response and an Offer." Theological Education 5 (Winter 1969):67-72.

438. Bonthius, Robert H. "Theological Education for Revolutionary Response." Drew Gateway 39 (Autumn 1968):50-65.

439. Boomershine, Tom. "The Rich and the Poor in Theological Education," Motive 30 (February 1970):20-30.

440. Boon, Harold Watson. "The Development of the Bible College or Institute in the United States and Canada since 1880 and Its Relationship to the Field of Theological Education in America." Ed.D. dissertation, New York University, 1950.

441. Boon, H. W. "How It All Began." Christian Life 21 (June 1959):36-7.

442. Boorstin, Daniel J. "Universities in the Republic of Letters." Perspectives in American History 1 (1967):369-79.

443. Booth, Gotthard. "Unconscious Motivation in the Choice of the Ministry as Vocation." Pastoral Psychology 9 (December 1958):18-24.

444. Booth, William. In Darkest England and the Way Out. London: International Headquarters of the Salvation Army, 1890.

445. Boozer, J. "Three Revolutions or One? [Pre-Seminary Education]." Journal of Bible and Religion 34 (April 1966).

446. Born, P. "Qualifications for the Gospel Ministry." Lutheran Quarterly 9 (October 1879):603-12.

447. Borrowman, Merle L. "The Professional Education of Teachers: A Search for the Golden Mean." Theological Education 5 (Spring 1969):222-39.

448. Bosch, David J. "Theological Education in Missionary Perspective." Missiology 10 (January 1982):13-34.

449. Bostrom, Harvey Rader. "Contributions to Higher Education by the Society for the Promotion of Collegiate and Theological Education at the West, 1843-1874." Ph.D. dissertation, New York University, 1960.

450. Bosworth, Edward I. "The School for Religious Leadership." Religious Education 2 (October 1907):127-34.

451. Bosworth, Edward Increase. "Seminaries and Non-College Students." Religious Education 16 (June 1921):153-7.

452. Bouma, Gary D. "Samuel W. Blizzard's Contribution to Ministry Studies and Theological Education." Pastoral Psychology 28 (Spring 1980):199-208.

453. Boutwell, Charles Rodney. "The Relationship between Early Parental Influences and Empathy in Theological Students." Ph.D. dissertation, University of Tennessee, 1964.

454. Bowden, Henry Warner. Church History in the Age of Science: Historiographical Patterns in the United States 1876-1918. Chapel Hill: University of North Carolina Press, 1971.

455. Bowden, Henry Warner. "Science and the Idea of Church History, an American Debate." Church History 36, no. 3 (1967):308-26.

456. Bowen, Elias. "Education for the Ministry." Christian Advocate (New York) 15 (December 9, 1840):65.

457. Bowen, Elias. A Sermon on Ministerial Education, Delivered before the Oneida Annual Conference, at Wilkes-Barre, August 16, 1843. Utica, N.Y.: R. W. Roberts, Printer, 1845.

458. Bower, William Clayton. "Building a Theological Curriculum around the Problems of the Student." Religious Education 23 (June 1928):546-50.

459. Bower, William Clayton. Through the Years: Personal Memoirs. Lexington, Ky.: Transylvania College Press, 1957.

41

460. Bower, W. C. "Training of the Ministry for a
     New World Order." Religious Education 40
     (January 1945):12-18.

461. Bowie, Mary Ella. Alabaster and Spikenard:
     The Life of Iva Durham Vennard. Chicago:
     Chicago Evangelistic Institute, 1947.

462. Bowman, C. M. "Minister's Training - One Pew
     View." Religion In Life 22, no. 1 (1952):
     58-71.

463. Bowman, C. V. "Ansgarius College." Swedish-
     American Historical Bulletin 2 (August
     1929):19-30.

464. Bowman, J. C. "(Theological Professor
     Instructed.)" Reformed Church Review 47
     (1900):153+.

465. Bowman, Mary Jo and Deeter, Allen C. "Peace
     Witness in Our Time." Brethren Life and
     Thought 23 (Winter 1978):6-63.

466. Bowman, R. D. "Some Needs of the Post-War
     World and Their Implications for the
     Seminary Curriculum." Christian Education
     26 (June 1943):256-62.

467. Bowman, S. L. "Inspiration and Infalli-
     bility." Methodist Review 71 (March
     1889):169-85.

468. Boyd, Carpenter W. "(Education for the
     Ministry.)" Hibbert Journal 3 (1905):433+.

469. Boyd, Malcolm. As I Live and Breathe: Stages
     of an Autobiography. New York: Random
     House, 1969.

470. Boyers, Auburn Archie. "Changing Conceptions
     of Education in the Church of the
     Brethren." Ed. D. dissertation, University
     1957):27.

471. Boyle, Leonard E. Pastoral Care, Clerical
     Education and Canon Law. Variorum, 1981.

472. Braaten, Carl E. "The Contextual Factor in
     Theological Education." Dialog 21 (Summer
     1982):169-74.

473. Bradbury, John W. "What are Ecumenical Pressures Doing to the Seminaries?" Christianity Today 10 (December 3, 1965): 15-17.

474. Bradley, C. F. "(Best Training for Christian Ministry.)" Quarterly Review of the Methodist Episcopal Church, South 46 (1886):911+.

475. Bradley, Ian. The Call to Seriousness: The Evangelical Impact on the Victorians. London: Cape; New York: Macmillan, 1976.

476. Bradley, J. C. "Continuing Education for Religious Educators." Religious Education 63 (September-October 1968).

477. Bradley, John. "The Nature of the Ministry We Seek." National Council Outlook 7 (June 1957):27.

478. Bradley, W. L. "Ethics and Apologetics in the New Curriculum." Hartford Quarterly 4 (Spring 1964).

479. Bradley, W. L. "Thoughts on the Teaching of Theology in Our Contemporary Setting." Hartford Quarterly 4 (Autumn 1963):33-44.

480. Bradshaw, Vinton David. "Supervised Concurrent Field Education at Christian Theological Seminary." Th.D. dissertation, Boston University School of Theology, 1972.

481. Branson, Mark L. "Evangelism and Social Ethics: Some Practical Implications. 1. Church, University and Seminary." Perkins School of Theology: Journal 35 (Winter-Spring 1982):17-20.

482. Branson, Mark L. "TSF Membership Survey and TSF Bulletin." TSF Bulletin 4 (October 1980):2-4.

483. Brash, William Bardsley. The Story of Our Colleges, 1835-1935: A Centenary Record of Ministerial Training in the Methodist Church. London: Epworth, 1935.

484. Brastow, L. O. "(Appeal of Theological School to Christian Men of Wealth.)" Yale Divinity Quarterly 2 (1906):27+.

485. Brastow, Lewis O. "Ministerial Training."
     New Englander 54 (February 1891):160.

486. Brauch, Manfred T. "Head and Heart Go to
     Seminary." _Christianity Today_ 19 (June 20,
     1975):11-12.

487. Brauer, Jerald C. "Lutheranism in American
     Theological Education." _Concordia Theo-
     logical Monthly_ 36 (June 1965):373-84.

488. Brauer, Jerald Carl. "Protestant Theological
     Education." _Christian Century_ 73 (April
     25, 1956):503-6.

489. Braver, Jerald C. and Malone, Edward F.
     "Planning for the Future: A Key Question.
     Why Keep the AATS." _Theological Education_
     4 (Spring 1968):728-34.

490. "Breaking the Pattern [Chicago]." _Time_ 66
     (October 24, 1955):46+.

491. Breasted, Charles. _Pioneer to the Past: The
     Story of James Henry Breasted._ New York:
     Charles Scribner's Sons, 1943.

492. Breasted, James Henry. _The Oriental Institute
     of the University of Chicago: A Beginning
     and a Program_. Chicago: University of
     Chicago Press, 1922.

493. Breckinridge, William Lewis. _Theological
     Seminaries in the West_. Louisville: Hull
     & Bro., 1850.

494. Breed, David Riddle. "Bible Institutes of the
     United States." _Biblical Review_ 12 (July
     1927):372-8.

495. Breimeier, Kenneth H. "The Fieldwork Program
     at Concordia Seminary." _Concordia Theo-
     logical Monthly_ 35 (December 1964):735-9.

496. Brekke, Milo L. "Instrumentation to Assess
     Readiness for Ministry." Paper presented
     at the 60th Annual Meeting of the American
     Educational Research Association, San
     Francisco, April 19-23, 1976. (ERIC
     Document)

497. Brekke, Milo L., Schuller, David S., and
     Strommen, Merton P. "Readiness for

Ministry: Report on the Research."
Theological Education 13 (Autumn 1976):22-
30.

498. Bremer, Paul L. "The Aims and Nature of the
Work in New Testament at the Reformed Bible
College." In _The New Testament Student and
Bible Translation_. Edited by J. H.
Skilton. Phillipsburg, N.J.: Presbyterian
and Reformed Pub. Co., 1978.

499. Brenner, D. "A Progression into Light: The
Hartford Seminary by Richard Meier &
Partners." _Architectural Record_ 170
(January 1982):65-73.

500. Brenner, Scott Francis. "Nevin and the
Mercersburg Theology." _Theology Today_ 12
(April 1955):43-56.

501. Brent, John. "Two New Ministries." _Munsey's
Magazine_ 27 (1902):908-12.

502. Brereton, Virginia Lieson. "The Invisible
Women: Workers and Wives." _Theological
Education_ 8 (Summer 1972):252-6.

503. Brereton, Virginia Lieson. "Protestant
Fundamentalist Bible Schools, 1882-1940."
Ph.D. dissertation, Columbia University,
1981.

504. Bretscher, Paul Martin. "Lutheran Education
and Philosophy." _Concordia Theological
Monthly_ 28 (April 1957):250-74.

505. Bridge, J. D. "Methodism, Theological
Seminary, Etc." _Zion's Herald_ 10
(September 18, 1839):149.

506. Bridges, Charles. _The Christian Ministry:
With an Inquiry into the Causes of Its
Inefficiency_. New York: Robert Carter &
Brothers, 1859.

507. Bridges, R. "Change in Climate." _Vital
Speeches_ 12 (May 1, 1946):437-8.

508. Bridston, Keith R. "The Cosmos and the Ego."
Religion In Life 28 (1958-9):34-45.

509. Bridston, Keith R. "Discussions on
Theological Education: An Ecumenical

Survey." <u>Encounter</u> 18 (Spring 1957):152-66.

510. Bridston, Keith R. "Form and Function in the Education of Ministers." <u>Theological Education</u> 4 (Autumn 1967):543-55.

511. Bridston, Keith R. and Culver, Dwight W., eds. <u>The Making of Ministers: Essays on Clergy Training Today</u>. Minneapolis: Ausburg Publishing House, 1964.

512. Bridston, Keith R. <u>Pre-Seminary Education: Report of the Lilly Endowment Study</u>. Minneapolis, Augsburg Publishing House, 1965.

513. Bridston, Keith R. "Theological Education for the Pacific Northwest, Survey and Proposal." Pacific Northwest Council on Theological Education, Portland, Oregon, 1965.

514. Bridston, Keith. <u>Theological Training in the Modern World</u>. Geneva: Worlds's Student Christian Federation, 1945.

515. Bridston, Keith R. "The Trivial and the Ultimate: A Report on the Case-Study Institute." <u>Theological Education</u> 9 (Autumn 1972):58-66.

516. <u>A Brief Outline of the Mode of Instruction Pursued by the Rev. John M. Mason, D.D. in the Theological Seminary Lately under His Care in the City of New-York</u>. New York: John P. Haven, 1828.

517. Briggs, C. A. "The Alienation of Church and People." <u>Forum</u> 16 (1893):366-78.

518. Briggs, Charles Augustus. <u>Biblical Study: Its Principles, Methods and History</u>. New York: Charles Scribner's Sons, 1883.

519. Briggs, C. A. "A Critical Study of the History of the Higher Criticism with Special Reference to the Pentateuch." <u>Presbyterian Review</u> 4 (1883):69-130.

520. Briggs, Charles Augustus. <u>History of the Study of Theology</u>. New York: Charles Scribner's Sons, 1916.

521. Briggs, Charles Augustus. "Is the Christian Religion Declining?" Popular Science Monthly 56 (February 1900):423-30.

522. Briggs, C. A. "A Plea for the Higher Study of Theology." American Journal of Theology 8 (July 1904):433-51.

523. Briggs, Charles A. "The Scientific Study of Holy Scripture." Independent 51 (November 30, 1899):3206-10.

524. Briggs, C. A. "Theological Education and Its Needs." Forum 12 (1892):634-45.

525. Briggs, Charles Augustus. Whither? A Theological Question for the Times. New York: Charles Scribner's Sons, 1889.

526. Briggs, Emilie Grace. "The Deaconess as a Missionary." Homiletic Review 66 (August 1913):108-12.

527. Briggs, Emilie Grace. "The Deaconess as Pastor's Assistant." Homiletic Review 65 (June 1913):458-63.

528. Briggs, Emilie Grace. "The Restoration of the Order of Deaconesses." Biblical World 41 (June 1913):382-90.

529. Briggs, G. W. "Theological Curriculum, the Christian and the World [bibliog.]." Review of Religion 12 (November 1947):5-28.

530. Briggs, Kenneth A. "Broadened Ministry Sought by Jersey Seminarians." New York Times 130 (May 23, 1981):11.

531. Briggs, Kenneth A. "Convicts in New York Study to be Ministers." New York Times 132 (December 4, 1982):13 (national ed.), 29 (late city ed.).

532. Bright, John. "The Academic Teacher and the Practical Needs of the Clergy." Theological Education 1 (Autumn 1964):35-52.

533. Brightman, Lloyd A. and Malette, Theodore A. "The Impact of the Seminary Experience on the Marital Relationship." Journal of Pastoral Care 31 (March 1977):56-60.

534. Briner, Lewis A. "The New Presbyterian System
     of Evaluating Candidates for Ordination."
     Theological Education 7 (Winter 1971):92-
     101.

535. "Bringing the Seminary to the Church."
     Christian Century 99 (March 10, 1982):273-
     4.

536. Briscoe, D. Stuart et al. "Impossible Dream:
     Can Seminaries Deliver." Christianity
     Today 21 (February 4, 1977):18-21.

537. Brittain, Raymond F. "The History of the
     Associate, Associate Reformed and United
     Presbyterian Theological Seminaries in the
     United States." Ph.D. dissertation, Uni-
     versity of Pittsburgh, 1945.

538. Broadus, John Albert. Favorite Sermons of
     John A. Broadus. Edited by Vernon Latrelle
     Stanfield. New York: Harper, 1959.

539. Broadus, John A. Memoir of James Petigru
     Boyce: Late President of the Southern
     Baptist Theological Seminary, Louisville,
     Ky. New York: A.C. Armstrong & Son, 1893.

540. Broadus, John Albert. "Ministerial Educa-
     tion." In his Sermons and Addresses, pp.
     198-215. 2d ed. Baltimore: H. M. Wharton
     & Co., 1887.

541. Broadus, John A. "Reforms in Theological
     Education." Baptist Quarterly Review 7
     (1885):431-42.

542. Broadus, L. A., Jr. "Three Years of
     Dedication [College of the Bible,
     Lexington]." College of the Bible
     Quarterly 40 (January 1963):53-8.

543. Broadus, Loren. "What in the World Does
     Theology Have To Do with Leadership."
     Lexington Theological Quarterly 11 (July
     1976):73-84.

544. Broadwell, Robert E. "Government Aid - Buried
     Treasure." Theological Education 16
     (Spring 1980):442-4.

545. Brockway, Duncan. "Reading and Library Habits
     of Connecticut Pastors." ATLA Proceedings

28 (1974):125-7.

546. Brodhead, C. D. "Dr. J. H. Franklin Heads
     Crozer." Christian Century 51 (November
     14, 1934):1467.

547. Bronson, Benjamin Franklin and Cole, Jirah
     Delano, eds. The First Half Century of
     Madison University (1819-1869). New York:
     Sheldon & Co., 1872.

548. Bronson, Oswald Perry. "The Origin and
     Significance of the Interdenominational
     Theological Center." Ph.D. dissertation,
     Northwestern University, 1965.

549. Bronson, Oswald P. "Significance of the
     Interdenominational Theological Center."
     Journal of the Interdenominational Theo-
     logical Center 2 (Fall 1974):1-7.

550. Bronson, William White. A Memorial of the
     Rev. Bird Wilson. Philadelphia: J. B.
     Lippincott, 1864.

551. Brooks, Charles. A Statement of Facts from
     Each Religious Denomination in New England,
     Respecting Ministers' Salaries. Boston,
     1854.

552. Broome, C. Richard. "The Computer: For
     Seminaries?" Theological Education 7
     (Autumn 1970):28-37.

553. Brown, A. "(Wanted - A Chair of Tent-Making
     in Education for Ministry.)" Atlantic
     Monthly 84 (1899):794+.

554. Brown, Alva Ross. Faith, Prayer, Work: Being
     I. The Story of Johnson Bible College,
     II. Choice Quotations from Ashley S.
     Johnson. Kimberlin Heights, Tenn? 1935?

555. Brown, Alva Ross. Standing on the Promises.
     Knoxville, Tenn.: Printed by S.B. Newman &
     Co., 1928.

556. Brown, Arlo Ayres. "Pretheological Courses in
     College [Methodist Episcopal Church]."
     Christian Education 11 (January 1928):244-
     56.

557. Brown, Arthur W. Always Young for Liberty: A Biography of William Ellery Channing. Syracuse, N.Y.: Syracuse University Press, 1956.

558. Brown, C. B. "Theological Students Today: A Student's Perspective." Union Seminary Quarterly Review 14 (March 1959):32-6.

559. Brown, C. S. "Old Problem and a New Experiment." Christian Century 44 (January 20, 1927):77-9.

560. Brown, Charles Reynolds. My Own Yesterdays. New York: Century Co., 1931.

561. Brown, Cynthia Stokes. "The American Discovery of the German University: Four Students at Göttingen, 1815-1822." Ph.D. dissertation, Johns Hopkins University, 1964.

562. Brown, Dale W. "We Have Seen the Enemy and They Is Us." Post American 4 (April 1975):26-8.

563. Brown, Daniel Alan. "A Comparative Analysis of Bible College Quality." Ph.D. dissertation, University of California, Los Angeles, 1982.

564. Brown, Esther Lucile. Lawyers, Law Schools and the Public Service. New York: Russell Sage Foundation, 1948.

565. Brown, Francis. Introduction to Old Testament and Semitic Studies in Memory of William Rainey Harper. Chicago: University of Chicago Press, 1908.

566. Brown, Francis. "The Study of Theology in New York City." Columbia University Quarterly 12 (June 1910):261-7.

567. Brown, Harold O. J. "Can a Seminary Stand Fast." Christianity Today 19 (February 14, 1975):7-9.

568. Brown, Ira V. "The Higher Criticism Comes to America, 1880-1900." Journal of the Presbyterian Historical Society 38, no. 4 (1960):193-212.

569. Brown, Jerry Wayne. _The Rise of Biblical Criticism in America, 1800-1870._ Middletown, Conn.: Wesleyan University Press, 1969.

570. Brown, L. D. et al. "Interorganizational Information Sharing: A Successful Intervention that Failed: Consortium of Theological Schools." _Journal of Applied Behavioral Science_ 10 (October 1974):533-54.

571. Brown, Robert McAfee. "Robert McAfee Brown Remembers Henry Pitney Van Dusen." _Journal of Presbyterian History_ 56 (Spring 1978): 62-78.

572. Brown, Robert Ousley. "Curricular Change at the Pittsburgh Theological Seminary: A Critical Analysis of Challenge and Change." Ph.D. dissertation, University of Pittsburgh, 1980.

573. Brown, Sterling Wade. _The Changing Function at Disciple Colleges._ Chicago, 1939.

574. Brown, William Adams. _The Case for Theology in the University._ Chicago: University of Chicago Press, 1938.

575. Brown, William Adams. "A Century of Theological Education and After." _Reformed Church Review_ 5 (January 1926):18-38. (Same) _Journal of Religion_ 6 (July 1926):363-83.

576. Brown, William Adams. _The Church in America._ New York: Macmillan Co., 1922.

577. Brown, William Adams. "The Common Problems of Theological Schools." _Journal of Religion_ 1 (May 1921):282-95.

578. Brown, William Adams. _The Education of American Ministers._ New York: Institute of Social and Religious Research, 1934.

579. Brown, William Adams. _The Seminary and the Church. Address Delivered at the Opening of the Seminary Seventy-Eighth Academic Year, 1913._ New York, 1913.

580. Brown, William Adams. "The Seminary of Tomorrow." _Harvard Theological Review_ 12

(April 1919):165-78.

581. Brown, William Adams. A Teacher and His
     Times: A Story of Two Worlds. New York:
     Charles Scribner's Sons, 1940.

582. Brown, William Adams. Theological Education.
     New York: Macmillan, 1914.

583. Brown, William Adams. "Untrained Clergy."
     American Scholar 5 (May 1936):339-46.

584. Browne, Rev. George. The History of the
     British and Foreign Bible Society, From ...
     1804, to ... 1854. 2 v. London: The
     Society, 1859.

585. Browning, Don. "The Disciples Divinity House
     and the University." Criterion 17 (Autumn
     1978):4-7.

586. Browning, Don S. "Method in Religious Living
     and Clinical Education." Journal of
     Pastoral Care 29, no. 3 (1975):157-67.

587. Brownrigg, Joseph Wayne. "Film Study in
     Seminaries Accredited by the Association of
     Theological Schools in the United States
     and Canada." Th.D. dissertation, Boston
     University School of Theology, 1976.

588. Brownson, James Irwin. A History of the
     Western Theological Seminary at Allegheny
     City, Pa.: Being an Address Delivered in
     the Third Presbyterian Church of
     Pittsburgh...On the Occasion of the Alumni
     Re-union, April 17th, 1872. N.p., n.d.

589. Brubaker, L. E., Jr. "What Are You Doing
     Here, Elijah? [Address to National
     Association of Biblical Instructors,
     December 1959]." Journal of Bible and
     Religion 28 (April 1960):161-6.

590. Bruce, Archibald. Introductory and Occasional
     Lectures: For Forming the Minds of Young
     Men Intending the Holy Ministry, to
     Theological and Useful Learning, Religion
     and Good Manners. Whitburn, 1797.

591. Bruder, E. E. "Clinical Pastoral Training in
     Preparation for the Pastoral Ministry."
     Journal of Pastoral Care 16 (Spring

1962):25-33.

592. Bruder, E. E. "Clinical Training and the
     Student." Journal of Pastoral Care 6, no.
     1 (1952):13-16.

593. Bruder, E. E. "Minister's Authority in
     Pastoral Care [Inaugural Address at Wesley
     Theological Seminary]." Pastoral
     Psychology 13 (October 1962):17-24.

594. Bruder, E. E. "New Directions in Clinical
     Pastoral Training." Journal of Religion
     and Health 10, no. 2 (1971):121-37.

595. Bruder, E. E. "Overview of Clinical Pastoral
     Education." Pastoral Psychology 16 (May
     1965):13-20.

596. Bruder, E. E. "Present Emphases and Future
     Trends in Clinical Training for Pastoral
     Counseling." Pastoral Psychology 11 (April
     1960):33-43.

597. Bruder, E. E. and Barb, M. L. "Survey of Ten
     Years of Clinical Pastoral Training at
     Saint Elizabeths Hospital." Journal of
     Pastoral Care 10 (Summer 1956):86-94.

598. Bruder, E. E. "Theological Considerations in
     Clinical Pastoral Education." Journal of
     Pastoral Care 8, no. 3 (1954):135-46.

599. Bruder, E. E. "Time of Challenge [Continuing
     Education]." Pastoral Psychology 16 (May
     1965):5-7.

600. Bruder, E. E. "Training and the Mental
     Hospital Chaplain." Journal of Pastoral
     Care 11 (Fall 1957):136-45.

601. Brueggemann, Walter. "An Attempt at an Inter-
     disciplinary M. Div. Curriculum." Theo-
     logical Education 13 (Spring 1977):137-45.

602. Brueggemann, Walter Albert. "Ethos and Ecu-
     menism: The History of Eden Theological
     Seminary, 1925-1970." Ph.D. dissertation,
     Saint Louis University, 1974.

603. Bruggink, Donald J. "The Historical Back-
     ground of Theological Education." Reformed
     Review 19 (May 1966):2-17.

604. Bruins, Elton John. "The New Brunswick Theo-
     logical Seminary, 1884-1959." Ph.D. dis-
     sertation, New York University, 1962.

605. Brunger, Ronald A. "Albion College: The
     Founding of a Frontier School." Michigan
     History 51, no. 2 (1967):130-53.

606. Brunner, Edmund de Schweinitz. Church Life in
     the Rural South. New York: Negro Univer-
     sities Press, 1969. (Reprint of the 1923
     edition.)

607. Brunson, Alfred. The Gospel Ministry: Its
     Characteristics and Qualifications. New
     York: Printed for the Author, 1856.

608. Brunson, Alfred. "Ministerial Qualifica-
     tions." Northwestern Christian Advocate 2
     (May 17, 1854):77.

609. Brush, J. W. "Yoked in Fellowship: A
     Reminiscence of Andover Newton Theological
     School." Foundations 6 (October 1963):336-
     42.

610. Bryan, D. C. "Frontiers of Pastoral Clinical
     Education." Journal of Bible and Religion
     24 (October 1956):275-80.

611. Bryan, Katharine Courtney. "Student Per-
     ceptions Concerning the Utilization of
     Andragogical Concepts in Selected Process
     Elements within The Learning Environment of
     Southwestern Baptist Theological Seminary."
     Ed.D. dissertation, Southwestern Baptist
     Theological Seminary, 1980.

612. Bryan, William Jennings. In His Image. New
     York: Fleming H. Revell Co., 1922.

613. Bryant, Robert H. "Seizing of a Seminary -
     Part II." Christian Century 92 (June 11-
     18, 1975):589-90.

614. Bryce, James. The American Commonwealth. 3d
     ed. New York and London: Macmillan & Co.,
     1895, Vol. 2.

615. Buchanan, James David. The Professional. New
     York: Coward, McCann & Geoghegan, 1972.

616. Buche, Elwyn. "A Study of Broad Goals and
     Strategies for Bible College Students among
     Selected Bible Colleges." Ed.D. disserta-
     tion, Illinois State University, 1976.

617. Buckham, J. W. "Changing Ideals in Theo-
     logical Education." Religious Education 4
     (June 1909):237-9.

618. Buckham, John Wright. "Modern Theological
     Education." Bibliotheca Sacra 64 (January
     1907):135-47.

619. Buckley, Cathryn. "The Everett Institute
     [Baptist]." North Louisiana Historical
     Journal 8, no. 3 (1977):119-24.

620. "Building the Kingdom [Harvard Divinity
     School]." Time 64 (October 18, 1954):50+.

621. Buker, Raymond B. and Ward, Ted, comps. The
     World Directory of Mission Related Educa-
     tional Institutions. South Pasadena,
     Calif.: William Carey Library, 1972.

622. Bullard, Ward. "A Central Theological
     Seminary for Our Church." Christian
     Advocate and Journal (New York) 29
     (February 2, 1854):1.

623. Bullock, Frederick William Bagshawe. A
     History of Training for the Ministry of the
     Church of England in England and Wales from
     1800 to 1874. St. Leonard's-on-Sea: Budd
     & Gillatt, 1955.

624. Bunce, Charles M. "Concord at Concordia?"
     Christianity Today 13 (March 14, 1969):37.

625. Burder, Henry Forster. Mental Discipline:
     Or, Hints on the Cultivation of
     Intellectual and Moral Habits: Addressed
     Particularly to Students in Theology and
     Young Preachers. New York: Leavitt, 1830.

626. Burge, Charles Douglas. "Attitudes of
     Chaplains in the United States Army in
     Europe Toward Clinical Pastoral Education."
     Ph.D. dissertation, United States Inter-
     national University, 1982.

627. Burghardt, Walter J. "The Impact of Ecumen-
     ical Developments for Theological

Education: A Roman Catholic View."
Theological Education 3 (Winter 1967):298-307.

628. Burkhart, R. A. "Therapy and Training of Pastors." _Christianity Today_ 5 (July 3, 1961):5-7.

629. Burkholder, J. L. "Harvard's Merrill Fellowship Program." _Theological Education_ 1 (Summer 1965):213-25.

630. Burkholder, J. L. "Patterns of Continuing Education: Harvard's Merrill Fellowship Program." _Theological Education_ 1 (Summer 1965):215-18.

631. Burnett, Marshall Emmett. "United Methodist Ministers in the Mississippi Conference and Their Perceived Continuing Education Needs." Ed.D. dissertation, University of Southern Mississippi, 1981.

632. Burnham, F. W. "Scot Gives 43rd Sprunt Lectures [Union Theological Seminary in Virginia]." _Christian Century_ 71 (April 7, 1954):437.

633. "Burning Issue in the American Church." _Current Literature_ 41 (July 1906):73-4.

634. Burns, William Henry. _Answer to Criticism of Crisis in Methodism._ N.p., 1910.

635. Burr, Nelson R. "The Church's Librarians, the Historians and the Layman." _Historical Magazine of the Protestant Episcopal Church_ 37 (September 1968):311-18.

636. Burrell, P. S. "(Growing Reluctance of Able Men to Enter the Ministry.)" _Hibbert Journal_ 1 (1903):713+.

637. Burrows, M. "Bible in the Theological Curriculum." _Journal of Religion_ 15 (October 1935):379-88.

638. Burton, Ernest D. "The Demand for Men and Women of Education in the Orient." In _Students and the World-Wide Expansion of Christianity_, pp. 400-4. Edited by Fennell P. Turner. Student Volunteer Movement for Foreign Missions. International

Convention. 7th, Kansas, Mo., 1913-1914.
New York: SVMFM, 1914.

639. Burton, Ernest DeWitt. "Place of the New
Testament in a Theological Curriculum."
American Journal of Theology 16 (April
1912):181-95.

640. Burton, Ernest De Witt and Mathews, Shailer.
Principles and Ideals for the Sunday
School: An Essay in Religious Pedagogy.
Chicago: University of Chicago Press,
1907.

641. Burton, Ernest D. "The Supply of Educated Men
for the Ministry." Biblical World 29 (June
1907):447-50.

642. Burton, Ernest De Witt. "What Should the
Churches Demand of the Theological
Schools?" Biblical World 25 (New Series)
(January 1905):20-9.

643. Busing, Paul F. W. "Reminiscences of
Finkenwalde." Christian Century 78
(September 20, 1961):1108-11.

644. Bustanoby, Andre. "Guidelines for Prospective
Seminarians." Christianity Today 19
(February 14, 1975):11-12.

645. Butterfield, Jeanne A. and Hunter, George I.
Education for Supervised Ministries.
Newton Centre, Mass.: Boston Theological
Institute, 1980.

646. Butterfield, K. L. "Education of Ministers
for the Country Parish." Religious
Education 5 (December 1910):438-43.

647. Buxbaum, Melvin H. "Benjamin Franklin and
William Smith: Their School and Their
Dispute." Historical Magazine of the
Protestant Episcopal Church 39 (December
1970):361-82.

648. Buzzell, Sid S. "Preparation for Church
Leadership: Trends in Students' Leadership
Orientation after one Year in Dallas
Theological Seminary (Texas)." Ph.D.
dissertation, Michigan State University,
1983.

649. Byers, A. P. et al. "Recalled Early Parent-
     Child Relations, Adult Needs and Occupa-
     tional Choice: A Test of Roe's Theory:
     FRI and EPPS Tests [bibliog.]." Journal of
     Counseling Psychology 15 (July 1968):324-8.

650. Cable, David Blaine. "The Development of the
     Accrediting Function of the Americal Asso-
     ciation of Theological Schools, 1918-1938."
     Ph.D. dissertation, University of
     Pittsburgh, 1970.

651. Cabot, Richard Clarke. "Adventures on the
     Borderland of Ethics: A Plea for a
     Clinical Year in the Course of Theological
     Study." Survey 55 (December 1, 1925):274-
     7.

652. Cabot, Richard C. "Ethics and Business."
     Survey 56 (April 1, 1926):18.

653. Cabot, Richard Clarke. "Ethics and Educa-
     tion." Survey 56 (June 1, 1926):321-2.

654. Cabot, Richard Clarke. "Ethics and Social
     Work." Survey 56 (September 1, 1926):572-
     6.

655. Cabot, Richard C. "Ethics and the Medical
     Profession." Survey 55 (March 1, 1926):
     618.

656. Cabot, Richard C. "That Clinical Year."
     Survey (February 1, 1926):567.

657. "Cabot Proposes Clinical Year for Ministers."
     Christian Century 42 (December 24,
     1925):1618.

658. Cadbury, Henry Joel. "New Testament Scholar-
     ship: Fifty Years in Retrospect." Journal
     of Bible and Religion 28 (April 1960):194-
     8.

659. Caddy, James. "Committee on Standards of
     Accreditation: Accreditation Guidelines
     for the Doctor of Ministry and the Theo-
     logical Librarian." ATLA Proceedings 31
     (1977):34-44.

660. Caemmerer, Richard R. "No Continuing City: A
     Memoir of Change toward Deepening and
     Growth in Jesus Christ." Currents in

Theology and Mission 5 (October 1978):268-315.

661. Caemmerer, Richard Rudolph, ed. Toward a More Excellent Ministry. St. Louis: Concordia Publishing House, 1964.

662. Caldwell, Georgine G. "Continuing Education for Protestant Clergy in the USA: With Some Implications for the Situation in Taiwan." Taiwan Journal of Theology no. 2 (1980):155-66.

663. Calhoun, Daniel Hovey. Professional Lives in America, 1750-1850. Cambridge: Harvard University Press, 1965.

664. Calhoun, David Bays. "The Last Command: Princeton Theological Seminary and Missions (1812 - 1862). Ph.D. dissertation, Princeton Theological Seminary, 1983.

665. Calhoun, J. R. "By These Paths: Avenues of Pre-Theological Study." Encounter 18 (Spring 1957):174-81.

666. Calhoun, Robert Lowry. "Role of Historical Theology." Journal of Religion 21 (October 1941):444-54.

667. Calian, Carnegie S. "Effects of Faculty Unionization on Seminary Governance as Seen by a Faculty Member." Theological Education 12 (Autumn 1975):26-8.

668. Calian, Carnegie Samuel. "The Grassroots Theologian." Theological Education 5 (Summer 1969):373-9.

669. Calitis, J. "Speaking for the Class of 1965." Harvard Divinity Bulletin 29 (July 1965):103-6.

670. Calkins, Raymond. The Life and Times of Alexander McKenzie. Cambridge, Mass.: Harvard University Press, 1935.

671. Callahan, Daniel J. The Role of Theology in the University. Milwaukee: Bruce Publishing Co., 1967.

672. Calvin Seminary, Grand Rapids. Semi-Centennial Volume: Theological School and

Calvin College, 1876-1926. Grand Rapids, Mich.: Semi-Centennial Committee, 1926.

673. The Cambridge History of the Bible.
      Cambridge: University Press, 1963-   .
      Vol. 2: The West from the Reformation to
      the Present Day, edited by S.L. Greenslade.

674. Campbell, Alexander. "Bethany College."
      Millenial Harbinger 7 (Series 3) (1850):
      291-3.

675. Campbell, Alexander. "The Clergy - No. IV."
      In The Christian Baptist, pp. 34-6. 10th
      ed. Cincinnati: American Christian Pub-
      lication Society, 1854.

676. Campbell, Alexander. "School of the
      Preachers." Millennial Harbinger 6 (1835):
      478-9.

677. Campbell, Doak S. "The Crisis in Baptist
      Higher Education." Review and Expositor
      64, no. 1 (1967):31-40.

678. Campbell, Ernest T. "The Formation of
      Ministers for the Late 20th Century:
      Community on Campus." Theological Educa-
      tion 2 (Autumn 1965):3-8.

679. Campbell, George. Lectures on Systematic
      Theology, Pulpit Eloquence, and the
      Pastoral Character. London: Thomas Tegg,
      Richard Griffin & Co., 1840.

680. Campbell, George. Lectures on the Pastoral
      Character. Edited by James Fraser.
      London: Black, Parry, & Kingsbury, 1811.

681. Campbell, Jerry D. and Hickcox, Michael A.
      "Video Usage in the Seminary Setting."
      ATLA Proceedings 29 (1975):101-27.

682. Campbell, T. C. "Reflections on Confrontation
      at the Christian Theological Union."
      Theological Education 6 (Summer 1970).

683. Campbell, Thomas C. "Implications of the
      Seminary Population Data: A Sociologist's
      View." Theological Education 1 (Spring
      1965):176-9.

684. Canfield, James Hulme. The Training of the
     Clergy: From the Standpoint of a Layman,
     what Constitutes Adequate Preparation for
     the Priesthood of the Protestant Episcopal
     Church. Pittsburgh, 1903.

685. Cannon, James. Bishop Cannon's Own Story:
     Life As I Have Seen It. Durham, N.C.:
     Duke University Press, 1955.

686. Capen, E. W. "Kennedy School of Missions."
     Missionary Review of the World 43 (August
     1920):702-3.

687. Capen, Edward Warren. The Kennedy School of
     Missions. Hartford, Conn.: Hartford
     Seminary Foundation, 1936.

688. Capron, S. B. "House-to-House Visitation."
     In Christianity Practically Applied, vol.
     2, pp. 96-8. Evangelical Alliance for the
     United States of America. Conference.
     Chicago, 1893. New York: Baker & Taylor,
     1894.

689. Cardwell, Sue Webb. "The Development of
     Persistence Scales Using Items of the
     Theological School Inventory." Ph.D.
     dissertation, Indiana University, 1978.

690. Cardwell, Sue Webb. "The MMPI as a Predictor
     of Success among Seminary Students."
     Ministry Studies 1 (August 1967):3-20.

691. Cardwell, Sue Webb and Hunt, Richard A.
     "Persistence in Seminary and in Ministry."
     Pastoral Psychology 28 (Winter 1979):119-
     31.

692. Cardwell, Sue. "The Theological School
     Inventory: After Ten Years." Journal of
     Pastoral Care 28, no. 4 (1974):267-79.

693. Cardwell, Sue Webb. "Why Women Fail/Succeed
     in Ministry: Psychological Factors."
     Pastoral Psychology 30 (Summer 1982):153-
     62.

694. Carey, James William. "A History of the
     Western Baptist Theological Institution,
     Covington, Kentucky." Ph.D. dissertation,
     Southern Baptist Theological Seminary,
     1905.

695. Carlan, M. M. "Missouri Synod: Still the Church Militant." Commonweal 100 (May 3, 1974):208-12.

696. Carlson, Edgar M. "The University: Pro and Con." Lutheran Quarterly 18 (November 1966):325-8.

697. Carlson, Mable Dosia. "Pre Ministerial Students: Selected Characteristics Differentiating from Migrating Candidates." Ph.D. dissertation, University of Pittsburgh, 1967.

698. Carmickle, L. "Survey of Bible College Libraries." Christian Life 14 (April 1971):5.

699. The Carnegie Foundation for the Advancement of Teaching. Sixth Annual Report of the President and of the Treasurer, 1911, pp. 94-107.

700. Carnell, Edward John. "Orthodoxy: Cultic vs. Classical." Christian Century 77 (March 30, 1960):377-9.

701. Carney, Frederick S. "Interdisciplinary Seminars in Ethics and Law." Journal of Bible and Religion 33, no. 3 (1965):241-6.

702. Carpenter, Joel A. "Fundamentalist Institutions and the Rise of Evangelical Protestantism, 1929-42." Church History 49 (March 1980):62-75.

703. Carr, Aute L. "The Federated Theological Faculty of the University of Chicago." Theological Education 4 (Summer 1968, Suppl. 1):61-80.

704. Carr, Aute L. "The Interdenominational Theological Center." Theological Education 4 (Summer 1968, Suppl. 1):33-46.

705. Carr, John Crosbie. "The MMPI, Ministerial Personality and the Practice of Ministry." Ph.D. dissertation, Northwestern University, 1980.

706. Carr, John Lynn. "Immersing for Ministry: Education and Evangelism in Church and Seminary." Theological Education 15

(Spring 1979):146-54.

707. Carrell, William D. "American College
     Professors: 1750-1800." History of Educa-
     tion Quarterly 8, no. 3 (1968):289-305.

708. Carrigan, R. L. "Psychotherapy and the Theo-
     logical Seminary." Journal of Religion and
     Health 6 (April 1967):91-8; (Same) Drew
     Gateway 36, nos. 1-2 (1965-66):28-35.

709. Carroll, David W. "Initial Psychological
     Prediction as Related to Subsequent
     Seminary Performance." Ph.D. dissertation,
     Fordham University, 1967.

710. Carroll, Jackson W. "Continuity and Change in
     Theological Education." Religion in Life
     40, no. 3 (1971):315-30.

711. Carroll, Jackson. "Project Transition: An
     Assessment of ATS Programs and Services."
     Theological Education 18 (Fall 1981):45-
     165.

712. Carroll, Jackson Walker. "Seminaries and
     Seminarians: A Study of the Professional
     Socialization of Protestant Clergymen."
     Ph.D. dissertation, Princeton Theological
     Seminary, 1970.

713. Carr-Saunders, Alexander Morris and Wilson,
     Paul Alexander. The Professions. London:
     Frank Cass, 1964.

714. Carter, Charles W. "Culture and Theological
     Education." Wesleyan Theological Journal
     14 (Fall 1979):77-81.

715. Carter, Paul Allen. The Decline and Revival
     of the Social Gospel: Social and Political
     Liberalism in American Protestant Churches,
     1920-1940. Hamden, Conn.: Archon Books,
     1971.

716. Carter, Paul Allen. The Spiritual Crisis of
     the Gilded Age. Dekalb: Northern Illinois
     University Press, 1971.

717. Cartwright, Peter. Autobiography. New York:
     Carlton & Porter, 1857.

718. Carver, William Owen. "Dr. Fuller in Seminary Leadership." Review and Expositor 48 (January 1951):5-12.

719. Carver, William Owen. Out of His Treasure: Unfinished Memoirs. Nashville: Broadman Press, 1956.

720. Carver, William O. "William Heth Whitsitt: The Seminary's Martyr." Review and Expositor 51 (October 1954):449-69.

721. Case, S. J. "Rehabilitation of Church History in Ministerial Education." Journal of Religion 4 (May 1924):225-42.

722. "Case Study in Theological Education." Theological Education 1 (Spring 1974):entire issue.

723. Casey, Thomas. "Seminary and Parish Training." American Ecclesiastical Review 144 (1961):372-6.

724. Cash, William Levi. Relation of Personality Traits to Scholastic Aptitude and Academic Achievement of Students in a Liberal Protestant Seminary. Ann Arbor: University Microfilms, 1954.

725. Cashdollar, Charles D. "Pursuit of Piety: Charles Hodge's Diary, 1819-1820." Journal of Presbyterian History 55 (Fall 1977):267-84.

726. Caspersen, H. C. "Augsburg Seminarium." Symra; a Norwegian-American Quarterly 6 (1910):163-84.

727. Cass, William D. "Theological Seminary." Zion's Herald 10 (August 7, 1839):125.

728. Cassady, Maynard Lamar. "A Comparative Study of Two Generations of Theological Graduates in Union Theological Seminary, New York." Ph.D. dissertation, Teachers College, Columbia University, 1935.

729. Cassler, H. H. "Lutheran Clinical Pastoral Education Today." Lutheran Quarterly 19 (May 1967):152-62.

730. Cassler, Henry H. "Lutheran Involvement in Clinical Pastoral Education in the U.S.A." Lutheran World 22, no. 4 (1975):299-302.

731. Casteel, J. L. "College Speech Training and the Ministry." Quarterly Journal of Speech 31 (February 1945):73-7.

732. Cathey, Robert. "Afro-American Studies at Princeton Theological Seminary, 1977-1981." TSF Bulletin 5, no. 2 (Nov. - Dec. 1981): 13-14.

733. Catholic Church. Pope, 1939-   (Pius XII) Sedes Sapientiae (31 May 1956) English. The Apostolic Constitution, Sedes Sapientiae... on the Religious, Clerical and Apostolic Training to be Imparted to Clerics...." Washington: Catholic University of America Press, 1957.

734. Catir, Norman Joseph, Jr. "Berkeley's Successful Failure: A Study of George Berkeley's Contribution to American Education." Historical Magazine of the Protestant Episcopal Church 33 (March 1964):65-82.

735. Catlin, H. D. J. "Is Our Present Seminary Hebrew Worth While?" Biblical World 32 (September 1908):205-10.

736. Cato, John David. "The Counter-Cultural Student and Theological Education." Foundations 13 (October - December 1970): 360-8.

737. Cave, Alfred. Introduction to Theology: Its Principles, Its Branches, Its Results & Its Literature. 2d ed. Edinburgh: T & T Clark, 1896.

738. Cavers, David F. "Legal Education in Time of Change." Theological Education 5 (Spring 1969):170-92.

739. Cecil, Anthony C. The Theological Development of Edwards Amasa Park: Last of the "Consistent Calvinists." Chambersburg, Pa.: American Academy of Religion (Distributed by Scholars Press, Missoula, Mont., 1974).

740. Celsus. "Our Illiterate Students." *Christian Century* 43 (February 25, 1926):255-6.

741. "Centennial Edition [Western Theological Seminary of the Reformed Church in America]." *Reformed Review* 19 (May 1966):2-71.

742. Center for Applied Research in the Apostolate, Washington, D.C. *US Catholic Institutions for the Training of Candidates for the Priesthood.* Washington, 1971.

743. "Center for Theological Studies Established in Rochester." *Christian Century* 84 (October 25, 1967):1342.

744. Cephas. "Theological Seminaries." *Christian Advocate* (Western edition) 1 (December 19, 1834):133.

745. Chadwick, J. W. "Harvard Divinity School." *New England Magazine* 11 (New Series) (February 1895):740-55.

746. Chadwick, Owen. *The Secularization of the European Mind in the Nineteenth Century.* New York: Cambridge University Press, 1975.

747. Chadwick, Owen. *The Victorian Church.* 2 vols. New York: Oxford University Press, 1966-70.

748. Chafer, L. S. "Why Substitutes? [Curriculum]." *Bibliotheca Sacra* 97 (October 1940):385-6.

749. Chalinor, R. H. "Student Evaluation of Clinical Training." *Journal of Pastoral Care* 3, nos. 3-4 (1949):36-8.

750. Chalmers, T. "On the Use of Text Books in Theological Education; Advice to Students on the Conduct and Prosecution of Their Studies." In his *Posthumous Works,* vol. 9, pp. ix, xxii. New York: Harper, 1855-60.

751. Champion, Leonard George. "Reflections upon the Present Curriculum of Theological Colleges." *Baptist Quarterly* 19 (April 1962):270-6.

752. "A Chance for a New Sort of Theological Educa-
      tion." Christian Century 46 (October 30,
      1929):1333.

753. Chandler, Douglas R. "Enthusiasm vs. Educa-
      tion? Early Methodist Preachers in New
      England." Duke Divinity School Review 34
      (Autumn 1969):188-95.

754. Chandler, Douglas R. Pilgrimage of Faith: A
      Centennial History of Wesley Theological
      Seminary, 1882-1982. Cabin John, Md.:
      Seven Locks Press, 1984.

755. Chandler, R. "Melodyland School: The
      Spirit's Tune: First Charismatic
      Institution." Christianity Today 17 (July
      20, 1973):42.

756. Chandler, R. "Preus on Concordia: No
      Progress Reports." Christianity Today 15
      (February 26, 1971):48.

757. Channing, W. E. "Extracts from Observations
      on the Proposition for Increasing the Means
      of Theological Education at the University
      in Cambridge." In his Works, vol. 5, pp.
      363-71. 16th ed. Boston: Crosby, Nichols
      & Co., 1859.

758. Channing, William Ellery. Observations on the
      Proposition for Increasing the Means of
      Theological Education at the University of
      Cambridge. Cambridge: Printed by Hilliard
      & Metcalf, 1816.

759. Chapell, Bryan. "Scramble for Students is on
      as Seminary Boom Days Fade." Christianity
      Today 24 (October 10, 1980):92+.

760. Chapman, Kathryn Nelson. "An Identification
      and Review of Components Necessary in a
      Master Degree Program Designed for the
      Professional Development of the Minister to
      Children in the Southern Baptist Conven-
      tion." Ed.D. dissertation, Saint Louis
      University, 1983.

761. Chappell, W. L. "Training Women for City,
      Home and Foreign Missionary Service."
      Religious Education 11 (December 1916):508-
      11.

762. Chave, Ernest J. "Religious Education in a
     Liberal Seminary." *Journal of Religion* 29
     (April 1949):124-35.

763. Cheek, John Lambuth. *The Translation of the
     Greek New Testament in America: A Phase of
     the History of American Criticism and
     Interpretation*. Chicago, 1942.

764. Chesham, Sallie. *Born to Battle: The Salva-
     tion Army in America*. Chicago: Rand
     McNally & Co., 1965.

765. "Chicago at 100: Chicago's Divinity School."
     Time 87 (March 25, 1966):74+.

766. Chicago Christians for Socialism. "Process
     Report and Critique on Theological Educa-
     tion." *Radical Religion* 4, no. 3-4
     (1979):43-5.

767. Child, Frank Samuel. *The Colonial Parson of
     New England*. New York: Baker & Taylor
     Co., 1896.

768. Childers, R. D. and White, W. F. "Personality
     of Select Theological Students: Marlowe-
     Crowne Social Desirability Scale
     [bibliog.]." *Personnel and Guidance
     Journal* 44 (January 1966):507-10.

769. Chiles, Robert Eugene. *Theological Transition
     in American Methodism: 1790-1935*. New
     York: Abingdon Press, 1965.

770. Chitty, Arthur Ben. "College of Charleston:
     Episcopal Claims Questioned, 1785--."
     *Historical Magazine of the Protestant
     Episcopal Church* 37 (December 1968):413-16.

771. Chitty, Arthur Ben. "Griswold College, 1859-
     1897 Davenport, Iowa." *Historical Magazine
     of the Protestant Episcopal Church* 37
     (March 1968):73-5.

772. Chitty, Arthur Ben. "Heirs of Hopes: Histor-
     ical Summary of the University of the
     South." *Historical Magazine of the
     Protestant Episcopal Church* 23 (September
     1954):258-65.

773. Chitty, Arthur Ben. "Racine College Racine,
     Wisconsin--1852-1933." *Historical Magazine*

of the Protestant Episcopal Church 37 (June 1968):135-38.

774. Chitty, Arthur Benjamin. Reconstruction at Sewanee: The Founding of the University of the South and Its First Administration, 1857-1872. Sewanee, Tenn.: University Press, 1954.

775. Chivers, Walter Richard. "Religion in Negro Colleges." Journal of Negro Education 9 (January 1940):5-12.

776. Chorley, E. Clowes. "The Oxford Movement in the Seminary." Historical Magazine of the Protestant Episcopal Church 5 (September 1936):177-201.

777. Christ Seminary - Seminex. "For the Ordination of Women: A Study Document Prepared by the Faculty." Currents in Theology and Mission 6 (June 1979):132-43.

778. Christensen, Carl W. "The Role of the Psychiatric Consultant to a Seminary." Journal of Pastoral Care 9 (Spring 1955):1-7; Boisen, A. T. "Reply." 9 (Autumn 1955):166.

779. Christensen, C. W. et al. "Some Aspects of Training Pastoral Counselors." Journal of Pastoral Care 22 (December 1968):212-22.

780. Christian Century. "D. Min. Degree after Ten Years: A Symposium." Christian Century 93 (February 4-11, 1976):96-111.

781. Christie, Francis Albert. The Makers of the Meadville Theological School, 1844-1894. Boston: Beacon Press, 1927.

782. Christopher Study Week. 2d, New York, 1964. Apostolic Renewal in the Seminary in Light of Vatican Council II. Edited by James Keller and Richard Armstrong. New York: Christophers, 1965.

783. Church, Robert. "Economists as Experts: The Rise of an Academic Profession in the United States, 1870-1920." In The University in Society. Edited by Lawrence Stone. Princeton, N.J.: Princeton University Press, 1974.

784. "Church and Assembly Line: Seminarians Summer Jobs." Time 62 (September 7, 1953):74.

785. "Church and Ministry." Christian Century 73 (July 25, 1956):869-71.

786. "Church and Office Bridge a Gap: Church and Industry Institute's Internship Program." Business Week (September 26, 1970):52.

787. "Church Reform: Training for Holy Orders." Church Quarterly Review 62 (April 1906):1-21.

788. Clague, J. G. "Theological Studies." Encounter 25 (Summer 1964).

789. The Claims and Opportunities of the Christian Ministry: John R. Mott, Editor. New York: Association Press, 1913.

790. "Claims of Biblical Theology to a Place in Our Theological Schools." Bibliotheca Sacra 38 (1881):188-99.

791. Clapp, R. "Keeping the Faith Downtown [Moody Bible Institute]." Christianity Today 26 (August 6, 1982):32-4.

792. Clapp, Roger Ross. "A Study of the College Environments of Two Selected Groups of Accredited, Interdenominational Bible Colleges." Ed.D. dissertation, University of Tennessee, 1971.

793. Clark, C. A. "Specialized Seminary Training for the Rural Minister." Review and Expositor 52 (July 1955):336-42.

794. Clark, Calvin Montague. History of Bangor Theological Seminary. Boston, New York: Pilgrim Press, 1916.

795. Clark, Davis Wasgatt. "Education for the Ministry." Christian Advocate 15 (November 18, 1840):53; (December 23, 1840):76.

796. Clark, Davis Wasgatt. Mental Discipline, with Reference to the Acquisition and Communication of Knowledge, and to Education Generally. New York: Lane & Tippett, 1847.

797. Clark, Elmer Talmage. The Small Sects in
      America. Rev. ed. New York: Abingdon
      Press, 1957?

798. Clark, Francis Edward. Memories of Many Men
      in Many Lands: An Autobiography. Boston:
      United Society of Christian Endeavor, 1922.

799. Clark, Francis Edward. Ways and Means for the
      Young People's Society of Christian
      Endeavor: A Book of Suggestions for the
      Prayer-Meeting, the Committee, and all
      Lines of Work Adopted by Christian Endeavor
      Societies. Boston: D. Lothrop Co., 1890.

800. Clark, Francis Edward. Young People's Prayer-
      Meetings in Theory and Practice. Chicago:
      Funk & Wagnalls, 1887.

801. Clark, Henry Balsley. "Tradition, Impotence
      and the Seminary." Duke Divinity School
      Review 33 (Spring 1968):75-81.

802. Clark, Henry William. History of English Non-
      Conformity from Wiclif to the Close of the
      Nineteenth Century. 2 v. London: Chapman
      & Hall, 1911.

803. Clark, John Alonzo. The Pastor's Testimony.
      4th ed. Philadelphia: W. Marshall & Co.,
      1836.

804. Clark, Kenneth Willis. "Four Decades of the
      Divinity School." Duke Divinity School
      Review 32 (Spring 1967):160-83.

805. Clark, Lynn Fred and McGloshen, Thomas Hilton,
      Jr. "Fostering Pastoral Counseling Effec-
      tiveness by In-Service Education." College
      Student Journal 9 (December 1975):328-32.

806. Clark, N. M. "Putting Religion to the Test
      [Chicago University. Divinity School]."
      American Magazine 109 (June 1930):50-1.

807. Clark, R. A. and Baldinger, A. H. "Seminar in
      Psychiatry for Theological Students."
      Mental Hygiene 30 (January 1946):110-13.

808. Clark, Robert Eugene. "Graduate Programs in
      Professional Christian Education in Church
      Related Colleges, Universities and
      Seminaries." Ed.D. dissertation,University

71

of Denver, 1968.

809. Clark, Sereno Dickenson. The New England
      Ministry Sixty Years Ago: The Memoir of
      John Woodbridge, D. D. Boston: Lee &
      Shepard, 1877.

810. Clark, Thomas D. "A History of Baptist
      Involvement in Higher Education." Review
      and Expositor 64, no. 1 (1967):19-30.

811. Clark, Thomas March. Reminiscences. New
      York: Thomas Whittaker, 1895.

812. Clark, W. H. "Do Seminaries Teach Religion?"
      Christian Century 82 (April 28, 1965):520-
      2+.

813. Clark, Walter Houston. "The Oxford Group:
      Its History and Significance." New York:
      Bookman Associates, 1951.

814. Clark, William Keith. "An Analysis of
      Contemporary Speech Education in American
      Protestant Seminaries." Ph.D. disserta-
      tion, Purdue University, 1960.

815. Clark, William K. "Speech Education in
      Protestant Seminaries, 1958-59 - 1968-69
      [bibliog.]." Speech Teacher 19 (September
      1970):173-6.

816. Clark, W. K. "Speech Education in the
      Seminaries." Speech Teacher 16 (January
      1967):61-3.

817. Clark, William K. "Speech Pedagogy in the
      Seminaries: The Spoken word vs. the Spoken
      Word." Encounter 24 (Spring 1963): 190-5.

818. Clarke, Adam. A Letter to a Preacher, on His
      Entrance into the Work of the Ministry.
      New York: N. Bangs & T. Mason for the
      Methodist Episcopal Church, 1820.

819. Clarke, Adam and Coke, Thomas. The Preacher's
      Manual: Including Clavis Biblica and A
      Letter to A Methodist Preacher ... Also
      Four Discourses on the Duties of a Minister
      of the Gospel. New York: T. Mason & G.
      Lane, 1837.

820. Clarke, Emily (Smith). _William Newton Clarke: A Biography_. New York: Charles Scribner's Sons, 1916.

821. Clarke, M. F. "Navy and the Seminaries." _Christian Century_ 60 (June 16, 1943):720.

822. Classical Conference, Ann Arbor, Michigan, 1908. _Value of Humanistic Particularly Classical, Studies as a Preparation for the Study of Theology, from the Point of View of the Profession_. University of Michigan, 1908.

823. "Classical Learning Not an Essential Prerequisite to the Christian Ministry." _Quarterly Review of the Methodist Episcopal Church, South_ 1 (July 1847):347-58.

824. _A Classification of Institutions of Higher Education, Revised Edition. A Report of the Carnegie Council on Policy Studies in Higher Education_. Berkeley, Calif.: Carnegie Council on Policy Studies in Higher Education, 1976.

825. Clayton, Gordon Maxwell. "An Analysis of Clinical Pastoral Training Using a Systems Approach: An Analysis of Six Programs of Clinical Pastoral Training at Saint Elizabeths Hospital with Emphasis on the Methodology of Supervision and Its Effects on Clinical Pastoral Learning." Th.D. dissertation, Graduate Theological Union, 1971.

826. Clebsch, William A. "The Founding of the Episcopal Theological Seminary of the Southwest." _Historical Magazine of the Protestant Episcopal Church_ 27 (September 1958):246-52.

827. Clebsch, William A. "Mission of the Church as the Context of Theological Education." _Canadian Journal of Theology_ 4 (October 1958):246-54.

828. Cleland, J. S. "Training for the Ministry in View of Changing Academic Standards." _Bibliotheca Sacra_ 87 (April 1930):219-26.

829. "Clergy Found Underpaid and Badly Trained." _News Week_ 3 (March 3, 1934):30.

830. "The Clergyman's Training: Has It Moved with the Times?" Times Educational Supplement (November 25, 1949):821.

831. Clinard, T. N. "Suggestion for Required Pre-Seminary Studies." Religion In Life 36 (Summer 1967):216-22.

832. Clinard, Turner N. "An Appeal for Film Direction and Specific Guidelines." Theological Education 4 (Autumn 1967):586-8.

833. "Clinical Pastoral Training as a Religious Experience." Journal of Pastoral Care 5, no. 1 (1951):31-5.

834. "Clinical Pastoral Training Programs and Member Seminaries by Region." Journal of Pastoral Care 15 (Winter 1961):225-30.

835. Clippenger, J. A. "Attitudes toward Pastoral Training of Sixty-One Outstanding Pastors." Religious Education 48 (March 1953):113-16.

836. Clutter, Ronald Thomas. "The Reorientation of Princeton Theological Seminary 1900-1929." Th.D. dissertation, Dallas Theological Seminary, 1982.

837. Clyde, J. D. "Should Primary Responsibility Rest on the Seminary? No!" Theological Education 1 (Summer 1965):229-32.

838. Coates, T. The Making of a Minister: The Training of Ministers in the Missouri Synod: A Historical Study and Critical Evaluation. Portland, Ore.: Concordia College, 195? (Mimeographed.)

839. Coates, T. "Theological Education: The Ecumenical Dimension." Concordia Theological Monthly 43 (May 1972):314-23.

840. Cobb, James Harrel and Jennings, Louis B. A Biography and Bibliography of Edgar Johnson Goodspeed. Chicago: University of Chicago Press, 1948.

841. Cobb, John B. "The Integration of Objective Studies and Practical Theology." Iliff Review 38 (Winter 1981):51-63.

842. Cobb, S. "(Education for Ministry.)" Univer-
     salist and General Review 22 (1865):293+.

843. Cobb, W. "West Point of Fundamentalism (Moody
     Bible Institute)." American Mercury 16
     (January 1929):104-12.

844. Cobble, James Forrest, Jr. "The Influence of
     the Doctor of Ministry Program and Its
     Expanded Clientele on the Program Content,
     Instructional Practice, and Perceived
     Mission of McCormick Theological Seminary."
     Ed.D. dissertation, University of Illinois
     at Urbana-Champaign, 1981.

845. Coburn, John B. "Anglican Theological
     Education: Some Reflections Following a
     Visit to England and Their Implications for
     the Episcopal Church." Anglican Theologi-
     cal Review 48 (1966):131-56.

846. Coburn, J. B. "Seminary Cooperation in
     Greater Boston." Christian Century 85
     (June 5, 1968):766-8.

847. Coburn, J. B. "The Seminary in Ten Years
     [Episcopal Theological School, Cambridge,
     Mass.]." Union Seminary Quarterly Review
     22 (May 1967):337-9.

848. Coburn, John B. "Theological Education: One
     Perspective and Two Proposals." Address at
     150th Anniversary, Harvard Divinity School,
     April 20, 1966.

849. Cocking, Herbert. "Bible College Accredita-
     tion by the North Central Association:
     1970-1980." Ph.D. dissertation, University
     of Michigan, 1982.

850. Cockrum, L. V. "Personality Traits and
     Interests of Theological Students
     [bibliog.]." Religious Education 47
     (January 1952):28-32.

851. Cockrum, L. V. "Predicting Success in
     Training for the Ministry [bibliog.]."
     Religious Education 47 (May 1952):198-202.

852. Codman, John. Dr. Codman's Speech in the
     Board of Overseers of Harvard College, Feb.
     3, 1831. Cambridge? 1831.

853. Coe, George A. "The Education of Ministers."
Religious Education 5 (December 1910):454-
7.

854. Coe, George A. "The Religious Breakdown of
the Ministry." Journal of Religion 1
(January 1921):18-29.

855. Coe, George Albert. "The Theological
Seminary: The Laboratory Method in the
Department of Religious Education."
Religious Education 7 (October 1912):420-4.

856. Coffin, Charles. "Importance of a Thoroughly
Educated Ministry for the Western States."
American Quarterly Register 2 (1830):74-7.

857. Coffin, Henry Sloane. A Half Century of Union
Theological Seminary, 1896-1945. New York:
Charles Scribner's Sons, 1954.

858. Coffin, Henry Sloane. "Is There a Religious
Breakdown of the Ministry?" Journal of
Religion 1 (March 1921):187-9.

859. Cogswell, William. Letters to Young Men
Preparing for the Christian Ministry.
Boston: Perkins & Marvin, 1837.

860. Cogswell, William. The Theological Class
Book. Boston: Crocker & Brewster, 1831.

861. Cole, S. G. "Place of Religious Education in
the Seminary Curriculum." Religious Education 22 (February 1927):105-17; "Criticisms
and Comments." 22 (February 1927):117-23.

862. Cole, Stewart Grant. The History of Fundamentalism. New York: R. R. Smith, 1931.

863. Coleman, C. D. "The Christian Methodist
Episcopal Church: The Rationale and Poli-
cies upon Which Support of Its Colleges Is
Predicated." Journal of Negro Education 29
(Summer 1960):315-18.

864. Coleman, Paul Robert. "The Life and Works of
John McNaugher." Ph.D. dissertation, University of Pittsburgh, 1961.

865. Coleman, Richard J. "Biblical Inerrancy: Are
We Going Anywhere." Theology Today 31
(January 1975):295-303.

866. Colgate University, Hamilton, N. Y. The First
     Half Century of Madison, University, (1819-
     1869) Or, the Jubilee Volume, Containing
     Sketches of Eleven Hundred Living and
     Deceased Alumni; With Fifteen Portraits of
     Founders, Presidents and Patrons. New
     York: Sheldon & Co., 1872.

867. Collard, Ernest William. "History of Wartburg
     Theological Seminary: With Biographical
     Sketches of the Professors." B.D. thesis,
     Wartburg Theological Seminary, 1952.

868. "College Courses for Future Ministers at
     Columbia University." Christian Century 43
     (May 13, 1926):626-7.

869. College of the Bible, Lexington, Ky. That
     There May Be More Ministers. Lexington,
     Ky., 1957.

870. College Theology Society. To Be a Man.
     Edited by George Devine. Englewood Cliffs,
     N.J.: Prentice-Hall, 1969.

871. Colley, James M. L. "Ninety Years of Shattuck
     School." Historical Magazine of the
     Protestant Episcopal Church 17 (September
     1948):251-73.

872. Collins, Varnum Lancing. Princeton. New
     York: Oxford University Press, 1914.

873. "Colloquies on Seminary Education: The
     Growing Edges of the Theological
     Disciplines." Encounter 25 (Summer
     1964):291-313.

874. Colson, Edna Meade. "The Negro Teachers'
     College and Normal School." Journal of
     Negro Education 2 (July 1933):284-98.

875. Colston, L. G. "Studies in Culture and
     Personality." Encounter 25 (Summer 1964).

876. Colvin, Gerald Franklin. "The Relationship of
     Social Intelligence, Creative Problem
     Solving Behavior, and other Selected
     Variables to Performance Criteria for Pre-
     Seminary Theology Majors." Ph.D. disserta-
     tion, University of Georgia, 1980.

877. Colwell, Ernest Cadman. "Closing the Gap between College and Seminary." _Journal of Bible and Religion_ 26 (April 1958):107-10.

878. Colwell, Ernest Cadman. "New Testament Scholarship in Prospect." _Journal of Bible and Religion_ 28 (April 1960):199-203.

879. Colwell, Ernest Cadman. "Plea for More General Education for the Minister." _Journal of Religion_ 23 (April 1943):103-9.

880. Colwell, Ernest Cadman. "Seminaries in the University for the Church." _Lutheran Quarterly_ 18 (November 1966):322-4.

881. Colwell, E. C. "Ten Commandments for a Theological School." _Christian Century_ 75 (April 23, 1958):494.

882. Colwell, Ernest Cadman. "A Tertium Quid: The Church's Seminary and the University." _Theological Education_ 1 (Winter 1965):96-103.

883. Colwell, Ernest Cadman. "Theological Education: Isolation or Interaction?" Claremont, California, Southern California School of Theology Bulletin, 1958.

884. Colwell, Ernest Cadman. "Toward Better Theological Education." _Journal of Religion_ 20 (April 1940):109-23.

885. "Colwell Warns Churches of Trends in Seminaries." _Christian Century_ 62 (July 18, 1945):828-9.

886. Combs, Kermit Stephen, Jr. "The Course of Religious Education at the Southern Baptist Theological Seminary, 1902-1953: A Historical Study." Ed.D. dissertation, Southern Baptist Theological Seminary, 1978.

887. Come, Arnold B. et al. "Report of the Consultation of Pacific Coast Seminaries on the Pacific Basin Theological Network, San Anselmo, California." _Southeast Asia Journal of Theology_ 19, no. 1 (1978):105-8.

888. Come, Donald Robert. "The Influence of Princeton on Higher Education in the South before 1825." _William and Mary Quarterly_ 2

(3rd series) (1945):359-96.

889. "Comeback for Seminaries in the U.S." U.S. News 80 (January 5, 1976):53-5.

890. Comfort, Richard Obee. "Education for the Rural Ministry." Pastoral Psychology 10 (October 1959):37-43.

891. "Coming Schools of Missions, 1933." Missionary Review of the World 56 (May 1933):268.

892. Conard, James M. "Personality Qualifications for Entrance to Six Theological Seminaries in Kentucky." Th.M. thesis, Southern Seminary, 1957.

893. "Concordia Seminary May Lose AATS Accreditation." Christian Century 89 (June 28, 1972):706.

894. "Concordia Seminary (Missouri)" AAUP Bulletin 61 (April 1975):49-59.

895. Concordia Theological Seminary, Springfield, Ill. Concordia Theological Seminary: A Century of Blessing, 1846-1946. Springfield, Ill., 1946?

896. "Concordia's Dispute Is Extended [Concordia Seminary]." Christianity Today 16 (May 12, 1972):37.

897. Cone, James H. "Black Power, Black Theology, and the Study of Theology and Ethics." Theological Education 6 (Spring 1970):202-15.

898. Conference of Baptist Theological Seminaries. Boston and Newton Centre, Mass., 1918. Conference of Baptist Theological Seminaries Held in Boston and Newton Centre, Massachusetts, March Twelve and Thirteen, Nineteen Hundred and Eighteen, at the Invitation of the Newton Theological Institution. Chicago: University of Chicago Press, 1918.

899. Conference of Theological Schools. Harvard University, August 13-16, 1918. "Harvard Conference a Milestone in Christian Unity." Christian Register 97 (August 22, 1918):801-9.

900. Conference on Judaism and the Christian
     Seminary Curriculum, Chicago, 1965.
     Judaism and the Christian Seminary
     Curriculum. Edited by J. Bruce Long.
     Chicago: Loyola University Press, 1966.

901. "Congratulations to Vanderbilt University."
     Outlook 106 (April 11, 1914):787-8.

902. Conn, Harvie M. "Theological Education and
     the Search for Excellence." Western Theo-
     logical Journal 41 (Spring 1979):311-63.

903. Conrad, David Holmes. Memoir of Rev. James
     Chisholm. New York: Protestant Episcopal
     Society for the Promotion of Evangelical
     Knowledge, 1857.

904. "The Constitution and Associate Statutes of
     the Theological Seminary in Andover."
     Panoplist 1 (New Series) (January
     1809):371-4.

905. "Constitution of the Society for the Promotion
     of Theological Education in Harvard Univer-
     sity: With a Circular Address, 1825."
     Christian Examiner 2 (1825):57-65.

906. "Consultation on Continuing Education for the
     Ministry." 1st, Andover Newton Theological
     School, Newton Centre, Mass., June 15-18,
     1964. (ERIC Document)

907. Continental Pietism and Early American
     Christianity. Edited by Ernest F.
     Stoeffler. Grand Rapids, Mich.: Wm. B.
     Eerdmans Publishing Co., 1976.

908. Continuing Quest: Opportunities, Resources
     and Programs in Post-Seminary Education.
     Edited by James B. Hofrenning. Minneapolis:
     Augsburg Publishing House, 1970.

909. Convocation of Methodist Theological Facili-
     ties. 1st, Nashville, 1959. The Ministry
     in the Methodist Heritage. Edited by
     Gerald O. McCulloh. Nashville: Dept. of
     Ministerial Education, Division of Educa-
     tional Institutions, Board of Education,
     Methodist Church, 1960.

910. Conway, Moncure Daniel. Autobiography. 2
     vols. Boston: Houghton, Mifflin Co.,

1904, Vol. 1.

911. Conwell, Russell Herman. Life of Charles
    Haddon Spurgeon. Philadelphia: Edgewood
    Publishing Co., 1892.

912. Cook, Ann, comp. City Life, 1865-1900: Views
    of Urban America. New York: Praeger,
    1973.

913. Cook, Harvey Toliver. Education in South
    Carolina under Baptist Control. Green-
    ville, S.C., 1912?

914. Cook, Joseph. "Fourth Year of Theological
    Study." Bibliotheca Sacra 27 (April 1870):
    244-61.

915. Cook, Thomas C. "Gerontology in Seminary
    Training: Overview and Introduction."
    Theological Education 16, Special Issue no.
    3 (Winter 1980):275-9.

916. Cook, Walter L. Bangor Theological Seminary:
    A Sesquicentennial History. Orono, Me.:
    University of Maine Press, 1971.

917. Cooke, Bernard J. "Essentials in Theological
    Curriculum." Theological Education 5
    (Autumn 1968):15-22.

918. Cooke, Bernard J. Ministry to Word and Sacra-
    ments. Philadelphia: Fortress Press,
    1976.

919. Cooke, George Alfred. The Present and the
    Future of Methodism: An Examination of the
    Teachings of Prof. Borden P. Bowne.
    Boston, n.d.

920. Cooper, Jack. "A Decade of Continuing Educa-
    tion at Princeton Theological Seminary."
    Reformed World 31 (September 1971):314-18.

921. Cooper, O. H. "Contributions of the Baptist
    Church to the Cause of Education."
    National Education Association. Proceed-
    ings and Addresses (1900):87-94.

922. Cooper, O. H. "Contributions of Religious
    Organizations to the Cause of Education."
    National Education Association. Proceed-
    ings and Addresses (1900):87-94.

923. "Cooperating Affiliation between Theological
      Seminaries of Different Denominations."
      Current Opinion 57 (September 1914):193.

924. "Cooperation in Theological Education: 1973."
      Theological Education 10 (Fall 1973):entire
      issue.

925. "Cooperation in Theological Instruction."
      Independent 72 (January 11, 1912):106-7.

926. "Cooperative Rehabilitation Training in Three
      Neighboring Divinity Schools, Berkeley,
      California." Education for Victory 2
      (January 20, 1944):22.

927. Cope, Henry Frederick. Efficiency in the
      Sunday School. New York: Hodder &
      Stoughton, 1912.

928. Cope, Henry Frederick. "The Professional Or-
      ganization of Workers in Religious Educa-
      tion." Religious Education 16 (June
      1921):162-7.

929. Copeland, Robert M. "The Reformed Presby-
      terian Theological Seminary in Cincinnati
      1845-1849." Cincinnati Historical Society
      Bulletin 31 (Fall 1973):151-63.

930. Copher, Charles B. "Perspectives and Ques-
      tions: The Black Religious Experience and
      Biblical Studies." Theological Education 6
      (Spring 1970):181-8.

931. Corey, Stephen Jared. Fifty Years of Attack
      and Controversy: The Consequences among
      Disciples of Christ. Des Moines: Committee
      on Publication of the Corey Manuscript,
      1953.

932. Cornwall Collective. Your Daughters Shall
      Prophesy: Feminist Alternatives in Theo-
      logical Education. New York: Pilgrim
      Press, 1980.

933. "Correspondence." Outlook 63 (December 23,
      1899):982-3.

934. Corwin, Edward Tanjore. A Manual of the Re-
      formed Church in America (Formerly Ref.
      Prot. Dutch Church), 1628-1902. 4th ed.
      New York: Board of Publication of the

Reformed Church in America, 1902.

935. Costen, Melva Ruby Wilson. "A Comparative Description of Curricular Offerings in Church Music Degree Programs at Accredited Protestant Theological Seminaries in the United States." Ph.D. dissertation, Georgia State University - College of Education, 1978.

936. Cotner, John H. "An Evaluation of the Academic Status and the Methodological and Ideological Orientation of the Psychology of Religion and Pastoral Counseling in American Seminaries." Ph.D. dissertation, University of Southern California, 1952.

937. Cotten, Carroll Cresswell. "The Imperative Is Leadership: A Study of Education for the Professional Ministry of the Christian Church [Disciples of Christ]." Ph.D. dissertation, Stanford University, 1975.

938. Coulson, John, ed. Theology and the University: An Ecumenical Investigation. Baltimore: Helicon Press, 1964.

939. "Council for Clinical Training, Inc. Clinical Pastoral Training Programs and Member Seminaries by Region, 1966." Journal of Pastoral Care 19 (Winter 1965):211-19.

940. "Course of Study." Christian Advocate (Nashville) 29 (New Series) (October 23, 1869):3.

941. "Course of Study." Christian Advocate (New York) 41 (January 25, 1866):26.

942. Courtenay, Bradley Calvin. "Selected Characteristics of Southern Baptist Ministers as Related to Patterns of Attendance in Continuing Education." Ed.D. dissertation, University of Georgia, 1976.

943. Covell, Ralph R. and Wagner, C. Peter. An Extension Seminary Primer. South Padadena, Calif.: William Carey Library, 1971.

944. Cowan, John Franklin. New Life in the Old Prayer-Meeting. New York: Fleming H. Revell Co., 1906.

83

945. Cox, Claire. The New-Time Religion.
     Englewood Cliffs, N.J.: Prentice Hall,
     1961.

946. Cox, F. A. "Preparation for the Work."
     Bibliotheca Sacra 101 (April 1944):210-26.

947. Cox, Harvey. "The Significance of the Church-
     World Dialogue for Theological Education."
     Theological Education 3 (Winter 1967):270-
     9.

948. Cox, James Herman, Jr. "Valued Characteris-
     tics of Bible College Presidents: Percep-
     tions of Trustees." Ph.D. dissertation,
     Ohio State University, 1981.

949. Cracknell, Kenneth. "Theological Education in
     Missionary Perspective: A Response from
     Britain to David J. Bosch." Missiology 10
     (April 1982):229-43.

950. Cragg, Gerald Robertson. Puritanism in the
     Period of the Great Persecution, 1660-1688.
     Cambridge [Eng.] University Press, 1957.

951. Cragg, Gerald R. "Training the Ministry - the
     Older Tradition." Andover Newton Quarterly
     8 (March 1968):223-34.

952. Craig, C. T. "Pre-Theological Training."
     Christian Education 15 (November 1931):130-
     8.

953. Craig, Henry Knox. Toil and Triumph: A
     Memorial of the Character, Work and Closing
     Days of Rev. Wheelock Craig. New Bedford:
     Tabor Bros., 1870.

954. Craig, John G. "Comments on 'I Graduate from
     Seminary.'" Religious Education 36
     (1941):166-74.

955. Cramer, A. E. "Responsibilities of a Semin-
     ary." Alliance Witness 115 (March 5,
     1980):9-10.

956. Crandall, Phineas. "The Ministry We Need."
     Zion's Herald 10 (October 16, 1839):165.

957. Crandall, Phineas. "Theological Seminary."
     Zion's Herald 10 (August 7, 1839):125.

84

958. Cranston, Earl. "Historical Backgrounds in College and Seminary." Journal of Bible and Religion 26 (April 1958):111-4.

959. Cranston, M. W. "U.S.C. School of Religion Moves." Christian Century 73 (July 18, 1956):855-6.

960. Cremin, Lawrence A. American Education: The Colonial Experience, 1607-1783. New York: Harper & Row, 1970.

961. Cremin, Lawrence Arthur, Shannon, David A. and Townsend, Mary Evelyn. A History of Teachers College, Columbia University. New York: Columbia University Press, 1954.

962. Crespy, G. "Spiritual Formation." Study Encounter 3, no. 4 (1967):187-8.

963. Cressy, Benjamin Cothen. Appeal in Behalf of the Indiana Theological Seminary. Boston: Printed by Pierce & Parker, 1832.

964. "The Crime of the Higher Criticism." Methodist Review 72 (November 1890):898-907.

965. "Crisis in Leadership." Christian Century 60 (February 10, 1943):158-9.

966. Crismon, Leo T. "The History and Growth of Theological Education among Southern Baptists [1822-1958]." Quarterly Review (Bap.) 18 (July-September 1958):3-10.

967. Crismon, Leo T. "The Southern Baptist Theological Seminary Library: Making an Ideal Live [1859-1959]." Review and Expositor 57 (April 1960):219-38.

968. Criswell, G. E. and Gebhart, J. E. "In Service Clinical Pastoral Education." Journal of Pastoral Care 23 (December 1969):237-40.

969. Crites, S. D. "Whence the Theological Doldrums?" Christian Scholar 47 (Spring 1964):3-6.

970. "Critical Issues: 1972." Theological Education 9 (Autumn 1972):entire issue.

971.	"(A Criticism on Theological Seminaries.)"
	Outlook 63 (1899):732+.

972.	Crocker, J. H. "(Training School for Ministers
	in the Northwest.)" Unitarian Review 30
	(1888):527+.

973.	Croft, Frederic Ashbrook. "Competencies in
	Adult Education of Selected Episcopal
	Priests, with Implications for the Seminary
	Curriculum." Ph.D. dissertation, Indiana
	University, 1964.

974.	Crofoot, Kenneth Stanley. "A Survey of
	Programs of Clinical Pastoral Education in
	the Protestant Denominations of the United
	States as a Preparation for Pastoral
	Counseling." Ph.D. dissertation, George
	Washington University, 1959.

975.	Cross, F. L. "Graduate Ordinand." Church
	Quarterly Review 124 (July 1937):285-301.

976.	Cross, Frank Moore and Wright, George Ernest.
	"Study of the Old Testament at Harvard."
	Harvard Divinity Bulletin 25 (April-July
	1961):14-20.

977.	Cross, M. K. "An Insufficient and Defective
	Ministry." Congregational Quarterly 7
	(1865):160-3.

978.	Cross, William Mastin. "Occupational
	Aspirations and Expectations of Seminary
	Students." Ph.D. dissertation, South
	Dakota State University, 1971.

979.	Cross, William M. "Perceived Influences on
	Occupational Choice of Seminarians."
	Concordia Theological Quarterly 44 (January
	1980):3-16.

980.	Crothers, S. M. "Colonel in the Theological
	Seminary." In Among Friends, pp. 194-221.
	New York: Houghton, Mifflin, 1910.

981.	Crum, T. B. "Bible College Education." In
	Accreditation in Higher Education, pp. 80-
	4. United States. Office of Education.
	Washington, 1959.

982.	Crum, T. B. "Bible Colleges Today."
	Christian Life 21 (June 1959):32-5.

86

983. Crum, Terrelle B. "Pre-Seminary Education
      from the View of the Bible College." Theo-
      logical Education 1 (Spring 1965):169-75.

984. Cully, Iris V. "Feminism and Ministerial
      Education." Christian Century 96 (February
      7-14, 1979):141-6.

985. Cully, K. B. "Discipline of Christian
      Education." Religious Education 61
      (November 1966):453-8.

986. Culpepper, Hugo H. "The Legacy of William
      Owen Carver." International Bulletin of
      Missionary Research 5 (July 1981):119-22.

987. Culver, Dwight W. "So Nobody Knows!"
      Christian Century 80 (January 23,
      1963):111-12.

988. Culver, E. T. "Man, Cosmology and the Earl
      Lectures [Pacific School of Religion]."
      Christian Century 85 (March 20, 1968):373-
      4.

989. Culver, Maurice E. "The Changing Shape of
      Theological Education at Asbury Theological
      Seminary." Asbury Seminarian 21 (October
      1967):12-19.

990. Culver, M. E. "Theological Education and the
      Church in Our Time." Asbury Seminarian 19
      (January 1965):41-9.

991. Cumberland Presbyterian Church. A Circular
      Letter Addressed to the Societies and
      Brethren of the Presbyterian Church
      Recently under the Care of the Council by
      the Late Cumberland Presbytery, In Which
      There is a Correct Statement of the Origin,
      Progress, and Termination, of the
      Difference, Between the Synod of Kentucky,
      and the Former Presbytery of Cumberland.
      Russellville, Ky.: Printed by Matthew
      Duncan at the Office of the Farmer's
      Friend, 1810.

992. Cummings, Anson Watson. The Early Schools of
      Methodism. New York: Phillips & Hunt,
      1886.

993. Cummins, Evelyn A. "The Beginnings of the
      Church in Ohio and Kenyon College."

> Historical Magazine of the Protestant
> Episcopal Church 6 (September 1937):276-98.

994. Cuninggim, J. L. "A Better System of Minis-
      terial Training for the Church." Methodist
      Review 62 (1913):309-22.

995. Cuninggim, J. L. "Making a Ministry." Bibli-
      cal World 42 (September 1913):158-60.

996. Cuninggim, Merrimon. "Blueprint for Break-
      through." Christian Century 77 (April 20,
      1960):470+.

997. Cuninggim, Merrimon. "Changing Emphases in
      the Seminary Curriculum." Journal of Bible
      and Religion 23 (April 1955):110-18.

998. Cuninggim, M. "Integration in Professional
      Education [Perkins School of Theology]."
      Annals of the American Academy of Political
      and Social Science 304 (March 1956):109-15.

999. Cuninggim, Merrimon. "The New Curriculum at
      Perkins." Christian Century 71 (April 28,
      1954):514-15.

1000. Cuningham, Charles E. Timothy Dwight, 1752-
      1817, A Biography. New York: MacMillan
      Co., 1942.

1001. Cunliffe-Jones, Hubert. "Selection and
      Training of Candidate for the Ministry."
      Expository Times 73 (October 1962):4-6.

1002. Cunningham, John T. University in the Forest:
      The Story of Drew University. Florham
      Park, N.J.: Afton Publishing Co., 1972.

1003. Cunningham, William. The Cure of Souls:
      Lectures on Pastoral Theology Delivered in
      the Lent Term 1908 in the Divinity School,
      Cambridge, and Other Addresses. Cambridge:
      At the University Press, 1908.

1004. Cuny, Ronald Edward. "The Attitudes of Clergy
      and Laity towards Ministerial Continuing
      Education with Their Church's Support for
      Continuing Education." Ed.D. dissertation,
      Indiana University, 1982.

1005. "Current Issues with Professional Schools:
      Theology." College and University 53

(Summer 1978):441-2.

1006. "Current News Stories from UEA Reporters."
       United Evangelical Action 5 (July 1,
       1946):11.

1007. Curry, D. "(Education for Christian Minis-
       try.)" Quarterly Review of the Methodist
       Episcopal Church, South 45 (1885):597+.

1008. Curry, James. History of the San Francisco
       Theological Seminary of the Presbyterian
       Church in the U.S.A., and Its Alumni
       Association. Vacaville, Calif.: Reporter
       Publishing Co., 1907.

1009. Curtis, K. "Strategy at the Front of the Bus:
       Black Seminarians." Christianity Today 13
       (December 6, 1968):41.

1010. Cushing, Christopher. "The Supply of
       Ministers." Congregational Quarterly 14
       (January 1872):28-44.

1011. Cushman, Robert E. "Fifty Years of Theology
       and Theological Education at Duke." Duke
       Divinity School Review 42 (Winter 1977):3-
       22.

1012. Cushman, R. E. "How Can They Hear without a
       Well-Trained Preacher." Duke Divinity
       School Bulletin 28 (November 1963):171-8.

1013. Cushman, R. E. "Is the Medium the Message?"
       Duke Divinity School Review 35 (Winter
       1970):28-31.

1014. Cushman, Robert E. "Objectives of Theological
       Education - And Impediments." Duke
       Divinity School Bulletin 26 (February
       1962):3-16.

1015. Cushman, Robert Earl. "Obsolescence and the
       Wisdom of God." Duke Divinity Review 35
       (Winter 1970):3-9.

1016. Cushman, Robert E. "Pre-Seminary Education
       and the Theological School." Theological
       Education 1 (Spring 1965):143-8.

1017. Cushman, Robert E. "Theological Education: A
       Reconsideration of Its Nature in Light of
       Its Objective." Duke Divinity School

Review 33 (Winter 1968):3-13.

1018. Cushman, R. E. "Worship, Our Ministry." Duke Divinity School Review 35 (Autumn 1970): 139-45.

1019. Cutshall, Elmer Guy. "The Doctrinal Training of the Traveling Ministry of the Methodist Episcopal Church of the United States." Ph.D. dissertation, University of Chicago, 1922.

1020. Cutshall, E. G. "Types and Tendencies in Theological Education." In Church Looks Ahead: American Protestant Christianity, An Analysis and a Forecast, pp. 329-39. Edited by Charles Edwin Schofield. New York: Macmillan, 1933.

1021. Cuyler, Theodore Ledyard. How To Be a Pastor. New York: Baker & Taylor, 1890.

1022. Dabney, V. "Place of Social Studies in Theological Education." Education 60 (February 1940):350-3.

1023. Dace, Thomas. The Introductory Lecture upon the Study of Theology and of the Greek New Testament. London, 1829.

1024. Daedalus. The Professions in America. Boston: Houghton Mifflin, 1965.

1025. Dahl, G. "Shall Prospective Ministerial Students Study Bible while in College?" Christian Education 15 (October 1931):38-45.

1026. Dahlberg, Edwin. "Edwin Dahlberg in Conversation: Memories of Walter Rauschenbusch: Transcribed by John E. Skoglund." Foundations 18 (July-September 1975):209-18.

1027. "Dallas at Forty." Christianity Today 9 (March 12, 1965):51-2.

1028. Dallmann, Roger Howard. "Springfield Seminary." Concordia Historical Institute Quarterly 50 (Fall 1977):106-30.

1029. Dammers, A. H. "Where Should Missionary Recruits Be Trained?" International Review of Missions 44 (April 1955):185-6.

1030. Dana, Daniel. A Remonstrance Addressed to the Trustees of Phillips Academy, On the State of the Theological Seminary under Their Care. Boston: Crocker & Brewster, 1853.

1031. Dana, M. "Training the Rural Minister." International Journal of Religious Education 7 (January 1931):30.

1032. "Dangerous Mission [Theological Students]." Christian Century 83 (May 18, 1966):641-2.

1033. Daniel, Robert Norman. Furman University: A History. Greenville, S.C.,: Furman University, 1951.

1034. Daniel, Robert Prentiss. "Relationship of the Negro Public College and the Negro Private and Church-Related College." Journal of Negro Education 29 (Summer 1960):388-93.

1035. Daniel, W. Harrison. "The Genesis of Richmond College, 1843-1860." Virginia Magazine of History and Biography 83, no. 2 (1975):131-49.

1036. Daniel, W. Harrison. "Madison College, 1851-1858: A Methodist Protestant School." Methodist History 17 (January 1979):90-105.

1037. Daniel, William Andrew. The Education of Negro Ministers. New York: George H. Doran Co., 1925.

1038. Daniel, William Andrew. "Negro Theological Seminary Survey." Ph.D. dissertation, University of Chicago, 1925.

1039. Daniels, George H. "The Process of Professionalization in American Science: The Emergent Period, 1820-1860." Isis 58 (Summer 1967):151-66.

1040. Danker, William J. "Missionary Training at Concordia Seminary." In Toward a More Excellent Ministry. Edited by Richard R. Caemmerer and Alfred O. Fuerbringer. St. Louis, Mo.: Concordia Theological Seminary, 1964.

1041. Danker, W. "Relationship between Graduate Theological Education and the Worldwide Mission of the Church." Concordia Theological Monthly 43 (May 1972):329-37.

1042. Dannelly, Clarence Moore. "The Development of Collegiate Education in the Methodist Episcopal Church, South, 1846-1902." Ph.D. dissertation, Yale University, 1933.

1043. D'Arcy, Paul F. and Kennedy, Eugene C. The Genius of the Apostolate: Personal Growth in the Candidate, the Seminarian, and the Priest. New York: Sheed & Ward, 1965.

1044. Darrah, T. S. "Speaking for the Class of 1939." Harvard Divinity Bulletin 28 (July 1964):109-12.

1045. Davidson, G. W. "Library versus the Streets?" Theological Education 6 (Autumn 1969):15-20.

1046. Davidson, N. C. "New Seminary Library [New Orleans Baptist Theological Seminary]." Library Journal 77 (September 1, 1952): 1373-4.

1047. Davidson, William J. "Seminary Work in Education: What Training in Education Should Be Required of all Seminary Graduates?" Religious Education 12 (1917):128-36.

1048. Davies, G. Henton. "Bristol Baptist College: Three Hundredth Birthday." Baptist History and Heritage 14 (April 1979):8-14.

1049. Davies, T. E. "Oversupply of Clergymen." Outlook 63 (December 23, 1899):982-3.

1050. Davis, Allen Freeman. American Heroine: The Life and Legend of James Addams. New York: Oxford University Press, 1973.

1051. Davis, Allen Freeman. Spearheads for Reform: The Social Settlements and the Progressive Movement, 1890-1914. New York: Oxford University Press, 1967.

1052. Davis, Charles Debrelle, III. "A Cognitive Modeling Approach for Increasing Assertive Behavior of Theological Students." Ph.D. dissertation, Boston University Graduate

School, 1981.

1053. Davis, Clifford E. and Wagner, Paula D. "A Guide for Counseling Church Workers." Church Occupations Counselor (UPC) (May 1967).

1054. Davis, Forest Kendali. "Conjunction over Harvard: Religion and the University Form a New Configuration." Journal of Higher Education 30 (May 1959):276-80.

1055. Davis, Grace Emeline (Tinker). Ozora S. Davis: His Life and Poems. Boston: Pilgrim Press, 1932.

1056. Davis, H. Grady. "Teaching of Homiletics: The Present Situation in American Seminaries." Encounter 22 (Spring 1961):197-207.

1057. Davis, Jackson. "The Outlook for the Professional and Higher Education of Negroes." Journal of Negro Education 2 (July 1933): 403-10.

1058. Davis, Jerome. A Life Adventure for Peace: An Autobiography. New York; Citadel Press, 1967.

1059. Davis, John Merle. "The Preparation of Missionaries for the Post-War Era." International Review of Missions 33 (July 1944):241-53.

1060. Davis, Murphy. "Seminary Quarter for Women at Grailville: Toward a Feminist Approach to Theological Education." Theological Education 11 (Winter 1975):67-74.

1061. Davis, Ozora Stearns. The Purpose and Unity of Theological Studies. Address at the Opening of the 68th Year of the Chicago Theological Seminary. October 1, 1925. Chicago, 1925.

1062. Dawley, Powell Mills. The Story of the General Theological Seminary: A Sesquicentennial History, 1817-1967. New York: Oxford University Press, 1969.

1063. Day, Clarence Burton. "Thomas Day Heresy Case in the Synod of California." Journal of

Presbyterian History 46 (June 1968):79-106.

1064. Day, Franklin D. "A Study of the Influence of
Stake Ecclesiastical leadership on the
Development of the Seminary and Institute
of Religion Program of the Church of Jesus
Christ of Latter-Day Saints." Ed.D.
dissertation, Brigham Young University,
1969.

1065. Day, G. M. "Among the Seminaries." Christian
Education 14 (May 1931):622-8, 787-9.

1066. Day, Gardiner M. "Can the Theolog Find
Employment?" Christian Education 17
(October 1933):41-4.

1067. Day, Gardiner, M. "Cooperation among the
Seminaries." Christian Education 13 (March
1930):414-16.

1068. Day, Gardiner M. "The Interseminary Movement:
As It Started." Christian Education 19
(February 1936):231-6.

1069. Day, Gardiner M. "Missions and Revolution in
Seminaries." Christian Education 16 (April
1933):223-7.

1070. Day, G. M. "Seminaries and the Church
Resistant." Christian Education 18
(December 1934):82-4.

1071. Day, Gardiner M. "Thought and Activity among
the Seminaries." Christian Education 18
(June 1935):320-4.

1072. Day, Henry N. "The Training of the Preacher."
American Biblical Repository 8, 2nd Series
(July 1842):71-90.

1073. Day, Thomas Franklin. "Theological Seminaries
and Their Critics." Presbyterian and
Reformed Review 11 (April 1900):298-308.

1074. Dayringer, Richard. "Goals in Clinical
Pastoral Education." Pastoral Psychology
22, no. 213 (1971):5-10.

1075. Dayton, Donald W. "Theodore Weld, Evangelical
Reformer: Recovering a Heritage, Part 8."
Post American 4 (March 1975):6-9.

94

1076. Dayton, Donald W. and Nelson, F. Burton. "The Theological Seminary and the City." In The Urban Mission. Edited by C. Ellison. Grand Rapids: Eerdmans, 1974.

1077. "Dean Deplores [Chicago University]." Newsweek 46 (October 17, 1955):78.

1078. "Death in the Family: Woodstock College, N.Y." Time 101 (January 22, 1973):47.

1079. Deats, P., Jr. "Pearly Gates Amendment and Congressional Images of Church and Ministry: Question of Draft Exemption for Ministerial Students." Christian Century 88 (April 21, 1971):486-7.

1080. De Blois, Austen K. "The Value to the Minister of the Study of Religious Education." Religious Education 1 (April 1906): 42-6.

1081. DeBoer, Lawrence P. "Seminary and University: Two Approaches to Theology and Religion." Journal of Bible and Religion 32 (October 1964):342-9.

1082. Decker, Arthur C. "Seventh Annual Inter-Seminary Conference." Religious Education 25 (April 1930):362-3.

1083. "Declining Enrollment Hits Southern Seminaries." Christian Century 79 (November 21, 1962):1409.

1084. "(Decrease in the Number of Theological Students.)" Biblical World 17 (1901):243+.

1085. Deedy, John. "News and Views: Seminary Enrollments in the US." Commonweal 96 (July 25, 1969):466-8.

1086. Deem, Warren H. "Another Word on Library Planning." Theological Education 5 (Winter 1969):95-8.

1087. Deem, W. H. and Van de Mark, G. "The 1970's: Alternatives for Change." Theological Education 4 (Summer 1968, Suppl. 2).

1088. Deem, Warren. "Observations of an Organization Birdwatcher." Theological Education 12 (Autumn 1975):63-7.

1089. Deffenbaugh, James T. "Three Classification
      Schemes for Use in a Judaeo-Christian Theo-
      logical Library: A Comparative Study."
      1975. (ERIC Document)

1090. Degen, Rainer. "A Further Manuscript of
      Barhebraeus' 'Creme of Wisdom': Princeton,
      Theological Seminary, MS Nestorian 25." In
      Oriens Christianus, 61. Edited by J.
      Molitor. 1977.

1091. Degregoris, Vincent. "An Investigation of
      Career Development in Graduate Theological
      Students: An Analysis of Retrospective
      Career Reports with Implications for
      Guidance in Admissions and Education."
      Ph.D. dissertation, Harvard University,
      1971.

1092. De Hueck, Catherine. Dear Seminarian.
      Milwaukee: Bruce, 1950.

1093. Deitz, Reginald W. "Eastern Lutheranism in
      American Society and American Christianity,
      1870-1914: Darwinism - Biblical Criticism
      - The Social Gospel." Ph.D. dissertation,
      University of Georgia, 1958.

1094. De Klerk, Peter. "A Bibliography of the
      Writings of the Professors of Calvin
      Theological Seminary." Calvin Theological
      Journal 16 (November 1981):251-2.

1095. De Klerk, Peter and Hilgert, Earle. Essays on
      Theological Librarianship: Presented to
      Calvin Henry Schmitt. Philadelphia:
      American Theological Library Association,
      1980.

1096. De Klerk, Peter. Renaissance, Reformation,
      Resurgence: Papers, Colloquium on Calvin
      and Calvin Studies, Calvin Theological
      Seminary, Grand Rapids, Mich., April 22-23,
      1976. Grand Rapids, Mich.: Calvin Theo-
      logical Seminary, 1976.

1097. Delk, E. H. "Function of a Modern Theological
      Teacher." Lutheran Quarterly 56 (October
      1926):365-73.

1098. Dell, William. The Trial of Spirits, Both in
      Teachers and Hearers. London: Reprinted
      and Sold by Mary Hinde, 1770.

1099. Demarest, D. D. "(The Theological School, A
       Practical Institution.)" Presbyterian and
       Reformed Review 2 (1891):30+.

1100. DeMille, George E. "One Man Seminary."
       Historical Magazine of the Protestant Epis-
       copal Church 38 (December 1969):373-9.

1101. DeMille, George E. and Gerlach, Don R.
       "Samuel Johnson at Yale: The Roots of Con-
       version, 1710-1722." Connecticut History
       17 (1976):15-41.

1102. Dempster, John. A Discourse on the Minis-
       terial Call. Concord: Jones & Cogswell,
       1854.

1103. Dempster, John. "The Importance, Especially
       to Ministers, of Studying the Scriptures."
       American Pulpit 2 (June 1846):27-37.

1104. Dempster, John. Lectures and Addresses,
       edited by D. W. Clark. Cincinnati: Poe &
       Hitchcock, 1864.

1105. Dempster, John. On Truth: An Address
       Delivered before the Literary Societies of
       the Methodist General Biblical Institute,
       Concord, N.H., November 2, 1852. Concord:
       For the Institute, 1852?

1106. Denison, John H. "The Defects of Ministerial
       Training." In Proceedings of the Second
       Convention of Christian Workers in the
       United States and Canada, pp. 17-27. New
       Haven, Conn.: 1887.

1107. "The Department of the Old Testament in the
       Seminary." Old Testament Student 4
       (November 1884):136-8.

1108. "A Desecration of Liberty." Christian Century
       79 (November 14, 1962):1375-6.

1109. Destler, Chester McArthur. American Radical-
       ism, 1865-1901. New London, Conn.:
       Connecticut College, 1946.

1110. "Devise Way to Give to Theological Education."
       Christian Century 71 (April 28, 1954):507.

1111. Devor, Richard C. "Training for Campus
       Ministry: Another View." Counseling and

Values 16 (Winter 1972):126-35.

1112. De Vries, Abraham. "Ignorant Preachers:
Study of Greek and Hebrew Made Optional."
Christianity Today 14 (January 2, 1970):8-
10.

1113. Deweese, Charles William. "The Contributions
of Albert Henry Newman to Baptist
Historiography." Baptist History and
Heritage 7, no. 1 (1972):2-14.

1114. De Witt, William Converse. The Work of the
Church in Theological Seminaries in the
United States of America. Published for
the Western Theological Seminary, Chicago,
by the Young Churchman Co., 1911.

1115. DeWolf, L. Harold. "Bowne: He Restored
Belief in God as a Person." Together 7
(June 1963):25-7.

1116. DeWolf, L. Harold. "Needed: All-Round
Pastoral Training." Pastoral Psychology 20
(March 1969):7-9.

1117. Dexter, E. G. "Training for Learned Professions." Educational Review 25 (January
1903):29-32.

1118. Dexter, E. G. "Training for the Ministry."
Harper's Weekly 47 (June 6, 1903):960-1.

1119. Dexter, Franklin Bowditch, ed. Documentary
History of Yale University, Under the
Original Charter of the Collegiate School
of Connecticcut 1701-1745. New Haven:
Yale University Press, 1916.

1120. Dexter, H. M. "(Congregational Theological
Seminaries in 1860.)" Congregational
Quarterly 2 (1860):186+.

1121. Dexter, Henry Martyn. The Congregationalism
of the Last Three Hundred Years...In Twelve
Lectures Delivered...in the Theological
Seminary at Andover, Mass., 1876-1879. New
York: B. Franklin, 1970.

1122. Dickey, Samuel. The Position of Greek in the
Theological Education of Today. N.p.,
1907.

1123. Dickey, Samuel. Preparation for Ministry in a
       New World...Being an Address Delivered at
       the Opening of McCormick Theological Semi-
       nary, Sept. 10, 1918. N.p., 1918.

1124. Dickinson, Baxter. "The Importance of an Able
       Ministry." American Quarterly Register 10
       (1838):412-14.

1125. Dictionary of American Biography. S.v.
       "Stuart, Moses."

1126. Diehl, Carl. American and German Scholarship,
       1770-1870. New Haven: Yale University
       Press, 1978.

1127. Dietze, C. E. "Seven Years of Development
       [College of the Bible, Lexington]."
       College of the Bible Quarterly 40 (January
       1963):42-5.

1128. Diffendorfer, R. F. "Training Tomorrow's
       Leaders." World Outlook 5 (May 1919):6.

1129. Diggle, John William. "Training of the
       Clergy." Contemporary Review 100 (November
       1911):661-70.

1130. Dike, S. W. "The Admission of the Study of
       Sociology to the Curriculum of Theological
       Seminaries." In Christianity Practically
       Applied, v. 2, pp. 461-5. Evangelical
       Alliance for the United States of America.
       New York: Baker & Taylor, 1894.

1131. Dike, S. W. "The Sociological Aspect of the
       Subject 'Country Church.'" In Christianity
       Practically Applied, v. 2, pp. 417-20.
       Evangelical Alliance for the United States
       of America. New York: Baker & Taylor,
       1894.

1132. Dillard, Lester Badgett. "Financial Support
       of Protestant Theological Education."
       Ph.D. dissertation, Indiana University,
       1973.

1133. Dillenberger, John. "The Graduate Theological
       Union in the San Francisco Bay Area."
       Journal of Bible and Religion 33 (January
       1965):49-52.

1134. Dillenberger, John. "Unravelling the Library
      Mystique." Theological Education 17
      (Autumn 1980):74-8.

1135. Dillistone, Frederick. "An English Critique."
      Theological Education 2 (Summer 1966):9-22.

1136. Dimer, Stephen. "The City and Its Univer-
      sity." Ph.D. dissertation, University of
      California (?), 1972.

1137. Directory. Vandalia, Ohio: Association of
      Theological Schools in the United States
      and Canada. (Issued annually since 1973;
      formerly, a biannual directory published as
      part of the Association's proceedings
      beginning in 1918).

1138. "Directory of Seminary Offerings." Christian
      Century 84 (April 26, 1967):537-63.

1139. "Directory of Theological Seminaries."
      Christian Century 79 (April 25, 1962):523-
      43.

1140. "Directory of U.S. Seminaries." Christian
      Century 78 (April 26, 1961):517-33.

1141. "Directory: Seminary Offerings." Christian
      Century 80 (April 24, 1963):533-57; 81
      (April 29, 1964):553-77.

1142. "Directory: Seminary Offerings." Christian
      Century 82 (April 28, 1965):529-56.

1143. "Directory: Seminary Offerings." Christian
      Century 83 (April 27, 1966):529-58.

1144. Dirks, Virgil Ralph. "Faculty/Staff and
      Student Perceptions of Public Relations
      Programs in the American Association of
      Bible Colleges." Ed.D. dissertation,
      University of Nebraska - Lincoln, 1977.

1145. Disciples of Christ. Study Commission on
      Ministerial Education. The Imperative Is
      Leadership. St. Louis: Bethany Press,
      1973.

1146. "Discord at Concordia: Ousting of President
      J. J. Tietjen [Concordia Seminary]." Time
      103 (February 4, 1974):54.

1147. "Discord in the Seminaries." _Time_ 59 (June 23, 1952):70.

1148. "The Discussion." _Outlook_ 63 (November 25, 1899):732-5.

1149. "Discussion Highlights [of Convocation on Theological Education as Professional Education]." _Theological Education_ 5 (Spring 1969):262-86.

1150. "Disturbed CRC Conservatives Create Alternative Seminary: Christian Reformed Church's Calvin to Get a Competitor." _Christianity Today_ 25 (September 4, 1981);68-9.

1151. Dittes, James E. and Powers, Charles W. "'Reason For Being' at Union and Yale." _Christian Century_ 87 (April 22, 1970):494-501.

1152. Dittes, James E. "Research on Clergymen: Factors Influencing Decisions for Religious Service and Effectiveness in the Vocation." _Religious Education Research Supplement_ 57 (July-August 1962):S141-S165.

1153. Dittes, James E. _Vocational Guidance of Theological Students: A Manual for Use of the Theological School Inventory_. Dayton, Ohio: Ministry Studies Board, 1964.

1154. "Divinity Ferments." _Newsweek_ 20 (July 13, 1942):58.

1155. "Division of Educational Institutions of the Methodist Episcopal Church." _School and Society_ 33 (June 27, 1931):854.

1156. Dix, William S. "The Princeton University Library in the Eighteenth Century." _Princeton University Library Chronicle_ 40, no. 1 (1978):1-102.

1157. "Do Southern Baptists Fear Liberty?" _Christian Century_ 77 (June 8, 1960):684; McElrath, W. N. "Reply." 77 (August 10, 1960):928-9.

1158. Dobbins, Gaines S. "The Contribution of the Southern Baptist Theological Seminary to Religious Education [1859-1956]." _Review and Expositor_ 53 (April 1956):174-86.

1159. Dobbins, Gaines Stanley. "Men Who Have Made Seminary History [Southern Baptist Theological Seminary]." Quarterly Review (Bap.) 18 (July-September 1958):30-46.

1160. Dobbins, Gaines S. "William Owen Carver, Missionary Pathfinder." Baptist History and Heritage 14, no. 4 (1978):2-6, 15.

1161. "Dr. Briggs on the Higher Criticism and Its Results." Bibliotheca Sacra 46 (April 1889):381-3.

1162. "Dr. Franklin Accepts Crozer Presidency." Christian Century 51 (March 28, 1934):412.

1163. "Dr. Garland's Communications." Christian Advocate (Nashville) 29, (New Series) (November 13, 1869):2.

1164. "Dr. Harper on Theological Seminaries." Outlook 61 (January 7, 1899):89.

1165. "Doctrinal Guidelines Rejected by Concordia Seminary Faculty." Christian Century 89 (April 26, 1972):475.

1166. Dodge, Ralph Edward. The Pagan Church: The Protestant Failure in America. Philadelphia: Lippincott, 1968.

1167. Doerksen, John George. "Mennonite Brethren Bible College and College of Arts: Its History, Philosophy, and Development." Ph.D. dissertation, University of North Dakota, 1968.

1168. "Does 'Advanced' Teaching Empty the Theological Seminaries?" Current Literature 45 (September 1908):297-8.

1169. "Does New Dean Intend New Policy at Yale?" Christian Century 66 (February 2, 1949): 133.

1170. Doggett, Laurence Locke. Man and a School: Pioneering in Higher Education at Springfield College. New York: Association Press, 1943.

1171. Dollar, George W. "A Bibliography of American Fundamentalism." Bibliotheca Sacra 119 (1962):20-7.

1172. Dombrowski, James. "Seminaries Discover a Social Problem." In his Early Days of Christian Socialism in America, pp. 60-73. New York: Columbia University Press, 1936.

1173. "Domesticity in Our Seminaries." Christian Century 75 (April 23, 1958):483-5; "Excerpt." Time 71 (April 28, 1958):71-2; "Discussion." Christian Century 75 (June 4, 1958):659-60, 670-2.

1174. Donahue, B. F. "Political Ecclesiology." Theological Studies 33, no. 2 (1972):294-306.

1175. Donaldson, William Jay. "An Investigation of Graduate Pastoral Counseling Programs in Selected Secular Universities and Schools of Theology." Ph.D. dissertation, Michigan State University, 1962.

1176. Doney, Carl Gregg. An Efficient Church. New York: Fleming H. Revell Co., 1907.

1177. Donlan, Thomas C. Theology and Education. Dubuque: W. C. Brown Co., 1952.

1178. Donohue, J. W. "Dreading to Leave an Illiterate Ministry: Analysis of George Lindbeck's Report Entitled University Divinity Schools." America 134 (March 27, 1976):258-60.

1179. Donovan, James Cornelius. "An Exploration of the Interrelationships of the Leadership Style and Adaptability of Bible College Presidents with Biographical Data." Ph.D. dissertation, Georgia State University, College of Education, 1982.

1180. "Doomed to Banality? [Editorial]." Dialog 4 (Winter 1965):6-7.

1181. Dorchester, Daniel. Concessions of "Liberalists" to Orthodoxy. Boston: D. Lothrop & Co., 1878.

1182. Dorey, F. D. "Negro College Graduates in Schools of Religion." Christian Education 29 (September 1946):350-8.

1183. Dorey, Frank D. "Negro College Graduates in Schools of Religion." Journal of Negro

Education 15 (October 1946):689-94.

1184. Dougherty, Thomas Edward, Jr. "An Appraisal
of a Death Education Process in Clinical
Pastoral Education." Th.D. dissertation,
Southern Baptist Theological Seminary,
1974.

1185. Douglas, Harlan Paul and de Brunner, Edmund.
The Protestant Church as a Social
Institution, (pp. 110-114). New York:
Harper & Bros., 1935, pp. 110-114.

1186. Douglass, H. P. "Employing Church and the
Training of Its Professional Ministers."
Religious Education 10 (October 1915):492-
9.

1187. Dowell, Spright. A History of Mercer
University, 1833-1953. Macon, Ga.: Mercer
University, 1958.

1188. Dowie, J. Iverne. "Town and Gown by the
Mississippi." In The Swedish Immigrant
Community in Transition: Essays in Honor
of Dr. Conrad Bergendoff, pp. 1-17. Rock
Island, Ill.: Augustana Historical
Society, 1963.

1189. Doyle, B. "Missouri Synod's Troubled Campus:
With Discussion [Concordia Seminary]."
Christianity Today 17 (November 24,
1972):20+, 40-1.

1190. Doyle, Laurence Alexander. "A Study of
Personnel Services in Bible Colleges."
Ed.D. dissertation, Boston University,
1963.

1191. Drake, Benjamin Michael. A Sketch of the Life
of Rev. Elijah Steele. Cincinnati:
Printed for the Author, at the Methodist
Book Concern, 1843.

1192. Dreier, William H. "Some Early and Current
Studies of Rural Churches." Paper
Presented at the Annual Meeting of the
Rural Sociological Society, San Francisco,
August 21-24, 1975. (ERIC Document)

1193. Drew University, Madison, N. J. The Teachers
of Drew, 1867-1942, Edited by James Richard

Jay. Madison, N.J.: Drew University, 1942.

1194. Driver, Tom F. "Seminary Education: New Purpose-In-Being." Union Seminary Quarterly Review 22 (May 1967):297-305.

1195. "Drought Hits the Halls of Divinity." Christian Century 88 (January 27, 1961):91-3.

1196. Drury, Clifford M. "Reminiscences of a Historian." Western Historical Quarterly 5, no. 2 (1974):132-49.

1197. Drury, Clifford Merrill. William Anderson Scott: "No Ordinary Man." Glendale, Calif.: Arthur H. Clark Co., 1967.

1198. Dudde, William A. "The Devotional Life of a Seminary Student." Christian Education 24 (June 1941):303-5.

1199. Duewel, Wesley L. "Supervision of Field Work in American Protestant Theological Seminaries." Ph.D. dissertation, University of Cincinnati, 1952.

1200. Duffy, John J. "Problems in Publishing Coleridge: James Marsh's First American Edition of 'Aids to Reflection.'" New England Quarterly 43, no. 2 (1970):193-208.

1201. Dugan, Richard Pierce. "The Theory of Education within the Bible Institute Movement at Selected Critical Times." Ph.D. dissertation, New York University, 1977.

1202. Duke, Robert W. "Seminary Worship." Theological Education 2 (Autumn 1965):42-6.

1203. Duke, Thomas Allen. "Attitudes, Interests and Experiences of Lutheran Seminary Interns, an Exploratory Study." Ph.D. dissertation, University of Minnesota, 1979.

1204. Dulles, John Foster. "The Significance of Theological Education." In The Spiritual Legacy of John Foster Dulles: Selections from his Articles and Addresses, pp. 213-16. Edited by Henry P. Van Dusen. Philadelphia: Westminster Press, 1960.

1205. Dunbar, W. H. "(Conservative Theological Teaching.)" _Lutheran Quarterly_ 35 (New Series) (1905):556+.

1206. Dunbar, W. H. "(Theological Training of Our Preachers.)" _Lutheran Quarterly_ 35 (New Series) (1905):1+.

1207. Duncan, Richard R. "The College of St. James nd the Civil War: A Casualty of War." _Historical Magazine of the Protestant Episcopal Church_ 39 (September 1970):265-86.

1208. Duncombe, David C. "Binocular Rivalry as an Indicator of Spiritual Growth in CPE." _Journal of Pastoral Care_ 31, no. 1 (1977):18-22.

1209. Duncombe, D. C. "Experiment in Interprofessional Education: A Model for Clinical Pastoral Education?" _Journal of Pastoral Care_ 24 (September 1970):202-4.

1210. Duncombe, David C. "Five Years at Yale: The Seminar on the Chronically Ill." _Journal of Pastoral Care_ 28, no. 3 (1974):152-63.

1211. Dunn, L. R. "Our Local Ministry." _Methodist Quarterly Review_ 17 (New Series) (October 1865):549-59.

1212. Dunn, Samuel. "Our Ministry." _Methodist Quarterly Review_ 19 (New Series) (October 1867):590-606.

1213. Durbin, John Price. "Theological Seminaries." _Christian Advocate_ (New York) 9 (August 29, 1834):3.

1214. Durnin, Richard G. "William Harris: Schoolmaster, Churchman and Columbia College President." _Historical Magazine of the Protestant Episcopal Church_ 35 (December 1966):387-94.

1215. "The Duty of the Theological Seminary in Reference to Bible Study." _Old Testament Student_ 5 (January 1886):234-5.

1216. Duvall, Sylvanus Milne. _The Methodist Episcopal Church and Education up to 1869._ New York: Teachers College, Columbia

University, 1928; reprint ed., New York: AMS Press, 1972.

1217. Duzen, N. W. "Table Talk at Catasauqua." Christian Century 72 (April 27, 1955):501+.

1218. Dwight, Henry Otis. The Centennial History of the American Bible Society. New York: Macmillan, 1916.

1219. Dwight, Theodore William. Argument for Egbert C. Smyth, Respondent before the Board of Visitors of Andover Theological Seminary. Boston: Rand Avery Co., 1887.

1220. Dwight, Timothy. "Duty of Preaching the Gospel." In his Sermons, v. 2, pp. 433-52. New Haven: H. Howe, Durry & Peck, 1828.

1221. Dwight, Timothy. The Nature and Danger of Infidel Philosophy, Exhibited in Two Discourses, Addressed to the Candidates for the Baccalaureate, In Yale College, September 9, 1797. New Haven: Printed by George Bunce, 1798.

1222. Dwight, Timothy. A Sermon Preached at the Opening of the Theological Institution in Andover: And at the Ordination of Rev. Eliphalet Pearson, September 28th, 1808. Boston: Farrand, Mallory & Co., 1808.

1223. Dwight, Timothy. Travels: In New England and New York. 4 vols. New Haven: T. Dwight, 1821 -   , v. 4, pp. 319-21.

1224. Dyer, Edward John. "A Description of Present Financial Practices and Policies of the Protestant Episcopal Church in the United States in Supporting Theological Education." Ed.D. dissertation, Temple University, 1965.

1225. Dyer, J. "(Theological Education in America.)" Penn Monthly 11 (1880):599+.

1226. Dykes, K. C. "Baptists and the Ministry: The Baptist Minister and the Baptist Union." Baptist Quarterly 18 (April 1959):54-62.

1227. Dyrness, E. C. "Fake Degrees in the Pulpit." Christianity Today 3 (May 11, 1959):8-10.

1228. Dyson, Walter. Howard University, the
      Capstone of Negro Education: A History,
      1867-1940. Washington: Graduate School,
      Howard University, 1941.

1229. Eagen, Larry John. "Institutional Planning
      Practices in Bible Colleges Accredited by
      the American Association of Bible
      Colleges." Ed.D. dissertation, Texas Tech
      University, 1980.

1230. Early, Tracy. "Seminary's Library a Trove for
      Bible Scholars [Union Theological Semi-
      nary]." Christian Science Monitor 71 (July
      9, 1979):14.

1231. Early, T. "Union Seminary and Student Power."
      Christian Century 86 (July 30, 1969):1024+.

1232. Early, Tracy. "Women Helping to Swell
      Seminary Enrollments." Christian Science
      Monitor 72 (June 12, 1980):7.

1233. Easley, J. A. "Statement on Pre-Theological
      Studies [Issued by the American Association
      of Theological Schools]." Journal of Bible
      and Religion 25 (July 1957):211-15.

1234. Eastman, Fred. "Dr. Cabot's Appeal to the
      Seminaries." Christian Work (December 26,
      1925):674-6.

1235. Eastman, F. "Father of the Clinical Pastoral
      Movement." Journal of Pastoral Care 5, no.
      1 (1951):3-7.

1236. Eastman, Fred. "Theological Education Today."
      Christian Century 52 (May 8, 1935):603-5.

1237. Eastman, F. "Theological Education Tomorrow."
      Christian Century 52 (May 15, 1935):637-9.

1238. Easton, Burton Scott. "America's Contribution
      to New Testament Science." Expository
      Times 42 (1930-31):265-9.

1239. Eaton, Anna Ruth. A Memorial of Rev. Horace
      Eaton, D. D. Boston: J. S. Cushing & Co.,
      1885.

1240. Eaton, Clement. "Professor James Woodrow and
      the Freedom of Teaching in the South."
      Journal of Southern History 28, no. 1

(1962):3-17.

1241. Ebeling, Gerhard. The Study of Theology.
Translated by Duane A. Priebe. Philadelphia: Fortress Press, 1978.

1242. Eberdt, Mary G. "Adapting Secular Post-
Graduate Education in Counseling to Meet
the Needs of Ministers." Counselor
Education and Supervision 9 (Winter
1970):122-5.

1243. Eberhardt, Charles Richard. The Bible in the
Making of Ministers: The Life Work of
William Webster White. New York: Associa-
tion Press, 1949.

1244. Eby, Frederick. Christianity and Education.
Dallas: Executive Board of the Baptist
General Convention of Texas, 1915.

1245. Eckardt, A. R., comp. "Bibliography: Pre-
Seminary Education and the Study of
Religion." Journal of Bible and Religion
34 (April 1966).

1246. Eckardt, A. Roy. "Pre-Seminary Education and
the Undergraduate Department of Religion."
Theological Education 1 (Spring 1965):149-
53.

1247. Ecob, J. H. "Freedom of Theological Teaching." New World 4 (September 1895):495-
505.

1248. Ecob, J. H. "Plea for Freedom of Theological
Teaching." Review of Reviews 12 (October
1895):477.

1249. "Ecumenical Campus." Christianity Today 98
(September 16, 1981):897.

1250. "Ecumenical Education for Ministers."
Christian Century 60 (June 9, 1943):686-7.

1251. "Ecumenical Move at Berkeley: Graduate Theological Union." America 117 (December 16,
1967):730.

1252. "Ecumenical Way of Learning: Manhattan's
Protestant Union Theological Seminary and
Fordham University Exchange Projects."
Time 87 (March 4, 1966):86.

109

1253. "Ecumenism in Theological Seminaries."
       Religious Education 62 (1967):200-2.

1254. Eddy, George Sherwood. A Century with Youth:
       A History of the Y.M.C.A. from 1844 to
       1944. New York: Association Press, 1944.

1255. Eddy, R. L. "Speaking for the Class of 1938."
       Harvard Divinity Bulletin 27 (July 1963):7-
       12.

1256. "Eden Observes Centennial." Christian Century
       67 (June 21, 1950):767-8.

1257. Edge, Findley B. "Gaines S. Dobbins: The
       Teacher." Review and Expositor 75 (Summer
       1978):371-82.

1258. (Editorial) Methodist Review 71 (July
       1889):579-83.

1259. Edman, V. R. "The Idea of a Christian
       College." United Evangelical Action 5
       (November 1, 1946):3.

1260. Edmundson, Daniel Lee. "A Historical and
       Comparative Survey of the Major
       Contemporary Theologies and the Extent of
       Their Influence upon the American
       Protestant Seminaries." Ph.D. disserta-
       tion, Bob Jones University, 1962.

1261. "An Educated Ministry." Christian Advocate
       (Nashville) 29 (New Series) (November 27,
       1869):1.

1262. "An Educated Ministry." Christian Advocate
       and Journal (New York) 29 (January 26,
       1854):1.

1263. "(Educated Ministry.)" Christian Review 18
       (1853):567+.

1264. "An Educated Ministry among Us." Christian
       Advocate (New York) 8 (July 18, 1834):186.

1265. "Educating for the Christian Ministry: A
       Symposium." Religious Education 40
       (January 1945):3-22.

1266. "Education and Its Money: School of Religion,
       Butler University, and Its Support from the
       Christian Foundation." Christian Century

58 (September 17, 1941):1136-7.

1267. "Education and Unity of Pursuit of the Christian Ministry." National Quarterly Review 5 (1862):106-18.

1268. "(Education for Christian Ministry.)" Quarterly Review of the Methodist Episcopal Church, South 46 (1886):577+.

1269. "(Education for Ministry.)" American Quarterly Register 12 (1840):98+.

1270. "(Education for Ministry.)" Andover Review 8 (1887):536+.

1271. "(Education for Ministry.)" Christian Review 2 (1837):260+.

1272. "(Education for Ministry.)" New Englander 1 (1843):126+.

1273. "(Education for Ministry in Georgia.)" Christian Review 2 (1837):579+.

1274. Education for the Ministry: Seminaries of the Disciples of Christ. Indianapolis: Board of Higher Education, 195?

1275. "Education in Theology [Editorial]." Theology Today 7 (July 1950):145-50.

1276. Education of American Ministers. 4 vols. New York: Institute of Social and Religious Research, 1934.

1277. "Educational Paradox: Academic Freedom and Theological Schools." Nation 87 (September 17, 1908):254-5.

1278. "Educational Qualifications for the Ministry." Methodist Quarterly Review 19 (New Series) (April 1867):221-36.

1279. Edwards, B. B. "History of American Colleges." American Quarterly Register 3 (May 1831):263-308.

1280. [Edwards, Bela Bates] "Influence of Eminent Piety on the Human Mind." American Quarterly Register 7 (August 1834):9-14.

1281. Edwards, Bela Bates. Memoir of the Rev. Elias Cornelius. Boston: Perkins, Marvin & Co., 1834.

1282. Edwards, B. B. "Reasons for the Study of the Hebrew Language." American Biblical Repository 12 (July 1838):113-32.

1283. Edwards, B. B. "Theological Education in the United States.)" Journal of Sacred Literature 4 (1850):145+.

1284. Edwards, Bela Bates. Writings of Professor B. B. Edwards, With a Memoir by Edwards A. Park. 2 vols. Andover: W. F. Draper, 1858.

1285. Edwards, David Lawrence, ed. Preparing for the Ministry of the 1970's: Essays on the British Churches. London: SCM Press, 1964.

1286. Edwards, Mary A. D. "To Know with Feeling [Seminary Class on Aging]." Theological Education 16, Special Issue no. 3 (Winter 1980):370-3.

1287. Edwards, O. C., Jr. "The Strange Case of the Diocesan Training Schools [Episcopalian]." Christian Century 97, no. 5 (1980):131-3.

1288. Edwards, Tilden H. "Spiritual Formation in Theological Schools: Ferment and Challenge: A Report of the ATS-Shalem Institute on Spirituality." Theological Education 17 (Autumn 1980):7-52.

1289. Eells, W. C. "Center of Population of Theological Education, 1870-1930." Christian Education 19 (April 1936):327-31.

1290. Eenigenburg, E. M. "New Curriculum at Western Seminary." Reformed Review 20 (December 1966):59-63.

1291. Eichelberger, James W. "The African Methodist Episcopal Zion Church: The Rationale and Policies upon Which Maintenance of Its Colleges Is Based." Journal of Negro Education 29 (Summer 1960):323-9.

1292. Eichelberger, James William. The Religious Education of the Negro. An Address

Delivered at the International Convention
of Religious Education, Toronto, Canada,
June 26, 1930. Chicago: Herald Press,
1931.

1293. Eighmy, John Lee. Churches in Cultural
Captivity: A History of the Social
Attitudes of Southern Baptists. Knoxville:
University of Tennessee Press, 1972.

1294. Eikmeier, Hermann. "The Lutheran Proseminary
in Steeden." Translated by John Theodore
Mueller. Concordia Historical Institute
Quarterly 29 (Winter 1957):137-53.

1295. Eiselen, F. C. "Correlation of Colleges and
Theological Seminaries." In Proceedings
... of the Annual Session January, 1931,
Held at the Claypool Hotel, Indianapolis,
Indiana, pp. 37-41. Methodist Episcopal
Church. Board of Education. Educational
Association. The Associaiton, 1931.

1296. Eiselen, Frederick Carl. The Theological
School of Today. Evanston, Ill.: Garrett
Biblical Institute, 1912.

1297. Elbrecht, Paul George. "Preferences Regarding
Programs of Theological Education as
Expressed by Lutheran Laymen." Ph.D.
dissertation, University of Alabama, 1970.

1298. Elder, J. D. "Meeting the Crisis of Negro
Leadership in the Church [Harvard]."
Harvard Divinity Bulletin 1 (New Series)
(Autumn 1967):17-18.

1299. "(Elective System in Theological Education.)"
Bibliotheca Sacra 36 (1879):367+.

1300. "11th Annual Pastors' Institute and Educational Conference, Chicago Theological
Seminary, July 27-August 8, 1942."
Publishers' Weekly 142 (August 8,
1942):380.

1301. Eliot, C. W. "(Education for Christian
Ministry.)" Princeton Review 11, Series 4
(1883):340+.

1302. Eliot, C. W. "On the Education of Ministers."
In his Educational Reform, p. 61. New
York: Century, 1898.

113

1303. Eliot, Charles W. "Theological Education at
       Harvard between 1816 and 1916." In
       Addresses Delivered at the Observance of
       the 100th Anniversary of the Establishment
       of Harvard Divinity School..., pp. 32-68.
       Harvard University Divinity School.
       Cambridge: Harvard University, 1917.

1304. Eliot, S. A. "(Theological Education.)"
       Christian Examiner and Theological Review 2
       (1825):57-64.

1305. Eller, Paul Himmel Evangelical Theological
       Seminary, 1873-1973, Shaping Ministry.
       Naperville, Ill.: Evangelical Theological
       Seminary, 1973.

1306. Ellerton, John, ed. A Manual of Parochial
       Work for the Use of the Younger Clergy.
       London: Society for Promoting Christian
       Knowledge, 1888.

1307. Elley, R. D. "Dignity of Man: A Clinical
       Note." Journal of Pastoral Care 10 (Spring
       1956):40-4.

1308. Ellinwood, Mary Gridley. Frank Field
       Ellinwood: His Life and Work. New York:
       Fleming H. Revell Co., 1911.

1309. Elliott, Charles. "Ministerial Culture."
       Central Christian Advocate 2 (April 26,
       1858):70.

1310. Elliott, Philip Ross Courtney. The Sociology
       of the Professions. New York: Herder &
       Herder, 1972.

1311. Elliott-Binns, Leonard Elliott. The Early
       Evangelicals. Greenwich, Conn.: Seabury
       Press, 1953.

1312. Ellis, Edward Earle. "Language Skills and
       Christian Ministry." Reformed Review 24
       (Spring 1971):162-3.

1313. Ellis, Edward Earle. "What Good are Hebrew
       and Greek?" Christianity Today 16 (May 26,
       1972):8-9.

1314. Ellis, John Tracy. Essays in Seminary Educa-
       tion. Notre Dame, Ind.: Fides Publishers,
       1967.

114

1315. Ellis, William E. "Edgar Young Mullins and the Crisis of Moderate Southern Baptist Leadership." Foundations 19 (April-June 1976):171-85.

1316. Ellison, Fay H. "Modest Proposal [On Placement of Women Seminarians]." Theological Education 11 (Winter 1975):106-11.

1317. Ellwanger, Walter H. "Lutheranism in Alabama and Other Parts of the South [Education for Black Ministerial Students]." Concordia Historical Institute Quarterly 48, no. 2 (1975):35-43.

1318. Elmer, Duane Harold. "Career Data as Indicators for Curriculum Development in Theological Education." Ph.D. dissertation, Michigan State University, 1980.

1319. Emerton, E. "Place of History in Theological Study." In Learning and Living: Academic Essays, pp. 309-25. Cambridge: Harvard University Press, 1921.

1320. Emerton, E. "Rational Education of the Modern Minister." In Learning and Living: Academic Essays, pp. 269-307. Cambridge: Harvard University Press, 1921.

1321. Emrick, E. H. "The Bethany They Remember." Brethren Life and Thought 11 (Summer 1966):4-36.

1322. Emswiler, Tom Jr. "Theological Education and Mass Communication." Theological Education 4 (Winter 1968):623-8.

1323. Encyclopedia of Southern Baptists, 1958 ed. S.v. "Boyce, J. P."

1324. Encyclopedia of Southern Baptists, 1958 ed. S.v. "Broadus, J. A."

1325. Encyclopedia of Southern Baptists, 1958 ed. S.v. "Manley, Jr., Basil."

1326. Encyclopedia of Southern Baptists. S.v. "Sandy Creek Church," by G. W. Paschal.

1327. Encyclopedia of Southern Baptists, 1958 ed. S.v. "Winkler, E.T."

1328. Encyclopedia of the Presbyterian Church in the United States of America, 1884 ed. S.v. "The German Theological School of Newark, N. J."

1329. Encyclopedia of the Social Sciences, 1931 ed. S.v. "Fundamentalism," by H. Richard Niebuhr.

1330. Engel, David E. "Educating the Layman Theologically." Theology Today 21 (1964):196-205.

1331. Engel, David E., ed. Pedagogy in Higher Education: Notes on the Continuing Education of a Theological Faculty. East Lansing, Mich.: Christian Faith & Higher Education Institute, 1964.

1332. Engelbrecht, A. "Teachers and Curriculum." Wartburg Seminary Quarterly 17 (November 1954):34-41.

1333. Engle, Gale Winston. "William Rainey Harper's Conception of the Structuring of the Functions Performed by Educational Institutions." Ph.D. dissertation, Stanford University, 1954.

1334. English, Eugune Schuyler. H. A. Ironside: Ordained of the Lord. Grand Rapids, Mich.: Zondervan, 1946.

1335. "English Bible in Theological Education." Biblical World 37 (April 1911):219-23.

1336. Enslin, M. S. "Future of Biblical Studies." Journal of Biblical Literature 65 (March 1946):1-12.

1337. Ensworth, George, Jr. "The Comparative Effect of Theological Belief and Intolerance on the Responses of First-Year Seminary Students in a Quasi-Interview Situation with Parishioners." Ph.D. dissertation, Michigan State University, 1967.

1338. "The Entire Faculty of Fuller Theological Seminary School of World Mission Has Sent a Letter to Reader's Digest." Christianity Today 24 (June 6, 1980):53.

1339. Episcopal Theological Seminary of the
       Southwest, Austin, Tex. The Mission of the
       Anglican Communion to Mexico and Central
       America. Edited by Das Kelley Barnett.
       Austin: Research Center in Christian
       Theology and Culture, 1961.

1340. Ericson, C. George. "A Century in Theologi-
       cal Education." Swedish Pioneer Historical
       Quarterly 22 (January 1971):21-33.

1341. Erling, Bernhard. "A Proposal for a Lutheran
       Graduate Seminary." Lutheran Quarterly 2
       (November 1950):450-3.

1342. "Ernest DeWitt Burton." Christian Century
       (June 4, 1925):723-4.

1343. "Establish Mental Health Curriculums for Theo-
       logical Students." Christian Century 73
       (September 5, 1956):1038.

1344. Estep, William R. "A. H. Newman and South-
       western's First Faculty." Southwestern
       Journal of Theology 21 (Fall 1978):83-98.

1345. Eubank, Earle. "Sociological Instruction in
       American Protestant Seminaries, 1936."
       Religious Education 32 (October-December
       1937):269-80.

1346. "Evangelical Education: Catholic Campuses
       Purchased by Evangelical (Bible) Schools."
       Christianity Today 14 (October 24, 1969):
       45.

1347. "Evanston Ringed by School Meets." Christian
       Century 71 (September 1, 1954):1044-6.

1348. Evenson, J. "New Leader, New Motif for New
       York Seminary." Christianity Today 13
       (March 28, 1969):42.

1349. Evenson, J. "Thinking Black in Newark:
       Philadelphia's Conwell School of Theology."
       Christianity Today 13 (November 22,
       1968):41.

1350. "(Events at the Divinity School [Chicago])."
       Criterion 9 (Winter 1970):4-27.

1351. Everett, Gill. A. T. Robertson, A Biography.
       New York: MacMillan Co., 1943.

117

1352. Evjen, J. O. "Basic Features of the Theological Curriculum." In Proceedings of the 1927 Convention, pp. 59-65. National Lutheran Educational Conference.

1353. Evjen, J. O. "Some Aspects of the Work and Requirements of a Graduate School of Theology [bibliog.]." Lutheran Quarterly 56 (January 1926):38-83.

1354. Evlee, Richard A. "Education for Christian Leadership in Bible Institutes and Bible Colleges." Ph.D. dissertation, State University of New York at Buffalo, 1953.

1355. Evoy, John J. "How Neurotic Is the New Breed?" Thought 41, no. 160 (1966):81-98.

1356. Ewin, Finis. "A Series of Letters, Containing a Reply to a Pastoral Letter of West Tennessee Presbytery. To Which Is Added an Address to the Congregations &c. under the Care of Cumberland Presbytery, By a Member of that Body." Russellville, Ky.: Printed for the Author, by Matthew Duncan, 1812.

1357. "Extracts from the Report on Education." American Quarterly Register 12 (1840):98-100.

1358. Fact Book on Theological Education. Vandalia, Ohio: Association of Theological Schools in the United States and Canada. (Issued annually since 1969).

1359. "Fact Book Reveals No Substantial Change in Seminary Enrollment." Christian Century 88 (June 16, 1971):740.

1360. "The Faculty of the Seminary." Chicago Lutheran Seminary Record 11 (April 1906):33-8.

1361. "Fading Big Five: Rockefeller Foundation Report." Time 107 (March 8, 1976):64.

1362. Failing, George E. "Developments in Holiness Theology after Wesley." In Insights into Holiness: Discussions of Holiness by Fifteen Leading Scholars of the Wesleyan Persuasion, pp. 11-31. Compiled by Kenneth Geiger. Kansas City, Mo.: Beacon Hill Press, 1962.

1363. Fairbairn, A. M. "Theology as an Academic
Discipline." Contemporary Review 51
(1887):196-219.

1364. Fairbairn, A. M. "Theology in the University
and in the Seminary." Outlook 52 (November
9, 1895):747-8; Christian Literature 14
(1896):169+.

1365. Fairbairn, Patrick. Pastoral Theology: A
Treatise on the Office and Duties of the
Christian Pastor. Edinburgh: T. & T.
Clark, 1875.

1366. Fairbank, John King, ed. The Missionary
Enterprise in China and America.
Cambridge: Harvard University Press, 1974.

1367. Fairbanks, Rollin J. "On Clinical Pastoral
Training." Christian Century 80 (April 24,
1963):556-9.

1368. Fairbanks, R. J. "One Seminary Looks at
Clinical Training." Journal of Pastoral
Care 18 (Winter 1964):208-12.

1369. Fairchild, J. H. "The True Principle of Theological Progress." Bibliotheca Sacra 41
(July 1884):573-85.

1370. Fairhurst, Alfred. Atheism in Our Universities. Cincinnati, Ohio: Standard
Publishing Co., 1923.

1371. Fallaw, Wesner. "Building 'the Seminary
Family.'" Christian Century 69 (April 30,
1952):526+.

1372. Fallaw, Wesner. The Case Method in Pastoral
and Lay Education. Philadelphia: Westminster Press, 1963.

1373. Fallaw, Wesner. "Governance of the Theological School." Theological Education 7
(Autumn 1970):38-46.

1374. "Falling off in the Number of Students for the
Ministry." American Magazine 66 (September
1908):512-3.

1375. Fallows, W. G. "Anglican Tradition of Sound
Learning." Modern Churchman 4 (New Series)
(October 1960):64-73.

1376. Falls, Helen E. "The Vocation of Home
       Missions 1845-1970." Baptist History and
       Heritage 7, no. 1 (1972):25-32.

1377. Fangmeier, R. A. "Seminary Drama and the God
       is Dead Theme." Christian Century 84 (June
       28, 1967):846-7.

1378. Farace, Charles. The History of Old Testament
       Higher Criticism in the United States.
       Chicago, 1939.

1379. Farber, Benjamin F. "The Seminary Student
       Yesterday and Today." Theology Today 13
       (1956):182-8.

1380. Farish, Hunter Dickinson. The Circuit Rider
       Dismounts: A Social History of Southern
       Methodism, 1865-1900. New York: Da Capo
       Press, 1969. [c 1938]

1381. Farley, Edward. "Can the Nonconservative
       Seminaries Help the Churches?" Christian
       Century 91 (February 6, 1974):126+.

1382. Farley, Edward. "The Reform of Theological
       Education as a Theological Task."
       Theological Education 17 (Spring 1981):93-
       117.

1383. Farmer, Herbert H. "Sense of Vocation in the
       Christian Ministry." Princeton Seminary
       Bulletin 55 (January 1962):12-18.

1384. Farmerie, Samuel A. "Carrier Seminary - A
       Short-Lived Methodist Educational Venture."
       Western Pennsylvania Historical Magazine 52
       (April 1969):129-39.

1385. Farris, Donn Michael. "The American Theo-
       logical Library Association." Special
       Libraries 58, no. 2 (1967):111-12.

1386. Fasti Academiae Mariscallanae Aberdonensis.
       Selections from the Records of the
       Marischal College and University MDXCIII -
       MDCCCLX. Edited by Peter John Anderson. 2
       vols. Aberdeen: Printed for the New
       Spalding Club, 1889.

1387. Faszer, Theodore Maurice. "The Preparation of
       Ministerial Students in Selected Seminaries
       To Plan and Lead Worship." Ed.D.

dissertation, University of South Dakota,
1979.

1388. Fatis, Michael. "Humanistic-Experiential
Models in Pastoral Counseling: A
Critique." Journal of Psychology and
Theology 7, no. 4 (1979):281-5.

1389. Faulkner, John Alfred. "Theological Education
in America in the Light of Recent Discussion." Methodist Review (January 1903):58-
64.

1390. Faulkner, John Alfred. "Theological Seminary
Orthodoxy: A Statement in History."
Methodist Review 86 (July 1904):629-32.

1391. Faulkner, John Alfred. "The Tragic Fate of a
Famous Seminary." Bibliotheca Sacra 80
(October 1923):449-64.

1392. Faunce, William Herbert Perry. The Educational Ideal in the Ministry. New York:
Macmillan, 1908.

1393. Faupel, D. William. "Budgeting Library Costs
in a Day of Shrinking Dollar Values." ATLA
Proceedings 34 (1980):95-8.

1394. Faust, D. E. "Pre-Seminary Training in Church
Colleges." Christian Education 20 (June
1937):380-4.

1395. "Federated Faculty Steals a March: Churches
Came before Foundations." Christian
Century 74 (March 6, 1957):283.

1396. Fehl, Noah Edward. "Case for Systematic
Theology (Anglican Theological Education)."
Anglican Theological Review 41 (January
1959):23-35.

1397. Feilding, Charles Rudolph. "Education for
Ministry [bibliog.]" Theological Education
3 (Autumn 1966):entire issue.

1398. Feilding, Charles. "Supervision as an Educational Method in Theological Education,
Including Continuing Education." American
Association of Theological Schools. Proceedings (1964):57-62.

1399.   Fellows, M. and Dickinson, C., eds. "Study of
        Sacred Music [Union Theological Seminary,
        NYC]." Etude 64 (August 1946):437+.

1400.   Felton, R. A. "Country Preacher Goes Back to
        School." World Outlook 6 (July 1920):29.

1401.   Felton, R. A. "Negro Pastors Go to Rural
        Colleges." Christian Century 60 (September
        22, 1943):1076.

1402.   Felton, Ralph Almon. New Ministers: A Study
        of 1978 Ministerial Students To Determine
        the Factors Which Influence Men To Enter
        the Ministry. Madison, N.J.: Dept. of the
        Rural Church, Drew Theological Seminary,
        1949.

1403.   Felton, Ralph Almon. "Untrained Negro
        Clergy." Christian Century 72 (February 2,
        1955):141-2.

1404.   "Female Seminarians." Christian Century 99
        (February 3-10, 1982):111.

1405.   Ferm, Vergilius Ture Anselm, ed. Contemporary
        American Theology: Theological Auto-
        biographies. 2 vols. New York: Round
        Table Press, 1932-33.

1406.   Fernlund, Jay Courtney. "An Analysis of the
        Internal Organizational Structure of the
        Educational Branches of Selected Bible
        Colleges." Ed.D. dissertation, Loyola
        University of Chicago, 1978.

1407.   Ferris, John L. and Gorrell, Donald K.
        "Educating Women for Ministry at the United
        Brethren Seminary (1874-1946)." In Women's
        Rightful Place, pp. 41-53. Edited by D.
        Gorrell. Dayton, Ohio: United Theological
        Seminary, 1980.

1408.   Ferris, Robert Weston. "The Emphasis on
        Leadership as Servanthood: An Analysis of
        Curriculum Commitments." Ph.D. disserta-
        tion, Michigan State University, 1982.

1409.   Fevold, Eugene L. The Lutheran Free Church:
        A Fellowship of American Lutheran
        Congregations, 1897-1963. Minneapolis:
        Augsburg Publishing House, 1969.

1410. "A Few Questions about Educating Preachers."
       Christian Advocate (Nashville) (August 15,
       1867):2.

1411. Fewster, Lowell H. "Marketing and Recruit-
       ment: Two Unholy Words and Their Possible
       Usefulness in Theological Education."
       Theological Education 16 (Spring 1980):457-
       64.

1412. Fey, Harold E. "First North American
       Interseminary Conference Meets in Oxford,
       Ohio." Christian Century 64 (July 2,
       1947):833.

1413. Fey, Harold Edward. Ministerial Education at
       Christian Theological Seminary.
       Indianapolis: Christian Theological
       Seminary, 1964?

1414. Fey, H. E. "Theological Schoolmen Meet in
       Chicago (AATS)." Christian Century 71
       (June 30, 1954):800.

1415. "Field Experience and Seminary Education."
       Theological Education 7 (Summer 1971):
       entire issue.

1416. "Field Work Policy for Theological Students."
       Christian Education 27 (June 1944):241-3.

1417. Fielder, Daniel William. "A Nomothetic Study
       of the Southern California School of
       Theology Seminarian." Th.D. dissertation,
       Southern California School of Theology,
       1964.

1418. Fiering, Norman S. "President Samuel Johnson
       and the Circle of Knowledge." William and
       Mary Quarterly 28 (3rd Series) (April
       1971):199-236.

1419. Fiering, Norman S. "Solomon Stoddard's
       Library at Harvard in 1664." Harvard
       Library Bulletin 20, no. 3 (1972):255-69.

1420. "Fifty, Going on Forward: Dallas Seminary."
       Christianity Today 18 (March 15, 1974):54.

1421. Fike, Jr., E. W. "The Shape of Ministry
       Tomorrow." Brethren Life and Thought 15
       (Winter 1970).

1422. Fillinger, Robert Earl. "A Study of Factors Affecting Teaching in Protestant Theological Seminaries." Ed.D. dissertation, Boston University School of Education, 1974.

1423. Findlay, James. "Agency, Denominations and the Western Colleges, 1830-1860: Some Connections between Evangelicalism and American Higher Education." Church History 50 (March 1981):64-80.

1424. Findlay, James F., Jr. Dwight L. Moody: American Evangelist, 1837-1899. Chicago: University of Chicago Press, 1969.

1425. Findlay, James. "Education and Church Controversy: The Later Career of Dwight L. Moody." New England Quarterly 39 (June 1966):210-32.

1426. Findlay, James. "Moody, 'Gapmen,' and the Gospel: The Early Days of Moody Bible Institute [bibliog.]." Church History 31 (September 1962):322-35.

1427. Findlay, James. "The SPCTEW and Western Colleges: Religion and Higher Education in Mid-Nineteenth Century America." History of Education Quarterly 17, no. 1 (1977):31-62.

1428. Findley, William Scott. "I'm Going to Be a Minister." Saturday Evening Post 221 (September 25, 1948):30+.

1429. Fink, Arthur S. "The Church and Its Ministry: Crisis and Renewal." McCormick Quarterly 17 (March 1964):35-42.

1430. Finney, Thomas M. The Life and Labors of Enoch Mather Marvin. St. Louis: James H. Chambers, 1880.

1431. "(Finney on Education for Ministry.)" Congregational Quarterly 20 (1878):401+.

1432. Fischer, Thomas R. A Report on Seminary Education: The Social Science Curriculum in Catholic Seminaries. St. Louis: B. Herder Book Co., 1967 [c 1966].

1433. Fisher, Daniel Webster. A Human Life: An Autobiography with Excursuses. New York: Fleming H. Revell Co., 1909.

1434. Fisher, G. P. "Systematic Training for the Ministry." New Englander 25 (1866):200-17.

1435. Fisher, James V. "A Reflection on Models." Theological Education 5 (Summer 1969):334-7.

1436. Fisher, J. V. "Rockefeller Anthropodicy." Harvard Divinity Bulletin 3 (New Series) (Fall 1969):17-19.

1437. Fisher, Miles Mark. "Negroes as Christian Ministers." Journal of Negro Education 4 (January 1935):53-9.

1438. Fisher, S. R. "Qualifications for the Christian Ministry." Mercersburg Quarterly Review 6 (1854):423-35.

1439. Fisk, W. "Education and Religion." Christian Advocate (New York) 9 (February 13, 1835):97.

1440. Fisk, Wilbur. "An Introductory Address, Delivered at the Opening of the Wesleyan Academy, in Wilbraham, Mass., Nov. 8, 1825." Methodist Magazine 9 (June 1826):213-23

1441. Fisk, Wilbur. The Science of Education. New York: M'Elrath & Bangs, Printers, 1832.

1442. Fitch, Robert E. "Mit Brennender Sorge." Christian Century 79 (April 25, 1962):544-6.

1443. Fite, J. David. "Continuing Education for Ministry." Southwestern Journal of Theology 15, no. 2 (1973):57-69.

1444. Fitzgibbon, C. "Philadelphia Divinity School: Zantzinger, Borie & Medary, Architects." Architectural Record 54 (August 1923):106-20.

1445. Fitzpatrick, T. Mallary. "Footnotes on Theological Education." Hartford Quarterly 8 (Summer 1968):7-28.

1446. "500 Seminary Students Meet in Rock Island:
Second Triennial National Conference of
Seminary Students." Christian Century 67
(January 11, 1950):37.

1447. Flatt, Bill. "Predicting Academic Success of
Graduate Students in Religion." Review of
Religious Research 14 (Winter 1973):110-11.

1448. Fleming, Donald. William H. Welch and the
Rise of Modern Medicine. Boston: Little,
Brown & Co., 1972.

1449. Fleming, Sandford. "Board of Education and
Theological Education, 1911-1963." Foundations 8 (January 1965):3-25.

1450. Fletcher, J. "INTER-MET: Bold Venture in
Theological Education." Thesis Theological
Cassettes 1, no. 12 (1970).

1451. Fletcher, John C. and Edwards, Tilden H.
"INTER-MET: On-the-Job Theological Education." Pastoral Psychology 22 (March
1971):21-30.

1452. Fletcher, John. "Trends in the Future of
Theological Education and Implications for
the D. Min." In Papers from the National
Symposium on Issues and Models of Doctor of
Ministry Programs. Edited by G. Douglass
Lewis. Hartford, Conn.: Hartford Seminary
Foundation, 1980.

1453. Fletcher, Robert Samuel. A History of Oberlin
College from Its Foundation through the
Civil War. Oberlin, Ohio: Oberlin
College, 1943.

1454. Flint, J. F. "(Psychology in Education for
Ministry.)" Biblical World 13 (New Series)
(1899):326+.

1455. Florell, John L. "After Fifty Years: Analysis of the National A CPE Questionnaire
1975." Journal of Pastoral Care 29, no. 4
(1975):221-32.

1456. Flournoy, Francis Rosebro. Benjamin Mosby
Smith, 1811-1893. Richmond: Richmond
Press, 1947.

1457. Flowers, J. Richard. (Seminary Professors as Models for Their Students). Crozer Voice 59 (April 1967):17-18.

1458. Flowers, Ronald B. "The Bible Chair Movement: An Innovation of the Disciples of Christ." Discipliana 26 (March 1966):8-13.

1459. Foley, Ruth Howard. "I Had Better Call You Joe." New England Galaxy 19, no. 4 (1978):43-8.

1460. "For More Ministers." Time 71 (June 2, 1958):67.

1461. "For the Soul of the World." Christian Century 67 (April 26, 1950):518-19.

1462. Ford, James Standley. "Clinical Pastoral Education and the Seminarian's Conscious Perception of his Vocation." Ph.D. dissertation, Iliff School of Theology, 1968.

1463. "Fordham-Union Link: Ecumenism in Practice." Times Educational Supplement 2654 (April 1, 1966):1002.

1464. Fortier, Charles Benedict. "A Study of Continuing Education Needs of Clergymen in Lafayette Parish, Louisiana, 1972." Ed.D. dissertation, Louisiana State University and Agricultural and Mechanical College, 1972.

1465. Fosdick, Harry Emerson. "Christian Ministry." Atlantic Monthly 143 (January 1929):24-30.

1466. Fosdick, Harry Emerson. The Living of These Days: An Autobiography. New York: Harper, 1956.

1467. Fosdick, Harry Emerson. The Modern Use of the Bible. New York: Macmillan Co., 1924.

1468. Foster, Arthur L. House Church Evolving. Chicago: Exploration Press, 1976.

1469. Foster, Charles I. An Errand of Mercy: The Evangelical United Front, 1790-1837. Chapel Hill: University of North Carolina Press, 1960.

1470. Foster, Frank Clifton. Field Work and Its
      Relation to the Curriculum of Theological
      Seminaries. Johnson City, Tenn.: Muse
      Whitlock Co., Printers, 1932.

1471. Foster, Frank Hugh. The Life of Edwards Amasa
      Park. New York: Fleming H. Revell Co.,
      1936.

1472. Foster, Frank Hugh. "The Limits of Theologi-
      cal Freedom." Bibliotheca Sacra 58 (April
      1901):209-41.

1473. Foster, G. B. "Contribution of Critical
      Scholarship to Ministerial Efficiency."
      American Journal of Theology 20 (April
      1916):161-78.

1474. Foster, George B. "The Theological Training
      for the Times." Biblical World 9 (New
      Series) (January 1897):23-5.

1475. Foster, O. D. "Canadian Theological Colleges
      and American Schools of Religion."
      Christian Education 5 (July 1922):281-303.

1476. Foster, O. D. "Student Attendance at
      Protestant Religious Training Schools in
      the U.S., Autumn Session, 1920." Christian
      Education 4 (April 1921):27-42.

1477. Foster, Randolph Sinks. A Treatise on the
      Need of the M.E. church with Respect to Her
      Ministry: Embodied in a Sermon, and
      Preached by Request before the New York
      East Conference, May 22, 1855. New York:
      Carlton & Phillips, 1855.

1478. "Foundations, Fortunes and Federated
      Faculties." Christian Century 73 (January
      4, 1956):4-5.

1479. Fountain, Charles Hillman. The Denominational
      Situation: Should Our Schools Be Investi-
      gated? Plainfield, N. J.: Printed by the
      Author, 1921.

1480. "Four Faiths, One School [Interdenominational
      Theological Center]." Ebony 16 (September
      1961):73+.

1481. Fowler, Bertha. "The Deaconess as the
      Pastor's Social Assistant." In The

Socialized Church, pp. 175-92. Edited by
Marion Worth Tippy. New York: Eaton &
Mains, 1909.

1482. Fowler, Bertha. "Historical Sketch of Folt's
Mission Institute [Methodist Training
School for Young Women for Home and Foreign
Missionary Work]." Herkimer County.
Historical Society Papers 5 (1923):152-9.

1483. Fowler, E. M. "P.S.R. (Pacific School of
Religion) Graduates Largest Class."
Christian Century 70 (July 15, 1953):826.

1484. Fowler, Newton B. "LTS as a Graduate
Professional School." Lexington Theological Quarterly 13 (October 1978):125-8.

1485. Fox, Roy S. "Educational Service Sharing: A
Conceptual and Methodological Framework and
Its Application to Two Seminaries." Ph.D.
dissertation, Northwestern University,
1978.

1486. Francke, August Hermann. Idea Studiosi
Theologiae, Oder, Abbildung eines der
Theologie Beflissenen, Wie Derselbe sich
zum Gebrauch und Dienst des Herrn und zu
Allem Guten Werck Gehöriger Maassen
Bereitet: Benebst einem Anhang, Bestehend
in einer Ansprache an die Studiosos
Theologiae zu Halle. 5th ed. Halle:
Wäysenhauses, 1758.

1487. Frank, Robert W. "The Religious Education of
the Minister." Religious Education 22
(November 1927):950-8.

1488. Franklin, Godfrey. "The Nature and Perceived
Adequacy of the Preparation for Counseling
of Selected Presbyterian and Reformed
Church Ministers in the United States."
Ph.D. dissertation, University of Alabama,
1983.

1489. Franzmann, Martin H. "Hear Ye Him: Training
the Pastor in the Holy Scriptures." In
Toward a More Excellent Ministry, pp. 81-
90. Edited by R. R. Caemmerer and A. O.
Fuerbringer. St. Louis: Concordia Publishing House, 1964.

1490. Fraser, Dorothy Bass. "Women with a Past: A
       New Look at the History of Theological
       Education." Theological Education 8
       (Summer 1972):213-24.

1491. Fraser, James Walter. "Pedagogue for God's
       Kingdom: Lyman Beecher and the Second
       Great Awakening." Ph.D. dissertation,
       Columbia University, 1975.

1492. Frederic, Harold. The Damnation of Theron
       Ware: Or, Illumination. Chicago: Herbert
       S. Stone & Co., 1898.

1493. Freeman, Arthur J. "Place of the Protestant
       Seminary in the Spiritual Development of
       the Minister." Moravian Theological
       Seminary: Bulletin (1967):21-30.

1494. Freeman, Zenas, comp. Manual of American
       Colleges and Theological Seminaries:
       Giving Statistical Statements of Their
       Origin, Endowments, Libraries, Students,
       Alumni, etc. with Supplementary Notes.
       Rochester: Steam Press of A. Strong & Co.,
       1856.

1495. "From Anxiety to Prayer for a State Mental
       Healther [Miles Turns to Ministry]." New
       York Times 129 (November 10, 1979):12.

1496. From Servitude to Service: Being the Old
       South Lectures on the History and Work of
       Southern Institutions for the Education of
       the Negro. 1905; reprint ed., New York:
       Negro Universities Press, 1969.

1497. Frost, Stanley Brice. "Reviewing Some Founda-
       tions: A Contribution from Canada."
       Theological Education 2 (Summer 1966):23-
       34.

1498. Frost, S. B. "Selection and Training of
       Candidates for the Ministry: Post-Graduate
       Theological Training." Expository Times 74
       (January 1963):112-14.

1499. Frost, Stanley Brice. "The Theologian and the
       World of Contemporary Thought." Theologi-
       cal Education 1 (Autumn 1964):3-14.

1500. Froyd, M. C. "Educational Significance of
       Field Work for Theological Study: Report

to the American Association of Theological
Schools on Seminary Field World Consultations Held during the Winter and Spring of
1962." Encounter 24 (Spring 1963):196-214.

1501. Froyd, Milton Carl. "Pre-Testing for the
Ministry." Christian Century 73 (June 27,
1956):769-70.

1502. Froyd, Milton C. "What Is Practical in
Theological Education?" Journal of
Religion 35 (1955):168-77.

1503. Froyd, Milton C. "What's Happening among
Governing Boards of Theological Schools."
Theological Education 8 (Winter 1972):137-
45.

1504. Fry, Charles Luther. The U.S. Looks at Its
Churches. New York: Institute of Social
and Religious Research, 1930.

1505. Fuchs, S. "Teaching Judaism to Lutheran
Seminarians." Christian Century 97 (April
30, 1980):486-7.

1506. Fuerbringer, A. O. "Mission of Concordia
Seminary." Concordia Theological Monthly
35 (December 1964):682-6.

1507. Fuhrmann, Earl Fred Albert. "Understanding
and Support of Science on the Part of
Clergy, Seminarians, and Youth of the
Lutheran Church-Missouri Synod." Ed.D.
dissertation, University of Colorado, 1971.

1508. Fukuyama, Yoshio. The Ministry in Transition:
A Case Study of Theological Education.
University Park: Pennsylvania State
University Press, 1972.

1509. Fuller, Andrew. The Complete Works of the
Rev. Andrew Fuller ... With a Memoir of His
Life. London: H. G. Bohn, 1959.

1510. Fuller, C. E. "God's Mercy in an Age of
Change [Fuller Theological Seminary]."
Christianity Today 3 (January 19, 1959):12-
13.

1511. Fuller, Carlos G. "Testing the Fledgling
Cleric." Christian Century 53 (December
23, 1936):1718-20.

1512. "Fuller Presidency." Christianity Today 7
      (March 1, 1963):34.

1513. Fullerton, William Young. C. H. Spurgeon: A
      Biography. London: Williams & Norgate,
      1920.

1514. Fulmer, Bob Gene. "Educational and Counseling
      Survey of Southern Baptist Pastors." Ph.D.
      dissertation, Southern Illinois University,
      1975.

1515. Fulton, John W. "Purpose of Theological
      Education." Moravian Theological Seminary:
      Bulletin (1963):25-9.

1516. Fund For Theological Education. "From Those
      Who Teach and Minister." Theological
      Education 9 (Summer 1973, Suppl.):entire
      issue.

1517. "Fund Given to Aid Study of Theology."
      Christian Century 71 (February 17,
      1954):195.

1518. "Fund Provided to Aid Theological Study."
      Christian Century 72 (January 26,
      1955):101.

1519. Funk, Henry D. "The Presbyterian Church and
      Education." Presbyterian Historical
      Society Journal 12, pt. 2 (July, October
      1925):193-224.

1520. Funk, Robert Walter. "Creating an Opening:
      Biblical Criticism and the Theological
      Curriculum." Interpretation 18 (October
      1964):387-406.

1521. Funk, Robert Walter. The Kerygma, the Church,
      and the Ministry. Madison, N. J.: Drew
      University, 1960.

1522. Funk, Robert W. "The Watershed of the
      American Biblical Tradition: The Chicago
      School, First Phase, 1892-1920." Journal
      of Biblical Literature 95 (March 1976):4-
      22.

1523. Furgeson, Earl H. "Implementing the Doctrine
      of the Ministry in Seminary Education."
      Journal of Pastoral Care 15 (Spring
      1961):13-24.

1524. Furman, Wood. A History of the Charleston Association of Baptist Churches in the State of South Carolina, With an Appendix Containing the Principal Circular Letters to the Churches. Charleston, S. C.: J. Hoff, 1811.

1525. Furness, C. Y. "Christian Social Workers [Philadelphia College of the Bible]." Christianity Today 10 (June 10, 1966):9-11.

1526. Furniss, Norman F. The Fundamentalist Controversy, 1918-1931. New Haven: Yale University Press, 1954.

1527. "Future Church Leaders Meet: Interseminary Movement." Christian Century 66 (December 14, 1949):1476.

1528. "Future Theological Student." Literary Digest 58 (September 7, 1918):37-8.

1529. Gable, Lee J. "A Unique Venture in Theological Education." United Church Herald 8 (January 15, 1965):14-15.

1530. Gaddis, Vincent H., and Huffman, Jasper A. The Story of Winona Lake: A Memory and a Vision. Winona Lake, Ind.: Winona Lake Christian Assembly, 1960.

1531. Gaebelein, Arno Clemens. Half a Century: The Autobiography of a Servant. New York: Publication Office "Our Hope," 1930.

1532. Gaebelein, Frank Ely. "The Bible College in American Education Today." School and Society 87 (May 9, 1959):223-5.

1533. Gallman, L. "Howard Plan." Adult Leadership 10 (November 1961):139-40.

1534. Gallman, L. "Theological Education of the Southern Baptist Ministry." Adult Leadership 12 (February 1964):229+.

1535. Galvin, Thomas J. "Library Collection: New Measures of Excellence." American Theological Library Association: Proceedings 32 (1978):69-78.

1536. Gamble, Connolly C., Jr. "Continuing Education and the Church's Ministry: A

Bibliographical Survey." Richmond, Va.:
Union Theological Seminary, 1967. (ERIC
Document)

1537. Gamble, Connolly C., Jr. "Continuing Education for Ministry: Personnel, Participation, and Evaluation." Richmond, Va.:
Union Theological Seminary, 1968. (ERIC
Document)

1538. Gamble, Connolly C. "Continuing Education for
Ministry - Perspectives and Prospects."
Address to the 8th Annual Meeting of SACEM,
June 16, 1975. (ERIC Document)

1539. Gamble, Connolly C. The Continuing Theologi-
cal Education of the American Minister.
Richmond, Va.: Union Theologi-cal
Seminary, 1960.

1540. Gamble, Connolly C. "Developing Goals for
Continuing Education." Theological
Education 12 (Spring 1976):195-200.

1541. Gamble, C. C. "Four Programs at Union in
Richmond [Continuing Education]."
Theological Education 1 (Summer 1965).

1542. Gamble, C. C. "Theological Schools and the
Minister's Continuing Education." Theological Education 1 (Summer 1965):197-204.

1543. Gambrell, Mary Latimer. Ministerial Training
in Eighteenth Century New England. New
York: Columbia University Press, 1937.

1544. Gandy, Samuel L. "Strategies in Individual
Competency Building [for Seminary Graduates
to Minister To All Ages]." Theological
Education 16, Special Issue no. 3 (Winter
1980):356-8.

1545. Gangel, Kenneth. "The Bible College: Past,
Present and Future." Christianity Today 24
(November 7, 1980):34-6.

1546. Gangel, Kenneth Otto. "A Study of the
Evolution of College Accreditation Criteria
in the North Central Association and its
Effects on Bible Colleges." Ph.D.
dissertation, University of Missouri-Kansas
City, 1969.

1547. Gannett, Ezra Stiles. An Address Delivered at the Semi-Centennial Celebration of the Cambridge Divinity School, July 17, 1867. Boston: Bowles, 1867.

1548. Gannett, Mary Lynn. "Students', Faculties' and Administrators' Perceptions of Student Personnel Services at Selected Colleges Accredited by The American Association of Bible Colleges." Ed.D. dissertation, Memphis State University, 1981.

1549. Gapp, Kenneth S. "The Theological Seminary Library [Princeton University, 1811-1953]." Princeton University Library Chronicles 15 (Winter 1954):90-100.

1550. "Garbage Problem? [Concordia Seminary]." Christianity Today 17 (October 13, 1972):49-50.

1551. Garber, Paul Neff. The Romance of American Methodism. Greensboro, N. C.: Piedmont Press, 1931.

1552. Gardiner, F. "The Bearing of Recent Scientific Thought upon Theology." Bibliotheca Sacra 35 (January 1878):46-75.

1553. Gardiner, F. "(Theological Education.)" Bibliotheca Sacra 34 (1877):37-51; 37 (1880):566+; 38 (1881):188+, 759+.

1554. Gardner, D. L. "Bay Area Blessed with Seminaries." Christian Century 74 (May 8, 1957):596+.

1555. Gardner, E. Clinton. "Interprofessional Seminar on the Role of the Professions: A Report." Theological Education 8 (Autumn 1971):36-45.

1556. Gardner, Freda A. "Memorial Minute of the Faculty of Princeton Theological Seminary." Princeton Seminary Bulletin 2 (New Series), no. 1 (1978):28-9.

1557. Garfield, J. "Charles Taylor as Dean [Episcopal Theological School, Cambridge]." Theological Education 2 (Summer 1966):5-8.

1558. Garland, L. C. "An Educated Ministry - No. 1." Christian Advocate (Nashville) 29 (New

Series) (October 9, 1869):1.

1559. Garland, L. C. "An Educated Ministry - No. 2." Christian Advocate (Nashville) 29 (New Series) (October 16, 1869):1.

1560. Garland, L. C. "An Educated Ministry - No. 3." Christian Advocate (Nashville) 29 (New Series) (October 23, 1869):1.

1561. Garland, L. C. "An Educated Ministry - No. 4." Christian Advocate (Nashville) 29 (New Series) (October 30, 1869):1.

1562. Garland, L. C. "An Educated Ministry - No. 5." Christian Advocate (Nashville) 29 (New Series) (November 6, 1869):1.

1563. Garland, L. C. "An Educated Ministry - No. 6." Christian Advocate (Nashville) 29 (New Series) (November 13, 1869):1.

1564. Garrett, James Leo, Jr. "Bureaucratic Governmental Regulation of Churches and Church Institutions." Journal of Church and State 21, no. 2 (1979):195-207.

1565. Garrett, Lewis. Strictures on a Pastoral Letter, Addressed to the Churches under the Care of the Presbytery of West-Tennessee. Nashville: Thomas Eastin, 1812.

1566. Garrett Biblical Institute, Evanston, Ill.: Semi-Centennial Celebration: Garrett Biblical Institute. Evanston, Ill., 1906.

1567. Garrettson, Freeborn. A Letter to the Rev. Lyman Beecher, Containing Strictures and Animadversions on a Pamphlet Entitled "An Address of the Charitable Society for the Education of Indigent Pious Young Men for the Ministry of the Gospel." Portland, Maine: F. Douglas, 1818.

1568. Garrison, J. F. "(Studies Needed by the Ministry.)" American Church Review 29 (1877):197+.

1569. Gasper, Louis. The Fundamentalist Movement. The Hague: Mouton & Co., 1963.

1570. Gates, Frederick Taylor. Chapters in My Life. New York: Free Press, 1977.

136

1571. Gates, Milo H. "Deans and Professors."
Historical Magazine of the Protestant
Episcopal Church 5 (September 1936):238-64.

1572. Gates, Owen H. "The Development of Old Testament Work in Theological Seminaries."
Bibliotheca Sacra 50 (January 1893):119-30.

1573. Gates, Owen Hamilton. "Graduate Courses for
Ministers." Biblical World 41 (May
1913):342-4.

1574. Gates, Owen H. "The Relation of the Seminary
to Previous Bible Study." Biblical World 8
(New Series) (October 1896):265-71.

1575. Gates, O. H. "Seminary and Democracy." Religious Education 13 (June 1918):193-206.

1576. Gatewood, Willard B. Preachers, Pedagogues
and Politicians: The Evolution Controversy
in North Carolina, 1920-1927. Chapel Hill:
University of North Carolina Press, 1966.

1577. Gay, George A. "Hispanic Ministries Education
at Fuller Theological Seminary." Theological Education 13 (Winter 1977):85-9.

1578. Gaydos, E. A. "Report on an Experiment [Theo-
logical Students]." NCEA Bulletin 65
(August 1968):47-53.

1579. Geary, Thomas F. "Personal Growth in CPE."
Journal of Pastoral Care 31, no. 1 (1977):
12-17.

1580. Geary, Thomas Francis. "Self-Actualization in
Clinical Pastoral Education." Ph.D. dissertation, California School of Professional Psychology, Los Angeles, 1975.

1581. Geer, Curtis Manning. The Hartford Theological Seminary, 1834-1934. Hartford, Conn.:
Case, Lockwood & Brainard Co., 1934.

1582. Geier, Woodrow A. "Sit-ins Prod a Community."
Christian Century 77 (March 30, 1960):379-
82.

1583. Geier, W. A. "Vanderbilt Congress: The
Chicago School." Christian Century 86
(April 9, 1969):491-4; Hansen, H. W.
"Reply." 86 (May 28, 1969):756.

1584. Geisler, Norman L. "The Concept of Truth in the Inerrancy Debate." Bibliotheca Sacra 137 (October-December 1980):327-39.

1585. "General Theological Seminary." Historical Magazine of the Protestant Episcopal Church 5 (September 1936).

1586. "Generation of Pioneers [Union Theological Seminary, NYC]." Outlook 139 (January 14, 1925):50-1.

1587. George, Denise. How To Be a Seminary Student and Survive. Nashville, Tenn.: Broadman Press, 1981.

1588. George Washington University, Washington, D.C. Office of the University Historian. Luther Rice, Founder of Columbian College. Washington, D.C., 1966.

1589. Gerber, Vergil, ed. Discipling through Theological Education: A Fresh Approach to Theological Education in the 1980's. Chicago: Moody, 1980.

1590. Gerberding, George Henry. The Lutheran Pastor. Philadelphia: Lutheran Pub. Co., 1902.

1591. Gerberding, George H. "Why Our English Lutheran Seminary Is Needed." Chicago Lutheran Seminary Record 5 (April 1900):42-4.

1592. Gerkin, Charles V. "Clinical Pastoral Education and Social Change." Journal of Pastoral Care 25, no. 3 (1971):175-81.

1593. Gerkin, Charles V. "Power and Powerlessness in Clinical Pastoral Education." Journal of Pastoral Care 34, no. 2 (1980):114-24.

1594. Gerlach, Barbara A., and Hewitt, Emily C. "Training Women for Ministry." Andover Newton Quarterly 17 (November 1976):133-42.

1595. Gerlach, Barbara A., Lykes, B. and Sandberg, J. "Women in the Seminaries: A Progress Report." Christian Century 92 (February 5-12, 1975):100-1.

138

1596. Gessell, John Maurice. "Clinical Pastoral
      Training and the Curriculum for Theological
      Education." Journal of Pastoral Care 22
      (September 1968):168-70.

1597. Gessell, John Maurice. "What the Theological
      Schools Might Expect from Clinical Pastoral
      Education." Journal of Pastoral Care 17
      (Autumn 1963):148-53.

1598. Gettemy, J. N. "Education for Ministry."
      Hartford Quarterly 4 (Spring 1964).

1599. Gettysburg Seminary. Special Collections.
      Schaeffer, Charles H. "Report of the
      German Professor, August 12, 1862."

1600. Getz, Gene Arnold. "A History of Moody Bible
      Institute and Its Contributions to Evan-
      gelical Education." Ph.D. dissertation,
      New York University, 1968.

1601. Getz, Gene A. MBI: The Story of Moody Bible
      Institute. Chicago: Moody Press, 1969.

1602. Gibbs, Mark. "They Deserve a First-Class
      Education." Theological Education 4
      (Autumn 1967):580-5.

1603. Giboney, Ezra P., and Potter, Agnes M. The
      Life of Mark A. Matthews. Grand Rapids,
      Mich.: Wm. B. Eerdmans, 1948.

1604. Gienapp, J. "Student Association: An
      Evaluation [Concordia Seminary]."
      Concordia Theological Monthly 35 (December
      1964):740-2.

1605. Gifford, Frank Dean. P.D.S.: A Centennial
      Address at Philadelphia (1857-1957). New
      York: Newcomen Society in North America,
      1957.

1606. Gilbert, George Blodgett. Forty Years a
      Country Preacher. New York: Harper &
      Bros., 1940.

1607. Gill, Jerry Wayne. "The Seminary Extension
      Department of the Seminaries of the
      Southern Baptist Convention." Ph.D.
      dissertation, New Orleans Baptist
      Theological Seminary, 1972.

1608. Gillan, W. Rush. Some Thought on Education in the Reformed Church...An Educated Ministry, by...George W. Richards, D.D.; Addresses Delivered before Potomac Synod...Oct. 18th, 1906. Philadelphia, Publication Board, 1906.

1609. Gillespie, Stephen W. "John Murray Forbes, 1807-1885: First Permanent Dean of the General Theological Seminary." Historical Magazine of the Protestant Episcopal Church 24 (December 1955):332-65.

1610. Gillett, R. W. "Report on the Chicago Urban Training Center." Harvard Divinity Bulletin 29 (July 1965):107-11.

1611. Gillette, David Anthony. "Role Expectations of the Baptist Pastor as Pastoral Counselor as Viewed by Pastors, Pastoral Students, and Faculty in Selected Pastoral Training Institutions." Ph.D. dissertation, University of Michigan, 1981.

1612. Gillette, Gerald W. "John A. Mackay: Influences on My Life." Journal of Presbyterian History 56, no. 1 (1978):20-34.

1613. Gilliam, Will D. "Robert Jefferson Breckinridge, 1800-1871. Part I." Register of the Kentucky Historical Society 72, no. 3 (1974):207-23.

1614. Gilliam, Will D., Jr. "Robert Jefferson Breckinridge, 1800-1971. Part II." Register of the Kentucky Historical Society 72, no. 4 (1974):319-36.

1615. Gillies, James Robertson. The Ministry of Reconciliation. London: A. & C. Black, 1919.

1616. Gilmore, George W. "The English Bible in Theological Seminaries." Biblical World 4 (New Series) (October 1894):287-90.

1617. Giltner, John Herbert. "Fragmentation of New England Congregationalism and the Founding of Andover Seminary." Journal of Religious Thought 20 (1963-4):27-42.

1618. Ginger, Ray, ed. The Nationalizing of American Life, 1877-1900. New York: Free

Press, 1965.

1619. Girling, Paul Alvin. "A Study of Values Held by American Theological Students." Ed.D. dissertation, University of Northern Colorado, 1968.

1620. Gladden, Washington, ed. Parish Problems: Hints and Helps for the People at the Churches. New York: Century Co., 1887.

1621. Glanding, W. M. B. "Educated Ministry: A Plea." Lutheran Quarterly 23 (New Series) (1893):258-73.

1622. Glasgow, W. Melancthon. History of the Reformed Presbyterian Church in America, pp. 753-5. Baltimore: Hill & Harvey, 1888.

1623. Glass, J. C., Jr. "Professional Churchman and Continuing Education." Adult Leadership 20 (April 1972):349-50.

1624. Glass, Joseph Dinson. "The Problem of Objectives in Religious Education, 1947-1965." Ph.D. dissertation, Yale University, 1966.

1625. Glasse, James D. Profession: Minister. Nashville: Abingdon Press, 1968.

1626. Glasse, James D. "Seminaries and Professional Education." Theological Education 8 (Autumn 1971):3-10.

1627. Glen, J. S. "Pastoral Responsibility of Theological Education." Scottish Journal of Theology 6 (December 1953):396-405.

1628. Glock, Charles Y. To Comfort and to Challenge: A Dilemma of the Contemporary Church. Berkeley: University of California Press, 1967.

1629. Glover, Willis Borders. Evangelical Noncomformists and Higher Criticism in the Nineteenth Century. London: Independent Press, 1955.

1630. "The Goals of Clinical Pastoral Training Reappraised." Journal of Pastoral Care 5 (Spring 1951):68-70.

141

1631. Gobbel, A. Roger. "Receiving and Constructing
       Knowledge and Understanding." Religious
       Education 77, no. 1 (1982):69-83.

1632. Godbey, A. H. "Some Relations of Semitic
       Studies to Divinity School Courses."
       Methodist Quarterly Review 77 (April
       1928):227-45.

1633. Godbold, Albea. The Church College of the Old
       South. Durham, N.C.: Duke University
       Press, 1944.

1634. Godfrey, W. Robert. "Essays in the History of
       American Presbyterianism: Jubilee Year of
       Westminster Theological Seminary."
       Westminster Theological Journal 42 (Fall
       1979):1-258.

1635. Godkin, E. L. "The Education of Ministers."
       Nation 12 (April 20, 1871):272-3.

1636. Goen, Clarence Curtis. "Changing Conceptions
       of Protestant Theological Education in
       America." Foundations 6 (October 1963):
       293-310.

1637. Goerner, Henry Cornell. "Contributions of the
       Southern Baptist Theological Seminary to
       World Missions, 1859-1959." Review and
       Expositor 56 (April 1959):133-43.

1638. Goetchius, Eugene Van Ness. "New Developments
       in Language Teaching." Theological Educa-
       tion 3 (Summer 1967):466-81.

1639. Goetchius, Eugene Van Ness and Landes, George
       M. "What Is Happening." Theological Edu-
       cation 3 (Summer 1967):448-65.

1640. Goheen, R. F. "Seminary and the University."
       Princeton Seminary Bulletin 54 (July
       1960):7-11.

1641. Going, Jonathan. "Baptist Literary and Theo-
       logical Institution [Written in 1819:
       Introduction by G. Peck]." Andover Newton
       Quarterly 16 (January 1976):173-87.

1642. Gold, V. R. "Theologian or Politician?
       [Faculty]." Dialog 1 (Autumn 1962):58;
       Knutson, K. S. "Reply." 58-60.

1643. "Golden Gate Baptist Theological Seminary,
      Marin County, California." Architect and
      Engineer 205 (June 1956):5.

1644. Gollock, Georgina A. "The Present Outlook on
      the Preparation of Missionaries." Inter-
      national Review of Missions 13 (July 1924):
      383-402.

1645. Goltermann, S. "Future of Theological
      Education." Concordia Theological Monthly
      39 (October 1968):597-606.

1646. Goode, William Josiah. "Encroachment,
      Charlatanism, and the Emerging Profession:
      Psychology, Sociology, and Medicine."
      American Sociological Review 25 (December
      1960):902-14.

1647. Goodling, R. A. and Webb, S. C. "Analysis of
      Faculty Ratings of Theology Students."
      Religious Education 54 (May 1959):228-33.

1648. Goodling, Richard A. "Clinical Pastoral
      Education in the Parish." Duke Divinity
      School Review 32 (Winter 1967):20-38.

1649. Goodloe, James C. IV. "Kenneth J. Foreman,
      Sr.: A Candle on the Glacier." Journal of
      Presbyterian History 57, no. 4 (1979):467-
      84.

1650. Goodloe, R. W. "Obligation of the Church to
      Create an Educated Ministry." Christian
      Education Magazine 18 (February 1928):10-
      18.

1651. Goodman, W. E. "The Doctor of Ministry
      Program." Asbury Seminarian 34 (October
      1979):23-32.

1652. Goodpasture, H. McKennie. "Robert E. Speer's
      Legacy." Occasional Bulletin of Missionary
      Research 2 (April 1978):38-41.

1653. Goodspeed, Edgar Johnson. As I Remember. New
      York: Harper, 1953.

1654. Goodspeed, E. J. "Divinity School of the
      University of Chicago." University of
      Chicago Magazine 7 (March 1915):133-41.

1655. Goodspeed, Thomas Wakefield. Ernest De Witt
      Burton: A Biographical Sketch. Chicago:
      University of Chicago Press, 1926.

1656. Goodspeed, Thomas Wakefield. William Rainey
      Harper, First President of the University
      of Chicago. Chicago: University of
      Chicago Press, 1928.

1657. Goodwin, H. M. "Dilemmas Confronting the
      Supervisor in Theological Education."
      Theological Education 5 (Summer 1969,
      Suppl. 1):503-8.

1658. Goodwin, H. M. and Dorfman, E. "Ministers
      Evaluate Their Training in Marriage
      Counseling." Journal of Religion and
      Health 4 (October 1965):414-20.

1659. Goodwin, William Archer Rutherfoord, ed.
      History of the Theological Seminary in
      Virginia and Its Historical Background. 2
      vols. New York: Edwin S. Gorham, 1923-24.

1660. Goodykoontz, Harry G. The Minister in the
      Reformed Tradition. Richmond, John Knox
      Press, 1963.

1661. Gordon, Adoniram Judson. How Christ Came to
      Church: The Pastor's Dream. A Spiritual
      Autobiography. With the Life Story and the
      Dream as Interpreting the Man, by A.T.
      Pierson. Philadelphia: American Baptist
      Publication Soc., 1895.

1662. Gordon, Ernest Barron. Adoniram Judson
      Gordon: A Biography. New York: Fleming
      H. Revell Co., 1896.

1663. Gordon, Ernest Barron. A Book of Protestant
      Saints. Chicago: Moody Press, 1946.

1664. Gordon, George Butler, III. "Personal and
      Theological Change as Influenced by
      Clinical Pastoral Education and the
      Supervisory Relationship." Th.D.
      dissertation, Iliff School of Theology,
      1980.

1665. "Gordon and Conwell Announce Betrothal."
      Christianity Today 13 (June 20, 1969):32.

144

1666. Gordon College of Theology and Missions.
      Gordon 75th Anniversary Year. Wenham,
      Mass.: Gordon College & Gordon Divinity
      School, 1964.

1667. "Gordon-Conwell Merger." Christianity Today
      13 (January 3, 1969):35.

1668. "Gordon Conwell Urban Center Future in Doubt."
      Christianity Today 14 (May 22, 1970):36.

1669. Gorman, John, and Tholin, Richard. "Public
      Schools as a Setting for Seminary Field
      Experience." In Explorations in Ministry.
      Edited by G. D. Lewis. New York: IDOC
      North America, 1971.

1670. Gorrell, Donald K. Women's Rightful Place:
      Women in United Methodist History. Dayton,
      Ohio: United Theological Seminary, 1980.

1671. Gosse, Edmund William. Father and Son:
      Biographical Recollections. New York:
      Charles Scribner's Sons, 1908.

1672. Gottlieb, David. "Processes of Socialization
      in the American Graduate School." Ph.D.
      dissertation, University of Chicago, 1960.

1673. Gotwald, F. G. "Pennsylvania German Lutherans
      and Higher Education." Lutheran Quarterly
      37 (July 1908):404-21.

1674. Gotwald, Luther A., Jr. "What's Really
      Avante-Garde? Clustered Seminaries? No!
      Ecumenical School of Theology? Yes!
      Theological Education 5 (Winter 1969):73-9.

1675. Gould, Joseph Edward. The Chautauqua Move-
      ment: An Episode in the Continuing Ameri-
      can Revolution. New York: State Univer-
      sity of New York, 1961.

1676. "Graduate and Professional Education." Col-
      lege and University 55 (Summer 1980):319-
      426.

1677. "Graduate and Professional Education."
      College and University 56 (Summer
      1981):303-417.

1678. "Graduate Chair in the Department of Homile-
      tics [Union Theological Seminary, NYC]."

Outlook 80 (June 3, 1905):265-6.

1679. "Graduate Study for the Rural Pastor."
Missionary Review of the World 52 (May
1929):390-2.

1680. The Graduate Theological Union: Its Partici-
pants and Their Ecclesiastical Heritage.
Berkeley: Graduate Theological Union
Guild, 1970.

1681. Graebner, August L. "Johann Michael Gottlieb
Schaller: A Biography." Concordia
Historical Institute Quarterly 54 (Spring
1981):2-29.

1682. Graebner, August L. "Theological Training in
the Early Lutheran Church of America."
Theological Quarterly 6 (1902):54-67, 79-
94.

1683. Graham, Ronald W. "The Galilean Accent -
Senior Communion, May 13, 1982." Lexington
Theological Quarterly 17 (July 1982):45-50.

1684. Grant, Alexander. The Story of the University
of Edinburgh during its First Three Hundred
Years. 2 vols. London: Longmans, Green &
Co., 1884.

1685. Grant, Frederick C. "Educating for the Ministry." Christendom 13 (1948):360-72.

1686. Grant, Gerald Charles. "Some Effects of Moral
Discussion on Clinical Pastoral Education
Students." Ed.D. dissertation, Boston
University School of Education, 1975.

1687. Grant, John Webster. Free Churchmanship in
England. London: Independent Press, 1955.

1688. Grant, Robert McQueen. "American New Testament Study, 1926-1956." Journal of
Biblical Literature 87 (March 1968):42-50.

1689. "Grants for Theological Education." Higher
Education 12 (February 1956):97-8.

1690. Graves, A. W. "Ecumenism in Theological
Seminaries." Religious Education 62 (March
1967):200-2+.

1691. Graves, Allen Wallace. "The Purpose and Place of Religious Education [School of Religious Education, Southern Baptist Theological Seminary]." Review and Expositor 54 (January 1957):79-95.

1692. Gray, James M. "The Awakening of American Protestantism." Bibliotheca Sacra 70 (October 1913):653-68.

1693. "Greek in Present Theological Education." Biblical World 31 (January 1908):68-9.

1694. Green, Ashbel. The Life of Ashbel Green. New York: Robert Carter & Bros., 1849.

1695. Green, Francis Marion. Hiram College and Western Reserve Eclectic Institute: Fifty Years of History, 1850-1900. Cleveland, Ohio: O.S. Hubbell Printing Co., 1901.

1696. Greene, William Brenton. "The Elective System in Our Colleges and the Curriculum of Our Theological Seminaries." Presbyterian and Reformed Review 11 (January 1900):66-88.

1697. Greenholt, Horner G. "Loehe's Lutheran Colonies in America." Lutheran Church Quarterly 11 (1938):413-19.

1698. Greenleaf, Robert K. Mission in a Seminary: A Prime Trustee Concern. Center For Applied Studies. Distributed by Windy Row Press, Peterborough, N.H., 1981.

1699. Greenleaf, Robert K. The Seminary as an Institution: The Work of the Trustee. Indianapolis: Lilly Endowment, 1980.

1700. Greenleaf, Robert K. Seminary as Servant: Essays on Trusteeship. Peterborough, N.H.: Windy Row Press, 1981.

1701. Greenleaf, Robert K. Servant: Retrospect and Prospect. Peterborough, N.H.: Windy Row Press, 1980.

1702. Gregory, Daniel Seely. Christ's Trumpet-Call to the Ministry. New York: Funk & Wagnalls Co., 1896.

1703. Gregory, Daniel Seely. The Presbyterian Church in Its Relations to Higher Education

147

and the Ministry. Lake Forest, Ill.: University Printing Co., 1882.

1704. Grice, Homer Lamar. "The Struggle To Get a Seminary [Establishment of Southern Baptist Theological Seminary, 1847-59]." Quarterly Review (Bap.) 18 (July-September 1958):25-9.

1705. Griffin, Edward Dorr. An Oration Delivered June 21, 1809. Boston: Farrand, Mallory & Co., 1809?

1706. Griffin, J. J. "Women in the Ministry: Southern Theological Students Join Liberation Forces [Union Theological Seminary in Virginia]." Christian Century 91 (September 18, 1974):855-7.

1707. Griffith, Gwilym O. "Reminiscences [Princeton Class 1909]." Princeton Seminary Bulletin 58 (February 1965):49-52.

1708. Griggs, Leverett. Letters to a Theological Student. Boston: American Tract Society, 1863.

1709. Grindal, Gracia. "Language of Worship and Hymnody: Tone." Worship 52 (November 1978):509-17.

1710. Grislis, E. "Lutheran Tradition and Theological Inquiry in Depth [Reply to H. E. Horn]." Lutheran Quarterly 19 (May 1967):185-7.

1711. Griswold, E. E. "A General Theological Seminary." Christian Advocate (New York) 29 (February 23, 1854):29.

1712. Groff, W. F. "Emerging Directions in Education for Ministry." Brethren Life and Thought 15 (Winter 1970).

1713. Groh, John E. "Ecumenism's Past and Future: Shifting Perspectives, an Interview with Bishop Stephen C. Neill." Christian Century 92 (June 4, 1975):568-72.

1714. Gross, John O. "The Bishops versus Vanderbilt University." Tennessee Historical Quarterly 22 (March 1963):53-65.

1715. Gross, John O. "Higher Education and Theo-
      logical Education." Christian Education 35
      (1952):229-41.

1716. Gross, John Owen. Methodist Beginnings in
      Higher Education. Nashville? 1959.

1717. Grossman, Maria. "The Boston Theological
      Library Consortium." Catholic Library
      World 42 (December 1970):219-24.

1718. Grossman, M. "Gifts to the Library:
      Collections from Distinguished Faculty
      [Harvard]." Harvard Divinity Bulletin 1
      (New Series) (Winter 1968):14-16.

1719. Grubbs, Jerry Cornelius. "A Study of Faculty
      Members and Students in Selected Midwestern
      Schools of Theology to Determine Whether
      Their Educational Orientation is Andragogi-
      cal or Pedagogical." Ed.D. dissertation,
      Indiana University, 1981.

1720. Gruber, L. Franklin. "Inaugural Address."
      Chicago Lutheran Seminary Record 34
      (January 1929):11+.

1721. Grudem, Wayne. "Letter to a Prospective
      Seminarian." Christianity Today 16 (August
      25, 1972):18-19.

1722. Grundman, Adolph H. "Northern Baptists and
      the Founding of Virginia Union University:
      The Perils of Paternalism." Journal of
      Negro History 63, no. 1 (1978):26-41.

1723. Guerry, Moultire. "Leonidas Polk and the
      University of the South." Historical
      Magazine of the Protestant Episcopal Church
      7 (December 1938):378-88.

1724. Guffin, Gilbert Lee, ed. What God Hath
      Wrought: Eastern's First Thirty-Five
      Years. Chicago: Judson Press, 1960.

1725. Gundry, Stanley N. Love Them in: The
      Proclamation Theology of D. L. Moody.
      Chicago: Moody Press, 1976.

1726. Gunn, Alexander. Memoirs of the Rev. John H.
      Livingston. New York: Wm. A. Mercein,
      Printer, 1829.

1727. Gunnemann, Louis H. "From Purpose to Curriculum." Theological Education 2 (Spring 1966):177-83.

1728. Gusfield, Joseph R. Symbolic Crusade: Status Politics and the American Temperance Movement. Urbana: University of Illinois Press, 1963.

1729. Gustafson, James M. "The Clergy in the United States." Daedalus 92 (Fall 1963):724-44.

1730. Gustafson, James M. "Theological Education as Professional Education." Theological Education 5 (Spring 1969):243-61.

1731. Gustavus, W. T. "The Ministerial Student: A Study in the Contradictions of a Marginal Role." Review of Religious Research 14, no. 3 (1973):187-93.

1732. Guthrie, Dwight Raymond. John McMillan: The Apostle of Presbyterians in the West, 1752-1833. Pittsburgh: University of Pittsburgh Press, 1952.

1733. Gwaltney, James A. "Spiritual Development through Designed Exercises in a Small Group Setting." Perkins School of Theology: Journal 28 (Summer 1975):1-24.

1734. Gynther, M. D. and Kempson, J. O. "Personal and Interpersonal Changes in Clinical Pastoral Training." Journal of Pastoral Care 12 (Winter 1958):210-19.

1735. Hadsell, John S. "We Heard the Church: Towards a Many-Celled Seminary [San Francisco Theological Seminary]." International Review of Mission 71 (April 1982):179-83.

1736. Hagenbach, Karl Rudolf. History of the Church in the Eighteenth and Nineteenth Centuries. Translated by John F. Hurst. New York: Scriber, 1869.

1737. Hague, William. Christian Greatness in the Scholar: A Discourse on the Life and Character of Rev. Irah Chase, D.D. Boston: Gould & Lincoln, 1866.

1738. Hague, William. *Life Notes: Or, Fifty Years' Outlook*. Boston: Lee & Shephard, 1888.

1739. Hahn, L. "Some Reflection upon the Theological Roots and Atmosphere of a Clinical Training Program." *Journal of Pastoral Care* 16 (Autumn 1962):173-6.

1740. Hahn, Stephen S. "Lexington's Theological Library, 1832-1859." *South Carolina Historical Magazine* 80, no. 1 (1979):36-49.

1741. Hahn, W. "Theological Education and the Nature of the Church." *Encounter* 18 (Spring 1957):167-73.

1742. Haight, Emily Suzanne. "Psychological Criteria for the Selection of Ministerial Candidates." Ph.D. dissertation, Northwestern University, 1980.

1743. Haines, A. B. "Colleges Re-educate for Christ's Return: Ambassador Colleges Supported by Radio Church of God." *Christian Century* 86 (February 19, 1969): 264.

1744. Haines, George Lamar. "The Princeton Theological Seminary, 1925-1960." Ph.D. dissertation, New York University, 1966.

1745. Hale, E. E. "The New England Ministry." *Lend A Hand* 9 (1892):412-15.

1746. Hale, J. R. "Future of Our Seminaries." *Lutheran Quarterly* 19 (November 1967):417-21.

1747. Hale, J. Russell. "Gettysburg Seminary: 150 Years." *Lutheran Historical Conference: Essays and Reports* 7 (1978):23-37.

1748. Hale, James Russell. "The Making and Testing of an Organizational Saga: A Case-Study of the Lutheran Theological Seminary at Gettysburg, Pennsylvania, with Special Reference to the Problem of Merger, 1959-1969." Ed.D. dissertation, Columbia University, 1970.

1749. Hall, Basil Douglas. *The Life of Charles Cuthbert Hall*. New York: Carlton Press, 1965.

1750. Hall, Charles Cuthbert. <u>The Ideal Minister.</u>
       <u>Atlantic Monthly</u> 100 (October 1907):448-58.

1751. Hall, Charles Cuthbert. <u>Notes of an Address</u>
       <u>before the Alumni of the Union Theological</u>
       <u>Seminary, in the Adams Chapel, 16 May,</u>
       <u>1905.</u> New York, 1905.

1752. Hall, Charles Cuthbert. <u>Qualifications for</u>
       <u>Ministerial Power: The Carew Lectures,</u>
       <u>1895.</u> Hartford, Conn.: Hartford Seminary
       Press, 1895.

1753. Hall, Charles Cuthbert. <u>The Seminary and the</u>
       <u>Ministry.</u> New York: Treasury Magazine
       Press, 1898.

1754. Hall, Charles Cuthbert. <u>Spiritual Experience</u>
       <u>and Theological Science: A Reconciliation:</u>
       <u>An Address Delivered at the Opening of the</u>
       <u>Sixty-Eighth Academic Year of the Union</u>
       <u>Theological Seminary, 24 September, 1903.</u>
       New York: DeVinne Press, 1904.

1755. Hall, Charles Cuthbert. "The Teaching of
       Theology." <u>Educational Review</u> 29 (January
       1905):85-101.

1756. Hall, Charles E., Jr. "New Thrusts for the
       Association For Clinical Pastoral Educa-
       tion." <u>Journal of Pastoral Care</u> 22
       (December 1968):203-5.

1757. Hall, Colby Dixon. <u>History of Texas Christian</u>
       <u>University.</u> Fort Worth: Texas Christian
       University Press, 1947.

1758. Hall, J. O. "Note on Relationships between
       Attitudes towards the Scientific Method and
       the Background of Seminarians." <u>Social</u>
       <u>Forces</u> 39 (October 1960):49-52.

1759. Hall, John. (Judge Hall's Address.) <u>American</u>
       <u>Quarterly Register</u> 7 (1835):168-75.

1760. Hall, Oswald. "The Stages of a Medical
       Career." <u>American Journal of Sociology</u> 53
       (March 1948):327-36.

1761. Hall, Robert. <u>The Works of the Rev. Robert</u>
       <u>Hall.</u> 4 vols. New York: Harper, 1848.

1762. Hallock, Donald H. V. "The Story of Nashotah." Historical Magazine of the Protestant Episcopal Church 11 (March 1942):3-17.

1763. Hallock, William Allen. Memorial of Rev. Wm. A. Hallock, D.D., First Secretary of the American Tract Society. New York: American Tract Society, 1882.

1764. Halmos, Paul. The Faith of the Counsellors. New York: Schocken Books, 1966.

1765. Halsey, Le Roy Jones. Address to the Alumni Society of the University of Nashville, on the Study of Theology as a Part of Science, Literature and Religion. Nashville: Printed by Cameron & Fall, 1841.

1766. Halsey, Le Roy J. A History of the McCormick Theological Seminary of the Presbyterian Church. Chicago: Published by the Seminary, 1893.

1767. Ham, Thomas Hale. "Research in Medical Education: Participation of Faculty and Students." Theological Education 2 (Spring 1966):211-18.

1768. Hamilton, Doyle. "Albert Venting Address." Southwestern Journal of Theology 23 (Fall 1980):84-6.

1769. Hamilton, James David. "An Evaluation of Professional Preparation for Pastoral Counseling." Ph.D. dissertation, University of Denver, 1959.

1770. Hamlin, R. B. Practical Work in Theological Seminaries. Philadelphia: Eastern Baptist Theological Seminary, 1936?

1771. Hamm, G. Paul. "An Historical Survey of the Relation among the Philosophy, Method, and Libraries of American Theological Education." Ph.D. dissertation, Golden Gate Baptist Theological Seminary, 1972.

1772. Hammer, Harvey M. "A Ministerial Training Program in Community Mental Health." Mental Hygiene 49 (October 1965):520-4.

1773. Hammett, Hugh B. "The Historical Context of
       the Origins of CPE." Journal of Pastoral
       Care 29, no. 2 (1975):76-85.

1774. Hammond, Al D. "From Bible College to
       Berkeley." Christian Standard 104 (August
       30, 1969):9-10.

1775. Hammond, J. D. "The Education of Ministers."
       Religious Education 5 (December 1910):451-
       4.

1776. Hamre, James. "Georg Sverdrup: A Theologian
       'In League with the Future.'" Lutheran
       Historical Conference 8 (1980):21-8.

1777. Hamre, James. "Georg Sverdrup Concerning
       Luther's Principles in America." Concordia
       Historical Institute Quarterly 43, no. 1
       (1970):15-22.

1778. Hamre, James S. "Georg Sverdrup's Concept of
       Theological Education in the Context of a
       Free Church." Lutheran Quarterly 22, no. 2
       (May 1970):199-209.

1779. Hamre, James. "Georg Sverdrup's Errand into
       the Wilderness: Building the Free and
       Living Congregation." Concordia Historical
       Institute Quarterly 53, no. 1 (1980):39-47.

1780. Hand, William J. "Principles and Techniques
       for Counseling Students in a Protestant
       Theological Seminary." Ph.D. dissertation,
       Temple University, 1960.

1781. Handy, Robert Theodore. "Do Not Let Your
       Minds Be Captured." Union Seminary
       Quarterly Review 19 (November 1963):5-9.

1782. Handy, Robert T. "Fundamentalism and
       Modernism in Perspective." Religion in
       Life (1954-55):381-94.

1783. Handy, Robert T. "The Influence of Canadians
       on Baptist Theological Education in the
       United States." Foundations 23 (January-
       March 1980):42-56.

1784. Handy, Robert T. "Involvement of Entire
       Faculty in Professional Education." In 9th
       Biennial Conference of the Association of
       Seminary Professors in the Practical

Fields, p. 5. 1966.

1785. Handy, Robert T. "Partnership of Faith and Learning." Andover Newton Quarterly 16 (January 1976):188-98.

1786. Handy, Robert T. "The Problem of Purpose in the Theological University." Theological Education 2 (Winter 1966):102-6.

1787. Handy, Robert T. "Studies in the Interrelationships between America and the Holy Land: a Fruitful Field for Interdisciplinary and Interfaith Cooperation." Journal of Church and State 13, no. 2 (1971):283-301.

1788. Handy, Robert T. "Theological Seminaries and Graduate Education in Religion." Council on the Study of Religion: Bulletin 7 (December 1976):6-7.

1789. Handy, Robert T. "Trends in Canadian and American Theological Education, 1880-1980." Theological Education 18 (Spring 1982):175-218.

1790. Handy, Robert T. We Witness Together: A History of Cooperative Home Missions. New York: Friendship Press, 1956.

1791. Hanly, D. J. "Professional Supervision of Pastoral Work." Theological Education 5 (Summer 1969, Suppl. 1):497-502.

1792. Hannah, John. A Letter to a Junior Methodist Preacher, Concerning the General Course and Prosecution of His Studies in Christian Theology. New York, 1839.

1793. Hannah, John D. "History of Bibliotheca Sacra." Bibliotheca Sacra 133 (July-September 1976):229-42.

1794. Hansen, Thorvald, and Rye, Stephen. School in the Woods: The Story of an Immigrant Seminary. Askov, Minn.: American Publishing, 1977.

1795. Hanson, H. E. "Concerning Internship: A Modest Proposal." Una Sancta 26 (August-September 1969):45-7.

1796. Happer, A. P. "Professorship of Missionary Instruction in Our Theological Seminaries." Bibliotheca Sacra 33 (1876):494-509.

1797. Harbison, Janet. "Making Modern Ministers: Where are Seminaries Heading?" Presbyterian Life (September 15, 1966):12-17.

1798. "Hard Times for Ph.D.'s." Christian Century 86 (December 31, 1969):1658.

1799. Hardesty, Nancy. "Women and the Seminaries." Christian Century 96 (February 7-14, 1979):122-3.

1800. Harding, Vincent. "Lyman Beecher and the Transformation of American Protestantism, 1775-1863." Ph.D. dissertation, University of Chicago, 1965.

1801. Hardy, Edward Rochie. "The Berkeley Divinity School: One Hundred Years, 1854-1954." Historical Magazine of the Protestant Episcopal Church 24, no. 1 (1955):15-38.

1802. Hardy, Edward Rochie, Jr. "The Organization and Early Years of the General Theological Seminary." Historical Magazine of the Protestant Episcopal Church 5 (September 1936):147-76.

1803. Hare Duke, M. "Clinical Theology." Frontier 6 (1963):210-12.

1804. Harford, Charles F., ed. The Keswick Convention: Its Message, Its Method and Its Men. London: Marshall Bros., 1907.

1805. Hargraves, J. Archie. "Blackening Theological Education." Christianity and Crisis 29 (April 14, 1969):93-8.

1806. Hargraves, J. Archie. "Seminary Must Go to the Streets, the Conditions, and the Systems." Drew Gateway 39 (Autumn 1968):32-46.

1807. Hargrove, Earl C. The Preachers are Coming! Lincoln, Ill., Lincoln Christian College Press, 1972.

1808. Harker, John Stanley. "The Life and Contributions of Calvin Ellis Stowe [1802-86]."

Abstracts of Doctoral Dissertations (University of Pittsburgh) 27 (1952):565-70.

1809. Harmelink, Herman. The Reformed Church in New Jersey (1660-1969). Synod of New Jersey, 1969.

1810. Harmon, Michelle. "The Clinical Pastoral Counselor and the Dialectic of Human Experience." Journal of Pastoral Care 29, no. 3 (1975):168-75.

1811. Harner, Nevin C. "The Reintegration of Christian Education within the Christian Community and Its Relevance for Theological Education." Religious Education 45 (July-August 1950):224-8.

1812. Harper, A. P. "A Professorship of Missionary Instruction in Our Theological Seminaries." Bibliotheca Sacra 33 (July 1876):494-509.

1813. Harper, Elsie Dorothy. The Past Is Prelude: Fifty Years of Social Action in the YWCA. New York, Bureau of Communications, National Board, YWCA, 1963.

1814. Harper, William Rainey. "Bible-Study in the Pastorate; Figures and Facts." Old Testament Student 6 (January 1887):131-5.

1815. Harper, William Rainey. (Editorial) Old Testament Student 8 (January 1889):161-3.

1816. Harper, William Rainey. "Ideals of Educational Work." In Journal of Proceedings and Addresses, pp. 987-98. National Educational Association, 1895.

1817. Harper, William Rainey. Introductory Hebrew Method and Manual. 12th ed. New York: Charles Scribner's Sons, 1896.

1818. Harper, William Rainey. Religion and the Higher Life. Chicago: University of Chicago Press, 1905.

1819. Harper, William Rainey. "Shall the Theological Curriculum Be Changed, and How?" American Journal of Theology 3 (January 1899):45-66.

157

1820. Harper, William Rainey. The Trend in Higher
      Education. Chicago: University of Chicago
      Press, 1905.

1821. Harper, William Rainey. "Why Are There Fewer
      Students for the Ministry?" World To-Day 8
      (January 1905):92-5.

1822. Harper, William Rainey. Why Should I Study
      the Bible? Chicago: American Institute of
      Sacred Literature, 1895.

1823. Harrell, David E. A Social History of the
      Disciples of Christ. Nashville: Disciples
      of Christ Historical Society, 1966-73.

1824. Harrelson, W. J. "Introduction [Teaching the
      Biblical Languages: The AATS Study]."
      Theological Education 3 (Summer 1967):437-
      40.

1825. Harriman, Frederick William. "Beneficiary
      Education for the Ministry." Church Review
      49 (June 1887):593-607.

1826. Harris, G. et al. "(Modifications in the
      Theological Curriculum.)" American Journal
      of Theology 3 (1899):324+.

1827. Harris, John Andrews. "Clerical Training,
      before and after Ordination." Church
      Review 42 (1883):97-112.

1828. Harrison, Beverly. "An Advocate's Guide to
      Seminary Discussions of 'The Woman
      Question!'" Theological Education 8
      (Summer 1972):225-32.

1829. Harrison, Paul M. "Scholarship in the Public
      Domain." Theological Education 3 (Spring
      1967):345-57.

1830. Harrison, Paul M. Theological Education and
      the United Church of Christ: A Draft
      Report Prepared for the Commission on
      Theological Education and the United Church
      of Christ. University Park, Pa.:
      Pennsylvania State University, Dept. of
      Religious Studies, 1967.

1831. Harrod, Howard L. "Formation of Ministers for
      Urban Society." Encounter 29 (Autumn
      1968):348-54.

1832. Hart, James Morgan. German Universities: A
      Narrative of Personal Experience, Together
      with Recent Statistical Information,
      Practical Suggestions, and a Comparison of
      the German, English and American Systems of
      Higher Education. New York: G. P.
      Putnam's Sons, 1874.

1833. Hart, John W. "The Controversy within the
      Presbyterian Church, U.S.A., in the 1920's
      with Special Emphasis on the Reorganization
      of Princeton Theological Seminary." B.A.
      thesis, Princeton University, 1978.

1834. Hart, John W. "Princeton Theological
      Seminary: The Reorganization of 1929."
      Journal of Presbyterian History 58, no. 2
      (1980):124-40.

1835. Harter, Terry Price. "A Critique of North
      American Protestant Theological Education
      from the Perspectives of Ivan Illich and
      Paolo Freire." Ph.D. dissertation, Boston
      University Graduate School, 1980.

1836. Hartford Theological Seminary, Hartford, Conn.
      A Memorial of the Semi-Centenary
      Celebration of the Founding of the
      Theological Institute of Connecticut.
      Hartford: Press of the Case, Lockwood &
      Brainard Co., 1884.

1837. Hartford Theological Seminary, Hartford, Conn.
      Theological Training for Women. Hartford,
      1892.

1838. Hartley, Loyde, and Schuller, David S.
      "Theological Schools." In American
      Denominational Organization, pp. 225-44.
      Edited by R. Scherer. Pasadena: William
      Carey Library, 1980.

1839. Hartranft, Chester David. The Aims of a
      Theological Seminary: An Address Delivered
      before the Alumni Association of the
      Theological Seminary, New Brunswick, N.J...
      June 7, 1977. New York: Board of Publica-
      tion of the Reformed Church in America,
      1878.

1840. Hartshorn, W. N. "Sunday Schools and the
      Negro." In Organized Sunday School Work in
      America, 1908-1911. International Sunday-

159

school Convention of the United States and
British American Provinces. 13th, San
Francisco, 1911. Chicago: Executive
Committee of the International Sunday
School Association, 1911.

1841. Hartshorne, H. "Theological Education and the
Churches." Religious Education 49
(September 1954):340-7.

1842. Hartshorne, H. "Theology and Life: Excerpts
from Address." Time 63 (May 3, 1954):58.

1843. Hartshorne, Hugh. "What Is Theological
Education? Journal of Religion 26 (October
1946):235-42.

1844. Hartt, Rollin Lynde. "Revolution in Divinity
School Training." Homiletic Review 92
(October 1926):277-80.

1845. Hartt, Rollin Lynde. "Where Do We Get Our
Preachers?" World's Work 50 (1925):103-8.

1846. Hartung, Bruce M. "Issues in Supervision
during a Training Year." Journal of
Pastoral Care 31, no. 3 (1977):172-7.

1847. Hartwick Seminary, Brooklyn. Annual Catalogue, Theological and Classical, 1875,
1895.

1848. Hartwick Seminary, Brooklyn. Memorial Volume
of the Semi-Centennial Anniversary of
Hartwick Seminary, Held Aug. 21, 1866.
Albany: J. Munsell, 1867.

1849. "Harvard and Chicago Have New Theology Deans."
Christian Century 72 (April 27, 1955):491.

1850. "Harvard-Andover Dissolution of Affiliation."
School and Society 24 (November 6, 1926):
572-3.

1851. Harvard College. The Testimony of the
President, Professors, Tutors, and Hebrew
Instructor of Harvard College in Cambridge,
against the reverend Mr. George Whitefield,
and His Conduct. Boston: Printed by T.
Fleet, 1744.

1852. "Harvard Divinity Reborn." Newsweek 39
(February 18, 1952):96.

160

1853. "Harvard Revival." Life 39-40 (December 26, 1955):106-10.

1854. "Harvard Steps Out." Time 59 (February 18, 1952):76+.

1855. "Harvard Strengthens Its Divinity School." Christian Century 69 (April 30, 1952):518-20.

1856. Harvard University Board of Overseers. Report of a Committee of the Overseers and Memorial of the Corporation of Harvard College on the Relations between the Theological School and the College. Boston: Printed by J. Wilson & Son, 1852.

1857. "Harvard's New Venture." Hibbert Journal 61 (October 1962):15.

1858. "Harvard's Theologian." Newsweek 43 (May 17, 1954):66.

1859. Haselden, Kyle. "The B.D. Frontier." Christian Century 78 (January 18, 1961):71.

1860. Haskell, Thomas L. The Emergence of Professional Social Science: The American Social Science Association and the Nineteenth-Century Crisis of Authority. Urbana: University of Illinois Press, 1977.

1861. Haslett, Samuel B. "The Pedagogical Bible School." Ph.D. dissertation, Clark University, 1901.

1862. Hassler, Simeon Oliver, III. "A Rationale for a Program of Clinical Pastoral Education in the Local Church." Th.D. dissertation, Southwestern Baptist Theological Seminary, 1976.

1863. Hatfield, Edwin Francis. The Early Annals of Union Theological Seminary in the City of New York. New York, 1876.

1864. Hatfield, Edwin Francis. Patient Continuance in Well-Doing: A Memoir of Elihu W. Baldwin. New York: Jonathan Leavitt, 1843.

1865. Hatt, Harold E. "Christian Experience, Systematic Theology, and the Seminary

Curriculum." Encounter 36 (Summer 1975):181-95.

1866. Haugk, Kenneth C. and Weber, Timothy T. "The DeBunking Exercise: Teaching Research Experientially in Pastoral Care and Counseling." Journal of Pastoral Care 34, no. 2 (1980):104-8.

1867. Havice, Doris Webster. "Chapters from 'Roadmap for a Rebel'." Union Seminary Quarterly Review 35 (Fall and Winter 1979-80):55-64.

1868. Hawkins, R. M. "Pre-Professional Training for Ministerial Students in Our Colleges." Bulletin of the Board of Education of the Methodist Episcopal Church, South 9 (August 1919):65-73.

1869. Hawley, C. A. "(Danish Theological Education in Iowa)." Church History 9 (1940):299+.

1870. Hay, C. E. "(Beneficiary of Education for Christian Ministry and its Effect.)" Lutheran Quarterly 15 (New Series) (1885):90+.

1871. Hay, J. Charles. "The Seminary Speaks to the Church about Trust, Freedom, and Support." Theological Education 15 (Spring 1979):123-8.

1872. Hayden, Roger. "What Are the Qualifications of a Gospel Minister?" Baptist Quarterly 19 (1962):352-8.

1873. Hazard, Caroline. Memoirs of the Rev. J. Lewis Diman, D. D. Boston: Houghton Mifflin, 1886.

1874. Hazelton, Roger. "The Face of Theological Education Today." Educational Record 46 (Summer 1965):217-22.

1875. Hazelton, Roger. "The Idea of a Seminary." Christian Century 74 (April 24, 1957):512-13.

1876. Hazelton, Roger. "Ministry as Servanthood." Christian Century 80 (April 24, 1963):521-4.

1877. "He Couldn't Say No: New York Theological
       Seminary to Specialize in Urban Ministry."
       Time 88 (August 5, 1966):70.

1878. Head, Eldred Douglas. "Scholarship in
       Spiritual Leadership." Christian Education
       28 (December 1944):112-20.

1879. Head, Mabel. "Opportunities Afforded in
       Special Institutions for Missionary
       Training." In The Fifth Report of the
       Board of Missionary Preparation (for North
       America) for 1915. Edited by Frank K.
       Sanders, New York, n.d.

1880. Headlam, A. C. "Study of Theology." In
       Oxford Lectures on University Studies,
       1906-1921. Oxford, 1924.

1881. Healy, Thomas F. "God's Stepson." American
       Mercury 20 (1930):293-301.

1882. Heard, William A. From Slavery to the
       Bishopric in the A.M.E. Church. 1924;
       reprint ed., New York: Arno Press, 1969.

1883. Heaton, Ada B., and Heaton, C. Adrian.
       "Recruiting for Academic Excellence in
       Theological Schools." Theological Educa-
       tion 11 (Spring 1975):133-257.

1884. Heaton, Richard L. "Ecumenical Expression in
       the Seminaries." National Council Outlook
       6 (February 1956):21.

1885. Heaton, Richard L. "The Student Christian
       Movement in the Seminaries." Christian
       Scholar 37 (September 1954):460-4.

1886. "Hebrew in the Seminary Elective." Old
       Testament Student 5 (November 1885):136-7.

1887. Heckman, Marlin Leroy. "A History of the
       Library of Bethany Biblical Seminary,
       Chicago, Illinois." Ph.D. dissertation,
       University of Chicago, 1963.

1888. Hefferlin, J. B. Lon, and Phillips, Ellis L.
       Information Services for Academic
       Administration. San Francisco, Jossey-
       Bass, 1971.

1889. Hefley, J. "Luther Rice: Upgrading a
       Seminary and Hoping to be Accredited."
       Christianity Today 27 (January 7, 1983):
       34+.

1890. Hefner, Philip J. "Doctorate for Ministers?"
       Dialog 5 (Spring 1966):86-7.

1891. Hefner, Philip J. The Future of the American
       Church: To Commemorate the 140th Anniver-
       sary of the Seminary. Philadelphia:
       Fortress Press, 1968.

1892. Heiges, Donald R. "Festschrift in Honor of
       Abdel Ross Wentz." Lutheran Theological
       Seminary, Gettysburg, Bulletin 48 no. 4
       (1968).

1893. Heilman, L. "(Objections to Education for
       Ministry.)" Lutheran Quarterly 8 (New
       Series) (1878):369+.

1894. Heinecken, Martin. "The Pre-Theological
       Curriculum." Lutheran Quarterly 2
       (November 1950):426-40.

1895. Heins, Henry Hardy. Throughout All the Years:
       The Bicentennial Story of Hartwick in
       America, 1746-1946. Oneonta, N.Y.: Board
       of Trustees, Hartwick College, 1946.

1896. Heintzen, E. H. "Fourscore and Ten."
       Springfielder 29 (Autumn 1965):3-5.

1897. Heintzen, Erich Hugo, III. "The Religious
       Attitudes and Interests of Seminary
       Students and Clergymen of the Lutheran
       Church - Missouri Synod." Ed.D. disserta-
       tion, University of North Dakota, 1971.

1898. Heisey, Paul Harold. "The Story of Lutheran
       Theological Education in America."
       Lutheran Church Review 46 (January
       1927):27-49.

1899. Helfaer, Philip Monroe. "The Psychology of
       Religious Doubt: Clinical Studies of
       Protestant Theological Students." Ph.D.
       dissertation, Harvard University, 1969.

1900. Helland, Andreas Andersen. Georg Sverdrup:
       The Man and His Message, 1848-1907.
       Minneapolis: Messenger Press, 1947.

1901. Hemenway, Francis Dana. _Life and Selected Writings of Francis Dana Hemenway._ Cincinnati: Cranston & Stowe, 1890.

1902. Henderlite, Rachel. "Religious Education as a Discipline: III. Theological Reflections on the Discipline of Religious Education." _Religious Education_ 62, no. 5 (1967):405-11.

1903. Henderson, G. D. _The Founding of Marischal College Aberdeen._ Aberdeen: University Press, 1947.

1904. Henderson, G. D. _Religious Life in Seventeenth-Century Scotland._ Cambridge: At the University Press, 1937.

1905. Henderson, Robert W. _The Teaching Office in the Reformed Tradition._ Philadelphia: Westminster Press, 1962.

1906. Hendrickson, Paul. "Leaving the Seminary." _New York Times_ 129, Section A (July 24, 1980):A19.

1907. Hendrickson, Paul. _The Seminary: A Search._ New York: Summit Books, 1983.

1908. Hendrix, Scott H. "Luther and the Climate for Theological Education." _Lutheran Quarterly_ 26, no. 1 (1974):3-11.

1909. Henery, Charles Robert. "Student Initiative in Spiritual Formation at the General Theological Seminary [1822-1845]." STM thesis, General Theological Seminary, 1973.

1910. Hennesey, J. "From One-Mile Tavern to Ecumenical Cluster." _America_ 134 (March 27, 1976):252-5.

1911. Henry, Carl F. "Committing Seminaries to the Word." _Christianity Today_ 20, no. 10 (1976):470-3.

1912. Henry, Carl F. H. "Committing Seminaries to the World." _Christianity Today_ 20 (February 13, 1976):6-9.

1913. Henry, Carl Ferdinand Howard. _Personal Idealism and Strong's Theology._ Wheaton, Ill.: Van Kampen Press, 1951.

1914. Henry, Carl F. H. "Preparing to Serve the Church." Christianity Today 25 (February 6, 1981):22-3.

1915. Henry, Carl F. "Teacher Training in Theological Seminaries." Religious Education 2 (June 1907):41-55.

1916. Henry, Stuart C. "The Lane Rebels: A Twentieth Century Look." Journal of Presbyterian History 49 (Spring 1971):1-14.

1917. Henry, Stuart Clark. Unvanquished Puritan: A Portrait of Lyman Beecher. Grand Rapids, Mich.: William B. Eerdmans Publishing Co., 1973.

1918. Herberg, Will. "Crisis at Drew." Christianity and Crisis 27 (February 20, 1967):25-7.

1919. Herbst, Jurgen. The German Historical School in American Scholarship: A Study in the Transfer of Culture. Ithaca, N.Y.: Cornell University Press, 1969.

1920. "Heresy of Union Seminary." Literary Digest 46 (June 14, 1914):1337-8.

1921. Herman, Abbott Philip. "The Motivating Factors Entering into the Choice of the Ministry; A Case Study of Ministerial Students." Ph.D. dissertation, University of Chicago, 1930.

1922. Herr, Vincent V. "Mental Health Training in Catholic Seminaries." Journal of Religion and Health 1 (January 1962):127-52.

1923. Herrick, E. C. "My Adventure in Homiletics." Homiletic Review 94 (October 1927):265-7.

1924. Herrick, Everett Carleton. Turns Again Home: Andover Newton Theological School and Reminiscences from an Unkept Journal. Boston: Pilgrim Press, 1949.

1925. Herring, Hubert. "Union Seminary Routs Its Reds." Christian Century 51 (June 13, 1934):799-801; "Discussion." 51 (June 27, 1934):865-6.

1926. Hershberger, John Kenneth. "An Experimental Study of the Influence of Child Abuse

Education on the Pastoral Counseling
Responses of Seminary Students." Ph.D.
dissertation, University of Iowa, 1981.

1927. Hertz, Karl H. "Planning Theological Education." Lutheran Quarterly 18 (November
1966):315-17.

1928. Hertzler, Silas. "Attendance in Mennonite and
Affiliated Colleges, 1966-67." Mennonite
Quarterly Review 42, no. 4 (1968):312-17.

1929. Herzog, F. "Black and White Together?
[Duke]." Duke Divinity School Review 34
(Spring 1969):115-20.

1930. Hester, Richard Loren. "Attitudes toward
Pastoral Authority among Selected
Theological Students." Th.D. dissertation,
Southern Baptist Theological Seminary,
1968.

1931. Heussman, John William. "The Literature Cited
in Theological Journals and Its Relation to
Seminary Library Circulation." Ph.D.
dissertation, University of Illinois at
Urbana-Champaign, 1970.

1932. Hevey, Jerome J. "Bringing the Seminary to
the Church." Christian Century 99 (March
10, 1982):273-4.

1933. Hewes, F. W. "Educated Ministry?" Outlook 51
(March 2, 1895):345.

1934. Hick, J. H. "Belief and Life: The
Fundamental Nature of the Christian Ethic
[Theological Students]." Encounter 20
(Fall 1959):494-516.

1935. Hickok, L. P. "Design of Theological
Seminaries." American Biblical Repository
11 (1838):187-203.

1936. Hiebert, Albert Arthur. "Expository and
Discovery Teaching of Systematic Theology:
An Analysis of the Instructional Models
Preferred by Teachers and Students of
Systematic Theology in Accredited Schools
of the American Association of Bible
Colleges." Ph.D. dissertation, New York
University, 1978.

167

1937. Hiemstra, William L. "History of Clinical
       Pastoral Training in the United States."
       Reformed Review 16 (May 1963):30-47.

1938. Higdon, E. K. "View Church Use of Formal
       Tests." Christian Century 72 (May 11,
       1955):579-80.

1939. Higgins, John Robert Stewart. "The
       Preparation of Ministers: A Study of the
       Process of Professional Growth in a Program
       of Clinical Pastoral Eduction." Ph.D.
       dissertation, Harvard University, 1970.

1940. Hildner, Ernest G. "Higher Education in
       Transition, 1850-1870." Journal of the
       Illinois State Historical Society 56, no. 1
       (1963):61-73.

1941. Hilgert, Earle. "Calvin Ellis Stowe: Pioneer
       Librarian of the Old West." Library
       Quarterly 50 (July 1980):324-51.

1942. Hill, D. S. Education and Problems of the
       Protestant Ministry. Worcester, Mass.:
       Clark University Press, 1908.

1943. Hill, David Spence. "The Education and
       Problems of the Protestant Ministry
       [bibliog.]." American Journal of Religious
       Psychology and Education 3 (May 1908):29-
       70.

1944. Hill, E. P. "City Missions and Theological
       Students." Missionary Review of the World
       35 (August 1912):601-5.

1945. Hill, James Langdon. Seven Sorts of Success-
       ful Services: Suggestive Solutions of the
       Sunday Evening Problem. New York: E. B.
       Treat & Co., 1904.

1946. Hill, Thomas. "Theology a Possible Science."
       Bibliotheca Sacra 31 (1874):1-29.

1947. Hill, William A. "Missions in the Theological
       Seminaries of the United States." Inter-
       national Review of Missions 23 (April
       1934):260-6.

1948. Hill, William A. "What Theological Schools
       Contribute to Missions." Missionary
       Reviews of the World 56 (December

1933):597-8.

1949.   Hillis, D.   "To Save a Seminarian: Internship Program." Christianity Today 14 (May
22, 1970):29-30.

1950.   Hiltner, S. "Clinical Education in Religion
and Mental Hygiene [bibliog.]." Religious
Education 38 (May 1943):152-9.

1951.   Hiltner, Seward and Ziegler, Jesse H. "Clini-
cal Pastoral Education and the Theological
Schools." Journal of Pastoral Care 15
(Autumn 1961):129-43.

1952.   Hiltner, Seward, ed. Clinical Pastoral
Training. New York: Commission on
Religion and Health, Federal Council of the
Churches of Christ in America, 1945.

1953.   Hiltner, S. "Debt of Clinical Pastoral
Education to Anton T. Boisen." Journal of
Pastoral Care 20 (September 1966):129-35.

1954.   Hiltner, Seward. "Fifty Years of CPE."
Journal of Pastoral Care 29, no. 2
(1975):90-8.

1955.   Hiltner, Seward. "Frontiers of Theological
Education." Encounter 23 (Autumn
1962):404-15.

1956.   Hiltner, S. "Influence of Clinical Training
upon the Clergyman's Work with Groups."
Christian Education 20 (June 1937):285-9.

1957.   Hiltner, Seward. "Psychological Tests for
Ministerial Candidates." Journal of
Pastoral Care 11 (1957):106-8.

1958.   Hiltner, Seward. "Teaching of Practical
Theology in the United States during the
Twentieth Century." Princeton Seminary
Bulletin 61 (Autumn 1967):61-75.

1959.   Hiltner, Seward. "Theology and Pastoral Care
in the United States." Theologische
Literaturzeitung 88 (July 1963):501-8.

1960.   Hine, Leland D. "Denomination Assists a
Seminary." Foundations 7 (January 1964):
63-76.

169

1961. Hinke, William J. "A Bibliography for Old Testament Study." Auburn Seminary Record 15 (September 10, 1919):147-92.

1962. Hinko, Edward N., and Paolino, Albert F. "Developing a Mental Health Seminar for Pastoral Counselors." Insight; Quarterly Review of Religion and Mental Health 2 (Summer 1963):21-4.

1963. Hinson, E. Glenn. "Historical Patterns of Lay Leadership in Ministry in Local Baptist Churches." Baptist History and Heritage 13, no. 1 (1978):26-34.

1964. Hinson, E. Glenn. "Morton T. Kelsey: Theologian of Experience." Perspectives in Religious Studies 9 (Spring 1982):5-20.

1965. Hinson, E. Glenn. "A Southern Baptist Context." Christian Century 94 (February 2, 1977):93-5.

1966. Hinton, John Howard. "On Completeness of Ministerial Qualification." Christian Review 3 (1838):254-63.

1967. "Historical Addresses Delivered at the Newton Centennial June, 1925." Institution Bulletin (Newton) 18, no. 2.

1968. The History of American Methodism. Edited by Emory Stevens Bucke. 3 vols. New York: Abingdon Press, 1964.

1969. Hoagland, N. S. "Summer School for Clergymen." Outlook 93 (October 30, 1909):517-8.

1970. Hobson, Charles Frank, Jr. "Transactional Analysis Applied to Scripture Reading and Sermon Delivery in a Seminary Preaching Class." Ed.D. dissertation, New Orleans Baptist Theological Seminary, 1978.

1971. Hockley, Robert E. "Clinical Pastoral Supervision: A Rationale." Journal of Christian Education 60 (1977):5-13.

1972. Hodge, C. "(Advice to Theological Students.)" Princeton Review 5 (1833):100+. New Englander 5 (1847):505+.

1973. Hodge, Charles. *Ministers: Their Education and Support.* Philadelphia: Presbyterian Board of Education, 1895.

1974. Hodge, Richard Morse. "The Education of Ministers." *Religious Education* 5 (December 1910):458-61.

1975. Hodges, George. *Henry Codman Potter: Seventh Bishop of New York.* New York: Macmillan Co., 1915.

1976. Hodgkin, Henry T. "The Special Preparation of Missionaries." *International Review of Missions* 1 (January 1912):108-24.

1977. Hodgson, Leonard. *The Bible and the Training of the Clergy.* London: Darton, Longman & Todd, 1963.

1978. Hoedemaker, Libertus A. "Hoekendijk's American Years." *Occasional Bulletin of Missionary Research* 1 (April 1977):7-10.

1979. Hoehn, Richard A. "Whitewashing Blackthink." *Lutheran Quarterly* 27, no. 3 (1975):220-9.

1980. Hoekendijk, Letty Russell. "Tradition as Mission." *Study Encounter* 6, no. 2 (1970):87-96.

1981. Hoffecker, Andrew. "Beauty and the Princeton Piety." In *Soli Deo Gloria: Essays in Reformed Theology.* Edited by R. C. Sproul. Phillipsburg, N.J.: Presbyterian and Reformed Pub. Co., 1976.

1982. Hofman, Hans, ed. *Making the Ministry Relevant.* New York: Scribner, 1960.

1983. Hofman, Hans. "Religion and Mental Health." *Journal of Religion and Mental Health* 1 (October 1962):319-36.

1984. Hofstadter, Richard. *Academic Freedom in the Age of the College.* New York: Columbia University Press, 1961 [c1955].

1985. Hofstadter, Richard and Hardy, C. DeWitt. *The Development and Scope of Higher Education in the United States.* New York: Columbia University Press, 1952.

1986. Hofstadter, Richard, ed. The Progressive
Movement, 1900-1915. Englewood Cliffs,
N.J.: Prentice-Hall, 1963.

1987. Hofstadter, Richard. "Pseudo-Conservatism
Revisited - 1965." In The Paranoid Style
in American Politics, and Other Essays.
New York: Alfred A. Knopf, 1965.

1988. Hoge, Dean R. and Faue, Jeffrey L. "Sources
of Conflict over Priorities of the
Protestant Church." Social Forces 52
(December 1973):178-94.

1989. Hoh, Paul J. "The Seminary and the Church's
Missionary Task." Lutheran Church
Quarterly 11 (1938):54-64.

1990. Hohlfeld, J. M. "A Theological Curriculum
with Ecumenical Dimensions." Hartford
Quarterly 4 (Spring 1964).

1991. Holbrook, C. A. "The Lilly Study: Challenge
to College and Seminary [Pre-Seminary
Education]." Journal of Bible and Religion
34 (April 1966).

1992. Holcomb, W. L. and Maes, J. L. "Functional
Roles, Professional Identity, and
Theological Curricula." Theological
Education 2 (Spring 1966).

1993. Holcomb, Walter L. "Preparing Ministers for
Leadership in Family Life Education:
Proposals for the Methodist Seminaries."
Ph.D. dissertation, Columbia University,
1950.

1994. Holder, Ray. "Centenary: Roots of a Pioneer
College (1838-1844)." Journal of
Mississippi History 42, no. 2 (1980):77-98.

1995. Holdich, Joseph. The Life of Wilbur Fisk,
D. D., First President of the Wesleyan
University. New York: Harper & Bros.,
1842.

1996. Holifield, E. Brooks. "Ethical Assumptions of
Clinical Pastoral Education." Journal of
Pastoral Care 34, no. 1 (1980):39-53.

1997. Holifield, E. Brooks. "Ethical Assumptions of
Clinical Pastoral Education." Theology

Today 36, no. 1 (1979):30-44.

1998. Holifield, E. Brooks. "History and Selfhood:
        An Historian's View." Journal of Pastoral
        Care 28, no. 3 (1974):147-51.

1999. Holifield, E. Brooks. "Mercersburg,
        Princeton, and the South: The Sacramental
        Controversy in the Nineteenth Century."
        Journal of Presbyterian History 54 (Summer
        1976):238-57.

2000. Holland, Fredric L. "Theological Education in
        Context and Change." D. Miss. disserta-
        tion, Fuller Theological Seminary, School
        of Psychology, 1978.

2001. Hollander, I. Fred. "Mental Health Teaching
        Materials for the Clergy." Journal of
        Religion and Mental Health 1 (July
        1962):113-282.

2002. Holley, Joseph Winthrop. You Can't Build a
        Chimney from the Top: The South through
        the Life of a Negro Educator. New York:
        William-Frederick Press, 1948.

2003. Hollis, Ernest V. and Taylor, Alice L. Social
        Work Education in the United States. New
        York: Columbia University Press, 1951.

2004. Holman, Charles T. "Extension Service in Mid-
        Western Theological Seminaries." Christian
        Education 21 (December 1937):116-21.

2005. Holman, C. T. "Pastors' Refresher Courses
        Successful." Christian Century 52 (August
        21, 1935):1066.

2006. Holman, C. T. "Pastors Throng Summer
        Schools." Christian Century 52 (August 7,
        1935):1022.

2007. Holmer, Paul Le Roy. "The Crisis in
        Rhetoric." Theological Education 7 (Spring
        1971):208-15.

2008. Holmes, Dwight Oliver Wendell. The Evolution
        of the Negro College. New York: Teachers
        College, Columbia University, 1934.

2009. Holmes, Dwight O. W. "Fifty Years of Howard
        University." Journal of Negro History 3

(April 1918):128-38; (October 1918):368-80.

2010. Holmes, Dwight Oliver Wendell. "The Negro
College Faces the Depression." Journal of
Negro Education 2 (January 1933):16-25.

2011. Holmes, John Haynes. I Speak for Myself: The
Autobiography of John Haynes Holmes. New
York: Harper & Bros., 1959.

2012. Holmes, O. "Baptist Fundamentalists Found
School [Eastern Baptist Theological
Seminary]." Christian Century 42 (May 28,
1925):712.

2013. Holmes, Urban T. III. "Strangeness of the
Seminary." Anglican Theological Review,
Suppl. Series no. 6 (June 1976):135-50.

2014. Holt, A. E. "Case Method and Teaching at
Chicago Theological Seminary." Religious
Education 23 (March 1928):207-12.

2015. Holt, A. E. "Training for Ministry in College
Community." Religious Education 8 (August
1913):250-2.

2016. Holzhammer, Robert Ernest. "The Formation of
the Domestic and Foreign Missionary
Society." Historical Magazine of the
Protestant Episcopal Church 40, no. 3
(1971):257-72.

2017. Hommen, Donovan Leroy. "An Assessment of the
Effects of a Community Mental Health Center
Laboratory Training - Education - Consulta-
tion Program in Bereavement Ministry for
Parish Clergymen." Ph.D. dissertation,
Boston University, 1972.

2018. Hommes, T. G. and Von Euw, C. K. "Mixed
Marriage [Boston Theological Institute]."
Harvard Divinity Bulletin 2 (New Series)
(Autumn 1968):18-20.

2019. Hommes, Tjaard G. "Supervision as Theological
Method." Journal of Pastoral Care 31, no.
3 (1977):150-7.

2020. Homrighausen, Elmer George. "Christian
Education after Ten Years of Ecumenical
Thinking." Religion in Life 19 (1950):176-
85.

174

2021. Homrighausen, E. G. "Making an Accredited
      Theological Curriculum." Christian
      Education 22 (June 1939):391-9.

2022. Homrighausen, Elmer G. "Reformed Faith and
      Its Call for a Competent Ministry."
      Reformed World 36, no. 3 (1980):117-21.

2023. Homrighausen, Elmer George. "Theological
      Education in the Service of the Church and
      the World." Princeton Seminary Bulletin 62
      (Autumn 69):21-36.

2024. Hoon, Paul W. "Training for the Parish
      Ministry." Religion In Life 28 (1958-
      9):13-24.

2025. Hooper, William Loyd. "The Master's Degree in
      Church Music in Protestant Theological
      Seminaries of the United States." Ph.D.
      dissertation, George Peabody College for
      Teachers, 1966.

2026. Hoover, Edwin A. "Pastoral Supervision as an
      Interpersonal Experience." Journal of
      Pastoral Care 31, no. 3 (1977):164-71.

2027. Hoover, H. D. "Prelude to the Teaching of
      Practical Theology." Lutheran Quarterly 56
      (October 1926):374-425.

2028. Hopewell, James F. "Guest Editorial [Theolog-
      ical Education]." International Review of
      Missions 56 (April 1967):141-4.

2029. Hopewell, James F. "Mission and Seminary
      Structure." International Review of
      Missions 56 (April 1967):158-63.

2030. Hopkins, Charles Howard. History of the
      Y.M.C.A. in North America. New York:
      Association Press, 1951.

2031. Hopkins, Garland Evans. "Seminary Heads Meet
      in Columbus." Christian Century 67 (June
      28, 1950):794.

2032. Hopper, M. T. "Where Go for Specialized
      Training?" International Journal of
      Religious Education 28 (March 1952):12-14.

2033. Hoppin, James Mason. Homiletics. New York:
      Fund & Wagnalls, 1883.

2034. Hoppin, James Mason. The Office and Work of the Christian Ministry. New York: Sheldon & Co., 1869.

2035. Hoppin, James Mason. Pastoral Theology. New York: Funk & Wagnalls, 1884.

2036. Hopson, George B. "The Beneficiary Education of Young Men for the Sacred Ministry." Church Review 47 (April 1886):417-31.

2037. Hordern, William F. "Renewal in the Seminary [Review Article]." Lutheran Quarterly 18 (November 1966):329-36.

2038. Horn, Henry E. "Jacobs Trilogy." Lutheran Quarterly 27 (May 1975):168-78.

2039. Horn, Henry E. "The University Environment and Future Seminary Life." Lutheran Quarterly 18, no. 4 (November 1966):307-14, 318-21.

2040. Horst, I. B. "The Fellowship in the Spirit: Immanental Grace in Seminary and Church Life [Anabaptists]." In De Geest in het Geding. Edited by I. B. Horst. Alphen aan den Rijn: H.D. Tjeenk Willink, 1978.

2041. Horton, D. "Church and University [Overlap in the Divinity School]." Harvard Divinity Bulletin 24 (October 1959):1-6.

2042. Horton, Douglas. "Harvard Divinity School in 1956." Harvard Divinity School Bulletin 21 (1955-56):137-50.

2043. Horton, Douglas. "Idea of a Theological Seminary." Hartford Quarterly 4 (Autumn 1963):7-15.

2044. Horton, Isabelle. "The Deaconess in Social Settlement Work." In The Socialized Church, pp. 147-73. Edited by Marion Worth Tippy. New York: Eaton & Mains, 1909.

2045. Horton, Isabelle. High Adventure: Life of Lucy Rider Meyer. New York: Methodist Book Concern, 1928.

2046. Horvath, W. J. "Parish or Perish." Christian Century 87 (June 24, 1970):790.

2047. Hotchkiss, Wesley A. "The Posture of the Church in Relationship to the Increasing Study of Religion in College and University." Theological Education 3 (Spring 1967):358-66.

2048. Hotter, Don W. "Some Changes Related to the Ordained Ministry in the History of American Methodism." Methodist History 13, no. 3 (1975):177-94.

2049. Houck, R. L., and Dawson, J. G. "Comparative Study of Persisters and Leavers in Seminary Training." Psychological Reports 42 (June 1978):1131-7.

2050. Hough, Joseph C., Jr. The Politics of Theological Education. Occasional Papers No. 37. Nashville, Tenn.: United Methodist Board of Higher Education and Ministry, 1981.

2051. Houghton, George G. "Lewis Sperry Chafer, 1871-1952." Bibliotheca Sacra 128 (1971):291-9.

2052. Hougland, Kenneth R. "How Much Does a D. Min. Program Cost." Theological Education 12 (Summer 1976):246-52.

2053. Housley, John B. "For Freedom in Seminaries [Letter]." Christian Century 72 (June 22, 1955):733.

2054. Houts, Donald C. "Ego Identity and Professional Preparation for Ministry." Journal of Pastoral Care 25, no. 1 (1971):12-23.

2055. Houts, Donald C. "Student Evaluation: Neglected Stepchild of Curriculum Revision." Theological Education 7 (Winter 1971):79-86.

2056. Houts, Donald Charles. "The Use of Ego Identity Measures in Evaluating a Seminary Curriculum." Ph.D. dissertation, Northwestern University, 1970.

2057. Houts, Richard F. "Learning To Be a Family." Christianity Today 24 (June 6, 1980):20-3.

2058. Houts, Richard Franklin. "A Survey of Field Education in Selected Seminaries Preparing

177

Parish Ministers of Education." D.R.E.
dissertation, Southern Baptist Theological
Seminary, 1971.

2059. Houts, William Franklin. "A Survey of Field
Education in Selected Seminaries Preparing
Parish Ministers of Education." D.R.E.
dissertation, Southern Baptist Theological
Seminary, 1971.

2060. Hovey, Alvah. Barnas Sears: A Christian
Educator. New York: Silver, Burdett &
Co., 1902.

2061. Hovey, Alvah. Historical Address Delivered at
the Fiftieth Anniversary of the Newton
Theological Institution, June 8, 1875.
Boston: Wright & Potter, 1875.

2062. Hovey, Alvah. "Reforms in Theological
Education." Baptist Quarterly Review 7
(1885):407-15.

2063. Hovey, George Rice. Alvah Hovey: His Life
and Letters. Philadelphia: Judson Press,
1928.

2064. "How Shall They Hear...?" Christian Century
78 (April 26, 1961):509.

2065. Howard, Harry Clay. Princes of the Christian
Pulpit and Pastorate. Nashville, Tenn.:
Cokesbury Press, 1928.

2066. Howard, Ivan Cushing. "Controversies in
Methodism over Methods of Education of
Ministers up to 1856." Ph.D. dissertation,
State University of Iowa, 1965.

2067. Howard, Victor B. "Sectionalism, Slavery and
Education, New Albany, Indiana Versus
Danville, Kentucky." Register of the
Kentucky Historical Society 68, no. 4
(1970):292-310.

2068. Howard, Victor B. "The Slavery Controversy
and a Seminary for the Northwest." Journal
of Presbyterian History 43 (December
1965):227-53.

2069. Howe, Daniel Walker. The Unitarian
Conscience: Harvard Moral Philosophy,
1805-1861. Cambridge: Harvard University

Press, 1970.

2070. Howe, George. A Discourse on Theological Education. New York: Leavitt, Trow & Co., 1844.

2071. Howe, George. History of the Presbyterian Church in South Carolina. 2 vols. Columbia, S.C.: Duffie & Chapman, 1870-1883, v. 2, pp. 561-3.

2072. Howe, Leroy T. (Special Issue in Honor of Retiring Dean Joseph D. Quillian, Perkins School of Theology). Perkins School of Theology: Journal 34 (Spring 1981):1-33.

2073. Howe, Reuel L. "Counseling the Theological Student." Journal of Clinical Pastoral Work 1 (Autumn 1947):11-17.

2074. Howe, R. L. "Institute for Advanced Pastoral Studies: A New Development." Journal of Pastoral Care 11 (Winter 1957):226-8.

2075. Howe, R. L. "Needs of the Church's Ministry Basic to Planning Continuing Education." Theological Education 1 (Summer 1965):205-12.

2076. Howe, R. L. "Pastoral Psychology: The Next 20 Years in Continuing Education." Pastoral Psychology 21 (February 1970):55-63.

2077. Howe, Reuel L. "The Role of Clinical Training in Theological Education." Journal of Pastoral Care 6 (Spring 1952):1-12.

2078. Howe, Reuel L. "Theological Education after Ordination." In Making the Ministry Relevant, pp. 133-69. Edited by Hans Hofmann. New York: Scribner, 1960.

2079. Hoyer, Louis Bach. "Theory of Ego Identity with Reference to the Young Pastor in Clinical Training." Ph.D. dissertation, Boston University, 1962.

2080. Hoyt, Arthur S. "Sociology in Theological Training." Homiletic Review 30 (November 1895):459-64.

179

2081. Hoyt, Benjamin R. "Address to Ministers and Members of the M. E. Church in New England." Zion's Herald 10 (May 8, 1839):74-5.

2082. Hoyt, Benjamin R. "Convention to Establish a Theological Seminary in New England." Zion's Herald 10 (May 1, 1839):70.

2083. Hsiao, Andrew K. H. "Theological Education and Christian Education." Theology and Life no. 2 (December 1979):14-29.

2084. Hsiao, Andrew K. H. "The Three Great Tasks of the Theological Seminary." Theology and Life (August 1978):1-6.

2085. Hubbard, David A. et al. "Parachurch Fallout: Seminary Students." Christianity Today 25 (November 6, 1981):36-7.

2086. Hubbard, David A. "Seminary Management from the President's Perspective: A Bicentennial Overview." Theological Education 13 (Autumn 1976):44-52.

2087. Hubbell, William K. "Henry Caswall (1810-1870) and the Backwoods Church." Historical Magazine of the Protestant Episcopal Church 29, no. 3 (1960):219-39.

2088. Hubble, G. "Reasons for Missionary Training." International Review of Missions 52 (July 1963):257-65.

2089. Huber, Donald L. "Capital and Wittenberg: Alternative Visions for Lutheran Theological Education in the Nineteenth Century." Trinity Seminary Review 4 (Spring 1982):26-31.

2090. Hudson, R. Lofton. "Preacher as Hero." Peabody Journal of Education 29 (March 1952):282-5.

2091. Huenemann, Reuben H. "Presidents: Administration in a New Era." Theological Education 6 (Spring 1970):232-4.

2092. Hugh, Martin. Puritanism and Richard Baxter. London: SMC Press, 1954.

2093. Hughes, Edwin Holt. I Was Made A Minister:
An Autobiography. New York: Abingdon,
Cokesbury, 1943.

2094. Hughes, Everett Cherrington. "Dilemmas and
Contradictions of Status." American
Journal of Sociology 50 (March 1945):353-9.

2095. Hughes, Everett C. et al. Education for the
Professions of Medicine, Law, Theology, and
Social Welfare. Berkeley, Calif.:
Carnegie Commission on Higher Education,
1973.

2096. Hughes, Everett C. "The Making of a Physi-
cian." Human Organization 14 (Winter
1956):21-5.

2097. Hughes, Everett Cherrington. Men and Their
Work. Glencoe, Ill.: Free Press, 1958.

2098. Hughes, George. "A Central Salvation
Seminary! The Great Need of Our Church."
Christian Advocate and Journal (New York)
29 (January 19, 1854):1.

2099. Hughley, J. Neal. "Theological Education:
Its Problems and Tasks." Journal of
Religious Thought 10 (1952-3):44-55.

2100. Hulbert, E. B. "The Morgan Park Period
[Memorials of William Rainey Harper]."
Biblical World 27 (March 1906):171-6.

2101. Hulbert, E. B. "The Relation of the Divinity
School to the University. To What Extent
Can the Divinity School Share the Advan-
tages of the University?" In Christianity
Practically Applied, v. 2, pp. 475-8.
Evangelical Alliance for the United States
of America. Conference. Chicago, 1893.
New York: Baker & Taylor, 1894.

2102. Hulick, William A. "Post-Seminary and
Inservice Education of Clergymen in the
Presbyterian Church, U.S.A." Ph.D.
dissertation, University of Pittsburgh,
1953.

2103. Hull, John. "Worship and Education." Educational Review 24 (November 1971):26-33.

181

2104. Hull, William E. "Theological Education and the 'Liberal Arts.'" Theological Education 12 (Winter 1976):134-6.

2105. Hulme, W. E. "Breakthrough: Dubuque's Experiment in Ecumenism: Cooperative Graduate Programs and Open Classes for Undergraduates." Christian Century 82 (September 29, 1965):1187-90.

2106. Hulme, W. E. "Seminary Student and His Family Life." Pastoral Psychology 11 (Summer 1960):33-8.

2107. Hultgren, Arland J. "Can We Not Afford Seminex." Dialog 18 (Spring 1979):146.

2108. Hultgren, Dayton D. "What Makes a Winning Proposal in Administrative Staff Development." Theological Education 16 (Autumn 1979):75-6.

2109. Humphrey, David C. "Colonial Colleges and English Dissenting Academies." History of Education Quarterly 12 (Summer 1972):184-97.

2110. Humphrey, Edna H. "Husband to Harriet [Calvin Ellis Stowe]." New England Galaxy 17, no. 4 (1976):9-14.

2111. Humphrey, Warren Benjamin. "An Analysis of Opinions of Bible College Administration Concerning Selected Issues of College Curriculum." Ed.D. dissertation, Syracuse University, 1965.

2112. "Hundred Years of Andover." Outlook 89 (June 20, 1908):359.

2113. Hunicutt, W. L. C. "Central University." Christian Advocate (Nashville) 32 (New series) (March 9, 1872):10.

2114. Hunt, Everett Lee. "The Teaching of Public Speaking in Schools of Theology." Quarterly Journal of Speech Education 10 (1924):369-73.

2115. Hunt, James D. "The Liberal Theology of Clarence R. Skinner." Journal of the Universalist Historical Society 7 (1967/68):102-20.

2116. Hunter, Doris and Hunter, Howard. "Neither Mail Nor Female." Christian Century 82 (April 28, 1965):527+; (Discussion) 82 (June 23, 1965):814.

2117. Hunter, Edith Fisher. Sophia Lyon Fahs: A Biography. Boston: Beacon Press, 1966.

2118. Hunter, George I. Supervision and Education-Formation for Ministry. Cambridge, Mass.: Episcopal Divinity School, 1982.

2119. Hunter, George I. Theological Field Education. Newton Centre, Mass.: Boston Theological Institute, 1977.

2120. Hunter, Margaret Adair. "Education in Pennsylvania Promoted by the Presbyterian Church, 1726-1837." Ed.D. dissertation, Temple University, 1937.

2121. Hunter, T. H. "More on Continuing Education." McCormick Quarterly 18 (March 1965):1-2.

2122. Hurd, John. "Observations about Good Proposals." Theological Education 16 (Autumn 1979):73-4.

2123. Hurlbut, Jesse Lyman. The Story of Chautauqua. New York: G. P. Putnam's Sons, 1921.

2124. Huseth, David Harlan. "A Descriptive Analysis of an Inservice Counselor Training Program for Ministers." Ph.D. dissertation, University of Oregon, 1973.

2125. Hutchins, Robert M. "The Place of Theological Education in a University." Christian Education 27 (December 1943):98-101.

2126. Hutchinson, P. "Battle of Princeton, 1925." Christian Century 42 (May 28, 1925):699-701.

2127. Hutchinson, William R. "Modernism and Missions." In The Missionary Enterprise in China and America, pp. 110-31. Edited by J. K. Fairbank. Cambridge: Harvard University Press, 1974.

2128. Hutchison, F. L. "Grant Spurs Yale Divinity Project." Christian Century 73 (January

25, 1956):124.

2129. Hutchison, William R. The Modernist Impulse in American Protestantism. Cambridge: Harvard University Press, 1976.

2130. Hutchison, William R. The Transcendental Ministers: Church Reform in the New England Renaissance. New Haven: Yale University Press, 1959.

2131. Huxtable, Ada Louise. "Moving into a New Realm [Hartford Seminary]." New York Times 131, Section 2 (September 27, 1981):D33.

2132. Huyck, Heather Ann. "To Celebrate a Whole Priesthood: The History of Women's Ordination in the Episcopal Church." Ph.D. dissertation, University of Minnesota, 1981.

2133. Hyde, William De Witt. "College and Seminary." Independent 61 (1906):264-8.

2134. Hyde, William D. "Reform in Theological Education." Atlantic Monthly 85 (January 1900):16-26.

2135. Hyslop, R. D. "Missions and the Missionary: A Study by the Ecumenical Fellows of the Program of Advanced Religious Studies, Union Theological Seminary, New York." International Review of Missions 53 (October 1964):459-66.

2136. Hyslop, R. D. "Right Men for the Ministry." Religious Education 40 (January 1945):3-7.

2137. "I Graduate from Seminary, with Comments." Religious Education 36 (July 1941):163-74.

2138. "I Like a Bible Institute!" Moody Monthly 59 (September 1958):80-2.

2139. "I Went to Seminary." Homiletic Review 107 (June-July 1934):446-9.

2140. "The Ideas of a Seminary." Christian Century 80 (April 24, 1963):518-20.

2141. "The Identity Crisis in Seminaries." Christian Century 94 (February 2, 1977):95-100.

2142. Igleheart, Glenn A. "Ecumenical Concerns among Southern Baptists." Journal of Ecumenical Studies 17, no. 2 (1980):49-61.

2143. Illick, Joseph E. "The Reception of Darwinism at the Theological Seminary and the College at Princeton, New Jersey. Part I. The Theological Seminary. Part II. The College." Journal of the Presbyterian Historical Society 38, no. 3 (1960):152-65 and no. 4:235-43.

2144. Imbler, John M. "By Degrees: The Development of Theological Education within the Disciples of Christ." S.T.M. thesis, Christian Theological Seminary, 1981.

2145. Imler, W. A. "Financial Aid for the Theological Student." Christian Century 84 (April 26, 1967):568+.

2146. "Importance of a Theological Institution." Panoplist 3 (December 1807):306-16.

2147. "Importance of an Educated Ministry." American Quarterly Register 3 (November 1830):105-7.

2148. "The Impossible Dream: Can Seminaries Deliver?" Christianity Today 21 (February 4, 1977):18-21.

2149. Indiana University, Indianapolis. Medical Center. "A Community Project in Religion and Mental Health." 1967. (ERIC Document)

2150. "Influence of Eminent Piety on the Intellectual Powers." Christian Review 5 (March 1840):1-22.

2151. Ingram, George H. "The Story of the Log College." Presbyterian Historical Society. Journal 12 (October 1927):487-511.

2152. Ingram, Osmond Kelly and Colver, Robert M. "Notes on the Graduating Classes of 1958-1967 of Duke Divinity School and Southeastern Baptist Theological Seminary." Duke Divinity School Review 36 (Spring 1971):100-11.

2153. Ingram, O. K. "Student Recruitment." Duke Divinity School Bulletin 28 (November

1963):188-98.

2154. Insko, W. Robert. "Benjamin Bosworth Smith,
Kentucky Pioneer Clergyman and Educator."
Register of the Kentucky Historical Society
69, no. 1 (1971):37-86.

2155. Inskow, W. Robert. "The Kentucky Seminary."
Kentucky Historical Society. Register 52
(July 1954):213-32.

2156. Institute for Religious and Social Studies.
Jewish Theological Seminary of America.
Patterns of Faith in America Today. Edited
by F. Ernest Johnson. New York: Institute
for Religious and Social Studies, 1957.

2157. "Institute of Pastoral Care, Inc. Clinical
Pastoral Training Centers, 1966." Journal
of Pastoral Care 19 (Winter 1965):220-7.

2158. "Integrity Schism, Neither, Both: Interview,
J.A.O. Preus [Concordia Seminary]."
Christianity Today 19 (October 25,
1974):11-12+.

2159. Interchurch World Movement of North America.
World Survey: Revised Preliminary State-
ment and Budget, 2 vols. New York:
Interchurch Press, 1920.

2160. International Sunday-School Convention of the
United States and British American
Provinces. Organized Sunday-School Work in
America, 1905-1908. Chicago: Exec. Comm.
of the International Sunday-School
Association, 1908.

2161. Inter-Professions Conference on Education for
Professional Responsibility, Buck Hill
Falls, Pa., 1948. Education for Profes-
sional Responsibility. Pittsburgh:
Carnegie Press, 1948.

2162. "Interseminary Movement As It Started."
Christian Education 19 (February 1936):231-
6.

2163. "Into the Thick of It, Or above the Battle?"
Literary Digest 55 (December 29, 1917):40.

2164. Irion, Paul E. "Practical Fields and Theological Education." In New Shape of Pastoral

186

Theology: S. Hiltner. Edited by William B. Oglesby. Nashville: Abingdon Press, 1969.

2165. Irwin, E. Robert. "An Analysis of the Church Music Curriculum of Selected Protestant Seminaries." Ph.D. dissertation, University of Rochester, 1967.

2166. Irwin, W. A. "What Is Theological Education? Reply." Journal of Religion 27 (January 1947):55.

2167. Isidro, G. "We Need Seminaries." Evangelical Missions Quarterly 4 (Fall 1967):26-31.

2168. "The Issue of Biblical Authority Brings a Scholar's Resignation [Case of J. R. Michaels]." Christianity Today 27 (July 15, 1983):35-6+.

2169. Istavridis, Vasil T. "Theological Education for Mission." Greek Orthodox Theological Review 13 (1968):7-14.

2170. Jackson, C. "Seminary Professor and New Testament Research." Journal of Religion 17 (April 1937):183-94.

2171. Jackson, F. J. F. "Education of the Clergy and Reunion." Constructive Quarterly 5 (June 1917):297-315.

2172. Jackson, G. E. "Conformity and Creativity in the Theological Seminary." Religious Education 55 (September 1960):330-5.

2173. Jackson, George A. "Is It Time for an Institute of Theology?" Andover Review 9 (June 1888):623-35.

2174. Jackson, Gordon E., Mitchell, Kenneth R. and May, William F. "Responses to E. Farley ['The Reform of Theological Education as a Theological Task' pp. 83-107]." Journal of Supervision and Training in Ministry 4 (1981):109-34.

2175. Jackson, James Conroy. "The Religious Education of the Negro in South Carolina prior to 1850." Historical Magazine of the Protestant Episcopal Church 36 (March 1967):35-61.

2176. Jacobs, H. E. "Seminary and the Lutheran Faith [Lutheran Theological Seminary, Gettysburg]." Lutheran Quarterly 56 (October 1926):460-7.

2177. Jacobs, Henry Eyster. Memoirs of Henry Eyster Jacobs: Notes on a Life of a Churchman. Edited by Henry E. Horn. 3 vols. Huntington, Pa.: Distributed by Church Management Service, 1974.

2178. Jacobs, Thornwell. Step Down, Dr. Jacobs. Atlanta: Westminster Publishers, 1945.

2179. Jacobus, M. W. "Student Aid and Minister Waste." Outlook 67 (February 16, 1901):409-12.

2180. Jagnow, Albert A. "The Broad Horizons of Wartburg Seminary." Wartburg Seminary Quarterly 17 (November 1954):41-7.

2181. Jagnow, Albert A. "Fruit of the Years [Wartburg Seminary]." Palimpsest 35 (June 1954):237-44.

2182. Jagnow, Albert A. "Growing Pains [Wartburg Seminary]." Palimpsest 35 (June 1954):221-8.

2183. James, A. "Problems of Clerical Education." World Today 46 (September 1925):880-4.

2184. James, Fleming. "The Increase and Training of Candidates for Holy Orders." Church Review 41 (1883):451-69.

2185. James, W. "Education of the Clergy." Fortnightly 182 (New Series 176) (November 1954):316-21.

2186. Jamison, William G. "Predicting Academic Achievement of Seminary Students." Review of Religious Research 6, no. 2 (1965):90-6.

2187. Jansen, David G. et al. "Clergymen as Counselor Trainees: Comparisons with Counselors Rated Most and Least Competent by Their Peers." Journal of Clinical Psychology 28 (October 1972):601-3.

2188. Jansen, Hugh M., Jr. "A Threatened Heresy Trial in the Twenties." Anglican

Theological Review 49, no. 1 (1967):17-44.

2189. Jantz, Harold Stein. "German Thought and
        Literature in New England, 1620-1820: A
        Preliminary Survey." Journal of English
        and Germanic Philology 41 (January 1942):1-
        45.

2190. Jantz, Harold S. "Samuel Miller's Survey of
        German Literature, 1803." Germanic Review
        16 (1941):269-77.

2191. Janzen, Leona Kaye. "Institutional Goal
        Perceptions among Selected Groups in Four
        Bible Colleges." Ed.D. dissertation, Drake
        University, 1978.

2192. Jaquith, H. C. "Recognition for the
        Minister." Christian Education 23 (June
        1940):334-7.

2193. Jefferson, Charles Edward. The Building of
        the Church. New York: Macmillan Co.,
        1910.

2194. Jefferson, Charles Edward. Quiet Hints to
        Growing Preachers In My Study. New York:
        Thomas Y. Crowell, 1901.

2195. Jefferson, Thomas. Crusade against Ignorance:
        Thomas Jefferson on Education. Edited by
        Gordon C. Lee. New York: Bureau of
        Publications, Teachers College, Columbia
        University, 1961.

2196. Jegen, Mary Carol Francis. "Religious
        Education as a Discipline: IV. Theolog-
        ical Reflections on the Discipline of
        Religious Education." Religious Education
        62, no. 5 (1967):411-18.

2197. Jelf, Richard William. Suggestions Respecting
        the Neglect of the Hebrew Language as a
        Qualification for Holy Orders. London:
        J.G. & F. Rivington, 1832.

2198. Jencks, C. and Riesman, D. "The Professional
        Schools." In The Academic Revolution, pp.
        199-256. Garden City, N.Y.: Doubleday,
        1968.

2199. Jencks, C. and Riesman, D. "Protestant
        Denominations and Their Colleges. In The

Academic Revolution, pp. 312-33. Garden
City, N.Y.: Doubleday, 1968.

2200. Jenkins, D. E. "Theological Education."
Modern Churchman 9 (New Series) (October
1965):6-14.

2201. Jenkins, David. "Market Place, Wilderness and
Mystery." Theology 85 (January 1982):1-3.

2202. Jennings, Louis B. The Bibliography and
Biography of Shirley Jackson Case.
Chicago, 1949.

2203. Jennings, Otho. "A Study of Christian Service
Training for Ministerial Students in
Accredited Bible Colleges." Ed.D.
dissertation, Michigan State University,
1960.

2204. Jenson, K. A. "Protestant Theological
Education in 1968." Theological Education
4 (Summer 1968, Suppl. 2).

2205. Jervey, Edward D. "LaRoy Sunderland and
Methodist Theological Education."
Christian Advocate 11 (August 10, 1967):11-
12.

2206. Jewett, Paul K. et al. "Vignettes of Seminary
Life." Christian Century 99 (February 3-
10, 1982):136-40.

2207. Jewett, Robert. "Gospel as Heresy: Concordia
Seminary in Exile." Christian Century 91
(March 27, 1974):336-40.

2208. Johann, Robert O. "New Strategies in Catholic
Seminary Training." Union Seminary
Quarterly Review 22 (May 1967):349-55.

2209. Johanson, Gregory J. "The Parish Revisited."
Journal of Pastoral Care 32, no. 3 (1978):
147-54.

2210. Johansson, C. J. "Bible School and the
Church." International Review of Missions
45 (October 1956):396-400.

2211. John Hopkins Morison: A Memoir. Boston:
Houghton, Mifflin & Co., 1897.

2212. John, R. T. "Study of the Characteristics of Former Minor Seminarians." NCEA Bulletin 64 (August 1967):58-61.

2213. John, W. C. "Higher Education, 1930-1936: Professional Education [bibliog.]." United States Office of Education. Bulletins 2, vol. 1, ch. 3 (1937):66-9.

2214. John, W. C. "Training Town and Country Pastors." School Life 27 (December 1941):96.

2215. Johns, John. A Memoir of the Life of The Right Rev. William Meade. Baltimore: Innes & Co., 1867.

2216. Johnson, Ben Sigel. "A Proposed Curriculum for the Master of Church Music Degree at Southeastern Baptist Theological Seminary, Wake Forest, North Carolina." Ed.D. dissertation, Columbia University, 1964.

2217. Johnson, Carl Ernest. "An Analysis of the Predictive Value of the Theological School Inventory at the Southern Baptist Theological Seminary." Ed.D. dissertation, Southern Baptist Theological Seminary, 1975.

2218. Johnson, Dale A. "Lutheran Dissension and Schism at Gettysburg Seminary, 1864." Pennsylvania History 33, no. 1 (1966):13-29.

2219. Johnson, Dale A. "The Methodist Quest for an Educated Ministry." Church History 51 (Summer 1982):304-20.

2220. Johnson, Dick. "Homosexuals and the Seminaries." ESA; Engage/Social Action 6 (August 1978):44-5.

2221. Johnson, E. H. "Minister's Degree: Reply." School and Society 33 (March 14, 1931):371-2.

2222. Johnson, E. H. "Personality Traits of Workers in the Field of Religion." Religious Education 38 (September 1943):325-9.

2223. Johnson, Emeroy and Wersell, Thomas W., eds. I Am at the Seminary: Twenty True Stories

        by Lutheran Pastors. Rock Island, Ill.:
        Augustana Press, 1958.

2224.   Johnson, G. H. "What Business Training Should
        a Minister Have?" Homiletic Review 89
        (March 1925):191-2.

2225.   Johnson, Herrick. The Ideal Ministry. New
        York: Fleming H. Revell Co., 1908.

2226.   Johnson, Inman. Of Parsons and Profs.
        Nashville: Broadman Press, 1959.

2227.   Johnson, James E. "Charles G. Finney and a
        Theology of Revivalism." Church History
        38, no. 3 (1969):338-58.

2228.   Johnson, Jesse. "Early Theological Education
        West of the Alleghenies." Bibliotheca
        Sacra 84 (October 1927):376-88.

2229.   Johnson, J. R. "Clinical Pastoral Education
        and Student Changes in Role Perception."
        Journal of Pastoral Care 21 (September
        1967):129-46.

2230.   Johnson, John Romig, Jr. "Perceptions of
        Pastoral Counseling among Seminary
        Students: A Study of Changes in Role
        Perception in Relation to Clinical Pastoral
        Education." Th.D. dissertation, Union
        Theological Seminary in the City of New
        York, 1966.

2231.   Johnson, Kathryn L. "The Mustard Seed and the
        Leaven: Philip Schaff's Confident View of
        Christian History." Historical Magazine of
        the Protestant Episcopal Church 50, no. 2
        (1981):117-70.

2232.   Johnson, Murray Lee. "Predictive Value of the
        MMPI as a Tool for Seminary Applicant
        Selection: A Longitudinal Study." Ph.D.
        dissertation, Heed University, 1975.

2233.   Johnson, Otis S. "Predictors of Social Action
        among Black Churches." Savannah State
        College, Georgia, 1977.

2234.   Johnson, Paul Emanuel. "Clinical Approach to
        Religion." Journal of Pastoral Care 15
        (Spring 1961):7-12.

2235. Johnson, Paul E. "Clinical Education of the Pastor." Christian Education 30 (March 1947):103-8.

2236. Johnson, Paul Emmanuel. "Clinical Pastoral Training at the Crossroads." Journal of Pastoral Care 16 (Summer 1962):65-71.

2237. Johnson, Paul E. "Early Experiences in Clinical Pastoral Education." Journal of Religion and Health 14, no. 2 (1975):79-81.

2238. Johnson, R. C. "Contextual Education in Pastoral Formation: Supervised Ministries at Asbury Theological Seminary." Asbury Seminarian 34 (October 1979):6-22.

2239. Johnson, R. L. "How the Theological School Prepares for Continuing Education." Theological Education 1 (Summer 1965):239-43.

2240. Johnson, Ray Marion. "Religious Life of Students in Theological Seminaries." Ph.D. dissertation, Yale University, 1932.

2241. Johnson, Sherman E. "Frederick Clifton Grant (1891-1974)." Anglican Theological Review 57 (January 1975):3-13.

2242. Johnson, Sherman E. "The Seminary President: Teacher of Students and Confidant of Trustees." Theological Education 1 (Autumn 1964):63-9.

2243. Johnson, Sherman Elbridge. "Theological Education." Anglican Theological Review 37 (January 1955):1-2.

2244. Johnson, Thomas Cary. The Life and Letters of Robert Lewis Dabney. Richmond: Presbyterian Committee of Publication, 1903.

2245. Johnston, J. O. "Theological Colleges." Contemporary Review 76 (September 1899):405-12.

2246. Johnstone, R. L. "Its Graduates Speak: The Seminary Listens [Concordia Seminary]." Concordia Theological Monthly 35 (December 1964):710-20.

2247. "Joining the Theologians for Thrift and Tolerance: Union of Seven Divinity

Schools." <u>Time</u> 84 (November 6, 1964):50-1.

2248. Jones, A. P. (Letter to 'Brother Campbell')
<u>Millennial Harbinger</u> 2 (New Series)
(1838):571-2.

2249. Jones, Edward Allen. "Morehouse College in
Business Ninety Years - Building Men."
<u>Phylon Quarterly</u> 18 (October 1957):231-45.

2250. Jones, George William. "Internships in the
Campus Ministry: An Exploration of
Teaching and Learning Based on Reports of
the Experiences of Selected Theological
Students Preparing to be Campus Ministers."
Ed.D. dissertation, Columbia University,
1965.

2251. Jones, Herbert L. "Staff Officers: To Be Or
Not To Be: Critical Questions in Planning
the Future of Your Seminary." <u>Theological
Education</u> 6 (Spring 1970):240-3.

2252. Jones, Howard Mumford. <u>The Age of Energy</u>.
New York: Viking, 1971.

2253. Jones, James A. "... And Some, Pastors ..."
<u>Theological Education</u> 2 (Summer 1966):58-
66.

2254. Jones, Jenkin Lloyd. "The Decline of the
Ministry." <u>Outlook</u> 80 (May 13, 1905):124-
8.

2255. Jones, Jenkin Lloyd. "Making a Choice of a
Profession: The Ministry." <u>Cosmopolitan
Magazine</u> 34 (1902-3):477-9.

2256. Jones, Kelsey A. "The Baccalaureate Degree
Program at INTER/MET." 1975 (ERIC
Document)

2257. Jones, Lawrence N. "Reflection on Theological
Education for the Whole Church." <u>Theologi-
cal Education</u> 14 (Spring 1978):93-9.

2258. Jones, Miles J. "Theological Education:
Education for Liberators." <u>Theological
Education</u> 7 (Spring 1971):184-9.

2259. Jones, M. J. "Why a Black Seminary?"
<u>Christian Century</u> 89 (February 2, 1972):
124+.

194

2260. Jones, Robert Tudur. Congregationalism in England, 1662-1962. London: Independent Press, 1962.

2261. Jones, Thomas Jesse. "Are Our Theological Seminaries Stagnating?" Outlook 92 (May 8, 1909):77-9.

2262. Jones, Tiberius Gracchus. Duties of Pastor to His Church. Charleston, S. C.: Southern Baptist Publication Society, 1853.

2263. Jordahl, Leigh D. "Happy Birthday, Gettysburg." Dialog 15 (Spring 1976):101-2.

2264. Jordan, Gerald Ray, Jr. "Mental Honesty and Seminary Recruitment." Christianity Today 8 (September 25, 1964):8-10.

2265. Jordan, Gilbert J. "Texas German Methodism in a Rural Setting." Perkins School of Theology: Journal 31 (Spring 1978):1-21.

2266. Jorjorian, Armen D. "The Meaning and Character of Supervisory Acts [Clinical Pastoral Education]." Journal of Pastoral Care 25, no. 3 (1971):148-56.

2267. Jorjorian, Armen. "Some Reflections on the Future of the Summer Quarter of Clinical Pastoral Training." Journal of Pastoral Care 13 (Fall 1959):155-9.

2268. Jud, Gerald John, Mills, Edgar W. and Burch, Genevieve W. Ex-Pastors: Why Men Leave the Parish Ministry. Philadelphia: Pilgrim Press, 1970.

2269. Judah, S. "Regional Cooperation and Bibliographic Control among San Francisco Bay Area Seminary Libraries [Graduate Theological Union]." Theological Education 6 (Autumn 1969):47-51.

2270. Judd, Orrin D. "An Historical Sketch of Colgate Rochester Divinity School." Colgate-Rochester Divinity School, 1963.

2271. Judson, Edward. The Institutional Church: A Primer in Pastoral Theology. New York: Lentilhon, 1899.

195

2272. Judson, Harry Pratt. "The Kind of Ministry We Need." _World's Work_ 50 (1925):438-40.

2273. Judy, Marvin T. "Professional Ministry: The Call, Performance, Morale, and Authority." _Perkins School of Theology: Journal_ 30 (Winter 1977):5-65.

2274. Judy, Marvin T. _Why Preach?_ Dallas: Perkins School of Theology, 1961.

2275. Junkin, Edward D. "Theological Education and Personal Growth." _Austin Seminary Bulletin: Faculty Edition_ 92 (March 1977):9-21.

2276. Jurji, E. J. "The Role of the History of Religions in College/University/Seminary Curricula." In _Ex Orbe Religionum_. By Kees W. Bolle, et al. Leiden: Brill, 1972.

2277. "Justification by Faith [Statement Adopted by the Faculty of Concordia Seminary, St. Louis]." _Concordia Theological Monthly_ 36 (October 1965):654-7.

2278. Kadel, William H. "Reflections on Administrative Life Style within a Church-Related Seminary." _Theological Education_ 12 (Autumn 1975):18-20.

2279. Kaiser, Leo M. "The Inaugural Address of Edward Wigglesworth as First Hollis Professor of Divinity." _Harvard Library Bulletin_ 27, no. 3 (1979):319-29.

2280. Kale, William Arthur. "Field Work at Duke: Its Educational Significance." _Duke Divinity School Review_ 33 (Autumn 1968):141-50.

2281. Kalish, Richard A. and Dunn, Lee. "Death and Dying: A Survey of Credit Offerings in Theological Schools and Some Possible Implications." _Review of Religious Research_ 17 (Winter 1976):134-40.

2282. Kameeta, Zephania. "Black Theology of Liberation." _Lutheran World_ 22, no. 4 (1975):276-8.

2283. Kaminska, Clyde William. "Importance of Recruitment Practices and Personal Influences on Student Choice of Pre-Ministerial Studies in the Lutheran Church - Missouri Synod." Ph.D. dissertation, Fordham University, 1974.

2284. Kaminska, Clyde W. "Where Have All the Young Men Gone." Springfielder 38 (March 1975):315-18.

2285. Kammen, Carol. "The Problem of Professional Careers for Women: Letters of Juanita Breckenridge, 1872-1893." New York History 55, no. 3 (1974):281-300.

2286. Kane, J. Herbert. "How to Develop a Missions Curriculum." Evangelical Missions Quarterly 5, no. 1 (1968):41-7.

2287. Kang, Young Woo. "Attitudes toward Blindness and Blind People among Theological and Education Students." Ph.D. dissertation, University of Pittsburgh, 1976.

2288. Kang, Young Woo and Masoodi, Bashir A. "Attitudes toward Blind People among Theological and Education Students." Journal of Visual Impairment and Blindness 71 (November 1977):394-400.

2289. Kania, W. "Healthy Defensiveness in Theological Students [bibliog.]." Ministry Studies 1 (December 1967):3-24.

2290. Kania, Walter. "An Investigation of the K Scale of the MMPI as a Measure of Defensiveness in Protestant Theological Seminary Students." Ph.D. dissertation, Michigan State University, 1965.

2291. Kansfield, Norman Jay. "Study the Most Approved Authors: The Role of the Seminary Library in Nineteenth-Century American Protestant Ministerial Education." Ph.D. dissertation, University of Chicago, 1981.

2292. Kantonen, Taito A. "Looking Forward in Lutheran Theological Education." Lutheran Church Quarterly 11 (April 1938):140-58.

2293. Kantzer, K. S. "Documenting the Dramatic Shift in Seminaries from Liberal to

Conservative." <u>Christianity Today</u> 27
(February 4, 1983):10-11.

2294. Kanzlemar, Joseph. "The Relationship of Mass
Media Courses in Ministerial Curriculum on
the Subsequent Behavior of Ministers."
Ed.D. dissertation, University of
Cincinnati, 1980.

2295. Kapp, Paul H. "Orientation Program for
Seminary Students." <u>Journal of Pastoral
Care</u> 29 (September 1975):193-5.

2296. Kapp, P. H. "Short-Term Clinical Pastoral
Education." <u>Journal of Pastoral Care</u> 18
(Autumn 1964):169-72.

2297. Katzenstein, M. E. "Enthusiastic Confirma-
tion." <u>Harvard Divinity Bulletin</u> 3 (New
Series) (Fall 1969):20-2.

2298. Kavanaugh, James J. "Missing Dimension."
<u>America</u> 112 (April 24, 1965):604.

2299. Kay, Jane Holtz. "Echo of the 1920's:
Architect Richard Meier Teams Up with the
Sun. [In His Cubist Design for Starkly
White Hartford Seminary]." <u>Christian
Science Monitor</u> 74 (January 22, 1982):15.

2300. Kayser, Elmer Louis. <u>Bricks Without Straw:
The Evolution of George Washington
University.</u> New York: Appleton-Century
Crofts, 1970.

2301. Keck, L. E. "Priorities for Theological
Education." <u>Lexington Theological
Quarterly</u> 10, no. 1 (1975):1-10.

2302. Kee, H. C. "Drew's Centennial under a Cloud."
<u>Christian Century</u> 85 (March 27, 1968):391-
4; "Discussion." 85 (June 5, July 31,
1968):755-6, 973.

2303. Keeley, Terry D., Burgin, James E. and Kenney,
Kevin. "The Use of Sensitivity Training in
a Unit of Professional Education." <u>Journal
of Pastoral Care</u> 25, no. 3 (1971):188-95.

2304. Keeter, Larry Gene. "Interseminary Commission
for Training for the Rural Ministry, 1929-
1965: An Analysis of a Voluntary Association and Its Influence on Theological

198

Education and the Rural Church." Ph.D.
dissertation, Boston University Graduate
School, 1971.

2305. Kegley, Charles W. "God Is Not Dead, But
Theology Is Dying." Intellect 103
(December 1974):177-80.

2306. Keightley, C. E. "Factors Related to
Persistence in Vocational Choice with
Particular Reference to the Methodist
Ministry." M.A. thesis, Northwestern
University, 1947.

2307. Keiter, Charles R. "Immigration in the
Nineteenth Century in its Relation to the
Lutheran Church in the U.S." Lutheran
Church Review 31 (April 1912):272-9; (July
1912):466-73.

2308. Keith, Jasper N. "The Association for CPE:
Who Needs It?" Journal of Pastoral Care
29, no. 3 (1975):202-3.

2309. Keller, Charles Roy. The Second Great
Awakening in Connecticut. New Haven: Yale
University Press, 1942.

2310. Keller, William S. "Clinical Experience As a
Background for the Pastoral Office."
Religious Education 30 (October 1935):112-
16.

2311. Kelleran, Marion M. "The Seminary Wife: Her
Role in Community." Theological Education
2 (Autumn 1965):38-41.

2312. Kelley, Alden D. "The Continuing Education
for the Ministry Movement." 1969. (ERIC
Document)

2313. Kelley, Alden Drew. "A Dean Looks at Clinical
Training." Journal of Pastoral Care 5
(1951):61-7.

2314. Kelley, A. D. "Looking Ahead with the
Seminaries." Christian Education 28
(December 1944):103-11.

2315. Kelley, D. C. "Ministerial Education:
Theological Schools." Christian Advocate
(Nashville) (June 20, 1867):1.

2316. Kelley, Dean M. Government Intervention in Religious Affairs. New York: Pilgrim Press, 1982.

2317. Kelley, Donald D. "Crisis at Bethesda [Curriculum, Media]." Religious Education 71, no. 5 (1976):527-34.

2318. Kelley, Elizabeth Burroughs. "John Burroughs' Student Days at Cooperstown." New York History 44, no. 3 (1963):275-82.

2319. Kellogg, Wendell. "Christian Ministers, Both Slaves and Spokesmen, Interseminary Conference is Told." National Council Outlook 7 (October 1957):7+.

2320. Kelly, Robert L. "The New Curriculum of the Oberlin Graduate School of Theology." Christian Education 12 (May 1929):491-4.

2321. Kelly, Robert L. "A New Theological Seminary Curriculum." Christian Education 10 (October 1926):5-10.

2322. Kelly, Robert Lincoln. "Tendencies in Theological Education in America." Journal of Religion 4 (January 1924):16-31.

2323. Kelly, Robert Lincoln. Theological Education in America: A Study of One Hundred Sixty-One Theological Schools in the United States and Canada. New York: George H. Doran Co., 1924.

2324. Kelly, R. L. "Theological Seminary Curriculum." Religious Education 21 (October 1926):501-4.

2325. Kelsey, Francis Willey. "Greek in the High School, and the Supply of Candidates for the Ministry." School Review 16 (November 1908):561-79.

2326. Kelsey, Francis Willey. "The State Universities and the Churches." In Proceedings of the Conference on Religious Education, Held at the University of Illinois, October 19, 1905.

2327. Kelso, James A. "A Student's Recollections of the Seminary, 1894-1896." Western Watch 1 (January 1, 1950):4-7; 2 (March 15,

1950):8-10.

2328. Kemp, Charles Frederick and Hunt, Richard A. Counselor's Manual for Use with Theological School Check List of Study Skills and Attitudes. St. Louis: Bethany Press, 1965.

2329. Kemper, R. G. "Academy's Opportunity." Christian Century 89 (December 20, 1972): 1289.

2330. Kendall, William Frederick. A History of the Tennessee Baptist Convention. Brentwood: Executive Board of the Tennessee Baptist Convention, 1974.

2331. Kennedy, Earl William. "William Brenton Greene's Treatment of Social Issues." Journal of the Presbyterian Historical Society 40, no, 2 (1962):92-112.

2332. Kennedy, Gerald Hamilton. While I'm on My Feet. New York: Abingdon Press, 1963.

2333. Kennedy, William B. "Learning in, with, and for the Church: The Theological Education of the People of God." Union Seminary Quarterly Review 36 Suppl. (1981):27-38.

2334. Kepler, T. S. "Pre-Theological Training." Religious Education 40 (January 1945):8-11.

2335. Kerby, J. et al. "Theological Seminary and Training for Social Work." National Conference of Social Work. Proceedings (1923):231-46.

2336. Kerr, Hugh Thomson. "Education in General and Theological Education." Theology Today 27 (January 1971):434-52.

2337. Kerr, Hugh T. "Not Like They Used to [Editorial, Limericks and Doggerel, Mostly Lampooning Teachers and Theologians]." Theology Today 32 (April 1975):1-9.

2338. Kerr, Hugh T. "Reflections on an Experiment." Improving College and University Teaching 22 (Summer 1974):195-7.

2339. Kerr, H. T. "Seminarian, Meet Theologian." Christian Century 92 (February 5,

1975):105-7.

2340.   Kerr, Hugh Thomson. "Seminarians and Self
        Directed Study." Princeton Seminary
        Bulletin 64 (March 1971):69-76.

2341.   Kerr, Hugh Thomson, ed. Sons of the Prophets:
        Leaders in Protestantism from Princeton
        Seminary. Princeton: Princeton University
        Press, 1963.

2342.   Kerr, Hugh T. "Teaching Methodology and
        Theological Education: A Prospectus."
        Princeton Theological Seminary, N.J., 1968.
        (ERIC Document)

2343.   Kett, Joseph F. Rites of Passage: Adoles-
        cence in America, 1790 to the Present. New
        York: Basic Books, 1977.

2344.   Keyser, Donald. "A History of Baptist Higher
        Education in the South to 1865." Th.D.
        dissertation, Southern Batist Theological
        Seminary, 1955.

2345.   Keyes, R. M. "Theological Education: Are We
        Doing the Right Things?" Evangelical
        Missions Quarterly 17 (April 1981):101-4.

2346.   Keysor, C. W. "Some Things I've Learned."
        Christianity Today 9 (November 6, 1964):18.

2347.   Kidder, D. P. "(Education for Ministry in
        M.E. Church.)" Bibliotheca Sacra 33
        (1876):558+.

2348.   Kidder, Daniel P. "Ministerial Education and
        Training in the Methodist Episcopal
        Church." Bibliotheca Sacra 33 (July
        1876):558-84.

2349.   Kidder, Maurice A. "Parish and Community: A
        Model for Post Ordination Training."
        Church In Metropolis 93 (Summer 1967):19-
        23.

2350.   Kieffaber, Alan. "Peace Studies at Bethany
        Theological Seminary." Brethren Life and
        Thought 23 (Winter 1978):45-6.

2351.   Kilde, Clarence. "Heresy in Milwaukee: An
        Interpretation." Christianity and Crisis
        15 (December 12, 1955):163-7.

2352. Kilpatrick, T. B. Suggested Courses of Study for Ministers. New York: Ryerson Press, 1933?

2353. Kim, Lester Edward. "A Critical Study of Selected Changes in Protestant Theological Students with Clinical Pastoral Education." Ph.D. dissertation, University of Southern California, 1960.

2354. Kimball, Charles Cotton. Manuscript Note-Books on Lectures at the Union Theological Seminary, New York, from 1859-1862. 6 vols. N.p., n.d.

2355. Kimball, R. C. "Theologian and the Gospel." Theology Today 21 (October 1964):324-33.

2356. Kimber, J. A. Morris. "Intersectional and Intrasectional Marriages in a Southern Bible College - 16 Years Later." Journal of Marriage and the Family 30 (August 1968):402-3.

2357. Kimble, Melvin A. "Education for Ministry with the Aging." In Ministry with the Aging. Edited by W. Clements, 1981.

2358. Kimble, Melvin Arnold. "The Relationship of Selected Self-Concept Characteristics of Theological Students to the Internship Year." Ph.D. dissertation, United States International University, 1975.

2359. Kinast, R. "Preparing Clergy for the New Laity." Theology Today 36 (October 1979):383-8.

2360. Kincheloe, Samuel C. "The Behavior Sequence of a Dying Church." Religious Education 24 (1929):329-45.

2361. "The Kind of Study the Bible Teachers Training School Stands for." Bible Magazine 1 (January 1913):2-3.

2362. King, C. W. "Motivations for Teaching in Bible Colleges." Religious Education 65 (September 1970):431-5.

2363. King, Henry Melville. Newton Theological Institution in the Last Fifty Years.

Newton Center, Mass.: The Institution, 1899.

2364. King, Larry L. "Bob Jones University." Harper's Magazine 232 (June 1966):51-8.

2365. King, P. M. "Learning from the Laity." Theology Today 36 (October 1979):368-74.

2366. King, William R. "Schools for Rural Pastors." Missionary Review of the World 53 (May 1930):380.

2367. Kinlaw, Howard McConneral. "Richard Furman as a Leader in Baptist Higher Education." Ph.D. dissertation, George Peabody College for Teachers, 1960.

2368. Kinsler, F. Ross. "Equipping God's People for Mission [Theological Education by Extension]." International Review of Mission 71 (April 1982):129-227.

2369. Kinsler, F. Ross. The Extension Movement in Theological Education: A Call to the Renewal of the Ministry. Pasadena: William Carey Library, 1978.

2370. Kinsler, F. R. "Theological Education by Extension: Service or Subversion?" Missiology 6 (April 1978):181-96.

2371. Kinsolving, Lester. "'Liberal' Charges Beset Baptist Seminary." Christian Century 84 (January 18, 1967):90-2.

2372. Kirk, James Stanley. "The Relationship of Personality Type to Choice of Academic Major in Seminary Education." Ph.D. dissertation, Boston University Graduate School, 1972.

2373. Kirk, K. E., ed. Study of Theology. New York: Harper, 1939.

2374. Kirk, R. "Balaam's Ass in the Seminary." National Review 17 (October 19, 1965):934.

2375. Kirk, R. "Shelton College and State Licensing of Religious Schools: An Educator's View of the Interface between the Establishment and Free Exercise Clauses." Law and Contemporary Problems 44 (Spring 1981):169-84.

2376. Kirkpatrick, H. F. "Training for the
      Ministry." Church Quarterly Review 135
      (October 1942):25-38.

2377. Kirsch, Elmer Edwin. "A Study of Fringe
      Benefits for Full-Time Faculty in Bible
      Colleges." Ed.D. dissertation, University
      of Southern California, 1972.

2378. Kitagawa, J. M. "Annual Report of the Dean
      [Chicago]." Criterion 9 (Autumn 1970):6-
      17.

2379. Kitagawa, Joseph M. "The Theological School
      as a Community of Scholarship: Some
      Reflections on the Views of William Rainey
      Harper." Criterion 19 (Spring 1980):9-14.

2380. Kitch, Edmund W., ed. Clinical Education and
      the Law School of the Future. Chicago:
      University of Chicago Law School, 1970.

2381. Klain, Zora. "Educational Activities of New
      England Quakers." Philadelphia: Westbrook
      Publishing Co., 1928.

2382. Klein, Easy. "Out of the Cloister." Change 6
      (February 1974):15-18.

2383. Klein, Ernst E. "Samuel H. Miller's Dialogue
      with Reality." Foundations 21, no. 1
      (1978):6-15.

2384. Klein, Harry Martin John. A Century of
      Education at Mercersburg, 1836-1936.
      Lancaster, Pa.: Lancaster Press, 1936.

2385. Klein, Harry Martin John. The History of the
      Eastern Synod of the Reformed Church in the
      United States. Lancaster, Pa.: Eastern
      Synod, 1943.

2386. Klein, Walter Conrad. Clothed with Salvation:
      A Book of Counsel for Seminarians.
      Evanston, Ill.: Seabury-Western Theologi-
      cal Seminary, 1953.

2387. Kleinman, S. and Fine, G. A. "Rhetorics and
      Action in Moral Organizations: Social
      Control of Little Leaguers and Ministry
      Students." Urban Life: A Journal of
      Ethnographic Research 8 (October 1979):275-
      94.

2388. Kleinman, Sherryl. "Changing Contexts, Rhetoric, and Socialization: The Making of the "New" Minister." Ph.D. dissertation, University of Minnesota, 1980.

2389. Kleinman, Sherryl. "Socialization through Rhetoric: 'Community' Talk and Problematic Control in a Seminary." University of North Carolina, Chapel Hill, 1981.

2390. Klemt, Calvin C. "AATS, Educational Techniques, and Seminary Libraries." Theological Education 5 (Summer 1969):357-64.

2391. Klever, Gerald L. "The Value Orientations and the Educational Participation of Clergymen - Progress Report." Paper presented at the National Seminar on Adult Education Research, Toronto, Feb. 9-11, 1969. (ERIC Document)

2392. Klever, Gerald Leroy. "Values and the Adult Educational Participation of Clergymen." Ph.D. dissertation, University of Chicago, 1974.

2393. Klick, Richard Coover. "The Female Diaconate in Recent American Lutheranism." S.T.D. thesis, Temple University, 1949.

2394. Kling, Frederick R. "A Study of Testing As Related to the Ministry." Religious Education 53 (May-June 1958):243-8.

2395. Klingberg, Haddon E., Jr. "An Evaluation of Sensitivity Training Effects on Self-Actualization, Purpose in Life, and Religious Attitudes of Theological Students." Ph.D. dissertation, Fuller Theological Seminary, School of Psychology, 1971.

2396. Klink, T. W. "Career of Preparation for the Ministry [bibliog.]." Journal of Pastoral Care 18 (Winter 1964):200-7.

2397. Klink, Thomas W. "Self-Evaluation Guides in Clinical Pastoral Education." Theological Education 5 (Summer 1969):365-72.

2398. Klink, T. W. "Supervision [bibliog.]." Theological Education 3 (Autumn 1966):176-217.

2399. Klink, T. W. "Supervision as a Routine Process in Professional Education for Ministry." Duke Divinity School Review 33 (Autumn 1968):155-73.

2400. Knight, Edward Hooker. "Requirements for Admission and Graduation in Lay Training Schools." Religious Education 7 (December 1912):558-64.

2401. Knight, F. H. "Theology and Education: Review of 'Case for Theology in the University.' by W. A. Brown. With Discussion." American Journal of Sociology 44 (March 1939):649-83.

2402. Knight, John L. et al. Foundations of Theological Education: The 1972 Willson Lectures, Wesley Theological Seminary, Washington, D.C. Washington, D.C.: Wesley Theological Seminary, 1972.

2403. Knights, W. A. "Gestalt Approach in a Clinical Training Group." Journal of Pastoral Care 24 (September 1970):193-8.

2404. Knights, Ward A., Jr. "Postgraduate Secular Education in Counseling for Clergymen: Proposals for Coordination." Counselor Education and Supervision 12 (September 1972):42-5.

2405. Knights, W. A. "Use of Self-Actualizing Group Therapy Techniques in Clinical Pastoral Training." Journal of Pastoral Care 20 (September 1966):163-5.

2406. Kniker, Charles Robert. "The Chautauqua Literary and Scientific Circle, 1878-1914: An Historical Interpretation of an Educational Piety in Industrial America." Ed.D. dissertation, Columbia University, 1969.

2407. Knoff, Gerald Everett. "The Yale Divinity School, 1858-1899." Ph.D. dissertation, Yale University, 1936.

2408. "A Knowledge of His Own Times Important to a Christian Minister." Christian Review 1 (March 1836):106-16.

2409. Knowles, James Davis. Importance of Theological Institutions. Boston: Lincoln & Edmands, 1832.

2410. Knowles, Rex Hanna. "Differential Characteristics of Successful and Unsuccessful Seminary Students. Ph.D. dissertation, University of Nebraska - Lincoln, 1968.

2411. Knox, John. History of the Reformation in Scotland. 2 vols. Edited by William Croft Dickinson. London: Nelson, 1949.

2412. Knox, John. Never Far from Home: The Story of My Life. Waco, Tex.: Word Books, 1975.

2413. Knox, L. L. "The Conference Course of Study." Daily Zion's Herald (May 12, 1852):33-4.

2414. Knubel, K. H. "Seminary and the Church [Lutheran Theological Seminary, Gettysburg]." Lutheran Quarterly 56 (October 1926):452-9.

2415. Knudson, Albert Cornelius. "Bowne in American Theological Education." Personalist 28 (July 1947):247-56.

2416. Koch, John B. "The Controversy within the Missouri Synod during the First Quarter of the Twentieth Century on the Nature of Justifying Faith." Concordia Historical Institute Quarterly 44, no. 1 (1971):18-31.

2417. Koester, Herman J. "A Participant's Report of the Controversy on Justifying Faith." Concordia Historical Institute Quarterly 44, no. 2 (1971):79-87.

2418. Kokkinakis, Athenagoras. "Holy Cross Greek Orthodox Theological School: Twenty Years of Progress, 1937-1957." Greek Orthodox Theological Review 3 (Summer 1957):15-22.

2419. Kollar, Nathan. "Action Training: A Methodology and a Theology." Theological Education 7 (Autumn 1970):57-65.

2420. Kornfield, W. J. "Challenge to Make Extension Education Culturally Relevant." Evangelical Missions Quarterly 12 (January 1976):13-22.

208

2421. Kortendick, James Joseph. The Library in the Catholic Theological Seminary in the United States. Washington: Catholic University of America Press, 1963.

2422. Kovach, Frank. "Bloomfield College and Seminary." Presbyterian Church in the U.S.A. Dept. of History. Journal 24 (June 1946):109-18.

2423. Kramer, William A. "A Teacher Examination in 1858." Concordia Historical Institute Quarterly 52, no. 3 (1979):125-7.

2424. Kratz, A. Roger. "Theological Education, Part of University Culture." Christian Education 15 (February 1932):295-300.

2425. Kraus, Clyde Norman. Dispensationalism in America: Its Rise and Development. Richmond: John Knox Press, 1958).

2426. Kretzmann, Paul Edward. "Methods of Teaching in Theological Seminaries." Lutheran Quarterly 55 (April 1925):121-31.

2427. Kreyche, G. F. "Ecumenism and Philosophy [bibliog.]" Christian Century 83 (April 27, 1966):521-4.

2428. Kriesel, H. Terry. "Training in Basic Pastoral Counseling Skills: A Comparison of a Microtraining Approach with a Skills Practice Approach." Journal of Pastoral Care 31, no. 2 (1977):125-33.

2429. Kring, W. D. "Speaking for the Class of 1940." Harvard Divinity Bulletin 29 (July 1965):99-102.

2430. Krolick, James Joseph. "Persistence and Non-Persistence in the Pre-Ministerial Curriculum at a Lutheran College." Ph.D. dissertation, University of Michigan, 1977.

2431. Kromminga, Carl G. "Education at Calvin Theological Seminary as Training for Ministry." Calvin Theological Journal 12 (April 1977):5-23.

2432. Kromminga, John H. "Calvin Seminary's Encounter with Ford Lewis Battles." Calvin Theological Journal 15 (November 1980):158-9.

2433. Krosnicki, Thomas A. "Seminary Liturgy
       Revisited." Worship 54 (March 1980):158-
       69.

2434. Krueger, John Frederick. "Theological Studies
       in German Universities." Lutheran Church
       Quarterly 6 (October 1933):353-70.

2435. Krug, Edward August. The Shaping of the
       American High School. 2 vols. New York:
       Harper & Row, 1964-72.

2436. Krusche, Werner. "Some Questions about
       Theological Education." International
       Review of Missions 56 (April 1967):164-6.

2437. Kucharsky, David E. "Seminary on the Spot
       [Concordia Seminary, St. Louis]."
       Christianity Today 16 (September 29,
       1972):38.

2438. Kuhn, Harold B. The Distinctive Emphasis of
       Asbury Theological Seminary. Wilmore, Ky.,
       1963.

2439. Kuiper, Barend Klaas. The Church in History.
       Grand Rapids, Mich.: National Union of
       Christian Schools, 1951.

2440. Kuist, Howard Tillman. These Words upon Thy
       Heart: Scripture and the Christian
       Response. Richmond, Va.: John Knox Press,
       1947.

2441. Kurtz, R. M. "School for Missionaries."
       Missionary Review of the World 44 (April
       1921):303-7.

2442. Lacher, J. H. A. "Nashotah House, Wisconsin's
       Oldest School of Higher Learning
       [bibliog.]." Wisconsin Magazine of History
       16 (December 1932):123-62.

2443. Lacy, Creighton. Frank Mason North: His
       Social and Ecumenical Mission. Nashville:
       Abingdon Press, 1967.

2444. Lacy, Creighton. "A New New Curriculum."
       Duke Divinity School Review 34 (Winter
       1969):10-18.

2445. Lacy, C. "You Have Wrought a Revolution
       [Duke]." Duke Divinity School Review 33

(Spring 1968):67-8.

2446. Ladd, G. T. et al. "Theological Education."
      Bibliotheca Sacra 36 (1879):182+, 367+,
      560+, 760+.

2447. Lake, Kirsopp. "American, English and Dutch
      Theological Education." Harvard Theologi-
      cal Review 10 (October 1917):336-51.

2448. Lamb, Francis Jones. "The Theological
      Seminary and Jural Science." Bibliotheca
      Sacra 72 (April 1915):283-97.

2449. Lamberti, Majorie. "Lutheran Orthodoxy and
      the Beginning of Conservative Party
      Organization in Prussia." Church History
      37 (December 1968):439-53.

2450. Lancaster Theological Seminary of the United
      Church of Christ. Addresses Delivered at
      the Inauguration of Rev. J. W. Nevin.
      Chambersburg, Pa.: Printed at the Office
      of Publication of the German Reformed
      Church, 1840.

2451. Lance, H. Darrell. "What Is Theological
      Research?" Theological Education 16
      (Spring 1980):465-71.

2452. Landes, George M. "Biblical Exegesis in
      Crisis: What Is the Exegetical Task in a
      Theological Context?" Union Seminary
      Quarterly Review 26, no. 3 (1971):273-98.

2453. Lane, Belden C. "Presbyterian Republicanism:
      Miller and the Eldership as an Answer to
      Lay-Clerical Tensions." Journal of
      Presbyterian History 56 (Winter 1978):311-
      24.

2454. Lane, C. S. "Religious Education at
      Hartford." Religious Education 10
      (February 1915):20-7.

2455. Lane Theological Seminary, Cincinnati, Ohio.
      History of the Foundation and Endowment of
      the Lane Theological Seminary. Cincinnati,
      1848.

2456. Laney, James T. "Identity Crisis in the
      Seminaries: Do Seminary Faculties Identify
      with the People of God or with Professional

Peer Groups." Christian Century 94
(February 2-9, 1977):95+.

2457. Langsley, D. G., Guldner, C. and Kritzer, H.
"Clinical Pastoral Training in an Emergency
Psychiatric Service." Journal of Religion
and Health 6 (April 1967):99-105.

2458. Lanmar, Geo. W. "A Theological Institution."
Christian Advocate and Journal (New York)
29 (March 16, 1854):1.

2459. Lansman, Quentin Charles. "An Historical
Study of the Development of Higher
Education and Related Theological and
Educational Assumptions in the Evangelical
United Brethren Church: 1800-1954." Ph.D.
dissertation, Northwestern University,
1969.

2460. Lapsley, James N. "Theological Curriculum for
the 1970's: A Critique." Theological
Education 5 (Winter 1969):99-102.

2461. Lard's Quarterly, Devoted to the Propagation
and Defense of the Gospel. Lexington, Ky.,
1863-   , Vol. 2.

2462. Larsen, L. P. "Theological Training."
International Review of Missions 27 (July
1938):377-85.

2463. Larson, Clifford E. "An Analysis of the
General Conceptions Underlying Bible
Institute Courses on How To Teach the
Bible." Ph.D. dissertation, University of
Southern California, 1955.

2464. Larson, Lynn S. "The Women's Movement and Men
in Seminary." Theological Education 8
(Summer 1972):241-6.

2465. Larson, Melvin Gunnard. Youth for Christ.
Grand Rapids, Mich.: Zondervan Publishing
House, 1947.

2466. Larson, W. D. "The Why of the Where to Place
Our Seminaries." Dialog 3 (Winter 1964):
57-9.

2467. Larue, Gerald A. "The American Expedition to
Hebron, 1964." Journal of Bible and
Religion 33, no. 4 (1965):337-9.

2468. Latourette, K. S. "Are Theological Schools Teaching Peace?" Christian Century 41 (November 13, 1924):1471-2.

2469. Latourette, Kenneth Scott. Beyond the Ranges: An Autobiography. Grand Rapids, Mich.: Eerdmanns, 1967.

2470. Laubach, Eugene E. "Inducting Theological Students into Ministry: A Description and Analysis of a Pilot Project in Ministry." Ed.D. dissertation, Columbia University, 1964.

2471. Laurence, Anya. "A New England Boyhood [Henry Ward Beecher]." New-England Galaxy 16, no. 3 (1975):28-33.

2472. Lawrence, Edward Alexander. The Life of Rev. Joel Hawes, D. D. Hartford: Hamersley & Co., 1871.

2473. Lawrence, H. J. "Duke Silent Vigil." Duke Divinity School Review 33 (Spring 1968):89-108.

2474. Lawrence, J. "On a Hill Far Away: Reflections on the Interseminary Church and Society Internship Program." Christian Century 86 (November 5, 1969):1419-20.

2475. Lawrence, W. F. "Hood Theological Seminary, Livingstone College, Salisbury, North Carolina 28144." AME Zion Quarterly Review 94 (April 1982):49-52.

2476. Lawrence, William. Memories of a Happy Life. Boston: Houghton Mifflin, 1926.

2477. Lawson, E. Thomas. "Implications for Theological Education in Seminaries of the Study of Religion in the University." Theological Education 3 (Spring 1967):396-402.

2478. Lawson, E. T. "Seminary, Department of Religion, and University [Reply to L.C.A. Lutherans]." Lutheran Quarterly 19 (February 1967):87-90.

2479. Lawyer, F. D. "On-the-Spot Design of a Graduate School for Religion." American School and University (1961):33-6.

2480. Laymen's Foreign Missions Inquiry. Commission
of Appraisal. Re-Thinking Missions: A
Laymen's Inquiry after One Hundred Years.
New York: Harper & Bros., 1932.

2481. Leach, Lena Mae. "A Survey of Music Programs
in Schools of the American Association of
Bible Colleges in Ohio and Contiguous
States." Ph.D. dissertation, Ohio State
University, 1983.

2482. Leavell, Roland Q. "Southern Baptist
Seminaries." Christian Century 72 (April
27, 1955):498-500.

2483. Leavell, Ullin Whitney. "Trends of
Philanthropy in Negro Education: A
Survey." Journal of Negro Education 2
(January 1933):38-52.

2484. Leavenworth, J. Lynn. "Toward Seminary
Merger." Christian Century 83 (April 27,
1966):527+.

2485. Leavenworth, L. "Advantages and Hazards for
the Seminary in Continuing Education."
Theological Education 1 (Summer 1965):233-
8.

2486. Le Bosquet, J. E. "Churches and the Theological Seminary." Journal of Religion 6
(November 1926):586-96.

2487. Lecky, Robert S. "Problems in the Theological
Capital." Christianity and Crisis 29
(April 14, 1969):102-3.

2488. Le Duc, Thomas Harold André. Piety and
Intellect at Amherst College, 1865-1912.
New York: Arno Press, 1969. (Reprint of
the 1946 ed.)

2489. Lee, Elizabeth Meredith. As among the
Methodists: Deaconesses Yesterday, Today
and Tomorrow. New York: Woman's Division
of Christian Service, Board of Mission,
Methodist Church, 1963.

2490. Lee, Henry Walsh. How Dry We Were:
Prohibition Revisited. Englewood Cliffs,
N.J.: Prentice-Hall, 1963.

214

2491. Lee, J. S. "Qualifications of the Ministry."
Universalist Quarterly and General Review 7
(April 1850):221-32.

2492. Lee, James Lucas. "An Exploratory Search for
Characteristic Patterns and Clusters of
Seminary Persisters and Leavers." Ph.D.
dissertation, University of Michigan, 1968.

2493. Lee, James L. "Seminary Persisters and
Leavers." Counseling and Values 16
(February 1971):39-45.

2494. Lee, James L. "Vocational Persistence and
Satisfaction among Clergy: A Review and
Analysis." Counseling and Values 20 (April
1976):143-9.

2495. Lee, James Michael. "Objective of the Roman
Catholic Seminary." Theological Education
2 (Winter 1966):95-101.

2496. Lee, James Michael and Putz, Louis J., eds.
Seminary Education in a Time of Change.
Notre Dame, Ind.: Fides Publishers, 1965.

2497. Lee, La Mont Robert. "The Effect of Modeling
on the Persistence of Change in Self-
Disclosure among Ministerial Students."
Ph.D. dissertation, Fuller Theological
Seminary, School of Psychology, 1974.

2498. Lee, Peter V. "The American Medical School:
A Case Study in Professional Education."
Theological Education 5 (Spring 1969):197-
214.

2499. Lefever, H. C. "Preparation of Missionaries,
1910 and 1960." International Review of
Missions 50 (October 1961):395-408.

2500. "Legal Setback [Southwestern Baptist
Theological Seminary to Submit Its
Employment Data]." Christianity Today 99
(April 28, 1982):504.

2501. Lehman, Edward C., Jr. "Correlates of
Placement of Women in Ministry: Half a
Replication." Brockport, State University
of New York, 1981.

2502. Lehman, Edward C., Jr. "Organizational
Resistance to Women in Ministry." State

215

University of New York, Brockport, 1980.

2503. Lehman, Edward C. "Placement of Men and Women in the Ministry." Review of Religious Research 22 (September 1980):18-40.

2504. Lehmann, P. "Harvard Colloquium: An Ecumenical Venture in the Grand Manner." Christianity and Crisis 23 (May 27, 1963):94-6.

2505. Leigh, Ronald Wilson. "Incongruities within the Literature Adopted for Teaching Apologetics at Schools Which are Members of the American Association of Bible Colleges." Ph.D. dissertation, New York University, 1980.

2506. Lenhart, Thomas E. and Norwood, Frederick A. "Checklist of Wesleyan and Methodist Studies: 1970-1975." Garrett-Evangelical Theological Seminary, 1976.

2507. "Leo XIII on Ecclesiastical Studies." American Catholic Quarterly Review 25 (1900):56-71.

2508. Leonard, Harriet V., comp. "Selected Bibliography on Theological Education." Duke Divinity School Review 33 (Winter 1968):54-5.

2509. Leonty, Metropolitan. "Theological Education in America." St. Vladimir's Seminary Quarterly 9 (1965):59-67.

2510. Lesick, Lawrence T. "The Founding of the Lane Seminary." Cincinnati Historical Society Bulletin 37, no. 4 (1979):236-48.

2511. Lesick, Lawrence Thomas. Lane Rebels: Evangelicalism and Anti-Slavery in Antebellum America. Studies in Evangelicalism, no. 2. Metuchen, N.J.: Scarecrow Press, 1980.

2512. Leslie, Robert C. "The National Conference: An Editorial." Journal of Pastoral Care 5 (Spring 1952):1-3.

2513. Leslie, Robert C. and Mudd, Emily Hartshorne, eds. Professional Growth for Clergymen through Supervised Training in Marriage

216

Counselling and Family Problems.
Nashville: Abingdon Press, 1970.

2514. "Letter to Harvard." Time 63 (January 18, 1954):98.

2515. "(Letter to a Theological Student.)" Dial 1 (1841):183+.

2516. Leuchtenburg, William Edward. The Perils of Prosperity, 1914-32. Chicago: University of Chicago Press, 1958.

2517. Levy, Charles S. Social Work Education and Practice 1898-1955. New York: Yeshiva University, 1968.

2518. Lewis, C. Douglass. Explorations in Ministry: A Report of the Ministry in the 70's Project. New York: IDOC North America, 1971.

2519. Lewis, C. Douglass, ed. Papers from the National Symposium on Issues and Models of Doctor of Ministry Programs. Hartford, Conn.: Hartford Seminary Foundation, 1980.

2520. Lewis, C. Douglass. "Participating in a Doctor of Ministry Program: Its Effect on the Pastor's Effectiveness and the Parish's Ministry." Pastoral Psychology 27 (Spring 1979):191-201.

2521. Lewis, C. Douglass. "The Role of Seminaries in Recruitment." Theological Education 5 (Summer 1969):321+.

2522. Lewis, C. Douglass. "Should Every Minister Have a Doctorate?" Christian Century 98 (February 4-11, 1981):137-8+.

2523. Lewis, Charles E. "The History of the Educational Activities of the Protestant Episcopal Church in Oregon." Oregon Historical Society. Quarterly 25 (June 1924):101-35.

2524. Lewis, E. "Professional Ministry." Atlantic Monthly 116 (November 1915):678-87.

2525. Lewis, Edwin. "The Problem of a Teacher of Theology." Christian Education 12 (January 1929):246-52.

2526. Lewis, Frank Grant. "A Sketch of the History of Baptist Education in Pennsylvania." Chester, Pa.: Crozer Theological Seminary, 1918.

2527. Lewis, H. G. "Bangor Elects Whittaker." Christian Century 69 (June 18, 1952):732+.

2528. Lewis, Kent Edward. "Counseling the Divorced: A Seminar Approach for In-Field Clergy." Ph.D. dissertation, Vanderbilt University Divinity School, 1979.

2529. Lewis, Robert E. "Ashbel Green, 1762-1848 - Preacher, Educator, Editor." Journal of the Presbyterian Historical Society 35, no. 3 (1957):141-56.

2530. Lex, James Joseph. "Attitude Change of Seminary Students Associated with a Course in Group Dynamics." Ed.D. dissertation, Indiana University, 1972.

2531. Lexington, Ky. College of the Bible. To Do and To Teach: Essays in Honor of Charles Lynn Pyatt. Lexington, 1953.

2532. Leypoldt, M. M. "Analysis of Seminary Courses in Christian Adult Education." Religious Education 60 (September 1965):395-402.

2533. Leypoldt, Martha M. "An Analysis of Seminary Courses Specifically Designed to Prepare Seminary Students to Assist Adults toward Christian Maturity through the Adult Education Program of a Local Church." Ed.D. dissertation, Indiana University, 1964.

2534. Leypoldt, Martha. "Seminaries around the Country Use Variety of Simulation Games." Simulation/Gaming/News 1 (March 1972):13-14.

2535. "Liberal Theology again Victorious [Union Theological Seminary, NYC]." Current Literature 28 (January 1905):5-6.

2536. "Liberty of Teaching in Theological Seminaries." Biblical World 25 (February 1905) (New Series):86-7.

2537. "Liberty of Theological Teaching." _Outlook_ 68
(May 18, 1901):151-4.

2538. "Library of the Mercer School of Theology."
Architectural Record 162 (July 1977):114-
16.

2539. Lightner, Robert Paul. _Neo-Evangelicalism._
2d ed. Des Plaines, Ill.: Regular Baptist
Press, 1965.

2540. Lile, A. T. "After While: The Brethren Style
[Bethany Biblical Seminary]." _Brethren
Life and Thought_ 8 (Summer 1963):48-53.

2541. "The Limitations of Biblical Criticism."
Methodist Review 72 (January 1890):109-15.

2542. Lincoln, C. F. "Lewis Sperry Chafer."
Bibliotheca Sacra 109 (1952):332-7.

2543. Lind, Christopher. _Priestly Studies in Modern
Papal Teachings._ Washington: Catholic
University of America Press, 1958.

2544. Lindbeck, George. "The Place of Scholarship
in a University Seminary." _Reflection_ 70
(March 1973):3-6.

2545. Lindbeck, George A. _University Divinity
Schools: A Report on Ecclesiastically
Independent Theological Education._ New
York: Rockefeller Foundation, 1976.

2546. Lindenthal, Jacob Jay. "The Delayed Decision
to Enter the Ministry: Some Issues and
Prospects." _Review of Religious Research_ 9
(Winter 1968):108-13.

2547. Lindenthal, Jacob Jay. "Entrance into the
Ministry at Two Points in Life: Some
Findings." _Journal for the Scientific
Study of Religion_ 7 (Fall 1968):284-5.

2548. Lindley, Denton Ray. _Apostle of Freedom._ St.
Louis: Bethany Press, 1957.

2549. Lindsay, L. R. "Letter from the Fringe: A
Defense of the NonPastoral Ministry."
Christian Century 83 (September 7,
1966):1075-7. "Discussion." 83 (October
26, 1966):1306.

2550. Lindsell, Harold. "The Decline of a Church and Its Culture." Christianity Today 25 (July 17, 1981):34-8.

2551. Lindsell, Harold. "Tensions in the Seminaries." Christianity Today 11 (May 12, 1967):5-8.

2552. Lindsell, Harold. "Whither Accreditation for Evangelical Seminaries?" United Evangelical Action 18 (June 1959):118+.

2553. Lindsell, Harold. "Who Is Right in the Missouri Synod Dispute." Christianity Today 19 (April 11, 1975):10-11.

2554. Lindskoog, Donald and Kirk, Roger E. "Some Life-History and Attitudinal Correlates of Self-Actualization among Evangelical Seminary Students." Journal for the Scientific Study of Religion 14 (March 1975):51-5.

2555. Lindskoog, Donald Philip. "Some Life History, Attitudinal, and Moral Development Correlates of Self-Actualization among Evangelical Seminary Students." Ph.D. dissertation, Baylor University, 1972.

2556. Lindsly, Philip. A Plea for the Theological Seminary at Princeton, N. J. Trenton, N.J.: George Sherman, 1821.

2557. Linebaugh, Dale E. and Devivo, Paul. "The Growing Emphasis on Training Pastor-Counselors in Protestant Seminaries." Journal of Psychology and Theology 9 (Fall 1981):266-8.

2558. Lippman, Hyman, Gerty, Francis and Boyd, David A., Jr. "Pastoral-Psychiatric Workshops." In Social Psychotherapy. Vol. 4: Progress in Psychotherapy, pp. 183-92. Edited by Jules H. Masserman and J. L. Moreno. New York: Grune & Stratton, 1959.

2559. "List of Books Recommended by Dr. Tappan to Theological Students." Panoplist 2 (December 1806):325-6.

2560. "Listening to the DEW Line." Christian Century 97 (February 6, 1980):126.

2561. "Literature in the Divinity School." _Time_ 90 (December 22, 1967):51.

2562. Litfin, A. Duane. "Seminary Costs: Up, Up, and Help." _Christianity Today_ 20 (February 13, 1976):10-12.

2563. Littell, Franklin H. "The Seminary Provides for Dialogue." _Theological Education_ 1 (Winter 1965):83-9.

2564. Littell, F. H. "Theological Education for a Pluralistic Society: The Seminary's Commitment to the Dialogue." _Encounter_ 25 (Summer 1964):273-82.

2565. Little, A. G. "The Relation of the Theological Seminaries to the Colleges." In _Christianity Practically Applied_. Evangelical Alliance for the United States of America. Conference. Chicago, 1893, v. 2, pp. 466-71. New York: Baker & Taylor, 1894.

2566. Littlejohn, Abram Newkirk. _The Christian Ministry at the Close of the Nineteenth Century_. New York: Thomas Whittaker, 1884.

2567. Littlejohn, Abram Newkirk. _Conciones ad Clerum (1879-1880)_. New York: Thomas Whittaker, 1881.

2568. Littlejohn, Carrie U. _History of Carver School of Missions and Social Work_. Nashville: Broadman Press, 1958.

2569. Litwak, Kenneth. "A Summary of Francis Andersen's 1980 Payton Lectures." _TSF Bulletin_ 4 (October 1980):9-10.

2570. Lively, Bruce Richard. "William Smith, The College and Academy of Philadelphia and Pennsylvania Politics 1753-1758." _Historical Magazine of the Protestant Episcopal Church_ 38 (September 1969):237-58.

2571. Livingston, John H. _An Address to the Reformed German Churches in the United States_...[to Convince Them of the Necessity of Resolving without Delay, to Establish a Theological Institution, as the First and

Indispensable Step to Preserve Their
Existence and Secure Their Respectability].
New Brunswick: Myer, 1819.

2572. Lloyd, B. M. "Key Issues in the Personal
Preparation of Clergy." Theological
Education 5 (Summer 1969, Suppl. 1):420-35.

2573. Lloyd, David D. "Proposal for a Preaching
Brotherhood." Christianity and Crisis 9
(April 18, 1949):45-7.

2574. Lloyd, Ralph Waldo. Maryville College: A
History of 150 Years, 1819-1969.
Maryville, Tenn.: Maryville College Press,
1969.

2575. Loehe, Wilhelm. Three Books about the Church.
Translated, edited, and with an Introduc-
tion by James L. Schaaf. Philadelphia:
Fortress Press, 1969.

2576. Loessner, Ernest J. "The Southern Baptist
Theological Seminary and Religious
Education." Review and Expositor 68
(Winter 1971):107-16.

2577. Loetscher, Lefferts A. "Founders' Dream Re-
Visited." Princeton Seminary Bulletin 67
(Winter 1975):20-5.

2578. Loetscher, Lefferts A. "A Kentuckian Comes to
Princeton Seminary." Princeton Seminary
Bulletin 2 (New Series), no. 3 (1979):251-
7.

2579. Logan, J. B. History of the Cumberland
Presbyterian Church in Illinois. Alton,
Ill.: Perrin & Smith, 1878.

2580. Logan, James C. "Toward a More Genuinely
Comprehensive Examination." Theological
Education 7 (Winter 1971):87-91.

2581. Logan, Rayford Whittingham. "The Evolution of
Private Colleges for Negroes." Journal of
Negro Education 27 (Summer 1958):213-20.

2582. Logan, Rayford Whittingham. Howard
University: The First Hundred Years, 1867-
1967. New York: New York University
Press, 1969.

2583. Long, C. H. "The Black Reality: Toward a
      Theology of Freedom [Chicago]." Criterion
      8 (Spring-Summer 1969):2-11.

2584. Long, Edward L. and Handy, Robert T. Essays
      in Honor of John Coleman Bennett.
      Philadelphia: Westminster Press, 1970.

2585. Long, Edward L. "Immediacy and Distance in
      Religion." Drew Gateway 48, no. 1
      (1977):4-11.

2586. Long, Edward L. "Preparing for Ministry: A
      Series of Talks Delivered in Craig Chapel,
      Drew Theological School, Sept. 1979." Drew
      Gateway 50, no. 1 (1979):25-37.

2587. Long, Rodney Herman. "Career Patterns of Top
      Level Administrators of Selected Four Year
      Evangelical Liberal Arts and Bible
      Colleges." Ph.D. dissertation, Florida
      State University, 1980.

2588. Longstaff, John Brett. "Anglican Origins of
      Columbia University." Historical Magazine
      of the Protestant Episcopal Church 9
      (September 1940):257-60.

2589. Lonsway, Francis A. "Experience-Oriented
      Learning in Theological Education."
      Theological Education 13 (Spring 1977):123-
      92.

2590. Lonsway, Francis A. Ministers for Tomorrow:
      A Longitudinal Study of Catholic
      Seminarians in Theology. Washington:
      Center for Applied Research in the
      Apostolate, 1972.

2591. "Looking with Favor on Fuller." Christianity
      Today 23 (October 6, 1978):50.

2592. Loomer, Bernard M. "The Divinity School: The
      Aim of Divinity Education." Divinity
      School Announcements (University of
      Chicago) (1950-51):2-4.

2593. Loomer, Bernard MacDougall. "Reflection on
      Theological Education." Criterion 4
      (Autumn 1965):3-8.

2594. Lortz, Joseph. The Reformation in Germany.
      Translated by Ronald Walls. 2 v. London:

Darton, Longman Todd; New York: Herder & Herder, 1968.

2595. Love, J. Brown. "Inter-Seminary Movement Grows in the Southwest." Christian Education 13 (April 1930):499-501.

2596. Love, Julian Price. In Quest of a Ministry. Richmond: John Knox Press, 1969.

2597. "Love in a Cold Climate [Bangor Theological Seminary." Christian Century 97 (February 6, 1980):164-7.

2598. Lovelace, Richard. "The Seminary as a Source of Renewal." Christianity Today 16 (January 21, 1972):6-9.

2599. Lowe, Martha Ann (Perry). Memoir of Charles Lowe. Boston: Cupples, Upham & Co., 1884.

2600. Lowndes, Robert S. "Theological Education and Field Education." Theological Education 5 (Summer 1969, Suppl. 1):445-54.

2601. Loy, Matthias. Essay on the Ministerial Office: An Exposition of the Scriptural Doctrine as Taught in the Evangelical Lutheran Church. Columbus, Ohio: Schulze & Gassmann, 1870.

2602. Loy, Matthias. Story of My Life. 3d ed. Columbus, Ohio: Lutheran Book Concern, 1905.

2603. Luccock, Robert Edward. "Seminary in Retrospect." Christian Century 67 (April 26, 1950):523-5.

2604. Luebke, Martin Frederick. "Inquiry into Admissions Policies and Their Relationship to Objectives in Protestant Theological Education." Ph.D. dissertation, University of Illinois at Urbana-Champaign, 1966.

2605. Luecke, Richard Henry. "Protestant Clergy: New Forms of Ministry, New Forms of Training [bibliog.]." Annals of the American Academy of Political and Social Science 387 (January 1970):86-95.

2606. Lueking, F. D. "Trial by Fire at Concordia [Seminary]." Christian Century 91

(February 6, 1974):116-17.

2607. Lugibihl, Walter H. and Gerig, Jared F. The Missionary Church Association: Historical Account of Its Origin and Development. Berne, Ind.: Economy Printing Concern, 1950.

2608. Lummis, Adair Trimble. "Especially Union? Educational Policy and Socialization in an Elite Boundary Professional School, Union Theological Seminary, New York." Ph.D. dissertation, Columbia University, 1979.

2609. Lund, L. D. "Role of Confidence in Seminary Education [Reply to H. E. Horn]." Lutheran Quarterly 19 (February 1967):91-3.

2610. Lundeen, Joel W. "The Archival Responsibility of Seminary and Church College Librarians." Lutheran Historical Conference 1 (1966):91-102.

2611. Lundquist, Carl Harold. "The Teaching of Preaching in Baptist Theological Seminaries of the United States." Ph.D. dissertation, Northern Baptist Theological Seminary, 1960.

2612. The Lutheran Cyclopedia, 1899 ed., s.v. "Ministerial Education," by Adolph Spaeth.

2613. Lutheran Educational Conference of North America, Washington, D.C. "What's Lutheran about Higher Education?" Proceedings of the 60th Annual Convention of the Lutheran Educational Conference of North America, St. Louis, Missouri, January 11-12, 1974. (ERIC Document)

2614. "Lutheran Seminarians Advocate Abolition of 4-D Exemption." Christian Century 87 (April 22, 1970):470

2615. Lutheran Theological Seminary, Philadelphia. Biographical Record of the Lutheran Theological Seminary at Philadelphia, 1864-1962. Edited by John A. Kaufmann. Philadellphia, 1964.

2616. Lutheran Theological Seminary, Philadelphia. The Philadelphia Seminary Biographical Record, 1864-1923. Edited by Luther D.

225

Reed. Mt. Airy, Philadelphia, 1923.

2617. Lyman, Albert Josiah. The Christian Pastor in the New Age: Comrade, Sponsor, Social Mediator. Lectures for 1909 on the George Shepherd Foundation, Bangor Theological Seminary. New York: Thomas Y. Crowell & Co., 1909.

2618. Lynch, F. "College Men and the Ministry." Outlook 50 (August 18, 1894):260-1.

2619. Lynch, Frederick. The New Opportunities of the Ministry. New York: Fleming H. Revell Co., 1912.

2620. Lynn, Robert W. and Wright, Elliott. The Big, Little School: Sunday Child of American Protestantism. New York: Harper & Row, 1971.

2621. Lynn, Robert W. "Discussion of the Paper." Theological Education 5 (Spring 1969):240-2.

2622. Lynn, Robert Wood. "Notes toward a History: Theological Encyclopedia and the Evolution of Protestant Seminary Curriculum, 1808-1968." Theological Education 17 (Spring 1981):118-44.

2623. Lyon, Robert W. "A Young Minister Looks at Biblical Studies." Asbury Seminarian 17 (Spring-Summer 1963):65-71.

2624. Lyons, John Frederick. "Cyrus Hall McCormick, Presbyterian Layman." Journal of the Presbyterian Historical Society 39, no. 1 (1961):14-29.

2625. Lyttle, C. "(Theology at Harvard Univ., 1636-1705)." Church History 5 (1936):301+.

2626. Mabee, Carlton. "Toussaint College: A Proposed Black College for New York in the 1870's [AME Zion]." Afro-Americans in New York Life and History 1, no. 1 (1977):25-36.

2627. McAllister, James Gray and Guerrant, Grace Owings. Edward O. Guerrant: Apostle to the Southern Highlanders. Richmond, Va.: Richmond Press, 1950.

2628. McAllister, James Gray. The Life and Letters of Walter W. Moore. Richmond, Va.: Union Theological Seminary, 1939.

2629. McAllister, L. G. "Historical Studies." Encounter 25 (Summer 1964).

2630. McAllister, Lester G. Thomas Campbell: Man of the Book. St. Louis: Bethany Press, 1954.

2631. MacAllister, P. E. "Dedication Ceremonies: CTS Library." Encounter 39 (Autumn 1978):447-51.

2632. McAlpine, Tom and Branson, Mark L. "News from TSF Chapters [Princeton, Yale, Harvard, Wesley, Perkins]." TSF Bulletin 5 (January-February 1982):9.

2633. McArthur, Harvey K. New Testament Sidelights: Essays in Honor of Alexander Converse Purdy. Hartford Seminary Foundation, 1960.

2634. McArthur, H. K. "Teaching the New Testament at Hartford - A Personal Confession." Hartford Quarterly 4 (Spring 1964).

2635. MacArthur, K. W. "Theological Education among the Dissenters, 1660-1811." Journal of Religion 21 (July 1941):265-84.

2636. McAsh, Edward Arthur. "A Study of Continuing Education Programs for the Ministry in the Theological Seminaries of the United Presbyterian Church in the USA." Ph.D. dissertation, Michigan State University, 1966.

2637. McAvoy, Thomas Timothy. "The Study of History and Clerical Education." American Ecclesiastical Review 127 (July 1952):19-24.

2638. McBirnie, William S., Jr. "A Study of the Bible Institute Movement." Ph.D. dissertation, Southwestern Baptist Theological Seminary, 1953.

2639. McCall, Duke K. "Baptist Ministerial Education." Review and Expositor 64 (Winter 1967):59-71.

2640. McCall, Duke K. "The Role of Southern
       Seminary in Southern Baptist Life." Review
       and Expositor 67 (Spring 1970):183-93.

2641. McCall, Duke K. "The Southern Baptist
       Theological Seminary One Hundred Years in
       Louisville." Baptist History and Heritage
       12 (October 1977):194-7+.

2642. McCall, Duke Kimbrough. "Southern Seminary
       and the Denomination." Review and
       Expositor 49 (July 1952):269-80.

2643. McCann, Richard V. The Churches and Mental
       Health. New York: Basic Books, 1962.

2644. McCann-Winter, Elva John Schertzer. "Clergy
       Education about Homosexuality: An Outcomes
       Analysis of Knowledge, Attitudes, and
       Counseling Behaviors." Ph.D. dissertation,
       University of Pennsylvania, 1983.

2645. McCarter, Neely D. and Little, Sara.
       "Readiness for Ministry and Curriculum
       Design." Theological Education 12 (Spring
       1976):151-7.

2646. McCaughey, Robert A. "The Transformation of
       American Academic Life: Harvard University
       1821-1892." Perspectives in American
       History 8 (1974):237-332.

2647. McCaw, John E. "Theological Faculty and
       University." Christian Century 76 (April
       22, 1959):471-2.

2648. McClain, D. C. "Bible College Library
       Standards." Christian Life 15 (October
       1971):8-10.

2649. McClellan, Graydon E. "One Ministry: Seabury
       Consultation on the Training of Negro
       Ministers." National Council Outlook 9
       (May 1959):6-8.

2650. McClellan, James F. "Seminary Training in
       Pastoral Counseling at Howard University."
       Ph.D. dissertation, Columbia University,
       1956.

2651. McCloy, Frank Dixon. "Bibliographical Survey:
       The History of Theological Education in
       America." Church History 31 (December

1962):449-53.

2652. McCloy, Frank Dixon. "The Founding of
Protestant Theological Seminaries in the
United States of America, 1784-1840."
Ph.D. dissertation, Harvard University,
1959.

2653. McCloy, Frank Dixon. "The History of
Theological Education in America." Church
History 31 (December 1962):449-53.

2654. McCloy, Frank Dixon. "John Mitchell Mason:
Pioneer in American Theological Education."
Journal of Presbyterian History 44, no. 3
(September 1966):141-55.

2655. McClure, James G. K. The Story of the Life
and Work of the Presbyterian Theological
Seminary, Chicago, Founded by Cyrus H.
McCormick. Chicago: Presbyterian
Theological Seminary, 1929.

2656. McConahay, John B. and Hough, Joseph C., Jr.
"Love and Guilt-Oriented Dimensions of
Christian Belief." Journal for the
Scientific Study of Religion 12 (March
1973):53-64.

2657. McConahay, John B. "Psychological Testing in
Evaluation and Guidance of Seminary
Students." Theological Education 7 (Winter
1971):109-20.

2658. McConahay, John B. and Hough, Joseph C., Jr.
"Symbolic Racism." Journal of Social
Issues 32 (Spring 1976):23-45.

2659. McConnell, C. M. "Educating the Farmer's
Preacher." Methodist Review 111 (January
1928):52-7.

2660. McConnell, C. M. "Qualifications of the
Country Preacher." Missionary Review of
the World 49 (July 1926):520-2.

2661. McConnell, Francis J. "Is There a Religious
Breakdown of the Ministry?" Journal of
Religion 1 (March 1921):192-4.

2662. McConnell, S. D. "The Education of
Preachers." World's Work 2 (1901):837-40.

2663. McConnell, S. D. "Theological Seminaries and the Decrease of the Ministry." Church Review 43 (1884):214-23.

2664. McConnell, Theodore A. "Theological Agendas for the 70's." Religious Education 65, no. 6 (1970):493-7.

2665. McConnell, Yaylor and Williams, Michael E. "Evaluating the Seminary Student." Explor 4, no. 2 (1978):63-73.

2666. McCord, James I. "Financing Theological Education." Christian Century 88 (January 27, 1971):106-7.

2667. McCord, James I. "Freedom and Liberation: Farewell Remarks to the Class of 1979." Princeton Seminary Bulletin 2 (New Series) no. 3 (1979):217-18.

2668. McCord, J. I. "Idea of a Reformed Seminary." Princeton Seminary Bulletin 53 (January 1960):5-9.

2669. McCord, J. I. "The Lilly Study and the Theological Seminary [Pre-Seminary Education]." Journal of Bible and Religion 34 (April 1966).

2670. McCord, James Iley. "Our Theological Responsibility." Encounter 30 (Winter 1969):17-24.

2671. McCord, James Iley. "Retrospect and Prospect." Princeton Seminary Bulletin 57 (October 1963):10-16.

2672. McCord, J. I. "Push at Princeton." Time 75 (April 11, 1960):56+.

2673. McCord, James Iley. "The Seminary and the Theological Mission." Theology Today 17 (October 1960):290-9.

2674. McCord, James I. "The Seminary Enterprise: An Appraisal." Theological Education 17 (Autumn 1980):53-8.

2675. McCord, James I. "Seward Hiltner's Contributions to the Life of the Churches and to Professional Theological Education." Pastoral Psychology 29 (Fall 1980):13-16.

2676. McCord, James Iley. "Theological Implications of the Relation of the Church and Theological School in America." Princeton Seminary Bulletin 54 (February 1961):4-11.

2677. McCord, James I. "Understanding of Purpose in a Seminary Closely Related to the Church." Theological Education 14 (Spring 1978):59-66.

2678. McCormick, Samuel Black. "One Hundred Years." Bulletin of the Western Theological Seminary 20 (April 1928):16-35.

2679. McCormick Theological Seminary, Chicago. Addresses at the Inauguration of Rev. David C. Marquis, D.D. as Professor of New Testament Literature and Exegesis, and of Rev. Herrick Johnson, D.D., LL.D., as Professor of Sacred Rhetoric and Pastoral Theology. Chicago: Spalding & Keefer, Printers, 1884.

2680. McCormick Theological Seminary, Chicago. Addresses at the Inauguration of Rev. Edward Lewis Curtis, Ph.D. as Professor of Old Testament Literature and Exegesis in the McCormick Theological Seminary. April 6, 1887. Chicago: Kittredge & Friott, 1887.

2681. McCormick Theological Seminary, Chicago. The Celebration of the Two Hundred and Fiftieth Anniversary of the Adoption of the Westminster Standards, and the Inauguration of the Rev. J. Ross Stevenson, as Professor of Ecclesiastical History. Chicago: Published by the Board of Directors, 1898.

2682. McCormick Theological Seminary, Chicago. A Defense against the Late Assaults upon the New Albany Theological Seminary. New Albany, Ind.: Warren, 1853.

2683. McCormick Theological Seminary, Chicago. Exercises in Connection with the Inauguration of James G.K. McClure, D.D., LL.D. as President of the McCormick Theological Seminary, Chicago, May 3, 1906. N.p., n.d.

2684. McCormick Theological Seminary, Chicago. Inaugural Addresses by Edwin Cone Bissell

231

and Augustus Stiles Carrier. Chicago, 1893.

2685. McCormick Theological Seminary, Chicago. Inaugural Addresses by Willis Green Craig and Andrew C. Zenos. Chicago: Young Men's Era Publishing Co., 1892.

2686. McCormick Theological Seminary Historical Celebration, In Recognition of the Eightieth Year of the Origin of the Seminary...November First and Second, Nineteen Hundred and Nine. Chicago, 1910.

2687. McCuistion, Fred. "Higher Education of Negroes." Journal of Negro Education 2 (July 1933):379-96.

2688. McCulloch, James Edward. "The Common Task of the Training School and the Theological Seminary." Religious Education 10 (October 1915):499-507.

2689. McCulloch, James Edward. "Co-ordinating Training Schools: The Principles of Correlation and Co-operation Applied to Training Schools for Religious and Social Workers." Religious Education 7 (December 1912):544-50.

2690. McCulloh, Gerald O. "Father of Methodist Theological Education: John Dempster." Christian Advocate 8 (August 27, 1964):12-13.

2691. McCulloh, Gerald O., ed. The Ministry in the Methodist Heritage. Convocation of Methodist Theological Faculties, 1st, 1959. Nashville: Dept. of Ministerial Education, Board of Education, Methodist Church, 1960.

2692. McCulloh, Gerald O. "Personnel Needs in the Ministry." Encounter 23 (1962):20-9.

2693. McCune, Shirley D. and Mills, Edgar W. "Continuing Education for Ministers: A Pilot Evaluation of Three Programs." National Council of Churches, New York, 1967. (ERIC Document)

2694. McDonnold, Benjamin Wilburn. History of the Cumberland Presbyterian Church. Nashville: Board of Publication of Cumberland

Presbyterian Church, 1888.

2695. McDowell, William Fraser. Dangers That Beset
Theological Students. New York: Inter-
national Committee of Young Men's Christian
Associations, 1903.

2696. McElwain, Frank Arthur, Norwood, Percy Varney
and Grant, Fredrick Clifton. "Seabury-
Western Theological Seminary: A History."
Historical Magazine of the Protestant
Episcopal Church 5 (December 1936):286-311.

2697. Macfarland, Charles Stedman. Across the
Years. New York: Macmillan Co., 1936.

2698. McFarland, H. Neill. "Seminary and University." Perkins School of Theology:
Journal 34 (Spring 1981):1-7.

2699. McGannon, J. Barry, ed. Christian Wisdom and
Christian Formation: Theology, Philosophy,
and the Catholic College Student. New
York: Sheed & Ward, 1964.

2700. McGarrah, Albert Franklin. A Modern Church
Program: A Study in Efficiency. New York,
Chicago: Revell, 1915.

2701. McGavran, Donald Anderson. "Advanced Education for Missionaries." Christianity Today
13 (September 26, 1969):115-17.

2702. McGehee, Larry Thomas. A Report of the New
Haven Disciples House Consultation on
Continuing Education for the Ministry. New
Haven, Conn.: New Haven Center for Con-
tinuing Education for the Ministry, 1965.

2703. McGiffert, A. C., Jr. "Greek Theologians-To-
Be in Protest." Christian Century 79 (May
23, 1962):662-3.

2704. McGiffert, A. C., Jr. "Mischievous Book:
Further Correspondence of A. C. McGiffert."
Union Seminary Quarterly Review 24 (Summer
1969):365-75.

2705. McGiffert, A. C., Jr. "Next Tasks in
Theological Education." Journal of
Religion 22 (October 1942):398-412.

2706. McGiffert, Arthur Cushman. "Theological Education." American Journal of Theology 15 (January 1911):1-19.

2707. Macgill, Stevenson. Considerations Addressed to a Young Clergyman, On Some Trials of Principle and Character Which May Arise in the Course of His Ministry. Glasgow: By the Author, 1809.

2708. McGill, William J. "The Belated Founding of Alma College: Presbyterians and Higher Education in Michigan, 1883-1886." Michigan History 57, no. 2 (1973):93-120.

2709. McGinnis, Robert Samuel, Jr. "A Model for Theological Education in Eighteenth Century America: Samuel Johnson, D.D. of King's College." D. Div. dissertation, Vanderbilt University Divinity School, 1971.

2710. McGlon, Charles Addis. "Preparing Men to Speak for God - Foreword to a Study in Educational Research [Speech Teaching at Southern Baptist Theological Seminary]." Southern Speech Journal 19 (May 1954):261-76.

2711. McGlon, Charles Addis. "Speech Education in Baptist Theological Seminaries in the United States, 1819-1943." Ph.D. dissertation, Columbia University, 1951.

2712. McGlothlin, William Joseph. Patterns of Professional Education. New York: G. P. Putnam's Sons, 1960.

2713. McGlothlin, William Joseph. The Professional Schools. New York: Center for Applied Research in Education, 1964.

2714. McGovern, A. I. "Dialogue with the Devil in Dubuque [Association of Theological Faculties in Iowa]." Dialog 8 (Spring 1969):136-8.

2715. McGuinness, R. M. "Seminary Education and Handicapped Persons." Momentum 12 (October 1981):31.

2716. Machen, John Gresham. The Attack upon Princeton Seminary: A Plea for Fair Play. Philadelphia, 1927.

234

2717. Machen, John Gresham. <u>Christianity and Liberalism</u>. New York: MacMillan Co., 1923.

2718. McIlwaine, Richard. <u>Hampden-Sidney College as an Educational Force from the War of the Revolution to the War between the States. An address in the Memorial Chapel, Hampden-Sidney, April 20, 1903</u>. Petersburg, Va.: Buchanan Mfg. Co., 1903.

2719. McIntosh, Hugh E. "How the Swedes Came to Paxton." <u>Swedish Pioneer Historical Quarterly</u> 30, no. 1 (1979):35-52.

2720. McIntosh, I. F. "Clinical Training in the Parish." <u>Pastoral Psychology</u> 17 (April 1966):43-51.

2721. McIntyre, J. "Structure of Theological Education." <u>Expository Times</u> 70 (April 1959):210-15.

2722. McKay, A. R. "President's Work: Enabling." <u>Theological Education</u> 1 (Spring 1965):185-6.

2723. McKay, A. R. "Some Deliberately Immoderate Observations on Theological Education." <u>Theological Education</u> 6 (Summer 1970).

2724. Mackay, J. A. "Seminary's Library Project." <u>Princeton Seminary Bulletin</u> 49 (October 1955):30-4.

2725. Mackay, John Alexander. "Some Questions Regarding Theological Education, With Special Reference to Princeton Seminary." <u>Princeton Seminary Bulletin</u> 49 (January 1956):3-12.

2726. Mackay, John Alexander. "Theological Triennium: For What?" <u>Princeton Seminary Bulletin</u> 52 (January 1959):5-14.

2727. Mackay, John Alexander. "Theology in Education." <u>Christian Century</u> 68 (April 25, 1951):521-3.

2728. McKelvey, Blake Faus. "Walter Rauschenbusch's Rochester." <u>Rochester History</u> 14 (October 1952).

235

2729. McKenzie, Alexander. "Memoir of Prof. Edwards Amasa Park." Massachusetts Historical Society. Proceedings (February 1901):444-67.

2730. McKenzie, Marna. "Going Back to Seminary: An Old Wife's Tale." Theological Education 8 (Summer 1972):257-9.

2731. Mackenzie, William Douglas, Jacobus, M. W., and Mitchell, E. K. On the Education of the Minister and on the Training for Various Forms of Christian Service. Hartford, Conn.: Printed for the Use of the Trustees, Hartford Theological Seminary, 1911.

2732. Mackenzie, William Douglas. "The Place of Latin and Greek in the Preparation for the Ministry." School Review 16 (June 1908): 370-83.

2733. Mackenzie, William Douglas. "The Standardization of Theological Education." Religious Education 6 (August 1911):253-61.

2734. Mackie, Steven G. "American Seminaries in World Perspective: A Draft Balance Sheet." Theological Education 5 (Autumn 1968):41-51.

2735. Mackie, Steven G. "Patterns of Ministry and the Purpose of a Theological School." Theological Education 2 (Winter 1966):82-8.

2736. Mackie, Steven. Patterns of Ministry: Theological Education in a Changing World London: Collins, 1969.

2737. McKim, Donald K. "Archibald Alexander and the Doctrine of Scripture." Journal of Presbyterian History 54 (Fall 1976):355-75.

2738. McKinney, Lois. "Why Renewal Is Needed in Theological Education." Evangelical Missions Quarterly 18 (April 1982):85-96.

2739. MacLean, G. E. "Present Standards of Higher Education in the United States." United States. Bureau of Education. Bulletins 4 (1913):70-4.

2740. McLean, George F. Christian Philosophy in the College and Seminary. Washington, D.C., 1966.

2741. Maclean, John. History of the College of New Jersey, From Its Origin in 1746 to the Commencement of 1854. 2 vols. Philadelphia: J. B. Lippincott & Co., 1877.

2742. McLean, John Knox. "The Presidency of Theological Seminaries." Bibliotheca Sacra 58 (April 1901):314-37.

2743. MacLeod, Donald. "Teaching Machines." Christian Century 78 (August 23, 1961): 1012.

2744. MacLeod, George Fielden. "Postscript to Chapter Five of Only One Way Left." Theological Education 1 (Winter 1965):81-2.

2745. McLinden, J. E. "Seminaries and Interinstitutional Cooperation." NCEA Bulletin 63 (February 1967):5-17.

2746. McLoughlin, William G. "Is There a Third Force in Christendom?" In Religion in America. Edited by William Gerald McLoughlin and Robert N. Bellah. Boston: Houghton Mifflin, 1968.

2747. McLoughlin, William Gerald. New England Dissent, 1630-1833: The Baptists and the Separation of Church and State. 3 vols. Cambridge: Harvard University Press, 1971.

2748. McMillan, G. Jarvis. "Video-Stimulated Recall in Pastoral Psychotherapy Training." Journal of Pastoral Care 28, no. 4 (1974):262-6.

2749. Macnab, D. I. "Thoughts on Pastoral Training and the Good Life." Journal of Pastoral Care 19 (Spring 1965):38-41.

2750. McNair, Malcolm Perrine, ed. The Case Method at the Harvard Business School: Papers by Present and Past Members of the Faculty and Staff. New York: McGraw-Hill, 1954.

2751. McNaugher, John. The History of Theological Education in the United Presbyterian Church

and Its Ancestries. Pittsburgh: United
Presbyterian Board of Publication & Bible
School Work, 1931.

2752. McNeill, John T. "Historical Types of Method
in the Cure of Souls." Crozer Quarterly 11
(July 1934):323-34.

2753. McNeill, John Thomas. A History of the Cure
of Souls. New York: Harper, 1951.

2754. McNett, James LeRoy. "Study of Public
Relations in Fund-Raising for American
Baptist Theological Institutions Based upon
a Study of Eighteen Institutions." Th.D.
dissertation, Central Baptist Theological
Seminary, 1971.

2755. McPheeters, Alphonso A. "The Origin and
Development of Clark University and Gammon
Theological Seminary, 1869-1944." Ph.D.
dissertation, University of Cincinnati,
1944.

2756. McPherson, H. W. "Spiritual Resources and
Obligations of the Council of Church Boards
of Education: Service to the Seminaries."
Christian Education 22 (April 1939):298-
303.

2757. McWilliams, T. S. "Attractions of the
Ministry to the College Man of Today."
Religious Education 14 (August 1919):260-2.

2758. Maddock, Richard, Kenny, Charles T. and
Middleton, Morris M. "Preference for
Personality versus Role-Activity Variables
in the Choice of a Pastor." Journal for
the Scientific Study of Religion 12
(December 1973):449-52.

2759. Madsen, William Lavern. "Multivariate Con-
sideration of Some Personality, Motivation,
Performance, and Persistence Variables in a
Selected Population of Theological Stu-
dents." Ph.D. dissertation, University of
Minnesota, 1973.

2760. Maehr, M. L. and Stake, R. E. "Value Patterns
of Men Who Voluntarily Quit Seminary
Training [bibliog.]." Personnel and
Guidance Journal 40 (February 1962):537-40.

238

2761. Magoun, George Frederic. <u>Asa Turner: A Home Missionary Patriarch and His Times.</u> Boston: Congregational Sunday School & Publishing Society, 1889.

2762. Magruder, Edith Mabel. <u>A Historical Study of the Educational Agencies of the Southern Baptist Convention, 1845-1945.</u> New York: Columbia University, Teachers College, 1951.

2763. Mahler, Henry Richard, Jr. "A History of Union Theological Seminary in Virginia, 1807-1865." Th.D. dissertation, Union Theological Seminary, 1951.

2764. Mahoney, John. "Seminary That Won't Quit." <u>Commonweal</u> 90 (August 8, 1969):478-9. "Reply." 90 (September 26, 1969):579+.

2765. Maier, Frederick C. "The 'Nature of the Ministry' Seminars: A Report and Evaluation." <u>McCormick Quarterly</u> 17 (March 1964):20-9.

2766. Maier, Paul L. <u>A Man Spoke, A World Listened: The Story of Walter A. Maier and the Lutheran Hour.</u> New York: McGraw-Hill, 1963.

2767. "Maine Band." <u>Congregationalist</u> 77 (1892): 464.

2768. "Make a Little Chamber...Clear Creek Mountain Preacher's Bible School." <u>Time</u> 57 (May 14, 1951):78.

2769. Malcom, Howard. <u>Theological Index: References to the Principal Works in Every Department of Religious Literature. Embracing Nearly Seventy Thousand Citations, Alphabetically Arranged under Two Thousand Heads.</u> Boston: Bould & Lincoln, 1868.

2770. Malcomson, William L. <u>Growing in Ministry: Reflections Based on Current Research.</u> Oakland, Calif.: Center for the Ministry, American Baptist Churches, 1981.

2771. Mallery, Frank Lynn. "An Evaluation of Ministerial Students and Development of a Model for Vocational Counseling of Upper

239

Level Ministerial Students at Pacific Union College, Angwin, California." Ph.D. dissertation, San Francisco Theological Seminary, 1973.

2772. Malone, Edward F. "A Response." Theological Education 4 (Spring 1968):732-4.

2773. Mampoteng, Charles. "The Library and American Church History." Historical Magazine of the Protestant Episcopal Church 5 (September 1936):225-37.

2774. Manhart, George Born. DePauw through the Years: A Brief Historical Sketch of Indiana (1837-1884) and DePauw University (1884 - . Greencastle, Ind.: DePauw University, 1958.

2775. Manker, Charles Clarence, Jr. "An Analysis of the Problem of Integration in the Curriculum of the Theological Seminary." Ph.D. dissertation, University of Kentucky, 1956.

2776. Mann, Arthur. Yankee Reformers in the Urban Age. Cambridge: Belknap Press of Harvard University Press, 1954.

2777. Manning, T. Clerical Education in Major Seminaries: Extract from a Thesis [bibliog.]." Los Angeles: T. Manning, 1946.

2778. Manross, William Wilson. "Growth and Progress since 1860." Historical Magazine of the Protestant Episcopal Church 5 (September 1936):202-24.

2779. Manschreck, Clyde L. "Strategies in Seminary and Continuing Education [in Gerontology]." Theological Education 16, Special Issue no. 3 (Winter 1980):352-3.

2780. Mant, Richard. The Clergyman's Obligations Considered: As to the Celebration of Divine Worship, Ministration of the Sacraments, Instruction of the Poor, Preaching, And Other Pastoral Duties: And as to His Personal Character and Conduct, His Occupations, Amusements, and Inter-course with Others. With Particular Reference to the Ordination Vow. 2d ed.

Oxford: J. Parker and J. G. & F.
Rivington, 1830.

2781. Manthei, D. W. "Area-Pastoral Counselor and
Pastoral Counselor Training." Lutheran
Quarterly 19 (November 1967):408-16.

2782. March, W. Eugene. "Biblical Theology,
Authority and the Presbyterians." Journal
of Presbyterian History 59 (Summer 1981):
113-30.

2783. March, Wallace Eugene. "Charles Hodge on
Schism and Civil Strife." Journal of the
Presbyterian Historical Society 39, no. 2
(1961):88-97.

2784. Margull, Hans Jochen. "Teaching Mission."
International Review of Missions 56 (April
1967):180-4.

2785. Maring, Norman H. "Baptists and Changing
Views of the Bible, 1865-1918."
Foundations 1 (July 1958):52-75; (October
1958):30-61.

2786. Markward, J. B. "Seminary and the Work of the
Home Field [Lutheran Theological Seminary,
Gettysburg]." Lutheran Quarterly 56
(October 1926):468-78.

2787. Marsden, George M. The Evangelical Mind and
the New School Presbyterian Experience: A
Case Study of Thought and Theology in
Nineteenth-Century America. New Haven:
Yale University Press, 1970.

2788. Marsh, Daniel L. "Methodism and Early
Methodist Theological Education."
Methodist History 1 (1962):3-13.

2789. Marsh, Herbert. A Course of Lectures,
Containing a Description and Systematic
Arrangement of the Several Branches of
Divinity: Accompanied with an Account...of
the Prayers...Which Has Been Made at
Different Periods, in Theological Learning.
Cambridge: W. Hilliard, 1812.

2790. Marsh, James. The Remains of the Rev. James
Marsh, D.D. Boston: Crocker & Brewster,
1843.

241

2791. Martin, A. "Needed: A Daring New Educational Path [Bible Colleges]." Church Growth Bulletin 14 (January 1978):172-4.

2792. Martin, Adkins Ron. "The Peace Witness of Bethany Bible School during World War I." Brethren Life and Thought 25 (Spring 1980):83-90.

2793. Martin, Alfred. "Christian Scholarship versus Intellectualism." Bibliotheca Sacra 118 (1961):142-7.

2794. Martin, Dennis. "Ashland College versus Ashland Seminary (1921-37): Prelude to Schism [Grace Theological Seminary]." Brethren Life and Thought 21 (Winter 1976):37-50.

2795. Martin, James Alfred, Jr. "The Graduate Study of Religion in a Seminary Environment." Journal of Bible and Religion 31 (October 1963):320-8.

2796. Martin, James P. "The Missing Q (Cue?) [Biblical Studies]." Lutheran Quarterly 22, no. 4 (1970):396-400.

2797. Martin, R. H. "An Evangelical Chair at Harvard?" Christianity Today 27 (February 4, 1983):14-20.

2798. Martin, Rodney T. "That All May Be Whole: Social Welfare Ministries Conference/Phewa Biennial, Louisville, 1981." Church and Society 71 (May-June 1981):3-70.

2799. Martin, Stanley H. "A Twenty-Year Survey of the Functional Aspects of Methodist Theological Education." Ph.D. dissertation, Boston University School of Education, 1954.

2800. Martin, W. C. "Speaking for the Class of 1963." Harvard Divinity Bulletin 27 (July 1963):13-15.

2801. Martin, W. Robert. "From Student to Ministry through Theological Education." Theological Education 16 (Spring 1980):448-54.

2802. Martin, W. Robert. "Ready or Not, Here They Come." Princeton Seminary Bulletin 63

(Winter 1970):21-31.

2803. Martin, W. Robert, Jr. "The Seminary as Testing Ground." Theological Education 8 (Autumn 1971):18-25.

2804. Martin, W. Robert, Jr. "Underrepresented Minorities: Speaking for Themselves [Black and Hispanic Seminarians]." Christian Century 97 (February 6-13, 1980):154-61.

2805. Marty, Martin E. "American Protestant Theology Today." Thought 41, no. 161 (1966):165-80.

2806. Marty, M. E. "The Baptist Inquisition." Christian Century 99 (May 5, 1982):551.

2807. Marty, Martin Emil. "Doctor of Ministry after Seven Years." Criterion 10 (Spring 1971): 19-21.

2808. Marty, M. E. "D. Min. Degree after Ten Years: A Symposium." Christian Century 93 (February 4, 1976):96+.

2809. Marty, Martin E. "FTE: High Purpose, Low Visibility [Fund For Theological Education]." Christian Century 98 (February 4-11, 1981):133-7.

2810. Marty, M. E. "Missouri's Exiles: Heartbreak, Ashes and Victory." Christian Century 91 (June 12, 1974):630-2.

2811. Marty, M. and Marty, S. "Moving out and Moving in [Concordia Seminary]." Christian Century 91 (April 17, 1974):422-5.

2812. Marty, Martin E. "No Radicalism Here: Faculty Survey." Christian Century 99 (August 18-25, 1982):843-5.

2813. Marty, M. E. "Plug for Seminex." Christian Century 91 (June 12, 1974):655.

2814. Marty, Martin E. "Reflections on William Rainey Harper." Criterion 18 (Autumn 1979):7-9.

2815. Marty, Martin E. "Response to Professor Cox-II." Theological Education 3 (Winter

243

1967):280-2.

2816. Marty, Martin E. and Clifford, M. Keith.
"Results of a Study of Field Placement of
Graduates." Criterion 7 (Winter 1968):33-
4.

2817. Marty, Martin E. "Seminary Enrollments 1962."
Christian Century 79 (November 7, 1962):
1360-2.

2818. Marty, Martin Emil. "Theological Education in
an Ecumenical Age: A Position Paper."
Criterion 4 (Autumn 1965):23-30.

2819. Marty, Martin E. "What the Old Boys Say
[Women in Theological Education]."
Christian Century 99 (February 3-10,
1982):107.

2820. Martyn, J. Louis. "Focus: Theological Education or Theological Vocation?" Union
Seminary Quarterly Review 29, nos. 3/4
(1974):215-20.

2821. Martyn, J. Louis. "Galatians 3:28, Faculty
Appointments and the Overcoming of
Christological Amnesia [Union Theological
Seminary, NYC, 1970]." Katallagete 8
(Summer 1982):39-44.

2822. Martyn, R. H. "See by the Way [General
Theological Library]." Christian Century
77 (November 23, 1960):1378.

2823. Mason, Arthur James. The Ministry of
Conversion. New York: Longmans, Green &
Co., 1912.

2824. Mason, H. C. "Changing Methods for Training
Ministers." United Evangelical Action 23
(June 1964):11-12+.

2825. Mason, J. M. and Proudfit, A. "Theological
Seminary." Panoplist 1 (January 1806):357-
61.

2826. Mason, John. Hints to Theological Students.
New York: Board of Publication of the
Reformed Protestant Dutch Church, 1856.

2827. Mason, R. et al. "Human Nature and
Authoritarianism in Seminary Students and

Counselor Trainees [bibliog.]." Personnel
and Guidance Journal 47 (March 1969):689-
92.

2828. Mason, Robert Lee, Jr. "A Comparative Study
of the Relationships between Seminary
Students and Counselor Trainees in Their
Perceptions of Human Nature and Tendencies
toward Authoritarianism." Ed.D. dissertation, University of Georgia, 1966.

2829. Massa, Conrad Harry. "Toward a Contemporary
Theology of Preaching." Ph.D. dissertation, Princeton Theological Seminary, 1960.

2830. Massey, Howard E., Sr. "A Descriptive Study
of How Students in Southwestern Baptist
Theological Seminary Obtain, Protect, and
Use Their Family Financial Resources."
Ed.D. dissertation, Southwestern Baptist
Theological Seminary, 1982.

2831. Masterman, Frederick J. "Some Aspects of the
Episcopate of William Heathcote De Lancey
First Bishop of the Diocese of Western New
York (1839-1865)." Historical Magazine of
the Protestant Episcopal Church 33, no. 3
(1964):261-77.

2832. Mathews, Donald G. "The Second Great
Awakening as an Organizing Process, 1780-
1830: An Hypothesis." American Quarterly
21 (Spring 1969):23-43.

2833. Mathews, S. "Awakened Church." World To-Day
16 (January 1909):57-61.

2834. Mathews, S. "Curriculum of a Theological
Seminary As Determined by the Social Task."
Religious Education 5 (April 1910):83-91.

2835. Mathews, Shailer. "The Function of the
Divinity School." Journal of Religion 13
(July 1933):253-68.

2836. Mathews, S. "(Ministerial Education.)" World
To-Day (Chicago) 6 (1904):789+.

2837. Mathews, Shailer. New Faith for Old: An
Autobiography. New York: Macmillan Co.,
1936.

245

2838. Mathews, Shailer. "The Rhetorical Value of the Study of Hebrew." Old Testament Student 7 (May 1888):276-80.

2839. Mathews, S. "State University and the Theological Seminary." Religious Education 4 (June 1909):179-86.

2840. Mathews, Shailer. "Theological Seminaries as Schools of Religious Efficiency." Biblical World 47 (February 1916):75-85.

2841. Mathews, Shailer. "Vocational Efficiency and the Theological Curriculum." American Journal of Theology 16 (April 1912):165-80.

2842. Mathis, Laura Anne. "Marital Satisfaction as a Function of Congruence on Holland's Types in Seminary Couples." Ph.D. dissertation, Rosemead Graduate School of Professional Psychology, 1977.

2843. Mathisen, James Albert. "The Moody Bible Institute: A Case Study in the Dilemmas of Institutionalization." Ph.D. dissertation, Garrett Evangelical Theological Seminary in cooperation with Northwestern University, 1979.

2844. Matthews, Arthur H. "Seminary Grant." Christianity Today 22 (January 27, 1978): 40-1.

2845. Matthews, J. B. "Red Infiltration of Theological Seminaries." American Mercury 77 (November 1953):31-6.

2846. Matthews, Lyman. Memoir of the Life and Character of Ebenezer Porter, D.D. Boston: Perkins & Marvin, 1837.

2847. Maurer, B. B. Continuing Education for Church Leaders at West Virginia University. Morgantown: West Virginia University, Center for Extension and Continuing Education, 1979.

2848. Maust, J. "Faculty Union Isn't a Social Hall." Christianity Today 24 (October 10, 1980):97-8.

2849. Maust, John. "Striking Activity at Dubuque Seminary." Christianity Today 24 (October

10, 1980):97-8.

2850. Maves, Paul B. "Spiritual Well-Being of the
       Elderly: A Rationale for Seminary Educa-
       tion." In Spiritual Well-Being of the
       Elderly, pp. 51-8. Edited by J. Thorson.
       Springfield, Ill.: Charles C. Thomas Pub.,
       1980.

2851. Maves, Paul B. "Theological and Biblical
       Foundations." Theological Education 16,
       Special Issue no. 3 (Winter 1980):313-16.

2852. Maxey, Margaret N. "To Catholic Women
       Contemplating Theological Education: 'Quo
       Vadis?'" Theological Education 8 (Summer
       1972):260-8.

2853. Maxwell, William. A Memoir of the Rev. John
       H. Rice, D.D. Philadelphia: J. Whetham,
       1835.

2854. May, James. The Proper Office and Spirit of
       the Ministry. Washington: Printed by
       W. Q. Force, 1844.

2855. May, M. A. "Theological Education." In
       Church Through Half a Century: Essays in
       Honor of William Adams Brown, By Former
       Students, pp. 249-64. Edited by S. M.
       Cavert and H. P. Van Dusen. New York:
       Scribner, 1936.

2856. Mayer, H. T. "Seminary and the Church
       [Concordia Seminary]." Concordia
       Theological Monthly 35 (December 1964):677-
       81.

2857. Mayer, Herbert T. Pastoral Care: Its Roots
       and Renewal. Atlanta: John Knox Press,
       1979.

2858. Mayfield, Gary K. and Dickerson, Ben E. "An
       Investigation of Seminarians' Attitudes
       toward the Elderly." Nacogdoches, Tex.:
       Stephen F. Austin State University, 1977.

2859. Mays, Benjamin E. Born to Rebel: An Autobio-
       graphy. New York: Charles Scribner's
       Sons, 1971.

2860. Mays, Benjamin E. "The Education of Negro
       Ministers." Journal of Negro Education 2

(July 1933):342-51.

2861. Mays, M. J. "Design of the Pre-Seminary Curriculum on a Liberal Arts Campus." Brethren Life and Thought 8 (Spring 1963):28-35.

2862. Mayse, Edgar C. "Ernest Trice Thompson: Presbyterian of the South." Journal of Presbyterian History 56, no. 1 (1978):36-46.

2863. Mead, George Whitefield. Modern Methods in Church Work. New York: Dodd, Mead & Co., 1897.

2864. Mead, L. B. "Seminary Community: A Critique." Christian Century 84 (April 26, 1967):563+.

2865. Mead, Sidney Earl. Nathaniel William Taylor, 1786-1858. Chicago: University of Chicago Press, 1942.

2866. Meade, William. Lectures on the Pastoral Office: Delivered to the Students of the Theological Seminary at Alexandria, Va. New York: Stanford & Swords, 1849.

2867. Meadows-Rogers, Arabella. "Men in Conversation about Men." Theological Education 11 (Winter 1975):112-24.

2868. "Meadville Theological School, Chicago: Views and Plans." Architectural Record 74 (November 1933):372-6.

2869. Means, John Jeffrey. "An Investigation of an Assessment Model for the Evaluation of the Capacity of Seminary Students to Utilize Clinical Pastoral Education as a Professional Learning Experience." Ph.D. dissertation, Northwestern University, 1980.

2870. "Meanwhile in the Seminaries ... [Results of Poll]." National Review 34 (August 6, 1982):975.

2871. Mears, David Otis. David Otis Mears, D. D.: An Autobiography, 1842-1893. Boston: Pilgrim Press, 1920.

2872. Mears, David Otis. Life of Edward Norris Kirk. Boston: Lockwood, Brooks & Co., 1877.

2873. Meeder, Andrew K. "The Pastor's Role: Supervised Field Work in Theological Education." Ph.D. dissertation, Wesley Theological Seminary, 1974.

2874. Mehl, John Edwards. "Motivation for Continuing Education among Protestant Parish Clergy." Ph.D. dissertation, University of Pittsburgh, 1976.

2875. Mehl, Warren R. "The Protestant Theological Library in America: Past, Present and Future." Theology and Life 7 (Autumn 1964):230-43.

2876. Meiburg, Albert L. "Conjoint Clinical Education: An Interdisciplinary Experiment." Journal of Pastoral Care 25, no. 2 (1971):116-21.

2877. Meiburg, Albert L. "Ministry with Older Persons." Theological Education 16, Special Issue no. 3 (Winter 1980):368-70.

2878. Meland, Bernard E. "Reminiscences and Reflections Concerning Wilhelm Pauck's Years in Chicago." Criterion 21 (Spring 1982):3-7.

2879. "Memorials of William Rainey Harper." Biblical World 27 (New Series) (March 1906):entire issue.

2880. "Men from Missouri." Time 61 (April 27, 1953):80+.

2881. Menendez, Albert J. "Uncle Sam's Seminaries and Church Colleges." Church and State 35 (March 1982):6-8.

2882. Mercer, L. P. "(Essential Qualifications for Ministry.)" New Church Review 8 (1901):1+.

2883. "Merger of Seminaries of the United Lutheran Church." Christian Education 16 (December 1932):92-3.

2884. Mergner, Julie. The Deaconess and Her Work. Translated from the German by Mrs. Adolph

249

Spaeth. Authorized by the Conference of
Lutheran Deaconess Mother Houses in
America. Philadelphia: General Council
Publication House, 1911.

2885. Methodist Church (United States). Division of
Educational Institutions. A Survey of Ten
Theological Schools Affiliated with the
Methodist Church, under the Auspices of the
Commission on Theological Education, the
Board of Education, and the Association of
Methodist Theological Schools. Nashville,
1948.

2886. Methodist Church (United States). Study
Commission on Theological Education. A
Study of Theological Education in the
Methodist Church 1952-1956. Nashville,
1956.

2887. Methodist Episcopal Church. The Doctrines and
Discipline of the Methodist Episcopal
Church. 17th ed. New York: John C.
Totten, Printer, 1814.

2888. Methodist Episcopal Church. The Doctrines and
Discipline of the Methodist Episcopal
Church, 1892. New York: Hunt & Eaton,
1892.

2889. Methodist Episcopal Church. The Doctrines and
Discipline of the Methodist Episcopal
Church, 1896. New York: Eaton & Mains,
1896.

2890. Methodist Episcopal Church. The Doctrines and
Discipline of the Methodist Episcopal
Church, 1900. New York: Eaton & Mains,
1900.

2891. Methodist Episcopal Church. The Doctrines and
Discipline of the Methodist Episcopal
Church, 1904. New York: Eaton & Mains,
1904.

2892. Methodist Episcopal Church. Doctrines and
Discipline of the Methodist Episcopal
Church, 1912. New York: Methodist Book
Concern, 1912.

2893. Methodist Episcopal Church. Doctrines and
Discipline of the Methodist Episcopal
Church, 1916. New York: Methodist Book

Concern, 1916.

2894. Methodist Episcopal Church. Board of
Education. The Board of Education of the
Methodist Episcopal Church: Analysis of
Statement. N.p., n.d.

2895. Methodist Episcopal Church. Board of
Education. Hand-Book and Report. New
York, 1896.

2896. Methodist Episcopal Church. Board of
Education. Quadrennial Report. New York,
1924.

2897. Methodist Episcopal Church. General Deaconess
Board. Directions and Helps: Course of
Study for Deaconesses. New York:
Methodist Book Concern, 1922.

2898. Methodist Episcopal Church, South. Doctrines
and Discipline of the Methodist Episcopal
Church, 1928. New York: Methodist Book
Concern, 1928.

2899. Methodist Episcopal Church, South. The
Doctrines and Discipline of the Methodist
Episcopal Church, South. Nashville, Tenn.:
Publishing House, Methodist Episcopal
Church South, 1938.

2900. Methodist Episcopal Church, South. Southern
Methodist Handbook, 1915, 1916. Edited by
Thomas Neal Ivey. Nashville, Tenn.: 1915.

2901. Methodist Episcopal Church, South. Educa-
tional Campaign Commission. Educational
Survey, Methodist Episcopal Church, South.
Edited by Elmer T. Clark. Nashville:
Educational Campaign Commission, 1918.

2902. Methodist Episcopal Church, South. General
Conferences. Journals of the 1846 and 1850
Conferences. Louisville, Ky.: Early,
1851.

2903. Methodist Episcopal Church, South. General
Conference. Journal. Nashville, Tenn.:
A. H. Redford, 1866.

2904. Methodist Episcopal Church, South. General
Conference. Journal. Nashville, Tenn.:
A. H. Redford, 1870.

251

2905. "Methodist Ministers' Education Shrinking."
        Christian Century 42 (November 12,
        1925):1422.

2906. "(Methodist Theological Schools.)" Methodist
        Review 56 (1896):618+.

2907. "Methods of Theological Teaching." Theologi-
        cal Education 9 (Spring 1973):entire issue.

2908. Metzger, Bruce Manning. "On the Study of
        Hebrew and Greek." Princeton Seminary
        Bulletin 54 (February 1961):26-33.

2909. Metzger, Walter P. Academic Freedom in the
        Age of the University. New York: Columbia
        University Press, 1961.

2910. Meyer, Carl S. "Concordia Seminary: For 125
        Years toward a More Excellent Ministry."
        Missouri Historical Review 59, no. 2
        (1965):210-22.

2911. Meyer, Carl S. "Concordia's Ante-Bellum Years
        in Saint Louis, 1849-1861." Concordia
        Historical Institute Quarterly 37 (January
        1965):129-42.

2912. Meyer, Carl S. "Greetings to the Perry County
        Lutherans on the 125th Anniversary of Their
        Coming to Missouri." Concordia Historical
        Institute Quarterly 37, no. 3 (1964):115-
        16.

2913. Meyer, Carl Stamm. Log Cabin to Luther Tower:
        Concordia Seminary during One Hundred and
        Twenty-five Years toward a More Excellent
        Ministry, 1839-1964. St. Louis: Concordia
        Publishing House, 1965.

2914. Meyer, Carl S. "Lutheran Immigrant Churches
        Face the Problems of the Frontier." Church
        History 29, no. 4 (1960):440-62.

2915. Meyer, Carl Stamm, ed. Moving Frontiers:
        Readings in the History of the Lutheran
        Church - Missouri Synod. St. Louis:
        Concordia Publishing House, 1964.

2916. Meyer, Carl S. "The School for Graduate
        Studies." Concordia Theological Monthly 35
        (1964):729-35.

2917. Meyer, J. Shelly. "The Growth and Resources of Training Schools." Religious Education 7 (December 1912):550-5.

2918. Meyer, Kenneth M. "Purpose of a Seminary Which Is Part of the Evangelical Movement." Theological Education 14 (Spring 1978):100-8.

2919. Meyer, Lucy Rider. "Deaconesses." In Christianity Practically Applied. Evangelical Alliance for the United States of America. Conference. Chicago, 1893, v. 2, pp. 70-95. New York: Baker & Taylor, 1894.

2920. Meyer, Lucy Jane (Rider). Deaconesses, Biblical, Early Church, European, American. Chicago: Message Publishing Co., 1889.

2921. M'Ferrin, J. B. "Methodist Itinerancy." Christian Advocate (Nashville) 29 (New Series) (October 23, 1869):1.

2922. Michaelson, Karin G. "Moving into the Mainstream: Report on the Evangelical Women's Conference at Fuller." Sojourners 7 (August 1978):7.

2923. Michaelson, Robert. "Religion and Academia." Theological Education 3 (Spring 1967):367-75.

2924. Michaelson, Robert. "Training of Teachers of Religion for College and University." Religion In Life 28 (1958-9):24-34.

2925. Micks, Marianne H. and Price, Charles P. Toward a New Theology of Ordination: Essays on the Ordination of Women. Alexandria, Va.: Virginia Theological Seminary, 1976.

2926. Middleton, R. G. "Yogi, Commissar and Christian." Christian Century 68 (March 29, 1950):396-7.

2927. "Midway Omelet Unscrambled." Christian Century 77 (May 18, 1960):595-6.

2928. Milburn, William Henry. Ten Years of Preacher-Life: Chapters from an

Autobiography. New York: Derby & Jackson, 1859.

2929. Miles, Matthew B., ed. Innovation in Education. New York: Bureau of Publications, Teachers College, Columbia University, 1964.

2930. Miller, A. L. "New Minds for Our Mission." Princeton Seminary Bulletin 54 (July 1960):16-22.

2931. Miller, Char. "'Teach Me O My God': The Journal of Hiram Bingham (1815-1816)." Vermont History 48, no. 4 (1980):225-35.

2932. Miller, Char. "'The World Creeps In': Hiram Bingham III and the Decline of Missionary Fervor." Hawaiian Journal of History 15 (1981):80-99.

2933. Miller, Donald E. "Simulation in Theological Education." Theological Education 13 (Spring 1977):175-83.

2934. Miller, Donald E. "Religious Education as a Discipline: V. Christian Education as a Contextual Discipline." Religious Education 62, no. 5 (1967):418-27.

2935. Miller, Douglas J. "Seminary Education Tomorrow: A Forecast." Christianity Today 19 (February 14, 1975):4-6.

2936. Miller, Edward Waite. The Beginnings of Auburn Seminary. N.p., n.d.

2937. Miller, G. L. and Ross, J. "Response to the Clergy Crisis: Why Set up a Paper Tiger [Bethany Theological Seminary]." Brethren Life and Thought 15 (Summer 1970):149-58.

2938. Miller, H. Earl. "The Old Seminary and the New, 1922-28." Concordia Historical Institute Quarterly 49 (Summer 1976):52-63.

2939. Miller, Howard. The Revolutionary College: American Presbyterian Higher Education 1707-1837. New York: New York University Press, 1976.

2940. Miller, J. B. "Studies in Christian Ministries." Encounter 25 (Summer 1964).

2941. Miller, J. Barrett. "Theology of William
Sparrow." Historical Magazine of the
Protestant Episcopal Church 46 (December
1977):443-54.

2942. Miller, Kelly. "The Higher Education of the
Negro Is at the Crossroads." Educational
Review 72 (December 1926):272-8.

2943. Miller, Marlin E. "Theological Reflections on
Allocating Scarce Church Funds for Theological Education." Theological Education
15 (Spring 1979):162-5.

2944. Miller, Ralph Llewellyn. "An Exploratory
Analysis of the Preferences of First-Year
Theological Students Designated as Liberal
and Conservative toward Directive and Non-
Directive Responses in the Pastor-
Parishioner Counseling Relationship."
Ph.D. dissertation, Michigan State
University, 1963.

2945. Miller, Randolph C. "The Discipline of
Theology: Seminary and University." In
Does the Church Know How To Teach. Edited
by K. Cully. New York: Macmillan, 1970.

2946. Miller, Randolph Crump. "For the World of
Tomorrow." Christian Century 81 (April 29,
1964):544-6.

2947. Miller, Robert Moats. How Shall They
Hearwithout a Preacher? The Life of Ernest
Fremont Tittle. Chapel Hill: University
of North Carolina Press, 1971.

2948. Miller, S. "(History of Princeton.)"
American Quarterly Register 10 (1838):31+.

2949. Miller, Samuel. A Brief History of the
Theological Seminary of the Presbyterian
Church, at Princeton, New Jersey: Together
with Its Constitution, By-Laws, Etc.
Princeton: Printed by John Bogart, 1838.

2950. Miller, Samuel. A Brief Retrospect of the
Eighteenth Century. Part the First; in
Three Volumes: Containing a Sketch of the
Revolutions and Improvements in Science,
Arts, and Literature, During that Period.
London: J. Johnson, 1805.

2951. Miller, Samuel. "Importance of an Educated
Ministry, Shown from Ecclesiastical
History." American Quarterly Register 4
(1832):85-95.

2952. Miller, Samuel. The Importance of Mature
Preparatory Study for the Ministry.
Andover: M. Newman, 1830.

2953. Miller, Samuel. Letters Concerning the
Constitution and Order of the Christian
Ministry: Addressed to the Members of the
Presbyterian Churches in the City of New
York... 2d ed. Philadelphia: J. Towar &
D. M. Hogan, 1830.

2954. Miller, Samuel. Letters on Clerical Manners
and Habits: Addressed to a Student in the
Theological Seminary, at Princeton, N.J.
New, rev. ed. Philadelphia: Presbyterian
Board of Publication, 1852.

2955. Miller, Samuel. The Life of Samuel Miller. 2
vols. Philadelphia: Claxton, Remsen &
Haffelfinger, 1869.

2956. Miller, Samuel H. "Church, Seminary, and
World: An Uneasy Frontier." Theological
Education 2 (Summer 1966):46-57.

2957. Miller, S. H. "Education for Insecurity."
Harvard Divinity Bulletin 29 (January
1965):27-34.

2958. Miller, S. H. "Experience of Consecration in
Professor and Student [in Theological
Schools]." Journal of Religious Thought 16
(Autumn-Winter 1958):27-34.

2959. Miller, Samuel H. "Field VI in the Divinity
School Curriculum." Harvard Divinity
Bulletin 20 (1954-5):71-4.

2960. Miller, Samuel Howard. "The Focus of
Theological Training." Harvard Divinity
Bulletin 24 (April 1960):1-8.

2961. Miller, Samuel H. "Needs of Theological
Education." School and Society 95 (March
18, 1967):174-5.

2962. Miller, Samuel H. "A Philosophy of Theological Education: Toward The Creation of

Meaningful Communities." Encounter 25
(Summer 1964):314-23.

2963. Miller, Samuel H. "The Prophetic Responsi-
bility of Theological Training." American
Association of Theological Schools.
Proceedings (1962):227.

2964. Miller, William Charles. "The Governance of
Theological Education: A Case Study of
Nazarene Theological Seminary, 1945 - 1976
[Missouri]." Ph.D. dissertation, Kent
State University, 1983.

2965. Milligan, R. "The Hiram Lectures."
Millennial Harbinger 37 (October 1866):451-
3.

2966. Mills, Beatrice Marie. "The Educational
Interests and Needs of Older Adults in
Selected Presbyterian Churches." Ed.D.
dissertation, Indiana University, 1968.

2967. Mills, C. S. "Ministerial Professional
Training." Religious Education 7 (October
1912):424-8.

2968. Mills, Edgar Wendell. Career Change among
Ministers: A Socio-Psychological Study.
Cambridge: Center for Research in Careers,
Graduate School of Education, Harvard
University, 1966.

2969. Mims, Edwin. History of Vanderbilt University. Nashville, Tenn.: Vanderbilt
University Press, 1946.

2970. Minear, Paul S. "The Impact of Ecumenical
Developments for Theological Education: A
Protestant View." Theological Education 3
(Winter 1967):308-16.

2971. "Ministerial Code of Ethics of Yale University
Divinity Students." School and Society 24
(December 4, 1926):699.

2972. "Ministerial Education." Christian Review 2
(June 1837):260-76.

2973. "Ministerial Education." Methodist Quarterly
Review 16 (New Series) (October 1864):533-
52.

2974. "Ministerial Education in Our Church."
Methodist Quarterly Review 54 (April
1872):246-67.

2975. "Ministers Are Not Quitters." Christian
Century 79 (December 5, 1962):1471-2.

2976. "Ministers in Foxholes?" Time 46 (December
31, 1945):52+.

2977. "Ministers of Tomorrow." Time 81 (February
22, 1963):69.

2978. "The Ministry." Universalist Quarterly and
General Review 10 (July 1853):275-93.

2979. "The Ministry and Social Reform." Independent
59 (1905):142-8.

2980. "Ministry for To-Day." Outlook 99 (October
14, 1911):364-5.

2981. "Ministry's Subterranean Shifts." Christian
Century 98 (February 4, 1981):141-5.

2982. Minnery, Tom. "Missouri Lutherans Clash over
Doctrinal Fine Point [Concordia Seminary,
St. Louis]." Christianity Today 25 (March
13, 1981):56-7.

2983. Minnery, T. "Nine Frustrated Faculty Leave
Luther Rice." Christianity Today 25
(December 11, 1981):49+.

2984. Minnery, Tom. "Short Cut Graduate Degrees
Shortchange Everybody." Christianity Today
25 (May 29, 1981):26-9.

2985. "Minnesota Bible College and the Village
Concept of Campus Planning." Minneapolis:
Minnesota Bible College, 1968. (ERIC
Document)

2986. Minor Seminary Conference. 11th, Catholic
University of America, 1960. Self-Evalua-
tion in the Minor Seminary. Edited by
Cornelius M. Cuyler. Washington: Catholic
University of America Press, 1961.

2987. "Minority Report of Committee on Education."
In Journal of the General Conference of the
Methodist Episcopal Church, South, pp. 240-
3. Edited by Thomas O. Summers.

Nashville: Publishing House of the
Methodist Episcopal Church, South, 1870.

2988. "Missionary Education in America." Missionary
Review of the World 44 (November 1921):832-
3.

2989. "Missionary Orientation Program Planned:
Ecumenical Training Center, Stony Point,
N.Y." Christian Century 77 (September 14,
1960):1045.

2990. Mitchell, H. G. "The New Old Testament."
Methodist Review 80 (July 1898):543-58.

2991. Mitchell, Henry H. "Black Power and the
Christian Church." Foundations (American
Baptist Historical Society) 11, no. 2
(1968):99-109.

2992. Mitchell, Henry H. "Issues and Perspectives:
The Practical Field and Its Relationship to
the Black Man's Practice of the Christian
Faith." Theological Education 6 (Spring
1970):216-24.

2993. Mitchell, H. H. "Key Term in Theological
Education for the Negro: Compensatory."
Christian Century 84 (April 26, 1967):530-
3.

2994. Mitchell, Hinckley Gilbert Thomas. For the
Benefit of My Creditors. Boston: Beacon
Press, 1922.

2995. Mitchell, James. "The Call to and Qualifications for the Ministry." In The Life and
Times of Levi Scott, D.D. One of the
Bishops of the Methodist Episcopal Church,
pp. 46-51. New York: Phillips & Hunt,
1885.

2996. Mitchell, Kenneth R. and Anderson, Herbert E.
"Simulated Families in a Training Session."
Journal of Supervision and Training in
Ministry 4 (1981):9-20.

2997. Miyakawa, Tetsuo Scott. Protestants and
Pioneers: Individualism and Conformity on
the American Frontier. Chicago: University of Chicago Press, 1964.

2998. Moats, Francis Ireland. "The Educational
       Policy of the Methodist Episcopal Church
       prior to 1860." Ph.D. dissertation, State
       University of Iowa, 1926.

2999. Moberg, David O. "Aging and Theological
       Education." Theological Education 16,
       Special Issue no. 3 (Winter 1980):283-93.

3000. "Modern Education of Ministers." Outlook 86
       (July 13, 1907):538-9.

3001. "Modern Instance [Berkeley Divinity School]."
       New Republic 23 (July 14, 1920):194-5.

3002. "Modifications in the Theological Curriculum."
       American Journal of Theology 3 (April
       1899):324-43.

3003. Moeller, Bernd. Imperial Cities and the
       Reformation. Edited and Translated by H.
       C. Erik Midelfort and Mark V. Edwards, Jr.
       Philadelphia: Fortress Press, 1972.

3004. Moeser, Donald H. et. al. "Faculty Papers in
       Memoriam Karl Barth." Lutheran Theological
       Seminary, Gettysburg, Bulletin 49, no. 2
       (1969):1-53.

3005. Moffatt, James. "Professor G. W. Bacon."
       Expository Times 43 (1931-32):437-42.

3006. Mohan, Robert Paul. "Seminarians and
       Service." America 114 (March 19,
       1966):384-5.

3007. Monnier, Charles M. "Seminary Speech
       Education in the 1970's: The Promise in
       Dr. Alvin Brightbill's Work." Brethren
       Life and Thought 16 (Summer 1971):185-91.

3008. Montgomery, John Warwick. "Theological
       Doctorates." Christianity Today 10
       (February 18, 1966):54-5.

3009. Montgomery, John Warwick. The Writing of
       Research Papers in Theology: An Intro-
       ductory Lecture with a List of Basic
       Reference Tools for the Theological
       Student. Ann Arbor? Mich., 1959.

3010. Montgomery, Riley Benjamin. The Education of
       Ministers of Disciples of Christ. St.

Louis, Mo.: Bethany Press, 1931.

3011. Montgomery, R. B. "Percentage of Theological
      Students Receiving Their Undergraduate
      Education at State Colleges and Universi-
      ties." Christian Education 26 (September
      1942):71-6.

3012. Moody, Granville. A Life's Retrospect: Auto-
      biography of Rev. Granville Moody. Edited
      by Sylvester Weeks. Cincinnati: Cranston
      & Stowe, 1890.

3013. Moore, Allen J. "Education for the Practice
      of Ministry." Religious Education 63
      (July-August 1968):294-300.

3014. Moore, A. J. "Role of Religious Education in
      Theological Education." Religious Educa-
      tion 60 (September 1965):375-80+.

3015. Moore, Arthur B. "Lilly Study and the Theo-
      logical Curriculum." Journal of Bible and
      Religion 34 (April 1966):146-51.

3016. Moore, A. B. B. "Pre-Seminary Education: A
      Canadian View." Theological Education 1
      (Spring 1965):159-63.

3017. Moore, E. Maynard. "Theological Education for
      a Revolutional Church." Theological
      Education 4 (Winter 1968):603-10.

3018. Moore, Ernest William. "An Historical Study
      of Higher Education and the Church of the
      Nazarene, 1900-1965." Ph.D. dissertation,
      University of Texas, 1966.

3019. Moore, G. F. "(Field of an Undenominational
      Theological School.)" Harvard Graduates'
      Magazine 11 (1903):201+.

3020. Moore, George Foot. "An Appreciation of
      Professor Toy." American Journal of
      Semitic Languages and Literatures 36
      (October 1919):1-17.

3021. Moore, George Foot. "Modern Theological
      Education." Independent 55 (September 17,
      1903):2211-4.

3022. Moore, G. V. "Seminary Extension Service."
      Christian Education 21 (April 1938):247-52.

3023. Moore, Leroy, Jr. "Academic Freedom: A Chapter in the History of the Colgate Rochester Divinity School." Foundations 10 (January-March 1967):64-79.

3024. Moore, LeRoy, Jr. "Another Look at Fundamentalism: A Response to Ernest R. Sandeen." Church History 37 (June 1968):195-202.

3025. Moore, Leroy, Jr. "The Rise of American Religious Liberalism at the Rochester Theological Seminary, 1872-1928." Ph.D. dissertation, Claremont Graduate School, 1966.

3026. Moore, Ralph R. "History of Baptist Theological Education in South Carolina and Georgia." Ph.D. dissertation, Southwestern Baptist Theological Seminary, 1949.

3027. Moore, Walter William. The Life & Letters of Walter W. Moore, Second Founder and First President of Union Theological Seminary. Richmond, Va.: Union Theological Seminary, 1939.

3028. Moore, Walter William. Preparation of the Modern Minister. 9 v. New York: YMCA, 1909.

3029. Moore, William Thomas. A Comprehensive History of the Disciples of Christ. New York: Fleming H. Revell Co., 1909.

3030. Moorhead, James H. "Joseph Addison Alexander: Common Sense, Romanticism and Biblical Criticism at Princeton." Journal of Presbyterian History 53 (1975):51-65.

3031. Moorland, Jesse Edward. The Demand and Supply of Increased Efficiency in the Negro Ministry. New York: Arno Press, 1969. (Reprint of 1909 edition).

3032. Moran, R. S. "Theological Seminaries in the M.E. Church." Christian Advocate and Journal (New York) 29 (January 26, 1854):1.

3033. "More Fog over St. Louis [Concordia Seminary]." Christianity Today 17 (February 2, 1973):26-7.

3034. "More Students for God." _Newsweek_ 38 (July 30, 1951):67.

3035. Morell, Parker. "Ministers in White; Theological Students as Hospital Interns." _Saturday Evening Post_ 215 (July 25, 1942):12+.

3036. Morentz, Paul E. "Image of the Seminary Wife." _Pastoral Psychology_ 12 (December 1961):46-52.

3037. Morgan, Carl Hamilton. "The Status of Field Work in the Protestant Theological Seminaries in the United States." Ph.D. dissertation, University of Pennsylvania, 1942.

3038. Morgan, Edmund S. "Ezra Stiles and Timothy Dwight." _Massachusetts Historical Society Proceedings_ 72 (1957-60):101-17.

3039. Morgan, F. Bruce. "Theological Education between East and West." _Theology Today_ 9 (April 1952):79-96.

3040. Morgan, Grant. "Seminary Memories." _Catholic World_ 125 (September 1927):810-16.

3041. Morison, Samuel Eliot. _The Founding of Harvard College_. Cambridge: Harvard University Press, 1935.

3042. Morison, Samuel Eliot. _Harvard College in the Seventeenth Century_. Cambridge, Mass.: Harvard University Press, 1936, vol. 1.

3043. Morrell, F. A. "A Central Theological Seminary." _Christian Advocate and Journal_ (New York) 29 (February 9, 1854):1.

3044. Morris, James. _The Preachers_. New York: St. Martin's Press, 1973.

3045. Morris, R. D. "Report to the Dean." _Journal of Pastoral Care_ 5, no. 1 (1951):27-30.

3046. Morris, William Stephen. _The Seminary Movement in the United States: Projects, Foundations and Early Development, 1833-1866_. Washington, D.C.: Catholic University of America, 1932.

263

3047. Morrison, C. C. "Communication." Christian Century 69 (July 23, 1952):854.

3048. Morrison, Clinton D., Jr. "Theological Education for Dual Occupations: Law and Ministry." Theological Education 7 (Spring 1971):180-3.

3049. Morrison, Clinton D. "Various Ministries and the Same Lord." McCormick Quarterly 17 (March 1964):10-19.

3050. Morrison, Hugh McE. An Appeal to the Presbyterian Church, in Behalf of Her Theological Seminaries, and Candidates for the Gospel Ministry. Columbia, S.C.: S. C. Morgan, 1858.

3051. Morro, William Charles. "Brother McGarvey": The Life of President J. W. McGarvey of the College of the Bible, Lexington, Ky.... St. Louis, Mo.: Bethany Press, 1940.

3052. Morro, W. C. "Graduate Dept. of Ministerial Education." Religious Education 7 (October 1912):375-8.

3053. Morse, Hermann N. "The Integration of Education for the Christian Ministry." American Association of Theological Schools. Proceedings (1948):99.

3054. Morse, Jedidiah. The True Reasons on Which the Election of a Hollis Professor of Divinity in Harvard College, Was Opposed at the Board of Overseers, Feb. 14, 1805. Charlestown: Printed for the Author, 1805.

3055. Morton, James P. "(Urban Training for the Ordained)." City Church 15 (January-February 1964):3.

3056. Moscheles, J. "Social Geography and Its Desirability in Schools of Divinity." Sociological Review 22 (October 1930):309-14.

3057. Moses, Jesse D. "The Intercultural Knowledge and Attitudes of Episcopal Seminary Students and the Implications for Seminary Education." Ph.D. dissertation, University of Southern California, 1955.

3058. Moss, Robert V., Jr. "Contexts for Theological Education in the Next Decade." Theological Education 5 (Autumn 1968):3-14.

3059. Mosteller, James D. "Something Old, Something New: The First 50 Years of Northern Baptist Theological Seminary." Foundations 8 (January 1965):26-48.

3060. Mostert, J. "Unheralded Halls of Higher Learning [Bible Colleges]." Christian Life 31 (June 1969):34-5+.

3061. Mostert, J. "What You Need to Know about Bible Colleges." Christian Life 30 (April 1969):57-9.

3062. Mott, John Raleigh. Addresses and Papers. New York: Association Press, 1946-7.

3063. Mott, John Raleigh. Confronting Young Men with the Living Christ. New York: Association Press, 1923.

3064. Mott, John Raleigh. The Future Leadership of the Church. New York: Student Department, Young Men's Christian Association, 1908.

3065. Mottu, H. "Theological Education in Ecumenical Perspective." Ecumenical Review 33 (April 1981):166-77.

3066. Moulton, Arthur W. A Memoir of Augustine Heard Amory. Salem, Mass.: Newcomb & Gauss, 1909.

3067. Moulton, G. The Bible as Literature. New York: Thomas Crowell & Co., 1896.

3068. Moulton, Richard Green. The Literary Study of the Bible. Boston: D. C. Heath & Co., 1895.

3069. Moxcey, Mary E. Some Qualities Associated with Success in the Christian Ministry. Columbia University Teachers College. Contributions to Education, no. 122. 1922. Reprint ed., AMS Press, 1972.

3070. Mudge, Lewis Seymour. Why Is the Church in the World? Philadelphia? Board of Christian Education, United Presbyterian

Church in the United States of America, 1967.

3071. Muelder, Walter G. "Recruitment of Negroes for Theological Studies." In The Black Church in America. Edited by M. Hart Nelsen, Raytha L. Yokley and Anne K. Nelsen. New York: Basic Books, 1971.

3072. Mueller, Peter Dietrich. "Kansas Vicarage [Concordia Seminary, Mo.]." Concordia Historical Institute Quarterly 49, no. 2 (1976):72-87.

3073. Mueller, William A. A History of Southern Baptist Theological Seminary. [Greenville, S.C. and Louisville, Ky., 1859-1959]. Nashville: Broadman Press, 1959.

3074. Mueller, William A. The School of Providence and Prayer: A History of the New Orleans Baptist Theological Seminary. New Orleans: Printed by the New Orleans Baptist Theological Seminary, 1969.

3075. Muilenburg, James. "Old Testament Scholarship: Fifty Years in Retrospect." Journal of Bible and Religion 28 (April 1960):173-81.

3076. Muller, James Arthur. The Episcopal Theological School, 1867-1943. Cambridge, Mass.: Episcopal Theological School, 1943.

3077. Mulligan, Joseph E. "Better Than Looking On." America 122 (May 2, 1970):468-9.

3078. Mullins, E. Y. "Training the Ministry for Civic Leadership." Religious Education 9 December 1914):558-60.

3079. Mullins, Isla May (Hawley). Edgar Young Mullins: an Intimate Biography. Nashville, Tenn.: Sunday School Board of the Southern Baptist Convention, 1929.

3080. "(Multiplication of Theological Seminaries.)" Bibliotheca Sacra 36 (1879):760+.

3081. Mumford, Thomas James, comp. Memoir of Samuel Joseph May. Boston: Roberts Bros., 1874.

3082. Mundy, Paul et al. "The Minor Seminarian: Social Class and Academic Achievement [bibliog.]." *Journal of Experimental Education* 40 (Summer 1972):65-9.

3083. Munger, Edith Marguerite. "Personality, Motivation, and Experience--Their Effect on Persistence in a Theological Seminary." Ph.D. dissertation, Fuller Theological Seminary, School of Psychology, 1974.

3084. Munger, T. T. "Divinity School and the University." *Outlook* 70 (March 22, 1902):728-33.

3085. Munson, W. T. "(Education for Ministry.)" *National Quarterly Review* 5 (1862):106+.

3086. Muntz, E. E., Jr. "Opinions of Divinity and Law Students on Social Class." *Journal of Educational Sociology* 34 (January 1961): 221-9.

3087. Murch, James DeForest. Cooperation without Compromise: A History of the National Association of Evangelicals. Grand Rapids, Mich.: Eerdmans, 1956.

3088. Murch, James DeForest. "Ecumenical Seminaries." *Christian Standard* (November 23, 1968):7-8.

3089. Murphy, David M. "Theological Curriculum for the 1970's: A Dean's Evaluation." *Theological Education* 5 (Winter 1969):103-11.

3090. Murphy, Michael J. "Church Speaks to Seminary." *Theological Education* 15 (Spring 1979):92-6.

3091. Murray, John Lovell. "An Adventure in Missionary Preparation." *International Review of Missions* 31 (April 1942):193-8.

3092. Murray, J. L. "Missionary Preparation in North America." *International Review of Missions* 14 (October 1925):586-97.

3093. Muskingum College, New Concord, Ohio. William Rainey Harper Memorial Conference, 1937. The William Rainey Harper Memorial Conference, Held in Connection with the

267

Centennial of Muskingum College, New
Concord, Ohio, October 21-22, 1937. Edited
by Robert N. Montgomery. Chicago: University of Chicago Press, 1938.

3094. Muzzey, Artemas Bowers. The Value of the
Study of Intellectual Philosophy to the
Minister: An Essay, Read before the
Cambridge Association of Ministers, Feb. 9,
1869. Boston: Edwards S. Coombs, 1869.

3095. Myers, Rawley. This Is the Seminary.
Milwaukee: Bruce Publishing Co., 1953.

3096. Myers, W. C. "Process in a First-Year
Pastoral Training Program." Theological
Education 5 (Summer 1969, Suppl. 1):479-85.

3097. Myklebust, Olav Guttorm. The Study of
Missions in Theological Education: An
Historical Inquiry into the Place of World
Evangelisation in Western Protestant
Ministerial Training, With Particular
Reference to Alexander Duff's Chair of
Evangelistic Theology. Oslo: Egede
Instituttet, Hovedkommisjon Land og Kirke,
1955-

3098. Nadal, B. H. "Educational Qualifications for
the Ministry." Methodist Quarterly Review
19 (New series) (April 1867):221-36.

3099. Nader, Ralph. "Law Schools and Law Firms."
New Republic 161 (October 11, 1969):20-3.

3100. Nash, Charles S. "Training of the Spiritual
Life in Theological Seminaries." In
Christianity Practically Applied. Evangelical Alliance for the United States of
America. Conference. Chicago, 1893, v. 2,
pp. 482-3. New York: Baker & Taylor,
1894.

3101. "The Nashotah Liturgy." Historical Magazine
of the Protestant Episcopal Church 29
(December 1960):287-301.

3102. National Academy of Education. Committee on
Educational Research. Research for
Tomorrow's Schools. New York: Macmillan,
1969.

268

3103. National Association of Evangelicals.
Christian Education in a Democracy: The
Report of the N.A.E. Committee. By Frank
E. Gaebelein. New York: Oxford University
Press, 1951.

3104. National Consultation on Continuing Education
for the Ministry. Proceedings. Edited by
Henry B. Adams. Chicago, 1965. (ERIC
Document)

3105. National Consultation on the Negro in the
Christian Ministry. One Ministry. New
York: Office of Publication and Distribu-
tion, for The Department of the Ministry,
National Council of the Churches of Christ
in the United States of America, 1959.

3106. National Council of Churches. Dept. of
Ministry. "Study Opportunities for
Ministers, January 1968 to January 1969."
New York: Council Press for the Dept. of
Ministry, National Council of Churches,
1968.

3107. National Council of the Churches of Christ in
the United States of America. Committee on
Theological Study and Teaching. The Study
of Religion in College and University and
Its Implications for Church and Seminary.
New York? Dept. of Higher Education,
National Council of Churches, 1967.

3108. National Council of the Churches of Christ in
the United States of America. Dept. of the
Ministry. Study Opportunities for
Ministers, March 1966 to March 1967. New
York, 1966.

3109. National Council of the Churches of Christ in
the United States of America. Division of
Foreign Missions. Committee on Missionary
Personnel. New Trends in Missionary
Training in the United States. New York:
Division of Foreign Missions, NCCC, 1957.

3110. National Council of the Churches of Christ in
the United States of America. Division of
Foreign Missions. Committee on Missionary
Personnel. Recruiting, Selection and
Training of Missionaries in North America.
New York: Division of Foreign Missiions,
NCCC, 1957.

3111. "Nature of the Ministry." National Council Outlook 7 (June 1957):17-18.

3112. Naumann, William Henry. "Theology and German-American Evangelicalism: The Role of Theology in the Church of the United Brethren in Christ and the Evangelical Association." Ph.D. dissertation, Yale University, 1966.

3113. Nauss, Allen. "Personality Changes among Students in a Conservative Seminary." Journal for the Scientific Study of Religion 11 (December 1972):377-88.

3114. Nauss, A. "Personality Stability and Change among Ministerial Students [bibliog.]." Religious Education 67 (November 1972):469-75.

3115. Naylor, Natalie A. "The Theological Seminary in the Configuration of American Higher Education: The Ante-Bellum Years." History of Education Quarterly 17 (Spring 1977):17-30.

3116. Naylor, Robert E. "Southwestern and Evangelism [Founders' Day Message, 12 March 1976]." Southwestern Journal of Theology 19 (Fall 1976):81-94.

3117. Neal, Bart Courtney. "A Study of Accountability in Secular Education in the United States to Determine Possible Principles for Theological Education among Southern Baptists." Ed.D. dissertation, New Orleans Baptist Theological Seminary, 1981.

3118. "Necessary Qualifications for the Christian Ministry." Outlook 105 (October 11, 1913):293-4.

3119. "Needs of Theological Education." School and Society 95 (March 18, 1967):174-5.

3120. Neely, H. A. "(Qualifications for the Ministry.)" American Church Review 27 (1875):481+.

3121. Neely, Thomas Benjamin. The Church Lyceum: Its Organization and Management. New York: Phillips & Hunt, 1882.

270

3122. "Negro on the Board [Union Theological Seminary, NYC]." Time 39 (June 1, 1942):57.

3123. Nelson, C. Ellis. "Church Education and the Teaching of Religion in the Public Domain." Theological Education 3 (Spring 1967):384-95.

3124. Nelson, C. Ellis. "The Relation of Seminary Training to Congregational Education." Religious Education 63 (July-August 1968):301-8.

3125. Nelson, Carl Ellis. Using Evaluation in Theological Education. Nashville: Discipleship Resources, 1975.

3126. Nelson, David Theodore. Luther College, 1861-1961. Decorah, Ia.: Luther College Press, 1961.

3127. Nelson, E. Clifford and Fevold, Eugene L. The Lutheran Church among Norwegian-Americans: A History of the Evangelical Lutheran Church. 2 vols. Minneapolis: Augsburg Publishing House, 1960.

3128. Nelson, E. Clifford. "Lutheran Identity in the USA, Historically Considered." Dialog 16 (Fall 1977):249-56.

3129. Nelson, E. Clifford, ed. The Lutherans in North America. Philadelphia: Fortress Press, 1975.

3130. Nelson, J. Robert. "The Church's Intellectual Center." Christian Century 75 (April 23, 1958):489-91.

3131. Nelson, J. Robert. "The Seminary: Academy and Chapel." Theological Education 1 (Autumn 1964):53-62.

3132. Nelson, J. R. "Theological Education of Homo Ecumenicus." Ecumenical Review 15 (January 1963):164-72.

3133. Nelson, John Oliver. "Archibald Alexander, Winsome Conservative (1772-1851)." Journal of the Presbyterian Historical Society 35 (March 1957):15-32.

3134.   Nelson, John Oliver. "Trends toward a
        Relevant Ministry." Christian Century 67
        (April 26, 1950):525-7.

3135.   Nelson, John Oliver. "Vocation, Theism and
        Testing." Pastoral Psychology 9 (December
        1958):33-40.

3136.   Nelson, Kenneth Arlyn. "Richard Clarke Cabot
        and the Development of Clinical Pastoral
        Education" Ph.D. dissertation, University
        of Iowa, 1970.

3137.   Nelson, Robert E. "Trusteeship: The Tradi-
        tion of Voluntary Action." Theological
        Education 12 (Autumn 1975):57-63.

3138.   Nelson, Rudolph L. "Fundamentalism at
        Harvard: The Case of Edward John Carnell."
        Quarterly Review (Methodist) 2 (Summer
        1982):79-98.

3139.   Nelson, W. S. "Theological Education for
        Ministers." Southern Workman 61 (December
        1932):504-9.

3140.   Nettleton, Douglas. "Social Welfare
        Ministries Conference: A Seminarian's
        Report." Church and Society 71 (May-June
        1981):60-1.

3141.   Neuhaus, Richard John. "Freedom for
        Ministry." Christian Century 94 (February
        2, 1977):81-6.

3142.   Neuner, J. "Ecumenical Formation in
        Seminaries." Clergy Monthly 32, no. 1
        (1968):6-16.

3143.   Neville, Graham. "Training for a Prophetic
        Ministry." Theology 61 (August 1958):324-
        7.

3144.   Nevin, John Williamson. My Own Life: The
        Earlier Years. Papers of the Eastern
        Chapter, Historical Society of the
        Evangelical & Reformed Church, No. 1.
        Lancaster, Pa., 1964.

3145.   Nevins, John F. A Study of the Organization
        and Operation of Voluntary Accrediting
        Agencies. Washington, D.C.: Catholic
        University of America Press, 1959.

3146. "A New Approach to the Problem of Clerical Recruitment." Christian Century 72 (October 19, 1955):1197-8.

3147. "New Buildings of the Union Theological Seminary." Biblical World 37 (February 1911):137-9.

3148. "New Degrees: Cosmetic Changes? Doctor of Ministry Degree." Christian Century 93 (February 4, 1976):84.

3149. "New Departure at Union Seminary." Christian Century 71 (May 19, 1954):604.

3150. New England Deaconess Association, Boston. Annual Report, 1906.

3151. New England Deaconess Association, Boston. Annual Report, 1910.

3152. New England Deaconess Association, Boston. Annual Report, 1912.

3153. New England Deaconess Association, Boston. Annual Report, 1916.

3154. New England Deaconess Association, Boston. Annual Report, 1917.

3155. New England Deaconess Home and Training School, Boston. Annual Report, 1889-90.

3156. New England Deaconess Home and Training School, Boston. Annual Report, 1890-91.

3157. New England Deaconess Home and Training School, Boston. Annual Report, 1891-92.

3158. "New Entry and a Change of Name: Center for Theological Studies." Christianity Today 23 (February 16, 1979):44+.

3159. "New Home [Union Theological Seminary, NYC]." Outlook 96 (December 10, 1910):802-3.

3160. "New Life in the Seminaries." Christian Century 64 (February 19, 1947):230-2.

3161. "New Lutheran School of Theology [Chicago]." Dialog 1 (Autumn 1962):11.

3162. "New Note at Harvard." Christian Century 70
       (October 14, 1953):1158-60.

3163. New Schaff-Herzog Encyclopedia of Religious
       Knowledge, 11th ed. S.v. "The History of
       Theological Education," by Ferdinand Cohrs
       and Henry K. Rowe.

3164. The New Schaff-Herzog Encyclopedia of Reli-
       gious Knowledge, 1950 ed. "Theological
       Libraries."

3165. New Schaff-Herzog Encyclopedia of Religious
       Knowledge, 11th ed. S.v. "Theological
       Seminaries."

3166. "A New School of Evangelism and World Mission
       Is Planned for Asbury Theological
       Seminary." Christianity Today 24 (January
       4, 1980):64.

3167. "New Style Theological Education [at Meadville
       Theological School]." Hibbert Journal 62
       (Summer 1964):192-4.

3168. "New Trends for Seminaries." America 113
       (November 27, 1965):660.

3169. New York. General Theological Seminary of the
       Protestant Episcopal Church in the United
       States. Proceedings Relating to the
       Organization of the General Theological
       Seminary of the Protestant Episcopal Church
       in the United States of America... New
       York: D. Dana, 1854.

3170. New York (State). Education Dept. Profes-
       sional Education in U.S. Theology. 1899.

3171. Newby, James R. "Try a Community Seminary."
       Christian Ministry 13 (May 1982):34+.

3172. Newell, Altus. "The Formation of a Profes-
       sional Baptist Ministry in the South, 1800-
       1860." A Research Paper Presented to Dr.
       Penrose St. Ament, The Southern Baptist
       Theological Seminary, in Partial Fulfill-
       ment of the Requirements of the Course
       Church History, October 19, 1971.

3173. Newell, James Altus. "A Strategy for
       Seminary-Related Continuing Education for
       Pastors." Ph.D. dissertation, Southern

Baptist Theological Seminary, 1974.

3174. Newell, Neal Curtis, Jr. "The Development of
Composite Minnesota Multiphasic Personality
Inventory Profiles on Fall 1976 Incoming
Students at Southwestern Baptist Theologi-
cal Seminary and Comparisons of Profiles
Based upon Sex, Marital Status and School
of Study." Ed.D. dissertation, South-
western Baptist Theological Seminary, 1977.

3175. Newhall, Fales H. "Ministerial Education."
Methodist Quarterly Review 16 (New Series)
(October 1864):533-52.

3176. Newhall, Jannette E. "There Were Giants in
Those Days: Pioneer Women and Boston
University." Nexus 7 (November 1963):17-
23, 41-42.

3177. Newman, Albert Henry. A History of the
Baptist Churches in the United States. New
York: Christian Literature Co., 1894.

3178. Newman, Stewart A. W. T. Connor: Theologian
of the Southwest. Nashville: Broadman
Press, 1964.

3179. Newman, William M. "Role Conflict in the
Ministry and the Role of the Seminary: A
Pilot Study." Sociological Analysis 32
(Winter 1971):238-48.

3180. "News and Views: Plans to Involve Seminarians
in Peace Corps Opposed." Commonweal 86
(September 22, 1967):562.

3181. "News: Roundup: Seminaries." Christian
Century 84 (April 26, 1967):572-4.

3182. Newton, Joseph Fort. Some Living Masters of
the Pulpit. New York: Doran, 1923.

3183. "Newton Theological Institution." American
Baptist Magazine 6 (New Series) (April
1826):128-9.; (October 1826):308.

3184. Newton Theological Institution, Newton Center,
Mass. Addresses Delivered at the Inauguration of George Edwin Horr. Imprinted for
the Trustees of the Newton Theological
Institution, 1909.

275

3185. Newton Theological Institution. Newton
Center, Mass. Historical Addresses
Delivered at the Newton Centennial, June,
1925. Newton Centre, Mass.: For the
Institution, 1926.

3186. Newton Theological Institution, Newton Center,
Mass. Newton Seminary and the Christian
Ministry. Newton Centre, Mass.: 1913.

3187. Nicholl, Grier. "The Image of the Protestant
Minister in the Christian Social Novel."
Church History 37 (September 1968):319-34.

3188. Nichols, J. H. "Art of Church History."
Church History 20 (March 1951):3-9.

3189. Nichols, J. H. "Theological Education at
Princeton." Princeton Seminary Bulletin 63
(December 1970):41-3.

3190. Nichols, J. Randall. "Great D. Min. Experiment." Theology Today 34 (January 1978):
431-5.

3191. Nichols, J. Randall. "The 'Matter' with
Homiletics: A Proposal for Preaching
Education." Anglican Theological Review 63
(April 1981):139-52.

3192. Nichols, J. Randall. "What Is the Matter with
the Teaching of Preaching?" Anglican
Theological Review 62 (July 1980):221-38.

3193. Nichols, James Hastings. "History in the
Theological Curriculum." Journal of
Religion 26 (1946):183-9.

3194. Nichols, James Hastings. "Protestantism and
Theological Education." American Association of Theological Schools. Proceedings
(1952):110-17.

3195. Nichols, James Hastings. "Theological
Education as Preparation for Teaching and
Research." Theological Education 7 (Spring
1971):197-200.

3196. Nichols, Robert Hastings. Presbyterianism in
New York State. Philadelphia: Published
for the Presbyterian Historical Society by
Westminster Press, 1963.

3197. Nicholson, Joseph William and Mays, Benjamin
Elijah. The Negro's Church. 1933;
reprint ed., New York: Russell & Russell,
1969.

3198. Nicholson, Stephen David. "Locus of Control
as a Function of Seminary Training." M.A.
thesis, North Texas State University, 1982.

3199. Nickel, Ronald Paul. "Professional Autonomy
in the Denominational Seminary: A Vulner-
ability Model." Ph.D. dissertation,
Washington University, 1977.

3200. Nicole, Roger. "Adventures and Discoveries of
a Book Rat." American Theological Library
Association. Proceedings 29 (1975):95-100.

3201. Niebuhr, Helmut Richard; Williams, Daniel Day
and Gustafson, James M. The Advancement of
Theological Education. New York: Harper,
1957.

3202. Niebuhr, Helmut Richard. "The Main Issues in
Theological Education." Theology Today 11
(January 1955):512-27.

3203. Niebuhr, Helmut Richard and Williams, Daniel
D., eds. The Ministry in Historical
Perspectives. New York: Harper, 1956.

3204. Niebuhr, Helmut Richard; Williams, Daniel Day
and Gustafson, James M. The Purpose of the
Church and Its Ministry: Reflections on
the Aims of Theological Education. New
York: Harper, 1956.

3205. Niebuhr, Helmut Richard. "Seminary in the
Ecumenical Age." Princeton Seminary
Bulletin 54 (July 1960):38-45.

3206. Niebuhr, Helmut Richard. The Social Sources
of Denominationalism. New York: Meridian
Books, 1957. (First published in 1929.)

3207. Niebuhr, Helmut Richard. "Why Restudy Theological Education?" Christian Century 71
(April 28, 1954):516+.

3208. Niebuhr, Reinhold. "Minute on the Death of
Dr. Coffin." Union Seminary Quarterly
Review 10 (January 1955):5-7.

3209. Niedner, Frederick. "Walther's Pastoral Theology: An Appreciation." Concordia Theological Monthly 32 (October 1961):627-31.

3210. Nielsen, Charles Merritt. "A Modest Proposal for Theological Education." Christianity Today 17 (May 25, 1973):4-6.

3211. Nielsen, E. W. "Towards Excellence in Theological Education." Southeast Asia Journal of Theology 6-7 (April-July 1965):95-108.

3212. Nieting, Lorenz. "Sermon [To a Congregation of Seminarians]." Dialog 16 (1977):46-8.

3213. Nippold, Friedrich Wilhelm Frantz. Handbuch der Neuesten Kirchengeschichte. 5 vols. Berlin: Wiegand & Schotte, 1889-1906, vol. 5.

3214. Njuguna, Isaac. "A Dialogical Interpretation of Clinical Pastoral Education Supervision." Ph.D. dissertation, Louisville Presbyterian Theological Seminary, 1979.

3215. Noble, David W. The Paradox of Progressive Thought. Minneapolis: University of Minnesota Press, 1958.

3216. Nock, A. J. "Value to the Clergyman of Training in the Classics." School Review 16 (June 1908):383-90.

3217. Nolde, Otto Fred. "Christian Education in the Theological Seminary." Lutheran Church Quarterly 5 (January 1932):1-18.

3218. Nolde, O. F. Department of Christian Education in the Theological Seminary. University of Pennsylvania, 1929.

3219. Noll, Mark A. "The Founding of Princeton Seminary." Western Theological Journal 42, no. 1 (Fall 1979):72-110.

3220. Noll, Mark A. "Jacob Green's Proposal for Seminaries [with text of Letter to J. Bellamy, Nov. 22, 1775]." Journal of Presbyterian History 58 (Fall 1980):210-22.

278

3221. "A Nondenominational Michigan Bible College Finally Closed This Fall." Christianity Today 24 (November 7, 1980):88.

3222. Norris, Beauford A. "Philosophy of Ministerial Education." Encounter 17 (Autumn 1956):403-11.

3223. Norris, Beauford A. "Seminary Climate." Encounter 25 (Summer 1964):309-13.

3224. Norris, John F. "A Central Theological Seminary." Christian Advocate and Journal (New York) 29 (March 23, 1854):1.

3225. Norris, Larry Richard. "A Study of Selected Characteristics of Continuing Theological Education in the Seminaries of the United Methodist Church." Ph.D. dissertation, Michigan State University, 1979.

3226. Norris, Richard A., Jr. "The Episcopal Church and Theological Education: Some Remarks." Anglican Theological Review, Suppl. Series, no. 2 (1973):88-95.

3227. Northcutt, Jesse J. "Preparation for Ministry: Recent Developments." Southwestern Journal of Theology 15 (Spring 1973):51-6.

3228. Northcutt, J. J. "Walter Thomas Conner, Theologian of Southwestern." Southwestern Journal of Theology 9 (Fall 1966):81-9.

3229. Northern Baptist Board of Education. Theological Education in the Convention. Philadelphia: American Baptist Publishing Society, 1945.

3230. Northfield, H. D. "Training of Men Missionaries." International Review of Missions 46 (January 1957):59-67.

3231. "Northwest Needs New Seminary." Christian Century 74 (July 17, 1957):861.

3232. Norton, Andrews. Inaugural Discourse: Delivered before the University in Cambridge, August 10, 1819. Cambridge: Printed by Hilliard & Metcalf.

3233. Norton, Fred Lewis, ed. <u>A College of</u>
<u>Colleges, Led by D. L. Moody.</u> New York:
        Fleming H. Revell Co., 1889?

3234. Norwood, Frederick Abbott. <u>Dawn to Midday at</u>
       <u>Garrett.</u> Evanston, Ill.: Garrett-
       Evangelical Theological Seminary, 1978.

3235. Norwood, Frederick Abbott. "The Shaping of
       the Methodist Ministry." <u>Religion in Life</u>
       43 (Autumn 1974):337-51.

3236. Norwood, Frederick Abbott. "Some Newly
       Discovered Unpublished Letters, 1808-1825."
       <u>Methodist History</u> 3, no. 4 (1965):3-24.

3237. Norwood, Percy V. "Jubilee College,
       Illinois." <u>Historical Magazine of the</u>
       <u>Protestant Episcopal Church</u> 11 (June
       1942):44-58.

3238. "Not All Is Golden at Golden Gate." <u>Christian</u>
       <u>Century</u> 83 (May 25, 1966):672-3.

3239. "A Notable Movement Toward Protestant Unity."
       <u>School and Society</u> 58 (July 10, 1943):22.

3240. Nottingham, W. J. "Third World First: The
       Relation of Theological Education to World
       Mission." <u>Lexington Theological Quarterly</u>
       4 (October 1969):97-114.

3241. Nouwen, Henri J. M. "Anton T. Boisen and
       Theology through Living Human Documents."
       <u>Pastoral Psychology</u> 19 (September 1968):49-
       63.

3242. Nouwen, Henri J. M. "Education to the
       Ministry." <u>Theological Education</u> 9 (Autumn
       1972):48-57.

3243. Nouwen, Henri J. M. "Training for Campus
       Ministry." <u>Counseling and Values</u> 16
       (Winter 1972):114-24.

3244. Novak, Michael. "Post-Seminary Thoughts."
       <u>Commonweal</u> 83 (October 8, 1965):9-12.
       (Discussion) 83 (October 29, 1965):111+;
       (November 5, 1965):166-7.

3245. Novak, Steven J. <u>The Rights of Youth:</u>
       <u>American Colleges and Student Revolt, 1798-</u>
       <u>1815.</u> Cambridge: Harvard University

Press, 1977.

3246. Novotny, D. "Awarded to Bangor Seminary."
       Christian Century 78 (August 30, 1961):10-
       36.

3247. Noyce, Gaylord B., ed. Education for
       Ministry: Theology, Preparedness, Praxis:
       15th Biennial Meeting, Association for
       Professional Education for Ministry.
       Toronto: Trinity College, 1978.

3248. Ntwasa, S. "Training of Black Ministers
       Today." International Review of Missions
       61 (April 1972):177-82.

3249. Nunnally, Stuart. "Education for a Pastoral
       Ministry." Religion In Life 31 (1962):515-
       18.

3250. Nuttall, Geoffrey Fillingham. Richard Baxter.
       London: Nelson, 1965.

3251. Nuttall, Geoffrey Fillingham. Richard Baxter
       and Philip Doddridge. London: Oxford
       University Press, 1951.

3252. Nyce, Dorothy Yoder. "Grieving People [CPE]."
       Journal of Pastoral Care 36, no. 1 (1982):
       36-46.

3253. Nyholm, Paul C. The Americanization of the
       Danish Lutheran Churches in America.
       Copenhagen: Institute for Danish Church
       History: Distributed by Augsburg
       Publishing House, Minneapolis, 1963.

3254. Nykamp, R. A. "Field Education: An Oppor-
       tunity for Reflection on the Ministry."
       Reformed Review 19 (March 1966):50-7.

3255. Nykamp, R. A. "Use of Reality Practice in a
       Pastoral Counseling Course." Theological
       Education 5 (Summer 1969, Suppl. 1):486-96.

3256. Oates, Stephen B. "The Intellectual Odyssey
       of Martin Luther King." Massachusetts
       Review 22, no. 2 (1981):301-20.

3257. Oates, W. E. "Counseling by Seminarians."
       Journal of Pastoral Care 8, no. 3
       (1954):154-9.

3258. Oates, W. E. "In Relation To Theological
Education." Pastoral Psychology 21
(February 1970):49-55.

3259. Oates, W. E. "Professor as Bishop." Journal
of Pastoral Care 15 (Summer 1961):65-71.

3260. Oates, Wayne E. "Seminary Training in Mental
Health for Parish Clergymen." In Community
Mental Health. Edited by Howard J.
Clinebell. Nashville: Abingdon Press,
1970.

3261. O'Boyle, Thomas F. "Spiritual Quest: The
Ministry Attracts Professionals Seeking a
More Fulfilling Life: A Dentist Turns
Seminarian, Psychiatrist Is Chaplain:
Money Can Be a Problem: From U.S. Steel to
the Pulpit." Wall Street Journal (October
22, 1982):1.

3262. O'Brian, John Lord. "What Future for Our
Divinity School? [1721-1952]." Harvard
Alumni Bulletin 54 (February 9, 1952):383-
6.

3263. O'Brian, R. E. "Minister's Degree." School
and Society 33 (January 17, 1931):87-9;
(Revised) Religious Education 27 (January
1932):66-9.

3264. O'Brian, Robert E. "The Preacher's Degree."
Religious Education 27 (January 1932):66-9.

3265. O'Brien, David J. American Catholics and
Social Reform: The New Deal Years. New
York: Oxford University Press, 1968.

3266. O'Brien, Elmer J. "The Center for the Study
of Evangelical United Brethren History."
In Women's Rightful Place. Edited by
Donald K. Gorrell. Dayton, Ohio: United
Theological Seminary, 1980.

3267. O'Brien, Elmer J. "Challenges and Diffi-
culties for the Independent Seminary
Library." American Theological Library
Association. Proceedings 29 (1975):71-5.

3268. O'Brien, Elmer J. "The Methodist Collections
at Garrett Theological Seminary."
Methodist History 8, no. 3 (1970):28-37.

3269. Oden, T. C. "Christian Ethics amid Pietistic Culture-Protestantism." Christian Century 83 (April 27, 1966):525-6+.

3270. Oden, Thomas C. "Seminary and Preseminary Education: Analysis of Two A.A.T.S. Reports." Christian Century 84 (April 26, 1967):536.

3271. O'Donoghue, Joseph. "Reforming the Seminaries." Commonweal 81 (November 6, 1964):194-6. "Discussion." 81 (December 11, 1964):391-2. "Discussion." 81 (January 6, 1965):466+.

3272. Oetting, E. R. et al. "Problems in Program Evaluation: A Ministers' Workshop." Mental Hygiene 53 (April 1969):214-17.

3273. Oetting, W. "Function of Historical Theology in the Theological Training Program." Concordia Theological Monthly 34 (July 1963):401-8.

3274. Offermann, H. "The Church, the Seminary, and the Study of Theology." Lutheran Church Quarterly 18 (1945):10-18.

3275. Offermann, H. "Faith, Theology and Theological Education." Lutheran Church Quarterly 8 (1935):398-410.

3276. Offermann, H. "Place of Biblical Criticism in a Lutheran Seminary." Lutheran Church Quarterly 10 (October 1937):396-410.

3277. Olbricht, Thomas H. "Charles Hodge as an American New Testament Interpreter." Journal of Presbyterian History 57, no. 2 (Summer 1979):117-33.

3278. "Old Union Theological Seminary." Architectural Record 22 (August 1907):151-4.

3279. Olsen, W. A. "Assets and Liabilities: The Bible Institute Comes of Age." Christianity Today 5 (February 27, 1961):29-30.

3280. Olson, Adolf. "Educational Work among the Swedish Baptists of America." Swedish Historical Society of America Yearbook 11 (1926):125-40.

3281. Olson, A. and Olson, V. A. Seventy-Five
Years. [Bethel Theological Seminary, St.
Paul, Minn.]. Chicago: Conference Press,
1946.

3282. Olson, D., ed. "Urban Perspective on Pastoral
Education: Participation of Evangelical
Seminaries in the Seminary Consortium for
Urban Pastoral Education: Interviews."
Christianity Today 22 (June 2, 1978):17-21.

3283. Olson, L. "Students of the Philadelphia
Divinity School Learn about Hospitals and
Nursing." Public Health Nursing 37
(February 1945):92.

3284. Olson, Oscar Nils. The Augustana Lutheran
Church in America 1860-1910. Vol. 2: The
Formative Period. Rock Island, Ill.:
Augustana Book Concern, 1950-

3285. Olson, Richard Allan. "Training Environment
and Conceptual Level in Lutheran Theological Internship." Ed.D. dissertation,
Columbia University, 1970.

3286. "On Clerical Education, in Relation to Sacred
Literature." Journal of Sacred Literature
5 (New Series) (October 1853):76-102.

3287. "On Learning, as a Qualification for the
Exercise of the Christian Ministry."
Congregational Magazine 1 (New Series)
(1837):483-90.

3288. "On the Education of Pious Youth for the
Gospel Ministry." Panoplist 3 (October
1807):211-13.

3289. Oosterzee, Johannes Jacobus van. Practical
Theology: A Manual for Theological
Students. Translated and Adapted to the
Use of English Readers by Maurice J. Evans.
2d ed. London: Hodder & Stoughton, 1889.

3290. "Opportunities for Study, Training and
Experience in Pastoral Psychology - 1955."
Pastoral Psychology 5 (January 1955):22-40.

3291. "Opportunities for Study, Training and
Experience in Pastoral Psychology - 1956."
Pastoral Psychology 6 (January 1956):23-49.

3292. "Opportunities for Study, Training and
Experience in Pastoral Psychology - 1958."
Pastoral Psychology 8 (January 1958):17-31.

3293. "Opportunities for Study, Training and
Experience in Pastoral Psychology - 1961."
Pastoral Psychology 11 (January 1961):11-
27.

3294. "Opportunities for Study, Training, Experience
and Continuing Education in Pastoral
Psychology." Pastoral Psychology 15
(February 1964):48-52.

3295. "Opportunities for Study, Training, and
Experience in Pastoral Psychology - 1965."
Compiled by National Council of the
Churches of Christ in the U.S.A. Department
of Ministry, Vocation, and Pastoral
Services. Pastoral Psychology 15 (January
1965):15-38.

3296. "Opportunities for Study, Training, and
Experience in Pastoral Psychology - 1967-
68." Compiled by the Department of
Ministry, Vocation, and Pastoral Services
of the National Council of the Churches of
Christ in the U.S.A. Pastoral Psychology
17 (January 1967):7-23.

3297. "Opportunities for Study, Training, and
Experience in Pastoral Psychology, 1969-
1970." Pastoral Psychology 20 (January
1969):8-26.

3298. "Optional Studies in the Seminary." Old
Testament Student 4 (April 1885):379.

3299. "Original Papers in Relation to a Course of
Liberal Education." American Journal of
Science and Arts 15 (January 1829):297-351.

3300. Orlans, Harold. Private Accreditation and
Public Eligibility. Lexington, Mass.:
D.C. Heath & Co., 1975.

3301. O'Rourke, D. K. "Dissimilar Field Placements
in the Pastoral Training Seminar: A Way of
Instructing in the Pastoral Contract."
Theological Education 5 (Summer 1969,
Suppl. 1):455-63.

3302. O'Rourke, David K. "Double Messages in
       Seminary Training." Theological Education
       5 (Summer 1969, Suppl 1):411-19.

3303. Orr, J. Alvin. "The Spirit of the Theological
       Teacher." Bibliotheca Sacra 81 (April
       1924):144-51.

3304. Orr, James Edwin. The Flaming Tongue: The
       Impact of Twentieth Century Revivals.
       Chicago: Moody Press, 1973: pp. 65-100.

3305. Orsy, Ladisias M. "Theology, University and a
       Brave New World." America 124 (June 12,
       1971):606-8.

3306. Orth, G and Kraemer, R. "Cooperative Venture
       [Evanston Theological Seminary, Naperville,
       Illinois]." Library Journal 79 (December
       15, 1954):2371-4.

3307. "Orthodoxy at Andover." Outlook 71 (July 19,
       1902):751-2.

3308. Osborn, Albert. John Fletcher Hurst: A
       Biography. New York: Eaton & Mains, 1905.

3309. Osborn, Eric. "Methods and Problems in
       Patristic Study." Union Seminary Quarterly
       Review 36 (Fall 1980):45-54.

3310. Osborn, Ronald E. "Portrait of a Churchman:
       The Ministry of O. L. Shelton." Encounter
       20, no. 2 (1959):132-67.

3311. Osborn, Ronald Ed., ed. The Reformation of
       Tradition. St. Louis, Mo.: Bethany Press,
       1963.

3312. Osgood, Howard. "President Harper's
       Lectures." Bibliotheca Sacra 52 (April
       1895):323-4.

3313. Osterhaven, M. Eugene et al. "Training
       Scribes for the Kingdom of Heaven: In
       Celebration of Cook Center for Theological
       Research." Reformed Review 35 (Spring
       1982):127-61.

3314. Ottensmeyer, Hilary. "Blueprint for
       Seminaries" America 113 (December 18,
       1965):780-1.

3315. Ottersberg, Gerhard. "Education: The Wartburgs." Palimpsest 35 (June 1954):229-36.

3316. Ottman, Ford Cyrinde. J. Wilbur Chapman: A Biography. Garden City, N.Y.: Doubleday, Page & Co., 1920.

3317. "Our Local Ministry." Methodist Quarterly Review 17 (New Series) (October 1865):549-59.

3318. "Our Ministry." Methodist Quarterly Review 19 (New Series) (October 1867):590+.

3319. "Our Schools of Theology." Methodist Review 78 (July 1896):618-20.

3320. "Our Theological School." Christian Advocate (Nashville) 29 (New Series) (December 25, 1869):1.

3321. "Our Theological School." Christian Advocate (Nashville) 30 (New Series) (February 19, 1870):1.

3322. Outler, A. C. "Fund for Evangelical Scholars [Foundation For Theological Education]." Christian Century 97 (February 6-13, 1980):138-40.

3323. "Outlines of a Theological Institution." Panoplist 3 (January 1808):345-8.

3324. "The Oversupply of Clergymen." Outlook 63 (September 23, 1899):222-5.

3325. Owen, W. M. "Preparing Ministers for Leadership of Musical Services." Religious Education 12 (October 1917):377-80.

3326. Owens, David Benton, ed. These Hundred Years: The Centennial History of Capital University. Columbus, Ohio: Capital University, 1950.

3327. Oxenden, Ashton. The Pastoral Office: Its Duties, Difficulties, Privileges, and Prospects. New York, 1857.

3328. Oxtoby, F. B. "Differences in Biblical Teaching in College and Seminary."

Religious Education 14 (August 1919):256-60.

3329.   Oxtoby, G. C.   "Seminaries Look to the
        Future." Christian Century 73 (July 25,
        1956):879+.

3330.   Ozment, Steven E.   The Reformation in the
        Cities: The Appeal of Protestantism to
        Sixteenth-Century Germany and Switzerland.
        New Haven: Yale University Press, 1975.

3331.   Pacala, Leon. "Reflection on the State of
        Theological Education in the 1980's."
        Theological Education 18 (Fall 1981):9-43.

3332.   Packard, Joseph, Jr. "Theological Seminary of
        Virginia." Church Review 47 (1886):105-12.

3333.   Padovano, Anthony T. "Modern Seminarian."
        Catholic World 206 (February 1968):219-22.

3334.   Page, Robert J. "Lengthening the Ropes and
        Strengthening the Stakes in Smaller
        Schools." Theological Education 2 (Autumn
        1965):23-7.

3335.   Pagett, Betty S., comp. "Women in Theological
        Education: Selected Resources." Theolog-
        ical Education 8 (Summer 1972):278-81.

3336.   Paine, Gregory Lansing. "John Burroughs and
        the Cooperstown Seminary." New York
        History 44, no. 1 (1963):60-77.

3337.   Painter, Gerald L. and Brown, Raymond Bryan.
        "Student Power and Governance." Theologi-
        cal Education 7 (Autumn 1970):47-8.

3338.   Palfrey, John G. "An Address Delivered before
        the Society for Promoting Theological
        Education." Christian Examiner 11
        (September 1831):84-99.

3339.   Palfrey, John G. "Education for the
        Ministry." Christian Examiner 11
        (September 1881):84-99.

3340.   Pallone, N. J. and Banks, R. R. "Vocational
        Satisfaction among Ministerial Students:
        Seventh Day Adventists." Personnel and
        Guidance Journal 46 (May 1968):870-5.

3341. Palmer, Albert Wentworth. Albert W. Palmer:
       A Life Extended. Edited by Margaret Palmer
       Taylor. Athens, Ohio: Lawhead Press,
       1968.

3342. Palmer, Albert Wentworth. "How Can a Theo-
       logical Seminary Best Serve the Present
       Age." Chicago Theological Seminary
       Register 20 (November 1930):1-10.

3343. Palmer, Albert W. "The Threat to the
       Protestant Ministry." Christian Century 60
       (March 31, 1943):386-7.

3344. Palmer, Benjamin Morgan. The Life and Letters
       of James Henry Thornwell. New York: Arno
       Press, 1969. (Reprint of the 1875 ed.)

3345. Palmer, George Herbert. The Autobiography of
       a Philosopher. Boston: Houghton Mifflin
       Co., 1930.

3346. Palmer, Lester D. "Field Education:
       Immediate Equipping for Ultimate Building."
       College of the Bible Quarterly 41 (January
       1964):1-7.

3347. Pangburn, Jessie May. The Evolution of the
       American Teachers College. New York:
       Teachers College, Columbia University,
       1932.

3348. "Parachurch Fallout: Seminary Students."
       Christianity Today 25 (November 6,
       1981):36-7.

3349. "Parish Ministry Losing Lure." Christian
       Century 80 (December 11, 1963):1537.

3350. Park, Edwards Amasa. "Introductory Essay on
       the Religious Influence of Theological
       Seminaries." In Writings of...William
       Bradford Homer, pp. [xi]-lix. By William
       Bradford Homer. Boston: T. R. Marvin,
       1849.

3351. Park, Edwards Amasa. "Life and Services of
       Professor B. B. Edwards." Bibliotheca
       Sacra 9 (October 1852):783-821.

3352. Park, Edwards Amasa. Memoir of Nathaniel
       Emmons: With Sketches of His Friends and
       Pupils. Boston: Congregational Board of

Publication, 1861.

3353. Park, Edwards Amasa. "Moses Stuart." In his
Memorial Collection of Sermons, pp. 179-
217. Boston: Pilgrim Press, 1902.

3354. Park, Edwards Amasa. Sketch of the Life and
Character of Prof. Tholuck. Edinburgh:
Thomas Clark, 1840.

3355. Park, Edwards A. "What Can Be Done for
Augmenting the Number of Christian
Ministers?" Bibliotheca Sacra 28 (January
1871):60-97.

3356. Park, William Edwards. "The Andover
Question." Bibliotheca Sacra 64 (January
1907):168-79.

3357. Parker, Duane Frank. "Development of a
Nationally Accredited Clinical Pastoral
Education Program." Ph.D. dissertation,
Kansas State University, 1979.

3358. Parker, Everett C. "Biblical Seminary Controversy." Christian Century 80 (March 20,
1963):380-2.

3359. Parker, Everett C. "Testing Ministerial
Candidates." Christian Century 80 (January
2, 1963):28-9.

3360. Parker, Harold M., Jr. "A New School
Presbyterian Seminary in Woodford County."
Register of the Kentucky Historical Society
74 (1976):99-111.

3361. Parker, Harold M., Jr. "A School of the
Prophets at Maryville." Tennessee Historical Quarterly 34, no. 1 (1975):72-90.

3362. Parker, John. "The Biblical Institute."
Christian Advocate (New York) 29 (February
2, 1854):17.

3363. Parks, Mitzi Alice Harrington. "A Descriptive
Study of Clinical Pastoral Education
Programs in Public Residential Institutions
for the Mentally Retarded." Ed.D. dissertation, University of Maryland, 1978.

3364. Parmenter, M. F. "Awakening of Chinese Souls:
Stories of Women in the Bible Teachers'

290

Training School." <u>Missionary Review of the World</u> 47 (April 1924):278-86.

3365. Parmenter, M. F. "Training Bible Teachers for China." <u>Missionary Review of the World</u> 46 (February 1923):104-8.

3366. Parsons, E. Spencer. "We Minister Where the Faith of the Church, the Learning of the University, and the Experiences of the World Converge." <u>Criterion</u> 6 (Summer 1967):27-9.

3367. Parsons, Mike. "Warfield and Scripture." <u>Churchman: A Quarterly Journal of Anglican Theology</u> 91 (July 1977):198-220.

3368. Paschal, George Washington. <u>History of Wake Forest College</u>. 3 vols. Wake Forest, N.C.: Wake Forest College, 1935.

3369. "Pastoral Training under Tutors: Requirements of the Presbyterian Church in America." <u>Christianity Today</u> 22 (October 7, 1977):61-3.

3370. "Pastors and Morals." <u>Journal of Pastoral Care</u> 2 (Winter 1948):36-9.

3371. "The Pastors' Institute of the Divinity School of the University of Chicago." <u>School and Society</u> 44 (July 4, 1936):7-8.

3372. <u>The Pastor's Manual, A Selection of Tracts... on Pastoral Duty</u>. Hudson, Ohio: Sawyer, Ingersoll, & Co., 1852.

3373. Paterson, Samuel White. "The Centenary of Clement Clarke Moore - Poet of Christmas Eve." <u>Historical Magazine of the Protestant Episcopal Church</u> 32, no. 3 (1963):211-20.

3374. Paton, David Macdonald. "Bridgebuilding: Seminary, Pulpit, Pew." <u>Christian Century</u> 73 (April 25, 1956):510+.

3375. "Patterns of Continuing Education." <u>Theological Education</u> 1 (Summer 1965):213-25.

3376. Patterson, R. M. "The Supply of Ministers." <u>Presbyterian Review</u> 1 (July 1880):526-48.

3377. Patterson, Samuel White. The Pact of
       Christmas Eve: A Life of Clement Clarke
       Moore, 1779-1863. New York: Morehouse-
       Gorham Co, 1956.

3378. Patterson, W. Morgan. "An Installation
       Address: Theological Education and the
       Baptist Experience." Presented October 12,
       1976, Golden Gate Baptist Seminary, Mill
       Valley, California. (Mimeographed)

3379. Patterson, W. Morgan. "Baptist Growth in
       America: Evaluation of Trends." Baptist
       History and Heritage 14, no. 1 (1979):16-
       26.

3380. Patterson, W. Morgan. "Changing Preparation
       for Changing Ministry." Baptist History
       and Heritage 15 (January 1980):14-22+.

3381. Patterson, W. Morgan, ed. Professor in the
       Pulpit: Sermons Preached... by the Faculty
       of Southern Baptist Theological Seminary.
       Nashville: Broadman, 1963.

3382. Patterson, Wendell K. "Central Seminary Now
       Is All American Baptist." Christian
       Century 73 (May 30, 1956):672-3.

3383. Pattison, E. M. "Functions of the Clergy in
       Community Mental Health Centers." Pastoral
       Psychology 16 (May 1965):21-6.

3384. Pattison, Thomas Harwood. For the Work of the
       Ministry. Philadelphia: American Baptist
       Publication Society, 1907.

3385. Pattison, Thomas Harwood. The History of
       Christian Preaching. Philadelphia:
       American Baptist Publication Society, 1903.

3386. Patton, Carl S. "The American Theological
       Scene Fifty Years in Retrospect." Journal
       of Religion 16 (October 1936):445-62.

3387. Patton, Cornelius Howard and Field, Walter T.
       Eight O'Clock Chapel: A Study of New
       England College Life in the Eighties.
       Boston: Houghton Mifflin Co., 1927.

3388. Patton, F. L. "(Education for Christian
       Ministry.)" Princeton Review 12 (Series 4)
       (1883):48+.

3389. Patton, F. L. "(Philosophy in the Curriculum of Theological Education.)" *Princeton Review* 9 (Series 4) (1882):103+.

3390. Patton, Glenn. "The College of William and Mary, Williamsburg and the Enlightenment." *Journal of the Society of Architectural Historians* 29, no. 1 (1970):24-32.

3391. Patton, John H. "Pastoral Care in the 1980's." *Journal of Pastoral Care* 34 (March 1980):1-61.

3392. Paul, Winston. "The Place and Value of Laymen in Theological Education." *Theological Education* 5 (Winter 1969):80-3.

3393. Paulsell, William O. "Knowing Whom We Have Believed [Installation Address, Lexington Theological Seminary, Nov. 12, 1981]." *Lexington Theological Quarterly* 17 (July 1982):19-30.

3394. Paulson, Ross E. *Women's Suffrage and Prohibition: A Comparative Study of Equality and Social Control.* Glenview, Ill.: Scott, Foresman, 1973.

3395. Payne, Earnest Alexander. *Studies in History and Religion.* London: Lutterworth Press, 1942.

3396. Pazmino, Robert William. "The Educational Thought of George W. Webber, Theological Educator, and Issues in Theological Education." Ed.D. dissertation, Columbia University Teachers College, 1981.

3397. Peabody, Francis G. "The Proportion of College-Trained Preachers." *Forum* 18 (1894):30-41.

3398. Peabody, Francis Greenwood. *Reminiscences of Present-Day Saints.* New York: Houghton Mifflin Co., 1927.

3399. Pearce, J. Winston. *Campbell College: Big Miracle at Little Buies Creek, 1887-1974.* Nashville, Tenn.: Broadman, 1976.

3400. Pears, Thomas Clinton. "Colonial Education among Presbyterians [1718-55]." *Presbyterian Historical Society. Journal* 30

(June - September 1952):115-26, 165-74.

3401. Pears, Thomas Clinton. Documentary History of
William Tennent and the Log College.
Philadelphia: Department of History
(Presbyterian History Society) of the
Office of the General Assembly of the
Presbyterian Church in the United States of
America, 1940.

3402. Pearson, Eliphalet. "Thoughts on the Importance of a Theological Institution."
Panoplist 3 (December 1807):307-16.

3403. Pearson, Roy Messer. "Excitement in the
Seminaries." Christian Century 75 (April
23, 1958):487-9.

3404. Pearson, R. M. "Ministers of the Ministering
Community [Inaugural Address as Dean of
Andover Newton Theological School]."
Pastoral Psychology 7 (May 1956):17-22.

3405. Pearson, Roy. "Trouble in the Seminaries."
Christian Century 85 (April 24, 1968):512-
15.

3406. Pease, G. Outline of Bible School Curriculum.
University of Chicago, 1908?

3407. Pease, K. R. "Paul Tillich Archive
[Harvard]." Harvard Divinity Bulletin 1
(New Series) (Winter 1968):14-16.

3408. Peck, George. "An Address Delivered before
the Literary Society of the Oneida
Conference, September 28, 1834." Methodist
Magazine and Quarterly Review 18 (1836):47-
69.

3409. Peck, John and Lawton, John. An Historical
Sketch of the Baptist Missionary Convention
of the State of New York: Embracing a
Narrative of the Origin and Progress of the
Baptist Denomination in Central and Western
New York. Utica, N. Y.: Printed by
Bennett & Bright, 1837.

3410. Peck, John Mason. Forty Years of Pioneer
Life: Memoirs of John Mason Peck. Edited
by Rufus Babcock. Carbondale: Southern
Illinois University Press, 1965. (Reprint
of the 1864 ed).

3411. Pegues, Albert W. <u>Our Baptist Ministers and Schools</u>. 1892. Reprint ed., Johnson Reprints, 1970.

3412. Pelikan, J. "Theological Library and the Tradition of Christian Humanism." <u>Concordia Theological Monthly</u> 33 (December 1962):719-23.

3413. "Pending Seminary Merger." <u>Christian Century</u> 99 (May 5, 1982):529.

3414. Peritz, Ismar J. "The Combination Course in Arts and Theology." <u>Christian Education</u> 15 (October 1931):46-53.

3415. Perry, E. F. "The Lilly Study: An Unfulfilled Promise." <u>Journal of Bible and Religion</u> 34 (April 1966).

3416. Perry, James H. <u>A Defence of the Present Mode of Training Candidates for the Ministry of the Methodist Episcopal Church: Being a Review of a Sermon Entitled 'A Treatise on the Need of the Church with Respect to Her Ministry,'</u> Preached by R. S. Foster, D.D. New York: Carlton & Phillips, 1855.

3417. Perry, Martha A. "Modeling and Instructions in Training for Counselor Empathy." <u>Journal of Counseling Psychology</u> 22 (May 1975):173-9.

3418. Peters, F. C. "Counseling and Pastoral Training." <u>Bibliotheca Sacra</u> 126 (October - December 1969):291-9.

3419. Peters, John Leland. <u>Christian Perfection and American Methodism</u>. New York: Abingdon Press, 1956.

3420. Peters, John Punnett. <u>The Old Testament and the New Scholarship</u>. New York: Macmillan Co., 1902.

3421. Petersen, Lorman M. "Theological and Higher Education at Springfield, Illinois." <u>Lutheran Historical Conference</u> 6 (1977): 134-59.

3422. Peterson, Frank Louis. "Why the Seventh-Day Adventist Church Established and Maintains a Negro College." <u>Journal of Negro</u>

Education 29 (Summer 1960):284-8.

3423. Peterson, George E. The New England College
in the Age of the University. Amherst:
Amherst College Press, 1964.

3424. Peterson, Stephen L. "Towards a Cooperative
Library Collection Development Program."
American Theological Library Association:
Proceedings 32 (1978):83-103.

3425. Peterson, Walter F. "Effects of Faculty
Unionization on Seminary Governance as Seen
by a President." Theological Education 12
(Autumn 1975):24-6.

3426. Petrie, John Clarence. "The Making of a Left-
Wing Parson." American Mercury 88 (January
1959):87-8.

3427. Pfabe, Jerrald Kort. "Theodore Graebner:
Apologist for Missouri Synod Lutheranism."
Ph.D. dissertation, St. Louis University,
1972.

3428. Pfleiderer, Otto. "The Duty of Scientific
Theology to the Church of Today." Andover
Review 17 (1892):133-46.

3429. Pheasant, Clayton N. "Working out the
Relationship: The Move Toward a Church-
College Alliance." Brethren Life and
Thought 27 (Winter 1982):6-14.

3430. Phelps, Austin. Men and Books. New York:
Charles Scribner's Sons, 1882.

3431. Phenix, Philip R. "A Functional Approach to
the Understanding of Ministry." Theological Education 4 (Autumn 1967):528-42.

3432. Phillips, Charles Henry. The History of the
Colored Methodist Episcopal Church in
America: Comprising Its Organization,
Subsequent Development, and Present Status.
2d ed. Jackson, Tenn.: Publishing House
C.M.E. Church, 1900.

3433. Phillips, Clifton J. "The Student Volunteer
Movement and Its Role in China Missions,
1886-1920." In The Missionary Enterprise
in China and America, pp. 91-109. By John
King Fairbank. Cambridge: Harvard

296

University Press, 1974.

3434. Phillips, William James. "A Systems Approach to Clergy Continuing Education Utilizing Media." Th.D. dissertation, Boston University School of Theology, 1976.

3435. Phillips Seminary Faculty. "A Plea for Multiple Strategies in Theological Education." Theological Education 5 (Winter 1969):112-18.

3436. Philputt, James McBride. "That They May All Be One:" Autobiography and Memorial of James M. Philputt. St. Louis: Christian Board of Publication, 1933.

3437. "(Physical Science in the Theological Seminary.)" Bibliotheca Sacra 39 (1882):190-7.

3438. "The Pie Was Cut Just Right." Christian Century 73 (January 4, 1956):5.

3439. Piepkorn, Arthur Carl. "The Primitive Baptists of North America." Baptist History and Heritage 7, no. 1 (1972):33-51.

3440. Pierce, Bessie Louise. A History of Chicago. Vol. 3: The Rise of a Modern City, 1871-1893. New York: Knopf, 1957.

3441. Pierce, P. F. and McTyeire, H. N. "A Note from Bishops Pierce and McTyeire." Christian Advocate (Nashville) 32 (New Series) (May 18, 1872):9.

3442. Pierce, R. D. "Legal Aspects of the Andover Creed [bibliog.]." Church History 15 (March 1946):28-47.

3443. Pierson, Arthur Tappan. The Crisis of Missions: Or, The Voice Out of the Cloud. New York: Robert Carter & Bros., 1886.

3444. Pierson, Arthur Tappan. Evangelistic Work in Principle and Practice. New York: Baker & Taylor Co., 1887.

3445. Pierson, Arthur Tappan. George Müller of Bristol and His Witness to a Prayer-Hearing God. New York: Baker & Taylor Co., 1899.

3446. Pierson, Arthur Tappan. The Story of Keswick and Its Beginnings. London: Marshall Bros., n.d.

3447. Pierson, Delavan Leonard. Arthur T. Pierson: A Spiritual Warrior, Mighty in the Scriptures; A Leader in the Modern Missionary Crusade. New York: Fleming H. Revell Co., 1912.

3448. Pierson, Robert Dwight. "A Study of the Effect of Protestant Seminary Christian Education upon the Attitudes of Closed Mindedness, Prejudice and Intrinsic Values." Ed.D. dissertation, Oklahoma State University, 1975.

3449. Pierson, Roscoe M. "The Autobiography of Walter Scott, 1796-1861." Lexington Theological Quarterly 16 (October 1981):146-8.

3450. Pieters, Albertus. "The League of Evangelical Students." Moody Monthly 32 (November 1931):113.

3451. Pinnock, Clark H. "Evangelical Theology: Conservative and Contemporary." Christianity Today 23 (January 5, 1979):23-9.

3452. Pinnock, Clark H. "Liberals Knock the Center out of Theological Education." Christianity Today 26 (February 5, 1982):32-3.

3453. Pino, Christopher J. "Interpersonal Needs, Counselor Style and Personality Change among Seminarians during the 1970's." Review of Religious Research 21 (Summer 1980):351-67.

3454. Pirazzini, Agide. Training of Ministerial and Lay Workers among the Italian People in America by the Italian Department of the Bible Teachers Training School of New York City." N.p., 1911?

3455. Pittenger, N. "Teaching Theology Today." Religion In Life 39 (Autumn 1970):396-406.

3456. Pittenger, William Norman. "Theological Students Today." Christian Century 84 (April 26, 1967):527-9.

3457. Pittenger, William Norman. "Today's Theological Student." Christian Century 71
(April 28, 1954):512-13.

3458. Plantz, Samuel. The History of Education in
the Methodist Episcopal Church, 1892 to
1917. New York: Board of Education of the
Methodist Episcopal Church, 1918.

3459. Platt, James M. and Hodge, Archibald A.
Addresses at the Inauguration of Rev.
Archibald A. Hodge, D.D. as Professor of
Didactic, Polemic and Historical Theology
in the Western Theological Seminary:
Comprising The Charge to the Professor, by
Rev. James M. Platt; and The Inaugural
Address, by Rev. Archibald A. Hodge, D.D.
Pittsburgh: Printed by James McMillin,
1864.

3460. Platt, Nancy Van Dyke and Moss, David M.
"Influence of the Alcoholic Parent on
Episcopal Seminarians' Ministry to
Alcoholics." Journal of Pastoral Care 31
(March 1977):32-7.

3461. "(Plea for Higher Theological Education.)"
Bibliotheca Sacra 36 (1879):182+.

3462. "Please Reconsider, Cardinal Cushing!"
Christian Century 83 (April 13, 1966):453-
4.

3463. Ploch, Donald R. "Higher Education: Faculty
as Professionalization and Change Agents.
Final Report." 1972. (ERIC Document)

3464. Plowman, E. E. "March in Missouri: Concordia
and Seminex Spring-Term Registration."
Christianity Today 18 (April 12, 1974):42-
4.

3465. Plowman, E. E. "Pressure in Pittsburgh:
United Presbyterian School." Christianity
Today 18 (January 4, 1974):53-5.

3466. Plumer, William S. Hints and Helps in
Pastoral Theology. New York: Harper &
Bros., 1874.

3467. Podhoretz, Norman. "Jewish Culture and the
Intellectuals: The Process of Redis-
covery." Commentary 19 (May 1955):451-7.

3468. Poehler, Willy August. "An Appraisal of Two Types of Pre-Ministerial Training Programs of the Lutheran Church-Missouri Synod." Ph.D. dissertation, University of Minnesota, 1954.

3469. Poethig, Richard P. "Developing a Theology for Metropolitan Ministry: Papers, Responses, Case Studies, Discussion, Findings, Evaluation." Institute on the Church in Urban-Industrial Society: Occasional Papers 7 (1977):1-45.

3470. Pohly, Kenneth Holt. "The Clinical Method in Theological Education." D.Div. dissertation, Vanderbilt University Divinity School, 1969.

3471. Poindexter, A. M. "(Scriptural Theory of Education for Ministry.)" Baptist Quarterly 5 (1871):87+.

3472. Poling, James N. "Beginning Thoughts on a Theological Method for Ministry." Pastoral Psychology 30 (Summer 1982):163-70.

3473. Pollock, John Charles. Billy Graham: The Authorized Biography. London: Hodder & Stoughton, 1966.

3474. Pollock, John Charles. The Keswick Story: The Authorized History of the Keswick Convention. London: Hodder & Stoughton, 1964.

3475. Polthoff, Harvey H. "When Experience Is Lifted to the Level of Devotion." Iliff Review 38 (Fall 1981):3-7.

3476. Pond, E. "(History of Bangor Theological Seminary.)" American Quarterly Register 14 (1842):27+.

3477. Pond, Enoch. The Young Pastor's Guide. Bangor, Me.: E. F. Duren, 1844.

3478. Poole, Stafford. "Diocesan Priest and the Intellectual Life: Excerpt from Seminary in Crisis." Commonweal 82 (April 9, 1965): 78-81.

3479. Poole, Stafford. Seminary in Crisis. New York: Herder & Herder, 1965.

3480. Poole, S. "Tomorrow's Seminaries." America
       110 (January 18, 1964):86+; (Discussion)
       110 (March 28, 1964):423+, (May 23, 1964):
       723-9.

3481. Poore, John Byron. "Attitudes of Selected
       Bible College Students in Mississippi and
       Alabama Related to Death and Dying." Ed.D.
       dissertation, Mississippi State University,
       1982.

3482. Pope, Liston. "The Bridston - Culver Report:
       Pre-Seminary Education." Theological
       Education 1 (Spring 1965):139-42.

3483. Pope, Liston. "Dilemmas of the Seminaries."
       Christian Century 67 (April 26, 1950):520-
       2.

3484. Pope, Liston. "Trends in the Seminaries."
       Christianity and Crisis 12 (1952):113-4.

3485. Pope, R. M. "College of the Bible [History]."
       College of the Bible Quarterly (Lexington)
       38 (April 1961):4-27.

3486. Pope, Richard Martin. "The Seminary as a
       Learning Community." Lexington Theological
       Quarterly 5 (April 1970):33-41.

3487. Porteous, Alvin C. "The Seminary and the
       Racial Crisis." Christian Century 81
       (January 29, 1964):147-8.

3488. Porter, Anthony Toomer. Led On! Step by
       Step: Scenes from Educational, and
       Plantation Life in the South, 1828-1898.
       New York: G. P. Putnam's Sons, 1898.

3489. Porter, C. L. "Biblical Studies." Encounter
       25 (Summer 1964).

3490. Porter, Earl W. Trinity and Duke, 1892-1924:
       Foundations of Duke University. Durham,
       N. C.: Duke University Press, 1964.

3491. Porter, Ebenezer. "Terms of Admission to the
       Theological Seminary, Andover." American
       Quarterly Register 5 (August 1832):93-4.

3492. Porter, Ebenezer, comp. The Young Preacher's
       Manual, or a Collection of Treatises on
       Preaching. Boston: Charles Ewer, 1819.

3493. Porter, Edward G. "The Andover Band in
       Maine." Andover Review 19 (March
       1893):198-207.

3494. Porter, Frank C. "The Ideals of Seminaries
       and the Needs of the Churches." New World
       9 (1900):25-31.

3495. Porter, James. Hints to Self-Educated
       Ministers. New York: Phillips & Hunt,
       1879.

3496. Porter, W. D. "Planning for Foreign Students
       in Theological Education." Theological
       Education 6 (Summer 1970):306-8.

3497. Posey, Walter Brownlow. The Baptist Church in
       the Lower Mississippi Valley 1776-1845.
       Lexington: University of Kentucky Press,
       1957.

3498. Potter, Charles Francis. The Preacher and I:
       An Autobiography. New York: Crown
       Publishers, 1951.

3499. Potter, James H. "Reminiscence and Reflection
       [Hartford Seminary Foundation]." Hartford
       Quarterly 6 (Spring 1966):31-9.

3500. Potts, David Bronson. "Baptist Colleges in
       the Development of American Society, 1812-
       1861." Ph.D. dissertation, Harvard
       University, 1967.

3501. Potts, M. D. "The Extended Unit: A Viable
       Alternative [in Clinical Pastoral
       Education]." Journal of Supervision and
       Training in Ministry 4 (1981):49-56.

3502. Potvin, R. H. and Suziedelis, A. "Seminarians
       of the Sixties." NCEA Bulletin 66 (August
       1969):44-9.

3503. Powell, Milton, comp. The Voluntary Church:
       American Religious Life, 1740-1865, Seen
       through the Eyes of European Visitors. New
       York: Macmillan, 1967.

3504. Powell, Noble Cilley. The Post-Ordination
       Training of the Clergy. The Twenty-Fifth
       Annual Hale Memorial Sermon, Delivered
       January 26, 1939. Evanston, Ill.:
       Seabury-Western Theological Seminary, 1939.

302

3505. Powell, Robert C. "Mrs. Ethel Phelps Stokes Hoyt [1887-1952] and the Joint Committee on Religion and Medicine [1923-1936]: A Brief Sketch." Journal of Pastoral Care 29, no. 2 (1975):99-105.

3506. Powell, Ruth Marie. Lights and Shadows: The Story of the American Baptist Theological Seminary, 1924-64. Nashville? 1965.

3507. Powers, Bruce Postell. "An Investigation of Teacher-Training for Graduate Students at the Southern Baptist Theological Seminary." Ed.D. dissertation, Southern Baptist Theological Seminary, 1971.

3508. Powers, Charles W. and Hornbeck, David W. "Seminary Social Action: A Report and Some Reflections." Theological Education 4 (Winter 1968):611-18.

3509. Pratt, Harry E. "Peter Cartwright and the Cause of Education." Illinois State Historical Society Journal 28 (January 1936):271-8.

3510. Pratt, Magee. "The Surplus of Congregational Ministers." Outlook 63 (1899):162-3.

3511. "Preaching: Hodgepodge or the Gospel?" Christian Century 72 (April 27, 1955):493-5.

3512. Pregnall, William Stuart. "The Role of Lay People in Theological Field Education." Ph.D. dissertation, University of the South, 1977.

3513. Pregnall, William S. and Hampton, Elizabeth E. "Training Field Education Supervisors." Theological Education 11 (Summer 1975):308-14.

3514. Prentiss, George Lewis. The Bright Side of Life: Glimpses of It Through Fourscore Years. Asbury Park, N. J.: Press of M., W. & C. Pennypacker, 1901.

3515. Prentiss, George Lewis. The Union Theological Seminary in the City of New York: Historical and Biographical Sketches of Its First 50 Years. New York: A. D. F. Randolph & Co., 1889.

303

3516. Prentiss, George Lewis. The Union Theological
Seminary in the City of New York: Its
Design and Another Decade of Its History.
With a Sketch of the Life and Public
Services of Charles Butler, LL.D. Asbury
Park, N.J.: M., W. & C. Pennypacker, 1899.

3517. Presbyterian Church in the U.S.A. Board of
Education. Address of a Committee of the
Board of Education under the Care of the
General Assembly, to the Members of the
Presbyterian Church, in the United States
of America. Philadelphia: J. W. Allen,
1824.

3518. Presbyterian Church in the U.S.A. Board of
Education. Address of the Board of
Directors of the Presbyterian Education
Society, to the Christian Public, Oct.
1831. New York: Sleight & Robinson, 1831.

3519. Presbyterian Church in the U.S.A. Board of
Education. Annual Report of the Board of
Education of the General Assembly of the
Presbyterian Church, May 1832. Phila-
delphia: Russell & Martin, 1832.

3520. Presbyterian Church in the U.S.A. Board of
Education. Annual Report of the Board of
Education of the General Assembly of the
Presbyterian Church, May 1833. Phila-
delphia: Russell & Martin, 1833.

3521. Presbyterian Church in the U.S.A. Board of
Education. Annual Report of the Board of
Education of the General Assembly of the
Presbyterian Church in the USA, Presented
May, 1839. Philadelphia: Published for
the Board, 1839.

3522. Presbyterian Church in the U.S.A. Committee
of Conference with the Theological
Seminaries. The Committee of Conference of
the General Assembly to the Board of
Directors of the Union Theological Seminary
Concerning the Compact of 1870. N.p.,
1892.

3523. Presbyterian Church in the U.S.A. General
Assembly. Acts and Proceedings of the
General Assembly of the Presbyterian Church
in the United States of America A.D. 1789.
Philadelphia: Jane Aitken, 1803.

3524. Presbyterian Church in the U.S.A. General
Assembly. A Letter ... Accompanied with a
Plan Adopted by the Assembly for the
Establishment of a Theological School ....
Philadelphia: Printed by J. Aitken, 1810.

3525. Presbyterian Church in the U.S.A. General
Assembly. The Plan of a Theological
Seminary Adopted by the General Assembly
... Together with the Measures Taken by
Them to Carry the Plan into Effect.
Philadelphia: J. Aitken, 1811.

3526. Presbyterian Church in the U.S.A. General
Assembly. Report of a Committee of the
General Assembly ... Exhibiting the Plan of
a Theological Seminary. New York: Printed
by J. Seymour, 1810.

3527. Presbyterian Church in the U.S.A. General
Assembly. Report of the Committee
Appointed to Devise Ways and Means of
Raising Funds for the Theological
Seminary.... Philadelphia: Printed by
Thomas & William Bradford, 1816.

3528. Presbyterian Church in the United States.
Report of a Survey of the Colleges and
Theological Seminaries of the Presbyterian
Church in the United States, 1941-1942
[bibliog.]. Louisville: Presbyterian
Church in the U.S., 1942.

3529. Presbyterian Church in the U.S. Committee of
Christian Education. Report of a Survey of
the Colleges and Theological Seminaries of
the Church [1941-1942]. Louisville:
Presbyterian Church, 1942.

3530. "Presbyterians and Union Seminary."
Independent 74 (May 29, 1913):1169-70.

3531. "Prescription for Seminaries: Six Yale
Seminarians." Christianity and Crisis 27
(1967):136-9.

3532. "Pre-Seminary Preparation and Study in
Religion." Journal of Bible and Religion
34 (April 1966).

3533. "Pre-Seminary Preparation and Study in
Religion [Official Statement of Policy by
the National Association of Biblical

Instructors]." Journal of Bible and
Religion 27 (April 1959):139-42.

3534. "Presidents or Deans of Schools of Theology."
        In Educational Directory, 1930, pp. 75-8.
        United States. Office of Education, 1930.

3535. Preus, David W. "The American Lutheran
        Church's Expectations re Sound Teaching."
        Theological Education 15 (Spring 1979):97-
        101.

3536. Preus, J. A. O. "Editorial [on Concordia
        Theological Seminary, Springfield, Ill.]."
        Springfielder 28 (Summer 1964):3-6.

3537. Preus, J. A. O. "Interview with Preus
        [Concordia Theological Seminary]."
        Christianity Today 17 (October 27,
        1972):44.

3538. Preus, Robert D. "Response [to 'Teaching
        Theology in a Pluralistic Society,'
        Wartburg Seminary Faculty, pp. 100-103]."
        Lutheran Theological Journal 15 (December
        1981):103-6.

3539. "Preus versus Tietjen [Concordia Seminary]."
        Christianity Today 17 (October 27,
        1972):27.

3540. Price, Charles P. "Clifford Leland Stanley:
        Teacher and Theologian." Anglican
        Theological Review (Suppl. Series) no. 7
        (November 1976):19-30.

3541. Price, J. L. "The Lilly Study and College
        Work in Religion." Journal of Bible and
        Religion 34 (April 1966).

3542. Price, Orlo J. "The Theological Seminary and
        the Needs of the Modern Church." Religious
        Education 11 (October 1916):409-18.

3543. Price, W. W. "Alliance School of Theology and
        Missions." Alliance Witness 114 (March 21,
        1979):9-10.

3544. Price, W. W. "Graduate Education: Growing."
        Alliance Witness 117 (March 17, 1982):7-9.

3545. Priest, J. "Has the Old Passed Away?
        [Curriculum]." Hartford Quarterly 4

(Spring 1964).

3546. Priest, J. F. "Theological Seminary: School or Church?" Hartford Quarterly 3 (Winter 1962):67-71.

3547. Priestley, David T. "Doctrinal Statements of German Baptists in North America." Foundations 22, no. 1 (1979):51-71.

3548. Prince, Albert Taylor, Jr. "A History of Gammon Theological Seminary." Microfilm Abstracts (New York University) 9, no. 1 (1949):95-6.

3549. Princeton Theological Seminary. The Centennial Celebration of the Theological Seminary of the Presbyterian Church in the United States of America at Princeton, New Jersey, May Fifth - May Sixth - May Seventh, Nineteen Hundred and Twelve. Princeton: At the Theological Seminary, 1912.

3550. "Princeton's Own." Newsweek 59 (May 14, 1962):95.

3551. Pringle, H. F. "That's How Preachers Are Made." Saturday Evening Post 225 (May 23, 1953):28+.

3552. Pritchett, Henry S. "The Progress and Tendencies of Theological Education from a National Point of View." In Sixth Annual Report of the President of the Carnegie Foundation for the Advancement of Teaching, October, 1911.

3553. "Private Instruction for the Ministry." Bibliotheca Sacra 38 (1881):369-83.

3554. "Problems of Theological Education." Biblical World 31 (March 1908):163-6.

3555. Proctor, Robert Allen, Jr. "A Study of Attitude Changes in Theological Students during One Year of Seminary Training." Ed.D. dissertation, Temple University, 1961.

3556. Proctor, Samuel D. "The Social Philosophy of John C[oleman] Bennett." Journal of Religious Thought 11 (Spring - Summmer

1954):93-104.

3557. "The Professional Education of Ministers."
Andover Review 8 (November 1887):536-40.

3558. Professional Growth for Clergymen, Through
Supervised Training in Marriage Counseling
and Family Problems. Nashville: Abingdon
Press, 1970.

3559. "Professional Schools Workshop: Theology."
College and University 53 (Summer
1978):440.

3560. "Prologue and Protest [Concordia Seminary]."
Christianity Today 17 (August 31, 1973):45.

3561. "Propaedeutics, Hermeneutics & Halieutics."
Christian Century 47 (January 8, 1930):38-
9.

3562. "Prophetic Inquiry and the Danforth Study."
Christian Century (February 7, 1979):128-
31.

3563. "A Proposed Revision of the Theological
Seminary Curriculum." School and Society
24 (July 10, 1926):38.

3564. Protestant Episcopal Church in the U.S.A.
General Convention. Joint Commission on
Theological Education. Theological Studies
and Examinations: A Syllabus, 1948. New
York: National Council of the Protestant
Episcopal Church, 1948.

3565. Protestant Episcopal Church in the U.S.A.
Massachusetts (Diocese). Commission on the
Ministry. Continuing Education for Minis-
try: A Catalog of Resources. Boston:
Protestant Episcopal Diocese of Massa-
chusetts, 1973.

3566. Protestant Episcopal Church in the U.S.A.
National Council. Dept. of Christian
Education. Commission on the Ministry.
Guide to Candidates for Holy Orders, Based
on the Canons of 1919. Milwaukee:
Morehouse Publishing Co., 1920.

3567. Protestant Episcopal Church in the U.S.A.
Special Committee on Theological Education.
Ministry for Tomorrow: Report. New York:

Seabury Press, 1967.

3568. "Protestant Seminaries Expect Record Enrollment." Christian Century 68 (August 8, 1951):909.

3569. "Protestant Theological Students in the United States." Biblical World 37 (February 1911):140-2.

3570. Pruyser, Paul W. "Impact of the Psychological Disciplines on the Training of Clergy." Pastoral Psychology 19 (October 1968):21-32.

3571. Pruyser, Paul W. "The Psychological Disciplines in Theological Education." Concordia Theological Monthly 34 (August 1963):472-8.

3572. Pryor, Thomas M. et al. "Proceedings: Town and Country Church Institute (38th, Urbana, Illinois, January 29-31, 1968). The Church and Community Development." Urbana: University of Illinois, Cooperative Extension Service, 1968. (ERIC Document)

3573. Pusey, Nathan M. "Address to the Harvard Divinity School." Christianity and Crisis 13 (1953):149-52.

3574. Pusey, N. "Doubts and the Divinity School: Summary of Address." Time 88 (October 7, 1966):94.

3575. Pusey, N. M. "Faith's Waning Power To Enthrall [Harvard]." Christianity Today 11 (May 12, 1967):6-7.

3576. Pusey, N. M. "Responsibility of Laymen in Theological Education." Drew Gateway 35, no. 2 (1965):77-82.

3577. "Put Seminary Eggs in Fewer Baskets: Policy Regarding Baptist Seminaries." Christian Century 82 (November 3, 1965):1341.

3578. Pyatt, C. L. "Experimental Course in Anti-Semitism [College of the Bible, Lexington, Ky.]." Christian Education 21 (December 1937):98-9.

309

3579. Pyburn, Richard Earl. "Selected Seminary
       Student Pastors and Their Churches: A
       Transactional Analysis." S.T.D. disserta-
       tion, Southern Baptist Theological
       Seminary, 1971.

3580. "(Qualifications for the Ministry.)" Boston
       Review 4 (1864):421+.

3581. "(Qualifications for the Ministry.)"
       Christian Review 3 (1838):254+.

3582. "(Qualifications for the Ministry.)" Spirit
       of the Pilgrims 6 (1833):268+, 456+.

3583. "The Quality of Teaching." Christian Century
       95 (February 1, 1978):92-3.

3584. Quanbeck, Warren A., Fevold, Eugene L. and
       Frost, Gerhard E. Striving for Ministry:
       Centennial Essays Interpreting the Heritage
       of Luther Theological Seminary.
       Minneapolis: Augsburg, 1977.

3585. "Quarterly Meeting of the Board of Directors
       of the Am. Ed. Society." American
       Quarterly Register 1 (January 1828):55-6.

3586. Quebedeaux, Richard. The Young Evangelicals:
       Revolution in Orthodoxy. New York: Harper
       & Row, 1974.

3587. Queen, Christopher. "Student Initiated Change
       in Theological Schools." In Ministry in
       the Seventies. Edited by J. Biersdorf.
       New York: IDOC North America, 1971.

3588. Queener, E. L. "Psychological Training of
       Ministers." Pastoral Psychology 7 (October
       1956):29-34.

3589. Quello, D. Y. "Comparative Investigation of
       the Personality Profiles of CPE and Non-CPE
       Theological Students [bibliog.]." Journal
       of Pastoral Care 24 (December 1970):240-3.

3590. Query, W. T. "Changes in Scores on California
       Psychological Inventory among Seminarians:
       What Happened to the Class of '68?"
       Psychological Reports 45 (August 1979):129-
       30.

3591. "(Question of Theological Education.)"
Reformed Church Review 47 (1900):248+.

3592. "Questions of the Two Edwardses for Their
Pupils in Theology." Bibliotheca Sacra 39
(1882):367-82.

3593. Quick, Charles W. "Teaching Law in the Theological School." Journal of Religious
Thought 13 (Autumn/Winter 1955-56):52-62.

3594. Quillian, Joseph D. "Basis of Dialogue
between Church and Seminary." Theological
Education 12 (Spring 1976):158-68.

3595. Quincy, Josiah. The History of Harvard
University. 2 vols. Cambridge: John
Owen, 1840.

3596. Quint, A. H. "(Congregational Theological
Seminaries in 1861.)" Congregational
Quarterly 3 (1861):199+.

3597. Quint, A. H. "(Congregational Theological
Seminaries in 1865-66.)" Congregational
Quarterly 8 (1866):293+.

3598. Quint, A. H. "(Congregational Theological
Seminaries in 1866-67.)" Congregational
Quarterly 9 (1867):276+.

3599. Quint, A. H. "(Congregational Theological
Seminaries in 1869-70.)" Congregational
Quarterly 12 (1870):291+.

3600. Quint, A. H. "(Congregational Theological
Seminaries in 1871-72.)" Congregational
Quarterly 14 (1872):294+.

3601. Quint, A. H. "(Congregational Theological
Seminaries in 1872-73.)" Congregational
Quarterly 15 (1873):294+.

3602. Quint, A. H. "(Congregational Theological
Seminaries in 1873-74.)" Congregational
Quarterly 16 (1874):304+.

3603. Quint, A. H. "(Congregational Theological
Seminaries in 1874-75.)" Congregational
Quarterly 17 (1875):350+.

3604. Quint, A. H. "(Congregational Theological
Seminaries in 1877-78.)" Congregational

Quarterly 20 (1878):334+.

3605. Quint, A. H. "(Congregational Theological
Seminaries in U.S.)" Congregational
Quarterly 1 (1859):181+.

3606. Raab, Earl, ed. Religious Conflict in
America: Studies of the Problems beyond
Bigotry. Garden City, N.Y.: Anchor Books,
1964.

3607. Raber, Chester Alden. "A Clinical Method of
Teaching Pastoral Care." Ph.D. disserta-
tion, Southern Baptist Theological
Seminary, 1963.

3608. Raftery, Elizabeth Brainerd. "Berkeley's
Three Founders." Berkeley Divinity School
Bulletin 195 (Summer 1966).

3609. Ragsdale, Bartow Davis. Story of Georgia
Baptists. Vol. 1: Mercer University,
Penfield Period and Related Interests.
Atlanta: By the Author, Auspices the
Executive Committee of the Georgia Baptist
Convention, 1932.

3610. Raible, Peter. "Confidential Memo from a
Seminary Dean." Christian Century 89
(February 2, 1972):135-7.

3611. Raines, R. A. "With Billy Graham at Yale."
His 18 (October 1957):28-32.

3612. Rambo, Lewis R. "TSF: A Quest to be
Conservative and Contemporary: Theological
Students Fellowship Serves the Needs of
Evangelicals in Pluralistic Settings."
Christian Century 97 (February 6-13,
1980):161-3.

3613. Ramm, Bernard L. "What's Happening in Our
Seminaries?" Eternity 21 (June 1970):24-6.

3614. Rampley, Lester Claude. "Preparation for
Professional Participation within a Destiny
- People." Lexington Theological Quarterly
5 (April 1970):23-32.

3615. Ramsdell, E. T. "Comprehensive Examinations
for the B. D. Degree." Journal of Bible
and Religion 17 (January 1949):19-22.

3616. Ramsden, William E. "The Processes and
       Effects of a Training Group in Clinical
       Pastoral Education." Ph.D. dissertation,
       Boston University, 1960.

3617. Ramsey, Paul. "Academic Freedom at Louisville
       [Letter to the Editor]." Christian Century
       75 (September 3, 1958):998-9.

3618. Ramsey, Paul. "The Status and the Advancement
       of Theological Scholarship in America."
       Christian Scholar 47 (Spring 1964):7-23.

3619. Ramsey, Robert Paul. "Theological Studies in
       College and Seminary." Theology Today 17
       (January 1961):466-84.

3620. Ranck, Henry Haverstick. The Life of the
       Reverend Benjamin Bausman. Philadelphia:
       Publication & Sunday School Board of the
       Reformed Church in the United States, 1912.

3621. Rand, Earl W. "The Negro Private and Church
       College at Mid-Century." Journal of Negro
       Education 22 (Winter 1953):77-9.

3622. Randall, M. W. "Our Curriculum Is to Blame
       [Bible Colleges]." Church Growth Bulletin
       14 (January 1978):169-72.

3623. Rankin, R. "Rockefeller Brothers Theological
       Fellowship Program." Christian Scholar 37
       (December 1954):558-9.

3624. Rankin, W. Robert. "Strengthening the
       Ministry." Christian Century 72 (April 27,
       1955):496-8.

3625. Ranson, Charles Wesley. "Address of the
       Reverend Charles Wesley Ranson on the
       Occasion of His Installation." Drew
       Gateway 35 (1965):83-90.

3626. Ranson, Charles W. "How the Theological
       Education Fund Began." In A Vision for
       Man, pp. 130-42. Edited by S. Amirtham.
       Madras: Christian Literature Society,
       1978.

3627. Ranson, C. W. "Theological Education Fund."
       International Review of Missions 47
       (October 1958):432-8.

3628. Ranson, Charles Wesley. "Theology and the Higher Learning." Hartford Quarterly 8 (Winter 1968):15-24.

3629. Raphaeli, Ruth. "The Development of Materials for Teaching Reading Comprehension in Biblical Hebrew." Ed.D. dissertation, Columbia University Teachers College, 1981.

3630. Raskopf, Roger William. "A Comparison of Correlates of Vocational Maturity Found in Episcopal Seminary Students Preparing for the Ministry as a Second Career with Those Found in Students Preparing for the Ministry as Their First Career." Ph.D. dissertation, St. John's University, 1975.

3631. Ratcliff, Charles, Jr. "A Study of the Social Objectives of the Member Schools of the American Association of Bible Colleges." Ed.D. dissertation, University of Cincinnati, 1978.

3632. Ratcliffe, E. B. "Accrediting of Professional Schools." School Life 25 (March 1940):175.

3633. Rauscher, William V. "Christianity and Parapsychology." Journal of the Academy of Religion and Psychological Research 3 (July 1980):170-9.

3634. Ray, Charles. The Life of Charles Haddon Spurgeon. London: Ibister & Co., 1903.

3635. Ray, Joel Dillard. "A Study of the Curriculum Development of the New Orleans Baptist Theological Seminary." Ph.D. dissertation, New Orleans Baptist Theological Seminary, 1960.

3636. Rayburn, Carole A. "The Need for Counseling and Consulting for Women in Seminaries." Paper presented at the 88th Annual Convention of the American Psychological Association, Montreal, Canada, September 1-5, 1980. (ERIC Document)

3637. Rayburn, Carole A. "Some Reflections of a Female Seminarian: Woman, Whither Goest Thou?" Paper Presented at the Convention of the American Psychological Association, New York, N.Y., September 1, 1979. (ERIC Document)

3638. Raymond, Lowell W. "For an Effective
Ministry." Christianity Today 12 (January
19, 1968):8.

3639. Reading, L. J. "Social Sciences and the Work
of the Churches. X. The Understanding of
Group Behavior in Clergy In-Service
Training." Expository Times 81 (September
1970):356-9.

3640. "Real Preparation for the Ministry." Outlook
85 (April 27, 1907):916-7.

3641. "Reality in the Pulpit." Journal of Pastoral
Care 5 (Fall 1951):45.

3642. Recker, R. "Concept of the Missio Dei and
Instruction in Mission at Calvin Seminary."
Calvin Theological Journal 11 (November
1976):181-98.

3643. "Record Seminary Enrollment." Christianity
Today 13 (December 1968):41-2.

3644. "Redbook Should Blush." Christian Century 78
(October 25, 1961):1260-1.

3645. Redekop, Calvin. "The Seminary as Participant
Observer." Theological Education 2 (Spring
1966):203-9.

3646. Reed, Alfred Zantzinger. Present-Day Law
Schools in the United States and Canada.
New York, 1928.

3647. Reed, Andrew and Matheson, James. A Narrative
of the Visit to the American Churches, by
the Deputation from the Congregational
Union of England and Wales. 2 vols. New
York: Harper & Bros., 1835.

3648. Reed, Kenneth Eugene. "Psychological Testing
in Supervision of Clinical Pastoral
Training." Ph.D. dissertation, Boston
University, 1963.

3649. Reese, David Meredith. "Brief Strictures on
the Rev. Mr. Sunderland's 'Essay on
Theological Education.'" Methodist
Magazine and Quarterly Review 17 (January
1835):105-17.

3650. Reese, D. M. and Sunterland, L. "(Theological
       Education.)" American Methodist Magazine
       17 (1835):85+, 204+, 347+.

3651. Reese, David M. "Theological Education."
       Methodist Magazine and Quarterly Review 6
       (New Series) (July 1835):347-52.

3652. Reeves, Floyd Wesley and Russell, John Dale.
       College Organization and Administration: A
       Report Based upon a Series of Surveys of
       Church Colleges. Indianapolis: Board of
       Education, Disciples of Christ, 1929.

3653. Reeves, F. W. "Colleges of the Disciples of
       Christ." Christian Education 12 (April
       1929):433-8.

3654. Reeves, Michael Dan. "An Analysis of Selected
       Factors which Present Potential Problems in
       the Transition from Seminary Training to
       Vocational Christian Service." Ed.D. dis-
       sertation, Southwestern Baptist Theological
       Seminary, 1982.

3655. "Reform in the Seminaries: Carrying out New
       Spirit of Freedom in the Catholic church."
       Time 87 (April 15, 1966):60.

3656. "Reformation Research Finds an Angel
       [Concordia Seminary]." Christian Century
       74 (October 23, 1957):1252.

3657. Reformed Church in America. Board of
       Education. Address of the Board of Educa-
       tion to the Reformed Dutch Churches. New
       York, 1828.

3658. Reformed Church in America. General Synod.
       The Acts and Proceedings of the General
       Synod of the Reformed Protestant Dutch
       Church in North America. (1771-1812).
       Vol. 1. New York: Board of Publication of
       the Reformed Protestant Dutch Church, 1859.

3659. Reformed Church in the United States.
       Addresses Delivered at the Inauguration of
       Rev. J. W. Nevin as Professor of Theology
       in the Theological Seminary of the German
       Reformed Church, Mercersburg, Pa., May
       20th, 1840. Chambersburg, Pa.: Printed at
       the Office of Publication of the German
       Reformed Church, 1840.

3660. Reformed Church in the United States. Minutes and Letters of the Coetus of the German Reformed Congregations in Pennsylvania, 1747-1792. Together with Three Preliminary Reports of Rev. John Phillip Boehm, 1734-1744. Philadelphia: Reformed Church Publishing Board, 1903.

3661. "Reforming Seminaries." America 122 (April 18, 1970):402.

3662. "Reforms in Theological Education." Baptist Quarterly Review 7 (1885):407-42.

3663. Rehmer, Rudolph. "Lutherans in Pioneer Indiana." Concordia Historical Institute Quarterly 40, no. 1 (1967):13-29.

3664. Reid, C. H. "Some Basic Assumptions for Continuing Education." Christian Century 87 (April 22, 1970):472-4.

3665. Reid, Clyde H. "Supervising Seminary Field Work." Christian Century 80 (April 24, 1963):528-30.

3666. Reid, Fred William. "An Evaluation of the Impact of Clinical Pastoral Education upon the Personality of the Minister." Ph.D. dissertation, University of North Carolina at Chapel Hill, 1972.

3667. Reid, H. M. B. The Divinity Professors in the University of Glasgow 1640-1903. Glasgow: Maclehose, Jackson & Co., 1923.

3668. Reid, Ira De A. "The Church and Education for Negroes." In Divine White Right. By Trevor Bowen. New York: Harper & Bros., 1934.

3669. Reid, Ira. "The Negro Baptist Ministry: An Analysis of Its Professions, Preparation, and Practices." Philadelphia: Haverford College, 1951. (Mimeographed.)

3670. Reinbold, John Clifford. "An Analysis of Changes in Attitudes of Participants in Selected Clergy Economic Education Programs." Ed.D. dissertation, Indiana University, 1965.

3671. Reinwald, C. "(Lutheran Ministerial Education in the Maryland Synod.)" Lutheran Quarterly 33 (New Series) (1903):117+.

3672. Reisinger, Donald D. and Osborn, Ronald E., eds. "20th Anniversary Celebration Edition [Disciples Seminary Foundation, Claremont, California] Impact no. 5 (1980):1-37.

3673. Reisinger, Donald D. and Osborn, Ronald E. "20th Anniversary Celebration Edition [Disciples Seminary Foundation, Claremont, Calif.]." Impact no. 6 (1981):1-44.

3674. "The Relation of Congregational Churches to Their Theological Seminaries." Andover Review 4 (September 1885):247-56.

3675. "The Relevance of Clinical Pastoral Education: A Symposium." Southwestern Journal of Theology 9 (Spring 1967):53-66.

3676. "Religion and Psychiatry." Christian Advocate 7 (December 1963):19.

3677. Religion and the American Revolution. Edited by Jerald C. Brauer. Philadelphia: Fortress Press, 1976.

3678. "Religion at Harvard." America 90 (October 17, 1953):60.

3679. "Reminiscences of America - No. V. Provision for the Ministry." Congregational Magazine 2 (New Series) (1838):485-91.

3680. "Renewing the Ministry, Prescription for Reforming Seminary Training." Commonweal 94 (April 16, 1971):125-6.

3681. Renfer, Rudolf Albert. "A History of Dallas Theological Seminary." Ph.D. dissertation, University of Texas, 1959.

3682. "Reorganization of the Departments of Religious Education at Union Theological Seminary and Teachers College." Religious Education 17 (December 1922):464-5.

3683. "Report of Committee on Education, No. 2." In Journal of the General Conference of the Methodist Episcopal Church, South, pp. 233-6. Edited by Thomas O. Summers.

Nashville: Publishing House of the
Methodist Episcopal Church, South, 1870.

3684. "Report of the Commission on Theological
Education, With Correspondence." In
Official Report of the Proceedings of the
25th Meeting. General Conference of
Unitarian and Other Christian churches.
Boston: G. H. Ellis, 1914.

3685. "Report of the Committee on Theological
Institutions." Zion's Herald 10 (July 31,
1839):121.

3686. Repp, Arthur Christian, ed. "The Period of
Planting 1847-1864." In 100 Years of
Christian Education, pp. 33-63. River
Forest, Ill.: Lutheran Education Associa-
tion, 1947.

3687. Repp, Arthur C. "Some Directives for the
Education of a More Excellent Ministry."
Concordia Theological Monthly 35 (December
1964):701-9.

3688. Repp, A. "Task of the Theological Professor."
Concordia Theological Monthly 43 (May
1972):308-13.

3689. Repp, A. C. "Tribute to an Evangelical
Ministry [Alfred Ottomar Fuerbringer]."
Concordia Theological Monthly 40 (June,
July - August 1969):330-6.

3690. Resolution Adopted by the Western Section of
the American Association of Theological
Seminaries." Christian Century 60 (May 26,
1943):639.

3691. "Resources Planning in Theological Education."
Theological Education 4 (Summer 1968):751-
833 (entire issue).

3692. "Responses to Proposals re Resources
Planning." Theological Education 5 (Winter
1969):65-118, (entire issue).

3693. Reuter, Alan C. "The Praxis of Preaching: An
Essay on Method." Trinity Seminary Review
3 (Spring 1981):9-13.

3694. "Rev. Ebenezer Porter, D. D., Late President
of the Theological Seminary, Andover."

319

American Quarterly Register 9 (August
1836):9-16.

3695. A Review of Dr. Dana's Remonstrance Respecting
Andover Theological Seminary. Boston:
Crocker & Brewster, 1853.

3696. Review of Half Century of Union Theological
Seminary, 1896-1945, by H. S. Coffin.
Newsweek 43 (May 31, 1954):50.

3697. "Reviews of Mental Discipline, by Henry
Forster Burder and Letters on Clerical
Manners and Habits, by Samuel Miller."
Christian Examiner 4 (1827):324-33.

3698. "Revised Course [Yale University Divinity
School]." School and Society 22 (November
28, 1925):677.

3699. "Revolt in the Seminary: St. John's
Seminary." Newsweek 67 (April 18,
1966):68-9.

3700. Reynolds, C. H. and Cupples, J. E.
"Chronology of Vietnam Protest at Harvard
Divinity School." Harvard Divinity Bul-
letin 1 (New Series) (Winter 1968):9-11.

3701. Rian, Edwin Harold. The Presbyterian Conflict. Grand Rapids, Mich.: William B.
Eerdmans Publishing Co., 1940.

3702. Rice, Frank Bertran, Jr. "Selected Factors
Associated with Faculty Recruitment and
Mobility among Bible Colleges." Ph.D.
dissertation, Washington State University,
1973.

3703. Rice, John H. "Ministerial Character and
Preparation Best Adapted to the Wants of
the United States, and of the World, in the
Nineteenth Century." American Quarterly
Register 1 (1829):209-16.

3704. Rich, M. "Beyond Seminary: Movement for
Continuing Education of Ministers."
Christian Century 82 (July 7, 1965):877-8.

3705. Rich, Mark. The Rural Church Movement.
Columbia, Mo.: Juniper Knoll Press, 1957.

3706. Rich, Mark. "Training for the Urban
       Ministry." Christian Century 81 (January
       29, 1964):148-9.

3707. Rich, Noah Glendean. "A Description of
       Personality Characteristics and Interests
       of Assemblies of God Pastors and Minis-
       terial Students." Ph.D. dissertation,
       United States International University,
       1981.

3708. Richard, J. W. "(Ministerial Training for the
       Times.)" Lutheran Quarterly 7 (New Series)
       (1977):477+.

3709. Richard, R. L. "New Breed Seminarians."
       America 112 (February 6, 1965):194.
       "Discussion." 112 (April 17, 1965):529+.

3710. Richard Meier & Partners. "A Progression into
       Light: The Hartford Seminary." Architec-
       tural Record 170 (January 1982):65-73.

3711. Richards, George Warren. History of the
       Theological Seminary of the Reformed Church
       in the United States, 1825-1934, Evangeli-
       cal and Reformed Church, 1934-1952.
       Lancaster, Pa., 1952.

3712. Richards, George Warren. "The Mercersburg
       Theology - Its Purpose and Principles."
       Church History 20 (September 1951):42-55.

3713. Richards, G. W. "Spirit of the Seminary
       [Theological Seminary of the Reformed
       Church in the United States]." Reformed
       Church Review 5 (January 1926):74-85.

3714. Richards, James McDowell, Jr. "Prediction of
       Academic Achievement in a Protestant
       Theological Seminary." Educational and
       Psychological Measurement 17 (Winter
       1957):628-30.

3715. Richardson, Caroline Francis. English
       Preachers and Preaching, 1640-1670. New
       York: Macmillan Co., 1928.

3716. Richardson, Cyril C. "Church History Past and
       Present [Its Teaching at Union, NYC, 1849-
       1949]." Union Seminary Quarterly Review 5
       (November 1949):5-15.

3717. Richardson, C. C. "Veritas - Unitas - Caritas." Union Seminary Quarterly Review 17 (November 1961):61-9.

3718. Richardson, Fredrick. "American Baptists' Southern Mission [Higher Education for Blacks]." Foundations 18, no. 2 (1975):136-45.

3719. Richardson, Harold Wellington. "A Study of the Readiness of American Baptist Theological Students Holding Opposing 'Fundamentalist' and 'Modernist' Theological Views to Associate in Religious Groups with Those Differing from Themselves." Ph.D. dissertation, University of Michigan, 1952.

3720. Richardson, J. F. and Richardson, A. "Training for the Ministry." Church Quarterly Review 156 (October-December 1955):367-71.

3721. Richardson, Jack. "Kemper College of Missouri." Historical Magazine of the Protestant Episcopal Church 30 (June 1961):111-26.

3722. Richardson, N. E. "Extension Service in Theological Seminaries." Christian Education 21 (October 1937):25-30.

3723. Richardson, Robert. Memoirs of Alexander Campbell. 2 vols. Philadelphia: J. B. Lippincott & Co., 1868-70.

3724. Richey, Russell E. "Liberalism, Theological Education and the Churches." Drew Gateway 42 (Winter 1972):78-90.

3725. Richmond. Union Theological Seminary. Centennial General Catalogue of the Trustees, Officers, Professors and Alumni of Union Theological Seminary in Virginia, 1807-1907. Edited by Walter W. Moore and Tilden Scherer. Richmond, Va.: Printed by Whittet & Shepperson, 1908.

3726. Riday, George Emil. "A Comparative Study of the Counseling Methods Employed by the Graduates of Andover Newton Theological School and Eastern Baptist Theological Seminary." Ph.D. dissertation, University of Michigan, 1956.

3727. Ridder, Herman J. "Theological Education and Today's Mission of the Church." Reformed Review 17 (December 1963):3-15.

3728. Ridder, H. J. "Western Seminary and the Churches' Need for Ministers." Reformed Review 19 (March 1966):5-9.

3729. Rieman, Elizabeth Glick. "The Feasibility of Enhancing Marriage through Experiential Theology in the Seminary Setting." Review of Religious Research 21 (Summer 1980):369-70.

3730. Riesman, David. "Toward an Anthropological Science of Law and the Legal Profession." American Journal of Sociology 57 (September 1951):121-35.

3731. Rigdon, V. Bruce and Will, J. E. "Needed: New Modes For Internationalizing Theological Education." Christian Century 87 (April 22, 1970):501-5.

3732. Riggan, G. A. "Theology in the New Curriculum." Hartford Quarterly 4 (Spring 1964).

3733. Riggs, James F. "Relation of the Seminary to Foreign Missions." In Christianity Practically Applied, v. 2, pp. 448-53. Evangelical Alliance for the United States of America. Conference. Chicago, 1893. New York: Baker & Taylor, 1894.

3734. "Rights and Freedom of Students as Members of the Academic Community." Theological Education 4 (Winter 1968):647-53.

3735. Riley, Theodore Myers. A Memorial Biography of the Very Reverend Eugene Augustus Hoffman. 2 vols. Jamaica, N.Y.: Privately Printed at the Marion Press, 1904.

3736. Riley, Thomas James. "Standardizing Training Institutions for Religious and Social Workers." Religious Education 7 (December 1912):555-8.

3737. Ringenberg, William C. "A Brief History of Fort Wayne Bible College." Mennonite Quarterly Review 54 (April 1980):135-55.

3738. Ripley, G. "Letter to a Theological Student."
       In The Dial: A Magazine for Literature,
       Philosophy, and Religion, v. 1, pp. 183-7.
       Russell & Russell, 1961.

3739. Rising, Richard L. "Confrontation at the
       Christian Theological Union." Theological
       Education 6 (Summer 1970):260-70.

3740. Rising, Richard L. "Theological Education: A
       Bird's Eye Perspective." Theological
       Education 6 (Autumn 1970):49-56.

3741. Riss, Paul. "A Study of the Critical
       Requirements of Teachers in the Lutheran
       Seminaries in the United States of
       America." Ph.D. dissertation, New York
       University, 1969.

3742. Rist, M. "Iliff Theological School Library."
       Library Journal 81 (December 1, 1956):2786-
       9.

3743. Roark, Dallas M. "J. Gresham Machen: The
       Doctrinally True Presbyterian Church."
       Journal of Presbyterian History 43 (June-
       September 1965):124-38, 174-81.

3744. Robbins, Jhan and June. "The Surprising
       Beliefs of Our Future Ministers." Redbook
       117 (August 1961):36+.

3745. Robbins, Sarah (Stuart). Old Andover Days:
       Memories of a Puritan Childhood. Boston:
       Pilgrim Press, 1908.

3746. Roberts, David E. "Case of the Union
       Students." Christian Century 57 (October
       30, 1940):1340-2.

3747. Roberts, Edward Howell. "Ecumenical Educa-
       tion." Christian Century 70 (April 29,
       1953):506-8.

3748. Roberts, Harry Walter. "The Rural Negro
       Minister: His Educational Status."
       Journal of Negro Education 17 (1948):478-
       87.

3749. Roberts, J. D. "Black Theological Education:
       Programming for Liberation." Christian
       Century 91 (February 6, 1974):117-18.

3750. Roberts, J. Deotis. "Where Do We Go from Here
[Interdenominational Theological Center,
Atlanta]." AME Zion Quarterly Review 93
(July 1981):26-32.

3751. Roberts, Oral. The Call: An Autobiography.
Garden City, N.Y.: Doubleday & Co., 1972.

3752. Roberts, Preston. "Two Experiments in
Correlation: The Field of Religion and Art
at Chicago." Christian Scholar 40 (1957):
339-45.

3753. Roberts, W. H. "(Methods of Control of
Presbyterian Theological Seminaries.)"
Presbyterian and Reformed Review 4
(1893):94+.

3754. Roberts, Walter Nelson. "The Idea of a
Theological School: Educating a Ministry
of Quality." Encounter 18 (Spring 1957):
182-7.

3755. Roberts, William Lloyd. "The Supervisory
Alternative to the Custodial Contract in
the Educational Ministry." Th.D. dissertation, Princeton Theological Seminary,
1970.

3756. Robertson, Archibald Thomas. Life and Letters
of John Albert Broadus. Philadelphia:
American Baptist Publication Society, 1901.

3757. Robins, H. B. "Re-organizataion of the
Theological Seminary in the Light of the
Needs of Today." Religious Education 15
(February 1920):29-32.

3758. Robins, Henry B. "The Theological Curriculum
and A Teaching Ministry." American Journal
of Theology 22 (October 1918):465-78.

3759. Robins, H. B. "Theological Education and the
Previous Question." Biblical World 44
(October 1914):248-52.

3760. Robinson, Edward. "Theological Education in
Germany." Biblical Repository 1 (1831):1-
51, 201-26, 409-51, 613-37.

3761. Robinson, Edward and Smith, Eli. Biblical
Researches in Palestine, and in the
Adjacent Regions. 3 vols. Boston:

Crocker & Brewster, 1856.

3762. Robinson, Ezekiel Gilman. *Ezekiel Gilman Robinson: An Autobiography*. Edited by E. H. Johnson. New York: Silver, Burdett & Company, 1896.

3763. Robinson, George Livingstone. *Autobiography of George L. Robinson*. Grand Rapids, Mich.: Baker Book House, 1957.

3764. Robinson, George Livingstone. *The Decalogue and Criticism: Or, The Place of the Decalogue in the Development of the Hebrew Religion. Inaugural Address... McCormick Theological Seminary, Chicago, Ill., May 3, 1899*. Chicago: R. R. Donnelley, 1899.

3765. Robinson, Ira E., Gersmehl, Carol A. and Smith, C. Neil. "A Study of Religious Meanings among Pastors, Seminarians, and Laymembers." University of Georgia, Athens, 1977.

3766. Robinson, James Herman. *Road without Turning: The Story of Reverend James H. Robinson: An Autobiography*. New York: Farrar, Straus & Co., 1950.

3767. Robinson, John A. T. "The Teaching of Theology for the Ministry." *Theology* 61 (December 1958):486-95.

3768. Robinson, William Childs. *Columbia Theological Seminary and the Southern Presbyterian Church: A Study in Church History, Presbyterian Polity, Missionary Enterprise, and Religious Thought*. Decatur, Ga.: Dennis Lindsey Printing Co, 1931.

3769. Rockefeller, John D., Jr. "The Christian Church: What of Its future?" *Saturday Evening Post* 190 (February 9, 1918):16-37.

3770. Rockefeller, John Davison. *Random Reminiscences of Men and Events*. Garden City, N. Y.: Doubleday, Doran & Company, 1933.

3771. Rockwell, William Walker. "Theological Libraries in the United States." *Religion in Life* 13 (1943-44):545-55.

3772. Rogers, C. "Black Theological Education: Successes and Failures." *Christian Century* 88 (January 27, 1971):129-31.

3773. Rogers, C. A. "What Is Christian Ministry?" *Duke Divinity School Review* 33 (Spring 1968):82-8.

3774. Rogers, Donald B. "Enhancing Learner Awareness through Feedback Instruments." *Theological Education* 13 (Spring 1977):158-67.

3775. Rogers, Jack Bartlett. *Confessions of a Conservative Evangelical.* Philadelphia: Westminster Press, 1974.

3776. Rogers, K. H. "Preparation for an Effective Pastoral Ministry." *Journal of Pastoral Care* 10 (Autumn 1956):161-9.

3777. Rohlfs, Claus H. *Contextual Education: Internship.* Occasional Papers no. 35. Nashville, Tenn.: United Methodist Board of Higher Education and Ministry, 1981.

3778. Rohlfs, Claus H. "History of the Development of the Perkins Intern Program." *Perkins School of Theology: Journal* 31 (Winter 1978):1-31.

3779. "The Role of Rural Social Science in Theological Education [With Particular Application to the Town and Country Ministry of the Methodist Church]." Evanston, Ill.: Garrett Theological Seminary, 1969. (ERIC Document)

3780. "Role of the Theological Seminary in Modern Culture." *College of the Bible Quarterly* 39 (January 1962):30-7.

3781. Ronning, N. N. "Red Wing Seminar - Hauges Synodes College Og Presteskole." *Symra; a Norwegian-American Quarterly* 6 (1910):38-50.

3782. "Roof Raising at Clear Creek Mountain Preachers Bible School." *Newsweek* 37 (May 14, 1951):94.

3783. Rooks, Charles Shelby. "The Black Church: Its Implications for Lutheran Theological

Education." <u>Concordia Theological Monthly</u>
40 (November 1969):682-91.

3784. Rooks, Charles Shelby, ed. "The Black
Religious Experience and Theological
Education for the Seventies." <u>Theological
Education</u> 6 (Spring 1970, Suppl.):entire
issue.

3785. Rooks, C. S. "Crisis in Church Negro Leadership." <u>Theology Today</u> 22 (October 1965):
323-35.

3786. Rooks, Charles Shelby. "Crisis in Theological
Education." <u>Theological Education</u> 7
(Autumn 1970):16-27.

3787. Rooks, C. S. "Cross to Bear [Goal of
Excellence for Black Seminarians]."
<u>Journal of Religious Thought</u> 20, no. 2
(1963-64):131-5.

3788. Rooks, Charles S. "'Dream, Dream, Dream.'"
<u>Theological Education</u> 15 (Spring 1979):135-
40.

3789. Rooks, C. Shelby. "The Image of the Ministry
as Reflected in the Protestant Fellowship
Program." <u>Journal of Religious Thought</u> 18
(1961-62):137-48.

3790. Rooks, Charles S. "A New Day Dawns [Address
Given at Dedication of Howard University
Divinity School]." <u>Journal of Religious
Thought</u> 38 (Spring-Summer 1981):5-11.

3791. Rooks, Charles Shelby. "Response to Paul
Holmes." <u>Theological Education</u> 7 (Spring
1971):215-18.

3792. Rooks, C. Shelby. "Response to President
Bennett - II." <u>Theological Education</u> 3
(Winter 1967):294-7.

3793. Rooks, C. S. "Shortage of Negro Theological
Students." <u>Christianity and Crisis</u> 25
(February 22, 1965):20-3.

3794. Rooks, C. S. "Theological Education and the
Black Church." <u>Christian Century</u> 86
(February 12, 1969):212-16.

3795. Rooks, C. S. "Theological Reflection in an Uncertain Age." Theology Today 36 (July 1979):220-7.

3796. Rooks, C. Shelby. "Why a Conference on the Black Religious Experience?" Theological Education 6 (Spring 1970):173-80.

3797. Rooy, Sidney H. "Theological Education for Urban Mission." In Discipling the City, pp. 175-207. Edited by Roger S. Greenway. Grand Rapids: Baker Book House, 1979.

3798. Ropes, C. J. H. "The Importance and the Method of Bible Study." New Englander 41 (September 1882):567-87.

3799. Ropes, C. J. H. "The Literary Work of Joseph Henry Thayer." American Journal of Theology 6 (April 1902):285-93.

3800. Ropes, James Hardy. "The New Testament in the Theological School." Christian Education 13 (October 1929):38-43.

3801. Ropes, J. H. "Theological Education at Harvard." Harvard Alumni Bulletin 17 (January 13, 1915):260-4.

3802. Roscoe, James Ernest. A Short History of Theological Education. London: Mitre Press, 1948.

3803. Roscoe, John T. and Girling, Paul A. "American Theological Students: A Survey of Their Value Commitments." Paper Presented at the Annual Meeting of the American Educational Research Association, Los Angeles, February 1969. (ERIC Document)

3804. Roscoe, John T. and Girling, Paul A. "Survey of Values of American Theological Students [Bibliog]." Review of Religious Research 11 (Spring 1910):210-18.

3805. Rose, Stephen C. "Listening to the World's Alarm Bells." Union Seminary Quarterly Review 22, no. 4 (1967):307-18.

3806. Ross, Ian. "Theological Education and Student Reaction in the United Kingdom." Theological Education 4 (Winter 1968):640-6.

3807. Rossman, Parker. "The Clergyman's Needs for
        Continuing Education." N.d. (ERIC
        Document)

3808. Rossman, P. "Should Primary Responsibility
        Rest on the Seminary? Yes." Theological
        Education 1 (Summer 1965):226-9.

3809. Roth, Gary G. "Wake Forest College and the
        Rise of Southeastern Baptist Theological
        Seminary, 1945-1951." Baptist History and
        Heritage 11 (1976):69-79.

3810. Rothstein, William G. American Physicians in
        the Nineteenth Century: From Sects to
        Science. Baltimore: Johns Hopkins
        University Press, 1972.

3811. Rottenberg, I. C. "Tendencies and Trends in a
        Century of Theological Education at Western
        Theological Seminary." Reformed Review 20
        (December 1966):22-4+.

3812. Rouch, Mark A. Competent Ministry: A Guide
        to Effective Continuing Education.
        Nashville: Abingdon Press, 1974.

3813. Rouch, Mark A. "A System Model for Continuing
        Education for the Ministry." Educational
        Technology 9 (June 1969):32-8.

3814. "Roundtable on Seminaries: Measuring the
        Vital Signs." United Evangelical Action 37
        (Fall 1978):14-17.

3815. Rouner, Leroy S. "Knocking Seminaries'
        'Knack' Courses: Notes on Theory and
        Practice in Theological Education."
        Christian Century 93 (February 4-11,
        1976):112-15.

3816. Rowatt, George Wade, Jr. "Pastoral Research:
        A Research Model for Pastoral Ministry
        Using Selected Seminary Student Ministers."
        Th.D. dissertation, Southern Baptist
        Theological Seminary, 1974.

3817. Rowatt, G. Wade. "What Is Pastoral Research?"
        Review and Expositor 79, no. 3 (1982):503-
        11.

3818. Rowe, Henry K. History of Andover Theological
        Seminary. Newton, Mass., 1933.

3819. Rowe, Kalloch Henry. History of Andover Theological Seminary. Newton, Mass., 1933.

3820. Rowe, Kenneth E. "New Light on Early Methodist Theological Education." Methodist History 10 (October 1971):58-62.

3821. Rowen, Samuel Frederick. "Curriculum Foundations, Experiences and Outcomes: A Participatory Case Study in Theological Education." Ph.D. dissertation, Michigan State University, 1981.

3822. Rowland, S. J., Jr. "Students in Search of Faith." New York Times Magazine (November 30, 1958):47+.

3823. Rowland, W. "Finance Your Graduate Study." International Journal of Religious Education 42 (December 1965):7+.

3824. Rozwenc, Edwin Charles and Roehm, A. Wesley, eds. The Status Revolution and the Progressive Movement. Boston: Heath, 1963.

3825. Ruben, Paul. "Consortium of the Seminaries." Change 4 (June 1972):21-3.

3826. Rudnick, Milton L. Fundamentalism and the Missouri Synod: A Historical Study of Their Interaction and Mutual Influence. St. Louis: Concordia Publishing House, 1966.

3827. Ruesink, David Charles. "A Study of the Seminary Student's Perception of Practitioner Roles to be Performed by the Minister." Ph.D. dissertation, North Carolina State University at Raleigh, 1967.

3828. Ruether, Rosemary Radford. "The Feminist Critique in Religious Studies." Soundings: An Interdisciplinary Journal 64 (Winter 1981):388-402.

3829. Ruether, Rosemary Radford. "Pastoral Education for New Communities." Theology Today 26 (July 1969):187-94.

3830. Rumford, Douglas. "What To Expect of a Seminary Graduate." Christianity Today 25 (February 6, 1981):24-5.

3831.   Rumpf, O. J.   "Theological Education for
        Laymen: Lay School of Theology at Eden
        Theological Seminary, Webster Groves, Mo."
        International Journal of Religious
        Education 38 (March 1962):18-19.

3832.   Runyon, T.   "Theology and Praxis at the Oxford
        Institute."   Christian Century 99
        (September 15-22, 1982):916.

3833.   Ruoss, George Martin.   A World Directory of
        Theological Libraries.   Metuchen, N.J.:
        Scarecrow Press, 1968.

3834.   Rupp, G.   "Cambridge Centenary: The Selwyn
        Divinity School, 1879-1979."   Historical
        Journal 24 (June 1981):417-28.

3835.   Rupp, W.   "(Place of Social Science in
        Theological Seminaries.)"   Reformed Church
        Review 48 (1901):558+.

3836.   Russell, Charles Allyn.   Voices of American
        Fundamentalism: Seven Biographical
        Studies.   Philadelphia: Westminster Press,
        1976.

3837.   Russell, Letty M.   "Clerical Ministry as a
        Female Profession."   Christian Century 96
        (February 7, 1979):125-6.

3838.   Russell, Letty M.   "Education as Exodus."
        Mid-Stream 19 (January 1980):3-9.

3839.   Russell, Letty Mandeville.   "Tradition as
        Mission: Study of a New Current in
        Theology and Its Implications for
        Theological Education."   Th.D. disserta-
        tion, Union Theological Seminary in the
        City of New York, 1969.

3840.   Rust, Eric C.   "Theological Emphases of the
        Past Three Decades."   Review and Expositor
        78 (Spring 1981):259-70.

3841.   Rutschman, Laverne.   "Anabaptism and
        Liberation Theology."   Mennonite Quarterly
        Review 55 (July 1981):255-70.

3842.   Ryan, John Henry.   "The Teaching of Oral
        Interpretation in Roman Catholic Seminaries
        in the United States."   Ph.D. dissertation,
        University of Missouri-Columbia, 1973.

3843. Ryan, Michael Daniel. "Theology at Drew: Between Its Past and Future." Drew Gateway 41 (Winter 1971):70-82.

3844. Ryan, Richard. "Problem of the Ex-Seminarian." Catholic World 186 (October 1957):28-33.

3845. Ryrie, C. C. "Bible Colleges Gain Stature." United Evangelical Action 20 (June 1961):131-2.

3846. Rystrom, John Kenneth. "The Control and Support of Higher Education in the Lutheran Church in America." Ph.D. dissertation, University of Minnesota, 1955.

3847. "SBC Seminary Growth." Christian Century 99 (January 6, 1982):9.

3848. Saarinen, Martin F. "Survey of Pastors' Concerns in Continuing Education." Columbia, S.C.: Lutheran Theological Southern Seminary, 1972.

3849. Sailer, T. H. P. "What Is the Purpose of a Missionary Institute?" Missionary Review of the World 53 (June 1930):455.

3850. Saint Andrews As It Was and As It Is: Being the Third Edition of Dr. Grierson's Delineations, Containing Much Curious and Valuable Information Never Before Printed. Cupar: Printed by G. S. Tullis, 1838.

3851. Salisbury, W. Seward. "Some Theoretical and Methodological Problems in a Comparative Study of Finnish and American Protestant Seminarians." State University College, Oswego, N.Y., 1969.

3852. Salomon, Richard G. "Philander Chase, Norman Nash, and Charles Bullfinch: A Study in the Origins of Old Kenyon." Historical Magazine of the Protestant Episcopal Church 15 (September 1946):209-31.

3853. Salvation Army. Living Epistles: Sketches of the Social Work of the Salvation Army. London, 1903.

3854. Salzman, S. F. "The Theology of Wartburg Seminary." Wartburg Seminary Quarterly 17

(November 1954):12+.

3855. Sampey, John Richard. Memoirs of John R. Sampey. Nashville, Tenn.: Broadman, 1947.

3856. "A Sample Constitution of the Evangelical Students Union [American Baptist Seminary of the West]." TSF Bulletin 4 (November 1980):8-9.

3857. Samuelson, Glenn Waldemar. "A Study in Curriculum Planning at Bethel Theological Seminary." Ed.D. dissertation, University of Maryland, 1960.

3858. Sandeen, Ernest R. "Defining Fundamentalism: A Reply to Professor Marsden." Christian Scholar's Review 1 (Spring 1971):227-33.

3859. Sandeen, Ernest R. "The Lively Experiment: A Review Article." Journal of Religion 44, no. 4 (1964):328-34.

3860. Sandeen, Ernest Robert. The Origins of Fundamentalism: Toward a Historical Interpretation. Philadelphia: Fortress Press, 1968.

3861. Sandeen, Ernest R. "The Princeton Theology: One Source of Biblical Literalism in American Protestantism." Church History 31 (1962):307-21.

3862. Sandeen, Ernest Robert. The Roots of Fundamentalism: British and American Millenarianism, 1800-1930. Chicago: University of Chicago Press, 1970.

3863. Sandeen, Ernest R. "Toward a Historical Interpretation of the Origins of Fundamentalism." Church History 36, no. 1 (1967):66-83.

3864. Sanders, C. F. "The Standard of Ministerial Scholarship." Lutheran Quarterly 28 (1898):419-29.

3865. Sanders, Frank Knight. "Training Missionaries: The Missionary Training Schools in the Field and at the Home Base: Their Respective Tasks." Religious Education 14 (December 1919):369-73.

3866. Sanders, Robert Stuart. History of Louisville
Presbyterian Theological Seminary, 1853-
1953. Louisville, Ky.: Louisville Presbyterian Theological Seminary, 1953.

3867. Sanders, Robert Stuart. "The Louisville Pres-
byterian Theological Seminary [1853-1953]."
Filson Club Historical Quarterly 27
(October 1953):321-6.

3868. Sanderson, Paul David. "A Descriptive
Analysis of Supervision in Clinical
Pastoral Education." Ph.D. dissertation,
Boston University Graduate School, 1977.

3869. Sandusky, Fred William. "The Admissions
Practices and Procedures to the Bachelor of
Divinity Program of Studies of the
Accredited Protestant Theological
Seminaries in the United States." Ed.D.
dissertation, Duke University, 1964.

3870. Sandusky, F. "Applications for Admission to
the Accredited Protestant Theological
Seminaries in the United States." College
and University 40 (Winter 1965):153-6.

3871. Sargent, Barbara. "Love in a Cold Climate
[Bangor Theological Seminary, Maine]."
Christian Century 97 (February 6-13,
1980):164-7.

3872. Sartain, Geraldine. "Mending Broken Lives:
Recounting a Visit to Riker's Island."
National Council Outlook 7 (October
1957):9-10.

3873. Sastrow, Bartholomäus. Social Germany in
Luther's Time. Westminster: A. Constable,
1902.

3874. "Satellite Abandoned: Christian Missionary
Alliance." Christianity Today 14 (June 19,
1970):36-7.

3875. Satterwhite, John Henry. "An Evaluation of
Hood Theological Seminary in the Light of
Its History." Ph.D. dissertation, Boston
University, 1957.

3876. Savage, Doris M. "The Rochester Theological
Seminary in the Old United States Hotel."
Rochester History 31 (July 1969):1-23.

335

3877. Savage, Peter. "My Crisis in Theological
       Education." Evangelical Missions Quarterly
       12, no. 1 (1976):25-30.

3878. Savage, William E. "Faith and Fruition in
       Finance." Asbury Seminarian 16 (Spring-
       Summer 1962):34-6.

3879. Scarborough, Lee Rutland. A Modern School of
       the Prophets: A History of the South-
       western Baptist Theological Seminary...Its
       First Thirty Years, 1907-1937. Nashville,
       Tenn.: Broadman Press, 1939.

3880. Schaaf, David Schley. The Life of Philip
       Schaff. New York: Charles Scribner's
       Sons, 1897.

3881. Schaaf, James Lewis. "Wilhelm Lhöhe's Rela-
       tions to the American Church: A Study in
       the History of Lutheran Mission." Doctoral
       dissertation, Evangelisch-Theologischen
       Fakultät der Ruprecht-Karl-Universität
       Heidelberg, 1961.

3882. Schaff, Philip. America: A Sketch of Its
       Political, Social, and Religious Character.
       Cambridge: Belknap Press of Harvard
       University Press, 1961.

3883. Schaff, Philip. Germany: Its Universities,
       Theology, and Religion. Philadelphia:
       Lindsay & Blakiston, 1857.

3884. Schaff, Philip. Theological Propaedeutic: A
       General Introduction to the Study of
       Theology: A Manual for Students. 2 v.
       New York: Charles Scribner's Sons, 1892-
       1893.

3885. Schaff, Philip. The Theology for our Age and
       Country. New York: Rogers & Sherwood,
       1872.

3886. Schaper, Richard L. "The Challenge of the New
       Student." Christianity and Crisis 29
       (April 14, 1969):91-2.

3887. Schaper, R. L. "Theological Student: A New
       Breed." Lutheran World 17, no. 3 (1970):
       274-9.

3888. Scharlemann, E. K. and Scharlemann, M. H. "A 'Hospitant' to the Seminary." *Concordia Historical Institute Quarterly* 49, no. 1 (1976):23-8.

3889. Scharlemann, Martin H. "Taped Interviews with the Rev. Dr. Ernst K. Scharlemann; Pt. 1: Hospitant to the Seminary, Pt. 2: A Foreigner Goes Native, Pt. 3: The Mob is Coming." *Concordia Historical Institute Quarterly* 49 (Spring 1976):23-8; (Summer 1976):64-71; (Fall 1976):123-30.

3890. Schauffler, A. F. "The Training of Theological Students in Mission Work." In *Proceedings of the Second Convention of the International Christian Workers Association*, pp. 116-21. New Haven, 1887.

3891. Schauffler, Grace Leavitt. *Fields of the Lord: The Story of Schauffler College (1886-1957)*. Oberlin, Ohio, 1957.

3892. Scheets, F. K. "Educating Priests After the Seminary." *America* 120 (May 3, 1969):526-8.

3893. Schelling, F. E. "(Seminary Method.)" *American* (Philadelphia) 16 (1888):407+.

3894. Scherer, Ron. "Bad Times Get Some Clergy To Study Economics." *Christian Science Monitor* 74 (May 13, 1982):10.

3895. Schieffelin, Samuel. *Words to Christian Teachers and Students for the Ministry*. 6th ed. Philadelphia: American Sunday School Union, 1888.

3896. Schilling, S. P. "Value of Clinical Training in the Ministry." *Christian Education* 19 (June 1936):376-82.

3897. Schleiermacher, Friedrich. *Brief Outline of the Study of Theology*. Edinburgh: T & T Clark, 1850.

3898. Schlicher, J. J. "Beginning and Early Years of the Mission House [bibliog.]." *Wisconsin Magazine of History* 25 (September 1941):51-72.

3899. Schlicher, J. J. "Mission House in the
       Eighties." Wisconsin Magazine of History
       25 (December 1941):187-209.

3900. Schmelling, W. D. Ministers and Laymen of the
       EUB Church. Dayton: United Theological
       Seminary, 1958.

3901. Schmemann, Alexander. "Response to Professors
       Burghardt and Minear: An Orthodox View."
       Theological Education 3 (Winter 1967):317-
       18.

3902. Schmemann, Alexander. "Thoughts for the
       Jubilee." St Vladimir's Theological
       Quarterly 13 (1969):95-102.

3903. Schmidt, G. Daniel et al. "Faculty
       Perceptions of Clergy in Counselor
       Education Programs." Counselor Education
       and Supervision 13 (June 1974):294-7.

3904. Schmidt, Gail R. "A Dream of the Rood."
       Dialog 18 (Spring 1979):103-7.

3905. Schmidt, George P. "Reminiscences of
       Concordia Seminary in the Early Twentieth
       Century." Concordia Historical Institute
       Quarterly 43, no. 2 (1970):79-82.

3906. Schmidt, J. "Foreign Missions in Our
       Seminaries." Lutheran Quarterly 15 (May
       1963):144-50.

3907. Schmidt, Stephen A. Powerless Pedagogues: An
       Interpretive Essay on the History of the
       Lutheran Teacher in the Missouri Synod.
       River Forest, Ill.: Lutheran Education
       Association, 1972.

3908. Schmitt, Calvin H. "Reflections on the
       Changing Role of the Library in a
       Theological Seminary." Reformed Review 35
       (Spring 1982):152-6.

3909. Schmitt, Calvin H. Self-Appraisal Guide. New
       Haven, Conn.: ATLA Library Development
       Program, 1962.

3910. Schmitthenner, John W. "The Origin and
       Educational Contribution of Hartwick
       Seminary." Ph.D. dissertation, New York
       University, 1934.

3911. Schmotter, James W. "The Irony of Clerical
        Professionalism: New England's
        Congregational Ministers and the Great
        Awakening." American Quarterly 31, no. 2
        (1979):148-68.

3912. Schmucker, Samuel Simon. The American
        Lutheran Church: Historically, Doc-
        trinally, and Practically Delineated, In
        Several Occasional Discoveries. 5th ed.
        Philadelphia: E. W. Miller, 1852.

3913. Schmucker, Samuel Simon. An Inaugural
        Address, Delivered Before the Directors of
        the Theological Seminary of the General
        Synod of the Evangelical Lutheran Church.
        Carlisle, Pa.: Printed by Tizzard &
        Crever, 1826.

3914. "Scholarship and the Ministry." Christian
        Century 54 (June 1, 1937):736-7.

3915. Scholl, George. "Ministerial Education."
        Lutheran Quarterly Review 20 (1890):395-
        404.

3916. Schomer, Howard. "Theology For All the
        People." Christian Century 76 (April 22,
        1959):475-7.

3917. Schomer, Howard. "Understanding Other
        Communities Around the Seminary Community."
        Theological Education 2 (Autumn 1965):28-
        33.

3918. "School of the Preachers." Evangelist of the
        True Gospel 6 (New Series) (January 1838):
        14-15.

3919. "Schools of the Methodist Episcopal Church."
        School and Society 9 (April 19, 1919):471-
        2.

3920. "Schools of Theology." In American Educa-
        tional Directory, 1930, pp. 718-23. Edited
        by H. L. Patterson. North Chicago, Ill.:
        Educational Directories, 1931.

3921. "Schools of Theology." In American Educa-
        tional Directory, 1936, pp. 718-23. Edited
        by H. La F. Patterson.

3922. "Schools of Theology." In American Educational Directory, 1937, pp. 718-23. Edited by H. La F. Patterson.

3923. "Schools of Theology." In American Educational Directory, 1940, pp. 718-23. Edited by H. L. Patterson.

3924. "Schools of Theology." In American Educational Directory, 1941, pp. 718-23. Edited by H. L. Patterson.

3925. "Schools of Theology." In Patterson's American Educational Directory, 1950, pp. 727-32. North Chicago: Educational Directories.

3926. "Schools of Theology." In Patterson's American Educational Directory, 1951, pp. 574-7. North Chicago: Educational Directories.

3927. "Schools of Theology." In Patterson's American Education, pp. 551-5. North Chicago: Educational Directories, 1956-57.

3928. "Schools of Theology [Mercer Memorial School of Theology]." Overview 1 (September 1960):83.

3929. "Schools of Theology: Name of Institution, Location, and President or Dean." In Educational Directory, 1931, pp. 83-6. United States. Office of Education, 1931.

3930. "Schools of Theology: Name of Institution, Location, and President or Dean." In Educational Directory, 1932, pp. 92-5. United States. Office of Education, 1932, pt. 2.

3931. Schreiter, Robert. "Two Consultations on Christianity and Religious Pluralism [Union Theological Seminary, Richmond, and Princeton Theological Seminary, October 1979]." Journal of Ecumenical Studies 17 (Winter 1980):210-11.

3932. Schroderbek, Charles G. "Sacred-Secular Definitions of the Priest's Role and Perseverance in the Seminary: Study of a Missionary Order of Men." Ph.D. dissertation, Catholic University of

America, 1970.

3933. Schroeder, W. Widick and Obenhaus, Victor.
Religion in American Culture: Unity and
Diversity in a Midwestern County. New
York: Free Press of Glencoe, 1964.

3934. Schroth, Raymond A. "End of Woodstock."
Commonweal 97 (January 26, 1973):364-5.

3935. Schuette, Conrad Herman Lewis. Before the
Altar: Or, A Series of Annotated
Propositions on Liturgics. Columbus, Ohio:
Lutheran Book Concern, 1894.

3936. Schuller, David S. "The Association of
Theological Faculties in Iowa (Dubuque): A
Descriptive-Evaluative Study." Theological
Education 4 (Summer Suppl. 1968):22-32.

3937. Schuller, David S. "Basic Issues in Theological Education." Theological Education 17
(Spring 1981):89-181.

3938. Schuller, D. "Called to Service and to
Seminary." Concordia Theological Monthly
41 (December 1970):726-31.

3939. Schuller, David S. "Case Method in Theological Education." Theological Education 4
(Autumn 1967):573-9.

3940. Schuller, David S. "Crisis and Renewal."
Concordia Theological Monthly 40, no. 1
(1969):3-12.

3941. Schuller, D. S. "A Critique of Theological
Education in the Light of Changing American
Culture." Concordia Theological Monthly 35
(December 1964):687-700.

3942. Schuller, D. S. "Formation of Clergy for
Ministry Today." Lutheran World 17, no. 3
(1970):231-44.

3943. Schuller, David S. "Graduate Theological
Union." Theological Education 4 (Summer
1968, Suppl. 1):3-21.

3944. Schuller, David S., ed. "Mission, Spirituality and Scholarship." Theological
Education 17 (Autumn 1980):1-84.

341

3945. Schuller, David S. "A New Degree Program...
But the World is Still Messed Up." Theological Education 6 (Summer 1970):291-315.

3946. Schuller, David S., et al. "Readiness for
Ministry: Significance for Church and
Seminary." Theological Education 12
(Spring 1976):143-205.

3947. Schuller, David S., et al. Readiness for
Ministry. Vandalia, Ohio: Association of
Theological Schools in the United States
and Canada, 1977?

3948. Schuller, David S., et al. Readiness for
Ministry, Volume II Assessment. Vandalia,
Ohio: Association of Theological Schools
in U.S., 1976.

3949. Schuller, D. S. "Reading Programs in Theology
[Concordia Seminary, St. Louis]." Concordia Theological Monthly 37 (October
1966):582.

3950. Schuller, D. S. "Theological Education:
Crisis and Renewal." Concordia Theological
Monthly 40 (January 1969):3-12.

3951. Schuller, David S. "The Toronto Graduate
School of Theological Studies." Theological Education 4 (Summer 1968, Suppl.
1):47-60.

3952. Schuller, David S. "University Religion
Departments: Challenge to Theological
Seminaries." Asbury Seminarian 21 (October
1967):20-3.

3953. Schuller, D. "Your Job, My President..."
Concordia Theological Monthly 43 (May
1972):303-7.

3954. Schultz, R. J. "Responsible Supervision
[bibliog.] [Concordia Theological Seminary,
Springfield, Illinois]." Springfielder 34
(June 1970):2-5.

3955. Schulz, Delphin Leo. "The Development and
Implementation of a Model for Curriculum
Revision for the System of Colleges and
Seminaries of the Lutheran Church -
Missouri Synod." Ph.D. dissertation, Saint
Louis University, 1974.

3956. Schurman, Paul G. and Ronkos, Charles G. "Continuing Education in Pastoral Counseling for Parish Clergy." Journal of Pastoral Care 29, no. 3 (1975):190-2.

3957. Schwalm, Vernon Franklin. "Bethany Biblical Seminary and the Church." Brethren Life and Thought 1 (Spring 1956):22-30.

3958. Schwalm, Vernon Franklin. "The Historical Development of the Denominational Colleges of the Old Northwest to 1870." In Abstracts of Theses, Humanistic Series, v. 5, pp. 299-306. University of Chicago. Chicago: University of Chicago Press, 1928.

3959. Schwartz, Gordon Grant. "A Study of Students' Theological Learning in a Unit of Clinical Pastoral Education." Ph.D. dissertation, Colgate Rochester Divinity School (Bexley Hall) Crozer Theological Seminary, 1974.

3960. Schwartz, Jack Wayne. "The State of Church Music Education for Ministerial Students in Protestant Seminaries in the United States." D.M.A. dissertation, University of Southern California, 1975.

3961. Schweitzer, Albert. The Quest of the Historical Jesus: A Critical Study of Its Progress From Reimarus to Wrede. London: A. & E. Black, 1910.

3962. Scotchmer, Paul F. "Today's Seminary Students: Back to Basics." Christianity Today 23 (February 2, 1979):16-19.

3963. Scott, Donald Eugene. "A Study of Factors Related to Cooperative Activities among the National Boards Responsible for Higher Education in the Three Major Lutheran Churches in North America." Ph.D. dissertation, University of Denver, 1973.

3964. Scott, Donald M. From Office to Profession: The New England Ministry, 1750-1850. Philadelphia: University of Pennsylvania Press, 1978.

3965. Scott, Ernest Findlay. Recent Developments in New Testament Study. Address Delivered before the Union Seminary Alumni Club. New

York: For Union Theological Seminary,
1920.

3966. Scott, H. M. "Relation of the Seminary to the
Foreign Population." In Christianity
Practically Applied. Evangelical Alliance
for the United States of America. Con-
ference. Chicago, 1893, v. 2, pp. 442-7.
New York: Baker & Taylor, 1894.

3967. Scott, Laura. "Additional Aids for
Ministerial Training." Concordia
Theological Monthly 35 (December 1964):743-
6.

3968. Scott, Leland Howard. "Methodist Theology in
America in the Nineteenth Century." Ph.D.
dissertation, Yale University, 1954.

3969. Scott, Marshal L. "Nature of the Ministry,
Historical and Social Background."
McCormick Quarterly 17 (March 1964):3-9.

3970. Scott, M. L. "Presbyterian Institute of
Industrial Relations [Continuing
Education]." Theological Education 1
(Summer 1965).

3971. Scott, Marshal L. "Training For an Industrial
Society." Theology Today 13 (July
1956):189-99.

3972. Scott, Nathan A. "A Neglected Aspect of the
Theological Curriculum." Journal of
Religious Thought 7 (1950):38-46.

3973. Scott, O. "Theological Education." Zion's
Herald 10 (April 10, 1839):59.

3974. Scott, O. "Theological Institution." Zion's
Herald 10 (December 11, 1839):197.

3975. Scovel, Raleigh Don. "Orthodoxy in Princeton:
A Social and Intellectual History of
Princeton Theological Seminary." Ph.D.
dissertation, University of California,
Berkeley, 1970.

3976. Searcy, J. B. "History of Baptist Schools and
Colleges in Arkansas." Arkansas Historical
Association. Publications 2 (1908):307-27.

3977. Sears, Barnas. _An Educated Ministry: An Address Delivered Before the N.Y. Baptist Union for Ministerial Education, At Its Anniversary, Held in Rochester, July 12, 1853._ New York: Lewis Colby & Co., 1853.

3978. Seaton, Craig E. "The Christian College as a Source of Students for Selected Theological Seminaries." La Mirada, Calif.: Biola College, 1970. (ERIC Document)

3979. Seely, Paul H. "The Lecture and Superficial Scholarship." _Theological Education_ 4 (Winter 1968):619-22.

3980. Seelye, Samuel Taylor and Stowe, Calvin E. _Discourses by Rev. Samuel T. Seelye, D.D., and Rev. Calvin E. Stowe, D.D., Delivered at Lowell, Mass., and Hartford, Conn., Before the Society for the Promotion of Collegiate and Theological Education at the West._ New York: John A. Gray & Green, Printers, 1864.

3981. Segler, Franklin M. "Areas of Strategic Insight Which Aid Maturity in Ministerial Students." _Southwestern Journal of Theology_ 5 (Autumn 1963):73-84.

3982. Selbie, W. B. "The Theological Colleges and Religious Education: A Plea for Reform of the Colleges." _Hibbert Journal_ 40 (July 1942):311-19.

3983. Selden, William K. _Accreditation: A Struggle Over Standards in Higher Education._ New York: Harper, 1960.

3984. "Selecting Ministers For Tomorrow." _National Council Outlook_ 6 (June 1956):22.

3985. "Selective Service Defers Pre-Theological Students." _Christian Century_ 6 (May 31, 1944):660.

3986. "Self-education." _Zion's Herald_ 10 (June 5, 1839):91.

3987. Seligman, D. "Seminarian Economics [Survey of Professors in Christian Theology Schools]." _Fortune_ 106 (July 26, 1982):27.

3988. Sellers, James. "Our Reluctant Laity and the
       Seminaries." Christian Century 81 (April
       29, 1964):551+.

3989. Sellers, O. R. "The Condition of the Post-War
       World and Its Implications for the Seminary
       Curriculum." Christian Education 26 (June
       1943):263-8.

3990. Sellers, Ovid R. The Fifth Quarter Century of
       McCormick: The Story of the Years 1929-
       1954 at McCormick Theological Seminary.
       Chicago: McCormick Theological Seminary,
       1955.

3991. Sellers, Ovid Rogers. Hebrew and Homiletics.
       Chicago: McCormick Theological Seminary,
       1924.

3992. "Seminarian Preacher Award Won by Naperville
       Student." Christian Century 68 (June 6,
       1951):676.

3993. "Seminarians and the Draft." Christian
       Century 85 (March 13, 1968):316-17.

3994. "Seminarians and Vietnam." Christian Century
       84 (December 13, 1967):1605.

3995. "Seminarians Speak." Christian Century 76
       (April 22, 1959):498+.

3996. "Seminaries." Commonweal 108 (October 23,
       1981):580-1.

3997. "Seminaries and Seminarians." Brownson's
       Quarterly Review 2 (1861):97-117.

3998. "Seminaries and Universities." Lutheran
       Quarterly 18, no. 4 (1966):307-14, 318-21.

3999. "Seminaries at the Crossroads." Christianity
       Today 16 (April 14, 1972):24.

4000. "Seminaries for the 70's (AATS)." Christian-
       ity Today 12 (July 5, 1968):41-2.

4001. "Seminaries Glum Over Gays." Christianity
       Today 23 (December 15, 1978):42.

4002. "Seminaries in Trouble with the Artists:
       Lennox Library and Robie House." Christian
       Century 74 (March 27, 1957):389.

4003. "Seminaries: Joining the Theologians For
Thrift and Tolerance." Time 84 (November
6, 1964):50-1.

4004. "Seminaries Look to the Future." Christian
Century 73 (July 25, 1956):879-80+.

4005. "Seminaries Merge." Christian Century 99 (May
12, 1982):560.

4006. "Seminaries: Right on the Premises." Time 82
(December 27, 1963):53.

4007. "Seminaries Up For Review." Christian Century
98 (October 14, 1981):1016.

4008. "Seminaries Welcoming More Women." Christianity Today 19 (February 14, 1975):41.

4009. "Seminary and Community." Christian Century
74 (April 24, 1957):509-11.

4010. "Seminary Backed on Denial of Degree to
Homosexual." New York Times 128 (May 19,
1979):6.

4011. "Seminary Enrollment." Christianity Today 14
(January 16, 1970):34-5.

4012. "Seminary Enrollments Continue Climb."
Christianity Today 20 (May 21, 1976):34-5.

4013. "Seminary for a Baptist College: Bethel
College and Seminary." Architectural
Record 140 (August 1966):110-11.

4014. "Seminary Librarians Consider Common
Problems." Library Journal 72 (February
15, 1947):297-8.

4015. "Seminary of the Future? [Union Theological
Seminary, NYC]." Newsweek 79 (June 19,
1972):90.

4016. "Seminary Professors Resign: Southeastern
Seminary, Wake Forest, N.C." Christian
Century 82 (January 27, 1965):101-2.

4017. "Seminary Setbacks: The Other Half of the
Story." Christian Century 89 (October 25,
1972):1055-6.

4018. "Seminary Starts Church Growth Department."
       Church Growth Bulletin 8 (September
       1971):173-4.

4019. "Seminary: Symposium." Christianity Today 19
       (February 14, 1975):4-9+.

4020. "Seminary's 150 Years [Princeton Theological
       Seminary]." Time 79 (April 27, 1962):46.

4021. "Seminary's Role in World Evangelism."
       Christianity Today 20 (February 13, 1976):
       36.

4022. "Seminex Will Graduate Its Last Class Next
       Spring." Christianity Today 27 (January
       21, 1983):27-8.

4023. Senn, Frank C. "Teaching Worship in
       Seminaries: A Response [To J. F. White,
       pp. 304-18]." Worship 55 (July 1981):325-
       32.

4024. Senn, Frank C. "Where Have All the Prophets
       Gone?" Dialog 20 (Spring 1981):84-5.

4025. Senn, Frank C. "Worship, Doctrine, and Life:
       Liturgical Theology, Theologies of Worship,
       and Doxological Theology." Currents in
       Theology and Mission 9 (February 1982):11-
       21.

4026. Sergeant, Maurice. "A Plan for Designing an
       Integrating Curriculum for Ministerial
       Students at Anderson College and
       Theological Seminary and the School of
       Theology, Anderson, Indiana." Ph.D.
       dissertation, Columbia University, 1953.

4027. Servotte, H. "Spiritual Formation." Study
       Encounter 3, no. 4 (1967):185-7.

4028. Setchko, E. S. "Toward an Informed Laity."
       Christian Century 77 (May 18, 1960):603-4.

4029. Seton, Celeste Andrews. "Helen Gould Was My
       Mother-in-Law." Ladies Home Journal 70
       (August 1953):30+; (September 1953):56+;
       (October 1953):52+.

4030. Settle, Edwin Theodore, Jr. "Classroom
       Procedure in Theological Education." Ph.D.
       dissertation, Yale University, 1931.

4031. Sewall, J. S. "Education for the Pulpit."
New Englander 36 (1877):671-93.

4032. Sewell, George. "Morris Brown College:
Legacy of Wesley John Gaines." Crisis 88,
no. 3 (1981):133-6.

4033. Sewell, James. "A Central Theological
Seminary for our Church." Christian
Advocate and Journal (New York) 29 (January
5, 1854):1.

4034. Sewell, O. T. "The Problem of the Country
Church." In Christianity Practically
Applied. Evangelical Alliance for the
United States of America. Conference.
Chicago, 1893, v. 2, pp. 405-11. New York:
Baker & Taylor, 1894.

4035. Shaffer, Kenneth M. "Library Cooperation and
Education for Ministry." Brethren Life and
Thought 25 (Winter 1980):58-61.

4036. Shahan, Robert Reed. "The Long-Range Planning
Process in a Theological School Using the
Techniques of Systems Analysis and Organi-
zation Development." Ph.D. dissertation,
Garrett-Evangelical Theological Seminary in
coop. with Northwestern University, 1979.

4037. Shailer Mathews Selections...From the Memorial
Service Held in Joseph Bond Chapel, the
University of Chicago. Chicago? 1941?

4038. Shanks, T. J., ed. A College of Colleges:
Led by D. L. Moody, and Taught by Prof.
Henry Drummond. New York: Fleming H.
Revell Co., 1887.

4039. Shannon, David Thomas. "Faculty Perception of
Governance of Seminaries of the United
Presbyterian Church, USA, 1974-1975."
Ph.D. dissertation, University of
Pittsburgh, 1975.

4040. Shannon, David T. "Theological Education as
Education for Ministry." Theological
Education 7 (Spring 1971):171-6.

4041. Shapiro, David S. et al. The Mental Health
Counselor in the Community: Training of
Physicians and Ministers. Springfield,
Ill.: Charles C. Thomas, 1968.

4042. Shapiro, David S., Maholick, Leonard T. and
       Robertson, Richard N. "Mental Health
       Training for Ministers." American Journal
       of Public Health 57 (March 1967):518-22.

4043. Shapiro, David S., Robertson, Richard N. and
       Maholick, Leonard T. "Training Ministers
       for Mental Health Work." Journal of
       Pastoral Care 16 (Fall 1962):149-56.

4044. Sharp, A. R. "Study of Protestant Under-
       graduate Pre-Theological Education in the
       United States." College of the Bible
       Quarterly 41 (July 1964):26-40.

4045. Sharp, Allan Rhinehart. "A Study of
       Protestant Undergraduate Pre-Theological
       Education in the United States." Ed.D.
       dissertation, Duke University, 1963.

4046. Sharpe, Dores Robinson. Walter Rauschenbusch.
       New York: MacMillan Co., 1942.

4047. Shaull, Millard Richard. "The Challenge to
       the Seminary." Christianity and Crisis 29
       (April 14, 1969):81-6.

4048. Schaull, Richard. "Response to President
       Bennett - I." Theological Education 3
       (Winter 1967):291-3.

4049. Shaver, Erwin L. "The Attitudes of Theo-
       logical Seminaries and Other Training
       Schools Toward the Training of Directors."
       Religious Education 42 (1947):16-24.

4050. Shaw, Henry K. Hoosier Disciples: A
       Comprehensive History of the Christian
       Churches (Disciples of Christ) in Indiana.
       St. Louis: Bethany Press, for The
       Association of the Christian Churches in
       Indiana, 1966.

4051. Shaw, William. The Evolution of an
       Endeavorer: An Autobiography. Boston:
       Christian Endeavor World, 1924, pp. 388-
       417.

4052. Shawchuck, Norman Lee. "The Process of
       Merging Two Seminaries." Ph.D. disserta-
       tion, Northwestern University, 1974.

4053. Sheatsley, Clarence Valentine. The Story of the First Lutheran Seminary of the West, 1830-1930. Columbus, Ohio: Lutheran Book Concern, 1930.

4054. Shedd, William G. T. Homiletics and Pastoral Theology. 2d ed. New York: Scribner, 1867.

4055. Sheldon, Charles M. "Some Experiments Worth Trying in the Ministry." Andover Review 16 (September 1891):265-72.

4056. Shelley, Bruce. "Sources of Pietistic Fundamentalism." Fides et Historia 5 (Spring 1973):68-78.

4057. Shen, P. "Reflections on Clinical Training: A Meditation." Journal of Pastoral Care 11 (Summer 1957):101-3.

4058. Sheneman, Lloyd E. "Doctor of Ministry: Once More To Serve." Theological Education 12 (Summer 1976):227-37.

4059. Sheneman, Lloyd E. "Effect of Church Relationships on Seminary Governance: A Lutheran Perspective." Theological Education 12 (Autumn 1975):47-51.

4060. Shepherd, J. "Adman in the Pulpit: Future Dual-Vocation Episcopal Priest." Look 29 (December 14, 1965):M14+.

4061. Sheridan, Harold J. "College Preparation for Theological Study." Christian Education 26 (June 1943):251-5.

4062. Sheridan, Wilbur Fletcher. The Sunday Night Service: A Study in Continuous Evangelism. Cincinnati: Jennings & Pye, 1903.

4063. Sherrill, Henry Knox. Among Friends. Boston: Little, Brown & Co., 1962).

4064. Sherrill, Lewis J. "American Association of Theological Schools." Christian Education 20 (February 1937):207-10.

4065. Sherrill, Lewis J. "The Status of Theological Education." Christian Education 19 (February 1936):219-30.

4066. Sherwood, Elisha Barber. <u>Fifty Years on the Skirmish Line</u>. Chicago: Fleming H. Revell Co., 1893.

4067. Shewmaker, William O. "The Training of the Protestant Ministry in the United States of America, Before the Establishment of Theological Seminaries." In <u>Papers of the American Society of Church History</u>, 2nd series, vol. 6, edited by Frederick William Loetscher. American Society of Church History. New York: G. P. Putnam's Sons, 1921.

4068. Shimel, William A. "Continuing Education Interests of Wisconsin Town and Country Clergymen." Ph.D. dissertation, University of Wisconsin, 1968.

4069. Shiras, Alexander. <u>Life and Letters of Rev. James May</u>. Philadelphia: Protestant Episcopal Book Society, 1865.

4070. Shires, Henry H. "History of the Church Divinity School of the Pacific." <u>Historical Magazine of the Protestant Episcopal Church</u> 11 (June 1942):179-88.

4071. Shirley, James K. "The Teaching of Oral Reading in the Protestant Theological Seminaries." Ph.D. dissertation, Wayne State University, 1966.

4072. Shissler, Henry Harrison. "An Experiment in Attitudinal Outcomes Resulting from Seminary Courses in The Church and Community." Ph.D. dissertation, Pennsylvania State University, 1956.

4073. Shockley, Grant S. "Development of the Status and In-Service Education of Negro Methodist Accepted Supply Pastors." Ph.D. dissertation, Columbia University, 1953.

4074. Shockley, Grant S. "Living out the Gospel in Seminary Life [Interdenominational Theological Center]." <u>Christian Century</u> 94 (February 2-9, 1977):90-1.

4075. Shockley, Grant S. "National Church Bodies and Interdenominational Theological Education." <u>Theological Education</u> 15 (Spring 1979):155-61.

4076. Shoemaker, Samuel Moor. "Where Goes the 'Glow'?" Christian Century 70 (April 29, 1953):508+.

4077. Short, Kenneth Richard M. "Baptist Training for the Ministry: The Francis Wayland Barnas Sears Debate of 1853." Foundations 11 (July-September 1968):227-34.

4078. Shorten, A. Lloyd. "The Church Speaks to its Seminaries on Preparing of Christian Education Specialists." Theological Education 15 (Spring 1979):109-12.

4079. "Should Every Minister Have a Doctorate?" Christian Century 98 (February 4, 1981):137-40.

4080. "Should Ministers Know Life?" Outlook 92 (May 8, 1909):75-82.

4081. "Should Theologians View Their Task as a Whole?" Christian Century 67 (June 28, 1950):779.

4082. Shriver, Donald W. "The Accountability of Theological Education to the Mission of the Church." Theological Education 17 (Autumn 1980):59-73.

4083. Shriver, Donald W. "Heart's Love Uttered with the Mind's Conviction [Inaugural Address]." Union Seminary Quarterly Review 32 (Fall 1976):3-16.

4084. Shriver, Donald W. et al. "How the Seminaries Link Piety and Learning: A Symposium by Administrators and Faculty Members." Christian Century 94 (February 2-9, 1977):87-95, 105-113.

4085. Shriver, Donald W. "Purpose in a School Faced with Mission to the City." Theological Education 14 (Spring 1978):87-92.

4086. Shriver, D. W., Jr. "Toward a Public Sense of Pastoral Care." Christian Century 94 (February 2, 1977):87-8.

4087. Shriver, G. H., Jr. "Southern Baptist Seminaries Challenged." Christian Century 84 (May 3, 1967):601-2.

4088. Shriver, George H., ed. <u>American Religious Heretics Formal & Informal Trials</u>. Nashville: Abingdon Press, 1966.

4089. Shryock, Richard Harrison. <u>Medical Licensing in America,, 1650-1965</u>. Baltimore: Johns Hopkins Press, 1967.

4090. Shuffelton, Frank. <u>Thomas Hooker, 1586-1647</u>. Princeton, N. J.: Princeton University Press, 1977.

4091. Shurden, Walter B. "The Pastor as Denominational Theologian in Southern Baptist History." <u>Baptist History and Heritage</u> 15, no. 3 (1980):15-22.

4092. Sigmund, Fred L. "The English Bible: Its Place in the Seminary." <u>Old and New Testament Student</u> 10 (June 1890):343-7.

4093. Simmons, James Barlow. <u>Schools for Colored Preachers</u>. New York: American Baptist Home Mission Society, n.d.

4094. Simmons, M. D., Jr. and Parker, H. J. "Attitude and Personality Traits of Ministerial Students: The Influence and Control of Reference Group Phenomena." <u>Religious Education</u> 63 (July 1968):309-14.

4095. Simmons, Milton Delbert, Jr. "The Relationship of Personality Characteristics to Attitudes of Ministerial Students." Ph.D. dissertation, University of Oklahoma, 1967.

4096. Simms, Paris Marion. <u>The Bible in America</u>. New York: Wilson-Erickson, 1936.

4097. "Simon Magus, 1932 Model: Spurious Degrees of Doctor of Divinity." <u>Christian Century</u> 49 (June 29, 1932):821.

4098. Simons, Joseph Bernard. "Congruence between Self and Religious Role Percepts: A Descriptive Study of Satisfaction with the Religious Life among Seminarians in Differential Stages of Preparation for the Priesthood." Ph.D. dissertation, University of Notre Dame, 1966.

4099. Simpson, Albert Benjamin. <u>The Challenge of Missions</u>. New York: Christian Alliance

Publishing Co., 1926.

4100. Simpson, Albert Benjamin. Christ in the
Bible. New York: Word, Work & World
Publishing Co., 1888-.

4101. Simpson, Albert Benjamin. The Four-Fold
Gospel. New York: Christian Alliance
Publishing Co., 1925.

4102. Simpson, Albert Benjamin. The Gospel of the
Kingdom: A Series of Discourses on the
Lord's Coming. New York: Christian
Alliance Publishing Co., 1890.

4103. Simpson, John. An Essay on the Impropriety of
the Usual Mode of Teaching Christian
Theology. London: Printed by Wilks &
Taylor, 1803.

4104. Simpson, Samuel. "Early Ministerial Training
in America." Papers of the American
Society of Church History 2, 2nd Series
(1910):115-29.

4105. Sims, David Henry. "Religious Education in
Negro Colleges and Universities." Journal
of Negro History 5 (April 1920):166-207.

4106. Sims, Marg Sophia Stephens. The Natural
History of a Social Institution - The Young
Women's Christian Association. New York:
Womans Press, 1936.

4107. Sims, Mary Sophia Stephens. The YWCA: An
Unfolding Purpose. New York: Woman's
Press, 1950.

4108. Sinclair, Andrew. Prohibition: The Era of
Excess. London: New English Library,
1965.

4109. Singer, D. "Seminarians: Out of the
Classroom, Into the Pulpit: Interviews."
Christianity Today 22 (February 10,
1978):13-19.

4110. Singer, H. Douglas. "The Need for Instruction
in Mental Hygiene in Medical, Law and
Theological Schools." Mental Hygiene 3
(January 1919):24-32.

4111. "Singing Seminarians: Five Students of Montforts' Major U.S. Seminary." _Newsweek_ 71 (May 27, 1968):105.

4112. Singleton, George A. _The Autobiography of George A. Singleton._ Boston: Forum Publishing Co., 1964.

4113. Singleton, Harold Craig. "The Ministry of Music as a Profession: A Study of Selected Graduates of the Southern Baptist Theological Seminary School of Church Music." D.M.A. dissertation, Southern Baptist Theological Seminary, 1980.

4114. Sisk, Glenn. "The Negro Colleges in Atlanta." _Journal of Negro Education_ 33, no. 4 (1964):404-8.

4115. Sitterly, Charles Fremont. _The Building of Drew University._ New York: Methodist Book Concern, 1938.

4116. Sizemore, Alva Don. "The History of Christian Normal Institute, Grayson, Kentucky." B.D. thesis, Butler University, 1944.

4117. Sizemore, Douglas Reece. "Longitudinal Data and Alternate Criteria in the Prediction of Academic Achievement and Success of Graduate Theological Students." Ph.D. dissertation, University of Northern Colorado, 1974.

4118. Skelly, John J. "Institutional Goals and Financial Development in a Protestant Seminary: A Historical Study." S.T.D. dissertation, San Francisco Theological Seminary, 1981.

4119. _Sketches of Life in the Hartford School of Religious Education, 1885-1935._ Edited by Karl Ruf Stolz. Hartford: Printed by Case, Lockwood & Brainard Co., 1935.

4120. Skillrud, H. C. "Fruits of Merger [Lutheran School of Theology, Chicago]." _Theological Education_ 3 (Spring 1967):424-6.

4121. Skillrud, Harold Clayton. _LSTC: Decade of Decision: A History of the Merger of the Lutheran School of Theology at Chicago with Special Emphasis on the Decade 1958-1968._

Chicago: Lutheran School of Theology at Chicago, 1969.

4122. Skilton, John H. New Testament Student and Theology. Phillipsburg, N.J.: Presbyterian and Reformed Pub. Co., 1976.

4123. Skinner, Ellouise W. "An Historical Sketch of Music at Union [NYC, 1835-1951]." Union Seminary Quarterly Review 7 (March 1952): 19-22.

4124. Skinner, Ellouise W. Sacred Music at Union Theological Seminary, 1836-1953: An Informal History. New York: Union Theological Seminary, 1953.

4125. Slater, John Rothwell. Rhees of Rochester. New York: Harper & Brothers, 1946.

4126. Slater, Nelle. "Faithful Participation in Seeking To Know [Inaugural Address, Christian Theological Seminary]." Encounter 43 (Autumn 1982):331-6.

4127. Slattery, Charles Lewis. Alexander Viets Griswold Allen, 1841-1908. New York: Longmans, Green & Co., 1911.

4128. Slavens, Thomas P. "The Development of the Library of the Union Theological Seminary in the City of New York." Library History Review (India) 1, no. 2 (1974):84-93.

4129. Slavens, T. P. "Librarianship of Charles Augustus Briggs." Union Seminary Quarterly Review 24 (Summer 1969):357-63.

4130. Slavens, Thomas P. "The Librarianship of Henry B. Smith, 1851-77." Library History Review [India] 1, no. 4 (1974):1-41.

4131. Slavens, Thomas Paul. "The Library of Union Theological Seminary in the City of New York, 1836 to the Present." Ph.D. dissertation, University of Michigan, 1965.

4132. Slavens, Thomas P. "A Theological Storm Center. Implications for Developing Theological Libraries." Special Libraries 61 (Jul/Aug 1970):275-9.

4133. Slavens, Thomas P. "William Walker Rockwell and the Development of the Union Theological Seminary Library." Journal of Library History 11, no. 1 (1976):26-43.

4134. Slayton, Wilfred George. "A Comparison of Successful and Unsuccessful Bible College Students with Respect to Selected Personality Factors." Ph.D. dissertation, University of Arizona, 1965.

4135. Sloan, Douglas. "Samuel Stanhope Smith." In The Scottish Enlightenment and the American College Ideal, pp. 146-84. New York: Teachers College Press, Columbia University, 1971.

4136. Slocum, William F. "Reconstruction in Theological Education." Forum 28 (January 1900):571-8.

4137. Sloper, D. W. "Expanding the Professional Development of Ordinands." Journal of Christian Education 66 (December 1979):39-51.

4138. Slosson, E. E. "Plea for a Scientific Theology." Scientific Monthly 17 (December 1923):621-2.

4139. Sloyan, Gerard S. "Religious Studies in Roman Catholic Colleges and Universities." Theological Education 3 (Spring 1967):376-83.

4140. Slusser, G. H. "Training for an Educational Ministry." Hartford Quarterly 4 (Spring 1964).

4141. Sly, Virgil A. "Education for Mission: Implications of the Church's World Mission for Theological Education." Lexington Theological Quarterly 4, no. 3 (1969):86-95.

4142. Smiley, David Leslie. "Two Hundred Years of Baptist Education [in the South, 1749-1959]." Quarterly Review (Baptist) 19 (January-March 1959):7-12.

4143. Smith, A. H. "Charge to the Professors-Elect of Hamma Divinity School." Lutheran Quarterly 54 (April 1924):145-52.

4144. Smith, Alson J. "What's Right With the Ministry." American Mercury 69 (1949):399-406.

4145. Smith, Alvin W. Covenanter Ministers, 1930-1963, pp. 323-5. Pittsburgh: Guttendorf Press, 1964.

4146. Smith, C. S. Development of Protestant Theological Education in China in the Light of the Education of the Clergy in Europe and America. Shanghai: Kelly & Walsh, 1941.

4147. Smith, D. "On the Importance of a Well Instructed Ministry." Methodist Magazine and Quarterly Review 21 (July 1839):267-75.

4148. Smith, Dana Prom. The Education Servant. Philadelphia: Board of Christian Education, United Presbyterian Church, U.S.A., 1967.

4149. Smith, Edward L. "The Band Idea in Home Missions." Home Missionary 65 (October 1892):310-12.

4150. Smith, Elwyn A. "The Evolution of Purpose in American Theological Education." Theological Education 2 (Winter 1966):64-9.

4151. Smith, Elwyn A. "The Forming of a Modern American Denomination." Church History 31 (1962):74-99.

4152. Smith, Elwyn Allen. The Presbyterian Ministry in American Culture: A Study in Changing Concepts, 1700-1900. Philadelphia: Westminster Press, 1962.

4153. Smith, Elwyn Allen. "What Is a Seminary For?" Christian Century 73 (April 25, 1956):506-7.

4154. Smith, Eugene Lewis. "The Contribution of Clinical Training to the Counseling Resources of the Clergyman." Ph.D. dissertation, New York University, 1945.

4155. Smith, Gerald Birney, ed. A Guide to the Study of the Christian Religion. Chicago: University of Chicago Press, 1916.

4156. Smith, Gerald Birney. "Is There a Religious
       Breakdown of the Ministry?" Journal of
       Religion 1 (March 1921):190-2.

4157. Smith, G. B. Practical Theology: A Neglected
       Field in Theological Education. University
       of Chicago, 1903.

4158. Smith, Gerald Birney. "Training Christian
       Ministers." Religious Education 23
       (September 1928):684-9.

4159. Smith, G. B. "Wernle's Introduction to
       Theological Study." American Journal of
       Theology 17 (January 1913):104-7.

4160. Smith, H. M. Training of the Clergy. New
       York: Macmillan, 1919.

4161. Smith, Harmon L. "The Need For Visions."
       Duke Divinity School Review 42 (Fall
       1977):178-87.

4162. Smith, Harmon L. and Westerhoff, John H.
       "Teaching Moral Theology." Duke Divinity
       Review 45, no. 3 (1980):47-59.

4163. Smith, Harold S. "The Life and Works of J. R.
       Graves (1820-1893)." Baptist History and
       Heritage 10, no. 1 (1975):19-27.

4164. Smith, Henry Boynton. Henry Boynton Smith:
       His Life and Work. Edited by His Wife.
       New York: A. C. Armstrong & Son, 1881.

4165. Smith, Henry Preserved. "Francis Brown: An
       Appreciation." American Journal of Semitic
       Languages and Literatures 33 (January
       1917):75-88.

4166. Smith, Henry Preserved. "Thirty Years of
       Biblical Study." Biblical World 39 (April
       1912):235-42.

4167. Smith, Horace Greeley. The Story of Garrett:
       1853-1953. Evanston, Ill.: Garrett
       Biblical Institute, 1954.

4168. Smith, Howard Wayne. "The Function of a
       Theological Seminary." Crozer Quarterly 26
       (October 1949):33-5.

4169. Smith, J. R. "Education of a Professor."
       Nation 108 (May 10, 1919):751-2.

4170. Smith, Jerry Ray. "The Professional
       Preparation of Theological Students in the
       Seminaries of the Lutheran Church in
       America in the Use of Educational Commun-
       ication and Mass Media." Ed.D disserta-
       tion, Temple University, 1973.

4171. Smith, John. Lectures on the Nature and End
       of the Sacred Office, and on the Dignity,
       Duty, Qualifications, and Character of the
       Sacred Order. Philadelphia: Sorin & Ball,
       1843.

4172. Smith, John Merlin Powls. "Value of the Old
       Testament in the Theological Curriculum."
       Biblical World 53 (July 1919):372-82.

4173. Smith, Kenneth and Sweet, Leonard. "Shailer
       Mathews: A Chapter in the Social Gospel
       Movement." Foundations 18, no. 3 (1975):
       219-37; no. 4:296-320; 19, no. 1 (1976):53-
       68; no. 2:152-70.

4174. Smith, Kirk Lamb. "Raising the Level of
       Pastoral Competency." Review and Expositor
       47 (July 1950):344-50.

4175. Smith, R. O. "Personality and Cultural
       Factors Affecting the Religion of One
       Hundred and Forty Divinity Students."
       Religious Education 43 (March 1948):106-11.

4176. Smith, Rockwell Carter. The Role of Rural
       Social Science in Theological Education:
       With Particular Application to the Town and
       Country Ministry of the Methodist Church.
       Evanston, Ill., 1969.

4177. Smith, Samuel Stanhope. Sermons of Samuel
       Stanhope Smith, D.D. To Which is Prefixed a
       Brief Memoir of His Life and Writings. 2
       vols. Philadelphia: S. Potter & Co.,
       1821.

4178. Smith, Timothy Lawrence. Called Unto
       Holiness: The Story of the Nazarenes.
       Kansas City, Mo.: Nazarene Publishing
       House, 1962.

4179. Smith, Timothy L. Uncommon Schools:
       Christian Colleges and Social Idealism in
       Midwestern America, 1820-1950. Reprinted
       for the author by the Indiana Historical
       Society, 1978.

4180. Smith, Wilbur Moorehead, comp. An Annotated
       Bibliography of D. L. Moody. Chicago:
       Moody Press, 1948.

4181. Smith, Wilbur Moorehead. A Voice for God:
       The Life of Charles E. Fuller. Boston: W.
       A. Wilde Co., 1949.

4182. Smith, William Martin. Servants Without Hire:
       Emerging Concepts of the Christian Ministry
       in the Campbell-Stone Movement. Nashville:
       Disciples of Christ Historical Society,
       1968.

4183. Smylie, James H. "American Religious Bodies,
       Just War, and Vietnam." Journal of Church
       and State 11, no. 3 (1969):383-408.

4184. Smylie, James H. "The Burden of Southern
       Church Historians: World Mission, Regional
       Captivity, Reconciliation [Union,
       Richmond]." Journal of Presbyterian
       History 46 (December 1968):274-307.

4185. Smylie, James H. "Presbyterians and the
       American Revolution: A Documentary
       Account." Journal of Presbyterian History
       52 (Winter 1972):303-481.

4186. Smyth, Egbert Coffin. Value of the Study of
       Church History in Ministerial Education: A
       Lecture Delivered to the Senior Class of
       Andover Theological Seminary. Andover:
       Warren F. Draper, 1874.

4187. Snider, Kenneth Lavern. "Field Education
       Experiences as an Element in Theological
       Seminary Preparation for the Parish
       Ministry as Perceived by Parish Ministers."
       Ph.D. dissertation, Michigan State
       University, 1968.

4188. Snowden, James Henry. "The Scientific Spirit
       in Theological Study and Teaching."
       Biblical World 49 (May 1917):275-80.

4189. Snyder, G. R. "Theological Seminaries in Our Church." Christian Advocate (New York) 29 (July 13, 1854):109; (July 20, 1854):113-14.

4190. Snyder, Graydon F. "Present Trends in Theological Education." Brethren Life and Thought 23 (Summer 1978):165-8.

4191. Snyder, J. A. "New Model for Clinical Pastoral Training." Pastoral Psychology 20 (December 1969):7-13.

4192. Snyder, Ross. "Boisen Heritage in Theological Education." Pastoral Psychology 19 (September 1968):9+.

4193. Snyder, R. D. "Psychiatry and the Seminary Curriculum." Lutheran Church Quarterly 11 (October 1938):376-84.

4194. Snyder, Ross. "Religious Education as a Discipline: II. Toward Foundations of a Discipline of Religious Education." Religious Education 62, no. 5 (1967):394-404.

4195. Snyder, R. "Religious Education in the Theological School." Journal of Religion 30 (July 1950):180-9.

4196. Soares, Theodore Gerald. "History of the Religious Education Association." Religious Education 23 (1928):621-33.

4197. Soares, T. G. "Practical Theology and Ministerial Efficiency." American Journal of Theology 16 (July 1912):426-43.

4198. Soares, T. G. "Professional Reading Course on the Preaching Task of the Modern Minister." Biblical World 47 (February - June, 1916): 124-32, 200-6, 272-8, 344-50, 414-20.

4199. Society For Promoting Theological Education. An Account of the Society, Formed in Boston, July 17, 1816, With the Constitution, Rules. Boston, 1816.

4200. Solanki, Anilkumar Daniel. "Nature and Role of Trustees in Theological Institutions [Indiana, Michigan and Ohio]." Ph.D. dissertation, Ohio State University, 1982.

4201. Solt, Leonard Franklin. "The Rise and Development of the Protestant Theological Seminary to 1860." M.A. thesis, Oberlin College, 1954.

4202. "Some Implications of the ACLS Study for Education in the Theological Seminaries." Theological Education 8 (Winter 1972):83-131.

4203. "Some Models for Theological Education." Theological Education 9 (Winter 1973): entire issue.

4204. "Some Problems of Theological Education." Biblical World 31 (March 1908):163-6.

4205. Sommerfield, Richard. "Social Class Background and Professional Aspiration: A Study of Selected Pre-Theological Students." Lutheran Quarterly 15 (1963):345-52.

4206. Sonne, N. H. "Principles for the Selection of Religious Books: Seminary Book Selection." Library Journal 83 (January 15, 1958):123-8.

4207. Sonne, N. H. "Salinger and John the Baptist: ATLA Annual Conference." Library Journal 88 (September 1, 1963):3031-3.

4208. Sontag, Frederick. "Pre-Seminary Education and Undergraduate Arts and Sciences." Theological Education 1 (Spring 1965):154-8.

4209. Sontag, F. "Socrates in the Seminary [Theological Students]." Religion In Life 31 (Autumn 1962):537-43.

4210. Soper, David Wesley. Highways to Faith: Autobiographies of Protestant Christians. Philadelphia: Westminster Press, 1954.

4211. Soper, E. D. "The Place of a School of Theology in a Unified Educational Program [Methodist Episcopal Church, South]." Christian Education Magazine 17 (May 1927):23-30.

4212. Soper, Edmund Davison. "The Study of Religion in the Training of Missionaries." Inter-

national Review of Missions 11 (July 1922):
406-20.

4213. "Sophisticated Technology for a Lutheran
Seminary: Lutheran School of Theology,
Chicago." Architectural Record 144
(September 1968):174-9.

4214. Sorenson, Randall C. "Evangelical
Seminarians' Philosophies of Human Nature
and Theological Beliefs." Journal for the
Scientific Study of Religion 20 (March
1981):33-8.

4215. Southard, Samuel. "How Men Decide for the
Ministry." Pastor 17 (February 1954):6-7.

4216. Southard, S. "Spiritual Development of
Successful Students." Journal of Religion
and Health 4 (January 1965):154-63.

4217. Southern Baptist Theological Seminary,
Louisville, Ky. Southern Baptist Theological Seminary: The First Thirty Years,
1859-1889. Edited by John R. Sampey.
Baltimore: Wharton, Barron & Co., 1890.

4218. "Southern Baptists Open Seminaries to
Negroes." Christian Century 68 (April 11,
1951):453.

4219. "Southern Baptists Rebuke Their Seminaries."
Christian Century 79 (June 20, 1962):770.

4220. Southworth, Franklin Chester. "The Organization of Summer Courses for the Ministry."
Religious Education 16 (June 1921):157-61.

4221. Spain, Rufus B. At Ease in Zion: Social
History of Southern Baptists, 1865-1900.
Nashville: Vanderbilt University Press,
1967.

4222. Spalding, John F. The Best Mode of Working a
Parish Considered in a Course of Lectures.
Milwaukee: Young Churchman Co., 1888.

4223. Spangler, James T. "The Philosophy of Dallas
Seminary." Bibliotheca Sacra 100 (1943):
199-207.

4224. Spaude, Paul William. The Lutheran Church
Under American Influence. Burlington,

365

Iowa: Lutheran Literary Board, 1943.

4225. Spaulding, F. L. "Training of the Minister in
       University Communities." Religious Educa-
       tion 8 (August 1913):252-5.

4226. Speare, Edward Ray. Interesting Happenings in
       Boston University's History, 1839 to 1951.
       Boston: Boston University Press, 1957.

4227. Spears, Philip Yates. "A Critical Analysis of
       the Role of Southern Baptist Colleges and
       Universities in Decisions for Church-
       Related Vocations." Ed.D. dissertation,
       Southwestern Baptist Theological Seminary,
       1982.

4228. "(Special Short Course of Theological
       Education.") Bibliotheca Sacra 36
       (1879):560+.

4229. Speer, R. E. "What the Church Has a Right to
       Expect from Its Seminaries." Christian
       Education 30 (June 1947):198-201.

4230. Speller, John L. "Alexander Nicoll and the
       Study of German Biblical Criticism in Early
       Nineteenth-Century Oxford." Journal of
       Ecclesiastical History 30 (October 1979):
       451-9.

4231. Spence, Andrew Emmett, Jr. "A Study of
       Student Personnel Services in Accredited
       Bible Colleges and Attitudes of Presidents
       toward These Services." Ph.D. disserta-
       tion, University of Southern Mississippi,
       1968.

4232. Spence, H. "They're Training a New Kind of
       Parson [Iliff School of Theology]."
       Saturday Evening Post 222 (November 26,
       1949):32-3+.

4233. Sperry, W. L. "The Standards of Religious
       Training." Saturday Review of Literature
       11 (July 21, 1934):3.

4234. Sperry, W. L., ed. "Two Letters from Students
       of Harvard Divinity School Sent in 1834 to
       the Two Most Conspicuously Liberal Theolog-
       ical Schools in Europe, Manchester College,
       England, and the Protestant Seminary in
       Geneva." Harvard Theological Review 34

366

(April 1941):145-59.

4235. Spicer, James E. "Place of Field Experience
        in Theological Education: Clues from
        Pastoral Theology." In New Shape of
        Pastoral Theology: S. Hiltner. Edited by
        W. B. Oglesby.

4236. Spielmann, Richard M. Bexley Hall: 150 Years
        A Brief History. Rochester: Colgate
        Rochester Divinity School/Bexley
        Hall/Crozer Theological Seminary, 1974.

4237. Spiers, Duane Edwin. "A Study of the
        Predictive Validity of a Test Battery
        Administered to Theological Students."
        Ph.D. dissertation, Purdue University,
        1965.

4238. Spindle, Richard Lee. "A Study of the
        Competency-Based Approach to Education and
        Its Utilization in Structuring a Bible
        College Model for Christian Education."
        Ed.D. dissertation, Southwestern Baptist
        Theological Seminary, 1976.

4239. "Spirit of Sixth Avenue: Proposals for
        Seminary Reform." Newsweek 65 (May 3,
        1965):85.

4240. Spitz, C. Thomas. "Theological Education and
        the Special Ministries." Concordia Theo-
        logical Monthly 36 (July 1965):385-97.

4241. Spofford, W. B., Jr. "Content in Extensive
        Training." Journal of Pastoral Care 7, no.
        2 (1953):97-101.

4242. Spofford, W. B., Jr. "Question of Extensive
        Training." Journal of Pastoral Care 7, no.
        1 (1953):33-6.

4243. Sprague, E. "Theological Seminary." Zion's
        Herald 10 (September 4, 1839):141.

4244. Sprague, William Buell. Annals of the
        American Pulpit: Or, Commemorative Notices
        of Distinguished American Clergymen of
        Various Denominations. 9 vols. New York:
        Robert Carter & Bros., 1857-69, vols. 3, 4.

4245. Sprague, William Buell. Lectures on Revivals
        of Religion: With an Introductory Essay by

367

Leonard Woods. 2nd ed. New York: Daniel
Appleton & Co., 1833.

4246. Sprague, William Buell. The Life of Jedidiah
Morse. New York: A.D.F. Randolph & Co.,
1874.

4247. Sprecher, Samuel. An Inaugural Address,
Delivered Before the Directors of
Wittenburg College. Springfield, Ohio:
Printed by Halsey & Emerson, 1849.

4248. Spring, Gardiner. Personal Reminiscences of
the Life and Times of Gardiner Spring. 2
vols. New York: Charles Scribner & Co.,
1866, vol. 1.

4249. Spring, Gardiner. The Power of the Pulpit.
New York: Baker & Scribner, 1848.

4250. Sproat, John G. The Best Men: Liberal
Reformers in the Gilded Age. London and
New York: Oxford University Press, 1968.

4251. "Squabble with a Landlord: Winona Institute
for Continuing Theological Education."
Christianity Today 12 (July 5, 1968):42.

4252. "Squeeze at the Seminaries." Newsweek 77 (May
31, 1971):85.

4253. "Squeeze Play: Resignation of R. J. Arnott."
Newsweek 69 (January 30, 1967):61.

4254. St. Amant, Clyde Penrose. "Theological
Education and the Denominational Seminary."
Review and Expositor 57 (April 1960,
Suppl.):239-56.

4255. Stach, John F. "The Changing Character of
Concordia College, Ft. Wayne, Ind., as
Reflected in Synodical Resolutions, 1847-
1953." Concordia Historical Institute
Quarterly 26 (1953):115-18.

4256. Stafford, William S. Domesticating the
Clergy: The Inception of the Reformation
in Strasbourg, 1522-1524. Missoula, Mont.:
Scholars Press, 1976.

4257. "Stagnation of Theological Seminaries."
Biblical World 34 (July 1909):3-7.

368

4258. Stalcup, Gordon Elwood. "A Study of
       Relationships between Academic Counseling
       Preparation, Perceived Value of Counseling
       Activities, and Time Spent in Counseling
       Activities by Memphis Clergy." Ed.D.
       dissertation, Memphis State University,
       1977.

4259. Stalker, James. The Preacher and His Models.
       London, New York: Hodder & Stoughton,
       1891.

4260. "Standardization of the Bachelor of Divinity
       Degree." Auburn Seminary Record 12
       (1916):436-57.

4261. "Standards for Methodist Academies, Colleges
       and Universities." School and Society 21
       (May 23, 1925):617.

4262. Standridge, Larry Allen. "An Analysis of
       Teaching in the Extension Centers of the
       Southern Baptist Seminaries." Ph.D.
       dissertation, Ohio State University, 1971.

4263. Stanfield, V. L., ed. "John A. Broadus [1827-
       95]." Quarterly Review (Bap.) 16 (July
       1956):52-60.

4264. Stange, Douglas C. "Bishop Daniel A. Payne
       and the Lutheran Church." Lutheran
       Quarterly 16, no. 4 (1964):354-9.

4265. Stange, Douglas C. "History of the
       Association of Lutheran Seminarians."
       Lutheran Quarterly 16 (May 1964):164-7.

4266. Stanger, Frank B. "Julian C. McPheeters, My
       Friend and Administrative Comrade." Asbury
       Seminarian 16 (Spring-Summer 1962):26-30.

4267. Stanger, Frank B. "Reflections on Admini-
       strative Life Style within an Evangelical
       Multidenominational Seminary." Theological
       Education 12 (Autumn 1975):20-3.

4268. Stanger, Frank Bateman. "Role of a Confes-
       sional Seminary in Theological Education."
       Asbury Seminarian 21 (October 1962):3-11.

4269. Starbuck, Edwin Diller and Holt, Arthur
       Erastus. "Theological Seminaries and
       Research." Religious Education 23 (May

1928):404-06.

4270. Starbuck, Winifred. "The Scattergood
      Seminary." Palimpsest 43 (August
      1962):327-33.

4271. Starratt, F. A. "Demands of Democracy upon
      the Theological Seminary." Religious
      Education 13 (June 1918):207-10.

4272. Starratt, F. A. "The Demands of the Rural
      Church Upon the Theological Curriculum."
      American Journal of Theology 22 (October
      1918):479-96.

4273. Stasheff, Edward. Methodist Research Project
      in Preaching: a Study of Current Develop-
      ments in the Teaching of Preaching in
      America and the United Kingdom. Indian-
      apolis: Indiana Area of the Methodist
      Church, 1963.

4274. "State of Union." Time 100 (October 9,
      1972):84.

4275. "Statement on Pre-Seminary Studies, the
      American Association of Theological
      Schools." Journal of Bible and Religion 34
      (April 1966).

4276. Stave, Douglas Tennyson. "Curricular Change
      in Selected Bible Institutes and Bible
      Colleges." Ed.D. dissertation, University
      of Oregon, 1962.

4277. Stealey, Sydnor Lorenzo. "Per Centennial
      Seminary Ideals." Review and Expositor 56
      (April 1959):119-32.

4278. Stearns, Lewis F. Henry Boynton Smith.
      Boston: Houghton Mifflin & Co., 1892.

4279. Stearns, W. A. "Education and Supply of
      Ministers in Different Ages and Countries:
      United States." Bibliotheca Sacra 8 (April
      1851):263-7.

4280. Stebbins, M. C. "Speculative Theology in Our
      Theological Seminaries." Bibliotheca Sacra
      44 (July 1887):504-11.

4281. Steckel, Clyde J. "Convocation Sermon:
      Nourishing the People of God." Theological

Markings no. 10 (Winter 1980):5-8.

4282. Steckel, Clyde J. and White, Donald R.
      "Introductory Theological Interpretation as
      Competency-Based Education." _Theological
      Education_ 13 (Spring 1977):184-94.

4283. Steele, Daniel. "Non-Classical Methodist
      Theological Schools." _Methodist Quarterly
      Review_ 68 (May 1886):454-9.

4284. Steele, Robert E. "Toward the Development of
      Adequate Training Programs for Urban
      Ministry." _Journal of Psychology and
      Theology_ 6, no. 4 (1978):291-7.

4285. Steen, Robert S. "Any Comeback, Union?
      [Letter to the Editor]." _Christian Century_
      81 (January 29, 1964):149.

4286. Steere, D. A. "Experiment in Supervisory
      Training." _Journal of Pastoral Care_ 23
      (December 1969):202-17.

4287. Steere, David Alden. "A New Pastoral
      Theology: A Study of Its Redefinition in
      the Clinical Pastoral Education Movement
      According to the Biblical Concept of
      Shepherding." Th.D. dissertation, Union
      Theological Seminary in the City of New
      York, 1966.

4288. Stein, E. V. "Pastoral Psychology's Scylla
      and Charybdis." _Journal of Pastoral Care_
      17 (Summer 1963):81-4.

4289. Steiner, Bernard Christian. _The History of
      Education in Connecticut._ Washington,
      D.C.: Government Printing Office, 1893.

4290. Stelzle, C. "Jebusites Versus Chicagoites."
      Outlook 92 (May 8, 1909):75-7.

4291. Stelzle, C. "Preparation of Ministers for
      Social Work: The Preparation in the
      Seminary." _(National) Conference of
      Charities and Correction. Proceedings_
      (1911):233-7.

4292. Stelzle, Charles. _A Son of the Bowery._ New
      York: George H. Doran Co., 1926.

4293. Stendahl, K. "Afterthoughts and Forethoughts
        [Student Demonstration at Harvard]."
        Harvard Divinity Bulletin 3 (New Series)
        (Fall 1969):1-5.

4294. Stendahl, K. "Convocation Address 1968."
        Harvard Divinity Bulletin 2 (New Series)
        (Autumn 1968):3-6.

4295. "Stepchild Seminaries." Christian Century 77
        (April 20, 1960):459-60.

4296. Stephens, Bruce M. "Frederick Huidekoper
        (1817-1892): Philanthropist, Scholar, and
        Teacher." Pennsylvania Magazine of History
        and Biography 103, no. 1 (1979):53-65.

4297. Stephens, Bruce M. "Liberals in the
        Wilderness: The Meadville Theological
        School, 1844-1856." Pennsylvania History
        42, no. 4 (1975):291-302.

4298. Stephens, Bruce M. "Mail Order Seminary:
        Bishop John Heyl Vincent and the Chautauqua
        School of Theology." Methodist History 14
        (July 1976):252-9.

4299. Stephens, Bruce M. "Samuel Miller, 1769-1850,
        Apologist for Orthodoxy." Princeton
        Seminary Bulletin 67 (Winter 1975):33-47.

4300. Stephens, Bruce M. "Watchman on the Walls of
        Zion: Samuel Miller and the Christian
        Ministry." Journal of Presbyterian History
        56, no. 4 (1978):296-309.

4301. Stephenson, George Malcolm. The Religious
        Aspects of Swedish Immigrations.
        Minneapolis: University of Minnesota
        Press, 1932.

4302. Stern, E. M. "Now It's the Clerical Intern."
        Christian Century 57 (July 10, 1940):876-8.

4303. Stern, George G. "Assessing Theological
        Student Personality." Journal of Pastoral
        Care 8 (Summer 1954):76-83.

4304. Stettner, John Willard. "A Study of Older
        Candidates for the Ministry." Ph.D.
        dissertation, Iliff School of Theology,
        1967.

4305. Stevens, Abel. Life and Times of Nathan
Bangs, D.D. New York: Carlton & Porter,
1863.

4306. Stevens, F. L. "German Theology and the
German University." New Englander 54,
(March 1891):259-88.

4307. Stevens, G. B. "Professor Phelps' 'Theory of
Preaching'." New Englander 41 (1882):120-
8.

4308. Stevens, George B. "Some Present Day
Conditions Affecting Theological
Education." New World 9 (December
1900):674-86.

4309. Stevens, V. "U.S. Seminary Profile."
National Council Outlook 6 (February
1956):20.

4310. Stevenson, D. E. "Bacon College Story: 1836-
1865 [bibliog.]." College of the Bible
Quarterly (Lexington) 39 (October 1962):5-
56.

4311. Stevenson, D. E. "College of the Bible
[Lexington) Idea." College of the Bible
Quarterly 40 (January 1963):5-9.

4312. Stevenson, Dwight Eshelman. Lexington
Theological Seminary, 1865-1965. St.
Louis: Bethany Press, 1964.

4313. Stevenson, Dwight E. "Models of Governance."
Theological Education 12 (Autumn 1975):29-
35.

4314. Stevenson, Herbert F., ed. Keswick's
Authentic Voice: Sixty-Five Dynamic
Addresses Delivered at the Keswick
Convention, 1875-1957. London: Marshall,
Morgan & Scott, 1959.

4315. Stevenson, J. R. "Greetings - Theological
Seminary of the Presbyterian Church,
Princeton, New Jersey." Reformed Church
Review 5 (January 1926):57-8.

4316. Stewart, Charles W. "How Effective Are Our
Marriage Ministries: A Critical Survey."
Pastoral Psychology 25 (Summer 1977):260-
71.

4317. Stewart, Charles, et al. "Living Issues in
       CPE: A Dialogue." Journal of Pastoral
       Care 29, no. 3 (1975):148, 156.

4318. Stewart, Charles William. Person and
       Profession: Career Development in the
       Ministry. Nashville, Tenn.: Abingdon
       Press, 1974.

4319. Stewart, Charles W. "The Relevance of
       Clinical Pastoral Training for Theological
       Education." In Fall Conference of the
       Institute of Pastoral Care, pp. 61-75.
       Framingham, Mass., 1959.

4320. Stewart, Charles W. "A Study of the Results
       of a Program of Continuing Education for
       Protestant Clergy." Institute for Advanced
       Pastoral Studies, Bloomfield Hills, Mich.,
       n.d. (ERIC Document)

4321. Stewart, Charles W. "Training Pastoral
       Supervisors for Seminary Field Education."
       Journal of Pastoral Care 25, no. 1
       (1971):24-32.

4322. Stewart, H. L. "Are Universities a War-
       Casualty? [Curriculum]." Hibbert Journal
       46 (January 1948):164-9.

4323. "Stewarts as Christian Stewards: A Sketch of
       Milton and Lyman Stewart of California
       [Bible Institue of Los Angeles]." Mission-
       ary Review of the World 47 (August 1924):
       595-602.

4324. Stibbitz, G. "Problem of Religious Education
       as It Relates Itself to the Theological
       Seminary." Reformed Church Review 2 (April
       1923):123-8.

4325. Stiles, Ezra. The Literary Diary of Ezra
       Stiles. 3 vols. Edited by Franklin
       Bowditch Dexter. New York: Charles
       Scribner's Sons, 1901.

4326. Stiles, Joseph. "Toward a Recovery of a
       Functional Approach to Theological
       Education." Review and Expositor 59 (July
       1962):340-55.

4327. "Still Small Voice: Missouri Synod Clergy
       Dissent [Concordia Seminary]." Christian

Century 90 (September 12, 1973):879.

4328. Stinnette, C. R., Jr. "Program in Psychiatry and Religion after Four Years." Union Seminary Quarterly Review 15 (May 1960):295-302.

4329. Stipe, C. E. "Anthropology in the Bible Institute and Bible College Curriculum." Practical Anthropology 3 (March 1956):19-30.

4330. "Stir at the Centers of Theological Education." Survey 32 (July 25, 1914):434-5.

4331. Stocker, M. N. "Draft the Theologues?" Christian Century 70 (October 21, 1953):1204.

4332. Stokes, A. P., Jr. University Schools of Religion. New Haven: Yale University, 1914.

4333. Stokes, Anson Phelps. "University Schools of Religion: A Study of Theological Education in the United States." Religious Education 9 (August 1914):323-35.

4334. Stollberg, Dietrich and Klessman, Michael. "Fifty Years of 'Something Else': a Half Century of Clinical Pastoral Education Seen from a German Perspective." Lutheran World 22, no. 4 (1975):293-8.

4335. Stone, Barton W. The Biography of Eld. Barton Warren Stone. New York: Arno Press, 1972. (Reprint of the 1847 ed.)

4336. Stone, John Timothy. "I Went to Seminary, Too." Homiletic Review 108 (July 1934):3-5.

4337. Stone, Lawrence. "Princeton's Roots: An Amalgam of Models." Princeton Alumni Weekly (September 12, 1977):16-21.

4338. Stonehouse, Ned Bernard. J. Gresham Machen: A Biographical Memoir. Grand Rapids: Eerdmans Publishing Co., 1954.

4339. Storr, Richard J. The Beginnings of Graduate Education in America. Chicago: University of Chicago Press, 1953.

4340. Storr, Richard J. Harper's University: The Beginnings. A History of the University of Chicago. Chicago: University of Chicago Press, 1966.

4341. Storrs, Richard Salter. Memoir of the Rev. Samuel Green. Boston: Perkins & Marvin, 1836.

4342. Story, Cullen I. K. "J. Gresham Machen: Apologist and Exegete." Princeton Seminary Bulletin 2 (New Series), no. 2 (1979):91-103.

4343. Stott, John R. W. "Seminarians Are Not Tadpoles." Christianity Today 25 (February 6, 1981):54-5.

4344. Stowe, Everett McKinery. Theological Schools and Family Life Education. New York: World Council of Christian Education and Sunday School Association, 1960.

4345. Stowe, Walter H. "American Church History in Our Theological Seminaries." Historical Magazine of the Protestant Episcopal Church 25 (March 1956):5.

4346. Stowe, Walter H. "Nashotah House Is Now an Accredited Seminary." Historical Magazine of the Protestant Episcopal Church 24 (December 1955):330.

4347. Stowe, Walter H. "Theological Education in the United States." Historical Magazine of the Protestant Episcopal Church 24 (March 1955):6-12.

4348. Stoyanoff, Karen Braatz. "An Evaluation of an Experiential Education Project: To Develop a Model of Evaluation for Use in Field Education in a Seminary, Using Trans-actional Analysis To Analyze Data Relating to Interpersonal Interaction; And To Describe the Experiential Education Received by Students Participating in the Project." Ph.D. dissertation, Northwestern University, 1978.

4349. "Strange Case of the Diocesan Training Schools [Episcopal Church]." Christian Century 97 (February 6-13, 1980):131-3.

4350. "Stransky, Wilmore: Editors at Large [Union Theological Seminary, NYC]." Christian Century 87 (April 22, 1970):468.

4351. Street, R. B. "Speaking for the Class of 1914." Harvard Divinity Bulletin 28 (July 1964):103-8.

4352. Street, Watson T. "The Evolution Controversy in the Southern Presbyterian Church with Attention to the Theological and Ecclesiastical Issues Raised." Journal of the Presbyterian Historical Society 37, no. 4 (1959):232-50.

4353. Street, Watson T. "Thomas Smith: Presbyterian Bookman." Journal of the Presbyterian Historical Society 37, no. 1 (1959): 1-14.

4354. Strempke, Vernon L. "Caring for the Aging." Theological Education 16, Special Issue no. 3 (Winter 1980):381-4.

4355. Strempke, V. L. "Future Organizational Structures for Clinical Pastoral Education." Journal of Pastoral Care 15 (Autumn 1961):170-1.

4356. Strempke, Vernon L. "Teaching Ministry in Seminaries." In Dynamic Interpersonalism for Ministry. Edited by Orlo Strunk. Nashville: Abingdon Press, 1973.

4357. Striving for Ministry: Centennial Essays Interpreting the History of Luther Theological Seminary. Edited by Warren A. Quanbeck, Eugene L. Fevold and Gerhard E. Frost. Minneapolis: Augsburg Publishing House, 1977.

4358. Strobel, Walter Robert. "Personal and Academic Problems of Bachelor of Divinity Degree Candidates at a Large Metropolitan Theological Seminary: A Descriptive Study." Ed.D. dissertation, Columbia University, 1966.

4359. Strobridge, George Egerton. Biography of The Rev. Daniel Parish Kidder. New York: Printed by Hunt & Eaton, 1894.

4360. Strong, Augustus Hopkins. The Church and the
       University ... to Which is Appended a
       Detailed Argument and Plan for the
       Establishment of a University in the City
       of New York, Under the Control of Baptists.
       Rochester: E. R. Andrews, Printer, 1889.

4361. Strong, A. H. Outlines of Systematic Theology
       Designed for the Use of Theological
       Students. Philadelphia? American Baptist
       Publishing Society, 1908.

4362. Strong, Augustus H. "Reforms in Theological
       Education." Baptist Quarterly Review 7
       (1885):415-24.

4363. Strong, James. "Central Theological Seminary
       for Our Church." Christian Advocate and
       Journal (New York) 28 (December 22,
       1853):1.

4364. Strong, James. "Theological Seminaries in Our
       Church." Christian Advocate (New York) 29
       (May 4, 1954):69.

4365. Strong, Josiah. "The Plans and Purposes of
       the Evangelical Alliance for the United
       States." In Proceedings of the Second
       Convention of the International Christian
       Workers Association, pp. 76-84. New Haven,
       1887.

4366. Stroup, H. W. "Patterns of Continuing
       Education: S.T.M. Program at Gettysburg."
       Theological Education 1 (Summer 1965):220-
       2.

4367. Stroup, H. W. "S.T.M. Program at Gettysburg
       [Continuing Education]." Theological
       Education 1 (Summer 1965).

4368. Strunk, Orlo. "Clinical Pastoral Training:
       Experiment in Theological Education."
       School and Society 83 (May 26, 1956):183-6.

4369. Strunk, Orlo. Dynamic Interpersonalism for
       Ministry: Essays in Honor of Paul E.
       Johnson. Nashville: Abingdon Press, 1973.

4370. Strunk, Orlo T., Jr. and Reed, Kenneth E.
       "The Learning of Empathy: A Pilot Study
       [CPE]." Journal of Pastoral Care 14
       (Spring 1960):44-8.

4371.   Strunk, Orlo. "Men, Motives and the
        Ministry." Religious Education 54
        (September 1959):429-34.

4372.   Strunk, O., Jr. "Preministerial Student's
        Education." Religious Education 56
        (September 1961):351-4.

4373.   Strunk, Orlo, Jr. "Relationships of Psycho-
        logy of Religion and Clinical Pastoral
        Education." Pastoral Psychology 22, no.
        217 (1971):29-35.

4374.   Strunk, O., Jr. "Theological Students: A
        Study in Perceived Motives [bibliog.]."
        Personnel and Guidance Journal 36 (January
        1958):320-2.

4375.   Stuart, Moses. "Letter to the Editor: On the
        Study of the German Language." Christian
        Review 6 (September 1841):446-71.

4376.   Stuart, Moses. (Letter to the Secretary of
        the American Education Society). American
        Quarterly Register 1 (April 1829):193-204.

4377.   Stuart, Moses. "Sacred and Classical
        Studies." American Quarterly Register 3
        (February 1831):161-6.

4378.   Stubblefield, Jerry M. "The Ecumenical Impact
        of E. Y. Mullins." Journal of Ecumenical
        Studies 17, no. 2 (1980):94-102.

4379.   "Student Enrollment in Theological Schools."
        Theological Education 4 (Winter 1968):654-
        7.

4380.   "Student Revolt Hits the Seminaries."
        Christianity Today 13 (March 28, 1969):25.

4381.   "Student Support for Concordia's Faculty
        [Concordia Seminary]." Christian Century
        91 (January 2, 1974):7.

4382.   "A Student's Diary: 1860-1862." Auburn
        Seminary Record 10 (1914-15):462-9.

4383.   "Study of Languages Cognate with Hebrew."
        Bibliotheca Sacra 39 (1882):555-67.

4384.   Study of Theological Education in the United
        States and Canada. Theological Education

in America. New Haven, Conn.: 1954-55.

4385. Stuenkel, Walter William. "The Dropout Factor
in the Cost of Ministerial Training in the
Lutheran Church - Missouri Synod." Ph.D.
dissertation, Marquette University, 1966.

4386. Stump, J. P. "Financing Continuing Education." Theological Education 1 (Summer
1965):244-6.

4387. Stump, Joseph. "The Church and the Theolog-
ical Seminary." In Proceedings of the 1927
Convention, pp. 71-9. National Lutheran
Educational Conference.

4388. Sturm, F. G. "Global Exchange in Theological
Study." Christian Century 79 (April 25,
1962):521+.

4389. Sturm, F. G. "Logos and Logic in Renewed
Rapport." Christian Century 78 (May 10,
1961):587-9.

4390. Sturtevant, J. M. "The Education of Indigent
Young Men for the Ministry." American
Biblical Repository 10 (2nd Series)
(October 1843):462-86.

4391. Stylites, S. "Little Annie Oakley."
Christian Century 71 (November 17,
1954):1392.

4392. Stylites, S. "Many Mansions." Christian
Century 74 (July 31, 1957):911.

4393. Styons, Melvin D. "A Study to Develop and
Evaluate a Competency-Based Introductory
Counseling Course for a Bible College."
Ed.D. dissertation, Nova University, 1978.

4394. "Subscription to Its Creed." Outlook 66
(December 1, 1900):773-4.

4395. "Sucker List Is Working Again: D.D. Degrees
by Mail." Christian Century 48 (April 22,
1931):533.

4396. Suelflow, August R. "Essays and Reports,
Sixth Biennial Meeting, Wartburg Theological Seminary, Dubuque, Iowa, 19-21 Oct.
1972." Lutheran Historical Conference:
Essays and Reports 5 (1974):1-229.

4397. Suelflow, August R. "Lutheran Historical
Conference: Essays and Reports, 8th
Biennial Meeting, Philadelphia, Pa.,
October 21-23, 1976." Lutheran Historical
Conference: Essays and Reports 7 (1978):1-
170.

4398. Suelflow, August R. "Lutheran Historical
Conference: Essays and Reports, 9th
Biennial Meeting, Dubuque, Iowa 2-4
November 1978." Lutheran Historical
Conference: Essays and Reports 8 (1980):1-
136.

4399. Suelflow, August R. "Preserving Church
Historical Resources." American Archivist
28, no. 2 (1965):239-46.

4400. Suelflow, Roy A. "A Gutachten for Pastor
Sieker." Concordia Historical Institute
Quarterly 54, no. 1 (1981):30-3.

4401. Suelflow, Roy Arthur. "The History of
Concordia Seminary, St. Louis, 1847-1865."
Concordia Historical Institute Quarterly 24
(July 1951):49-68; (October 1951):97-124.

4402. Sugeno, Frank E. et al. "Annual Meeting Held
at the Episcopal Theological Seminary of
the Southwest, Austin, Texas." Historical
Magazine of the Protestant Episcopal Church
46 (September 1977):361-75.

4403. "Suggestion toward Filling Tomorrow's Empty
Pulpits." Christian Century 61 (May 3,
1944):549.

4404. Sullivan, J. B. "Changing Seminary Mystique."
Momentum 10 (October 1979):35-8+.

4405. Summers, Thomas A. "Story Day in CPE."
Journal of Supervision and Training in
Ministry 4 (1981):37-48.

4406. Sunderland, La Roy. "Essay on a Theological
Education." Methodist Magazine and
Quarterly Review 16 (1834):423-37.

4407. Sunderland, La Roy. "Theological Education."
Methodist Magazine and Quarterly Review 6
(New Series) (April 1835):204-21.

4408. Sunderland, Ronald Harry. "A Study of
Relationships of Dogmatism, Self-
Actualization, Values, and State-Trait
Anxiety, in Students Entering a Clinical
Pastoral Education Program." Ed.D.
dissertation, University of Houston, 1978.

4409. "The Supply of Educated Men for the Christian
Ministry [Editorial]." Biblical World 37
(February 1911):75-7.

4410. Survey 57 (February 15, 1927):624.

4411. "Survey of Methodist Episcopal Institutions."
School and Society 30 (October 12,
1929):514-15.

4412. "Survey of Theological Education." School and
Society 31 (February 15, 1930):222.

4413. "A Survey of Theological Schools." School and
Society 20 (August 16, 1924):208-9.

4414. Susskind, Jacob L. "Samuel Miller's Intellectual History of the Eighteenth Century."
Journal of Presbyterian History 49, no. 1
(1971):15-31.

4415. Sutherland, Arthur E. The Law at Harvard: A
History of Ideas and Men, 1817-1967.
Cambridge: Belknap Press of Harvard
University, 1967.

4416. Sutherland, M. R. "Introductory Remarks to
the Convocation: A Theological School
Looks to the Sciences [Meadville Theological School]." Zygon 1 (March 1966):108-
10.

4417. Swanson, G. B. and Ward, J. "Seminaries Can't
Do It All." Christianity Today 26
(February 5, 1982):88.

4418. Swanson, Paul Reginald. "Some Effects of
Clinical Pastoral Education on a Group of
Theological Students and Pastors." Ph.D.
dissertation Boston University Graduate
School, 1962.

4419. Swanson, Richard A. "Knowledge and Attitudes
Relating to Human Sexuality among Theolog-
ical Students." Ed.D. dissertation,
University of Southern California, 1980.

4420. Sweeney, James Earl. "Professional Competencies for Church Ministry as Perceived by Seminary Faculties, Church Lay Leaders, and Seminary Seniors." Ph.D. dissertation, Oregon State University, 1979.

4421. Sweet, H. H. "Theological Schools Affiliated with State Universities." Religious Education 8 (August 1913):259-63.

4422. Sweet, Leonard I. "The University of Chicago Revisited: The Modernization of Theology, 1890-1940." Foundations 22 (October-December 1979):324-51.

4423. Sweet, Louis Matthews. "The Study of the English Bible." Bible Magazine 1 (January 1913):8-20.

4424. Sweet, Louis Matthews. The Study of the English Bible. New York: Association Press, 1914.

4425. Sweet, William Warren. Indiana Asbury-DePauw University 1837-1937: A Hundred Years of Higher Education in the Middle West. New York: Abingdon Press, 1937.

4426. Sweet, William Warren. Methodism in American History. Rev. ed. Nashville: Abingdon Press, 1954.

4427. Sweet, William Warren. Religion and the Development of American Culture, 1765-1840. New York: Charles Scribner's Sons, 1952.

4428. Sweet, William Warren, ed. Religion on the American Frontier. 4 vols. New York: H. Holt & Co., 1931-9.

4429. Sweet, William Warren. "The Rise of Theological Schools in America." Church History 6 (September 1937):266-73.

4430. Sweeting, George. "Bible Colleges and Institutes: Chronicling the Vision of a Century." Christianity Today 26 (February 5, 1982):38-41.

4431. Sweetser, Seth. The Ministry We Need. Boston: American Tract Society, 1873.

4432. Swidler, Jacob Samuel. "The Development and Evaluation of the Master of Arts Program in Pastoral Marriage Counseling at the University of Detroit." Ed.D. dissertation, Columbia University, 1968.

4433. Swift, A. L. "New York City, A Theological Laboratory [Union Theological Seminary]." School and Society 21 (April 18, 1925):459-62.

4434. Swift, Elisha Pope. Duties and Responsibilities of the Professoral Office in Theological Seminaries. Pittsburgh: Printed by Johnson & Stockton, 1828.

4435. Swift, David E. "Thomas Jefferson, John Holt Rice, and Education in Virginia, 1815-25." Journal of Presbyterian History 49, no. 1 (1971):32-58.

4436. Sykes, S. W. "Theological Study: The Nineteenth Century and After." In The Philosophical Frontiers of Christian Theology, pp. 95-118. Edited by B. Hebblethwaite and S. Sutherland. Cambridge, 1982.

4437. Sylvester, H. "Negro Seminary." Commonweal 33 (April 11, 1941):615-16.

4438. "A Symposium on Bible-Study in the Theological Seminaries." Old Testament Student 5 (April 1886):321-34; (May 1886):353-65.

4439. Taggart, Morris. "A Study of Attitude Change in a Group of Theological Students." Ph.D. dissertation, Northwestern University, 1962.

4440. Takayama, K. Peter and Michel, Jerry B. "The Emergence of a New Seminary in a Congregationally Organized Denomination." Memphis State University, Tennessee, 1979.

4441. Talbert, Horace. The Sons of Allen. Together with a Sketch of the Rise and Progress of Wilberforce University, Wilberforce, Ohio. Xenia, Ohio: Aldine Press, 1906.

4442. Talbot, Gordon Gray. "A Study of the Accrediting Association of Bible Colleges from 1947 through 1966." Ph.D.

dissertation, New York University, 1968.

4443. Talley, John Daniel, Jr.. "A Homiletics Manual for the Bible College Student." Ph.D. dissertation, Western Conservative Baptist Seminary, 1979.

4444. Tanis, James Robert. "The Library and Its Role in the Divinity School." Harvard Divinity Bulletin 26 (January 1962):19-22.

4445. Tapp, Robert B. "The Place of the Non-Christian Religions in American Protestant Seminary Education." Ph.D. dissertation, University of Southern California, 1953.

4446. Tappert, Theodore Gerhardt. History of the Lutheran Theological Seminary at Philadelphia 1864-1964. Philadelphia: Lutheran Theological Seminary, 1964.

4447. Tappert, Theodore Gerhardt. "Lutherans in the Great Economic Depression." Lutheran Quarterly 7 (May 1955):145-54.

4448. Task Force on the Church and Higher Education, UPCUSA. "The Church's Mission in Higher Education." Journal of Presbyterian History 59 (Fall 1981):440-65.

4449. "The Task of Correlation: An Editorial." Journal of Pastoral Care 6 (Fall 1952):53-4.

4450. Tatnall, E. C. "As Others See Us: Ecumenical Scholarship Exchange Students." National Council Outlook 6 (June 1956):10-11+.

4451. Tavuchis, Nicholas. Pastors and Immigrants: The Role of a Religious Elite in the Absorption of Norwegian Immigrants. The Hague: Martinus Nijhoff, 1963.

4452. Taylor, Charles L. "Do Churches Support the Seminaries?" Christian Century 79 (April 25, 1962):548-9.

4453. Taylor, C. L. "Educated Ministry." College of the Bible Quarterly 40 (January 1963):46-52.

4454. Taylor, Charles L. "The Location of Theological Schools." Theological Education 2

(Winter 1965):104-9.

4455. Taylor, Charles L. "Selection and Training of Candidates for the Ministry: The Training of American Ministers." Expository Times 73 (1962):363-6.

4456. Taylor, Charles L. "Seminaries and Universities in Partnership." Princeton Seminary Bulletin 54 (July 1960):12-15.

4457. Taylor, Charles L. "The Situation in 1958." Religion In Life 28 (1958-9):5-13.

4458. Taylor, C. L. "Theological Education, Protestant." In Accreditation in Higher Education, pp. 212-14. United States. Office of Education. Washington, 1959.

4459. Taylor, C. L. "Year with A.A.T.S." Christian Century 76 (April 22, 1959):477+.

4460. Taylor, Charles L. "Why a University Involvement?" Lutheran Quarterly 18, no. 4 (1966):307-14, 318-21.

4461. Taylor, D. E. "Ecumenical Opportunity." Christian Century 73 (January 25, 1956):115.

4462. Taylor, D. M. "Clinical Pastoral Training." Journal of Pastoral Care 16 (Spring 1962):34-40.

4463. Taylor, Frederick Howard. J. Hudson Taylor: A Biography. Chicago: Moody Press, 1965.

4464. Taylor, Graham. "Field Work: Its Educational Value and Relation to the Financial Aid of Students." In Christianity Practically Applied, v. 2, pp. 428-41. Evangelical Alliance for the United States of America. Conference. Chicago, 1893. New York: Baker & Taylor, 1894.

4465. Taylor, Graham. The Practical Training Needed for the Ministry of To-Day: Inaugural Address Oct. 10, 1888. Hartford, 1888.

4466. Taylor, Graham. "Sociological Training of the Ministry." In Christianity Practically Applied, v. 1, pp. 396-413. Evangelical Alliance for the United States of America.

386

Conference. Chicago, 1893. New York:
Baker & Taylor, 1894.

4467. Taylor, Harry T. Bloomfield College: The
First Century, 1868-1968. Bloomfield,
N.J.: Bloomfield College, 1970.

4468. Taylor, John Phelps. "The Place of the
English Bible in Modern Theological
Education." Andover Review 18 (December
1892):615-32.

4469. Taylor, Marvin J. "Accreditation as
Improvement of Theological Education."
Theological Education 15 (Autumn 1978):50-
7.

4470. Taylor, Marvin J. "The D. Min: History and
Typology [Responses, pp. 16-26]." In
Papers from the National Symposium on
Issues and Models of Doctor of Ministry
Programs. Edited by G. Douglass Lewis.
Hartford, Conn.: Hartford Seminary
Foundation, 1980.

4471. Taylor, Marvin J. "Pastor and Parish as Co-
Learners in the Doctor of Ministry Program:
An Experiment in Theological Education."
Theological Education 16, Special Issue no.
2 (Winter 1980):175-265.

4472. Taylor, Marvin J. "A Theological Faculties
Profile: A 1970-71 Survey of AATS
Schools." Theological Education 8 (Autumn
1971):57-72.

4473. Taylor, Mary Geraldine (Guinness). Borden of
Yale '09: "The Life That Counts." London,
Philadelphia: China Inland Mission, 1926.

4474. Taylor, Prince Albert, Jr. "A History of
Gammon Theological Seminary." Ed.D.
dissertation, New York University, 1948.

4475. Taylor, Raymond R. "A Century of the Philadelphia Divinity School, 1857-1957."
Historical Magazine of the Protestant
Episcopal Church 26 (September 1957):204-
23.

4476. Taylor, Raymond R. History of the Philadelphia Divinity School. Philadelphia, 1957.

387

4477. Taylor, W. S. "An Emerging Community of Theological Study." Theological Education 2 (Winter 1965):110-17.

4478. Taylor, William. The Model Preacher. Cincinnati: Swormstedt & Poe, 1859.

4479. Taylor, William M. "The Heroic Spirit in the Christian Ministry." Presbyterian Review 10 (July 1889):444-55.

4480. Taylor, William Mackergo. The Ministry of the Word. New York: Anson D. F. Randolph & Co., 1876.

4481. "The Teaching Ministry." Biblical World 15 (March 1900) (New Series):164-8.

4482. "Teaching the Arts in Seminaries." Christian Century 97 (February 6, 1980):133-5.

4483. "Teeing off with TEE [Theological Education by Extension]." Christianity Today 17 (April 27, 1973):43-4.

4484. "Television Preacher Jerry Falwell's Liberty Baptist Seminary Lost Its Dean in a Doctrinal Dispute over Calvinism." Christianity Today 24 (February 22, 1980):49.

4485. Telfer, Walter A. and Handspicker, Meredith B. "Teaching Parishes: Partners in Theological Education." Andover Newton Quarterly 17 (November 1976):109-17.

4486. Telfer, Walter A. "The Teaching Parish Program: Participatory Education." Andover Newton Quarterly 14, no. 4 (1974):267-71.

4487. Tennent, Gilbert. The Danger of an Unconverted Ministry, Considered in a Sermon on Mark VI.34. 2nd ed. Boston: Printed by Rogers & Fowle, 1742.

4488. Tenney, Merrill C. "How College-Seminary Work Can Best Fit Together." Evangelical Missions Quarterly 5, no. 1 (1968):20-5.

4489. Terrien, Samuel. "On the Future of Theological Education." Religion In Life 49 (Winter 1980):488-99.

4490. Terry, Milton Spenser. "Biblical Scholars of
       the United States in 1882." Biblical World
       39 (April 1912):225-34.

4491. Te-Selle, Sallie McFague. "Between Athens and
       Jerusalem: The Seminary in Tension."
       Christian Century 93 (February 4-11,
       1976):89-93.

4492. Tetlow, J. A. "Readiness for Ministry:
       Project of the Association of Theological
       Schools." America 128 (March 25,
       1978):233-6.

4493. Tewksbury, Donald G. The Founding of American
       Colleges and Universities before the Civil
       War. New York: Arno Press & The New York
       Times, 1969. (First published in 1932).

4494. Tharp, J. Clifford, Jr. Statistical Factors
       Related to Establishing a New SBC Seminary.
       Nashville: Sunday School Board of the
       Southern Baptist Convention, 1979.

4495. That Clinical Year: A Symposium." Survey 55
       (January 1, 1926):432-3.

4496. Thayer, J. Henry. "The American School in
       Syria." Biblical World 6 (New Series)
       (October 1895):307-08.

4497. Thayer, Joseph Henry. The Change of Attitude
       towards the Bible: A Lecture Given under
       the Auspices of the Boston Board of the
       American Institute of Sacred Literature,
       February 17, 1891. Boston: Houghton,
       Mifflin & Co., 1891.

4498. "Theologians to Leave if Race Ban Holds."
       Christian Century 69 (June 25, 1952):740.

4499. "Theologians Wanted." Time 80 (July 20,
       1962):52.

4500. "Theological Co-operation." Outlook 107 (July
       25, 1914):689-90.

4501. "Theological Curriculum for the 1970's."
       Theological Education 4 (Spring 1968):
       entire issue.

4502. "Theological Curriculum for the 70's." Theo-
       logical Education 5 (Winter 1969):99-111.

4503. "Theological Default in American Seminaries."
Christianity Today 8 (September 11, 1964):
28-9.

4504. "Theological Education." Christian Advocate
(Western edition) 1 (March 6, 1835):178.

4505. "Theological Education." Christian Century 68
(April 25, 1951):518.

4506. "Theological Education." Methodist Magazine
and Quarterly Review 17 (January 1835):85-
105.

4507. "Theological Education." Union Seminary
Quarterly Review 22 (May 1967):297-365.

4508. "Theological Education 1958." Christian
Century 75 (April 23, 1958):487-94.

4509. "Theological Education 1968." Christian
Century 85 (April 24, 1968):512+.

4510. "Theological Education 1969." Christian
Century 86 (April 23, 1969):541+.

4511. "Theological Education 1970." Christian
Century 87 (April 22, 1970):472+.

4512. "Theological Education 1971." Christian
Century 88 (January 27, 1971):91+.

4513. "Theological Education 1972." Christian
Century 89 (February 2, 1972):111+.

4514. "Theological Education 1973." Christian
Century 90 (February 7, 1973):140+.

4515. "Theological Education 1974: Symposium."
Christian Century 91 (February 6,
1974):116-17+.

4516. "Theological Education 1975: Symposium."
Christian Century 92 (February 5,
1975):100-12+.

4517. "Theological Education 1976: Symposium."
Christian Century 93 (February 4,
1976):84+.

4518. "Theological Education 1977: Symposium with
Editorial Comment." Christian Century 94
(February 2, 1977):76-7, 81-95+.

4519. "Theological Education 1978: Symposium with Editorial Comment." Christian Century 95 (February 1, 1978):92-3, 98-106+.

4520. "Theological Education 1979: Symposium with Editorial Comment." Christian Century 96 (February 7, 1979):115, 122-30+.

4521. "Theological Education 1982: Focus on Women." Christian Century 99 (February 3-10, 1982):107, 109-11+.

4522. "Theological Education 1983." Christian Century 100 (February 2-9, 1983):83-4, 90-8+.

4523. "Theological Education - A Special Course of Theological Study for Those Who Have Had No College Training." Bibliotheca Sacra 36 (July 1879):560-79.

4524. "Theological Education - Advantages of Private Instruction." Bibliotheca Sacra 38 (October 1881):759-73.

4525. "Theological Education - An Appeal for Higher Theological Training." Bibliotheca Sacra 36 (January 1879):182-91.

4526. "Theological Education: Annual Review of Current Issues, Books and Seminary Programs." Christian Century 74 (April 24, 1957):509-18.

4527. "Theological Education as Professional Education." Theological Education 5 (Spring 1969):entire issue.

4528. Theological Education as Professional Education: The Report of a Convocation Sponsored by the Episcopal Theological School during Its Centennial Year Observance. Edited by Olga Craven, Alden L. Todd and Jesse H. Ziegler. Dayton, Ohio: American Association of Theological Schools, 1969.

4529. Theological Education Association of Mid-America. TEAM-A Serials: A Union List of the Serials Holdings of the Theological Education Association of Mid-America. Louisville: TEAM Libraries at the Southern Baptist Theological Seminary, 1972.

4530. "Theological Education - Diversities in the Curriculum of Our Theological Schools." Bibliotheca Sacra 37 (July 1880):566-76.

4531. "Theological Education in a World Context." Theological Education 9 (Summer 1973): entire issue.

4532. "Theological Education in America [bibliog.]." Religion In Life 28 (Winter 1958-59):5-44.

4533. "Theological Education in 1925." Christian Education 9 (January 1926):99-144.

4534. "Theological Education of Laymen Needed." Christian Century 74 (May 22, 1957):644-5.

4535. "Theological Education: Physical Science in the Theological Seminary." Bibliotheca Sacra 39 (January 1882):190-6.

4536. "Theological Education - Private Instruction for the Ministry." Bibliotheca Sacra 38 (April 1881):369-83.

4537. "Theological Education - Questions of the Two Edwardses for their Pupils in Theology." Bibliotheca Sacra 39 (April 1882):367-81.

4538. "Theological Education Takes New Step." Christian Century 77 (September 7, 1960): 1014.

4539. "Theological Education - The Claims of Biblical Theology to a Place in Our Theological Schools." Bibliotheca Sacra 38 (January 1881):188-98.

4540. "Theological Education: The Elective System in Theological Seminaries." Bibliotheca Sacra 36 (April 1879):367-72.

4541. "Theological Education: The Multiplication of Theological Seminaries." Bibliotheca Sacra 36 (October 1879):760-71.

4542. "Theological Education - The Study of Languages Cognate with Hebrew." Bibliotheca Sacra 39 (July 1882):555-66.

4543. "Theological Faculty to End Federation." Christian Century 77 (May 11, 1960):565.

4544. "(Theological Institutions in America.)"
Congregational Magazine 21 (1839):98+,
154+.

4545. "(Theological Institutions in the United
States.)" American Quarterly Register 6
(1834):34+.

4546. "Theological Library Boom: Annual Conference." Library Journal 89 (August
1964):2965.

4547. "Theological Scholarship at Princeton."
American Journal of Theology 17 (January
1913):94-102.

4548. "Theological Scholarships at Harvard." School
and Society 17 (March 31, 1923):351.

4549. The Theological School and Calvin College.
Semi-Centennial Volume: Theological School
and Calvin College, 1876, 1926. Grand
Rapids: Theological School and Calvin
College, 1927.

4550. "Theological Seminaries." Independent 71
(July 6, 1911):53-4.

4551. "(Theological Seminaries.)" Old and New 4
(1871):66+.

4552. "Theological Seminaries." Outlook 63 (October
21, 1899):436-9; "Discussion." 63
(November 25, 1899):732-5.

4553. "(Theological Seminaries and Congregational
Churches.)" Andover Review 4 (1885):247+.

4554. "(Theological Seminaries, Are They in Danger
of Overtraining?)" Andover Review 12
(1889):91+.

4555. "(Theological Seminaries in the United
States.)" American Education Society.
Quarterly Register and Journal 1
(1829):118, 220+.

4556. "Theological Seminaries Return the Fire."
Homiletic Review 89 (January 1925):3-10.

4557. "(Theological Seminaries - Security of Their
Trust Funds.)" Reformed Church Review 44
(1897):252+.

4558. "Theological Seminaries Stand Together."
Christian Century 70 (January 21, 1953):68.

4559. "Theological Seminaries under Fire."
Homiletic Review 88 (September, November
1924):181-5, 347-54.

4560. Theological Seminary of the Reformed Church in
America, New Brunswick, N.J. Biographical
Record, Theological Seminary, New Bruns-
wick, New Jersey, 1784-1934. Compiled by
John Howard Raven. New Brunswick? 1934.

4561. Theological Seminary of the Reformed Church in
America, New Brunswick, N.J. Biographical
Record, Theological Seminary, New Bruns-
wick, 1784-1911. Compiled by John Howard
Raven. New Brunswick, N.J., 1912.

4562. Theological Seminary of the Reformed Church in
America, New Brunswick, N.J. Centennial of
the Theological Seminary of the Reformed
Church in America, 1784-1884. New York:
Board of Publication of the Reformed Church
in America, 1885.

4563. Theological Seminary of the Reformed Church in
America, New Brunswick, N.J. Fortieth
Anniversary of the Inauguration of the Rev.
Samuel M. Woodbridge, D.D., LL.D., as
Professor in the Theological Seminary of
the Reformed (Dutch) Church in America at
New Brunswick, 1857-1897. Printed for the
Alumni Association, 1898.

4564. Theological Seminary of the Reformed Church in
America, New Brunswick, N.J. The One
Hundred Fiftieth Anniversary of the
Founding of New Brunswick Theological
Seminary, - October Second and Third,
Nineteen Hundred Thirty-Four. New
Brunswick, N.J., 1934.

4565. "Theological Seminary Receives Large Gift."
Christian Century 80 (December 18,
1963):1569.

4566. "Theological Students Today." Religion In
Life 31 (Autumn 1962):497-536.

4567. Theological Study Today: Addresses Delivered
at the Seventy-Fifth Anniversary of the
Meadville Theological School, June 1-3,

1920. Chicago: University of Chicago Press, 1921.

4568. "Theological Training and the War." Religious Education 13 (October 1918):374-5.

4569. "Theology and Graduate Religion: The Struggle for Coherence." Christian Century 89 (February 2, 1972):111-12.

4570. "Theology and Religious Education: Symposium [bibliog.]." Religious Education 53 (September 1958):412-46.

4571. "Theology Comes Alive: Summer School at University of San Francisco." America 113 (August 28, 1965):198.

4572. Theology in Modern Education: A Creative Encounter. Edited by Laurence Bright. London: Darton, Longman & Todd, 1965.

4573. "Theology in the Headlines: Suspension of President John H. Tietjen [Concordia Seminary]." America 130 (February 9, 1974):82.

4574. "Theology in the University." Christian Century 60 (November 17, 1943):1326-8.

4575. "Theology: Literature in the Divinity School." Time 90 (December 22, 1967):51.

4576. Theron, Daniel Johannes. "Some Thoughts on the Study of the Biblical Languages." Princeton Seminary Bulletin 49 (May 1956):22-5.

4577. Thielicke, H. "Spiritual Exercise for Theologs." Translated by C. L. Taylor. Encounter 23 (Autumn 1962):387-403.

4578. Thiessen, Henry Clarence. "Should New Testament Greek Be 'Required' in our Ministerial Training Courses?" Bibliotheca Sacra 91 (January 1934):34-45.

4579. "Thinking of Seminary." His 21 (November 1960):10-13.

4580. Thirkield, Wilbur P. "The Training of Ministers and Physicians for the Negro Race." In Education and National

Character, pp. 157-66. Chicago: Religious
Education Association, 1908.

4581. This Ministry: The Contribution of Henry
Sloane Coffin. Edited by Reinhold Niebuhr.
New York: Charles Scribner's Sons, 1945.

4582. Thoburn, James Mills. Life of Isabella
Thoburn. Cincinnati: Jennings & Pye,
1903.

4583. Tholuck, Friedrick August Gottreu. "Theological Encyclopaedia and Methodology: Translated from the Unpublished Lectures of
Prof. Tholuck of Halle by Edwards A. Park."
Bibliotheca Sacra 1 (1844):178-217, 332-67,
552-78, 726-35.

4584. Thomas, Carey S. "Bible Training Schools and
Bible Evangelism." Moody Monthly 33 (July
1933):490-1.

4585. Thomas, Clifford William. "A Descriptive
Study of Ministerial Education in the
Wesleyan Church." Ed.D. dissertation,
Michigan State University, 1968.

4586. Thomas, George B. "Questioning the Present
State of Black Theological Education." AME
Zion Quarterly Review 92 (October 1980):27-
35.

4587. Thomas, J. R. "Evaluations of Clinical
Pastoral Training and Part-Time Training in
a General Hospital." Journal of Pastoral
Care 12 (Spring 1958):28-38.

4588. Thomas, James S. The Intentional Development
of the Black Ministry. Occasional Papers
No. 29. Nashville, Tenn.: United
Methodist Board of Higher Education and
Ministry, 1979.

4589. Thomas, John Lawrence. Religion and the
American People. Westminster, Md.: Newman
Press, 1963.

4590. Thomas, John T., Stein, Leonard I. and Klein,
Marjorie H. "Comparative Evaluation of
Changes in CPE Students in Different
Clinical Settings Measured by the Adjective
Check List and Experience Scale." Journal
of Pastoral Care 36 (Summer 1982):181-93.

4591. Thomas, O. C. "Psychological Pressures on the
      Seminarian." Journal of Pastoral Care 16
      (Summer 1962):95-7.

4592. Thomas, Owen Clark. Introduction to Theology.
      Cambridge: Greeno, Hadden, 1973.

4593. Thomas, Owen Clark. "A Preliminary Raising of
      Issues." Theological Education 5 (Spring
      1969):139-43.

4594. Thomas, Owen C. "Professional Education and
      Theological Education." Theological Educa-
      tion 4 (Autumn 1967):556-65.

4595. Thomas, Owen C. "Some Issues in Theological
      Education." Theological Education 5
      (Summer 1969):346-56.

4596. Thomas, Robert A. "Theological Education for
      the Seventies." Encounter 33 (Summer
      1972):257-64.

4597. Thomas, Robert A. "There and Then; Here and
      Now." Encounter 36 (Spring 1975):139-48.

4598. Thomas, William Henry Griffith. The Work of
      the Ministry. London: Hodder & Stoughton,
      1913.

4599. Thomas, William Holcombe. "Some Educational
      History of Alabama Methodism." Montgomery:
      Paragon Press, 1908.

4600. Thompson, A. C. "(Education for the
      Ministry.)" Hartford Seminary Record 7
      (1897):20+.

4601. Thompson, C. G. "Theological Seminaries: An
      Evaluation." Methodist Quarterly Review 74
      (July 1925):413-21.

4602. Thompson, Charles Henry. "The Problem of
      Negro Higher Education." Journal of Negro
      Education 2 (July 1933):257-71.

4603. Thompson, Dean K. "Moral Duty and Divine
      Grace: A Union Seminary Case Study."
      Religion in Life 45 (Spring 1976):82-8.

4604. Thompson, Dean K. "Robert McAfee Brown
      Remembers Henry Pitney Van Dusen." Journal
      of Presbyterian History 56, no. 1

(1978):62-78.

4605. Thompson, Dean K. "World War II, Interven-
      tionism, and Henry Pitney Van Dusen."
      Journal of Presbyterian History 55, no. 4
      (1977):327-45.

4606. Thompson, Ernest Trice. Presbyterians in the
      South. 3 vols. Richmond, Va.: John Knox
      Press, 1963-73.

4607. Thompson, Ernest Trice. "Union Theological
      Seminary [Richmond, 1812-1951]." Common-
      wealth (Va.) 19 (February 1952):15-18.

4608. Thompson, Henry Adams. Biography of Jonathan
      Weaver...a Bishop in the Church of the
      United Brethren in Christ... Dayton:
      United Brethren Publishing House, 1901.

4609. Thompson, H. A. School of the Prophets.
      Dayton, Ohio: United Brethren Pub. House,
      1908?

4610. Thompson, J. Earl. "Abolitionism and Theolog-
      ical Education at Andover." New England
      Quarterly 47 (June 1974):238-61.

4611. Thompson, J. Earl. "Church History Comes to
      Andover: The Persecution of James
      Murdock." Andover Newton Quarterly 15
      (March 1975):213-27.

4612. Thompson, J. Earl, Jr. "Lyman Beecher's Long
      Road to Conservative Abolitionism." Church
      History 42, no. 1 (1973):89-109.

4613. Thompson, Jorgen Sogn. "A Study of the
      Relationships between Certain Measured
      Psychological Variables and Achievement in
      the First Year of Theological Seminary
      Work." Ph.D. dissertation, University of
      Minnesota, 1956.

4614. Thompson, Lewis O. The Prayer-Meeting and Its
      Improvement. Chicago: F. H. Revell Co.,
      1873.

4615. Thompson, Owen F. Sketches of the Ministers
      of the Reformed Presbyterian Church of
      North America from 1888 to 1930, pp. 416-
      18. Blanchard, Iowa, 1930.

4616.   Thompson, Robert C. "A Research Note on the
        Diversity among American Protestants: A
        Southern Baptist Example." Review of
        Religious Research 15 (Winter 1974):87-92.

4617.   Thompson, W. D. "Teaching Speech to the
        Clergy: A Bibliography." Speech
        Monographs 31 (August 1964):350-4.

4618.   Thompson, W. J. "Theological Seminary and the
        Liberals Arts College." In The Liberal
        Arts College Movement, pp. 156-63. Edited
        by Archie M. Palmer. Conference of Liberal
        Arts Colleges, Chicago, March 18-20, 1930.
        New York: Printed by J. J. Little & Ives
        Co., 1930.

4619.   Thompson, W. O. A Report on a Survey of the
        Theological Seminaries and the Assembly's
        Training School of the Presbyterian Church
        in the United States, July 1928.
        Louisville, Ky.: Dept. of Christian Educa-
        tion of the Presbyterian Church in the
        United States, 1928.

4620.   Thornburg, Hershel Dean. "An Analysis of the
        Attitudes of Ministerial Students Enrolled
        in Post Baccalaureate Schools of Religion
        toward Sex as Measured by the Sex Attitude
        Inventory." Ed.D. dissertation, University
        of Oklahoma, 1968.

4621.   Thornton, Edward Everett. "A Critique of
        Clinical Pastoral Education." Ph.D. dis-
        sertation, Southern Baptist Theological
        Seminary, 1961.

4622.   Thornton, E. E. "Ministerial Drop-Outs: A
        Note." Journal of Pastoral Care 14
        (Summer 1960):117-8.

4623.   Thornton, E. E. "Place of Clinical Pastoral
        Education in New Plans of Theological
        Education." Journal of Pastoral Care 20
        (March 1966):16-23.

4624.   Thornton, Edward E. Professional Education
        for Ministry: A History of Clinical
        Pastoral Education. Nashville: Abingdon
        Press, 1970.

4625.   Thornton, Edward E. "Radical Reformation of
        the Seminaries." Pastoral Psychology 20

(January 1969):57-60.

4626. Thornton, Edward E. "Some Hard Questions for Clinical Pastoral Educators." Journal of Pastoral Care 22 (December 1968): 194-202.

4627. Thornton, E. E. "Training for Pastoral Care and Its Ecumenical Dimension." Pastoral Psychology 18 (June 1967):23-8.

4628. "(Thorough Course of Education for Ministry.)" American Education Society. Quarterly Register and Journal 1 (1829):145+.

4629. Thorp, Willard, ed. The Lives of Eighteen from Princeton. Princeton: Princeton University Press, 1946.

4630. Thorson, James A. and Cook, Thomas C. Spiritual Well-Being of the Elderly. National Intradecade Conference, Atlanta, Georgia, 1977. Springfield, Ill.: Charles C. Thomas, 1980.

4631. "Thoughts on the Importance of a Liberal Education to a Minister." Panoplist and Missionary Magazine 9 (1813):70-3.

4632. "Thoughts on the State of Theological Science and Education in Our Country." Bibliotheca Sacra 1 (November 1844):735-68.

4633. "Three-Wing Academic Complex for Theology School [Lutheran School of Theology, Chicago]." American School and University 40 (April 1968):71.

4634. Thrift, Charles T., Jr. "The History of Theological Education in the Methodist Episcopal Church, South, 1845-1915." Master's thesis, Duke University, 1933.

4635. Thurman, W. Peyton. "The Training of Ministers [Old Problems - New Solutions]." Review and Expositor 59 (July 1962):365-78.

4636. Thurston, Branson Luther. "A Comparison of Selected Psychological Health Factors and Perceptions of Administrative Procedures in Those Ministers and Seminary Students Perceiving the Administrative Role to be More Integral to an Effective Ministry and in Those Perceiving That Role to be Less

400

Integral." Ed.D. dissertation, Syracuse
University, 1970.

4637. Thwing, C. F. "College and the Ministry:
With Letters from Seven College
Professors." Outlook 48 (October 7,
1893):625-7.

4638. Thwing, C. F. and Warfield, B. B. "(Improvement of Theological Seminaries.)"
Christian Literature 13 (1895):135+.

4639. Thwing, Charles Franklin. The Ministry: An
Appeal to College Men. Boston: Pilgrim
Press, 1916.

4640. Thwing, Charles. The Working Church. New
York: Fleming H. Revell, 1888.

4641. Tietjen, J. H. "In God for the World
[Concordia Seminary, St. Louis]." Concordia
Theological Monthly 41 (January 1970):3-9.

4642. Tietjen, J. H. "Style and the Mission
[Concordia Seminary, St. Louis]."
Concordia Theological Monthly 41 (December
1970):693-700.

4643. Tietjen, J. "Theological Education in
Ecumenical Perspective." Concordia
Theological Monthly 45 (January 1974):8-10.

4644. Tietjen, John H. Which Way to Lutheran Unity?
A History of Efforts to Unite the Lutherans
of America. St. Louis: Concordia
Publishing House, 1966.

4645. Tiffany, Henry W. "The Service and Servants
of the Seminary." Review and Expositor 48
(April 1951):191-203.

4646. Tiffin, Gerald C. "The Changing Years [Bible
College]." Christianity Today 13, no. 12
(1969):533-4.

4647. Tiffin, Gerald Clay. "The Interaction of the
Bible College Movement and the Independent
Disciples of Christ Denomination." Ph.D.
dissertation, Stanford University, 1968.

4648. Tilden, William Phillips. The Work of the
Ministry: Lectures Given to the Meadville
Theological School, June, 1889. Boston:

401

Geo. H. Ellis, 1890.

4649. "Timothy Lin." Christianity Today 24 (March 21, 1980):45.

4650. Tinder, D. "Three Other Seminaries in the Bay Area." Christianity Today 23 (February 2, 1979):19.

4651. Tinney, J. S. "Ferment at Central Baptist." Christianity Today 15 (May 21, 1971):46.

4652. Tippett, Alan. "Anthropology: Luxury or Necessity for Missions?" Evangelical Missions Quarterly 5, no. 1 (1968):7-19.

4653. Tipple, Ezra Squier, ed. Drew Theological Seminary, 1867-1917. Cincinnati: Methodist Book Concern, 1917.

4654. Tiryakian, Edward A. "Sociological Reflections on Theological Education." Duke Divinity School Review 33 (Spring 1968):69-74.

4655. Titzel, J. M. "(Qualifications for Ministry.)" Reformed Quarterly Review 34 (1887):33+.

4656. "To Build a Better Bible College: It Has Become an Evangelical Substitute for a Four-Year Liberal Arts Education." Christianity Today (February 5, 1982):14-16.

4657. "To Fill Empty Pulpits." Newsweek 43 (February 22, 1954):71.

4658. "To Save a Seminarian." Christianity Today 14 (May 22, 1970):29-30.

4659. Todd, John. John Todd: The Story of His Life. Compiled and edited by John E. Todd. New York: Harper & Bros., 1876.

4660. Todt, Heinz Edward. "The Purpose of the Theological Faculties of Continental Universities." Theological Education 2 (Winter 1966):76-81.

4661. Tolles, Bryant Franklin, Jr. "Ammi Burnham Young and the Gilmanton Theological Seminary." Old-Time New England 61

(October-December 1970):47-54.

4662. Tolles, Bryant F., Jr. "The New Hampton Institute Building (1853) at Fairfax (Vermont)." Vermont History 45, no. 3 (1977):169-72.

4663. Tolman, Frank L. "The Study of Sociology in Institutions of Learning in the United States." American Journal of Sociology 7 (May 1902):797-838.

4664. Tolson, G. T. "Theological Education." In Religious Progress on the Pacific Slope: Addresses and Papers at the Celebration of the Semi-Centennial Anniversary of Pacific School of Religion, Berkeley, California, pp. 108-24. Berkeley, Calif.: Pacific School of Religion, 1917.

4665. Tomlinson, Everett Titsworth. "Coddling Theological Students." Worlds Work 10 (May 1905):6151-4.

4666. "Tomorrow's Empty Pulpits." Christian Century 61 (April 26, 1944):518-19.

4667. Torbet, Robert George. "Baptist Theological Education: An Historical Survey." Foundations 6 (October 1963):311-35.

4668. Torbet, Robert George. A History of the Baptists. Rev. ed. Valley Forge, Pa.: Judson Press, 1963.

4669. Torrey, Charles Cutler. "The Beginnings of Oriental Study at Andover." American Journal of Semitic Languages and Literatures 13 (July 1897):249-66.

4670. Torrey, R. A. "The English Bible: Instruction in Its Use in Personal Work." In Christianity Practically Applied, v. 2, pp. 479-81. Evangelical Alliance for the United States of America. Conference. Chicago, 1893. New York: Baker & Taylor, 1894.

4671. Torrey, Reuben Archer. How to Work for Christ. Chicago, New York: Fleming H. Revell Co., 1901.

4672. Torrey, Reuben Archer. The Importance and
      Value of Proper Bible Study: How Properly
      to Study and Interpret the Bible. New
      York: George H. Doran Co., 1921.

4673. "Toward Fewer and Better Seminaries."
      Christian Century 84 (September 13, 1967):
      1147; "Discussion." 84 (November 1, 1967):
      1403.

4674. Towne, Edgar A. "A 'Singleminded' Theologian:
      George Burman Foster at Chicago." Founda-
      tions 20 (1977):36-59, 163-80.

4675. Towne, Edgar A. "Theological Education: The
      Risk of Caring." Encounter 38 (Winter
      1977):12-19.

4676. Townsend, Luther Tracy. The Sword and
      Garment. Boston: Lee & Shepard, 1874.

4677. Toy, Crawford Howell. Modern Biblical
      Criticism. Boston: American Unitarian
      Association, n.d.

4678. Tozer, Aiden Wilson. Wingspread, Albert B.
      Simpson: A Study in Spiritual Attitude.
      Harrisburgh, Pa.: Christian Publication,
      1943.

4679. Trachsel, Marlene D. "Survival and Attrition
      among Seminarians." Ed.D. dissertation,
      Marquette University, 1973.

4680. Tracy, David W. "Catholic Presence in the
      Divinity School." Criterion 11 (Winter
      1972):29-31.

4681. "Traditional or Creative Theological
      Education." Biblical World 35 (May
      1910):291-5.

4682. "Training Clergymen in Urban Mental Health."
      Mental Health News Digest (August 1967):33.

4683. "Training for a More Meaningful Ministry:
      Clinical Pastoral Training." National
      Council Outlook 9 (February 1959):24-6.

4684. "Training for the Rural Ministry." School and
      Society 30 (November 2, 1929):596-7.

4685. "(Training of the Christian Ministry, before and after Ordination.)" American Church Review 42 (1883):97+.

4686. "The Training of the Young Preacher." Christian Advocate (New York) (January 12, 1928):49.

4687. "Training the Young Prophets of Methodism." Christian Advocate (New York) (February 18, 1926):209.

4688. Trakatellis, Demetrios. "Suggestions for Our Theological Task Today and Tomorrow." St. Vladimir's Theological Quarterly 25, no. 3 (1981):183-90.

4689. "Transfusion at Harvard." Newsweek 45 (April 25, 1955):56.

4690. Travis, James L., III. "The Professional Resocialization of Clergymen in Clinical Pastoral Education." Ph.D. dissertation, Emory University, 1974.

4691. Travis, T. "Ministerial Gauntlet." Independent 65 (September 24, 1908):707-12.

4692. Traynham, Warner R. "Black Studies in Theological Education: The Camel Comes of Age." Harvard Theological Review 66, no. 2 (1973):257-71.

4693. Treese, Donald H. "Some Objections [Reply to C. Walters-Bugbee, 'Seminaries In Search of Support' May 13: Rejoinder]." Christian Century 98 (July 1-8, 1981):715-16.

4694. Trent, William Johnson. "The Relative Adequacy of Sources of Income of Negro Church-Related Colleges." Journal of Negro Education 29 (Summer 1960):356-67.

4695. Tribble, Harold Wayland. "Edgar Young Mullins." Review and Expositor 49 (April 1952):125-38.

4696. "Tributes to Professor Edwards A. Park." Massachusetts Historical Society. Proceedings (June 1900):189-95.

4697. Trinterud, Leonard J., comp. Elizabethan Puritanism. New York: Oxford University

Press, 1971.

4698. Trinterud, Leonard J. The Forming of an
American Tradition: A Re-examination of
Colonial Presbyterianism. Philadelphia:
Westminster Press, 1949.

4699. Tripp, K. F. "Growth in Christ through
Sacraments." Theological Education 4
(Winter 1968):634-9.

4700. Troeger, Thomas H. "We Had to Sacrifice the
Woman." Christian Century 98 (February 4,
1981):108-11.

4701. Trost, Theodore Louis. "Continuing Theologi-
cal Education for Protestant Clergymen."
Ed.D. dissertation, Teachers College,
Columbia University, 1962.

4702. Trotter, F. Thomas. "The Church's Stake in
the Seminaries." Christian Century 89
(February 2, 1972):112-14.

4703. Trotter, F. Thomas. "Generation of Leaders."
Christian Century 92 (April 23, 1975):404-
5.

4704. Trotter, F. Thomas. "The Seminaries: Survival and Revival." Christian Century 92
(February 5-12, 1975):102-3.

4705. Trotter, F. Thomas. "The Seminary as the
Church's School." Theological Education 15
(Spring 1979):105-8.

4706. Trotter, F. Thomas. "A Visit with Bishop
Ting." Christian Century 96 (August 29 -
September 5, 1979):813-14.

4707. Trotti, John B. "Dealing with Pain: Preser-
vation, Automation, Interpretation and
Negotiation [in Theological Libraries]."
Theological Education 17 (Autumn 1980):79-
84.

4708. Trotti, John Boone. "The Theological Library:
In Touch with the Witnesses." Reformed
Review 35, no. 3 (1982):157-61.

4709. Trotti, John Reporter. "Workshop on Doctor of
Ministry Programs." ATLA Proceedings 30
(1976):65-73.

4710. Trout, Douglas G. and Douglas Trout Asso-
       ciates. Theological Education Resources of
       the United Presbyterian Church for the
       1970's: A Study for the Council on Theo-
       logical Education of the United Presby-
       terian Church in the United States of
       America. Washgington, D.C., 1970.

4711. Trueblood, David Elton. The Continued
       Education of Ministers. Lynchburg, Va.:
       Lynchburg College, 1955.

4712. Trueblood, D. Elton. "New Departure: A
       Quaker Seminary." Christian Century 80
       (April 24, 1963):53+.

4713. Trueblood, Roy Wallace. "Attitude Changes
       among First-Year Theological Students."
       Ph.D. dissertation, Northwestern
       University, 1972.

4714. Trumbull, Charles Gallaudet. The Life Story
       of C. I. Scofield. New York: Oxford
       University Press, 1920.

4715. "Truth in Learning: A Matter of Degrees."
       Christianity Today 25 (June 11, 1981):12-
       13.

4716. Trutter, Carl B. "Theologizing in Field
       Education." Theological Education 8
       (Autumn 1971):26-35.

4717. Tucker, Grayson Letcher. "A Group Process for
       the Professional Development of Semina-
       rians." S.T.D. dissertation, Southern
       Baptist Theological Seminary, 1970.

4718. Tucker, Robert Leonard. Builders of the
       Church New York: Abingdon Press, 1924.

4719. Tucker, William E. "Restudy of Possible
       Cluster Areas Required." Theological
       Education 5 (Winter 1969):84-7.

4720. Tucker, William Hugh. "Doctor of Ministry:
       Nontraditional Models of Advanced Inservice
       Professional Education." Ph.D. disserta-
       tion, University of Michigan, 1977.

4721. Tucker, William Jewett. "The Authority of the
       Pulpit in a Time of Critical Research and
       Social Confusion." Andover Review 16

(October 1891):384-402.

4722. Tucker, William Jewett. My Generation.
      Boston: Houghton Mifflin Co., 1919.

4723. Tucker, William Jewett. "The Newer Education
      and the Ministry." Biblical World 12
      (September 1898) (New Series):183-9.

4724. Tucker, William J. "Social Christianity - The
      Andover House Association." Andover Review
      17 (January 1892):82-8.

4725. Tucker, William Jewett. "Twenty-Five Years in
      Residence." Atlantic Monthly 119 (May
      1917):640-9.

4726. Tuckerman, Joseph. The Principles and Results
      of the Ministry at Large, in Boston.
      Boston: James Munroe & Co., 1838.

4727. Tufts, James H. "In a Seminary - Forty Years
      Ago and Now." Religious Education 25
      (March 1930):230-4.

4728. Tunis, John. "Social Science in the
      Theological Seminaries." Lend a Hand 16
      (1896):3-15.

4729. Turkington, Charles G. "Faith Is the Strength
      To Serve." Asbury Seminarian 17 (Spring-
      Summer 1963):8-16.

4730. Turkington, W. D. "Appreciation [Julian C.
      McPheeters]." Asbury Seminarian 16
      (Spring-Summer 1962):31-3.

4731. Turner, G. A. "Voices of Experience: Theo-
      logical Education Reviewed from the
      'Field'." Asbury Seminarian 21 (October
      1967):24-6.

4732. Turner, Paul Winston. "A Study of Attitudes
      of Selected Graduates of the Southern
      Baptist Theological Seminary toward
      Ministry: 1950-1970." S.T.D. disserta-
      tion, Southern Baptist Theological
      Seminary, 1972.

4733. Turner, S. "Promoters of Doubt or Builders of
      Faith?" Christianity Today 9 (May 7,
      1965):3-4.

4734. Turner, Samuel Hulbeart. Autobiography of the
       Rev. Samuel H. Turner, D.D. New York:
       A.D.F. Randolph, 1863.

4735. Turner, Samuel H. Remarks on a Late Editorial
       Article in the Churchman, Entitled, Results
       of the General Convention, Theological
       Seminary. And on Certain Other Articles
       Formerly Published in That Journal. New
       York: Harper & Brothers, 1845.

4736. Turney, Edmund. Ministerial Culture: Or, The
       Relation of Theological Education to the
       Work of the Ministry: An Address Delivered
       on Occasion of the First Anniversary of the
       Fairmount Theological Seminary, June 21,
       1854. Cincinnati: Anderson, Gates &
       Wright, 1857.

4737. Turrentine, S. B. "Methodism's Educational
       Mission in National Life." Methodist
       Review (South) 51 (1902):88-103.

4738. "12th Annual Conference, University of
       Chicago, 1943 [Pastors' Institute]."
       School and Society 58 (July 24, 1943):57.

4739. "Twenty-Five Seminaries Speaking for Them-
       selves." Outlook 92 (May 8, 1909):79-82.

4740. "Two Systems of Ministerial Education."
       Methodist Quarterly Review 32 (January
       1872):94-103.

4741. Tyng, Charles Rockland, ed. Record of the
       Life and Work of the Rev. Stephen Higginson
       Tyng, D.D. New York: E. P. Dutton &
       Fraser Co., 1890.

4742. Tyng, Stephen Higginson. The Importance of
       Uniting Manual Labour with Intellectual
       Attainments, in a Preparation for the
       Ministry. Philadelphia: Printed by W.
       Stavely, 1830.

4743. Tyng, Stephen Higginson. The Office and Duty
       of a Christian Pastor. New York: Harper &
       Bros., 1874.

4744. Udarbe, P. and Miller, R. C. "Christian
       Education and Theological Education."
       Religious Education 58 (January 1963):21-8.

4745.   Ulrich, Reinhard. "The School of Prophets: A
        Study of the Cultural and Theological
        Patterns in the Establishment and Early
        Development of the German Reformed Mission
        House in Wisconsin." Ph.D. dissertation,
        Lutheran School of Theology at Chicago,
        1963.

4746.   "Union Centenary." News Week 7 (May 16,
        1936):22.

4747.   "Union Seminary." Independent 69 (December 8,
        1910):1286-7.

4748.   "Union Seminary: An Ethical Dilemma."
        Christianity Today 13 (June 6, 1969):27.

4749.   "Union Seminary [NYC] to Implement Major
        Policy Changes." Christian Century 89
        (June 28, 1972):706.

4750.   Union Theological Seminary, New York (City).
        The Dedication of the New Buildings of the
        Union Theological Seminary in the City of
        New York, November 27, 28 and 29, 1910.
        New York, 1910?

4751.   Union Theological Seminary, New York (City).
        The Seminary: Its Spirit and Aims.
        Addresses Given at the Annual Dinner of the
        Alumni Held on May 13, 1907 and a Review of
        the Year 1906-1907. New York: Irving
        Press, 1907.

4752.   Union Theological Seminary, Richmond. The
        Days of Our Years, 1812-1962. Richmond,
        1962?

4753.   "Union's 100th." Time 27 (May 25, 1936):58-
        61.

4754.   Unitarian Universalist Association. Report of
        the Ministerial Education Commission.
        Boston: Unitarian Universalist Associa-
        tion, 1973.

4755.   Unitarian Universalist Association. Committee
        to Study Theological Education. A Compre-
        hensive Plan of Education for the Unitarian
        Universalist Ministry. Boston: Unitarian
        Universalist Association, 1962.

4756. United Church of Christ. Minutes, Reports and
      Miscellaneous Papers on the Subject of
      Theological Education, 1960-1975.

4757. United Church of Christ. General Synod.
      Advisory Committee on Theological Education
      of the Executive Council. A First Confi-
      dential Report to the Committee, by Ross W.
      Sanderson, Research Consultant. New York,
      1964.

4758. United Presbyterian Church in the U.S.A.
      Council on Theological Education. The
      Report on the Pastoral Function of the
      Minister and Theological Education.
      Prepared by the Subcommittee of the
      Curriculum Committee of the Council on
      Theological Education. Louisville:
      Presbyterian Theological Seminary, 1959.

4759. United Presbyterian Church in the U.S.A.
      Council on Theological Education. The
      United Presbyterian Enterprise of
      Theological Education. Philadelphia, 1959.

4760. U.S. Office of Education. Report of the
      Commissioner of Education for the Year
      1889-1890. Vol. 2: Curricula of Profes-
      sional Schools: Theology. Washington:
      Government Printing Office, 1893.

4761. U.S. Selective Service System. Theological
      School Enrollments: A Survey Study of the
      Effects of the War and of the Exemption of
      Theological Students from the Selective
      Draft on the Enrollment in Certain Theolog-
      ical and Divinity Schools, With an Analysis
      of Reports Received from 561 Recognized
      Theological Schools. Washington, D.C.,
      1947-.

4762. University of Edinburgh. A Catalogue of the
      Graduates of the Faculties of Arts, Divin-
      ity, and Law. Edinburgh: Printed by Neill
      & Co., 1858.

4763. "Upgrading the Seminaries: Episcopal Minis-
      terial Education Program." Time 90
      (September 8, 1967):82.

4764. Uphaus, Willard Edwin. Commitment. New York:
      McGraw-Hill, 1963.

4765. Uplegger, Francis J. "A Brief Review of Nearly Ninety Years of Life by the Grace of God." Concordia Historical Institute Quarterly 38, no. 3 (1965):146-50.

4766. "Uproar at Drew: Theological School." Time 91 (February 2, 1968):37.

4767. Urich, B. W. H. "Clinical Pastoral Education in a Local Parish [Readers' Forum]." Pastoral Psychology 18 (March 1967):54-5.

4768. Vail, Stephen M. "The 'Central Theological' and the 'Salvation Seminaries' Combined." Christian Advocate and Journal (New York) 29 (March 2, 1854):1.

4769. Vail, Stephen Montford. Ministerial Education in the Methodist Episcopal Church. Boston: J. P. Magee, 1853.

4770. Vaill, J. "(Theological Education in Connecticut 70 Years Ago.)" Congregational Quarterly 6 (1864):137+.

4771. Vair, D. "Students' Worship Service [at End of Clinical Pastoral Training]." Journal of Pastoral Care 10 (Summer 1956):103-4.

4772. Valentine, M. "Ministerial Education." Lutheran Quarterly Review 21 (1891):112-22.

4773. Valentine, M. "(Present Demands of the Study of Theology.)" Lutheran Quarterly 14 (New Series) (1884):596+.

4774. Van Antwerp, Eugene I. "New Foundation for Institutional Assessment." Theological Education 12 (Spring 1976):180-6.

4775. Van Antwerp, Eugene I. "So Who Listens?" Theological Education 5 (Summer 1969):328-33.

4776. Van Antwerp, E. "Spiritual Formation for Ministry." Concordia Theological Monthly 41 (December 1970):732-6.

4777. Van Baalen, J. K. "Minister as a Student." Christianity Today 6 (June 8, 1962):4-5.

4778. Van de Creek, Larry and Royer, Jerry. "Education for Inter-Disciplinary Teamwork."

Journal of Pastoral Care 29, no. 3
(1975):176-84.

4779. Vanderpool, Harold Young. "The Andover
Conservatives: Apologetics, Biblical
Criticism and Theological Change at Andover
Theological Seminary, 1808-1880." Ph.D.
dissertation, Harvard University, 1971.

4780. Vandever, William Tolbert, Jr. "An Educational History of the English and American
Baptists in the Seventeenth and Eighteenth
Centuries." Ph.D. dissertation, University
of Pennsylvania, 1974.

4781. Van Dusen, Henry Pitney. "For Henry Sloane
Coffin [1877-1954]: Minute to the New York
Presbytery." Union Seminary Quarterly
Review 10 (March 1955):19-23.

4782. Van Dusen, H. P. "Naval Chaplaincy Training
Program." Christian Century 60 (May 19,
1943):611; "Discussion." 60 (May 19-26,
June 9, 1943):599-601, 629-31, 695-6, 697.

4783. Van Dusen, Henry P. "Theological Education
for an Ecumenical Church." Christian
Century 69 (April 30, 1952):521-3.

4784. Van Dusen, Henry Pitney. "Theological Education in the Ecumenical Era." Princeton
Seminary Bulletin 56 (February 1963):4-11.

4785. Van Dusen, H. P. "Theological Students Today:
The President's Perspective." Union
Seminary Quarterly Review 14 (March
1959):25-32.

4786. Van Dyck, Nicholas B. "Sharpening Goals and
Evaluation in Field Education." Theological Education 12 (Spring 1976):169-79.

4787. Van Elderen, Bastiaan. "Archaeology, Biblical
Studies, Calvin Theological Seminary."
Calvin Theological Journal 11 (April
1976):61-74.

4788. Vannesse, Alfred and Neff, Therese. "Parental
Images and the Representation of God in
Seminarians and Women Religious." In The
Parental Figures and the Representation of
God. Edited by Antoine Vergote and Alvara
Tamayo. New York: Mouton, 1981.

413

4789. Van Nostrand, Manning Eugene. "The Call to
the Ministry from Another Career:
Perceptions of Christian Vocation Held by
Catholic and Protestant Seminarians."
Ph.D. dissertation, Boston University
Graduate School, 1970.

4790. Van Santvoord, C. "John Mitchell Mason."
Presbyterian Review 3 (1882):264-77.

4791. Van Vechten, Jacob. Memoirs of John M. Mason,
D.D., S.T.P. with Portions of His Corre-
spondence. New York: Robert Carter &
Bros., 1856.

4792. Van Zanten, John Wilson. "My Theological
Education and the Ministry Today." Union
Seminary Quarterly Review 12 (November
1956):41-5.

4793. Vaughan, J. "Theological Seminaries: Where
the Action Is Today." Christian Life 37
(June 1975):26-7+.

4794. Vaughan, R. P. "Seminary Training and
Personality Change." Religious Education
65 (January 1970):56-9.

4795. Vaux, K. L. "Tomorrow's Education in Medicine
and Ministry." Journal of Religion and
Health 9 (July 1970):285-91.

4796. Vayhinger, John M. "Implications of the
Seminary Population Data: A Psychologist's
View." Theological Education 1 (Spring
1965):180-4.

4797. Vedder, H. C. "(Reforms in Theological Education.)" Baptist Quarterly Review 7
(1885):323+.

4798. Vendettuoli, J. A., Jr. "History of the
Alumni Association of Harvard Divinity
School." Harvard Divinity Bulletin 21
(1955-56):101-26.

4799. Ventimig, J. C. "Career Commitment among
Continuing and Exiting Seminary Students."
Sociological Analysis 38, no. 1 (1977):49-
58.

4800. Ventimiglia, J. C. "Socialization and
Commitment among Seminarians: The Effects

of Career and Significant Other on Identification." University of Michigan, Ann Arbor, 1972.

4801. Verdesi, Elizabeth Howell. "The Professionally-Trained Woman in the Presbyterian Church: The Role of Power in the Achievement of Status and Equality." Ph.D. dissertation, Columbia University, 1975.

4802. Vichert, John Frederick. "Contribution of Church History to Ministerial Efficiency." Biblical World 48 (November 1916):277-82.

4803. Viertel, Weldon E. A Guide to Decentralized Theological Education. El Paso, Tex.: Carib Baptist Publications, 1979.

4804. Vieth, P. H. "Church, the Family, the Minister: A Yale Divinity School Course [bibliog.]." Journal of Social Hygiene 38 (April 1952):152-9.

4805. "View of Literary Institutions." American Quarterly Register 3 (November 1830):127-35.

4806. "View of the Theological Seminaries, 1833." American Quarterly Register 6 (1834):34.

4807. Vincent, John H. "A Non-Resident School of Theology." Methodist Review 79 (March 1897):195-208.

4808. Vincent, John H. "The Out-of-School Theological Seminary." Homiletic Review 23 (May 1892):406-11.

4809. Vincent, Leon Henry. John Heyl Vincent: A Biographical Sketch. New York: MacMillan Co., 1925.

4810. Vincent, Marvin Richardson. That Monster, the Higher Critic. New York: D. F. Randolph & Co., 1894.

4811. Vinet, Alexandre Rodolphe. Pastoral Theology: Or, The Theory of the Evangelical Ministry. Translated & edited by Thomas H. Skinner. 2d ed. New York: Inson, Blakeman, Taylor & Co., 1871.

4812. Virginia. General Assembly. The Act of
       Incorporation of the Trustees of the
       Protestant Episcopal Theological Seminary
       and High School in Virginia. The By-Laws
       of the Board of Trustees and Rules and
       Regulations for the Government of the
       Theological Seminary. N.p., 1904.

4813. Virkler, Henry A. "Counseling Demands, Pro-
       cedures, and Preparation of Parish
       Ministers: A Descriptive Study." Journal
       of Psychology and Theology 7 (Winter
       1979):271-80.

4814. Virkler, Henry A. "The Facilitativeness of
       Parish Ministers: A Descriptive Study."
       Journal of Psychology and Theology 8
       (Summer 1980):140-6.

4815. "Vitalizing Theological Scholarship."
       Biblical World 31 (June 1908):403-6.

4816. Vivian, C. T. "Theological Education and the
       Black Community [With Reply by C. W.
       Williams]." Criterion 8 (Spring-Summer
       1969):12-19.

4817. Vogt, Weldon. "A Survey Analysis and
       Evaluation of Some Psychological Tensions
       Encountered by Students of Southwestern
       Baptist Theological Seminary." Ph.D.
       dissertation, Southwestern Baptist
       Theological Seminary, 1962.

4818. Voight, A. G. "Centenary of the Southern
       Seminary." Lutheran Church Quarterly 4
       (January 1931):56-62.

4819. Voight, Andrew George. "The Theological
       Seminary and the Doctrine of the Ministry."
       Lutheran Church Quarterly (October 1928):
       470-6.

4820. "Voyage: Vision: Venture: Report of Task
       Force on Spiritual Development, the AATS."
       Theological Education 8 (Spring 1972):
       entire issue.

4821. Wach, Joachim. "Place of the History of
       Religions in the Study of Theology." In
       Types of Religious Experience, Christian
       and Non-Christian, pp. 3-29. University of
       Chicago Press, 1951.

4822. Wade, Louise Carroll. "The Graham Taylor
       Connection." Newberry Library Bulletin 3
       (October 1953):109-21.

4823. Wade, Louise C. Graham Taylor: Pioneer for
       Social Justice, 1851-1938. Chicago:
       University of Chicago Press, 1964.

4824. Wagner, C. P. "Extending Leadership Training
       for the Church in the Seventies." Journal
       of American Scientific Affiliation 24
       (September 1972):105-10.

4825. Wagner, Murray L. "For the Work of Ministry
       [Bethany Theological Seminary 25th Anniver-
       sary]." Brethren Life and Thought 25
       (Winter 1980):4-61.

4826. Wagner, Murray L. "Primitivist Reflections
       from the Electric Library." Brethren Life
       and Thought 25 (Winter 1980):55-7.

4827. Wagoner, Walter D. "Agenda for a Seminary
       Board Meeting." Christian Century 82
       (April 28, 1965):525-6.

4828. Wagoner, Walter Dray. "Audacity to Be
       Ordained." Christian Century 74 (April 24,
       1957):516-17.

4829. Wagoner, Walter D. Bachelor of Divinity:
       Uncertain Servants in Seminary and
       Ministry. New York: Association Press,
       1963.

4830. Wagoner, Walter D. "Discussion of the Paper."
       Theological Education 5 (Spring 1969):167-
       9.

4831. Wagoner, Walter D. "Ecumenicity and Seminary
       Archaism." Christian Century 79 (April 25,
       1962):516-18.

4832. Wagoner, Walter Dray. "Ministry: Image and
       Reality." Christian Century 77 (April 20,
       1960):464-6.

4833. Wagoner, Walter D. "A Model for Theological
       Education." Theological Education 2
       (Winter 1965):90-5.

4834. Wagoner, Walter. "Mona Lisa and Melchizedek
       [The Arts and the Training of Clergy]." In

Humanities, Religion and the Arts Tomorrow.
Edited by Howard Hunter. New York: Holt,
1972.

4835. Wagoner, Walter D. The Seminary: Protestant
and Catholic. New York: Sheed & Ward,
1966.

4836. Wagoner, W. D. "Seminary: Staging Area for
Career." Ministry Studies 3, no. 1
(1969):22-5.

4837. Wagoner, Walter D. "Time, Tide and Seminary
Priorities." Christian Century 83 (April
27, 1966):519-21.

4838. Wagoner, Walter D. "Uneasy Aggiornamento:
The Changing Profile of American Protestant
Seminaries." Christian Scholar 50 (Summer
1967):129-36.

4839. Wakefield, Gary A. "An Examination of the
Master's Degree Level Christian Education
Preparation Programs Offered by Selected
Seminaries and Divinity Schools." Ed.D.
dissertation, West Virginia University,
1983.

4840. Walcott, Dorothea K. "Field Work Experiences
with Children and Youth in Seminary
Training for the Ministry." Religious
Education 53 (1958):285-9.

4841. Walker, Edwin Carlton. "A History of Seventh-
Day Adventist Higher Education in the
United States." Ed.D. dissertation,
University of California, Berkeley, 1966.

4842. Walker, W. "Theological Seminaries and
Religious Education." Religious Education
7 (April 1912):6-16.

4843. Walker, W. H. "World War and the Future of
Theological Study in the English-Speaking
Lands." Biblical World 53 (May 1919):283-
9.

4844. Walker, Williston. "The Churches and Their
Seminaries." Hartford Seminary Record 9
(1898):291-5.

4845. Wall, James M., ed. "Theological Education
1980: Filling the Gaps." Christian

Century 97 (February 6-13, 1980):131-63.

4846. Wall, James M. "Theological Education 1981."
Christian Century 98 (February 4-11,
1981):98-140.

4847. Wall, James M. "What the Old Boys Say
[Women's Place in Theological Education]."
Christian Century 99 (February 3, 1982):
107-8.

4848. Wallis, Jim. "Special Section on Theological
Education." Sojourners 6 (August 1977):12-
26.

4849. Walls, William Jacob. The African Methodist
Episcopal Zion Church. Charlotte, N.C.:
A.M.E. Zion Pub. House, 1974.

4850. Walsh, F. A. Catechetics in the Seminary
Curriculum. New York: Benziger Bros.,
1937.

4851. Walsworth, Lowell Frank. "A Study of the
Level of Participation of Ministers in
Continuing Education in the West Michigan
Annual Conference of the United Methodist
Church and Its Relationship with Their
Perceived Management of Role Conflict."
Ph.D. dissertation, Michigan State
University, 1978.

4852. Walters-Bugbee, Christopher. "Across the
Great Divide: Seminaries and the Local
Church." Christian Century 98 (November
11, 1981):1154-9.

4853. Walters-Bugbee, Christopher. "Called to
Repentance: Churches and Their
Seminaries." Christian Century 99
(February 3-10, 1982):141-7.

4854. Walters-Bugbee, C. "Emphasizing the Congregation: New Directions for Seminaries."
Christian Century 99 (November 10,
1982):1131-6.

4855. Walters-Bugbee, Christopher. "Going Public:
Seminaries in Search of Support."
Christian Century 98 (May 13, 1981):538-43.

4856. Walters-Bugbee, Christopher. "Hard-Pressed
and Anxious: Seminaries Face the 80's."

Christian Century 98 (February 4, 1981):98-103.

4857. Walther, Carl Ferdinand Wilhelm. _Amerikanisch-Lutherische Pastoral Theologie_. St. Louis, 1872.

4858. Waltner, Erland. "Associated Mennonite Biblical Seminaries." _Mennonite Life_ 14 (April 1959):55-77.

4859. Walton, O. M. "Endeavor to Unite Church and Labor." _Christian Century_ 59 (March 18, 1942):358.

4860. Walton, Wesley S. "What We Need to Know about Law - Federal and State." _Theological Education_ 16 (Spring 1980):429-41.

4861. Walvoord, John F. _Truth for Today: Bibliotheca Sacra Reader: Commemorating 30 Years of Publication by Dallas Theological Seminary, 1934-1963_. Chicago: Moody Press, 1963.

4862. Walworth, Clarence Augustus. _The Oxford Movement in America: Or Glimpses of Life in an Anglican Seminary_. New York: Catholic Book Exchange, 1895.

4863. Walz, Edgar John Karl. "A Proposed Program of Business Education for the Ministerial Students of the Lutheran Church - Missouri Synod." Ed.D. dissertation, Indiana University, 1961.

4864. "Wanted: $42 million [Seven Theological Schools]." _Christianity Today_ 17 (March 16, 1973):28-9.

4865. "Wanted: Unselfish Service: Study by Association of Schools in the United States and Canada." _Christian Century_ 93 (March 31, 1976):300.

4866. Warch, Richard. _School of the Prophets: Yale College, 1701-1740_. New Haven, Conn.: Yale University Press, 1973.

4867. Warch, Richard. "The Shepherd's Tent: Education and Enthusiasm in the Great Awakening." _American Quarterly_ 30 (Summer 1978):177-98.

4868. Ward, A. Marcus. "The Theological Education Fund of the International Missionary Council." _International Review of Missions_ 49 (1960):137-47.

4869. Ward, Bullard. "A Central Theological Seminary." _Christian Advocate_ (New York) 29 (February 2, 1854):17.

4870. Ward, D. J. H. _Minister's Course_. Denver: Up The Divide Pub. Co., 1927.

4871. Ward, Elizabeth Stuart (Phelps). _Austin Phelps: A Memoir_. New York: Charles Scribner's Sons, 1891.

4872. Ward, Elizabeth Stuart (Phelps). _Chapters from a Life_. Boston and New York: Houghton, Mifflin & Co., 1897.

4873. Ward, Frank Gibson. "Religious Education in the Theological Seminaries." _Religious Education_ 10 (October 1915):426-41.

4874. Ward, H. F. "New Horizons in Professional Training." _Survey_ 60 (June 1, 1928):289-90.

4875. Ward, R. A. "Relevance of Ministerial Training [bibliog.]." _Religion In Life_ 25 (Winter 1955-56):55-64.

4876. Ward, T. and Rowen, S. F. "Significance of the Extension Seminary." _Evangelical Missions Quarterly_ 9 (Fall 1972):17-27.

4877. Ward, T. "Types of TEE." _Evangelical Missions Quarterly_ 13 (April 1977):79-85.

4878. Ward, William T. _Variety in the Prayer Meeting_. New York: Methodist Book Concern, 1915.

4879. Ware, H. "(Theological Education.)" _Christian Examiner and Theological Review_ 4 (1827):324-33.

4880. Ware, John. _Memoir of the Life of Henry Ware, Jr_. Boston: James Munroe & Fraser Co., 1846.

4881. Ware, Larry Gordon. "The Actual and Preferred Degree of Participative Management

Practiced in the Six Southern Baptist
Seminaries as Perceived by the Faculty and
Administration." Ed.D. dissertation,
Southwestern Baptist Theological Seminary,
1978.

4882. Ware, Orie S. "The Western Baptist
Theological Institute in Covington,
Kentucky [1834-55]." Christopher Gist
Historical Society. Papers (1949-50):43-9.

4883. Warfield, Benjamin B. "The Fundamental
Curriculum of the Seminary." Brief
Prepared for the Special Committee of the
Board of Directors of Princeton Theological
Seminary, 1906.

4884. Warfield, Benjamin B. "How Princeton Seminary
Got to Work." Journal of the Presbyterian
Society 9 (June 1918):256-67.

4885. Warfield, Benjamin B. Notes on Certain
Proposed Readjustments of the Curriculum.
N.p.: By the Author, 1914.

4886. Warfield, Benjamin B. "The Purpose of the
Seminary." Presbyterian (November 22,
1917):   .

4887. Warfield, B. B. "Shall our Theological
Seminaries Have a Curriculum?" Independent
8 (July 30, 1896):1025-6.

4888. Warfield, Benjamin B. "Spiritual Culture in
the Theological Seminary." Princeton Theological Review (January 1904):   .

4889. Warford, Malcolm Lyle. "Piety, Politics and
Pedagogy: An Evangelical Protestant Tradition in Higher Education at Lane, Oberlin,
and Berea, 1834-1904." Ed.D. dissertation,
Columbia University, 1973.

4890. Wargelin, J. "Finns in Michigan: Suomi
College." Michigan History Magazine 24,
no. 2 (1940):195-203.

4891. Warnecke, J. C. "Master Planning a Seminary
Campus [Golden Gate Theological Seminary]."
American School and University (1958):319-
26.

4892. Warner, Timothy Marcus. "A Study of the Place of General Education in the Bible College Curriculum." Ed.D. dissertation, Indiana University, 1967.

4893. Warren, William F. "Current Biblical Discussions - The Proper Attitude of Theological Faculties With Respect To Them." Methodist Review 81 (May 1899):368-81.

4894. Warren, W. F. "(Education for Ministry in M.E. Church.)" Quarterly Review of the Methodist Episcopal Church, South 32 (1872):246+.

4895. Warren, W. F. "(Two Systems of Education for Ministry.)" Quarterly Review of the Methodist Episcopal Church, South 32 (1872):94+.

4896. Warren, W. F. "What the New England Methodist Conference Has Done for Education in the South and West." New England Magazine 14 (New Series) (May 1896):351-4.

4897. Wartburg Theological Seminary. "Teaching Theology in a Pluralistic Society." Lutheran Theological Journal 15 (December 1981):100-3.

4898. Wartluft, David J. "Cooperative Ventures in Theological Libraries." Drexel Library Quarterly 6 (January 1970):27-43.

4899. Washburn, Henry Bradford. "The Theological School." Harvard Graduate Magazine 31 (March 1923):340-6.

4900. Wasson, Margaret. "Texas Methodism's Other Half [Methodist Women]." Methodist History 19 (July 1981):206-23.

4901. Waterman, Leroy. "A Half-Century of Biblical and Semitic Investigation." American Journal of Semitic Languages and Literatures 32 (July 1916):219-29.

4902. Watkin, Robert Nuckols, Jr. "The Forming of the Southern Presbyterian Minister: From Calvin to the American Civil War." Ph.D. dissertation, Vanderbilt University, 1969.

4903. Watkins, Janice Nutt. "A Comparison of Student Achievement in Harmony Review Courses Taught by the Personalized System of Instruction and by the Lecture-Discussion Method at Southwestern Baptist Theological Seminary." D.M.A. dissertation, Southwestern Baptist Theological Seminary, 1981.

4904. Watson, John; Dods, Marcus; Edwards, T. C.; Denney, James; Darlow, T. H.; Selby, T. G.; Nicoll, W. Robertson; and Stoddart, J. T. The Clerical Life: A Series of Letters to Ministers. New York: Dodd, Mead & Co., 1898.

4905. Watson, John. The Cure of Souls London: Hodder & Stoughton, 1896.

4906. Watson, Richard. Theological Institutes: Or, a View of the Evidences, Doctrines, Morals, and Institutions of Christianity. 2 vols. New York: Carlton & Porter, 1850.

4907. Watt, Hugh. New College, Edinburgh: A Centenary History. Edinburgh and London: Oliver & Boyd, 1946.

4908. Watts, John D. W. "Higher Education in Southern Baptist Foreign Missions." Baptist History and Heritage 11, no. 4 (1976):218-29.

4909. Watts, Michael R. The Dissenters. Vol. 1: From the Reformation to the French Revolution. Oxford [Eng.]: Clarendon Press, 1978 -   .

4910. Watts, Vera L. "Resource List for Seminary Registrars." Theological Education 16 (Spring 1980):455-6.

4911. Watts, Vera L. The Role and Function of the Seminary Registrar. Evanston, Ill.: Watts, 1977.

4912. Waugh, Barbara Rae. "The Evolution of a Women's Liberation Movement Group from 1970 to 1980: A Study of the Women's Program of a Theological Consortium." Ph.D. dissertation, Wright Institute, 1981.

4913. Way, Peggy Ann. "Visions of Possibility: Women for Theological Education."

Theological Education 8 (Summer 1972):269-
77.

4914. Wayland, Francis. The Apostolic Ministry: A
Discourse. Rochester: Sage & Bro., 1853.

4915. Wayland, Francis. Letters on the Ministry of
the Gospel. Boston: Gould & Lincoln,
1863.

4916. Wayland, Francis and Wayland, H. L. A Memoir
of the Life and Labors of Francis Wayland.
2 vols. New York: Sheldon & Co., 1867.
Vol. 1.

4917. Wayland, Francis. Thoughts on the Present
Collegiate System in the United States.
Boston: Gould, Kendall & Lincoln, 1842.

4918. Wayland, John Terrill. "The Theological
Department in Yale College, 1822-1858."
Ph.D. dissertation, Yale University, 1933.

4919. Weatherspoon, J. B. "My Image of a Theological Seminary: Founders Day Address, March
14, 1962." Southwestern Journal of
Theology 5 (October 1962):88-99.

4920. Weaver, Glenn. "The Society for the Increase
of the Ministry: A Brief Centennial
History." Historical Magazine of the
Protestant Episcopal Church 26 (December
1957):294-310.

4921. Weaver, William N. "Two Decades and Five
Generations of Students Later: 1950-1972."
Criterion 11 (Autumn 1971):11-16.

4922. Webb, Sam C. "Convergent-Discriminant
Validity of a Role Oriented Interest
Inventory." Educational and Psychological
Measurement 33 (Summer 1973):441.

4923. Webb, Sam C. "Development and Validity of the
Inventory of Religious Activities and
Interest Inventory." Paper Presented at
the American Personnel and Guidance
Association Convention in New Orleans,
Louisiana, March 22-26, 1970. (ERIC
Document)

4924. Webb, Sam C. et al. "Predicting Occupational
Choice by Clinical and Statistical

Methods." _Journal of Counseling Psychology_ 24 (March 1977):98-109.

4925. Webb, S. C. et al. "Prediction of Field Work Ratings in a Theological School [Candler School of Theology]." _Religious Education_ 53 (November 1958):534-8.

4926. Webb, Sam Clement and Goodling, R. A. "Test Validity in a Methodist Theology School." _Educational and Psychological Measurement_ 18 (Winter 1958):859-66.

4927. Webber, George W. "The Christian Minister and the Social Problems of the Day." _Theological Education_ 1 (Autumn 1964):15-34.

4928. Webber, George W. "Hispanic Ministry: New York Theological Seminary." _Theological Education_ 13 (Winter 1977):90-4.

4929. Webber, George W. "Hope for the Seminary: From Renewal to Mission." _Union Seminary Quarterly Review_ 22, no. 4 (1967):319-28.

4930. Webber, George W. "Innovation in Theological Education: Reflections from the United States [Focus on New York Theological Seminary]." In _Learning in Conflict: The Search for Innovative Patterns in Theological Education._ By Coe et al. Kent, Eng.: Theological Education Fund, 1973.

4931. Webber, George W. "Recruiting for the Protestant Ministry." _Christian Century_ 70 (April 19, 1953):504-6.

4932. Webber, George W. "The Struggle for Integrity [The American Church Experience over Last 30 Years]." _Review of Religious Research_ 23 (September 1981):3-21.

4933. Webber, George Williams. "Training for Urban Mission." _International Review of Missions_ 56 (April 1967):173-9.

4934. Webber, G. W. "Young Men and the Ministry." _Religion in Life_ 19, no. 1 (1949):29-39.

4935. Webber, W. B. "Hope for the Seminary: From Renewal to Mission [Union, NYC]." _Union Seminary Quarterly Review_ 22 (May 1967):319-28.

4936. Weber, William A. "Theological Education in the Reformed Church in America." Ph.D. dissertation, Yale University, 1934.

4937. Webster, Ransom L. "Geerhardus Vos (1862-1949): A Biographical Sketch." Westminster Theological Journal 40 (Spring 1978):304-17.

4938. Weddell, Sue. "Missionary Training in North America." International Review of Missions 33 (1944):368-75.

4939. Wedel, Theodore O. "Continuing Education Looks at Pre-Seminary Education." Theological Education 1 (Spring 1965):164-8.

4940. Wedel, Theodore O. "An Introduction to a Study of Patterns of Ministry and Theological Education." Theological Education 4 (Autumn 1967):523-7.

4941. Weed, Charles Allison. "American Baptists and an Education Ministry prior to 1850." Ph.D. dissertation, Crozer Theological Seminary, 1935.

4942. Weeks, Louis, III. "John Holt Rice and the American Colonization Society." Journal of Presbyterian History 46, no. 1 (1968):26-41.

4943. Weeks, Louis. "Stuart Robinson: Kentucky Presbyterian Leader." Filson Club Historical Quarterly 54, no. 4 (1980):360-77.

4944. Weeks, W. J. "Practical Training for Christian Work." Missionary Review of the World 58 (April 1935):186.

4945. Wehmeier, Waldemar W. "Calling a Pastor: How it Evolved in the Missouri Synod." Currents in Theology and Mission 4 (October 1977): 269-75.

4946. Weidman, Judy. "Financing Ministerial Education." Christian Century 92 (February 5-12, 1975):128-30.

4947. Weidner, R. F. "The Theological Education Needed in Our Times." Lutheran Church Review 15 (January 1896):79-84.

4948. Weigle, E. D. "The Ministry and Current
      Social Problems." Lutheran Quarterly 24
      (October 1984):467-80.

4949. Weigle, Luther A. "The War-Time Service of
      the Yale University Divinity School."
      Christian Education 26 (December 1942):107-
      12.

4950. Weigle, Luther Allan. "Who and What Determine
      the Educational Policies of the Theological
      Schools?" Educational Record 13 (July
      1932):201-11.

4951. Weil, Oscar A. "The Movement to Establish
      Lebanon Seminary, 1833-1835." Journal of
      the Illinois State Historical Society 59,
      no. 4 (1966):384-406.

4952. Weinlick, John R. "The Whitefield Tract."
      Transactions of the Moravian Historical
      Society 23, no. 2 (1979):51-74.

4953. Weis, James. "The Problem of Language
      Transition among Lutherans in Ohio, 1836-
      1858." Concordia Historical Institute
      Quarterly 39, no. 1 (1966):5-19.

4954. Weisenburger, Francis Phelps. Ordeal of
      Faith: The Crisis of Church-Going America,
      1865-1900. New York: Philosophical
      Library, 1959.

4955. Weiser, C. Z. "(External History of German
      Reformed Church.)" Mercersburg Review 23
      (1976):5+.

4956. Weiser, R. "A Want in the Lutheran Church Met
      by the Founding of the Missionary Insti-
      tute." Evangelical Review 10 (1858-
      59):332-47.

4957. Welch, Claude. Graduate Education in
      Religion: A Critical Appraisal. Missoula:
      University of Montana Press, 1971.

4958. Welch, Claude. Religion in the Undergraduate
      Curriculum: An Analysis and Interpreta-
      tion. Washington: Association of American
      Colleges, 1972.

4959. Welch, Claude. "Some Unsystematic Observa-
      tions [With Comments by J. F. Wilson and

R. T. Handy, pp. 5-7]." Council on the
Study of Religion: Bulletin 7 (December
1976):3-5.

4960. Welch, Herbert. As I Recall My Past Century.
New York: Abingdon Press, 1962.

4961. Weld, W. C. "Extension Education Seen as
Meeting Needs of Churches." Evangelical
Missions Quarterly (January 1974):48-52.

4962. Weld, Wayne. The World Directory of Theological Education by Extension. Pasadena,
Calif.: Fuller Theological Seminary, 1973.

4963. Wells, Amis Russel. Sunday-School Essentials.
Boston: W. A. Wilde Co., 1911.

4964. Wells, D. F. "Pastoral Ministry; Preparation." Christianity Today 17 (February 16,
1973):8-12.

4965. Wells, Donald Austin. "D. L. Moody and His
Schools: An Historical Analysis of an
Educational Ministry." Ph.D. dissertation,
Boston University, 1972.

4966. Wells, Frederic Palmer, ed. "Newbury
Seminary." In History of Newbury Vermont,
pp. 208-32. St. Johnsbury, Vt.:
Caledonian Co., 1902.

4967. Welsh, Wiley Alfred. "Research Leaves and
Scholarly Productivity." Lexington Theological Quarterly 3 (January 1968):29-32.

4968. Welsh, W. A. and Wilburn, Ralph G. "The
Seminary and Restructure." Lexington
Theological Quarterly 3, no. 2 (1968):33-
42.

4969. Welsh, W. A. "Seminary and the Local
Congregration." Lexington Theological
Quarterly 1 (January 1966):13-23.

4970. "Wendel Bequest [Drew Theological Seminary]."
School and Society 33 (April 4, 1931):454.

4971. Weng, Marjory R. "Passavant's Vision: A
History of the Chicago Lutheran Theological
Seminary, 1891-1951." Chicago Lutheran
Seminary Record 56 (October 1951):5-93.

4972. Wenger, Hobert Elwood. "Social Thought in
      American Fundamentalism, 1918-1933." Ph.D.
      dissertation, University of Nebraska,
      Lincoln, 1973.

4973. Wenley, Robert Mark. The Life and Work of
      George Sylvester Morris. New York:
      Macmillan Co., 1917.

4974. Wentz, A. R. "Bringing the Theological
      Curriculum Up-To-Date." In Proceedings of
      the 1927 Convention, pp. 37-47. National
      Lutheran Educational Conference.

4975. Wentz, Abdel R. et al. Essays in Honor of
      Carl Christian Rasmussen. Gettysburg:
      Lutheran Theological Seminary, 1965.

4976. Wentz, Abdel R. et al. "Festschrift in Honor
      of Harry Fridley Baughman." Lutheran
      Theological Seminary, Gettysburg, Bulletin
      47, no. 3 (1967).

4977. Wentz, Abdel Ross. Gettysburg Lutheran Theo-
      logical Seminary. 2 vols. Harrisburg,
      Pa.: Evangelical Press, 1964.

4978. Wentz, Abdel Ross. History of the Evangelical
      Lutheran Synod of Maryland of the United
      Lutheran Church in America 1820-1920.
      Harrisburg, Pa.: Printed for the Synod by
      the Evangelical Press, 1920.

4979. Wentz, Abdel Ross. History of the Gettysburg
      Theological Seminary of the General Synod
      of the Evangelical Lutheran Church in the
      United States and of the United Lutheran
      Church in America, Gettysburg, Pennsyl-
      vania, 1826-1926. Philadelphia: Printed
      for the Seminary by the United Lutheran
      Publication House, 1927?

4980. Wentz, Abdel Ross. "A New Strategy for
      Theological Education." Christian
      Education 20 (April 1937):291-318.

4981. Wentz, A. R. "Philosophic Roots of S. S.
      Schmucker's Thought." Lutheran Quarterly
      18 (August 1966):245-59.

4982. Wentz, Abdel Ross. Pioneer in Christian
      Unity: Samuel Simon Schmucker.
      Philadelphia: Fortress Press, 1967.

4983. Wentz, Frederick K. "Consortia: The Seminaries' Lifeline." Christian Century 98 (February 4, 1981):127-33.

4984. Wentz, Frederick K. "Take the Seminaries to the Candidates." Christian Century 92 (February 5-12, 1975):109-12+, 122; Johnson, E. A. "Reply." 92 (March 26, 1975):317.

4985. Wentz, Richard E. "Beware the Practics!" Christian Century 72 (May 11, 1955):571.

4986. Wentz, Richard E. "Is There a New Establishment of Religion?" Christian Century 84 (April 12, 1967):463-5.

4987. "Were Seminaries Refuges From Wartime Draft?" Christian Century 65 (January 28, 1948):100.

4988. Werling, Henry F. "The Student Personnel Programs in the Pretheological Colleges and Theological Seminaries in the Major Lutheran Bodies." Ph.D. dissertation, University of Wyoming, 1963.

4989. Wersell, Thomas W., ed. Why I Am at the Seminary: Forty-One True Stories by Theological Students. Rock Island, Ill.: Augustana Press, 1962.

4990. Wertenbaker, Thomas Jefferson. "The College of New Jersey and the Presbyterians." Journal of the Presbyterian Historical Society 36, no. 4 (1958):209-16.

4991. Wertenbaker, Thomas Jefferson. Princeton 1746-1896. Princeton: Princeton University Press, 1946.

4992. Westberg, Granger E. "American Academy of Parish Clergy: Why not?" Christian Century 82 (April 28, 1965):557-8.

4993. Westberg, Granger E. and Draper, Edgar. Community Psychiatry and the Clergyman. Springfield, Ill.: Charles C. Thomas, 1966.

4994. Westberg, Granger E. "The Need for Radical Changes in Theological Education." In The Ministry and Mental Health, pp. 167-82.

Edited by Hans Hofmann. New York:
Association Press, 1960.

4995. Westberg, Granger E. "The Role of the Clergyman in Mental Health." Pastoral Psychology
11 (May 1960):19-22.

4996. Westberg, Granger Ellsworth. "Theological
Education for Dual Occupations: Medicine
and Ministry." Theological Education 7
(Spring 1971):177-80.

4997. Westerhoff, John H., ed. "The Church's
Ministry in Higher Education." Papers and
Responses Presented at a Conference at Duke
Divinity School, January 1978. New York:
United Ministries in Higher Education in
New York, 1978.

4998. Westerhoff, John H. "Theological Education
and Models for Ministry." Saint Luke's
Journal of Theology 25 (March 1982):153-69.

4999. Westermeyer, Paul. "Prospects of Psalmody in
the American Church Today." Hymn 33 (April
1982):74-9.

5000. "Western Theological Seminary, Evanston,
Illinois, Armstrong, Furst and Tilton,
Architects." Architectural Record 70 (July
1931):7-12.

5001. Western Theological Seminary, Pittsburgh.
Bibliography. Pittsburgh: Western
Theological Seminary, 1918.

5002. "Westminster Seminary Fires Theologian."
Christianity Today 26 (January 1, 1982):49.

5003. "Westminster Seminary Officials Respond to a
Crunch for Space at Philadelphia Campus."
Christianity Today 24 (May 23, 1980):45.

5004. Wetherbe, Linda Ann. "Selected Variables
Associated with Sex Role Perceptions of
Protestant Seminary Students and Faculty."
Ed.D. dissertation, Northern Illinois
University, 1982.

5005. Weyerhaeuser, C. Davis. "Trustees: What
Price Conservatism?" Theological Education
6 (Spring 1970):234-6.

5006. "What a Newspaperman Learned by Going to a
Theological Seminary." Current Opinion 58
(February 1915):113.

5007. "What Are Ministers To Do in the Great Controversy of the Age." New Englander 2 (April
1844):222-32.

5008. "What Is the Matter with Our Theological
Schools?" Current Literature 43 (October
1907):410-11.

5009. "What Kind of Ministry? What Kind of
Training?" South East Asia Journal of
Theology 6-7 (April-July 1965):67-72.

5010. "What Must Be Done To Provide an Educated
Christian Ministry?" New Englander 1
(January 1843):126-39.

5011. "What Seminaries Don't Believe: Question of
Jesus' Bodily Resurrection." Christianity
Today 22 (November 4, 1977):29-31.

5012. "What Seminary Students Say About the
Theological Curriculum." Christian
Education 7 (May 1924):364-6.

5013. "What Would John Wesley Do about It? Union
Theological Students vs. Methodist Church's
Board of Missions." Christian Century 83
(October 19, 1966):1264; Hornbeck, D. W. et
al. "Reply." 83 (December 7, 1966):1506-
7.

5014. Wheeler, Barbara G. "Accountability to Women
in Theological Seminaries." Religious
Education 76 (July-August 1981):382-90.

5015. Wheeler, Benjamin Ide. The Abundant Life.
Edited by Monroe E. Deutsch. Berkeley,
Calif.: University of California Press,
1926.

5016. "Where Teachers are Taught." Newsweek 53
(June 29, 1959):95.

5017. "Where the Action Is: Need for Jesuit
Seminaries to Move to Urban Academic
Centers." Newsweek 70 (July 31, 1967):72.

5018. Wherry, Neal M. "Theological School Enrollments 1937-47, 1947-50: A Survey of 561

433

Recognized Theological Schools." National
Headquarters, Selective Service System,
Washington, D.C., 1950.

5019. White, Alex Sandri. Guide to Religious
Education: The Directory of Seminaries,
Bible Colleges, and Theological Schools
Covering the USA and Canada. 1965-66 ed.
Allenhurst, N.J.: Aurea Publications,
1965.

5020. White, Alex Sandri. Guide to Religious
Education: A Directory of Seminaries,
Bible Colleges, and Theological Schools
Covering the USA and Canada. New ed.
Allenhurst, N.J.: Aurea Publications,
1979.

5021. White, Charles L. The Churches at Work. New
York: Missionary Education Movement of the
United States and Canada, 1915.

5022. White, Gaylord S. "Social Training of Lay
Workers." Religious Education 8 (April
1913):83-7.

5023. White, James F. "Liturgical Scholars: A New
Outspokenness." Christian Century 98
(February 4-11, 1981):103-7.

5024. White, James F. "Liturgical Strategy: Four
Lines of Attack." Christian Century 96
(March 7, 1979):242-6.

5025. White, James F. "A Protestant Worship
Manifesto." Christian Century 99 (January
27, 1982):82-6.

5026. White, James F. "The Teaching of Worship in
Seminaries in Canada and the United
States." Worship 55 (July 1981):304-18.

5027. White, James F. "Teaching the Arts in
Seminaries." Christian Century 97
(February 6-13, 1980):133-5.

5028. White, Morton Gabriel. Social Thought in
America: The Revolt against Formalism.
London, New York: Oxford University Press,
1976.

5029. White, Richard C. "Dwight E. Stevenson,
Teacher of Preachers." Lexington

434

Theological Quarterly 10 (April 1975):1-6.

5030. White, Stanley. "The Facilities Afforded for Women Missionaries in Theological Seminaries." In The Fifth Report of the Board of Missionary Preparation (for North America) for 1915. Edited by Frank K. Sanders. New York, n.d.

5031. White, Wilbert W. "Bible Study Programs: The Book of Genesis." Bible Magazine 1 (January 1913):66-80.

5032. White, Wilbert W. "The History, Basic Principles and Aims of the Bible Teachers Training School." Bible Record (May 1910):181-8.

5033. White, William. Protestant Episcopal Theological Seminary: Address to Episcopalians. New York, T. and J. Swords, 1817.

5034. White, William Spottswood. Rev. William S. White...and His Times (1800-1873): An Autobiography. Edited by H. M. White. Richmond, Va.: Presbyterian Committee of Publication, 1891.

5035. Whitehead, James D. and Evelyn E. "Educational Models in Field Education." Theological Education 11 (Summer 1975):269-78.

5036. Whitehead, Priscilla Felisky, and McAlpine, Tom. "Evangelical/Liberal Theology - A False Dichotomy: Report on the Harvard/Gordon-Conwell Dialogue." TSF Bulletin 5 (March-April 1982):8-11.

5037. Whitesel, John A. "Parental Relationships of Theological Students in Reference to Dominance-Submission." Ph.D. dissertation, Boston University Graduate School, 1952.

5038. Whitlock, Glenn E. "The Choice of the Ministry as an Active or Passive Decision." Pastoral Psychology 12 (March 1961):47-53.

5039. Whitlock, Glenn E. Consultation with Pastors Seeking to Demit the Ministry. Pastoral Services Committee, Synod of California, Southern Area, 1966.

435

5040. Whitlock, Glenn E. From Call to Service: The Making of a Minister. Philadelphia: Westminster Press, 1968.

5041. Whittaker, Frederick William. "Called Again From the Nets." Christian Century 71 (November 3, 1954):1330.

5042. Whittaker, Frederick W. "Freedom's Holy Light." Theological Education 13 (Autumn 1976):7-15.

5043. Whittemore, George H., ed. Memorials of Horatio Balch Hackett. Rochester, 1876.

5044. "Whose Freedom? Nomination of A. J. Ehlen [Concordia Seminary]." Christianity Today 16 (July 28, 1972):25.

5045. Wicke, Myron F. A Brief History of the University Senate of the Methodist Church. Nashville, Tenn.: Department of Public Relations and Finance, Division of Educational Institutions, Board of Education, Methodist Church, 1956.

5046. Wickey, Gould. "Trends in Theological Education." Christian Education 29 (December 1946):447-59.

5047. Wickey, N. J. G. "Place of Evangelism in Seminaries." Christian Education 19 (June 1936):383-90.

5048. Wiederaenders, Robert C. In Remembrance of Reu, An Evaluation of the Life and Work of J. Michael Reu, 1869-1943. Dubuque: Wartburg Seminary Association, 1969.

5049. Wiederaenders, Robert C. "Wartburg Seminary Through 125 Years." Lutheran Historical Conference 8 (1980):94-101.

5050. Wiemer, Marlin James. "Dogmatism and Future Time Perspective in Seminary Students." Ph.D. dissertation, University of Minnesota, 1969.

5051. Wigfield, Paul. "Training for Christian Communication." Educational Television International 3 (April 1969):31-3.

5052. Wilbert, Warren Norman. "A Policy Statement for a Seminary-Based Program of Continuing Christian Education." Ed.D. dissertation, Indiana University, 1976.

5053. Wilbur, E. M. "Education and Success in the Ministry." Harvard Graduates' Magazine 22 (September 1913):61-8.

5054. Wilbur, Earl Morse. "Reminiscences of a Divinity School Graduate of the Class of 1890." Harvard Divinity School Bulletin 20 (1954-5):75-96.

5055. Wilbur, Theresa M. "The Young Women's Christian Association and the Problem of Religious Influence in Colleges." Religious Education 4 (April 1909):89-90.

5056. Wilburn, Ralph Glenn. "The Role of the Theological Seminary in Modern Culture." College of the Bible Quarterly 39 (January 1962):30-7.

5057. Wilburn, R. G. "Skeptically Religious Student [bibliog.]." Christian Education 30 (September 1947):239-47.

5058. Wilburn, Ralph Glenn. "Widening Horizons in Theological Education." College of the Bible Quarterly 38 (July 1961):1-10.

5059. Wilder, A. N. "New Testament Study in the Divinity School." Harvard Divinity Bulletin 25 (January 1961):9-16.

5060. Wilder, Amos Niven. "Theological Education Abroad: Discussions in England, France and Germany." Harvard Divinity School Bulletin 20 (1954-5):39-51.

5061. Wiles, C. P. "(Ministerial Education.)" Lutheran Quarterly 33 (New Series) (1903):393+.

5062. Wilke, Harold H. "Access to Professional Education." Theological Education 15 (Autumn 1978):18-32.

5063. Wilke, Harold H. "To Open the Door: Access to Professional Theological Education [for the handicapped]." Church and Society 69 (January-February 1979):42-55.

5064. Wilkinson, Carl Wesley, III. "The Life and Work of William Joseph McGlothlin." Ph.D. dissertation, Southern Baptist Theological Seminary, 1981.

5065. Willard, Louis C. "An Analysis of Paper Stability and Circulation Patterns of the Monographic Collection of Speer Library, Princeton Theological Seminary." In Essays on Theological Librarianship: Presented to Calvin Henry Schmitt. Edited by P. De Klerk. Philadelphia: American Theological Library Association, 1980.

5066. Willard, Samuel. Brief Directions to a Young Scholar Designing the Ministry for the Study of Divinity. Boston: Printed by J. Draper for T. Hancock, 1735.

5067. Willard, Warren Wyeth. Fire on the Prairie: The Story of Wheaton College. Wheaton, Ill.: Van Kampen Press, 1950.

5068. Willcox, Giles Buckingham. The Pastor Amidst His Flock. New York: American Tract Society, 1890.

5069. Willett, H. L. "Question Box: Is It Advisable for a Ministerial Student to Subject Himself to a Regular Theological Course in One of Our Leading Seminaries?" Christian Century 51 (February 21, 1934):259.

5070. William and Mary College, Williamsburg, Va. The History of the College of William and Mary from Its Foundation, 1660, to 1874. Richmond: J. W. Randolph & English, 1874.

5071. Williams, D. R. "Speaking for the Class of 1913." Harvard Divinity Bulletin 27 (July 1963):1-6.

5072. Williams, Daniel Day. The Andover Liberals: A Study in American Theology. New York: Octagon Books, 1970 [c1941].

5073. Williams, Daniel Day. "The Morphology of Commitment in Theological Education." Theological Education 5 (Autumn 1968):23-40.

5074. Williams, Daniel Day. "New Spirit in Theological Education." Union Seminary
Quarterly Review 11 (November 1955):33-8.

5075. Williams, Daniel Day. "What Psychiatry Means
to Theological Education." Journal of
Pastoral Care 18 (Autumn 1964):129-32.

5076. Williams, David Leonard. "A Comparison of the
Christian Religious Beliefs and Selected
Counseling Values of Pastoral and Secular
Counseling Students." Ed.D. dissertation,
Northern Illinois University, 1972.

5077. Williams, D. L. and Kremer, B. L. "Pastoral
Counseling Students: A Comparison."
Journal of Counseling Psychology 21 (May
1974):238-42.

5078. Williams, G. H. "Dean's Letter." Harvard
Divinity Bulletin 20 (1954-55):97-116.

5079. Williams, G. H. "Friends of God and Prophets:
Wisdom of Solomon 7:27 [Theological
Students]." Harvard Divinity Bulletin 30
(October 1965):1-24.

5080. Williams, George Huntston, ed. The Harvard
Divinity School: Its Place in Harvard
University and in American Culture.
Boston: Beacon Press, 1954.

5081. Williams, George H. "The Seminary in the
Wilderness: A Representative Episode in
the Cultural History of Northern New
England [Gilmanton Seminary, 1835-46]."
Harvard Library Bulletin 13 (Autumn
1959):369-400; 14 (Winter 1960):27-58.

5082. Williams, George H. "Translatio Studii: The
Puritans' Conception of Their First University in New England, 1636." Archiv für
Reformationsgeschichte 57, no. 1-2
(1966):7-288.

5083. Williams, George Huntston. Wilderness and
Paradise in Christian Thought. New York:
Harper, 1962.

5084. Williams, George Huntston. "The Wilderness
and Paradise in the History of the Church."
Chruch History 28, no. 1 (1959):3-24.

5085. Williams, Howard D. <u>A History of Colgate University, 1819-1969</u>. New York: Van Nostrand Reinhold Co., 1969.

5086. Williams, Walter George. "Theological Education in Retrospect and Prospect." <u>Journal of Bible and Religion</u> 28 (April 1960):167-72.

5087. Williams, William R. <u>The Prayers of the Church Needed for Her Rising Ministry: A Discourse Delivered in the Chapel of the Hamilton Literary and Theological Seminary, Before the New York Baptist Education Society at Their Annual Meeting, Tuesday, August 18, 1835</u>. New York: William Van Norden, Printer, 1835.

5088. Williamson, Arthur. "Evangelicals Study the Link between Social Action and Gospel [Reformed Bible College]." <u>Christianity Today</u> 26 (August 6, 1982):54+.

5089. Williamson, Donald S. "Inefficiency of Emotional Inhibition: A Seminary Faculty Takes a Thoughtful Second Look." <u>Duke Divinity School Review</u> 32 (Winter 1967):69-78.

5090. Willimon, William H. "What I Learned at School: Thoughts on Moving from Parish Ministry to Seminary Teaching and Back Again." <u>Christian Century</u> 98 (July 15-22, 1981):736-8.

5091. Willis, Gwendolen B. "Olympia Brown." <u>Universalist Historical Society Journal</u> 4 (1963):1-76.

5092. Willis, Wesley Robert. "An Adaptation of the Institution-Building Model and Field Test at Fort Wayne Bible College." Ed.D. dissertation, Indiana University, 1978.

5093. Wills, K. C. "Leslie Robinson Elliott, Librarian of Vision." <u>Southwestern Journal of Theology</u> 11 (Spring 1969):123-30.

5094. Wilmore, Gayraud S. "Black Pastors/White Professors: Dialogic Education [Lilly Endowment Project at Colgate Rochester, Bexley Hall/Crozer Theological Seminary]." <u>Theological Education</u> 16 Special Issue no.

1 (Winter 1980):83-169.

5095. Wilmore, Gayraud S. "Tension Points in Black
      Church Studies." Christian Century 96
      (April 11, 1979):411-13.

5096. Wilson, Carl Bassett. The Baptist Manual
      Labor School Movement in the United States:
      Its Origin, Development and Significance.
      Waco, Tex.: Baylor University, 1937.

5097. Wilson, Charles Reagan. "Robert Lewis Dabney:
      Religion and the Southern Holocaust."
      Virginia Magazine of History and Biography
      89, no. 1 (1981):79-89.

5098. Wilson, H. L. McGill. "On the Buildings of
      the Theological Seminary of the Presby-
      terian Church in the United States of
      America, 1817-1950." Princeton Seminary
      Bulletin 43 (Winter 1950?):24-7.

5099. Wilson, J. Christy, ed. Ministers in
      Training: A Review of Field Work
      Procedures in Theological Education...
      Princeton, N.J.: Directors of Field Work
      in the Theological Seminaries of the
      Presbyterian Church, U.S.A., 1957.

5100. Wilson, J. C. "Seminary Moves into the Church
      [Field Work]." Christianity Today 3 (May
      11, 1959):11-12.

5101. Wilson, Lon Ervin. "The Status of Speech and
      Homiletics in Bible Schools in the United
      States and Canada." Ph.D. dissertation,
      Northern Baptist Theological Seminary,
      1958.

5102. Wilson, Robert Allen. "An Evaluation of the
      Christian Education Curricula of Bible
      Colleges Supported by Christian Churches."
      D.R.E. dissertation, Southern Baptist
      Theological Seminary, 1972.

5103. Wilson, Samuel Tyndale. A Century of
      Maryville College, 1819-1919. Maryville,
      Tenn.: Directors of Maryville College,
      1916.

5104. Wimberly, Merritt. "A Gallery of Theologues."
      American Mercury 20 (1930):417-22.

5105. Winchester, Benjamin S. "The Issue in
       Theological Education." Outlook 90
       (September 5, 1908):23-7.

5106. Winehouse, Irwin. The Assemblies of God: A
       Popular Survey. New York: Vantage Press,
       1959.

5107. Winfield, Oscar Ahlenius. "The Control of
       Lutheran Theological Education." Ph.D.
       dissertation, Yale University, 1930.

5108. Winfield, Oscar Ahlenius. The Control of
       Lutheran Theological Education in America.
       Rock Island, Ill.: Augustana Book Concern,
       1933.

5109. Wingo, Robert Lewis. "A Study of the Need for
       Correlating the Courses in Religion in
       Texas Baptist Colleges and Southern Baptist
       Seminaries." Ph.D. dissertation, South-
       western Baptist Theological Seminary, 1963.

5110. Winkleman, Gerald Gene. "Polemics, Prayers,
       and Professionalism: The American
       Protestant Theological Seminaries from 1784
       to 1920." Ph.D. dissertation, State
       University of New York at Buffalo, 1975.

5111. Winn, Albert Curry. "Serious Questions About
       the RPC [Resources Planning Commission of
       AATS] Report." Theological Education 5
       (Winter 1969):88-91.

5112. Winner, I. "Theological Schools in Our
       Church." Christian Advocate and Journal
       (New York) 29 (June 1, 1854):85.

5113. Winner, I. "Theological Schools: The Views
       of the Bishops Thereon." Christian
       Advocate and Journal (New York) 29 (March
       30, 1854):1.

5114. Winner, I. "Theological Seminaries in Our
       Church: Mr. Strong's Logic." Christian
       Advocate (New York) 29 (June 1, 1854):85.

5115. Winter, Gibson. "Seminary in a Metropolitan
       Society." Princeton Seminary Bulletin 1
       (New Series) no. 4 (1978):201-12.

5116. Winter, Gibson. "Theological Education for
       Ministry: Central Issues in Curriculum

                          442

Construction." <u>Theological Education</u> 2
(Spring 1966):184-9.

5117. Winter, J. Allan and Mills, Edgar W.
        "Relationships among the Activities and
        Attitudes of Christian Clergymen: A
        Preliminary Report." New York: National
        Council of Churches, 1968. (ERIC Document)

5118. Winter, Ralph D. <u>Theological Education: A</u>
        <u>Bibliography</u>. Pasadena, Calif.: Fuller
        Theological Seminary, 1968.

5119. Winters, Charles L. "Theological Education in
        the Next Decade." In <u>Realities and</u>
        <u>Visions: The Church's Mission Today</u>, pp.
        125-33. Edited by Furman C. Stough and
        Urban T. Homes. New York: Seabury Press,
        1976.

5120. Wisbey, Herbert Andrew. <u>Soldiers without</u>
        <u>Swords: A History of the Salvation Army in</u>
        <u>the United States</u>. New York: Macmillan
        Co., 1955.

5121. Wise, C. A. "Call to the Ministry." <u>Pastoral</u>
        <u>Psychology</u> 9 (December 1958):9-17.

5122. Wise, Carroll Alonzo. "Education of the
        Pastor for Marriage Counseling." <u>Pastoral</u>
        <u>Psychology</u> 10 (December 1959):45-8.

5123. Wise, Carroll Alonzo. "Human Values in the
        Seminary." <u>Journal of Pastoral Care</u> 16
        (Summer 1962):89-90.

5124. Wise, Carroll A. "The Place of Clinical
        Training in the Department of Pastoral
        Theology." <u>Journal of Pastoral Care</u> 5
        (Spring 1951):46-52.

5125. Wise, Carroll Alonzo. "Project in the
        Pastoral Care of the Ill." <u>Journal of</u>
        <u>Pastoral Care</u> 20 (June 1966):101-2.

5126. Wise, C. A. "Relationship between Clinical
        Training and Field Work Supervision."
        <u>Journal of Pastoral Care</u> 8, no. 4
        (1954):189-94.

5127. Wishart, Alfred Wesley. "What Does the
        Pastorate Demand of the Seminary?"
        <u>Religious Education</u> 7 (April 1912):31-6.

443

5128. Wissink, Charles J. "Vocational Attitude Changes in First Year Seminary Students." Ph.D. dissertation, Princeton Theological Seminary, 1975.

5129. Witmer, John A. "Building upon the Foundation." Bibliotheca Sacra 131 (1974):3-13.

5130. Witmer, S. A. "Bible College Education." School and Society 80 (October 16, 1954):113-16.

5131. Witmer, Safara Austin. The Bible College Story: Education with Dimension. Manhasset, N.Y.: Channel Press, 1962.

5132. Witmer, S. A. "Bible Institutes Meet a Need." United Evangelical Action 20 (June 1961):134-5.

5133. Witschey, Warren Lee. "A Brief Biography of the Reverend John West Reger, D.D." West Virginia History 30, no. 3 (1969):548-58.

5134. Wittenbach, H. A. "Training of a Missionary." International Review of Missions 49 (October 1960):405-10.

5135. Wolbrecht, Walter F. "What a Protestant Church Wants its Seminaries to Be and to Do." Theological Education 2 (Winter 1966):89-94.

5136. Wolcott, Dorothea Kathryn. "An Appraisal of the Opportunities for Supervised Field Work in Christian Education with Children and Youth in the Seminary Training of the Ministry." Ph.D. dissertation, Northwestern University, 1957.

5137. Wolcott, Dorothea K. "Field Work Experiences with Children & Youth: In Seminary Training For the Ministry." Religious Education 53 (May-June 1958):285-9.

5138. Wolcott, L. T. "Missionary Training: The Communal Non-Academic Orientation." International Review of Missions 49 (October 1960):401-4.

5139. Wolf, C. Umhau. "Present Trends in Lutheran Seminary Training." Lutheran Church Quarterly 15 (1942):67-75.

5140. Wolf, Fred C., Jr. "Documentary History of the American Church: Benjamin Bosworth Smith, 'The West, A Field for Mission.'" Historical Magazine of the Protestant Episcopal Church 33, no. 1 (1964):83-92.

5141. Wolf, L. B. "Seminary and Foreign Missions." Lutheran Quarterly 56 (October 1926):479-91.

5142. Wolf, Richard Charles. "Recover our Protestant Heritage." Christian Century 69 (April 30, 1952):523-5.

5143. Wolf, William J. "Curriculum Revision at the Episcopal Theological School and Some Dynamics of its Acceptance." Theological Education 2 (Summer 1966):104-15.

5144. Wolff, Florence I. "Oral Reading of Scripture: Denominational Application and a Successful Lectures' Workshop Format." Paper Presented at the Annual Meeting of the Speech Communication Association, Chicago, December 1974. (ERIC Document)

5145. "Women and the Seminaries." Christian Century 96 (February 7, 1979):122-3.

5146. "Women Clergy: How Their Presence is Changing the Church: A Symposium on the Seminary Campus." Christian Century 96 (February 7-14, 1979):122.

5147. Women's Theological Coalition. "Doctoral Placement Service for Women in Religion." Theological Education 11 (Winter 1975):125-6.

5148. Wood, George T. "Specialized Training for the Ministry." Homiletical Review 98 (November 1929):348-51.

5149. Wood, James E. "A Baptist Seminary Resists the Equal Employment Opportunity Commission." In Government Intervention in Religious Affairs. Edited by D. Kelley. New York: Pilgrim Press, 1982.

5150. Wood, Paul H. "Student Personnel Services in Pacific Coast Schools of Ministerial Training." Ph.D. dissertation, Oregon State University, 1954.

5151. Woods, C. S. "Are Bible Schools and
Seminaries Doing the Job?" Eternity 7
(July 1956):14-15+.

5152. Woods, C. Stacey. "Inter-Varsity Fellowship:
Bringing Christ to the Campus." United
Evangelical Action 5 (July 1, 1946):7.

5153. Woods, Donald C. The Personality Adjustment
and Social, Economic, and Political
Attitudes of Liberal and Conservative
Ministerial Students. Ph.D. dissertation,
University of Chicago, 1956.

5154. Woods, Leonard. History of the Andover Theological Seminary. Boston: James R. Osgood
& Co., 1885.

5155. Woods, Robert A. "Social Christianity in the
Country." In Christianity Practically
Applied. Evangelical Alliance for the
United States of America. Conference.
Chicago, 1893, v. 2, pp. 412-16. New York:
Baker & Taylor, 1894.

5156. Woodson, Carter Godwin. The History of the
Negro Church. Washington, D.C.: Associated Publishers, 1921.

5157. Woodson, Carter Godwin. The Mis-education of
the Negro. Washington, D.C.: Associated
Publishers, 1932.

5158. "Woodstock to Manhattan: Catholic Attendance
at Protestant Seminaries." Time 91 (March
8, 1968):46.

5159. Woodward, F. C. "Methodism and Ministerial
Education." Southern Methodist Review (New
Series) (November 1886):208-17.

5160. Woodward, R. L. "Educational Values in Field
Work." Religious Education 40 (January
1945):18-22.

5161. Woolery, William Kirk. Bethany Years: The
Story of Old Bethany from Her Founding
Years through a Century of Trial and
Triumph. Huntington, W. Va.: Standard
Printing & Publishing Co., 1941.

5162. Woollcombe, Kenneth J. "The Purpose of Theological Schools in Great Britain."

Theological Education 2 (Winter 1966):70-5.

5163. Woolverton, John Frederick. "William Augustus Muhlenburg and the Founding of St. Paul's College." Historical Magazine of the Protestant Episcopal Church 29 (September 1960):192-218.

5164. Worcester, E. S. "History for Seventy-Five Years." In Recent Christian Progress, pp. 331-5. By Lewis Bayles Paton. Macmillan, 1909.

5165. Worcester, Elwood. Life's Adventure: The Story of a Varied Career. New York: Charles Scribner's Sons, 1932, pp. 76-80.

5166. "Work and Workers." Biblical World 8 (New Series) (December 1896):492-6.

5167. "World Council Arranges Seminarian Exchange." Christian Century 67 (October 11, 1950):1188.

5168. Wotherspoon, Henry Johnstone. The Ministry in the Church in Relation to Prophecy and Spiritual Gifts. London and New York: Longmans, Green & Co., 1916.

5169. Wren-Lewis, John. "A Layman Looks at Theological Education." Frontier 4 (1961):54-6.

5170. Wright, C. J. et al. "Reflections on Clinical Training." Pastoral Psychology 16 (September 1965):55-7.

5171. Wright, Conrad, comp. Religion in American Life. Boston: Houghton Mifflin, 1972.

5172. Wright, Edward, Jr. "Recruitment of Minority Groups." Theological Education 8 (Autumn 1971):11-17.

5173. Wright, George E. "History in Theological Education." Harvard Divinity Bulletin 27 (October 1962):1-16.

5174. Wright, George Ernest. "Old Testament Scholarship in Prospect." Journal of Bible and Religion 28 (April 1960):182-93.

5175. Wright, G. Frederick. "Dr. Briggs's 'Whither?'" Bibliotheca Sacra 47 (January 1890):136-53.

5176. Wright, George Frederick. Story of My Life and Work. Oberlin: Bibliotheca Sacra Co., 1916.

5177. Wright, G. Frederick. "The Work of the Seminary as Conditioned by its Location." In Christianity Practically Applied. Evangelical Alliance for the United States of America. Conference. Chicago, 1893, v. 2, pp. 421-7. New York: Baker & Taylor, 1894.

5178. Wright, H. Elliott. "The Seminary Scene: An Overview." Christianity and Crisis 29 (April 14, 1969):98-101.

5179. Wright, Helen M. "The Seminary Speaks to the Church about Opening Ministries for All Who Are Prepared." Theological Education 15 (Spring 1979):141-5.

5180. Wright, Henry Clarke. Human Life: Illustrated in My Individual Experience as a Child, a Youth and a Man. Boston: Bela Marsh, 1849.

5181. Wright, Richard Louis. "Language Standards and Communicative Style in the Black Church." Ph.D. dissertation, University of Texas at Austin, 1976.

5182. Wright, T. F. "(Training of the Christian Minister.)" New Church Review 3 (1896): 427+.

5183. Wuerffel, Leonhard C. "Gifts from the Lord of the Church." Concordia Theological Monthly 35 (December 1964):721-8.

5184. Wuerffel, Leonhard Carl. "A Study of Changes in a Theological Student's Concept of the Ministry during the Year of Internship." Ed.D. dissertation, Washington University, 1961.

5185. Wuthnow, Robert J. "New Forms of Religion in the Seminary." Review of Religious Research 12 (Winter 1971):80-7.

5186. Wyckoff, D. Campbell. "Religious Education as
      a Discipline: I. Toward a Definition of
      Religious Education as a Discipline."
      Religious Education 62, no. 5 (1967):387-
      94.

5187. Wynn, J. C. and Hunt, J. J. "Experiment in
      the Use of a Family Casework Agency as a
      Training Source for Pastoral Counseling."
      Marriage and Family Living 24 (November
      1962):381-3.

5188. Wynne, Edward James. "The Implications of
      Carl Michalson's Theological Method for
      Christian Education." Ph.D. dissertation,
      New York University, 1971.

5189. "Yale Divinity School Improvement." Outlook
      90 (September 19, 1908):100.

5190. "Yale Divinity School, New Haven, Conn.,
      Delano Aldrich, Architects." Architecture
      67 (May 1933):269-74.

5191. "Yale Divinity School Plans Expansion."
      Christian Century 73 (January 11, 1956):38.

5192. Yale University. The Centennial Celebration
      of the Founding of the Yale Divinity School
      Held in Connection with the Fourteenth
      Annual Convocation. New Haven, 1923?

5193. Yale University. Divinity School. Education
      for Christian Service, by Members of the
      Faculty of the Divinity School of Yale
      University: a Volume in Commemoration of
      Its One Hundredth Anniversary. New Haven:
      Yale University Press, 1922.

5194. Yates, Elizabeth. Howard Thurman: Portrait
      of a Practical Dreamer. New York: John
      Day Co., 1964.

5195. Yerkes, Royden Keith. "The Beginnings of the
      Graduate School of Theology of the
      University of the South." Historical
      Magazine of the Protestant Episcopal Church
      29 (December 1960):315-24.

5196. Yost, John K. "Hugh Latimer and the Reforma-
      tion Crisis in the Education of Preachers."
      Lutheran Quarterly 24 (1972):179-89.

5197. Young, Edward James. The Minister's Club,
      1870-1899: A Historical Sketch.
      Cambridge: Harvard University Press, 1900.

5198. Young, James Reed. "Relation of the Church
      and Clergy to Education in the American
      Colonies." Ph.D. dissertation, University
      of Chicago, 1916.

5199. Young, Lewis Charles. "The Relationship of
      Self-Acceptance to Acceptance of Others
      with Reference to Clinical Pastoral
      Training." Ph.D. dissertation, Boston
      University, 1965.

5200. The Young Minister's Companion: Or A
      Collection of Valuable and Scarce Treaties
      on the Pastoral Office. Boston: Samuel T.
      Armstrong, 1813.

5201. "Young Seminary: Federated Theological
      Faculty." Time 65 (April 18, 1955):80.

5202. Yrigoyen, Charles. "Emanuel Gerhart and the
      Mercersburg Theology." Journal of the
      Lancaster County Historical Society 82, no.
      4 (1978):199-221.

5203. Yrigoyen, Charles. "Emanuel V. Gerhart:
      Apologist for the Mercersburg Theology."
      Journal of Presbyterian History 57, no. 4
      (1979):485-500.

5204. Yurica, K. "Dissonance Jars the Melodyland
      Harmony." Christianity Today 23 (December
      1, 1978):46.

5205. Yurica, K. "Melodyland Lingers: Is the Song
      Ended?" Christianity Today 23 (December
      15, 1978):42.

5206. Zabriskie, A. C. "Clinical Pastoral Training:
      Implications [Letter to D. Vair]." Journal
      of Pastoral Care 10 (Summer 1956):101-2.

5207. Zappala, Anthony. "A Joint Venture of
      Psychiatrists and Clergy: The Pastoral
      Institute." Medical Annals of the District
      of Columbia 32 (June 1963):247-8, 254.

5208. Zenos, A. C. "Standards of Admission, Scho-
      larship, and Degrees." In Christianity
      Practically Applied. Evangelical Alliance

for the United States of America. Conference. Chicago, 1893, v. 2, pp. 454-9. New York: Baker & Taylor, 1894.

5209. Zentz, George H. "Goals and Issues in the Training of Pastoral Counseling Specialists." Ph.D. dissertation, Boston University Graduate School, 1974.

5210. Zerfoss, Karl P. "The Background and Experience of Theological Students." Ph.D. dissertation, Yale University, 1929.

5211. Zerner, Ruth. "Dietrich Bonhoeffer's American Experiences: People, Letters, and Papers from Union Seminary." Union Seminary Quarterly Review 31 (Summer 1976):261-82.

5212. Zerof, Herbert Goddard. "An Evaluation of a Short-Term Course in Teaching Clergymen Skills in Family Crisis Intervention Conducted in Conjunction with a Community Mental Health Center." Ed.D. dissertation, University of Pennsylvania, 1968.

5213. Ziebell, Thomas. "The Michigan Synod School of the Prophets in 1889." Concordia Historical Institute Quarterly 55 (Summer 1982):82-96.

5214. Ziegler, Howard J. B. "Frederick Augustus Rauch [1806-41], American Hegelian." Lancaster, Pa.: Franklin and Marshall College, 1953.

5215. Ziegler, Jesse H. "The AATS and Theological Education." Theological Education 2 (Summer 1966):67-83.

5216. Ziegler, Jesse H. "Academic Freedom and Faculty Tenure." Theological Education 12 (Winter 1976):85-136.

5217. Ziegler, Jesse H. "Administrative Staff Development in Theological Schools." Theological Education 16 (Spring 1980):419-71.

5218. Ziegler, Jesse Hunsberger. "Conservation and Change in Theological Education." St. Vladimir's Theological Quarterly 13 (1969):103-10.

5219. Ziegler, Jesse H. "A Continuation of the Dialogue on Facilities Planning." Theological Education 5 (Winter 1969):92-4.

5220. Ziegler, Jesse H., ed. "Continuing Education of Ministers." Theological Education 1 (Summer 1965):197-246.

5221. Ziegler, Jesse H., ed. "Dialog between Church and Seminary." Theological Education 15 (Spring 1979):89-165.

5222. Ziegler, Jesse H. "Education For Ministry in Aging: Gerontology in Seminary Training." Theological Education 16 Special Issue no. 3 (Winter 1980):271-414.

5223. Ziegler, Jesse Hunsberger. "Education in Pastoral Theology: Some American Approaches." Expository Times 74 (December 1962):69-72.

5224. Ziegler, Jesse H. "Education of the Ministry." College of the Bible Quarterly 41 (January 1964):8-18.

5225. Ziegler, Jesse H. "Ferment in Theological Education." Journal of Pastoral Care 20 (June 1966):65-73.

5226. Ziegler, J. H. "Identity of Pre-Seminary Students on the College Campus [bibliog.]." Brethren Life and Thought 8 (Spring 1963): 13-27.

5227. Ziegler, Jesse H. "Indications of Crisis in Theological Education." Theological Education 13 (Autumn 1976):40-3.

5228. Ziegler, Jesse H. "Issues in Accrediting." Theological Education 14 (Autumn 1977):5-51.

5229. Ziegler, J. H. "Lack of Communication in Theological Education." Theological Education 1 (Autumn 1964):1-2+.

5230. Ziegler, Jesse H. "Major Issues in the AATS 1970 Biennial Meeting." Theological Education 6 (Summer 1970):285-90.

5231. Ziegler, Jesse H. "Managerial Implications of Theological Education in the 1970's."

Theological Education 7 (Autumn 1970):9-15.

5232. Ziegler, Jesse H. "Nurture of the Ministry for the Minutes Before the Clock Strikes." College of the Bible Quarterly 38 (January 1961):37-43.

5233. Ziegler, Jesse H. "Reflections on Education for Ministry." Brethren Life and Thought 15 (Winter 1970):15-17.

5234. Ziegler, J. H. and Carr, A. L. "Salaries in AATS Schools: A Biennial Report." Theological Education 2 (Winter 1966):107-10.

5235. Ziegler, Jesse H. "The Search for Parameters and Priorities." Theological Education 7 (Spring 1971):157-62.

5236. Ziegler, Jesse H. "Selection and Training of Candidates for the Ministry: Education in Pastoral Theology: Some American Approaches." Expository Times 74 (1962-3): 69-72.

5237. Ziegler, Jesse H. "Shaping Education for the Ministry in the 1970's." Lexington Theological Quarterly 6 (April 1971):29-36.

5238. Ziegler, Jesse H. "Strategies in Seminary Curricula." Theological Education 16, Special Issue no. 3 (Winter 1980):349-51.

5239. Ziegler, Jesse H., ed. "Theological Education and Liberation Theology: A Symposium." Theological Education 16 (Autumn 1979):5-68.

5240. Ziegler, J. H. "Theological Education for a Changing Ministry." Theological Education 3 (Winter 1967):263.

5241. Ziegler, Jesse H. "Theological Education in a Changing Society." Southwestern Journal of Theology 9 (Spring 1967):31-41.

5242. Ziegler, J. H. "Vocation of the Professor of Christian Education in the Advancement of Theological Education: With Comments [bibliog.]." Religious Education 56 (November 1961):403-17.

5243. Ziff, Larzer. The American 1890s: Life and
      Times of a Lost Generation. New York:
      Viking Press, 1966.

5244. Zikmund, Barbara Brown. "Upsetting the
      Assumptions [Increased Numbers of Women in
      Theological Education]." Christian Century
      96 (February 7-14, 1979):127-8.

5245. Zimmerman, G. "Help Wanted: Ministers,
      Priests and Rabbis." Look 26 (November 20,
      1962):112+; "Discussion." Christian
      Century 79 (December 5, 1962):1471-2; 80
      (January 23, 1963):111-12.

5246. Zimmerman, J. S. "Christian Theological
      Approach to Clinical Pastoral Training."
      Journal of Pastoral Care 7, no. 2
      (1953):59-76.

5247. Zimmerman, J. S. "Relevance of Clinical
      Pastoral Training to Field Education."
      Journal of Pastoral Care 22 (March 1968):1-
      6.

5248. Zimmerman, J. S. "View from the Field: A
      Supervising Pastor's Experience in the In-
      Parish Pastoral Studies Program [Yale]."
      Theological Education 3 (Spring 1967):419-
      22.

5249. Zorn, Herbert M. "Are We Ready for Seminaries
      in Context." Currents in Theology and
      Mission 2 (October 1975):266-70.

SUBJECT INDEX

In a bibliography of this size, some kind of
subject or key-word index becomes necessary to make it
accessible to users. However, it was not at all easy
to index this bibliography, for two main reasons.
Often titles do not indicate what the work is really
about. And the subject and time period of the
bibliography is so extensive that I cannot claim
expertise in the areas covered. I was fortunate,
however, to be able to call upon Glenn Miller, whose
in-depth knowledge of the history of Protestant
theological education helped me in categorizing items
which I could not otherwise place. He also identified
the significant names and institutions. Inevitably,
some inaccuracies in the indexing remain, and these
are entirely my responsibility.

The theological schools are indexed under their
present names (except in the case of Andover Newton
and Colgate Rochester, which have headings for the
individual schools which later united). Schools
currently in existence are not cross-referenced by
denomination. It is assumed that a researcher
interested in Lutheran seminaries, for instance, would
first look under the general category "Lutherans -
Education" then look up the names of all Lutheran
seminaries currently in existence. However,
seminaries that are defunct have been listed by their

names, as well as under the general category
"Lutherans - Education", for example. Bible colleges
are indexed in the same fashion. Church colleges have
not been listed under individual names, but rather
under the general heading, "Colleges", and under the
denominations in which they fall.

I. BACKGROUND MATERIALS

Assemblies of God - General History

5106.

Baptists - General History

156. 174. 246. 250. 1026. 1226. 1524.
1963. 2330. 2785. 2806. 2991. 3177. 3409.
3439. 3497. 3500. 3547. 4668.

Bible, Study of

42. 238. 279. 304. 467. 518. 519. 523.
565. 568. 569. 658. 673. 725. 763. 840.
865. 878. 964. 1103. 1125. 1161. 1238.
1284. 1336. 1351. 1378. 1466. 1467. 1522.
1574. 1584. 1688. 1814. 1822. 1961. 2170.
2241. 2412. 2452. 2541. 2737. 2785. 2990.
3067. 3068. 3276. 3277. 3286. 3351. 3353.
3367. 3420. 3489. 3735. 3761. 3764. 3799.
3961. 4096. 4100. 4166. 4230. 4423. 4424.
4438. 4490. 4496. 4497. 4670. 4672. 4677.
4734. 4810. 4901. 5030. 5174. 5175. 5176.

Brethren - General History

465.

Christian and Missionary Alliance - General History

53. 1661.

Christian Churches - General History

675. 931. 1807. 1823. 2248. 2630. 2965.
3029. 3449. 3672. 3673. 3723. 4050. 4182.
4335.

Church History, Study of

165. 282. 399. 454. 455. 1892. 2190. 2231.
2383. 2862. 2878. 3656. 4299. 4300. 4369.

Church of the Nazarene - General History

4178.

Congregationalists - General History

206. 1121. 1617. 2260. 3510. 3911.

Episcopalians - General History

2132. 2241. 4920. 5140. 5165.

Europe - Religious History - 16th Century

2594. 3003. 3330. 3873. 4256.

Europe - Religious History - 17th Century

950. 1904. 2092. 3250. 3251. 3715. 4697.

Europe - Religious History - 18th Century

802. 3634. 4909.

Europe - Religious History - 19th Century

208. 237. 274. 444. 475. 746. 747. 802.
911. 1629. 1663. 1761. 1804. 2575. 3213.
3395. 3445. 3446. 3853. 3862. 4250. 4314.
4905. 4906. 4909.

Europe - Religious History - 20th Century

1285. 3395. 3474. 4314.

Homiletics, Study of

538. 1923. 2033. 2829. 3385. 3756. 4054.
4263. 4307.

Lutherans - General History

76. 77. 151. 695. 1093. 1188. 1409. 1590.
1697. 1710. 1897. 1900. 2307. 2393. 2416.
2417. 2449. 2553. 2601. 2602. 2912. 2914.
2915. 3127. 3128. 3129. 3256. 3284. 3427.
3663. 3781. 3826. 3881. 3912. 3935. 4224.
4264. 4301. 4397. 4398. 4447. 4451. (Cont.)

Lutherans - General History (Cont.)

4644. 4857. 4945. 4953. 4978. 4979.

Methodists - General History

242. 253. 323. 634. 769. 919. 1163. 1191.
1211. 1212. 1213. 1380. 1551. 1670. 1968.
2048. 2081. 2265. 2489. 2887. 2888. 2889.
2890. 2891. 2892. 2893. 2898. 2899. 2902.
2903. 2904. 2921. 3112. 3266. 3419. 3432.
3441. 3900. 3968. 4426. 4849. 4900.

Ministry, Study of

181.

Missionary Church - General History

2607.

Pastors

3. 4. 24. 46. 146. 167. 205. 229. 258.
271. 288. 312. 319. 346. 412. 506. 545.
551. 583. 607. 608. 628. 668. 679. 680.
705. 767. 789. 803. 809. 818. 819. 829.
854. 858. 933. 1020. 1049. 1066. 1152.
1227. 1300. 1306. 1365. 1383. 1460. 1465.
1473. 1504. 1590. 1615. 1625. 1661. 1702.
1729. 1745. 1750. 1845. 1872. 1876. 1905.
1973. 2034. 2065. 2090. 2192. 2221. 2253.
2254. 2255. 2262. 2268. 2272. 2273. 2274.
2319. 2365. 2394. 2476. 2494. 2518. 2524.
2566. 2573. 2596. 2605. 2617. 2619. 2661.
2692. 2707. 2758. 2770. 2780. 2854. 2866.
2877. 2968. 2975. 2976. 2979. 2980. 2981.
3044. 3069. 3134. 3141. 3182. 3187. 3203.
3264. 3272. 3324. 3327. 3343. 3349. 3366.
3370. 3372. 3376. 3384. 3397. 3426. 3430.
3431. 3472. 3477. 3492. 3638. 3654. 3679.
3697. 3773. 3817. 3864. 3964. 3969. 3984.
4055. 4080. 4144. 4156. 4171. 4174. 4222.
4244. 4259. 4281. 4318. 4319. 4371. 4403.
4431. 4451. 4478. 4479. 4480. 4487. 4598.
4622. 4623. 4624. 4657. 4666. 4691. 4721.
4726. 4738. 4743. 4811. 4828. 4832. 4904.
4914. 4915. 4927. 4945. 4992. 5007. 5015.
5039. 5068. 5117. 5121. 5197. 5200. 5232.
5245.

Presbyterians - General History

121. 270. 725. 991. 1063. 1197.1356. 1565.
1622. 1649. 1652. 1749. 1999. 2071. 2453.
2529. 2579. 2694. 2782. 2783. 2787. 2862.
3196. 3514. 3701. 3743. 3768. 4145. 4152.
4185. 4352. 4353. 4606. 4615. 4698. 4790.
4791. 4943. 5097.

Professions

106. 144. 308. 410. 411. 447. 564. 615.
652. 653. 654. 655. 663. 701. 707. 713.
738. 783. 1024. 1039. 1117. 1128. 1310.
1448. 1555. 1626. 1646. 1676. 1677. 1730.
1760. 1767. 1798. 1860. 2003. 2094. 2095.
2096. 2097. 2161. 2173. 2198. 2213. 2261.
2285. 2380. 2498. 2517. 2712. 2713. 2750.
3048. 3099. 3199. 3261. 3345. 3632. 3646.
3730. 3810. 4089. 4415. 4580. 4594. 4663.
4795. 4830. 4874. 5062.

Reformed Churches - General History

149. 275. 389. 500. 934. 1660. 1809. 2385.
3658. 3660. 4955. 5176.

Southern Baptists - General History

116. 262. 1157. 1160. 1293. 1326. 2142.
3379. 4221. 4616.

Theology, Study of

204. 273. 274. 314. 318. 401. 520. 521.
522. 525. 566. 666. 725. 737. 739. 743.
897. 969. 1241. 1351. 1363. 1471. 1472.
1499. 1552. 1710. 1842. 1878. 1880. 1946.
2035. 2173. 2305. 2379. 2451. 2656. 2729.
2793. 2865. 2945. 3009. 3158. 3313. 3428.
3451. 3592. 3618. 3628. 4138. 4188. 4592.
4674. 4696. 4815. 5011.

Unitarians/Universalists - General History

557. 2069. 2115. 2978. 5091.

United States - Church History - 19th Century

324. 688. 1131. 1176. 1620. 1736. 2130.
2271. 2439. 3121. 3647. 4062. 4640. 4954.
5120.

United States - Church History - 20th Century

405. 700. 918. 1166. 1174. 1185. 1429.
1468. 1628. 1945. 1988. 2193. 2194. 2360.
2439. 2550. 2700. 2798. 2833. 3070. 3206.
4184. 4718. 4859. 4878. 4932. 4999. 5021.
5120. 5168.

United States - Educational History

106. 291. 350. 411. 442. 614. 699. 707.
734. 796. 824. 888. 922. 960. 961. 1126.
1136. 1240. 1244. 1279. 1333. 1357. 1370.
1418. 1423. 1427. 1441. 1494. 1672. 1676.
1677. 1816. 1820. 1888. 1940. 1984. 1985.
2067. 2109. 2195. 2300. 2435. 2739. 2929.
3102. 3103. 3245. 3299. 3347. 3423. 3509.
4289. 4339. 4435. 4493. 4917.

United States - History - 19th Century

32. 75. 210. 261. 293. 912. 1109. 1618.
1675. 2343. 2406. 2719. 3440. 4805. 5243.

United States - History - 20th Century

1. 1986. 1987. 2252. 2343. 2490. 2516.
2658. 3215. 3824. 4108. 5028.

United States - Religious History

226. 244. 3311. 3882. 4090. 4245.

United States - Religious History - 18th Century

430. 907. 3503. 3677. 4245. 4427. 4867.

United States - Religious History - 19th Century

95. 216. 517. 568. 569. 576. 606. 633.
764. 799. 800. 862. 944. 1051. 1075. 1104.
1105. 1171. 1181. 1218. 1254. 1280. 1311.
1329. 1362. 1423. 1469. 1491. 1569. 1687.
1793. 1800. 2030. 2123. 2227. 2309. 2408.
2425. 2471. 2567. 2787. 2832. 2997. 3386.
3398. 3444. 3503. 3862. 3863. 3885. 4051.
4088. 4151. 4365. 4427. 4428. 4614. 4671.
4942. 5007. 5155. 5164.

United States - Religious History - 20th Century

57. 96. 158. 239. 612. 702. 715. 716.
764. 797. 945. 1015. 1051. 1171. (Cont.)

1254.	1329.	1334.	1362.	1526.	1530.	1569.
1576.	1687.	1692.	1728.	1782.	1793.	1813.
1980.	2030.	2129.	2156.	2316.	2425.	2465.
2467.	2539.	2585.	2717.	2746.	2776.	2805.
2823.	3024.	3062.	3087.	3265.	3269.	3304.
3386.	3467.	3473.	3586.	3606.	3775.	3836.
3840.	3841.	3858.	3860.	3861.	3933.	4052.
4056.	4088.	4183.	4210.	4589.	4972.	4986.
5142.	5152.	5171.				

II. MATERIALS RELATING TO THEOLOGICAL EDUCATION

Academic Freedom

9. 186. 243. 1247. 1248. 1277. 1984. 2536.
2537. 2909. 3023. 3617. 4153. 4893. 5216.

Accreditation

12. 94. 108. 255. 286. 650. 659. 849.
893. 1546. 1889. 2552. 3145. 3300. 3632.
3983. 4260. 4442. 4458. 4469. 5228.

Administration

150. 175. 325. 336. 667. 718. 948. 1000.
1179. 1512. 1557. 1571. 1849. 2031. 2086.
2091. 2108. 2111. 2242. 2251. 2278. 2587.
2604. 2722. 2742. 2964. 3038. 3425. 3534.
3610. 3652. 3869. 3953. 4039. 4059. 4231.
4267. 4313. 4881. 4910. 4911. 5150. 5217.
5231.

Architecture

499. 1444. 1643. 2299. 2538. 2868. 3147.
3278. 3390. 3710. 4013. 4891. 5098. 5190.

Assemblies of God - Education

3707.

Baptists - Education
(See also under names of Baptist institutions.)

103. 104. 112. 247. 248. 249. 251. 547.
619. 677. 694. 810. 820. 840. 866. 898.
913. 921. 1033. 1035. 1048. 1449. (Cont.)

Baptists - Education (Cont.)

```
1479.  1588.  1641.  1722.  1783.  1913.  1960.
2060.  2061.  2062.  2063.  2226.  2249.  2344.
2367.  2371.  2526.  2611.  2639.  2711.  2728.
2747.  2754.  2837.  3280.  3411.  3506.  3577.
3609.  3669.  3718.  3762.  3847.  3876.  3976.
3977.  4077.  4163.  4173.  4360.  4667.  4674.
4780.  4881.  4941.  5085.  5087.  5096.  5109.
5149.
```

Bible Colleges
(See also under names of individual Bible colleges.)

```
  11.   12.   68.   364.  380.  381.  382.  417.  440.
 461.  494.  498.  503.  555.  563.  616.  698.
 792.  849.  948.  981.  982.  983.  1144. 1167.
1179.  1190. 1201. 1229. 1334. 1346. 1354.
1406.  1531. 1532. 1545. 1546. 1548. 1774.
1861.  1936. 2111. 2138. 2191. 2203. 2210.
2356.  2362. 2377. 2463. 2481. 2505. 2542.
2638.  2648. 2768. 2791. 2792. 3060. 3061.
3221.  3279. 3406. 3481. 3622. 3631. 3702.
3736.  3845. 3862. 4101. 4102. 4134. 4231.
4238.  4276. 4329. 4393. 4430. 4442. 4443.
4584.  4646. 4647. 4656. 4678. 4714. 4892.
5032.  5101. 5102. 5130. 5131. 5132. 5151.
```

Black Americans

```
  52.  157.  167.  263.  379.  409.  548.  549.
 704.  732.  775.  863.  874.  897.  930.  1009.
1034.  1037. 1038. 1057. 1182. 1183. 1228.
1291.  1292. 1298. 1317. 1349. 1401. 1403.
1437.  1480. 1496. 1582. 1805. 1840. 1882.
1929.  1979. 2002. 2007. 2008. 2009. 2010.
2175.  2233. 2258. 2259. 2282. 2475. 2483.
2581.  2582. 2583. 2626. 2649. 2650. 2687.
2755.  2804. 2859. 2860. 2942. 2991. 2992.
2993.  3031. 3071. 3105. 3122. 3197. 3248.
3256.  3422. 3432. 3487. 3506. 3548. 3621.
3668.  3669. 3718. 3748. 3749. 3750. 3772.
3783.  3784. 3785. 3786. 3787. 3788. 3790.
3791.  3792. 3793. 3794. 3795. 3796. 3875.
4032.  4073. 4075. 4093. 4105. 4112. 4114.
4218.  4264. 4437. 4441. 4474. 4498. 4531.
4580.  4586. 4588. 4602. 4692. 4694. 4816.
4849.  5094. 5095. 5156. 5157. 5172. 5181.
5194.
```

Brethren - Education
(See also under names of Brethren institutions.)

395. 431. 470. 3429. 4190. 4609.

Canada - Theological Education

3951.

Christian and Missionary Alliance - Education
(See also under name of Christian and Missionary
Alliance institution.)

3874.

Christian Churches - Education
(See also under names of Christian Churches
institutions.)

114. 159. 343. 349. 418. 459. 543. 573.
585. 674. 676. 937. 1145. 1274. 1458.
1695. 1757. 2144. 3010. 3436. 3652. 3653.
3918. 4116. 4647. 5161.

Church and Seminary

332. 361. 424. 535. 579. 642. 706. 723.
784. 785. 786. 827. 880. 882. 885. 947.
990. 1014. 1041. 1070. 1114. 1186. 1258.
1381. 1564. 1650. 1735. 1741. 1753. 1841.
1871. 1891. 1914. 1932. 1989. 2023. 2040.
2257. 2333. 2414. 2474. 2486. 2675. 2676.
2677. 2756. 2856. 2943. 2956. 3017. 3090.
3130. 3140. 3179. 3204. 3274. 3348. 3374.
3494. 3535. 3542. 3579. 3594. 3724. 3727.
3765. 3794. 3917. 3946. 3957. 4059. 4072.
4075. 4078. 4082. 4153. 4219. 4229. 4387.
4448. 4452. 4471. 4485. 4486. 4553. 4702.
4705. 4844. 4852. 4853. 4854. 4961. 4969.
4997. 5090. 5100. 5127. 5135. 5179. 5221.

Church of the Nazarene - Education
(See also under name of Church of the Nazarene
institution.)

3018.

Clinical Pastoral Education
(See Pastoral Care)

Colleges

17.   52.   71.   91.   130.   154.   157.   191.   199.
259.   272.   276.   349.   353.   354.   357.   358.
360.   420.   463.   547.   573.   605.   672.   674.
717.   770.   771.   773.   866.   874.   993.   1033.
1034.   1035.   1036.   1048.   1078.   1170.   1187.
1207.   1259.   1291.   1394.   1433.   1546.   1633.
1695.   1716.   1743.   1757.   1994.   1995.   2008.
2010.   2199.   2249.   2364.   2375.   2422.   2488.
2565.   2574.   2581.   2718.   2774.   2881.   3103.
3126.   3328.   3368.   3387.   3390.   3399.   3429.
3500.   3609.   3621.   3652.   3653.   3721.   3891.
3958.   3978.   4032.   4114.   4179.   4227.   4425.
4467.   4637.   4694.   4889.   4890.   4917.   5055.
5067.   5070.   5103.   5161.

Congregationalists – Education
(See also under names of Congregationalist institutions.)

280.   977.   1000.   1010.   1120.   2846.   2865.
3596.   3597.   3598.   3599.   3600.   3601.   3602.
3603.   3604.   3605.   3674.   4246.   4440.   4544.
4553.   4661.   4822.   4823.   5081.   5083.   5084.

Continuing Education

21.   26.   27.   28.   29.   30.   31.   39.   61.   143.
202.   304.   309.   310.   311.   320.   329.   476.
599.   630.   631.   662.   743.   906.   908.   920.
942.   1004.   1331.   1398.   1443.   1464.   1536.
1537.   1538.   1539.   1540.   1541.   1542.   1623.
1969.   1982.   2004.   2005.   2006.   2074.   2075.
2076.   2078.   2102.   2121.   2239.   2312.   2349.
2391.   2392.   2485.   2513.   2636.   2693.   2702.
2779.   2847.   2874.   3055.   3104.   3106.   3108.
3173.   3225.   3272.   3371.   3375.   3434.   3504.
3559.   3565.   3572.   3639.   3664.   3670.   3704.
3807.   3812.   3813.   3848.   3892.   3894.   3970.
3971.   4068.   4073.   4220.   4251.   4320.   4366.
4367.   4386.   4571.   4685.   4701.   4711.   4851.
4939.   5039.   5052.   5220.

Cooperation

13.   292.   426.   477.   570.   846.   887.   898.
923.   924.   925.   926.   1067.   1068.   1071.
1082.   1252.   1412.   1485.   1527.   1554.   1717.
1790.   2018.   2105.   2162.   2247.   2269.   2474.
2484.   2595.   2714.   2745.   3111.   3306.   3424.
3825.   3936.   4035.   4388.   4500.   4529.   4558.
4719.   4898.   4983.

Curriculum

35. 89. 141. 164. 173. 340. 364. 415.
458. 466. 478. 529. 572. 587. 601. 732.
748. 751. 812. 875. 900. 915. 917. 973.
997. 996. 999. 1022. 1047. 1111. 1130.
1286. 1290. 1299. 1318. 1332. 1343. 1345.
1352. 1408. 1432. 1454. 1470. 1568. 1596.
1597. 1632. 1696. 1727. 1787. 1826. 1865.
1936. 1967. 1890. 1992. 2021. 2055. 2056.
2080. 2104. 2111. 2224. 2261. 2276. 2281.
2294. 2317. 2320. 2321. 2324. 2350. 2357.
2444. 2460. 2468. 2561. 2622. 2644. 2645.
2775. 2834. 2841. 2999. 3015. 3056. 3089.
3298. 3389. 3406. 3414. 3437. 3545. 3563.
3578. 3593. 3622. 3635. 3698. 3758. 3784.
3821. 3835. 3857. 3884. 3955. 3972. 3989.
4018. 4026. 4072. 4084. 4170. 4193. 4272.
4276. 4291. 4322. 4329. 4445. 4466. 4482.
4501. 4502. 4530. 4535. 4540. 4669. 4728.
4739. 4760. 4772. 4804. 4821. 4834. 4850.
4883. 4885. 4887. 4892. 4974. 5012. 5027.
5051. 5116. 5143. 5238.

Curriculum - Bible

115. 153. 269. 383. 384. 638. 639. 790.
930. 976. 1025. 1107. 1215. 1243. 1335.
1458. 1489. 1520. 1572. 1616. 1653. 1977.
2463. 2623. 2633. 2634. 2796. 3075. 3328.
3798. 3800. 3965. 4092. 4122. 4172. 4377.
4468. 4539. 4787. 5059.

Curriculum - Biblical Languages

265. 334. 383. 735. 1112. 1122. 1282.
1312. 1313. 1638. 1639. 1693. 1815. 1817.
1819. 1824. 1886. 2197. 2706. 2732. 2743.
2838. 2908. 3002. 3201. 3629. 3991. 4204.
4383. 4542. 4576. 4578.

Curriculum - Christian Education
(See Religious Education.)

Curriculum - Church History

200. 201. 268. 721. 1319. 2629. 2637.
3188. 3193. 3309. 3716. 4186. 4345. 4611.
4802. 5173.

Curriculum - Classics

396. 822. 823. 2732. 3216. 4377.

Curriculum - Homiletics

281. 404. 1056. 1678. 1970. 2611. 3191.
3192. 3511. 3693. 4198. 4273. 4443. 5101.

Curriculum - Music

296. 935. 1399. 2025. 2165. 2216. 2481.
3325. 3963. 4111. 4113. 4123. 4124.

Curriculum - Speech

285. 303. 731. 814. 815. 816. 817. 2114.
2710. 2711. 3007. 3842. 4071. 4617. 5101.
5144.

Curriculum - Theology

141. 172. 268. 404. 479. 671. 1364. 1755.
3273. 3289. 3732. 3767. 4122. 4159. 4162.
4280. 4282. 4361. 4539. 5223. 5236.

D. Min. Degrees

19. 23. 780. 844. 1452. 1651. 1890. 2052.
2519. 2520. 2522. 2807. 2808. 3008. 3148.
3190. 4058. 4079. 4395. 4470. 4471. 4709.
4720.

Directories

11. 88. 179. 381. 382. 621. 1137. 1138.
1139. 1140. 1141. 1142. 1143. 1358. 1494.
3534. 3565. 3833. 3920. 3921. 3922. 3923.
3924. 3925. 3926. 3927. 3929. 3930. 4962.
5019. 5020.

Ecumenism

292. 473. 509. 602. 627. 839. 899. 900.
923. 938. 1249. 1250. 1251. 1252. 1253.
1463. 1505. 1674. 1690. 1713. 1884. 1910.
1890. 2105. 2142. 2159. 2427. 2504. 2564.
2818. 2970. 3065. 3088. 3132. 3142. 3205.
3239. 3747. 3901. 3931. 4378. 4450. 4461.
4627. 4643. 4783. 4784. 4831. 4982. 5167.

Episcopalians - Education
(See also under names of Episcopal institutions.)

17. 298. 394. 400. 421. 647. 684. 770.
771. 773. 776. 845. 871. 973. 993. 1100.
1207. 1214. 1224. 1287. 1375. 1396. (Cont.)

Episcopalians - Education (Cont.)

2013. 2036. 2087. 2188. 2523. 2570. 2588.
2778. 2831. 2941. 3057. 3226. 3236. 3488.
3540. 3564. 3566. 3567. 3630. 3721. 3852.
4060. 4349. 4741. 4763. 4862. 4899. 5033.
5163.

Faculty

90. 167. 196. 197. 338. 464. 553. 581.
589. 667. 703. 1094. 1097. 1193. 1331.
1360. 1405. 1457. 1571. 1599. 1642. 1719.
1784. 2168. 2362. 2377. 2456. 2525. 2647.
2703. 2812. 2821. 2848. 2958. 3195. 3259.
3303. 3381. 3425. 3455. 3463. 3540. 3583.
3688. 3702. 3741. 3907. 3987. 4016. 4039.
4143. 4169. 4249. 4269. 4296. 4381. 4434.
4472. 4967. 5089. 5234.

Field Education

18. 51. 236. 267. 305. 306. 365. 367.
480. 495. 1199. 1397. 1415. 1416. 1470.
1500. 1669. 1795. 2059. 2119. 2238. 2250.
2280. 2589. 2600. 2873. 3037. 3254. 3301.
3346. 3512. 3513. 3665. 3778. 4187. 4235.
4302. 4321. 4348. 4464. 4716. 4731. 4786.
4822. 4823. 4840. 4925. 5035. 5099. 5100.
5126. 5136. 5137. 5160. 5247. 5248.

Financing

228. 544. 629. 1110. 1132. 1224. 1266.
1361. 1436. 1516. 1517. 1518. 1570. 1689.
1737. 2036. 2108. 2122. 2128. 2145. 2179.
2367. 2483. 2562. 2666. 2754. 2809. 2844.
2943. 3322. 3403. 3438. 3623. 3624. 3626.
3627. 3691. 3692. 3769. 3789. 3823. 3878.
4118. 4248. 4385. 4386. 4464. 4557. 4565.
4693. 4694. 4855. 4856. 4864. 4868. 4946.
4970.

Friends - Education

2381. 4712.

German Influence on American Theological Education

42. 221. 491. 1125. 1126. 1599. 1681.
1919. 2189. 2190. 3144. 3277. 3352. 3353.
3354. 3762. 3880. 3881. 3897. 4046. 4164.
4278. 4375. 4583. 5043. 5048.

Germany - Theological Education

124. 561. 643. 739. 1486. 1832. 1873.
2060. 2434. 3760. 3763. 3883. 4306.

Great Britain - Theological Education

129. 260. 385. 623. 830. 845. 1023. 1098.
1386. 1509. 1513. 1627. 1684. 1880. 1903.
2184. 2243. 2245. 2376. 2411. 2789. 3667.
3806. 3834. 3850. 3982. 4230. 4762. 4907.
5162.

Laity, Training of

322. 1053. 1297. 1330. 1372. 1963. 2400.
2966. 3392. 3454. 3576. 3831. 3916. 4028.
4349. 4534. 4944. 5022.

Libraries, Theological

22. 62. 98. 109. 110. 190. 292. 545. 635.
681. 698. 967. 1045. 1046. 1086. 1089.
1095. 1134. 1156. 1230. 1385. 1393. 1419.
1535. 1549. 1717. 1718. 1740. 1771. 1887.
1931. 1941. 2110. 2269. 2291. 2390. 2421.
2538. 2610. 2631. 2648. 2724. 2769. 2773.
2822. 2875. 3164. 3200. 3267. 3268. 3407.
3412. 3424. 3742. 3771. 3833. 3908. 3909.
4014. 4035. 4128. 4129. 4130. 4131. 4132.
4133. 4206. 4207. 4399. 4444. 4529. 4546.
4707. 4708. 4826. 4898. 5065. 5093. 5219.

Lutherans - Education
(See also under names of Lutheran institutions.)

7. 8. 54. 64. 107. 122. 152. 190. 191.
200. 201. 202. 203. 213. 283. 284. 287.
351. 353. 354. 355. 356. 358. 388. 422.
446. 463. 487. 504. 726. 728. 730. 838.
1028. 1203. 1205. 1206. 1294. 1297. 1317.
1340. 1341. 1353. 1360. 1505. 1507. 1591.
1621. 1673. 1681. 1682. 1746. 1776. 1777.
1778. 1779. 1794. 1847. 1869. 1870. 1893.
1894. 1896. 1898. 1908. 2037. 2038. 2089.
2223. 2283. 2292. 2351. 2423. 2430. 2478.
2612. 2613. 2614. 2766. 2878. 2883. 2938.
3126. 3209. 3276. 3285. 3315. 3326. 3421.
3468. 3535. 3671. 3686. 3741. 3783. 3846.
3888. 3889. 3907. 3954. 3955. 3963. 4053.
4059. 4170. 4247. 4265. 4385. 4400. 4460.
4765. 4772. 4773. 4863. 4890. 4897. (Cont.)

Lutherans - Education (Cont.)

4948. 4956. 4988. 5061. 5107. 5108. 5139.
5196. 5213.

Mennonites - Education

333. 1167. 1928. 4858.

Methodists - Education
(See also under names of Methodist institutions.)

15. 52. 157. 215. 220. 234. 256. 342.
474. 483. 505. 556. 605. 622. 685. 717.
727. 744. 753. 795. 863. 909. 941. 956.
957. 992. 994. 1019. 1036. 1042. 1115.
1155. 1216. 1261. 1262. 1264. 1268. 1278.
1291. 1295. 1309. 1384. 1410. 1430. 1439.
1440. 1482. 1477. 1558. 1559. 1560. 1561.
1562. 1563. 1711. 1716. 1792. 1868. 1882.
1993. 1994. 1995. 2066. 2082. 2098. 2113.
2205. 2219. 2306. 2315. 2347. 2348. 2413.
2458. 2459. 2506. 2690. 2691. 2774. 2788.
2799. 2885. 2886. 2894. 2895. 2896. 2897.
2900. 2901. 2905. 2906. 2928. 2974. 2987.
2995. 2998. 3032. 3043. 3098. 3175. 3224.
3225. 3235. 3236. 3268. 3317. 3318. 3319.
3320. 3321. 3362. 3408. 3416. 3458. 3509.
3548. 3683. 3685. 3777. 3779. 3820. 3919.
3973. 3974. 4032. 4033. 4073. 4147. 4176.
4189. 4211. 4243. 4261. 4273. 4283. 4298.
4305. 4363. 4364. 4411. 4425. 4441. 4504.
4506. 4599. 4608. 4634. 4687. 4740. 4737.
4768. 4769. 4809. 4851. 4869. 4894. 4895.
4896. 4926. 5045. 5112. 5113. 5114. 5159.

Missionary Education

219. 252. 290. 321. 419. 448. 686. 687.
761. 891. 943. 949. 1029. 1040. 1059.
1482. 1644. 1796. 1812. 1879. 1976. 2064.
2088. 2441. 2499. 2568. 2701. 2784. 2988.
2989. 3091. 3092. 3109. 3110. 3230. 3364.
3365. 3543. 3849. 3865. 3890. 4212. 4295.
4938. 4944. 4956. 5030. 5134. 5138.

Missions

8. 34. 253. 302. 584. 621. 638. 664. 719.
986. 1069. 1160. 1281. 1338. 1339. 1366.
1376. 1588. 1637. 1652. 1790. 1885. 1944.
1947. 1948. 1989. 2016. 2029. 2127. 2135.
2169. 2286. 2367. 2368. 2369. 2370. (Cont.)

Missions (Cont.)

2420. 2480. 2673. 2761. 3097. 3166. 3240.
3433. 3443. 3447. 3642. 3722. 3733. 3906.
4021. 4099. 4141. 4149. 4463. 4652. 4908.
5013. 5141.

Pastoral Care

25. 38. 55. 59. 60. 82. 126. 127. 166.
168. 171. 176. 179. 277. 299. 300. 313.
369. 379. 425. 426. 428. 429. 434. 471.
586. 591. 592. 593. 594. 595. 596. 597.
598. 599. 600. 610. 626. 651. 656. 657.
708. 729. 730. 749. 778. 779. 805. 807.
825. 833. 834. 936. 939. 968. 974. 1074.
1116. 1175. 1184. 1208. 1209. 1210. 1234.
1235. 1242. 1307. 1367. 1368. 1388. 1455.
1462. 1488. 1514. 1523. 1579. 1580. 1592.
1593. 1596. 1611. 1630. 1648. 1658. 1664.
1686. 1734. 1739. 1756. 1764. 1769. 1772.
1773. 1791. 1803. 1810. 1846. 1862. 1866.
1922. 1926. 1937. 1939. 1950. 1951. 1952.
1953. 1954. 1956. 1959. 1962. 1971. 1983.
1996. 1997. 1998. 2001. 2017. 2019. 2026.
2054. 2073. 2076. 2077. 2079. 2124. 2149.
2157. 2187. 2209. 2229. 2230. 2234. 2235.
2236. 2237. 2266. 2267. 2296. 2303. 2308.
2310. 2313. 2353. 2397. 2403. 2404. 2405.
2428. 2457. 2512. 2513. 2528. 2557. 2558.
2643. 2650. 2720. 2748. 2749. 2752. 2753.
2781. 2857. 2869. 2876. 2996. 3045. 3136.
3214. 3241. 3252. 3255. 3257. 3258. 3260.
3290. 3291. 3292. 3293. 3294. 3295. 3296.
3297. 3357. 3363. 3383. 3391. 3417. 3418.
3460. 3470. 3501. 3505. 3558. 3570. 3571.
3588. 3589. 3607. 3616. 3641. 3648. 3666.
3675. 3676. 3726. 3729. 3868. 3896. 3903.
3956. 3959. 4041. 4042. 4043. 4057. 4086.
4110. 4154. 4191. 4192. 4193. 4241. 4242.
4258. 4286. 4287. 4288. 4316. 4317. 4328.
4334. 4344. 4354. 4355. 4368. 4370. 4373.
4393. 4405. 4408. 4410. 4418. 4432. 4449.
4462. 4495. 4587. 4590. 4621. 4626. 4627.
4630. 4682. 4683. 4690. 4767. 4771. 4778.
4813. 4814. 4993. 4995. 4996. 5075. 5076.
5077. 5122. 5123. 5124. 5125. 5126. 5170.
5187. 5199. 5206. 5207. 5209. 5212. 5222.
5246. 5247.

Practics

82. 402. 406. 435. 532. 841. 1442. 1502.
1770. 1859. 1958. 2027. 2164. 2335. 2443.
2959. 2992. 3013. 3283. 3466. 3815. 3832.
4157. 4197. 4326. 4410. 4465. 4985.

Presbyterians - Education
(See also under names of Presbyterian institutions.)

45. 58. 69. 70. 79. 118. 183. 186. 187.
188. 189. 227. 516. 534. 537. 571. 963.
1073. 1308. 1328. 1433. 1456. 1519. 1603.
1612. 1613. 1614. 1703. 1732. 2068. 2120.
2422. 2574. 2708. 2718. 2737. 2751. 2939.
2953. 2966. 3050. 3220. 3316. 3360. 3361.
3369. 3400. 3517. 3518. 3519. 3520. 3521.
3522. 3523. 3524. 3525. 3526. 3527. 3528.
3529. 3530. 3753. 4039. 4148. 4164. 4165.
4278. 4448. 4467. 4619. 4710. 4758. 4759.
4781. 4902. 4990. 5083. 5084. 5103.

Pre-Seminary Education

20. 71. 223. 225. 297. 445. 512. 556.
665. 697. 731. 822. 831. 832. 868. 876.
877. 879. 952. 983. 1016. 1025. 1233.
1245. 1246. 1394. 1696. 1868. 1894. 1991.
2039. 2133. 2283. 2325. 2334. 2430. 2669.
2861. 3011. 3015. 3016. 3270. 3415. 3468.
3482. 3532. 3533. 3541. 3978. 4044. 4045.
4061. 4208. 4275. 4372. 4488. 4618. 4637.
4939. 4988. 5109. 5226.

Private Theological Instruction

48. 69. 240. 241. 1430. 1732. 2151. 2215.
2559. 2871. 2928. 3012. 3369. 3401. 3488.
3495. 3553. 3986. 4067. 4524. 4536. 4608.
4734. 4741. 4742. 4807. 4808. 5066.

Reform

264. 541. 559. 1017. 1087. 1382. 1806.
2062. 2134. 2174. 2444. 3021. 3271. 3587.
3655. 3661. 3662. 3680. 3757. 4136. 4239.
4362. 4625. 4638. 4797. 4872. 4994.

Reformed Churches - Education
(See also under names of Reformed institutions.)

147. 148. 178. 537. 1150. 1608. 1905.
2022. 2571. 2826. 3620. 3657. 3659. (Cont.)

Reformed Churches - Education (Cont.)

3711. 3712. 4655. 4745. 4936. 5214.

Religious Education

276. 321. 331. 450. 451. 476. 640. 760.
762. 808. 855. 861. 886. 927. 928. 985.
1080. 1158. 1292. 1487. 1624. 1691. 1811.
1840. 1902. 1915. 2020. 2083. 2160. 2175.
2196. 2222. 2361. 2454. 2532. 2533. 2549.
2576. 2620. 2688. 2689. 2731. 2863. 2917.
2924. 2934. 2940. 3014. 3123. 3124. 3217.
3218. 3448. 3507. 3682. 3736. 4049. 4078.
4105. 4194. 4195. 4196. 4238. 4324. 4481.
4570. 4744. 4839. 4842. 4873. 4963. 5019.
5020. 5102. 5136. 5186. 5188. 5242.

Roman Catholics - Education

16. 80. 671. 733. 742. 782. 938. 1043.
1432. 1881. 1922. 2208. 2212. 2421. 2495.
2496. 2507. 2543. 2590. 2699. 2745. 2986.
3040. 3077. 3082. 3168. 3314. 3333. 3462.
3478. 3479. 3480. 3655. 3699. 3842. 3844.
3892. 3932. 3996. 4098. 4139. 4572. 4680.
4835. 5017. 5158.

Rural Pastors

39. 373. 413. 646. 793. 890. 1031. 1192.
1400. 1401. 1606. 1679. 2214. 2304. 2366.
2659. 2660. 2768. 3705. 3748. 3779. 3782.
4034. 4176. 4272. 4684.

Southern Baptists - Education
(See also under names of Southern Baptist institutions.)

90. 173. 296. 391. 540. 541. 760. 942.
966. 986. 1187. 1315. 1323. 1324. 1325.
1327. 1514. 1534. 1607. 1965. 2053. 2482.
2762. 3026. 3079. 3117. 3172. 3227. 3229.
3368. 3378. 3380. 3399. 4087. 4142. 4218.
4219. 4227. 4262. 4494. 4908.

Teaching Methods

1422. 2014. 2338. 2342. 2426. 2534. 2907.
2933. 3583. 3645. 3939. 3979. 4030. 4262.
4903.

Testing

649.	683.	689.	690.	692.	705.	709.	768.
1455.	1501.	1511.	1938.	1957.	2232.	2290.	
2394.	2580.	2657.	3135.	3359.	3590.	3615.	
3648.	3714.	3774.	3946.	3947.	3948.	4237.	
4303.	4492.	4613.	4922.	4923.	4924.	4926.	
5148.							

Theological Education - Post-1860
(This heading covers general materials or materials
not easily fitting into another classification.)

2.	5.	34.	40.	41.	43.	44.	65.	66.	67.
73.	81.	97.	99.	100.	117.	120.	122.	128.	
131.	145.	162.	170.	194.	212.	214.	218.		
230.	289.	294.	307.	341.	347.	359.	362.		
363.	368.	370.	371.	372.	374.	377.	386.		
390.	393.	407.	414.	437.	438.	439.	441.		
452.	460.	462.	468.	472.	481.	485.	486.		
488.	501.	507.	508.	510.	511.	513.	514.		
515.	524.	536.	552.	562.	567.	575.	577.		
578.	580.	582.	613.	617.	618.	645.	660.		
678.	682.	710.	714.	722.	752.	766.	787.		
788.	801.	821.	828.	835.	837.	842.	853.		
873.	881.	883.	884.	889.	902.	946.	951.		
954.	955.	958.	965.	970.	971.	975.	980.		
987.	995.	1001.	1005.	1006.	1007.	1012.			
1013.	1020.	1064.	1065.	1083.	1085.	1088.			
1099.	1106.	1118.	1129.	1135.	1147.	1148.			
1149.	1154.	1168.	1172.	1173.	1177.	1180.			
1194.	1195.	1196.	1204.	1217.	1225.	1236.			
1237.	1260.	1265.	1275.	1276.	1289.	1296.			
1301.	1302.	1314.	1320.	1322.	1347.	1355.			
1369.	1371.	1377.	1389.	1392.	1411.	1421.			
1431.	1434.	1435.	1445.	1461.	1474.	1475.			
1478.	1497.	1498.	1508.	1515.	1521.	1529.			
1553.	1573.	1575.	1589.	1598.	1602.	1631.			
1635.	1636.	1640.	1645.	1657.	1685.	1712.			
1715.	1730.	1775.	1786.	1789.	1797.	1818.			
1825.	1827.	1835.	1838.	1843.	1844.	1874.			
1875.	1907.	1911.	1912.	1927.	1933.	1942.			
1943.	1955.	1964.	1974.	2000.	2015.	2024.			
2028.	2032.	2043.	2050.	2057.	2084.	2099.			
2118.	2136.	2140.	2141.	2148.	2163.	2166.			
2167.	2171.	2172.	2183.	2185.	2200.	2201.			
2204.	2206.	2293.	2298.	2301.	2314.	2322.			
2323.	2329.	2336.	2337.	2345.	2346.	2352.			
2355.	2359.	2373.	2374.	2382.	2388.	2389.			
2396.	2398.	2399.	2415.	2418.	2419.	2424.			
2436.	2446.	2447.	2448.	2462.	2466.	2487.			
2508.	2509.	2548.	2551.	2560.	2563.	2569.			
2572.	2593.	2598.	2603.	2609.	2621.	(Cont.)			

```
2651.  2653.  2662.  2663.  2664.  2670.  2674.
2688.  2715.  2721.  2723.  2727.  2733.  2734.
2735.  2736.  2738.  2744.  2764.  2777.  2795.
2801.  2803.  2815.  2820.  2824.  2836.  2840.
2845.  2850.  2851.  2855.  2864.  2867.  2870.
2881.  2882.  2916.  2918.  2926.  2931.  2932.
2935.  2946.  2957.  2960.  2961.  2962.  2963.
2967.  2984.  3000.  3019.  3022.  3028.  3039.
3049.  3052.  3053.  3058.  3078.  3080.  3085.
3094.  3095.  3096.  3118.  3119.  3120.  3125.
3139.  3143.  3160.  3163.  3165.  3170.  3171.
3181.  3194.  3198.  3202.  3207.  3211.  3222.
3223.  3231.  3242.  3243.  3244.  3247.  3249.
3263.  3275.  3302.  3310.  3329.  3331.  3334.
3339.  3388.  3405.  3413.  3435.  3452.  3461.
3471.  3483.  3484.  3486.  3508.  3546.  3552.
3554.  3557.  3561.  3562.  3591.  3613.  3614.
3619.  3633.  3640.  3644.  3708.  3720.  3731.
3740.  3753.  3755.  3759.  3766.  3776.  3780.
3808.  3814.  3829.  3838.  3839.  3859.  3877.
3893.  3895.  3902.  3904.  3914.  3915.  3934.
3937.  3938.  3941.  3942.  3950.  3966.  3980.
3988.  3998.  3999.  4002.  4003.  4004.  4005.
4006.  4007.  4009.  4017.  4019.  4024.  4031.
4036.  4040.  4047.  4048.  4052.  4065.  4076.
4081.  4097.  4137.  4140.  4146.  4150.  4155.
4158.  4160.  4168.  4202.  4203.  4225.  4228.
4233.  4240.  4252.  4253.  4254.  4257.  4271.
4277.  4309.  4330.  4347.  4356.  4384.  4389.
4391.  4392.  4404.  4412.  4413.  4417.  4420.
4436.  4453.  4454.  4455.  4456.  4457.  4477.
4483.  4489.  4491.  4503.  4507.  4508.  4509.
4510.  4511.  4512.  4513.  4514.  4515.  4516.
4517.  4518.  4519.  4520.  4522.  4523.  4525.
4526.  4527.  4532.  4533.  4537.  4538.  4541.
4550.  4551.  4552.  4554.  4556.  4559.  4568.
4569.  4575.  4579.  4593.  4595.  4596.  4597.
4601.  4635.  4649.  4650.  4654.  4673.  4675.
4676.  4681.  4686.  4688.  4703.  4704.  4706.
4715.  4723.  4727.  4729.  4733.  4774.  4782.
4792.  4793.  4803.  4819.  4824.  4833.  4835.
4836.  4837.  4838.  4841.  4843.  4845.  4846.
4848.  4860.  4870.  4875.  4876.  4877.  4886.
4919.  4929.  4940.  4947.  4950.  4957.  4959.
4964.  4968.  4980.  4998.  5008.  5009.  5016.
5018.  5042.  5046.  5047.  5053.  5056.  5060.
5069.  5073.  5074.  5086.  5104.  5105.  5110.
5111.  5115.  5118.  5119.  5151.  5166.  5169.
5177.  5178.  5182.  5185.  5208.  5218.  5224.
5225.  5227.  5229.  5233.  5235.  5237.  5239.
5240.  5241.  5249.
```

Theological Education - Pre-1860
(This heading covers general materials or materials
not easily fitting into another classification.)

14.   63.   72.   79.   182.   240.   241.   315.   330.
375.   403.   449.   456.   457.   493.   516.   575.
603.   856.   860.   914.   1072.   1102.   1124.
1263.   1267.   1269.   1270.   1271.   1272.   1273.
1283.   1304.   1438.   1494.   1543.   1567.   1759.
1935.   1966.   2070.   2146.   2147.   2150.   2154.
2228.   2409.   2635.   2651.   2652.   2653.   2709.
2825.   2951.   2952.   2972.   2973.   3046.   3115.
3287.   3288.   3308.   3338.   3350.   3402.   3580.
3581.   3582.   3649.   3650.   3651.   3703.   3802.
4103.   4104.   4201.   4270.   4279.   4390.   4406.
4407.   4429.   4436.   4545.   4555.   4628.   4631.
4632.   4662.   4770.   4806.   4879.   4952.   5010.
5133.   5198.

Theological Encyclopedia

4583.

Theological Students

16.   47.   49.   50.   83.   84.   85.   87.   92.   93.
163.   169.   177.   254.   257.   345.   351.   352.
427.   443.   453.   458.   482.   496.   497.   530.
531.   533.   558.   590.   625.   636.   641.   644.
648.   683.   689.   690.   691.   692.   709.   712.
724.   736.   740.   750.   759.   768.   784.   850.
851.   859.   870.   892.   978.   979.   1032.   1043.
1052.   1079.   1084.   1091.   1092.   1153.   1203.
1231.   1337.   1359.   1373.   1374.   1379.   1402.
1428.   1446.   1447.   1457.   1476.   1495.   1528.
1544.   1578.   1582.   1587.   1604.   1619.   1647.
1708.   1719.   1721.   1731.   1733.   1742.   1758.
1780.   1821.   1883.   1885.   1897.   1899.   1906.
1916.   1921.   1930.   1934.   1944.   1949.   1958.
1972.   2046.   2049.   2073.   2085.   2106.   2137.
2139.   2153.   2186.   2212.   2220.   2264.   2275.
2284.   2287.   2288.   2289.   2290.   2295.   2306.
2318.   2325.   2327.   2328.   2339.   2340.   2358.
2372.   2386.   2387.   2395.   2410.   2470.   2492.
2493.   2497.   2515.   2521.   2530.   2546.   2547.
2554.   2590.   2614.   2618.   2632.   2665.   2695.
2757.   2759.   2760.   2771.   2802.   2804.   2816.
2817.   2826.   2827.   2828.   2830.   2842.   2858.
2944.   2971.   2977.   3006.   3034.   3035.   3057.
3063.   3064.   3082.   3083.   3086.   3113.   3114.
3146.   3174.   3180.   3212.   3261.   3333.   3337.
3340.   3348.   3355.   3450.   3453.   3456.   3457.
3496.   3502.   3531.   3555.   3566.   3568.   (Cont.)

Theological Students (Cont.)

3569.	3579.	3587.	3590.	3612.	3630.	3643.
3700.	3707.	3709.	3734.	3738.	3739.	3744.
3746.	3803.	3804.	3806.	3816.	3827.	3830.
3844.	3851.	3856.	3869.	3870.	3872.	3886.
3887.	3962.	3981.	3985.	3992.	3993.	3994.
3995.	3997.	4001.	4010.	4011.	4012.	4094.
4095.	4098.	4109.	4117.	4134.	4175.	4205.
4209.	4214.	4215.	4234.	4237.	4265.	4293.
4303.	4304.	4331.	4336.	4343.	4358.	4374.
4379.	4380.	4382.	4409.	4419.	4439.	4499.
4505.	4566.	4591.	4620.	4636.	4639.	4658.
4665.	4679.	4713.	4717.	4732.	4761.	4775.
4777.	4785.	4788.	4789.	4794.	4796.	4799.
4800.	4817.	4828.	4829.	4865.	4921.	4931.
4934.	4984.	4987.	4989.	5004.	5006.	5013.
5037.	5038.	5040.	5050.	5057.	5063.	5079.
5128.	5153.	5158.	5167.	5172.	5184.	5210.

Theological Students - Spiritual Life

101.	962.	1198.	1288.	1493.	1909.	2240.
2958.	3100.	3475.	3822.	3944.	4027.	4074.
4084.	4216.	4577.	4699.	4776.	4888.	

Theses

6.	41.	64.	67.	84.	89.	130.	160.	173.
199.	215.	254.	267.	281.	294.	296.	304.	
306.	329.	364.	366.	423.	440.	449.	453.	
470.	480.	503.	537.	548.	563.	572.	587.	
602.	604.	611.	616.	626.	631.	648.	650.	
664.	689.	694.	697.	705.	712.	728.	760.	
792.	808.	814.	825.	836.	844.	849.	864.	
867.	876.	886.	892.	935.	936.	937.	942.	
948.	973.	974.	978.	1004.	1019.	1038.		
1042.	1052.	1064.	1091.	1093.	1132.	1136.		
1144.	1167.	1175.	1179.	1184.	1190.	1199.		
1201.	1203.	1224.	1229.	1260.	1297.	1318.		
1333.	1337.	1354.	1387.	1406.	1408.	1417.		
1422.	1462.	1464.	1485.	1488.	1491.	1507.		
1514.	1546.	1548.	1580.	1600.	1607.	1611.		
1624.	1664.	1672.	1686.	1719.	1742.	1748.		
1769.	1771.	1780.	1800.	1833.	1835.	1861.		
1862.	1887.	1897.	1899.	1909.	1921.	1926.		
1930.	1931.	1936.	1939.	1970.	1993.	2000.		
2017.	2025.	2056.	2058.	2059.	2066.	2079.		
2102.	2111.	2120.	2124.	2132.	2144.	2165.		
2191.	2203.	2216.	2217.	2230.	2232.	2240.		
2250.	2283.	2287.	2290.	2291.	2294.	2304.		
2306.	2344.	2353.	2358.	2367.	2372.	2377.		
2388.	2392.	2393.	2395.	2406.	2407.	(Cont.)		

Theses (Cont.)

2410.	2430.	2459.	2463.	2470.	2481.	2492.
2497.	2505.	2530.	2533.	2555.	2587.	2604.
2608.	2611.	2636.	2638.	2644.	2650.	2652.
2709.	2754.	2755.	2759.	2771.	2775.	2799.
2828.	2829.	2830.	2842.	2843.	2869.	2944.
2964.	2966.	3018.	3025.	3026.	3037.	3057.
3083.	3112.	3117.	3172.	3173.	3174.	3198.
3199.	3214.	3225.	3285.	3357.	3363.	3396.
3427.	3434.	3448.	3468.	3481.	3500.	3507.
3512.	3555.	3579.	3607.	3616.	3629.	3630.
3631.	3635.	3648.	3654.	3666.	3670.	3681.
3702.	3707.	3719.	3726.	3741.	3755.	3765.
3816.	3821.	3827.	3839.	3842.	3846.	3851.
3857.	3868.	3869.	3875.	3881.	3910.	3955.
3959.	3960.	3963.	3975.	4026.	4030.	4036.
4039.	4045.	4052.	4068.	4071.	4072.	4073.
4095.	4098.	4113.	4116.	4117.	4118.	4131.
4134.	4154.	4170.	4187.	4200.	4201.	4227.
4231.	4237.	4238.	4258.	4262.	4276.	4287.
4304.	4348.	4358.	4385.	4393.	4408.	4418.
4419.	4420.	4432.	4439.	4440.	4442.	4443.
4445.	4474.	4585.	4613.	4620.	4621.	4634.
4636.	4647.	4679.	4690.	4701.	4711.	4713.
4717.	4720.	4732.	4745.	4779.	4780.	4789.
4800.	4801.	4817.	4839.	4841.	4851.	4863.
4881.	4889.	4892.	4902.	4903.	4912.	4918.
4936.	4941.	4965.	4972.	4988.	5004.	5037.
5050.	5052.	5064.	5076.	5092.	5101.	5102.
5107.	5109.	5110.	5128.	5136.	5150.	5181.
5184.	5188.	5198.	5199.	5209.	5210.	5212.

Trustees

1373.	1503.	1698.	1699.	1700.	1701.	2964.
3122.	3137.	3337.	4200.	4248.	4827.	5005.

Unitarians/Universalists - Education

111. 278. 972. 2491. 3020. 3167. 3684.
4754. 4755.

United Church of Christ - Education
(See also under names of United Church of Christ
institutions.)

1830. 4756. 4757.

Universities and Colleges - Religion Courses

155. 172. 224. 574. 775. 1081. 1246. 1765.
1788. 1829. 2047. 2276. 2326. 2401. (Cont.)

Universities and Colleges - Religion Courses   (Cont.)

    2477. 2478. 2740. 2839. 2923. 2924. 3107.
    3305. 3752. 3952. 4139. 4571. 4574. 4958.
    5105.

University Divinity Schools
(See also under names of individual universities.)

    113. 132. 150. 574. 696. 1178. 2041. 2101.
    2125. 2479. 2544. 2545. 2698. 2835. 3084.
    4332. 4333. 4421. 4660.

Urban Pastors

    436. 1076. 1450. 1451. 1610. 1831. 1877.
    2214. 3055. 3282. 3469. 3706. 3797. 4085.
    4284. 4292. 4682. 4928. 4933.

Wesleyans - Education

    4585.

Women

    116. 180. 266. 348. 415. 416. 419. 423.
    502. 526. 527. 528. 533. 693. 761. 777.
    932. 984. 1050. 1060. 1232. 1316. 1404.
    1407. 1481. 1482. 1490. 1594. 1595. 1670.
    1706. 1799. 1828. 1837. 2044. 2045. 2116.
    2117. 2132. 2285. 2311. 2393. 2464. 2489.
    2501. 2502. 2503. 2730. 2819. 2852. 2884.
    2897. 2919. 2920. 2922. 2925. 3036. 3150.
    3151. 3152. 3153. 3154. 3155. 3156. 3157.
    3176. 3335. 3364. 3394. 3636. 3637. 3828.
    3837. 4008. 4029. 4106. 4107. 4521. 4582.
    4700. 4788. 4801. 4847. 4900. 4912. 4913.
    5014. 5030. 5055. 5091. 5145. 5146. 5147.
    5244.

Worship

    1018. 1202. 1387. 1709. 2103. 2433. 3101.
    3131. 4023. 4025. 4771. 5023. 5024. 5025.
    5026.

III. THEOLOGICAL SEMINARIES AND SCHOOLS, ASSOCIATIONS
AND BIBLE COLLEGES

(Denominations noted are general groupings as
classified by the Association of Theological
Schools.)

Academy of Parish Clergy

10.

Alliance Theological Seminary (Christian and
Missionary Alliance)

3543. 3544.

American Baptist Seminary of the West (Baptist)

3856.

American Education Society

93. 105. 1281. 3351. 3585. 4376. 4917.

Anderson College School of Theology (Churches of God)

4026.

Andover Newton Theological School

609. 1924. 3404. 3726.

Andover Theological Seminary

42. 133. 134. 135. 136. 137. 138. 139.
140. 141. 142. 176. 206. 207. 209. 211.
403. 670. 739. 798. 904. 1030. 1125. 1219.
1222. 1239. 1281. 1391. 1471. 1588. 1617.
1705. 1763. 1808. 1850. 1864. 1873. 2112.
2472. 2476. 2729. 2790. 2846. 3307. 3323.
3351. 3352. 3353. 3354. 3356. 3442. 3491.
3493. 3694. 3695. 3745. 3818. 4127. 4248.
4341. 4394. 4610. 4611. 4659. 4669. 4670.
4696. 4722. 4724. 4725. 4779. 4871. 4872.
4916. 5072. 5154. 5180.

Asbury Theological Seminary

6. 989. 2238. 2438. 3166. 4246. 4266.
4268. 4730.

Associate Theological Seminary (Presbyterian)

    118.

Association of Theological Schools in the United
States and Canada

    102. 177. 378. 489. 650. 711. 1137. 1233.
    1414. 1500. 1824. 2390. 2772. 3270. 3690.
    3945. 4000. 4064. 4275. 4459. 4492. 4820.
    5111. 5215. 5230. 5234.

Auburn Theological Seminary (Presbyterian)

    37. 183. 184. 185. 186. 187. 188. 189.
    1308. 2225. 2936. 4382.

Augustana Theological Seminary

    See Lutheran School of Theology at Chicago

Bangor Theological Seminary (United Church of Christ)

    794. 916. 953. 2527. 2597. 2767. 3246.
    3476. 3871. 4278. 5041.

Berkeley Divinity School (Episcopal)

    432. 1606. 1801. 3001. 3608.

Bethany Bible School (Brethren)

    2792.

Bethany Theological Seminary (Brethren)

    1321. 1887. 2350. 2540. 2937. 3957. 4825.

Bethel Theological Seminary (Baptist)

    3281. 3857. 4013.

Bexley Hall (Episcopal)

    4127. 4236.

Biblical Seminary

    See New York Theological Seminary

Bloomfield Seminary (Presbyterian-Defunct)

    2422.

Boston University (Methodist)

560. 1901. 2093. 2994. 3176. 3256. 4112.
4226.

Calvin Theological Seminary (Reformed)

672. 1094. 1096. 2431. 2432. 3642. 4549.
4787.

Candler School of Theology (Methodist)

4925.

Carrier Seminary (Methodist)

1384.

Central Baptist Theological Seminary (Baptist)

3382. 4651.

Chautauqua School of Theology (Defunct)

4298.

Chicago Theological Seminary (United Church of Christ)

1061. 2014. 3341. 3342. 3343.

Christ Seminary-Seminex (Lutheran)

33. 777. 2107. 2207. 2810. 2813. 3464.
4022.

Christian Theological Seminary (Christian Churches)

1266. 1413. 2631. 4126. 4565.

Church Divinity School of the Pacific (Episcopal)

469. 4070.

Clear Creek Mountain Preachers Bible School

3782.

Colgate Rochester Divinity School (Baptist)

301. 547. 866. 2270. 2728. 3023. 3025.
3762. 3876. 4046. 5085. 5194.

Colgate Rochester Divinity School/Bexley Hall/Crozer
Theological Seminary

5094.

Columbia Theological Seminary, Decatur, Ga.
(Presbyterian)

45. 3344. 3768.

Concordia Seminary, St. Louis (Lutheran)

9. 495. 624. 661. 756. 893. 894. 896.
1040. 1146. 1165. 1189. 1506. 1550. 1604.
2157. 2246. 2277. 2437. 2606. 2811. 2856.
2880. 2910. 2911. 2913. 2982. 3033. 3072.
3464. 3539. 3560. 3656. 3687. 3689. 3905.
3940. 3949. 3967. 4327. 4381. 4401. 4573.
4641. 4642. 5044. 5183.

Concordia Theological Seminary, Fort Wayne (Lutheran)

895. 1896. 3536. 3537. 3539. 3954. 4255.

Cooperstown Seminary (Defunct)

3336.

Crozer Theological Seminary (Baptist)

546. 1162.

Dallas Theological Seminary

648. 1027. 1420. 2051. 2542. 3681. 4223.
4714. 4861. 5129.

Disciples Divinity House

See University of Chicago

Drew University (Methodist)

119. 193. 1002. 1193. 1390. 1918. 2302.
2586. 2947. 3625. 3843. 4115. 4359. 4653.
4766. 4960. 4970.

Dubuque Seminary (Presbyterian)

2849.

Duke University (Methodist)

    804. 1011. 1929. 2152. 2280. 2445. 2473.
3490. 4161.

Eastern Baptist Theological Seminary (Baptist)

    1724. 2012. 3726.

Eden Theological Seminary (United Church of Christ)

    602. 1256. 3831.

Episcopal Divinity School (Episcopal)

    847. 1368. 1444. 1557. 1605. 3066. 3076.
3283. 4063. 4475. 4476. 4528. 5143.

Episcopal Theological Seminary of the Southwest
(Episcopal)

    408. 826. 1339. 4402.

Evanston Theological Seminary

    3306.

Everett Institute (Baptist)

    619.

Fairmount Theological Seminary (Defunct)

    4736.

Fort Wayne Bible College

    2607. 3737. 5092.

Foundation For Theological Education

    3322.

Fuller Theological Seminary

    94. 108. 1338. 1510. 1512. 1577. 2591.
4181.

Gammon Theological Center

    See Interdenominational Theological Center

Garrett-Evangelical Theological Seminary (Methodist)

245. 1305. 1566. 1901. 2690. 3234. 3268.
4167. 4359.

General Theological Seminary (Episcopal)

376. 550. 1062. 1585. 1609. 1802. 1909.
2822. 3169. 3373. 3377. 3396. 3735. 4734.
4735.

German Reformed Mission House, Wisconsin

4745.

German Theological School (Presbyterian)

1328.

Gilmanton Theological Seminary (Congregational -
Defunct)

4661. 5081.

Golden Gate Baptist Theological Seminary (Southern
Baptist)

263. 1643. 3238. 4891.

Gordon-Conwell Theological Seminary

1349. 1661. 1662. 1665. 1666. 1667. 1668.
2168. 5036.

Grace Theological Seminary

2794.

Graduate Theological Union

1133. 1251. 1680. 2269. 3943.

Hartford Seminary

217. 499. 813. 1581. 1836. 1837. 2131.
2299. 2454. 2731. 3499. 3710. 4119. 4289.
4600. 4822. 4823.

Hartwick Seminary (Lutheran - Defunct)

1847. 1848. 1895. 3910.

Harvard University

35. 36. 142. 326. 328. 433. 620. 629.
630. 669. 745. 757. 758. 848. 852. 905.
910. 976. 1003. 1044. 1054. 1255. 1298.
1303. 1419. 1547. 1718. 1849. 1850. 1851.
1852. 1853. 1854. 1855. 1856. 1857. 1858.
2011. 2042. 2069. 2211. 2279. 2297. 2429.
2504. 2514. 2599. 2625. 2646. 2797. 2800.
2959. 3020. 3041. 3042. 3054. 3081. 3138.
3162. 3232. 3262. 3344. 3407. 3573. 3574.
3575. 3595. 3678. 3700. 3799. 3801. 4199.
4234. 4293. 4294. 4351. 4415. 4444. 4548.
4689. 4798. 4880. 5036. 5054. 5071. 5078.
5080. 5082.

Hood Theological Seminary (Methodist)

2475. 3875.

Howard University

1228. 1533. 2009. 2582. 2650. 3790.

Iliff School of Theology (Methodist)

3742. 4232.

Indiana Theological Seminary

963.

Interdenominational Theological Center

548. 549. 704. 1480. 2755. 3548. 3750.
4074. 4075. 4474.

INTER/MET

2256.

Johnson Bible College

398. 554.

Lancaster Theological Seminary (United Church of Christ)

147. 148. 2384. 2450. 2538. 3659. 3711.
3712. 3713. 3880. 5202. 5203. 5214.

Lane Seminary

> See McCormick Theological Seminary

Lebanon Seminary

> 4951.

Lexington Theological Seminary (Christian Churches)

> 459. 542. 869. 1127. 1484. 1683. 1740.
> 2531. 3050. 3393. 3485. 3578. 4310. 4311.
> 4312. 5029. 5058.

Liberty Baptist Seminary (Baptist)

> 4484.

Louisville Presbyterian Theological Seminary
(Presbyterian)

> 3866. 3867.

Luther Northwestern Theological Seminary (Lutheran)

> 3584. 4357.

Luther Rice Seminary (Baptist)

> 1889. 2983.

Lutheran School of Theology at Chicago (Lutheran)

> 54. 64. 152. 191. 355. 1720. 3161. 4120.
> 4121. 4213. 4633. 4971.

Lutheran Theological Seminary at Gettysburg
(Lutheran)

> 1599. 1747. 1748. 1892. 2176. 2218. 2263.
> 2414. 2786. 3004. 3913. 4366. 4367. 4975.
> 4976. 4977. 4979. 4981. 5141.

Lutheran Theological Seminary at Philadelphia
(Lutheran)

> 2177. 2615. 2616. 4446.

Lutheran Theological Southern Seminary (Lutheran)

> 4818.

McCormick Theological Seminary (Presbyterian)

79.   315.   316.   317.   844.   1123.   1308.   1766.
1808.   1916.   2225.   2455.   2510.   2511.   2624.
2655.   2679.   2680.   2681.   2682.   2683.   2684.
2685.   2686.   2765.   3316.   3551.   3763.   3764.
3990.   4066.   4612.   4889.

Meadville/Lombard Theological School

See University of Chicago.

Melodyland School of Theology

755.   5204.   5205.

Mercer Memorial School of Theology (Defunct)

3928.

Mercersburg

See Lancaster Theological Seminary

Midwestern Baptist Theological Seminary (Southern Baptist)

1108.

Minnesota Bible College

2985.

Mission Home Seminary

See United Theological Seminary of the Twin Cities.

Moody Bible Institute

160.   791.   843.   1424.   1425.   1426.   1600.
1601.   2793.   2843.   3233.   4038.   4965.

Nashotah House (Episcopal)

125.   1762.   2442.   3101.   4346.

Nazarene Theological Seminary (Church of the Nazarene)

2964.

New Albany Theological Seminary

See McCormick Theological Seminary

New Brunswick Theological Seminary (Reformed)

604. 1726. 1839. 4560. 4561. 4562. 4563.
4564. 4822. 4823.

New Orleans Baptist Theological Seminary (Southern
Baptist)

263. 1046. 3074. 3635.

New York Theological Seminary

1348. 1877. 2440. 3358. 4928. 4930.

Newbury Seminary, Vermont

4966.

Newton Theological Institution (Baptist)

1737. 1738. 1785. 1967. 2060. 2061. 2063.
2363. 3183. 3184. 3185. 3186. 3498. 4077.
4125. 5043.

Northern Baptist Theological Seminary (Baptist)

3059.

Oberlin University

259. 1453. 2320. 3891. 4066. 4889.

Oral Roberts University

3751.

Pacific School of Religion

988. 1483. 2332. 4664.

Perkins School of Theology (Methodist)

86. 998. 999. 1733. 2072. 3778.

Philadelphia College of the Bible

1525.

Philadelphia Divinity School

See Episcopal Divinity School

Pittsburgh Theological Seminary (Presbyterian)

235. 572. 588. 864. 3465. 5001.

Princeton Theological Seminary (Presbyterian)

69. 74. 203. 238. 281. 295. 664. 685.
725. 732. 811. 836. 872. 888. 920. 1090.
1156. 1308. 1549. 1556. 1694. 1707. 1738.
1744. 1833. 1834. 1981. 1999. 2126. 2143.
2151. 2178. 2190. 2215. 2331. 2341. 2383.
2529. 2556. 2577. 2578. 2667. 2668. 2671.
2672. 2716. 2725. 2726. 2741. 2872. 2930.
2948. 2949. 2950. 2954. 2955. 3030. 3133.
3144. 3189. 3219. 3277. 3367. 3549. 3550.
3743. 3763. 3861. 3931. 3975. 4020. 4135.
4177. 4299. 4300. 4315. 4337. 4338. 4342.
4414. 4473. 4547. 4629. 4883. 4884. 4982.
4990. 4991. 5065. 5098.

Protestant Episcopal Theological Seminary in Virginia

78. 903. 1659. 1975. 2215. 2866. 3332.
4069. 4812.

Reformed Bible College

5088.

Reformed Presbyterian Theological Seminary, Cincinnati

929.

Rochester Theological Seminary

See Colgate Rochester Divinity School

Rock Spring Seminary (Baptist - Defunct)

3410.

San Francisco Theological Seminary (Presbyterian)

1008. 1735.

Scattergood Seminary

4270.

Seabury-Western Theological Seminary   (Episcopal)

2696.

Southeastern Baptist Theological Seminary   (Southern Baptist)

2152.   2216.   3809.   4016.

Southern Baptist Theological Seminary   (Southern Baptist)

263.   392.   538.   539.   718.   719.   720.   886.
967.   1158.   1159.   1257.   1351.   1637.   1691.
1704.   2217.   2576.   2640.   2641.   2642.   2710.
3073.   3381.   3473.   3507.   3617.   3756.   3855.
4113.   4217.   4263.   4378.   4645.   4695.   4732.
5064.

Southwestern Baptist Theological Seminary   (Southern Baptist)

231.   232.   233.   263.   611.   1113.   1344.   1768.
2500.   2830.   3116.   3174.   3178.   3228.   3879.
4817.   4903.   5093.

Springfield Seminary

1028.

Theological Education Fund

3626.   3627.   4868.

Theological Seminary of the German Reformed Church, Mercersburg, Pa.

See Lancaster Theological Seminary

Theological Seminary of the Protestant Episcopal Church, Kentucky

2155.

Trinity Lutheran Seminary   (Lutheran)

4143.

Union Theological Seminary, New York City

51.   195.   335.   336.   337.   338.   339.   344.
469.   571.   728.   857.   1151.   1230.   1231.
1239.   1252.   1399.   1466.   1586.   1678.   (Cont.)

Union Theological Seminary, New York City   (Cont.)

1749.	1751.	1754.	1781.	1863.	1867.	1920.
1925.	1978.	2135.	2231.	2354.	2412.	2469.
2535.	2584.	2608.	2704.	2821.	3122.	3147.
3149.	3159.	3208.	3210.	3278.	3396.	3436.
3515.	3516.	3556.	3682.	3696.	3716.	3717.
3746.	3805.	4015.	4083.	4085.	4123.	4124.
4128.	4129.	4130.	4131.	4133.	4164.	4165.
4274.	4278.	4285.	4350.	4433.	4581.	4603.
4604.	4605.	4746.	4747.	4748.	4749.	4750.
4751.	4753.	4781.	4935.	4973.	5013.	5211.

Union Theological Seminary in Virginia   (Presbyterian)

327.	632.	1541.	1706.	2244.	2627.	2628.
2763.	2853.	3027.	3530.	3725.	3931.	4184.
4435.	4607.	4752.	4942.	5034.	5097.	

United Theological Seminary   (Methodist)

1407.

United Theological Seminary of the Twin Cities
(United Church of Christ)

1727. 3898. 3899.

University of Chicago

114.	159.	165.	198.	366.	459.	490.	491.
492.	565.	585.	703.	765.	781.	806.	840.
1077.	1164.	1342.	1350.	1395.	1570.	1653.	
1654.	1655.	1656.	1849.	2100.	2202.	2241.	
2378.	2583.	2592.	2814.	2837.	2868.	2878.	
2879.	2927.	3047.	3093.	3167.	3312.	3371.	
3770.	4037.	4112.	4173.	4290.	4297.	4340.	
4416.	4422.	4543.	4567.	4648.	4674.	4823.	
5201.							

University of Southern California   (Methodist)

959. 1417.

University of the South   (Episcopal)

772. 774. 1723. 5195.

Vanderbilt University

901. 1714. 2969.

Virginia Seminary

See Protestant Episcopal Theological Seminary in Virginia

Virginia Union University (Baptist)

1722.

Wartburg Theological Seminary (Lutheran)

867. 2180. 2181. 2182. 3538. 3854. 4396.
4897. 5048. 5049.

Wesley Theological Seminary (Methodist)

754. 2402.

Western Baptist Theological Institution, Ky.
(Defunct)

694. 4882.

Western Theological Seminary (Reformed)

741. 1290. 2678. 3144. 3459. 3728. 3811.

Western Theological Seminary, Evanston, Illinois

5000.

Westminster Theological Seminary (Presbyterian)

1634. 3743. 4338. 4342. 4937. 5002. 5003.

Whitestown Seminary

387.

Xenia Theological Seminary

See Pittsburgh Theological Seminary

Yale University

114. 206. 211. 221. 222. 306. 309. 484.
734. 1000. 1058. 1101. 1119. 1151. 1169.
1210. 1220. 1221. 1222. 1223. 1281. 2128.
2407. 2469. 2697. 2761. 2865. 2971. 3005.
3038. 3341. 3531. 3611. 3698. 4325. 4764.
4804. 4866. 4871. 4918. 4949. 5189. 5190.
5191. 5192. 5193. 5248.

IV. INDIVIDUALS SIGNIFICANT IN THEOLOGICAL EDUCATION

Abbott, Lyman

    3. 4. 5.

Adger, John Bailey

    45.

Alexander, Archibald

    69. 70. 74. 2737. 3133.

Alexander, Joseph Addison

    3030.

Allen, Alexander Viets Griswold

    78. 4127.

Ames, Charles Gordon

    112.

Ames, Edward Scribner

    114. 159.

Bacon, G. W.

    3005.

Bangs, Nathan

    240. 241. 242. 4305.

Barnes, William W.

    233. 262.

Barth, Karl

    273. 274. 3004.

Bausman, Benjamin

    3620.

Baxter, Richard

    288.

Beecher, Henry Ward

314. 2471.

Beecher, Lyman

79. 315. 316. 317. 1491. 1567. 1800. 1917. 4612.

Bennett, John Coleman

335. 336. 337. 338. 339. 340. 341. 344. 2584. 3556.

Boisen, Anton T.

176. 425. 426. 427. 428. 429. 1953. 3241. 4192.

Borden (of Yale)

4473.

Bowne, Borden P.

919. 1115.

Breckinridge, Robert Jefferson

1613. 1614.

Broadus, John Albert

538. 539. 540. 541. 3756. 4263.

Brooks, Phillips

78.

Brown, Francis

565. 566. 4165.

Brown, Robert McAfee

571. 4604.

Burton, Ernest DeWitt

638. 639. 640. 641. 642. 1342. 1655.

Cabot, Richard Clarke

651. 652. 653. 654. 655. 656. 657. 3136.

Campbell, Alexander

674. 675. 676. 2248. 3723.

Cannon, Bishop

685.

Carnell, Edward John

700. 3138.

Cartwright, Peter

717. 3509.

Carver, William Owen

718. 719. 720. 986. 1160.

Case, Shirley Jackson

721. 2202.

Chafer, Lewis Sperry

748. 2051. 2542.

Channing, William Ellery

557. 757. 758.

Chapman, J. Wilbur

3316.

Chase, Irah

1737.

Clarke, James Freeman

433.

Clarke, William Newton

820.

Coffin, Henry Sloan

    857. 858. 3208. 4581. 4781.

Conner, Walter Thomas

    3178. 3228.

Cornelius, Elias

    1281.

Dabney, Robert Lewis

    2244. 5097.

DeLancey, William Heathcote

    2831.

Dempster, John

    245. 1102. 1103. 1104. 1105. 2690.

Dwight, Timothy

    1000. 1220. 1221. 1222. 1223. 3038.

Edwards, Bela Bates

    1279. 1280. 1281. 1282. 1283. 1284. 3351.

Ellinwood, Frank Field

    1308.

Emmons, Nathaniel

    3352.

Fisk, Wilbur

    1439. 1440. 1441. 1995.

Fosdick, Harry Emerson

    1465. 1466. 1467.

Foster, George Burman

    1473. 1474. 4674.

Fuerbringer, Alfred Ottomar
1506. 3689.

Fuller, Andrew
1509.

Fuller, Charles E.
1510. 4181.

Furman, Richard
2367.

Gaebelein, Arno Clemens
1531. 1532.

Gates, Frederick Taylor
1570.

Goodspeed, Edgar Johnson
840. 1653. 1654.

Gordon, Adoniram Judson
1661. 1662.

Graham, Billy
3473. 3611.

Grant, Frederick Clifton
1685. 2241.

Graves, J. R.
4163.

Green, Ashbel
1694. 2529.

Hackett, Horatio Balch
5043.

Hall, Charles Cuthbert

    1749. 1750. 1751. 1752. 1753. 1754. 1755.

Harper, William Rainey

    491. 565. 1164. 1333. 1656. 1814. 1815.
    1816. 1817. 1818. 1819. 1820. 1821. 1822.
    2100. 2379. 2814. 2879. 3093. 3312. 3770.
    4308. 4340.

Hodge, Archibald A.

    3459.

Hodge, Charles

    725. 1972. 1973. 2783. 3277.

Hoffman, Eugene Augustus

    3735.

Holmes, John Haynes

    2011.

Hovey, Alvah

    2060. 2061. 2062. 2063.

Ironside, H. A.

    1334.

Jacobs, Henry Eyster

    2176. 2177.

Johnson, Paul E.

    2234. 2235. 2236. 2237.

King, Martin Luther

    3256.

Knox, John

    2412.

McCormick, Cyrus Hall

    2624. 2655.

McGiffert, A. C.

    2703. 2704. 2705. 2706.

Machen, J. Gresham

    2716. 2717. 3743. 4338. 4342.

McMillan, John

    1732.

Maier, Walter A.

    2766.

Mason, John Mitchell

    516. 2654. 2825. 4790. 4791.

Mathews, Shailer

    2833. 2834. 2835. 2836. 2837. 2838. 2839.
    2840. 2841. 4037. 4173.

Mays, Benjamin E.

    2859. 2860.

Merrick, John Austin

    154.

Miller, Samuel

    2190. 2383. 2453. 2948. 2949. 2950. 2951.
    2952. 2953. 2954. 2955. 4299. 4300. 4414.

Mitchell, Hinckley Gilbert Thomas

    2994.

Moody, Dwight L.

    1424. 1425. 1426. 1725. 3233. 4038. 4180.
    4965.

Morse, Jedediah

    3054. 4246.

Mott, John R.

    789. 3062. 3063. 3064.

Mullins, Edgar Young

    1315. 3078. 3079. 4378. 4695.

Munger, Theodore Thornton

    206. 3084.

Murdock, James

    4611.

Naylor, Robert E.

    232. 3116.

Nevin, John Williamson

    3144.

Newman, A. H.

    1113. 1344. 3177.

North, Frank Mason

    2443.

Park, Edwards Amasa

    739. 1284. 1471. 2729. 3350. 3351. 3352.
    3353. 3354. 3355. 4696.

Pauck, Wilhelm

    2878.

Payne, Daniel A.

    4264.

Phelps, Austin

    3430. 4871.

Philputt, James M.

    3436.

Pierson, Arthur T.

    1661. 3443. 3444. 3445. 3446. 3447.

Porter, Ebenezer

    2846. 3491. 3492. 3694.

Ranson, Charles Wesley

    3625. 3626. 3627. 3628.

Rauschenbusch, Walter

    1026. 4046.

Rice, John H.

    2853. 3703. 4435. 4942.

Rice, Luther

    1588.

Roberts, Oral

    3751.

Robertson, A. T.

    1351. 3756.

Robinson, Ezekiel Gilman

    3762.

Rockwell, William Walker

    3771. 4133.

Sampey, John R.

    3855.

Schaff, Philip

    3882. 3883. 3884. 3885.

Schaller, Johann Michael Gottlieb
    1681.
Schmucker, Samuel Simon
    203. 3912. 3913. 4981. 4982.
Scofield, C. I.
    4714.
Scott, Walter
    3449.
Sears, Barnas
    2060. 3977. 4077.
Shaw, William
    4051.
Smith, Benjamin Mosby
    1456.
Smith, Henry Boynton
    4130. 4164. 4278.
Smith, Samuel Stanhope
    4135. 4177.
Speer, Robert E.
    1652. 4229.
Sprecher, Samuel
    4247.
Spring, Gardiner
    4248. 4249.
Spurgeon, Charles
    208. 911. 1513. 3634.

Stevenson, Dwight E.

    4310. 4311. 4312. 4313. 5029.

Stiles, Ezra

    3038. 4325.

Stone, Barton Warren

    4335.

Stowe, Calvin Ellis

    1808. 1941. 2110.

Stuart, Moses

    42. 1125. 3353. 4375. 4376. 4377. 4916.

Sverdrup, Georg

    1776. 1777. 1778. 1779. 1900.

Sweet, William Warren

    165. 4425. 4426. 4427. 4428. 4429.

Taylor, Graham

    4464. 4465. 4466. 4822. 4823.

Taylor, J. Hudson

    4463.

Taylor, Nathaniel William

    2865.

Tennent, William

    69. 3401.

Thayer, Joseph Henry

    3799. 4496.

Tholuck, Friedrich August Gottreu

    3354. 4583.

Thompson, Ernest Trice

2862. 4606.

Thornwell, James Henry

3344.

Thurman, Howard

5194.

Tittle, Ernest Fremont

2947.

Toy, Crawford

4677.

Turner, Samuel H.

4734. 4735.

Tyng, Stephen Higginson

4741. 4742. 4743.

Van Dusen, Henry Pitney

571. 4604. 4605. 4781. 4782. 4783. 4784.
4785.

Vincent, John Heyl

4807. 4808. 4809.

Ware, Jr., Henry

4880.

Wayland, Francis

4077. 4914. 4915. 4916. 4917.

Webber, George W.

3396. 4927. 4928. 4929. 4930. 4931. 4932.
4933. 4934.

Wentz, Abdel Ross

    1892. 4974. 4975. 4976. 4977. 4978. 4979. 4980. 4981. 4982.

Whitsett, William Heth

    720.

Wieman, Henry Nelson

    198. 366.

Wilson, Bird

    550.

Wright, George Frederick

    5175. 5176. 5177.

Young, Ammi Burnham

    4661.